"Heart to heart: this is the preaching that 'cuts us to the quick' and applies the balm of Gilead. And it is marvelously modeled in this book. Having appreciated every sermon I've heard from Joel Beeke, I am sure that you will discern a refreshing connection between doctrine, experience, and life in his writing."

Michael Horton, J. Gresham Machen Professor of Systematic Theology and Apologetics, Westminster Seminary California; Host, *White Horse Inn*; author, *Core Christianity*

"*Reformed Preaching* is unique for its emphasis on learning to preach experientially from the Reformers and their theological successors through the centuries. Joel Beeke convincingly shows that Reformed preaching is doctrinally sound, profoundly personal, and effectively practical. Far from being a contemporary model, this work presents the preaching of the Reformation, which encompasses head, heart, and hands, as the enduring way to proclaim Scripture. This is a very foundational understanding of the Reformation impact on the history of the church."

John MacArthur, Pastor, Grace Community Church, Sun Valley, California; President, The Master's University and Seminary

"Faithful preaching is intimately bound up with the heartbeat of faithful Christian living. The proof of this is seen throughout the history of the church. Wills, affections, lives, churches, and entire communities have been transformed when the proclamation of God's Word has reached beyond the mind to the heart. This was true during the Protestant Reformation, was repeated under the influence of the Puritans, and has been witnessed during times of revival. Joel Beeke mines the theology and practice of the great preacher-pastor-theologians of the past in a way that is guaranteed to bless and equip those who carry the baton for the generation they serve in the present and beyond."

Mark G. Johnston, Minister, Bethel Presbyterian Church, Cardiff, United Kingdom

"The ethos of this soul-satisfying book on preaching is not 'fast forward to the new and fanciful' but 'turn your affections back to the solid theological foundations of the past.' Too much modern-day preaching aims to attract the undiscerning hearer with exciting and flossy novelties. But godly church members hunger and thirst not for shallow novelty, but for real, solid, biblical preaching and genuine food for the soul. The author's message is to open up the excellencies of the model preachers of the past—from Luther and Calvin to the great Puritans and right down to the beloved Martyn Lloyd-Jones, who died in 1981. Here is a book ideally suited to the reader who longs for solid preaching in the pulpit for his soul. For this reason, this is also an ideal book to place in the hands of the serious student for the ministry."

Maurice Roberts, Former Editor, *The Banner of Truth* magazine; author, *The Thought of God* and *The Mysteries of God*

"A preacher who does not practice what he preaches is a hypocrite; a preacher who does not preach what he himself has practiced is a mere theorist. A good preacher gives to others the overflow of what he himself has taken in from God's Word. Effective preaching is from heart to heart, as suggested by the subtitle of Joel Beeke's *Reformed Preaching*. Preaching is more than simply a verbal book report; it is a God-ordained means of bringing God's truth to bear on the hearts and in the experience of the hearers. Beeke effectively underscores this powerful function of preaching both with models from past preachers and clear instructions for modern preachers. Beeke's passion for experiential preaching is obvious, exposing his heart to ours."

Michael P. V. Barrett, Vice President for Academic Affairs, Puritan Reformed Theological Seminary; author, *Complete in Him* and *Love Divine and Unfailing*

"Reformed preaching is simply ordinary preaching. Sermons that are faithful in their exposition and application to the hearers, rich in gospel content, Christ-centered in focus, and earnestly evangelistic in their calls to sinners to repent and entrust themselves to Jesus Christ—this is Reformed preaching. It is not long sermons and heavy preaching. It is the pulpit's pastoral and reviving ministry to the body of Christ, most frequently on the Lord's Day, generally to the assembly of the faithful, but mighty in addressing the world. It is delivering compassionate and heart-warming sermons, sometimes profoundly solemn sermons. It is, most of all, interesting, gripping preaching and life-changing pulpit fare; and once it has been heard, nothing else will ever satisfy an awakened soul that hungers for the living God. It is the believer's weekly feast. How does one preach like that? Read this book for starters. You will be enlightened and motivated, and you will especially become prayerful, longing for the spread of this kind of ministry throughout the whole world."

Geoffrey Thomas, Former Pastor, Alfred Place Baptist Church, Aberystwyth, Wales

"*Reformed Preaching* is grand, sweeping, and engaging. It is at once substantive theology, a church-historical survey, and a book of practical divinity on experiential, Reformed preaching. No one has written anything quite like it. Subtitled *Proclaiming God's Word from the Heart of the Preacher to the Heart of His People*, Beeke's book breathes the air of its theme. This book is excellent in every way; it is all doctrine and all application. *Reformed Preaching* challenges the church with the indispensable necessity of preaching that is biblical, doctrinal, and experiential, preaching that leads God's people to "taste and see that the LORD is good" (Ps. 34:8). While Beeke addresses ministers and hearers of the preached Word alike, as a gospel preacher, I found myself worshiping the triune God on every page and humbled in the dust with gratitude for the privilege of proclaiming God's truth. This is a book to be read over and over again. I pray that this volume will be widely and extensively read. I pray as well that *Reformed Preaching* may be a spark to revive the old Reformed commitment to experiential preaching in a new day."

David B. McWilliams, Senior Minister, Covenant Presbyterian Church, Lakeland, Florida

"It is said that 'a sermon is as good as a sermon does.' Joel Beeke's book will greatly help God's servants minister the Word to this end: to the head, heart, and life. Here he scripturally defines Reformed and experimental preaching, surveys its foremost exponents from church history, and searchingly persuades us of the need for this kind of preaching today. Reading this, no preacher can fail to be challenged—but also encouraged and helped—to preach this way more than ever before. With the Lord's blessing, this book will do untold good for ministers and churches everywhere. This is a much-needed and unique volume. I wholeheartedly commend it to ministerial students as required reading, and to all of us who proclaim the unsearchable riches of Christ."

> **John Thackway,** Pastor, Holywell Evangelical Church, North Wales;
> Editor, *Bible League Quarterly*

"As an able teacher and exemplary model of the best in pulpit ministry, Joel Beeke has much to say about the subject of preaching. In this book, we sit at his feet and learn what real biblical exposition is from this gifted expositor. If there was ever a season when the church needed to read this book, the time is now."

> **Steven J. Lawson,** President, OnePassion Ministries

"True Christian experience is always the experience that God and his Word are true. That truth is preeminently proclaimed through Spirit-anointed preaching. *Reformed Preaching* shows why preaching is a key of God's kingdom. This helpful survey of the history of a few dozen of the Reformed church's great preachers, from Ulrich Zwingli to Martyn Lloyd-Jones, illustrates how experiential preaching is used by the Holy Spirit to cause needy sinners to experience the vital truth of the gospel."

> **Henk van den Belt,** Special Chair in Reformed Theology, Faculty of Theology
> and Religious Studies, University of Groningen, The Netherlands

"It has been one of the great privileges of my life to teach homiletics alongside Joel Beeke at Puritan Reformed Theological Seminary for the past ten years. I've not only witnessed his expertise and passion for the subject, but I've also seen and felt the ministry-transforming effects of this upon my own preaching, as well as upon hundreds of students from all over the world. It's a joyful answer to prayer to see his lectures now in print for the benefit of thousands more preachers of the gospel."

> **David Murray,** Professor of Old Testament and Practical Theology,
> Puritan Reformed Theological Seminary; author, *Jesus on Every Page*;
> *Reset*; and *Exploring the Bible*

"I have yet to come across a preaching resource so helpful, poignant, biblical, and even devotional as Joel Beeke's *Reformed Preaching*. The breadth and depth of historical weight and confessional integrity make this book a superb volume for any pastor, teacher, or layperson. I will certainly be using this in both my preaching classes and pulpit preparation!"

> **Brian Cosby,** Senior Pastor, Wayside Presbyterian Church, Signal Mountain,
> Tennessee; Visiting Professor, Reformed Theological Seminary, Atlanta

"I am very pleased to endorse this book by Joel Beeke because it is an invaluable contribution to Reformed preaching. While some in the Reformed community tend to associate experiential preaching with pietism and mysticism, Beeke shows that generations of Spirit-anointed Reformed preachers have employed the biblical experiential method. Beeke's book represents the culmination of what has been on the author's mind for many years, namely, to come to a clear biblical understanding of what the gospel is and by whom, to whom, and especially *how* it is to be preached. This latest homiletical contribution by Beeke deserves to be read by all seminary professors, theological students, pastors, and all who are hungry for the true Bread of Life. 'The afflicted shall eat and be satisfied; those who seek him shall praise the LORD! May your hearts live forever' (Ps. 22:26)."

Cornelis (Neil) Pronk, Emeritus Pastor, Free Reformed Churches of North America

"If 'Reformed experiential preaching' sounds dull or dry, or just difficult, then you ought to read this book. As a true instructor, writing with real warmth and insight, Joel Beeke opens up enduring principles, spans the centuries to survey practitioners and identify patterns, and then earnestly urges us to the lively practice of such preaching. He carries us from the lecture room to the training ground and then sends us out into the field, humbled and yet hopeful, to preach from our hearts to the hearts of others."

Jeremy Walker, Pastor, Maidenbower Baptist Church, Crawley, United Kingdom; author, *Life in Christ*; *Anchored in Grace*; and *A Face Like a Flint*

"Having known Joel Beeke for nearly fifty years, both as a personal friend and as a fellow minister of the gospel, I can unhesitatingly affirm that Reformed preaching has been, and continues to be, the passion of his ministry. Frequently I have had the privilege of hearing him preach from his heart to the hearts of his audience, preaching the unsearchable riches of Christ to poor, needy, and guilty sinners in need of precisely such a Savior. I am therefore delighted that in *Reformed Preaching* he is passing on to the next generation of preachers what it means to preach Christ scripturally, doctrinally, and experientially, and how to effectively aim such preaching at the hearts of those who hear them—doing so in complete dependence upon the Spirit of Christ for explication and application. May many younger (and older!) ministers of the gospel benefit richly from the ripe fruit of Beeke's lifelong commitment to experiential preaching."

Bartel Elshout, Pastor, Heritage Reformed Congregation, Hull, Iowa; translator, *The Christian's Reasonable Service* and *The Christian's Only Comfort in Life and Death*

"In this latest book, Joel Beeke warmly welcomes us into his pulpit, his study, and even the place of his private prayers. To accept his invitation is to discover what it means for a sermon to offer both light and heat, and to learn how to preach the gospel as food for the hungry rather than as dessert for the deserving. In *Reformed Preaching*, Beeke introduces favorite figures from church history to form a composite picture of the experiential expositor. Even experienced expositors will find much to learn in this book from both the author and his friends."

Chad Van Dixhoorn, Professor of Church History, Westminster Theological Seminary

REFORMED PREACHING

Proclaiming God's Word from
the Heart of the Preacher
to the Heart of His People

Joel R. Beeke

WHEATON, ILLINOIS

Reformed Preaching: Proclaiming God's Word from the Heart of the Preacher to the Heart of His People

Copyright © 2018 by Joel R. Beeke

Published by Crossway
        1300 Crescent Street
        Wheaton, Illinois 60187

Cover design: Peter Voth

First printing 2018

Printed in the United States of America

All Scripture quotations are from the *King James Version* of the Bible.

All emphases in Scripture quotations have been added by the author.

Hardcover ISBN: 978-1-4335-5927-3
ePub ISBN: 978-1-4335-5930-3
PDF ISBN: 978-1-4335-5928-0
Mobipocket ISBN: 978-1-4335-5929-7

Library of Congress Cataloging-in-Publication Data

Names: Beeke, Joel R., 1952- author.
Title: Reformed preaching: proclaiming God's word from the heart of the preacher to the heart of his people / Joel R. Beeke.
Description: Wheaton, Illinois: Crossway, [2018] | Includes bibliographical references and index. |
Identifiers: LCCN 2017052039 (print) | LCCN 2018021742 (ebook) | ISBN 9781433559280 (pdf) | ISBN 9781433559297 (mobi) | ISBN 9781433559303 (epub) | ISBN 9781433559273 (hardcover) | ISBN 9781433559303 (ePub) | ISBN 9781433559297 (Mobipocket)
Subjects: LCSH: Preaching. | Reformed Church—Doctrines.
Classification: LCC BV4211.3 (ebook) | LCC BV4211.3 .B363 2018 (print) | DDC 251—dc23
LC record available at https://lccn.loc.gov/2017052039

Crossway is a publishing ministry of Good News Publishers.

LB		26	25	24	23	22	21	20	19	18
14	13	12	11	10	9	8	7	6	5	4	3	2	1

For
Paul Smalley
authentic friend, prayer partner,
faithful and able teacher's assistant—you
are appreciated far more than you know.

In preaching there is intended a communion of souls,
and a communication of somewhat from ours [as preachers]
unto theirs [as God's people].

Richard Baxter

Contents

PART 3: PREACHING EXPERIENTIALLY TODAY

Foreword

Sinclair B. Ferguson

Almost fifty years ago I took a yearlong course at university that consisted entirely of studying the great works in the Christian theological tradition, such as Irenaeus's *Adversus Haereses*, Augustine's *Confessions*, Athanasius's *De Incarnatione*, Anselm's *Cur Deus Homo*, Thomas Aquinas's *Summa Theologiae*, and so on through the centuries. The exam paper consisted of a series of lengthy quotations with this simple instruction: "Comment." Three of us were in the class with the professor, a well-known theologian. But because of my degree program, unlike my fellow students' exam papers, the quotations on my copy were left in the original languages. Exposition required translation. All this was a little daunting! But during that year I had discovered the study method John Calvin had employed as a young man: before he went to sleep he rehearsed in his mind everything he had learned that day, and did not get out of bed the next morning until he had gone over it again (it sounds simple, but try it!). I may know more now, but I suspect that was the last time I felt "in command" of my knowledge.

This long-forgotten memory unexpectedly came back to me just as I finished reading *Reformed Preaching*, for one of its most impressive features is that its author, Joel Beeke, really knows what he knows and is eager to share that knowledge. Moreover, whether or not he has pursued Calvin's study method, he has, in many respects, imitated Calvin's model of ministry. He shares Calvin's remarkable facility to mark, recall, and use the fruit of his prodigious reading. But also like the Genevan Reformer, he is simultaneously pastor of a large congregation, professor at (indeed, founder and president of) a theological seminary, church-man, scholar, prolific author, visionary, and driving force in a variety of Christian enterprises; at home, a loving and grateful husband, father, and brother; and at large, an important and loved member of an informal but real international network of brethren who share his vision.

Joel Beeke is uniquely qualified to write a book on Reformed experiential preaching. Very few have his breadth and depth of experience as a preacher—in terms of the sheer amount of preaching he has done, the decades during which he has expounded God's Word, the many countries he has visited in order to do so, and the wide variety of conferences he has addressed. Add to this his knowledge of the Puritan divines *as preachers* and the degree to which he has studied their goals, style, and methodology, and then include the fruitfulness of his own ministry (the litmus test, surely), and readers can be reassured that these pages will take them on a wonderful five-hundred-page journey in the company of an experienced guide to some of the most impressive preachers since the days of the Reformation. They will also find on page after page quotations or comments that (if the metaphor may be forgiven!) they can suck for the length of time a Queen Wilhelmina peppermint lasts during a Dutch sermon! For here, seamlessly joined together, are the insights of preaching giants coupled with the wisdom and experience of a contemporary exponent of Reformed experiential preaching. The whole book is an education in itself, and full of stimulation. Readers who are preachers may be well advised not only to read and inwardly digest its contents, but to mark those statements and quotations that particularly strike them—at least until they have marked more than half of the contents! I suspect that many who are called upon to give an occasional lecture on preaching (or for that matter an entire course) will be grateful to the author for providing them with so many apt quotations to epitomize and thrust home a salient point. But they will need to be on their guard lest their hearers mentally note, "Ah, that's *another* quote from Joel Beeke's book!"

Even for those of us who have never taught homiletics it is impossible to avoid the students' question, "Have you any words of wisdom for a beginning preacher?" I usually give the same answer: "*Listen with two heads to preachers*, especially those whose ministry is a help to you. With your own head take in for yourself all that exalts God, humbles sinners, directs you to Christ, enlivens you by the Spirit, thrills you with the truth, redirects your will, and captures your affections. But with the other head ask the question, 'What is he doing that humanly speaking makes his preaching so helpful? And what do I need to do, *given my different gifts, personality, and experience*, to build those same principles into my own preaching of God's Word?'" This is not a recipe for cloning or artificial mimicking in which we lose ourselves and distort God's gifts to us and in us, but an encouragement to *imitation* in the biblical sense, to recognize the biblical principles that should inform all preaching, to apply them to our own gifts and setting in both geography and history, and to seek, as Paul challengingly urges Timothy, to make sure that our progress is evident to all our hearers (1 Tim. 4:15).

When we make such progress, our congregations will be both *well-instructed* and *well-nourished*. I owe this way of putting things to friends who told me, some time after their minister had been called to another congregation, "Looking back now we realize that over the past years we were *well instructed*, but we feel *poorly nourished*." Their phrasing struck me as an apt analysis of one pitfall in preaching—exposition that is no more than educational instruction but never reaches the affections. No less an intellectual than Jonathan Edwards wrote by contrast that his goal in preaching was to reach the affections. Thus, he wrote in *Some Thoughts Concerning the Revival*:

> I should think myself in the way of my duty to raise the affections of my hearers as high as I possibly can, provided that they are affected with nothing but the truth, and with affections that are not disagreeable to the nature of what they are affected with. . . .
>
> Our people don't so much need to have their heads stored, as to have their hearts touched; and they stand in the greatest need of that sort of preaching that has the greatest tendency to do this.[1]

This is the chief characteristic of Reformed experiential preaching. One of its inevitable fruits is that it is so all-demanding on our whole being that those who engage in it themselves grow by it—and those they serve sense that they too are being nourished as well as instructed. We need all the help we can get to fulfill the grand apostolic challenge to make progress.

---

1. Jonathan Edwards, *Some Thoughts Concerning the Revival*, in *The Works of Jonathan Edwards*, vol. 4, *The Great Awakening*, ed. C. C. Goen (New Haven, CT: Yale University Press, 1972), 4:387–88.

Visits to other countries help us to see our own nations with fresh eyes. So, for preachers, visits to other places and times in the long history of preaching and preachers help us to reflect on what we ourselves are called to be and to do in our own places and times. *Reformed Preaching* provides just such a refreshing and renewing trip abroad, in literary form, and shows us sights to which we will want to return again as the years pass.

Such visits are important because, if my own experience is anything to go by, preaching does not get any easier as we grow older. Yes, from one point of view, it does: we have increased resources on which to draw and we have more experience. But these are ancillary to preaching; they are not *preaching itself*—that daunting, wonderful, mysterious, romantic, exciting, humbling-in-the-dust instrument that God has used throughout the centuries to call sinful men and women, young people, and boys and girls to faith in Jesus Christ. Over the years our sense of the privilege of preaching increases, but the task is never less daunting, and the awareness of our weakness and inadequacy only increases; the number of times we come to the conclusion of a message and feel we want to say, once more, "Sorry, Lord; forgive me," seems to grow exponentially! Of course! This is because no one needs to sit under our preaching more than we do. And if the Lord purposes to use our preaching, he also wants to make sure that the glory remains his. If we are growing as preachers, and realize with Robert Murray M'Cheyne that our people's greatest need is our personal holiness, then it should come as no surprise that even (perhaps especially) through our own preaching, the Spirit will constantly chip away at the deep, hidden, and most stubborn residual areas of our sinfulness. No matter how much we grow or how great our gifts, we will always be in the position of Isaiah—realizing that sin has entangled itself not only in our weaknesses and faults, but in the very best gifts God has given us. Those whose calling it is to speak God's Word, of all men, need to be brought to say, "I am a man *of unclean lips*" (Isa. 6:5).

There was a time in my native land of Scotland when the vast majority of twelve-year-old boys and girls knew the answer to the question, *"How is the word made effectual to salvation?"* It was Question 89 in The Shorter Catechism, penned by some of the Reformed experiential preachers of the seventeenth century whose writings and wisdom feature so largely in these pages. The answer? "The Spirit of God maketh the reading, but especially the preaching of the word, an effectual means of convincing and converting sinners, and of building them up in holiness and comfort, through faith, unto salvation."

Is this conviction still alive and well in the hearts of preachers today? These pages present a clarion call to return to believe it and live it out in our ministries, for this is the true apostolic tradition:

> Therefore seeing we have this ministry, as we have received mercy, we faint not; but have renounced the hidden things of dishonesty, not walking in craftiness, nor handling the word of God deceitfully; but by manifestation of the truth commending ourselves to every man's conscience in the sight of God. . . . For we preach not ourselves, but Christ Jesus the Lord; and ourselves your servants for Jesus' sake. For God, who commanded the light to shine out of darkness, hath shined in our hearts, to give the light of the knowledge of the glory of God in the face of Jesus Christ. But we have this treasure in earthen vessels, that the excellency of the power may be of God, and not of us. . . . For which cause we faint not. (2 Cor. 4:1–2, 5–7, 16)

Reformed Preaching represents a labor of immense love on the part of its author. It is a great gift to the company of preachers worldwide. It is a sure guide to places and times from which we can learn much. It is, perhaps especially, a gift from Joel Beeke to the coming generation of preachers. And it encourages us all to take a long hard look at the character and fruit of our own preaching, challenging us to keep on growing in this greatest of callings, and to become fruitful ministers of the Word of God. That at least has been my experience in reading it, and I feel sure it is the author's hope and prayer that it will be yours too.

Sinclair B. Ferguson
Chancellor's Professor of Systematic Theology,
Reformed Theological Seminary
Teaching Fellow, Ligonier Ministries

Preface and Acknowledgments

I have wanted to write this book for more than twenty years and have been pecking away at it for more years than that. Two reasons have driven me. First, Reformed experiential preaching—preaching from the preacher's heart to the hearts of God's people—has been sorely lacking in Reformed and evangelical churches in recent decades. Second, little has been written on this critical subject. Charles Bridges has a few great sections on it in his classic *The Christian Ministry*[1] and John Jennings has an excellent chapter in *The Christian Pastor's Manual*, edited by John Brown,[2] but no full-length book has been devoted to this specific subject. Recently, a few helpful books have been written on preaching to the heart,[3] but none have focused as narrowly on the subject of what was known as experimental or experiential preaching as this volume does.

The alert reader will have noticed already that the title of the book, *Reformed Preaching*, is different from the term I used in the paragraph above, Reformed *experiential* preaching. The title was chosen for the sake of simplicity, but the book's subtitle—*Proclaiming God's Word from the Heart of the Preacher to the Heart of His People*—is a good summary of what Reformed experiential preaching is. This term has a rich history and meaning, as I hope to show, so I will be using it throughout the book.

I have had the privilege of teaching a homiletics course on Reformed experiential preaching at Puritan Reformed Theological Seminary (PRTS) in Grand Rapids for the last twenty-five years. I also have taught various versions of it for doctor of ministry courses at the Master's Seminary

---

1. Charles Bridges, *The Christian Ministry* (London: Banner of Truth, 1967), 259–80.
2. John Brown, ed., *The Christian Pastor's Manual* (Ligonier, PA: Soli Deo Gloria, 1991), 47–62.
3. See, for example, Murray A. Capill, *The Heart Is the Target: Preaching Practical Application from Every Text* (Phillipsburg, NJ: P&R, 2014).

and Westminster Seminary California, as well as for master of divinity courses at Reformed Theological Seminary in Jackson, Mississippi, and for a number of seminaries around the globe. I am grateful for these opportunities and for how they have afforded me the time to revisit and rework my lecture material on numerous occasions.

Though not identical to my lectures, the chapters of this book are organized around the same three major divisions of the course. First, it considers what Reformed experiential preaching is. Second, it looks at a number of examples of experiential preaching, from Ulrich Zwingli, the first Reformed preacher in the sixteenth century, to Martyn Lloyd-Jones in the twentieth century. The book especially focuses on the English Puritan and Dutch Further Reformation preachers, since they specialized in experiential preaching. Finally, it examines how to cross the bridge from earlier centuries of Reformed experiential preaching to today's preaching in a number of areas, stressing how experiential preaching can best be done today.

The target audience for this book is not just preachers, theological students, and seminaries. I trust that educated church members who long for good preaching might find help in this volume and might draw upon it to lovingly encourage their pastors to preach to their hearts as well as to their minds. I have aimed at simplicity in writing so that the target audience might be as wide as possible. My prayer is that this book might help give Reformed experiential preaching a much-needed boost and support.

I have far too many people to thank for this book than I can mention in this brief space. I owe my emphasis on the experiential aspect of preaching first to my dear father, John Beeke (1920–1993), who often spoke to me as a child and a teenager about the saving work of the Holy Spirit experienced in the souls of God's people. My greatest debt, of course, is to the Holy Spirit himself, who convicted me of sin at the age of fourteen and drew me irresistibly, powerfully, and sweetly to Jesus Christ alone as my total salvation the following year. I trust that he has not ceased to do his work in my soul for the last half century, sanctifying me in some small measure especially through trials and afflictions, so that I hope and pray I can say with conviction, like John the Baptist, "He [Christ] must increase, but I must decrease" (John 3:30).

I am grateful to have learned much about God's leadings with his people from my first theological instructors, Rev. Jan C. Weststrate and Rev. William C. Lamain, both of whom emphasized various experiential dimensions of preaching. Many discussions with each of them about experiential themes have also been profitable for my soul. For my later PhD training at Westminster Seminary in Philadelphia in the early 1980s, I learned the most experientially from my good friend Sinclair B. Ferguson, both from his lectures and in private discussions. His friendship has been invaluable over the years, and I am so grateful for his willingness to write the foreword to this volume.

I owe a large debt to each of the three churches I have been privileged to pastor: the Sioux Center, Iowa, Netherlands Reformed Congregation (1978–1981), the Franklin Lakes, New Jersey, Netherlands Reformed Congregation (1981–1986), and the Grand Rapids Heritage Reformed Congregation, which I have had the privilege of serving as pastor since 1986. In all three churches, spiritual friendship and pastoral conversations with mature saints have been a great help in fostering within me a deep appreciation for the Reformed experiential heritage that has been handed down to us from faithful shepherds, especially many in the Reformation, Puritan, and Dutch Further Reformation eras. Thanks too to the staff of Reformation Heritage Books and to the faculty, staff, theological students, and alumni of PRTS for all the influence they've had on my spiritual nurturing. I feel that the brothers (and they are real brothers to me) surrounding me as faculty members are more gifted and godly than I am, and I owe much experientially to the sanctifying graces that exude from their lives. And a big thanks to Paul Smalley, my faithful teacher's assistant, who chased down the footnotes and did so much to make this a better book than it would have been without him. I also owe heartfelt thanks to Greg Bailey, Ray Lanning, and Phyllis TenElshof for their editorial assistance, and to Crossway Books for being such a joy to work with in seeing this book through the publication process.

I would be remiss in not expressing gratitude to God for granting me access to a wonderful collection of books, both in my own library and at PRTS, that convey the experiential Reformed emphasis throughout the centuries. In recent decades, the Puritan Resource Center has provided me with a storehouse of solid Reformed reading material. I have now been reading the Puritans for more than fifty years and have never grown tired of it. Their writings have done more for me perhaps than any other means of grace apart from Scripture itself. I can say with Martin Luther that some of "my best friends are dead ones," sitting on my shelf in the form of antiquarian books. Countless times I have been deeply moved by reading divines such as John Calvin, William Perkins, Thomas Goodwin, John Owen, John Bunyan, Anthony Burgess, Samuel Rutherford, Willem Teellinck, Wilhelmus à Brakel, and Herman Witsius, as well as women such as Mary Winslow, Ruth Bryan, and Anne Dutton. They, "being dead," yet speak (Heb. 11:4).

Finally, I am so grateful for my God-fearing family. How can I express in words what I owe to my dear mother—a great prayer warrior—who passed away in 2012 at the age of ninety-two, leaving a legacy of thirty-five grandchildren and ninety-two great-grandchildren. My two brothers, John and Jim, have been a special influence on my life experientially, as have my three children in different ways: Calvin, Esther, and Lydia. Each of them, together with spouses and our young grandchildren, have brought untold joy into my life. But no one has befriended me like my kind and precious wife, Mary. Because of her, I can affirm from experience Richard Baxter's definition of marriage: "It is a mercy to have a faithful friend that loves you entirely . . . to whom you may open your mind and communicate your affairs. . . . And it is a mercy to have so near a friend to be a helper to your soul and . . . to stir you up in the grace of God."[4]

May God graciously use this book to promote God-honoring preaching that addresses the real needs of his people—preaching that is not only biblically doctrinal, covenantal, historical-redemptive, and practical, but also biblically and warmly experiential both in its applicatory and discriminatory dimensions for the building up of the universal church.

---

4. Richard Baxter, as quoted in Leland Ryken, *Worldly Saints: The Puritans as They Really Were* (Grand Rapids, MI: Academie Books, 1986), 43.

PART 1

———————◎———————

Reformed Experiential Preaching Defined and Described

1

What Is Reformed Experiential Preaching?

Perhaps you have heard preaching that fills the head but not the heart. You come away better informed and educated, but little moved by God's glory to do God's will. In the worst case, such preaching puffs people up with knowledge. At its best, it is light without heat. You may also have heard preaching that touches the heart but not the head. Hearing it can be an emotionally moving experience. People leave the service excited, fired up, and feeling good. But they have zeal without knowledge. Like cotton candy, such preaching has lots of flavor but no nutritional value. It might bring people back for more (until they get sick), but it will not nurture life or develop maturity.

The greatest tragedy about these two abuses of preaching is that they sever the vital connection between truth and love in Christ: "But speaking the truth in love, [we] may grow up into him in all things, which is the head, even Christ" (Eph. 4:15). It's not just that we need both truth and love. Gospel truth has not reached its goal until it produces love. Love has no living roots without gospel truth. Therefore, the truth of Christ must be brought home to the heart by the Holy Spirit in order to produce love. That's the kind of preaching we need. That's what this book is about.

Reformed experiential preaching is not merely aesthetic, causing people to walk away thinking, "What a beautiful idea!" It is not merely informative, imparting knowledge about the Bible and theology. It is not merely emotional, warming hearts and producing strong feelings. It is not merely moralistic, instructing and exhorting in what is right and wrong. All of these elements are present in good preaching, but none of them is the heart of the matter.

Reformed experiential preaching uses the truth of Scripture to shine the glory of God into the depths of the soul to call people to live solely and wholly for God. It breaks us and remakes us. It is both exhilarating and humbling. Such preaching brings us face to face with the most glorious and delightful Being in the universe, and also face to face with our own profound wickedness. By such preaching, the holy God binds himself to sinful men heart to heart with a word of blood-bought grace.

What is Reformed experiential preaching? Let's look at it from a number of angles, then conclude by putting together a working definition.

Experiential (or Experimental) Preaching

Idealistic, Realistic, and Optimistic

The Reformers, such as John Calvin (1509–1564), talked about "experimental" Christianity.[1] Calvin paraphrases Psalm 27:9 this way: "Make me truly to experience that thou hast been near to me, and let me clearly behold thy power in saving me." He then comments, "We must observe the distinction between the theoretical knowledge derived from the Word of God and what is called the experimental knowledge of his grace." The latter is when "God shows himself present in operation," yet "he must first be sought in his Word."[2] Thus, Calvin believed that the truth of Scripture is foundational to Christianity, yet truth must be experienced in the form of "experimental knowledge." The Puritans used this same language. For example, William Perkins (1558–1602) said that the spiritual knowledge of God consists in an "experimental knowledge" of Christ's death and resurrection, "an effectual and lively knowledge, working in us new affections and inclinations."[3]

The word *experimental* comes from a Latin root meaning "to try, prove, or test." Calvin did not wonder whether Christianity would crash

---

1. Parts of this and the next few sections are revised and expanded from Joel R. Beeke, "Experiential Preaching," in *Feed My Sheep: A Passionate Plea for Preaching*, ed. Don Kistler (Morgan, PA: Soli Deo Gloria, 2002), 94–128. Used with permission.

2. John Calvin, *Commentaries of Calvin*, various translators and editors, 45 vols. (Edinburgh: Calvin Translation Society, 1846–1851; repr., 22 vols., Grand Rapids, MI: Baker, 1979) [Ps. 27:9].

3. William Perkins, *A Commentary on Galatians*, ed. Gerald T. Sheppard (1617; facsimile reprint, New York: Pilgrim Press, 1989), 270 [Gal. 4:8–11].

like an experimental airplane. The "experiment" envisaged is not testing the Bible, but testing *us* by the Bible. The root for *experimental* also shows up in the word *experiential*. Experimental preaching stresses the need to know the great truths of the Word of God by personal experience. It also tests our personal experience by the doctrines of the Bible. It brings truth to the heart to illuminate who we are, where we stand with God, how we need to be healed, and where we need to be headed.

On the day I left my six months of active duty with the Army Reserves to begin the follow-up years of weekend meetings and summer camps, a sergeant, knowing I might be called up one day, laid his large hand on my shoulder and said, "Son, if you ever have to fight in war, remember three things: first, how the battle ought to go ideally with the tactics you have been taught; second, how the battle really is going (which is often quite different from the ideal, as wars are bloody and seldom go the way that is expected); and third, the ultimate goal, victory for the American people."

This translates well into experiential (or experimental) preaching. Reformed experiential preaching explains how things ought to go in the Christian life (the ideal of Romans 8), how they actually go in Christian struggles (the reality of Romans 7), and the ultimate goal in the kingdom of glory (the optimism of Revelation 21–22). This kind of preaching reaches people where they are in the trenches and gives them tactics and hope for the battle.

Paul Helm writes of the need for experiential preaching:

> The situation [today] calls for preaching that will cover the full range of Christian experience, and a developed, experimental theology. The preaching must give guidance and instruction to Christians in terms of their actual experience. It must not deal in unrealities or treat congregations as if they lived in a different century or in wholly different circumstances. This involves taking the full measure of our modern situation . . . and entering with full sympathy into the actual experiences, the hopes and the fears, of Christian people.[4]

Discriminatory

Experimental preaching must be discriminatory. I am not referring to discrimination on the basis of skin color or ethnicity. Neither am I speaking of any form of bigotry and hatred. Discriminatory preaching aims to

---

4. Paul Helm, "Christian Experience," *Banner of Truth* 139 (April 1975): 6.

distinguish the Christian from the non-Christian so that people can diagnose their own spiritual conditions and needs. The preacher applies biblical truth to help his hearers test whether they belong to Christ and have his Spirit (Rom. 8:9; 2 Cor. 13:5).

Ministers use the "keys of the kingdom of heaven" (Matt. 16:19), entrusted to us by Christ, to open or shut the door of the kingdom by the preaching of the gospel of the forgiveness of sins (John 20:23). How does the preacher do that? The Heidelberg Catechism (Q. 84) says:

> Thus: when according to the command of Christ it is declared and publicly testified to all and every believer, that, whenever they receive promise of the gospel by a true faith, all their sins are really forgiven them of God for the sake of Christ's merits; and on the contrary, when it is declared and testified to all unbelievers, and such as do not sincerely repent, that they stand exposed to the wrath of God and eternal condemnation, so long as they are unconverted; according to which testimony of the gospel, God will judge them both in this and in the life to come.[5]

In a manner of speaking, through discriminatory preaching, the Holy Spirit brings judgment day near to the consciences of men, either to their vindication and joy or to their guilt and terror.

Preaching must also target the spiritual maturity and condition of the preacher's audience. This is no easy task, because many kinds of hearers are present. Archibald Alexander (1772–1851) writes: "The word of God should be so handled, that it may be adapted to Christians in different states and stages of the divine life; for while some Christians are like 'strong men,' others are but 'babes in Christ, who must be fed with milk, and not with strong meat.'"[6] Alexander goes on to explain how the Reformed preacher also should rightly divide the Word by making specific applications to the backsliding, the worldly minded, the afflicted, and the dying believer.[7]

Charles Bridges (1794–1869) presents three aspects of discriminatory preaching. First, preachers must distinctly "trace the line of demarcation between the Church and the world," he says. Ministers must bear in mind

---

5. Quoted in Joel R. Beeke, ed., *Doctrinal Standards, Liturgy, and Church Order* (Grand Rapids, MI: Reformation Heritage Books, 2003), 64.
6. Archibald Alexander, "Rightly Dividing the Word of Truth," in *The Princeton Pulpit*, ed. John T. Duffield (New York: Charles Scribner, 1852), 42.
7. Alexander, "Rightly Dividing the Word of Truth," 42–45.

that there are fundamentally two kinds of hearers before them—the saved and the unsaved. Bridges stresses the biblical support for this division:

> They are described by their state before God, as righteous or wicked (Prov. 14:32; Mal. 3:18)—by their knowledge or ignorance of the Gospel, as spiritual or natural men (1 Cor. 2:14–15)—by their special regard to Christ, as believers or unbelievers (Mark 16:16; John 3:18, 36)—by their interest in the Spirit of God, "being in the Spirit, or having not the Spirit of Christ" (Rom. 8:9)—by their habits of life, "walking after and minding, the things of the Spirit, or the things of the flesh" (Rom. 5:1, 5)—by their respective rules of conduct, the word of God, or "the course of this world" (Ps. 119:105; Matt. 25:46)—by the Masters whom they respectively obey, the servants of God, or the servants of Satan (Rom. 6:16)—by the road in which they travel, the narrow way or the broad road (Matt. 7:13–14)—by the ends to which their roads are carrying them, life or death—heaven or hell (Rom. 8:13; Matt. 25:46).[8]

Second, preachers must identify the line that separates the false professor (the hypocrite) from the true believer. Jesus himself draws that line sharply when he speaks of those who claim to belong to his professing church and who cry, "Lord, Lord, have we not prophesied in thy name? . . . and in thy name done many wonderful works?" only to hear his response: "I never knew you: depart from me, ye that work iniquity" (Matt. 7:22–23).

Of this second line of discrimination, Bridges writes: "Every part of the Christian character has its counterfeit. How easily are the delusions of fancy or feeling mistaken for the impressions of grace. The genuineness of the work of God must be estimated, not by the extent, but by the influence, of Scriptural knowledge—not by a fluency of gifts, but by their exercise in connexion with holiness and love."[9] David Brainerd (1718–1747) puts it this way: "Labor to distinguish clearly upon experiences and affections in religion, that you may make a difference between the 'gold' and the shining 'dross' (Prov. 25:4); I say, labor here, as ever you would be an useful minister of Christ."[10]

---

8. Charles Bridges, *The Christian Ministry* (London: Banner of Truth, 2006), 277.
9. Bridges, *The Christian Ministry*, 278.
10. Quoted in Jonathan Edwards, *The Life of David Brainerd*, in *The Works of Jonathan Edwards*, vol. 7, *The Life of David Brainerd*, ed. Norman Pettit (New Haven, CT: Yale University Press, 1984), 495.

Ministers need to help their hearers rightly examine themselves. Second Corinthians 13:5 says, "Examine yourselves, whether ye be in the faith; prove your own selves." Pastors must not assume or presume that all churchgoers, including children, are saved. They also are to avoid presumed church "unregeneration," as if only a few who have professed faith in Christ are truly saved. Rather, preachers are to present repeatedly before their people the biblical marks of those who have been born again and have come to Christ by way of saving faith and genuine repentance.

Third, Bridges says, preachers "must also regard the different individualities of profession within the Church."[11] Like Jesus, preachers must distinguish between the blade, the ear, and the full corn in the ear (Mark 4:28). Like Paul, they must differentiate between babes and adults in grace (1 Cor. 3:1). Like John, they must preach to various believers as little children, young men, and fathers in grace (1 John 2:12–14).

Alexander makes the case for discriminatory preaching. He writes: "The promises and threatenings contained in the Scriptures [must] be applied to the characters to which they properly belong. How often do we hear a preacher expatiating on the rich consolations of the exceeding great and precious promises of God, when no mortal can tell, from anything which he says, to whom they are applicable. In much of preaching, there is a vague and indiscriminate application of the special promises of the covenant of grace, as though all who heard them were true Christians, and had a claim to the comfort which they offer." After concluding that, in true preaching, "the saint and the sinner are clearly distinguished by decisive scripture marks, so that every one may have a fair opportunity of ascertaining to which class he belongs, and what prospects lie before him," Alexander goes on to lament:

> It is much to be regretted that this accurate discrimination in preaching has gone so much out of use in our times. It is but seldom that we hear a discourse from the pulpit which is calculated to afford much aid to Christians in ascertaining their own true character; of which will serve to detect the hypocrite and formalist, and drive them from all their false refuges. In the best days of the reformed churches, such discriminating delineation of character, by the light of Scripture, formed an important part of almost every sermon. But we are now more attentive to the rules of rhetoric than to the marks of true religion. How do Owen, Fla-

---

11. Bridges, *The Christian Ministry*, 279.

vel, Boston, and Erskine abound in marks of distinction between the true and false professor? And the most distinguished preachers of our own country,—the Mathers, Shepards, Stoddards, Edwardses, as also the Blairs, Tennents, Davies, and Dickinsons, were wise in so dividing the word of truth, that all might receive their portion in due season.[12]

In short, discriminatory preaching must remain faithful to God's Word. Grace is to be offered indiscriminately to all (Matt. 13:24–30); however, the divine acts, marks, and fruits of grace that God works in his people must be explained to encourage the elect to know themselves aright and to uncover the false hopes of the hypocrites. As Bishop Joseph Hall (1574–1656) says of the minister, "His wisdom must discern betwixt his sheep and wolves; in his sheep, betwixt the wholesome and unsound; in the unsound, betwixt the weak and the tainted; in the tainted, betwixt the natures, qualities, degrees of the disease, and infection; and to all these he must know to administer a word in season. He hath antidotes for all temptations, counsels for all doubts, evictions for all errors; for all languishings, encouragements."[13]

Robert Hall (1764–1831) says that it is difficult to decide "which we should most anxiously guard against, the infusion of a false peace, or the inflaming of the wounds which we ought to heal."[14] Little wonder, then, that Richard Baxter (1615–1691) warns preachers that when, as spiritual physicians, they apply the wrong spiritual medication to their parishioners, they can become murderers of souls, which has grave ramifications for eternity.[15] Preachers must be honest with every soul and strive to bring them and the touchstone of Holy Scripture together.

Such preaching teaches us that unless our religion is genuinely experienced, we will perish. Experience itself does not save us, but the Christ who saves us must be experienced personally as the foundation of our eternal hope (Matt. 7:22–27).

Applicatory

Experiential preaching is applicatory. It applies the text to every aspect of the listener's life, promoting religion that is not just a "form of godliness"

---

12. Alexander, "Rightly Dividing the Word of Truth," 40–42.
13. Joseph Hall, "To My Brother Mr. Sa. Hall," Epistle 5 in *The Works of the Right Reverend Joseph Hall*, ed. Philip Wynter (Oxford: Oxford University Press, 1863), 6:231.
14. Robert Hall, "On the Discouragements and Supports of the Christian Ministry," in *The Works of the Rev. Robert Hall* (New York: G. & C. & H. Carvill, 1830), 2:138.
15. Quoted in Bridges, *The Christian Ministry*, 280.

but also the "power" of God (2 Tim. 3:5). Robert Burns (1789–1869) says that experiential religion is "Christianity brought home to 'men's business and bosoms.'" He writes, "Christianity should not only be known, and understood, and believed, but also felt, and enjoyed, and practically applied."[16]

Paul was never content merely to declare the truth, so he could write to the Thessalonians that his "gospel came not unto you in word only, but also in power, and in the Holy Ghost, and in much assurance" (1 Thess. 1:5). To use Baxter's language, Paul wanted to screw the truth into the hearts and minds of men and women. Baxter writes, "It would grieve one to the heart to hear what excellent doctrine some ministers have in hand, while yet they let it die in their hands for want of close [searching] and lively [living] application."[17] If only it could be said of more ministers' preaching today what one might say of the preaching of Jonathan Edwards (1703–1758): all his doctrine was application and all his application was doctrine.

Application is the major emphasis of experiential preaching. The Reformers and Puritans spent many times more effort in application than in discrimination. Many preachers today fall far short in this area. They have been trained to be good expositors, but they have not been trained in the classroom or by the Holy Spirit to bring the truth home to the heart. That is why, when you hear certain preachers, you say to yourself: "Oh, he can really handle the Word of God well, but he stopped just when I thought he was starting. He didn't bring it home to me. I seem to have escaped the preacher's notice altogether. What should I do with the sermon now?"

Some preachers say, "Application is the Holy Spirit's job, not mine." But that is not the way the Bible handles truth. People need to be spoon-fed when you bring them the Word of God, not only in your exposition but also in your application. They need help to know what the truth implies for what they must do and how they must do it. If you read Calvin's sermons, you stand amazed at his constant attention to application. Take his book of sermons on Deuteronomy. It would not surprise me if ten to twenty times per sermon he says, "Now this is to teach us that," "This is how we are to handle that," or, "This is the way we are to live out that."

---

16. Robert Burns, introduction to the *Works of Thomas Halyburton* (London: Thomas Tegg, 1835), xiv–xv. The expression "come home to men's business and bosoms" comes from scientist and philosopher Francis Bacon (1561–1626) in his dedication to later editions of his *Essays*.

17. Richard Baxter, *The Reformed Pastor* (Edinburgh: Banner of Truth, 1974), 147.

Charles H. Spurgeon (1834–1892) exaggerates only slightly when he says, "Where the application begins, there the sermon begins."[18] However, the best preachers include application *throughout* their sermons, not only when concluding. Bridges writes:

> The method of perpetual application, where the subject will admit of it, is probably best calculated for effect—applying each head distinctly; and addressing separate classes [or groups] at the close with suitable exhortation, warning, or encouragement. The Epistle to the Hebrews [itself a series of sermons] is a complete model of this scheme. Argumentative throughout, connected in its train of reasoning, and logical in its deductions—each successive link is interrupted by some personal and forcible conviction; while the continuity of the chain is preserved entire to the end.[19]

The Puritan preachers, who learned from the Reformers, were masters of the art of application. This art is beautifully summarized in a short chapter titled "Of the Preaching of the Word" in the Directory for the Public Worship of God, composed by the Calvinistic and Puritan Westminster divines. They wrote, "He [the preacher] is not to rest in general doctrine, although never so much cleared and confirmed, but to bring it home to special use, by application to his hearers."[20] I will explore the wise counsel of the Westminster divines in a later chapter.

Finally, it needs to be said that applicatory preaching is often costly preaching. As has often been said, when John the Baptist preached *generally*, Herod heard him gladly. But when John applied his preaching *particularly* (criticizing Herod's adulterous relationship with his brother's wife), he lost his head (Mark 6:14–29). Both internally in a preacher's own conscience, as well as in the consciences of his people, a fearless application of God's truth will exact a price. And yet, how needful such preaching is! One day, every preacher will stand before God's judgment seat to give an account of how he handled God's Word among the flock of sheep entrusted to him. Woe to that preacher who has not striven to bring home the Word of God to the souls and consciences of his hearers.

---

18. Quoted in John A. Broadus, *A Treatise on the Preparation and Delivery of Sermons*, ed. Edwin C. Dargan (New York: A. C. Armstrong, 1898), 245.
19. Bridges, *The Christian Ministry*, 275.
20. *Westminster Confession of Faith* (Glasgow: Free Presbyterian Publications, 1994), 380.

Preachers, I urge you to remember that we are not to speak *before* people but *to* people. Application is not only critical, it is an essential part of true preaching and, in many respects, the main thing to be done. And those who fear God will want God's Word personally administered to them. As Daniel Webster says, "When I attend upon the teachings of the gospel, I wish to have it made a personal matter—*a personal matter—a personal matter.*"[21]

Biblical, Doctrinal, Experiential, and Practical

Experiential preaching, then, teaches that the Christian faith must be experienced, tasted, and lived through the saving power of the Holy Spirit. It stresses the knowledge of scriptural truth "which [is] able to make [us] wise unto salvation through faith which is in Christ Jesus" (2 Tim. 3:15). Specifically, such preaching teaches that Christ, the living Word (John 1:1) and the very embodiment of the truth, must be experientially known and embraced. It proclaims the need for sinners to experience God in the person of his Son. As John 17:3 says, "And this is life eternal, that they might know thee the only true God, and Jesus Christ, whom thou hast sent." The word *know* in this text, as elsewhere in the Bible, does not indicate mere casual acquaintance but a deep, abiding relationship. For example, Genesis 4:1 uses the word *know* to express marital intimacy: "And Adam knew Eve his wife; and she conceived, and bare Cain." Experiential preaching stresses the intimate, personal knowledge of God in Christ.

Biblical preaching must combine doctrinal, experiential, and practical elements. This subject was discussed by John Newton (1725–1807) and other evangelical ministers at one of their Eclectic Society meetings in London in 1798. John Clayton (1754–1843), an English independent minister, raised the question, "What are we to understand by doctrinal, experimental, and practical preaching?" He pointed out that doctrinal preaching by itself tends to produce argumentative thinkers, experiential preaching can overemphasize our inward feelings to the neglect of truth and action, and practical preaching may become man centered and self-righteous, belittling Christ and the gospel. Clayton said that all three components must have their place in preaching, quoting Thomas Bradbury (1677–1759) as say-

---

21. Quoted in "Funeral of Mr. Webster," *The New York Daily Times*, Oct. 30, 1852.

ing, "Religion is doctrinal in the Bible; experimental in the heart; and practical in the life."[22]

John Goode (1738–1790) said, "In the members of our flock, there would be sight, feeling, and obedience; and to produce these, all three—doctrinal, experimental, and practical preaching—must be combined in their proper proportion." Newton declared the organic and vital unity of these three, saying, "Doctrine is the trunk, experience the branches, practice the fruit." He warned that without the doctrine of Christ we say nothing more than pagan philosophers.[23]

Thomas Scott (1747–1821) also warned that there is a false way to handle each dimension of preaching: doctrines may not be biblical truth or may be only half-truths, which effectively are lies; experience may follow human prescriptions or be based on visions, impressions, or man-made schemes; and we may substitute mere morality for evangelical or gospel-empowered obedience.[24]

So we see that Reformed experiential preaching aims to bring together the doctrinal, experiential, and practical dimensions as one unified whole. Though we must humbly admit that in our sermons we often do not attain the kind of balance and completeness we strive for, we must stress that we cannot neglect any aspect of biblical preaching—doctrinal, experiential, and practical—without damaging the others, for each one flows naturally out of the others.

Walking with Our Triune God and Savior

Reformed experiential preaching grounded in the Word of God is God centered (theocentric) rather than man centered (anthropocentric). Some people accuse the Puritans of being man centered in their passion for godly experience. But as J. I. Packer argues, the Puritans were not interested in obsessing over their own experience but in entering into fellowship with the triune God. Packer writes, "The thought of communion with God takes us to the very heart of Puritan theology and religion."[25] The Puritans avoided "false mysticism" by approaching communion with God "objectively and theocentrically." They grounded the Christian's experience upon

---

22. Quoted in John H. Pratt, ed., *The Thought of Evangelical Leaders: Notes of the Discussions of The Eclectic Society, London, During the Years 1798–1814* (1856; repr., Edinburgh: Banner of Truth, 1978), 77–78.
23. Quoted in Pratt, ed., *Thought of Evangelical Leaders*, 79.
24. Quoted in Pratt, ed., *Thought of Evangelical Leaders*, 80.
25. J. I. Packer, *A Quest for Godliness: The Puritan Vision of the Christian Life* (Wheaton, IL: Crossway, 1990), 201.

the objective truth of how God saves sinners through Christ. They also shaped experience according to the form of the Trinity, relating to Father, Son, and Holy Spirit as the gospel reveals the triune God.[26]

This passion for fellowship with the triune God means that experiential preaching not only addresses the believer's conscience but also his relationship with others in the church and the world. If experiential preaching led me to examine only my experiences and my relationship with God, it would fall short of impacting my interaction with family members, church members, and others in society. Self-centered preaching produces self-centered hearers. Instead, true experiential preaching brings a believer into the realm of vital Christian experience, drawing him away from himself and promoting a love for God and his glory as well as a burning passion to declare that love to others around him. A believer so instructed cannot help but be evangelistic, since vital Christian experience and a heart for missions are inseparable.

In other words, my life is an open epistle of the grace of God. I want to speak to others about the Lord. It is an oxymoron to say that I am an experiential Christian and not be an evangelistic Christian. These two things belong together. When we preach experientially, and people experience the power of God unto salvation, the whole congregation becomes evangelistic. People learn to treasure truth so much that they want to share it. The Father, Christ, and his Spirit become real for them under experiential preaching. God's glory fills them and moves them so that they want to start evangelistic programs and talk to their unsaved relatives about Christ—out of the abundance of the heart the mouth speaks (Luke 6:45).

In sum, Reformed experimental preaching brings the entire range of Christian living into connection with the Savior of the world. Where Christ is truly known as Savior, he is also served as Lord. With the Spirit's blessing, the mission is to transform the believer in all that he is and does so that he becomes more and more like the Savior.

Bible-Based Experience

Experiential knowledge of God is never divorced from Scripture. According to Isaiah 8:20, all of our beliefs, including our experiences,

---

26. Packer, *Quest for Godliness*, 204; see John Owen, "Of Communion with God the Father, Son, and Holy Ghost," in *The Works of John Owen*, ed. William H. Goold (repr., Edinburgh: Banner of Truth, 1965), 2:1–274.

must be tested by the witness of Holy Scripture. Martin Luther (1483–1546) reputedly quipped that if we can't find our experiences in the Bible, they are not from the Lord but from the Devil. That is really what the word *experimental* intends to convey. Just as a scientific experiment tests a hypothesis against a body of evidence, so experimental preaching involves examining experience in the light of the Word of God.

Of course, there is also the danger that ministers may discriminate and apply the Bible, but not exegete and expound it. They fall into what I call *experientialism*, where experience becomes the savior (though often only implicitly). We do not preach experience, but Christ Jesus our Lord from the Holy Scriptures (2 Cor. 4:5). As a safeguard, we should always be preaching out of a particular text of Scripture, showing what God has said in it and how that truth applies to the hearers. However, I have heard ministers insert into every sermon a set form of what a sinner experiences when God converts him, whether the particular Scripture text being expounded taught it or not. Other preachers fall into a similar trap by constantly preaching some particular aspect of experience. This does not make it true experiential preaching!

An experiential preacher addresses the whole range of the Christian's experience by preaching through the whole range of Scripture. He knows how to draw out the Christian's experience from each particular text, be it in the area of misery, the area of deliverance, the area of thankfulness, or the area of wrestling with backsliding. The experiential preacher knows how Scripture promotes vital religion. This is what Paul refers to when he says that "all scripture," being breathed out by God through his Spirit, is "profitable for doctrine, for reproof, for correction, for instruction in righteousness" (2 Tim. 3:16).

When a preacher preaches this way, something resonates from the pulpit into the believer's soul. The believer who has a real relationship with God feels this preaching to be a great force of transformation—it moves him, challenges him, exhorts him, and molds him. He feels the reality of the Holy Spirit's unction in such preaching. Such preaching, then, becomes "the power of God unto salvation" (Rom. 1:16).

Such preaching stands by the gates of hell, as it were, to proclaim that those who are not born again shall soon walk through these gates to dwell forever in the homelessness of the abyss—unless they repent. But such preaching also stands at the gates of heaven, preaching that the regenerate, who by God's preserving grace persevere in holiness, will soon walk through into eternal glory and unceasing communion with God.

Ask for the Old Paths, Where Is the Good Way

As I will show in the chapters of the second part of this book, experiential preaching is part of the grand tradition flowing out of the revival of biblical godliness in the sixteenth-century Reformation. Until the mid-nineteenth century, many Reformed ministers preached experientially. Baptist minister and educator Francis Wayland (1796–1865) wrote in 1857:

> From the manner in which our ministers entered upon the work, it is evident that it must have been the prominent object of their lives to convert men to God. . . . They were remarkable for what was called experimental preaching. They told much of the exercises of the human soul under the influence of the truth of the gospel:
>
> - the feeling of a sinner while under the convicting power of the truth;
> - the various subterfuges to which he resorted when aware of his danger;
> - the successive applications of truth by which he was driven out of all of them;
> - the despair of the soul when it found itself wholly without a refuge;
> - its final submission to God, and simple reliance on Christ;
> - the joys of the new birth and the earnestness of the soul to introduce others to the happiness which it has now for the first time experienced;
> - the trials of the soul when it found itself an object of reproach and persecution among those whom it loved best;
> - the process of sanctification;
> - the devices of Satan to lead us into sin;
> - the mode in which the attacks of the adversary may be resisted;
> - the danger of backsliding, with its evidences, and the means of recovery from it.

Wayland concludes with these sad words: "These remarks show the tendency of the class of preachers which seems now to be passing away."[27]

How different experiential preaching is from what we often hear today. I live in a city with more than one hundred Reformed churches (perhaps more Reformed churches than any city other than Seoul, South Korea). But I would guess that if you gathered us all together and asked ministers to raise their hands if they preach Reformed experiential sermons, at least half would ask, "What is that?" Things have changed dramatically in Reformed circles since the mid-nineteenth century.

The Word of God is preached too often in a way that cannot transform listeners because the preacher fails to discriminate and to apply. Such preaching is reduced to a lecture, mere catering to what people want to hear, or the kind of subjectivism that is divorced from the foundation of scriptural truth. It fails to biblically explain what the Reformers and Puritans called vital religion: how a sinner must be stripped of his self-righteousness, driven to Christ alone for salvation, and led to the joy of simple reliance upon Christ. It fails to show how a sinner encounters the plague of indwelling sin, battles against backsliding, and gains victory by faith in Christ.

Experiential preaching, rightly understood, is transforming because it accurately reflects the vital experience of the children of God (Rom. 5:1–11), clearly explains the marks and fruits of the saving grace necessary for a believer (Matt. 5:3–12; Gal. 5:22–23), and sets before believer and unbeliever alike their eternal futures (Rev. 21:1–8) and their calling at the present hour.

That kind of preaching is very different from much contemporary preaching, which never deals with the experience of the soul. It always stays on a shallow level:

"You must believe."
"Yes, I believe."
"OK, you are a Christian."

This preaching does not talk about the experience of losing my life, dying to my own righteousness, and finding my life in the righteousness of Christ. Contemporary preaching, though not without some value,

---

27. Francis Wayland, *Notes on the Principles and Practices of Baptist Churches* (New York: Sheldon, Blakeman, and Co., 1857), 40–43. I have separated Wayland's paragraph into bullet points for easier reading.

often fails to transform people because of a lack of discrimination and application of truth to the heart.

Preaching to Satisfy Spiritual Taste Buds

Ultimately, Reformed experiential preaching is not just a homiletic method but a spiritual exercise of satisfying the appetite of the soul. The Scriptures use the language of sense perception to communicate that spiritual realities produce true experiences of the soul, not just mental ideas. The Bible says, "He that doeth good is of God: but he that doeth evil hath not seen God" (3 John 11; cf. 1 John 3:6). No one can see God in the literal sense of perceiving with the vision of the eyes (John 1:18; 1 John 4:12, 20). John is speaking of the vision of the soul, the seeing of God's grace and glory by faith in Christ (John 1:14).

Similarly, the Lord spoke of having "ears to hear,"[28] not referring to physical ears but "the hearing of faith" by the soul (Gal. 3:2, 5). The gospel is compared to the stench of death to the perishing, but to the sweet fragrance of life to the saved (2 Cor. 2:15–16). Only the Holy Spirit can produce spiritual senses that apprehend God in the Word.

Perhaps the most vivid sensory metaphor for spiritual experience is that of taste. Psalm 119:103 says: "How sweet are thy words unto my taste! yea, sweeter than honey to my mouth!" Jeremiah says, "Thy words were found, and I did eat them; and thy word was unto me the joy and rejoicing of mine heart: for I am called by thy name, O LORD God of hosts" (Jer. 15:16). We read in 1 Peter 2:2–3, "As newborn babes, desire the sincere milk of the word, that ye may grow thereby: if so be ye have tasted that the Lord is gracious."

Edwards writes that when God saves a person, he gives him "a real sense of the excellency of God, and Jesus Christ, and of the work of redemption, and the ways and works of God revealed in the gospel"—"the sense of the heart" that brings "pleasure and delight." He illustrates, "There is a difference between having a rational judgment that honey is sweet, and having a sense of its sweetness."[29]

Herman Hoeksema (1886–1965) explains the difference between theoretical knowledge and experiential knowledge in this manner:

---

28. Deut. 29:4; Matt. 11:15; 13:9, 43; Mark 4:9, 23; 7:16; Luke 8:8; 14:35.
29. Jonathan Edwards, "A Divine and Supernatural Light," in *The Works of Jonathan Edwards*, vol. 17, *Sermons and Discourses 1730–1733*, ed. Mark Valeri (New Haven, CT: Yale University Press, 1999), 413–14.

A dietitian may be able to analyze thoroughly every item on a menu and inform you exactly as to the number and kinds of vitamins each dish contains. But if he has cancer of the stomach, he cannot taste the food and enjoy it; neither is he able to digest it and derive the necessary strength from it. In contrast, a man with a hungry stomach may sit at the table with the dietitian, knowing absolutely nothing about vitamins; but he will order his meal, relish his food, and appropriate it to himself in such a way that he is refreshed and strengthened.[30]

Such is the difference between having bare intellectual knowledge about Christ, which any unbeliever might have, and knowing Christ in a personal and life-changing way, as only a believer can. Reformed experiential preaching is more than reading the menu to people and giving them a nutritional report. It is dishing out hot food in all its rich aromas and tastes to satisfy the hungry soul.

Preaching from Heart to Heart

Experiential preaching often grows out of the preacher's own experience of Christ in the midst of his sorrows and sins. It is one thing for you to preach about the intercession of Christ and ask, "Isn't it wonderful, congregation, that Jesus is at the right hand of the Father, interceding for you every single second?" That is not a bad statement. People might walk away and say, "Wasn't that wonderful? That's comforting." But how much richer is your preaching if you have experienced in the depths of your soul what it means to be brought to an end of your own prayer. You have been at your wit's end in a situation for which you couldn't find a solution. You have learned to cry to God Almighty, and God has assured you, through his Word, that his Son is at his right hand, interceding for you. If you have heart knowledge of that comfort, then you are going to preach it with far more power and energy than if you are preaching it only from head knowledge.

It is very hard to explain the difference in words, but I can tell you that I have experienced it. I preached about the intercession of Christ with much greater liberty after I felt so needy and helpless I hardly knew how to pray except to cling to the promise that "he ever liveth to make intercession for them" (Heb. 7:25). Then I was able to say, "Lord, if that

---

30. Herman Hoeksema, *Reformed Dogmatics*, 2nd ed. (Grandville, MI: Reformed Free Publishing Association, 2005), 2:75.

is true, then right now, when I can hardly pray and am at my wit's end, Thou art praying for me!" Comfort swept over me. Then I was able not merely to describe Christ's intercession from my head to my people's heads, but to preach it from my heart to their hearts.

A major element in this process is growing in humility. Our native pride constantly pushes away heart religion and replaces it with a superficial form of godliness lacking the power of true religion. We all by nature prefer either to reject the Bible entirely or merely clean the outside of the cup while the inside remains filthy. God must break into our whitewashed tombs with the gift of humility before we can truly experience his grace. A key aspect of Reformed experiential preaching is that the knowledge of God humbles the preacher and those to whom he preaches. Calvin points out that such humility arises directly from seeing the Lord as he is:

> Again, it is certain that man never achieves a clear knowledge of himself unless he has first looked upon God's face and then descends from contemplating Him to scrutinize himself. For we always seem to ourselves righteous and upright and wise and holy—this pride is innate in all of us—unless by clear proofs we stand convinced of our own unrighteousness, foulness, folly and impurity. Moreover, we are not thus convinced if we look merely to ourselves and not also to the Lord, who is the sole standard by which this judgment must be measured.[31]

We must constantly keep in view our depravity and Christ's righteousness. It is critical that these be contrasted so that we see the Savior in all his glory and beauty. As long as we declare over and over that his righteousness exceeds our unrighteousness and his holiness exceeds our perversity, then all our hope is in Christ. Nevertheless, it is critical for a preacher to stress our sinful depravity often in preaching, because the Holy Spirit uses such preaching to drive us to Christ repeatedly as the only remedy for our indwelling sin. Under such heart-convicting preaching, we see deeper into our souls' experience: our selfishness, pride, unbelief, and disobedience. We see more deeply who God is in all his riches, glory, beauty, and grace for sinners. Then we both preach experientially and live experientially.

---

31. John Calvin, *Institutes of the Christian Religion*, trans. Ford Lewis Battles, ed. John T. McNeill, Library of Christian Classics, vols. 20–21 (Philadelphia: Westminster, 1960), 1.1.2.

Conclusion: A Tentative Definition

So what then is Reformed experiential preaching? I have touched briefly on a number of its ingredients. It is preaching that:

- tests genuine Christian experience by the standard of biblical truth—idealistically, realistically, and optimistically;
- draws lines distinguishing between believers and unbelievers;
- makes frequent and wise application of truth to life;
- balances biblical, doctrinal, experiential, and practical elements;
- cultivates a life of communion with our God and Savior;
- builds experience upon the foundation of Holy Scripture, God's Word;
- goes beyond contemporary superficiality into the deep wisdom of old paths;
- offers food to satisfy the new spiritual sense of the believer's soul; and
- touches the heart with the bitterness of sin and the sweetness of grace.

You can see that there is a multidimensional richness to Reformed experiential preaching. Yet it is not that complicated. All these ingredients, when blended together and baked in the fires of the Spirit and suffering, produce a single, satisfying loaf of delicious bread.

I will examine these matters in more detail in the rest of this book. For now, I can offer the following tentative definition: Reformed experiential preaching is preaching that applies the truth of God to the hearts of people to show how things ought to go, do go, and ultimately will go in the Christian's experience with respect to God and his neighbors— including his family members, his fellow church members, and people in the world around him. Even more simply, we could say that the Reformed experiential preacher receives God's Word into his heart and then preaches it to the minds, hearts, and lives of his people. I am not saying that preachers who speak mostly from head knowledge are useless—far from it. They may accurately instruct people in God's truth. They may edify the church. We must remember that we do not change people by our experiences. The Holy Spirit changes people, and he can use even defective preaching of Christ (Phil. 1:15–18). But how much more can he use preachers whose hearts burn with love. If the Spirit intends to work in the hearers of the Word, he generally works first in the preacher of the

Word. That's why wise preachers so covet the prayers of God's people for the filling of the Holy Spirit that they may preach powerfully (Acts 4:8, 29–33; Eph. 6:18–20).

May the Holy Spirit fill you now, dear reader, and may he fill you more and more as you proceed through the rest of this book so that Christ will be magnified in the eyes of your faith, and in your life and ministry.

2

Preaching from Head to Heart

Words matter. A man was enjoying a visit with some friends one evening outside. As it got darker, the air grew chilly. He noticed that one woman did not have a coat or jacket on. Finally he asked her in genuine concern, "Aren't you getting cold?" The problem was that she did not hear the *c*. She thought he had said rather bluntly, "Aren't you getting *old?*" Needless to say, she did not react quite the way he expected.

Many a preacher has had the experience of thinking he said one thing only to discover later that people heard something quite different. We know that we must be careful with our words. In the last chapter, I used terms such as *heart knowledge, experimental,* and *experiential.* Before I go on, I need to explain what I mean by these words. Then we will be able to proceed with greater clarity to consider why Reformed experiential preaching is needed.

What Is the Difference between "Head" Knowledge and "Heart" Knowledge?

These are not the most academic or scholarly terms; rather, they are practical terms that people can understand. By "head" knowledge we mean knowledge that is strictly intellectual or theoretical, and by "heart" knowledge we mean knowledge that is brought home to our souls with power to produce fruit in our lives.

Scripture teaches us in a number of places that we need head knowledge. We cannot be saved without knowledge of the gospel. Paul writes:

"How then shall they call on him in whom they have not believed? and how shall they believe in him of whom they have not heard? and how shall they hear without a preacher? . . . So then faith cometh by hearing, and hearing by the word of God" (Rom. 10:14, 17). Christ came to give us knowledge and understanding of the truth (John 18:37; 1 John 5:20). We cannot float heart knowledge in the air. True heart knowledge is rooted in head knowledge.

Yet by itself, head knowledge is insufficient to save us or make us holy; the Spirit must apply truth to the heart. The heart is the source from which all our choices and actions flow. Proverbs 4:23 says, "Keep thy heart with all diligence; for out of it are the issues of life." All sin originates in the heart (Mark 7:21–23). The heart is the seat of saving faith: "For with the heart man believeth unto righteousness" (Rom. 10:10). Wisdom resides in the heart, as is evident from the biblical expressions "wise in heart" or "wise of heart" (Prov. 10:8; 11:29; 16:21).

We might say the difference is in depth and dominion. Christ compares the preaching of the Word to the sowing of seed (Matt. 13:1–23). Some seed falls on the packed-down earth of a pathway. The truth lies on the surface of the heart, but the heart does not receive it. This, as our Lord explains, refers to the one who "heareth the word of the kingdom, and understandeth it not" (v. 19). Satan snatches it away so that it makes no impression on the soil at all. Other seed falls on rocky soil and makes a good beginning. The heart receives the Word with some understanding and even "with joy" (v. 20). But the truth has no "root" (v. 21), which suggests that its impact does not reach the deep parts of the soul. As a result, suffering or persecution eradicates its influence.

Jesus presents a third case in which the seed falls among thorns, symbolizing "the care of this world" and "the deceitfulness of riches" (Matt. 13:22). The word *care* speaks of sinful affections, and *deceitfulness* of false beliefs. These weeds still dominate the heart and destroy the fruitfulness of the truth. By implication, when the seed falls on good soil and bears fruit, it has attained both depth and dominion in the heart of man. Our Lord says this is a kind of knowledge ("he that heareth the word, and understandeth it," v. 23) that the unsaved do not possess ("hearing ye shall hear, and shall not understand," v. 14).

So on the one hand, we must sow the seed. We must spread the truth. Without evangelistic preaching, people will not be saved. We cannot expect the kingdom to progress in the world without the preaching of the gospel any more than a farmer should expect a field to produce a crop of wheat without his sowing of wheat seed in it. People need head knowledge.

On the other hand, merely sowing the seed does not produce a crop. The land must be cleared, rocks removed, vegetation burned off, and the soil broken up. Jeremiah 4:3 says, "For thus saith the LORD to the men of Judah and Jerusalem, Break up your fallow ground, and sow not among thorns." Weeds must be pulled up before and after planting. The clouds must rain down water, and the sun must shine with heat. All these means give the seed deep roots and the ability to dominate so that it will produce living fruit from the heart.

We may also say that the difference between head and heart knowledge is akin to the difference between knowing something about a person and knowing him personally. The Bible sometimes uses the word *know* of factual knowledge (Gen. 27:2), but it often uses *know* to reflect a relationship, not just the possession of facts or information (Gen. 4:1). This is especially true of the relationship between the Lord and his people.[1]

Let me give you an illustration. A ministerial author who was very influential in my life walked into a bookstore in the Netherlands. He saw that the shop had his books for sale. He was curious about how his books were priced, so he picked one up and turned it over. Meanwhile, the store clerk came over and asked whether he knew the book's author. The minister said coyly, "I think I do." The clerk said that he also knew him. The author replied, "No, you don't know him." The clerk was puzzled, so the minister said: "If you knew the author, you would have greeted him when he walked in the door. I am the author!"

At that, the clerk turned red in the face and sputtered: "But I feel like I know you. I read your book."

"Yes," the author replied," but you don't know *me*."

Many people think that they know the Lord because they have read his Book, but they do not know him. And when he comes at judgment day, he will say to them, "I never knew you: depart from me, ye that work iniquity" (Matt. 7:23). Mere knowledge puffs up and has no power to save us or change our lives. Everything hinges on knowing the Lord with grateful love because we are known by him in his gracious love (1 Cor. 8:1–3; Gal. 4:9).

---

1. Gen. 18:19; Ex. 33:12, 17; Ps. 1:6; 9:10; Jer. 9:24; 22:16; 31:34; Dan. 11:32; Hos. 2:20; 5:4; 6:6; Matt. 7:23; 11:27; John 17:3; etc.

Furthermore, Christians can confuse increasing in knowledge about the Lord with increasing in godliness. There are university and seminary professors who can run circles around you with their knowledge of the Bible, theology, history, or ministry skills. There are pastors who have amazing insights into how to make churches into successful organizations. But they might have little heart knowledge and might even be spiritual midgets, if not hypocrites. It is entirely possible to increase in head knowledge and yet not increase in "the knowledge of his will in all wisdom and spiritual understanding; that ye might walk worthy of the Lord unto all pleasing" (Col. 1:9–10).

So what then is heart knowledge? It is that knowledge of God acquired as the result of a personal encounter with Christ by the work of the Spirit through the Word (2 Cor. 3:17–18; 4:6). This is what we call "saving knowledge." It is knowledge that stirs and transforms the heart. It bears fruit Godward. It tastes and sees that God is good, and leads us to the blessedness of trusting in him (Ps. 34:8). Heart knowledge is a God-worked appetite for God as he reveals himself in his Word. We read in Jeremiah 15:16a, "Thy words were found, and I did eat them; and thy word was unto me the joy and rejoicing of mine heart."

Heart knowledge is not a mystical feeling without content. Heart knowledge feasts on truth made real to the inner man. The joy of the believer is found in God himself (Ps. 144:15; 146:5). When we experience saving heart knowledge, then all the truths in the Bible become real and vivid to us. God becomes a dominating presence in, over, and around our lives. Sin becomes an unbearable burden and a loathsome evil. Christ becomes altogether lovely, and his saving work appears absolutely necessary. Grace is esteemed, embraced, and exulted in.

Head knowledge is not evil in itself. Most of the great Christian ministers and leaders of the Reformation and Post-Reformation eras were highly educated men. They valued a thorough Christian education. But this education must be sanctified by the Holy Spirit to our hearts. Head knowledge remains insufficient for our spiritual good without the Spirit's heart application. That is why the writers of previous centuries counseled people to seek to fill their heads with knowledge while seeking the Lord in hope that he would bless it to their hearts.

Preachers should ask themselves, "Am I preaching almost entirely to people's heads?" We dare not promote a cold intellectualism in the church. On the other hand, we should also ask, "Am I preaching so as to root heart experience in head knowledge?" If not, then we may be leading people into a dangerous form of mysticism that will ultimately replace the Bible with subjectivism and replace faith in the saving work of Christ with a quest for mere experience. The goal for biblical preaching is to build a bridge between head and heart so that knowledge and affection do daily commerce in the marketplace of the soul, each one commending the other to us for our growth in grace.

Is There a Difference between *Experimental* and *Experiential*?

Generally speaking, there is no difference between these terms. Both have been used to describe the Christian experience of God as he is revealed in the Bible. One old dictionary defined "experimental religion" as the "practical experience of the influence of religion upon the powers and operations of the soul."[2] However, this meaning of *experimental* is archaic and no longer found in the dictionary. Today in English we use the word *experiential* to describe such things. But the Reformed forefathers used *experimental* often, and understanding why they did so enriches our perspective on spiritual experience.

Both the words *experimental* and *experiential* have their roots in the idea of knowledge verified by testing something in real life. The term *experimental* (Latin *experimentalis*) comes from *experimentum*, meaning "trial." It was derived from the verb *experior*, "to try, test, or prove." This verb can also mean "to know by experience." It gave rise to the noun *experientia*, meaning "experiment or knowledge gained by testing something."

Thus, experiential preaching has a great deal of appeal to people. They are always looking for something that is real, that works, and that is not merely theoretical but capable of being experienced. At the same time, faithful believers seek to test or verify all things by the Bible.

John Calvin uses *experimental* (Latin *experimentalis*) and *experiential* (Latin *experientia*) interchangeably to refer to our testing of our experience of God for its reality according to the standards of Holy Scripture. The Bible is the measure of all experience, as Isaiah 8:20 says: "To the law and to the testimony: if they speak not according to this word, it is because there is no light in them."[3]

---

2. "Experimental," I.2.c, in *The Oxford English Dictionary* (Oxford: Clarendon Press, 1933), 3:431.
3. See Willem Balke, "The Word of God and *Experientia* according to Calvin," in *Calvinus Ecclesiae Doctor*, ed. Wilhelm H. Neuser (Kampen: Kok, 1978), 20–21.

Whereas faith gives us certainty that God's words are true, experience brings heavenly realities into the heart. Faith opens a window to see into heaven, but experiential knowledge brings a foretaste of heaven into the soul. Calvin says:

> But it is to be observed, that there are two kinds of knowledge—the knowledge of faith, and what they call experimental knowledge. The knowledge of faith is that by which the godly feel assured that God is true—that what he has promised is indubitable; and this knowledge at the same time penetrates beyond the world, and goes far above the heavens, that it may know hidden things; for our salvation is concealed; things seen, says the Apostle, are not hoped for (Rom. 8:24). It is then no wonder that the Prophet says, that the faithful shall then know that Christ has been sent by the Father, that is, by actual experience, or in reality: Ye shall then know that Jehovah has sent me.[4]

In another place, Calvin writes, "David not only asserts that God is good, but he is ravished with admiration of the goodness which he had experienced." There is an experience that only believers possess because it is the exercise of a new spiritual sense. The goodness of God fills the world, yet it is hidden to unbelievers, being reserved to "the experience of the saints, because they alone, as I have said, experience in their souls the fruit of divine goodness."[5]

This is not to say that faith and experience are different things. Rather, faith is the root of experience, and experience is the fruition of faith. Thus, Calvin writes of "the gracious experience of faith."[6] He also says that experimental (*experimentalis*) knowledge "makes the deepest impression."[7] Relying on God means that "we embrace with our whole hearts" the promises of God's grace and "endeavor to have the experience of his goodness pervading our whole minds." Then we are prepared to stand firm with strength in the face of our daily conflicts.[8]

So the goal of experimental or experiential preaching is to know the Lord personally in a way that is true to the Word. As soon as we abandon

---

4. John Calvin, *Commentaries of Calvin*, various translators and editors, 45 vols. (Edinburgh: Calvin Translation Society, 1846–1851; repr., 22 vols., Grand Rapids, MI: Baker, 1979) [Zech. 2:9], hereafter, *Commentary*.
5. *Commentary* [Ps. 31:19].
6. *Commentary* [Ps. 36:8].
7. *Commentary* [Ps. 66:5]. The French version reads "cognoissance d'experience et de prattique" ("knowledge of experience and practice").
8. *Commentary* [Ps. 31:24].

the Word, we fall into a false kind of mysticism. This is a very important point to remember, because when you start preaching experientially, someone is going to say to you: "Why do we need all this experience? Aren't you afraid it will end in experience for its own sake?" We reply, "No, because we always bring it to the Word of God to determine its authenticity and value."

Both words, *experimental* and *experiential*, have strengths and weaknesses. *Experimental* is the term found in the older books. Its strength is that it contains the word *experiment*. Immediately the idea of testing something comes to mind. Speaking of experimental Christianity can suggest that you are viewing your experiences through the microscope of Scripture and asking, "Are they true to the Word of God?"

However, the weakness of the term *experimental* is that few people understand it in this manner anymore. Instead, it communicates something that we do not want to say about Christianity or the preaching of the Word. One dictionary listed the following definitions of *experimental*: "based on untested ideas and not yet established or finalized; involving a radically new and innovative style; of or relating to scientific experiments; based on experience as opposed to authority or conjecture."[9] On the contrary, the preaching of the gospel is trustworthy in content and ancient in origin; it stands upon the absolute and unchanging authority of God's inerrant Word. It's not at all "experimental" in the modern sense.

Experiential is the more modern term in the sense in which we are using it. It brings to mind "experience" as opposed to mere talk or theory. For this reason, I almost always speak of Reformed *experiential* preaching, not *experimental* preaching. Some writers use the word *existential*, but I generally avoid it. I would not want to promote confusion between experiential Christianity and the various philosophies known as existentialism. So *experiential* seems to be the best word to describe preaching that speaks the Word from heart to heart.

There is a weakness to this word, however. *Experiential* does not communicate testing of the genuineness and maturity of our experience by an objective standard. It does not imply an experiment or trial. This aspect of the matter must be explained and added. We face a danger, therefore, that people will seize on the word *experiential* and run with it

---

9. "Experimental," *Oxford Dictionaries* (Oxford: Oxford University Press, 2012), http://oxford dictionaries.com/definition/experimental?region=us&q=experimental.

to pursue heart experiences with no truth content. They may say: "We don't need more teaching. We need experience."

Alternatively, people may take things in another direction, seeking guidance from unusual providences of God rather than following the way of the Word. This can lead to a sad bondage to superstition. One woman was wrestling with doubts about whether she should take the Lord's Supper. She sensed her sinfulness and questioned her salvation. She bowed down in prayer, seeking God's wisdom. When she stood up without a resolution, she looked out the window and saw smoke rising from her neighbor's window. She again knelt in prayer. When she got up this time, she saw no smoke. So she got down on her knees yet again and prayed, "Lord, if I look once more and see smoke, then I will take it as a sign I should receive the Supper." She arose and, behold, there was smoke. She felt that she had truly experienced God's guidance.

That's not what we mean by experiential Christianity. We must not wander into experientialism or superstition. It is far better for us to cling to the Scriptures as our life and to examine our lives by the Scriptures. The decision to partake of the Lord's Supper is not to be made by "putting out a fleece," but by searching our souls for the biblical marks (see the epistle to the Romans) of knowing by experience some degree of our sin and misery, our deliverance in Christ, and a yearning to live a lifestyle of gratitude and sanctification to God for such a deliverance (see the Heidelberg Catechism). This is true experiential Christianity. Reformed experiential preaching aims to foster it.

Again, these concerns lead us to self-examination. The preacher of the Word must ask: "Does my preaching help people to walk closely with God in real life? Or does it simply set up a beautiful world of ideas disconnected from their experiences?" People may feel that your preaching is disconnected from real life just because they are spiritually dead and have no communion with God. Or perhaps they are backslidden and have little communion with him. But believers growing toward maturity will resonate with experiential preaching. Ask, "Does my preaching find an echo in the experience of true believers?"

On the other hand, the preacher should ask: "Does my preaching cultivate a self-reflection by which people test their experience by the Scriptures? Or am I allowing people to embrace virtually anything as an experience of God's grace so long as they feel close to God?" We live in an age of experientialism—spirituality without boundaries, fixed content, or standards. We should constantly be shining the light of biblical truth into the souls of men and challenging them to consider whether their experiences are from the Spirit of Christ.

Why Is the Experiential Dimension of Preaching Necessary?

Why do people need to hear Reformed experiential preaching? Why is this ingredient in the ministry of the Word so important that leaving it out is like leaving the fizz out of soda pop or the cheese off of pizza? Hopefully this whole book will help to cultivate a growing appetite in you for experiential reality in the Christian life and the preaching of the Word. Here, however, let me offer a few specific reasons why this dimension is so important for the kingdom of God.

First, *the Bible enjoins experiential preaching.* Paul writes to Timothy, "I charge thee therefore before God, and the Lord Jesus Christ, who shall judge the quick and the dead at his appearing and his kingdom; preach the word; be instant in season, out of season; reprove, rebuke, exhort with all long suffering and doctrine" (2 Tim. 4:1–2). Paul's charge implies that ministers must preach out of the fear of the Lord, the sovereign King who will judge both us and our hearers. It is only in knowing the "terror of the Lord" that the preacher is enabled to "persuade men" (2 Cor. 5:11). This fear is not dread of wrath and punishment, of course, because Christ took our sins upon himself and gave us his righteousness (v. 21). But it is a fear of displeasing God that moves us to aim to obey him in all things (v. 9). The Word must grip us with the glory of the Lord or we will be content merely to tickle men's ears (2 Tim. 4:3–4). But through the fear of the Lord, we live and labor in hope of a crown to be given from "the Lord, the righteous judge" on the day of "his appearing" (v. 8).

Consider the elements Paul commands Timothy to include in his preaching. God requires preachers to teach "doctrine" and to apply it. To "reprove" aims at conviction, drawing verbal pictures of sins and errors with vivid color so that men recognize them as their own sins and see their ugliness. To "rebuke" means admonishing men to turn from wickedness back to God in true repentance. To "exhort" involves pressing the duties implicit in the truths of Scripture upon people and urging them to respond rightly, with faith and obedience.[10] This is not harsh or

---

10. George W. Knight III, *Commentary on the Pastoral Epistles*, New International Greek Testament Commentary (Grand Rapids, MI: Eerdmans, 1992), 454 [2 Tim. 4:2].

unloving preaching, but preaching "with all longsuffering." It is "gentle" and "patient" preaching (2 Tim. 2:24). Yet it is preaching that forcefully applies the truth.

Calvin says that we must not preach in the same way that "a man should teach in a school," that is, without searching application (indeed, there is no reason that school teaching need be devoid of application either; it's a matter of emphasis). At the same time, one must not neglect doctrine. Calvin preaches: "It must be done with doctrine: as if he said, when we exhort, we must stand upon good reason: for otherwise we should build in the air. So then, doctrine is (as it were) the groundwork, and then, threatenings, exhortations, and all the rest, is to go on with the building."[11]

The prophets also call for experiential preaching. We hear the Lord saying in Isaiah 40:1–2: "Comfort ye, comfort ye my people, saith your God. Speak ye comfortably to Jerusalem." In the context, this refers to the preaching of the gospel (v. 9; cf. 52:7–9). God commands that his servants speak truth to his people aimed to "comfort" them. Charles Spurgeon says: "It is our duty to reprove, to exhort, to invite, but it is equally our duty to console. The minister should ask God for the Spirit, that he may be filled with His influence as a comforter."[12]

Literally, to "speak comfortably" (Isa. 40:2) is to "speak to the heart." Therefore, God commands his servants to apply the gospel to the hearts of believers in a way that comforts them. Joseph Alexander (1809–1860) writes, "By speaking to the heart, we are to understand speaking so as to affect the heart or feelings, and also in accordance with the heart or wishes, i.e. what the person addressed desires or needs to hear."[13] Our greatest need is reconciliation with God, without which there is no peace (Isa. 57:21). Spiritual comfort arises from joyfully finding life and refreshment from the truth that God's anger is turned away and he has become our salvation (12:1–3).

Alec Motyer says that the repetition, "Comfort ye, comfort ye," communicates "emotional intensity." He writes that speaking to the heart not only suggests comforting but also "seeking to persuade, inviting to respond in love."[14] So here again we see preaching characterized as a

---

11. *Commentary* [2 Tim. 4:1–2].
12. Charles H. Spurgeon, Sermon #221, "Comfort Proclaimed," Sept. 21, 1856, in *The Spurgeon Archive*, https://www.spurgeon.org/resource-library/sermons/comfort-proclaimed.
13. Joseph A. Alexander, *The Later Prophecies of Isaiah* (New York: Wiley and Putnam, 1847), 2 [Isa. 40:2].
14. J. Alec Motyer, *The Prophecy of Isaiah: An Introduction and Commentary* (Downers Grove, IL: InterVarsity Press, 1993), 299 [Isa. 40:1–2].

man taking the truth into his heart to stir his own affections and then speaking it to the hearts of others to move them to respond in love.

Second, *Scripture exemplifies experiential preaching*. Consider the Beatitudes spoken by our Lord Jesus (Matt. 5:3–12). The first and last beatitudes state "for theirs is the kingdom of heaven." This is an example of spiritual discrimination, setting forth the marks of genuine Christians in distinction from people outside the kingdom, no matter how religious (cf. v. 20). At the center of the text, the fourth beatitude (v. 6) identifies the heartbeat of all true Christian experience, hungering and thirsting after righteousness, and the fifth beatitude (v. 7) displays the essence of all true Christian activity, showing mercy to others.

The apostle Paul also exemplified experiential preaching. It began with his own heart. He writes in Romans 1:9, "For God is my witness, whom I serve with my spirit in the gospel of his Son, that without ceasing I make mention of you always in my prayers." Paul devoted himself to communion with God in prayer. He dwelt constantly in God's presence, conscious that the divine eye was a "witness" to all his thoughts, words, and deeds (cf. 1 Tim. 5:21; 2 Tim. 4:1). And he carried his fellow Christians in his heart as he drew near to God.

Furthermore, notice Paul's phrase, "whom I serve with my spirit in the gospel of his Son." The word translated in this text as "serve" (Greek *latreuō*) is not the word for the work of a servant but for the devotional acts of a worshiper.[15] Paul preached like a priest offering a sacrifice in the temple for God's pleasure (Rom. 15:16). All believers are priests in Christ, yet we note that Paul especially spoke here of his ministry of the Word. He preached as "in the sight of God" (2 Cor. 4:2), as if he spoke while standing before the very throne of heaven.

When Paul preached to people, the Word affected his heart, and his heart affected his preaching of the Word. His preaching of the gospel was an act of worship that engaged his "spirit"—worship in spirit and truth. He preached with flaming love for God. Martyn Lloyd-Jones (1899–1981) writes, "He serves God, you see, in his spirit, in his inner man, in the very center of his life and being. . . . It was the deepest desire of his life and of his heart to serve God."[16] The doxologies in his epistles show that he could not speak of Christ without bursting forth in praise to God.[17] He preached

---

15. For example, see also Matt. 4:10; Luke 2:37; Acts 7:42; Rom. 1:25; Phil. 3:3.

16. D. Martyn Lloyd-Jones, *Romans: The Gospel of God, Exposition of Chapter 1* (Grand Rapids, MI: Zondervan, 1985), 207, 214 [Rom. 1:9].

17. For example, see Rom. 1:25; 9:5; 11:33–36; 16:25–27.

with compassionate love for people, sometimes even with tears in his eyes for the perishing.[18] He not only preached about the power of God; he preached with God's power working in him "mightily" (Col. 1:28–29).

We also see experiential preaching in the content of Paul's writing. The epistle to the Romans is renowned as a doctrinal treatise. But it is also richly experiential. Romans 5:3–5 says, "And not only so, but we glory in tribulations also: knowing that tribulation worketh patience; and patience, experience; and experience, hope: and hope maketh not ashamed; because the love of God is shed abroad in our hearts by the Holy Ghost which is given unto us." Here we have a remarkable series of connections made within Christian experience, all derived from the application to the soul of the doctrine of justification by faith in Christ alone (see Rom. 5:1, 6–8). Paul was not just talking about doctrine theoretically or analytically; he was glorying in Christ even as he spoke.

Romans 7 presents to us a man delighting in God's law yet groaning over his depravity: "O wretched man that I am!" (v. 24). Paul groaned in his preaching. Romans 8 unfolds the work of the Spirit who moves God's children to cry to God, "Abba, Father" (v. 15). The same chapter ends on an exultant note: "For I am persuaded, that neither death, nor life, nor angels, nor principalities, nor powers, nor things present, nor things to come, nor height, nor depth, nor any other creature, shall be able to separate us from the love of God, which is in Christ Jesus our Lord" (vv. 38–39).

Neither does the Old Testament omit experiential preaching. Jeremiah felt compelled to preach because the Word was as a fire in his bones (Jer. 20:9). Micah was "full of power by the spirit of the LORD" to preach against the sins of Jacob (Mic. 3:8). Who can read the Psalms without marveling at the variety and detail of experiences described there? In the midst of brilliant theology and warm doxology, the psalmists repeatedly laid bare their souls as their cries ascended heavenward. Here we find the darkest depths and the most glorious heights of knowing God, "my exceeding joy" (Ps. 43:4).

Throughout the Holy Scriptures, we find examples of godly people embracing the truth of Christ in their hearts and bringing it to bear on the experiences of others. That is the second reason why the experiential dimension is necessary in preaching.

---

18. Acts 20:19, 20, 31; 2 Cor. 2:4; Phil. 3:18; cf. Rom. 9:1–3.

Third, *real religion is more than notions in the mind or actions of the body.* Intellectualism makes Christianity into mere words and ideas. Moralism would make religion into a matter of good conduct. If we reduce Christianity to ideas and behavior, we cut the heart out of the faith. Christianity is more than words. In contrast to "the speech of them which are puffed up," Paul says, "the kingdom of God is not in word, but in power" (1 Cor. 4:19–20). It's more than external behavior. Paul also writes, "For the kingdom of God is not meat and drink; but righteousness, and peace, and joy in the Holy Ghost" (Rom. 14:17). The kingdom consists of the righteousness of Christ and the powerful work of the Spirit producing effects within our souls. Paul highlighted effects that we consciously experience: peace and joy.

What would be left of the Bible if we cut out all the references to affections of the heart? Not much. Jonathan Edwards says, "The Holy Scriptures do everywhere place religion very much in the affections; such as fear, hope, love, hatred, desire, joy, sorrow, gratitude, compassion and zeal."[19]

Above all else, the "fruit of the Spirit is love" (Gal. 5:22). God commands us to love him with all our heart, soul, and might (Deut. 6:5). If we fail to engage our hearts for his glory, then our religion is hypocrisy (Matt. 15:7–8). Edwards says: "The things of religion are so great, that there can be no suitableness in the exercises of our hearts, to their nature and importance, unless they be lively and powerful. In nothing is vigor in the actings of our inclinations so requisite, as in religion; and in nothing is lukewarmness so odious [offensive and disgusting]."[20]

Fourth, *without an experiential faith, we will perish forever.* Saving faith is a "faith which worketh by love" (Gal. 5:6), not a faith that "hath not works [and so] is dead" (James 2:17). Sometimes such experiential faith is called the fear of the Lord. In Jeremiah 32:40, the Lord makes this promise of salvation: "And I will make an everlasting covenant with them, that I will not turn away from them, to do them good; but I will put my fear in their hearts, that they shall not depart from me." This verse speaks of a glad yet trembling awe in light of the glory of Christ. After declaring the majesty and victory of the messianic King, the psalmist gives this evangelistic call to the nations: "Serve the LORD

---

19. Jonathan Edwards, *Religions Affections*, in *The Works of Jonathan Edwards*, vol. 2, *Religions Affections*, ed. John E. Smith (New Haven, CT: Yale University Press, 1959), 102.
20. Edwards, *Religions Affections*, in *Works*, 2:100.

with fear, and rejoice with trembling" (Ps. 2:11). The alternative is to face his wrath (v. 12).

In the same way, Peter writes of Christ, "Whom having not seen, ye love; in whom, though now ye see him not, yet believing, ye rejoice with joy unspeakable and full of glory: receiving the end of your faith, even the salvation of your souls" (1 Pet. 1:8–9). There is something ineffable about saving faith; even in its weakest moments, it engages the heart with love, joy, and longing for Christ. It springs from "the knowledge of God, and of Jesus our Lord," who multiplies "grace and peace" through "his divine power" operating in God's "great and precious promises" (2 Pet. 1:2–4).

We find Paul's definition of the true people of God in Philippians 3:3: "For we are the circumcision, which worship God in the spirit, and rejoice [or glory] in Christ Jesus, and have no confidence in the flesh." Paul was not saying that we are saved by our worship or joy. He sought to "be found in him [Christ], not having mine own righteousness, which is of the law, but that which is through the faith of Christ, the righteousness which is of God by faith" (v. 9). Salvation is entirely by Christ's righteousness received by faith.

We are not saved by our experience, or by having a certain degree of experience or depth of feeling. Nevertheless, God has bound up justifying faith with "the knowledge of Christ Jesus my Lord," a knowledge that has an "excellency" about it surpassing all things (Phil. 3:8). If we lack a glorious, transforming knowledge of Christ, we remain blinded by the god of this world and perishing in our sins (2 Cor. 3:18; 4:4–6).

Therefore, we need experiential preaching. God can work saving faith through mere teaching, indeed through the bare words of Scripture on the page, but ordinarily he ignites a burning heart with a burning preacher.

Does your preaching consist of theology on fire? Does biblical truth pass from the head to the heart in your religion, or is it stuck in the head?

3

Major Elements of Reformed Experiential Preaching

The church is amazing.[1] Its membership spans the globe. It is thousands of years old. At times, it rises up like a gracious bride, beautiful and longing for her groom. At other times, it goes to war against evil, taking up the sword of truth, the shield of faith, and the armor of love. Yet the church has also had its seasons of declension into shocking darkness, ugliness, and weakness. It always struggles against the deforming sicknesses of indwelling sin and false teaching. Sometimes it appears sick unto death. But Jesus Christ builds his church, and the gates of hell will not prevail against it (Matt. 16:18). The Son of Man still walks among the lampstands of his church (Rev. 1:13).

In the centuries following the deaths of the apostles, the church struggled and grew in its understanding of fundamental truths such as the deity of Christ and the Trinity. Yet it also increasingly succumbed to errors. Although true faith remained in its midst, the visible church in the Middle Ages turned increasingly away from trusting in Christ alone, looking instead to mere human beings as its ruling powers, authoritative teachers, and worthy intercessors for obtaining mercy from God. Bishops and popes sat on Christ's throne, tradition pushed aside Scripture, superstition corrupted worship, and Mary and the saints became the recipients of prayer and adoration. As the light of the gospel

---

1. Portions of this chapter are adapted from Joel R. Beeke, *Living for God's Glory: An Introduction to Calvinism* (Lake Mary, FL: Reformation Trust, 2008), chaps. 3, 19. Used with permission.

grew dimmer in the visible church, moral corruption and decay spread as a blight.

But in the sixteenth century, the Lord Jesus Christ granted his church an explosion of spiritual light and life. Through men such as Martin Luther, Ulrich Zwingli, Martin Bucer, Heinrich Bullinger, and John Calvin, God brought about the Reformation, which took the church back to its ancient roots. Many of these men are remembered today as theologians, but first and foremost they were preachers of the Word of God. Through their preaching, God raised up the Reformed movement— a movement that continues today. Whereas the church had become *deformed* from its apostolic pattern by human sin and corruption, God *reformed* the church by his Word and the Spirit.

Perhaps you are a minister in a denominationally Reformed church. Maybe you picked up this book but have no idea what *Reformed* means. In either case, you may be wondering what I mean by "Reformed experiential preaching." We have talked some about experiential preaching. But it is important to see how experiential preaching fits into the bigger picture of Reformed Christianity. Reformed preaching is not merely giving a sermon in a church of a particular denomination. Reformed preaching is declaring biblical truth to promote biblical spirituality as it was rediscovered in the Reformation of the sixteenth century.

Preaching Reformed Truth

The Reformed Christian faith is a wealth of wisdom. It is impossible to cram the richness of Reformed doctrine into a five-point outline, however helpful outlines may be for introducing basic ideas.[2]

Merely surveying the headings of the Westminster Confession of Faith (1647) reveals the confluence of many streams of truth: Holy Scripture, God and the holy Trinity, God's eternal decree, creation, providence, the fall of man into sin, God's covenant with man, Christ the Mediator, free will, effectual calling, justification, adoption, sanctification, saving faith, repentance unto life, good works, the persever-

---

2. The Canons of Dort, the basis of the so-called "Five Points of Calvinism," were not intended to sum up the Reformed faith but to respond to five objections raised by the Remonstrants or Arminians. Thus, they address only a narrow portion, albeit a critical one, of Reformed doctrine. This is why the Canons of Dort do not stand alone as the doctrinal standard of the Dutch Reformed churches, but are included with the Heidelberg Catechism and the Belgic Confession in the Three Forms of Unity. More representative of Reformed Christianity, but still only an outline, are the five *solas*: *sola Scriptura* ("Scripture alone"), *sola gratia* ("grace alone"), *solus Christus* ("Christ alone"), *sola fide* ("faith alone"), and *soli Deo gloria* ("for the glory of God alone").

ance of the saints, assurance of grace and salvation, the law of God, Christian liberty and liberty of conscience, religious worship and the Sabbath day, lawful oaths and vows, the civil magistrate, marriage and divorce, the church, the communion of saints, the sacraments of baptism and the Lord's Supper, church censures, synods and councils, the state of men after death, the resurrection of the dead, and the last judgment.

When you add the rich expositions of living for God (the Ten Commandments) and depending on God (the Lord's Prayer) found in the Reformed catechisms, it's clear that Reformed truth encompasses "all the counsel of God" that the faithful preacher must declare (Acts 20:27).

The preacher should always be seeking to grow in his understanding of the panorama of biblical truth. If you don't have much background in Reformed Christianity, I highly recommend that you read through the Heidelberg Catechism (1563) or the Westminster Shorter Catechism (1647). Don't rush through them. Get a good edition with the Scripture references printed in full and meditate on each question and answer with its Scripture proofs. Next, read through a Reformed confession of faith or one of the longer catechisms.[3]

If you are familiar with Reformed catechisms and confessions, dig deeper by reading an exposition of a catechism, such as Thomas Watson (c. 1620–1686) or John Brown (1722–1787) of Haddington on the Westminster Shorter Catechism,[4] or G. I. Williamson on the Heidelberg Catechism.[5] Next, read Reformed experiential theology, such as that

---

3. All the Westminster Standards, with full Scripture references, are contained in *Westminster Confession of Faith* (Glasgow: Free Presbyterian Publications, 1994). For the Heidelberg Catechism with full Scripture references, as well as other Dutch standards, see *The Psalter with Doctrinal Standards, Liturgy, Church Order, and Added Chorale Section*, ed. Joel R. Beeke (Grand Rapids, MI: Reformation Heritage Books, 2010); see also *Reformed Confessions Harmonized*, ed. Joel R. Beeke and Sinclair B. Ferguson (Grand Rapids, MI: Baker, 1999). Baptists may wish to consult *The Shorter Catechism: A Modest Revision for Baptists Today* (Grand Rapids, MI: Truth for Eternity, 1991); *The 1689 London Baptist Confession of Faith and the 1695 Baptist Catechism* (Birmingham, AL: Solid Ground, 2010).

4. Thomas Watson, *A Body of Divinity* (Edinburgh: Banner of Truth, 1965); *The Ten Commandments* (Edinburgh: Banner of Truth, 1965); *The Lord's Prayer* (Edinburgh: Banner of Truth, 1965); John Brown of Haddington, *Questions and Answers on the Shorter Catechism* (Grand Rapids, MI: Reformation Heritage Books, 2006). Baptists may consult Benjamin Beddome, *A Scriptural Exposition of the Baptist Catechism* (Birmingham, AL: Solid Ground, 2006); Samuel E. Waldron, *The 1689 Baptist Confession of Faith: A Modern Exposition* (Darlington, England: Evangelical Press, 1989).

5. G. I. Williamson, *The Heidelberg Catechism: A Study Guide* (Phillipsburg, NJ: P&R, 1993); see also the robust expositions of the Heidelberg Catechism by Zacharias Ursinus, George Bethune, and many other writers.

written by the men we will study in later chapters. I would especially recommend the masterful exposition of Christian doctrine and life by Wilhelmus à Brakel (1635–1711)—it is devotional theology at its best.[6]

However, as I speak about Reformed experiential preaching, I want to highlight two core elements of Reformed truth: preaching Christ and preaching God's sovereignty.

Preaching Christ

Reformed experiential preaching is Christ centered. That is, it focuses on God's living Word, Jesus Christ, made known in God's written Word, the Bible. William Perkins says, "Christ is the substance or subject matter of the whole Bible."[7] He writes: "Christ stands alone in the work of redemption, without colleague or partner, without deputy or substitute, whether we respect the whole work of redemption, or the least part of it. . . . There is no other name whereby we can be saved beside the name of Christ (Acts 4:12). Christ saves them perfectly that come unto him (Heb. 7:25). In him we are complete (Col. 2:10)."[8]

Preaching Christ is the only way to give solid comfort to suffering people. The Heidelberg Catechism opens with this beautiful statement:

> Question 1: What is thy only comfort in life and death?
> Answer: That I with body and soul, both in life and death, am not my own, but belong unto my faithful Savior Jesus Christ; who, with His precious blood, hath fully satisfied for all my sins, and delivered me from all the power of the devil; and so preserves me that without the will of my heavenly Father, not a hair can fall from my head; yea, that all things must be subservient to my salvation, and therefore, by His Holy Spirit, He also assures me of eternal life, and makes me sincerely willing and ready, henceforth, to live unto Him.[9]

In this manner, the Reformed faith invites us into sweet fellowship with the triune God through the blood of the faithful Savior. In Christ, sinners find assurance of eternal life and willingness to live for God. Therefore, we must preach Christ.

---

6. Wilhelmus à Brakel, *The Christian's Reasonable Service*, trans. Bartel Elshout, ed. Joel R. Beeke, 4 vols. (Grand Rapids, MI: Reformation Heritage Books, 2012).

7. William Perkins, *A Commentary on Galatians*, ed. Gerald T. Sheppard (1617; facsimile repr., New York: Pilgrim Press, 1989), 47 [Gal. 1:17].

8. Perkins, *A Commentary on Galatians*, 274 [Gal. 4:8–11].

9. See Beeke, ed., *Doctrinal Standards*, in *The Psalter*, 27 [second pagination].

To preach Christ is to preach the text of Scripture in its redemptive context. Biblical preaching flows out of the scriptural passage as it is expounded in accord with sound exegetical and hermeneutical principles. Jeremiah 3:15 says that God has given preachers to his people to "feed [them] with knowledge and understanding."

While Reformed preaching is rooted in grammatical and historical exegesis, it also involves spiritual, practical, and experimental application. In 1 Corinthians 2:10–16, Paul says that good exegesis is spiritual. Since the Spirit always testifies of Jesus Christ, sound exegesis finds Christ not only in the new covenant, but also in the old. It was said in the ancient world that all roads led to Rome; so the preaching of all texts today must lead ultimately to Christ.

Jesus himself says, "Search the scriptures; for in them ye think ye have eternal life: and they are they which testify of me" (John 5:39). Likewise, when he speaks with his disciples following the resurrection, Jesus says, "These are the words which I spake unto you, while I was yet with you, that all things must be fulfilled, which were written in the law of Moses, and in the prophets, and in the psalms, concerning me" (Luke 24:44).

The great theme and controlling contour of experiential preaching is Jesus Christ, for he is the supreme focus, substance, and goal of God's revelation. Therefore, a true Reformed preacher, like Paul, must be "determined not to know any thing among you, save Jesus Christ, and him crucified" (1 Cor. 2:2). Perkins says that the heart of all preaching is "to preach one Christ, by Christ, to the praise of Christ."[10] The New England divine Cotton Mather (1663–1728) puts it this way: "Let not the true bread of life be forgotten; but exhibit as much as you can of a glorious Christ unto them. Yea, let the motto upon your whole ministry be: *Christ is all.*"[11]

Christ must be the beginning, middle, and end of every sermon (Luke 24:27; 1 John 1:1–4). Preaching must exalt Christ for awakening, justifying, sanctifying, and comforting sinners (Eph. 5:14; 1 Cor. 1:30; Isa. 61:2). As John says: "In him was life; and the life was the light of men. . . . The Word was made flesh, and dwelt among us, (and we beheld his glory, the glory as of the only begotten of the Father), full of grace and truth" (John 1:4, 14; cf. Ps. 36:9; 119:130).

---

10. William Perkins, "The Arte of Prophecying," in *Works of William Perkins* (London: John Legatt, 1613), 2:762.

11. Cotton Mather, *Manuductio ad Ministerium: Directions for a Candidate to the Ministry* (Boston: for Thomas Hancock, 1726), 93.

Exegesis offers sound analysis of the words, grammar, syntax, and historical setting of Scripture. Experiential preaching does not minimize these aspects of interpretation, but neither is it content with them. A minister who presents only the grammatical and historical meaning of God's Word may be lecturing or discoursing, but he is not preaching. The Word must be applied spiritually. Spiritual exegesis is thus Christological, and, through Christ, it is theological, giving all glory to the triune God.

Reformed experiential preaching, then, teaches that the Christian faith must be experienced, tasted, and lived through the saving power of the Holy Spirit as the Spirit of Christ. It stresses the knowledge of scriptural truth, as the Bible is the Word of Christ, which is able to make us wise unto salvation through faith in Christ (2 Tim. 3:15). Specifically, such preaching teaches that Christ, the living Word (John 1:1) and the very embodiment of the truth, must be experientially known and embraced. It proclaims the need for sinners to experience who God is in his Son.

Such preaching is liberating—not only for the congregation but also for the preacher. How freeing and reassuring it is for ministers to know that what God blesses in the ministry is not their ingenuity, intellect, insight, or persuasiveness—though all their gifts must be used in dependence on the Holy Spirit. Rather, God blesses the proclamation of his Son in the preaching of his own Word to his glory and the salvation of sinners. Reformed ministers believe that they are but ambassadors of Christ, called to deliver the message that God has given them to declare. That is where they cast their anchors as they bring their congregations the Word of the living God week after week, in season and out of season (2 Tim. 4:2).

The insight of Calvin into Christ's threefold ministry as our Prophet, Priest, and King immeasurably enriches our preaching of Christ.[12] It helps us to see the manifold sufficiency of Christ to comfort us in every facet of our misery. As John Preston (1587–1628) observes, there is fullness in Christ for us. He preached before King James I of England that Christ our Prophet "is full of all treasures of wisdom and knowledge." All the apostles and prophets that ever spoke of God "received their light from this Sun." As a Priest, Christ is always heard by God, "full of

---

12. See John Calvin, *Institutes of the Christian Religion*, trans. Ford Lewis Battles, ed. John T. McNeill, Library of Christian Classics, vols. 20–21 (Philadelphia: Westminster, 1960), 2.15.1–6, hereafter, *Institutes*.

compassion to men" to hear their requests, and "full of merit" to obtain what he asks from God. As a King, he is "full of authority . . . full of strength to defend his servants, and resist his enemies, till he hath made them a footstool," and full of royal generosity to provide for his servants what they need and to richly reward their work.[13] We may truly preach Christ as all that anyone could ever need.

How does the offer of Christ function in experiential preaching? If Christ is the preeminent subject of preaching, and his righteousness is at the center of salvation, we must freely offer this righteousness and this Savior to sinners. We must call and command men to come to him. We must allure sinners to him by presenting Christ in his beauty, sufficiency, and mercy. Offering Christ to sinners is never an appendix tacked on to the end of the sermon. Proclaiming Christ is the heart of experiential preaching. The preaching of Christian experience is always subordinate to this greater goal of the offering of Jesus Christ and him crucified to sinners.

God calls out in Isaiah 55:1, "Ho, every one that thirsteth, come ye to the waters, and he that hath no money; come ye, buy, and eat; yea, come, buy wine and milk without money and without price." Scottish preacher William Guthrie (1620–1665) says: "Wherever he comes in the word of his gospel, he excludes none but those who exclude themselves. And so the promises are held out to all. . . . God offers the promises freely to all that will take them."[14]

New England Puritan Thomas Hooker (1586–1647) declares, "The Lord proclaims his mercy openly, freely offers it, heartily intends it, waits to communicate it, lays siege to the soul by his long sufferance: there is enough to procure all good, distrust it not: he freely invites, fear it not, thou mayest be bold to go: he intends it heartily, question it not: yet he is waiting and wooing, delay it not therefore, but hearken to his voice."[15]

When Christ is faithfully preached and held forth as the grand object of faith, we can expect the Holy Spirit to bless the preaching subjectively to the soul in the exercises of faith. What does the Holy Spirit like best in a preacher? The Spirit most delights in the preaching of Christ. The

---

13. John Preston, *The Fullness of Christ for Us* (London: by M. P. for Iohn Stafford, 1639), 5–7.

14. William Guthrie, sermon on Isaiah 44:3, in *A Collection of Lectures and Sermons . . . mostly in the time of the Late Persecution*, ed. J[ohn] H[owie] (Glasgow: J. Bryce, 1779), 25.

15. Thomas Hooker, *The Application of Redemption, By the effectual Work of the Word, and Spirit of Christ, for the bringing home of lost Sinners to God, The First Eight Books* (1657; facsimile repr., New York: Arno Press, 1972), 362–63.

Holy Spirit is the Spirit of Christ (Rom. 8:9). His whole task is to take the things of Christ and show them to us (John 16:13–14). Thus, the work of the Spirit in the hearts of men is directly connected to the knowledge of Christ (Eph. 3:16–19).

Do not be surprised that there is little experiential knowledge in congregations where the ministers do not often preach Christ. But where Christ is faithfully preached and freely offered, you will often find that, over a period of time, the Spirit cultivates rich Christian experience in those who hear. Thus, the Dutch sometimes ask about a minister, "*Is hij een Christus-prediker?*" ("Is he a Christ-preacher?") They are not asking merely whether he preaches the doctrines of Christ. They are asking, "Does he offer the riches of Christ and woo sinners to him?" There is no more important question.

Preaching the Sovereignty of God

To preach Christ is to preach the kingdom of God. It is to proclaim his sovereignty in creation, in providence, in grace, and in glory. *Sovereignty* means "rule"; hence, to speak of God's sovereignty is to refer to God's rule. God's sovereignty is his supremacy, his kingship, and his deity. His sovereignty shows him to be God, the incomprehensible Trinity who is nevertheless knowable insofar as he chooses to reveal himself to us. His sovereignty is exercised in all of his attributes, declaring him to be perfect in all respects and the possessor of all righteousness and holiness. He is the sovereignly gracious and omnipotent Jehovah, the Most High God who does his will in the army of heaven and among the inhabitants of the earth (Dan. 4:35). He cannot be reduced to spatial or temporal categories for human understanding and analysis.

Here we discover the true marrow of the Reformed faith. The Reformed Christian believes that God is the Lord of life and Sovereign of the universe, whose will is the key to history. He believes that God is free to accomplish his purposes independent of any force outside himself; that he knows the end from the beginning; that he creates, sustains, governs, and directs all things; and that his marvelous design will be fully and perfectly manifest at the end of the ages. "For of him, and through him, and to him, are all things: to whom be glory for ever" (Rom. 11:36).

I am not saying that every sermon must be about the sovereignty of God. Scripture must dictate our subject matter as we preach through the Bible. Speaking about preaching God's sovereignty and the doctrines of the Reformed faith, John Newton says, "I am more of a Calvinist than anything else; but I use my Calvinism in my writing and preaching as I use this sugar. I do not give it alone, and whole; but mixed, and diluted."[16] This is really the way God's sovereignty functions in Scripture. It is the constant backdrop for all that takes place in the foreground. Charles Hodge (1797–1878) says: "God's sovereignty is to all other doctrines what the granite formation is to the other strata of the earth. It underlies and sustains them, but it crops out only here and there. So this doctrine should underlie all our preaching, and should be definitely asserted only now and then."[17]

God's sovereignty is also the marrow of Reformed doctrine—provided we understand that this sovereignty is not arbitrary but is the sovereignty of the God and Father of our Lord Jesus Christ. B. B. Warfield (1851–1921) writes, "The Biblical writers find their comfort continually in the assurance that it is the righteous, holy, faithful, loving God in whose hands rests the determination of the sequence of events and all their issues."[18] The Heidelberg Catechism says:

> **Question 26:** What believest thou when thou sayest, I believe in God the Father, Almighty, Maker of heaven and earth?
> **Answer:** That the eternal Father of our Lord Jesus Christ (who of nothing made heaven and earth, with all that is in them; who likewise upholds and governs the same by His eternal counsel and providence) is for the sake of Christ His Son, my God and my Father; on whom I rely so entirely, that I have no doubt but He will provide me with all things necessary for soul and body; and further, that He will make whatever evils He sends upon me, in this valley of tears, turn out to my advantage; for He is able to do it, being Almighty God, and willing, being a faithful Father.[19]

This is balanced, genuine, defensible Calvinism. It is the faith expressed in Isaiah 9:6, which says that the government, or sovereignty, is upon the shoulder of him who is called "Wonderful, Counsellor, The mighty God, The everlasting Father, The Prince of Peace." In Christ, the warm and fatherly sovereignty of the God of the Scriptures

---

16. Quoted in William Jay, *The Autobiography of William Jay* (London: Banner of Truth, 1974), 272.
17. Charles Hodge, *Princeton Sermons* (Edinburgh: Banner of Truth, 1958), 6.
18. B. B. Warfield, *Biblical and Theological Studies* (Philadelphia: P&R, 1952), 324.
19. See Beeke, ed., *Doctrinal Standards*, in *The Psalter*, 37 [second pagination].

is vastly different from the cold and capricious sovereignty of other "gods." Fatherly sovereignty is in perfect harmony with all of God's attributes. The believer finds peace in the conviction that behind God's all-encompassing providence is the full acquiescence of the triune God. The sovereign grace and love that went to Calvary has the whole world in its hands. God's fatherly sovereignty in Christ is the essence of who God is.

To be Reformed means to be God centered. To preach Reformed truth is to help people to see God as the great King of grace, present and working at all times and places to carry out his wise plan of eternal love. As Warfield writes:

> It is this sense of God, of God's presence, of God's power, of God's all-pervading activity—most of all in the process of salvation—which constitutes Calvinism. . . . The Calvinist, in a word, is the man who sees God. . . . God in nature, God in history, God in grace. Everywhere he sees God in His mighty stepping, everywhere he feels the working of His mighty arm, the throbbing of His mighty heart.[20]

At the end of this book, we will consider in more depth how to preach divine sovereignty in a balanced way. At this point, this God-centered approach to all of life leads us to consider the great aim of Reformed preaching: that God should be glorified through the godliness of his people.

Preaching for Reformed Spirituality

From its earliest roots, the Reformed movement was a pursuit of holiness in personal, church, and national life. Building on the solid foundation of justification by faith alone, the Reformers labored together under the Spirit to construct a community of godliness by grace alone for the glory of God alone. They were not mere teachers and educators. Calvin writes, "Indeed, we shall not say that, properly speaking, God is known where there is no religion or piety."[21] The sole purpose for which he wrote his great work of theology was that people might be "shaped to true godliness."[22] Godliness or piety (Latin *pietas*) is reverential love for

20. B. B. Warfield, *Calvin as a Theologian and Calvinism Today* (London: Evangelical Press, 1969), 26–27.
21. *Institutes*, 1.2.1.
22. "Prefatory Address to King Francis I of France," in *Institutes*, 9.

God arising from God's grace and aiming to please him in all things.[23] Calvin calls piety "the soul of life."[24]

Preaching plays a crucial role in the growth of the church in godliness. Paul writes that the ascended Lord Jesus gives "pastors and teachers . . . for the edifying of the body of Christ" until every Christian reaches maturity, growing "unto a perfect man, unto the measure of the stature of the fulness of Christ" (Eph. 4:11–13). Calvin observes that God desires his people "to grow up into manhood" through "the preaching of the heavenly doctrine" by "the pastors."[25]

This Bible-based, God-centered impulse of Reformed spirituality lived on as the heartbeat of Puritanism. The Puritans built no walls between doctrine and life. William Ames (1576–1633) writes that theology is "the doctrine of living to God."[26] Reformed preaching aims at producing a people who, in union with Christ, "live unto God" (Gal. 2:19–20; cf. Rom. 6:11; 2 Cor. 5:15).

This view has implications for the preacher and the people.

The Holiness of the Preacher

Experiential preaching coincides with holy living. It is impossible to separate godly living from true experiential ministry. The holiness of a minister's heart is not merely an ideal; it is absolutely necessary for his work to be effective. Holiness of life must be his consuming passion.

The unique channels of experiential preaching are experiential preachers. Paul writes in 1 Thessalonians 2:4a, "But as we were allowed of God to be put in trust with the gospel, even so we speak." True ministers of the gospel speak as men approved by God to be entrusted with the gospel. God has tested their hearts and has found them to be fit vessels, sanctified by his grace to declare the riches of his grace.

How critical, then, is the question of what kind of men are approved by God and entrusted with the gospel as holy men of God? I will mention three characteristics:

---

23. *Institutes*, 1.2.1; see also "Calvin's Catechism (1538)," in James T. Dennison Jr., *Reformed Confessions of the Sixteenth and Seventeenth Centuries in English Translation, Volume 1, 1523–1552* (Grand Rapids, MI: Reformation Heritage Books, 2008), 410.

24. John Calvin, *Commentaries of Calvin*, various translators and editors, 45 vols. (Edinburgh: Calvin Translation Society, 1846–1851; repr., 22 vols., Grand Rapids, MI: Baker, 1979) [2 Pet. 1:3], hereafter, *Commentary*. Cf. Joel R. Beeke, introduction to *The Soul of Life: The Piety of John Calvin*, ed. Joel R. Beeke (Grand Rapids, MI: Reformation Heritage Books, 2009), 57.

25. *Institutes*, 4.1.5.

26. William Ames, *The Marrow of Sacred Divinity*, in *The Workes of the Reverend and Faithful Minister of Christ William Ames* (London: Iohn Rothwell, 1643), 1.1.1.

1. *They Are God-Fearing Gospel Believers.* Their lives pulsate with the power of the gospel. They are single-minded men who fear God rather than swivel-headed men who fear other people (1 Thess. 2:6). Fearing God, they esteem his smiles and frowns to be of greater weight and value than the smiles and frowns of men.

2. *They Manifestly Love the People to Whom They Minister.* Paul can say to the Thessalonians, "So being affectionately desirous of you, we were willing to have imparted unto you, not the gospel of God only, but also our own souls, because ye were dear unto us" (1 Thess. 2:8). There is no aloofness in the experiential preacher, no professional distance from the people. Richard Baxter writes: "The whole of our ministry must be carried on in a tender love to our people. . . . They should see that we care for no outward thing, neither wealth nor liberty nor honor nor life in comparison with their salvation."[27]

3. *Their Lives Manifest the Fruits of a Growing Experience of God.* James Stalker (1848–1927) writes: "A ministry of growing power must be one of growing experience. . . . Power for work like ours is only to be acquired in secret."[28] When a preacher ceases to grow in the grace and knowledge of the Lord, his preaching begins to stagnate. Stalker says: "The hearers may not know why their minister with all his gifts does not make a religious impression on them. But it is because he is not himself a spiritual power."[29]

Scripture says there should be no disparity between the character of a man who is called to proclaim God's Word and the content of his message. Jesus condemned the Pharisees and scribes for not practicing what they preached. He faulted them for the difference between their words and deeds, between what they professionally declared and how they personally acted in their daily lives. Professional clerics, more than anyone else, should consider the scathing words of Christ: "The scribes and the Pharisees sit in Moses' seat: all therefore whatsoever they bid you observe, that observe and do; but do not ye after their works: for they say, and do not" (Matt. 23:2–3). Ministers are called to be experientially holy in their private relationships with God, in their roles as husbands and fathers at home, and in their callings as shepherds among their people, just as they appear to be holy in the pulpit. There

---

27. Richard Baxter, *The Reformed Pastor* (Edinburgh: Banner of Truth, 1974), 117.
28. James Stalker, *The Preacher and His Models* (New York: A. C. Armstrong & Son, 1891), 53.
29. Stalker, *The Preacher and His Models*, 55.

must be no disjunction between their calling and living, their confession and practice.

Scripture says there is a cause-and-effect relationship between the character of a man's life as a Christian and his usefulness as a minister (2 Tim. 2:20–22). A minister's work is usually blessed in proportion to the sanctification of his heart before God. Ministers therefore must seek grace to build the house of God with sanctified lives as well as by sound experiential preaching and doctrine. Their preaching must shape their lives, and their lives must adorn their preaching.

Edward M. Bounds (1836–1913) writes: "The preacher is more than the sermon. . . . All the preacher says is tinctured, impregnated by what the preacher is. . . . The sermon is forceful because the man is forceful. The sermon is holy because the man is holy. The sermon is full of divine unction because the man is full of divine unction. . . . The sermon cannot rise in its life-giving forces above the man."[30] John Boys (1571–1625) summarizes it well when he quips, "He doth preach most that doth live best."[31] Ministers must be what they preach, not only applying themselves wholly to their texts but also applying their texts wholly to themselves. Otherwise, as John Owen (1616–1683) warns, "If a man teach uprightly and walk crookedly, more will fall down in the night of his life than he built in the day of his doctrine."[32]

The Holiness of the People

Whenever the Word and the Spirit break forth in Reformed experiential preaching, people are transformed. The Spirit is the Lord of reformation and revival. As Lord, he acts sovereignly and freely (John 3:8). He may act in small, quiet ways or he may suddenly rush upon men like a mighty wind. He may work upon thousands in a single day or he may touch just one hearer. But he is ever the Spirit of holiness, and his effects constantly bear the image of Jesus. This, then, must be the aim of preaching: a holy people for the glory of God.

Someone may object, "But what about conversions?" As I said earlier, Reformed preaching offers Christ to sinners and calls them to conversion. But the marks of true conversion are the seeds of holiness planted

---

30. E. M. Bounds, *Preacher and Prayer* (Chicago: Christian Witness Co., 1907), 8–9.

31. John Boys, *The Works of John Boys: An Exposition of the Several Offices* (Morgan, PA: Soli Deo Gloria, 1997), 25.

32. John Owen, "Eshcol: A Cluster of the Fruit of Canaan," in *The Works of John Owen*, ed. William H. Goold (Edinburgh: Banner of Truth, 1976), 13:57.

in the regenerate soul. Initial conversion is only the beginning of true spirituality; progressive sanctification is its growth.

Our sermons must train people to live unto God every day of the week. The holy life centers upon the Lord's Day, but it radiates outward to sanctify all of life unto the Lord—not just in devotions but in daily work, play, and rest. Reformed spirituality strongly affirms the holiness of ordinary life (Zech. 14:20–21). Hughes Oliphant Old writes:

> The Reformation was a reform of spirituality as much as it was a reform of theology. For millions of Christians at the end of the Middle Ages the old spirituality had broken down. For centuries spirituality had been cloistered behind monastery walls. . . . For Protestants spirituality became a matter of how one lived the Christian life with the family, out in the fields, in the workshop, in the kitchen, or at one's trade.[33]

This Reformed spirituality has massive implications for preaching, especially in the application of doctrine. The preacher is not to call people to a monastic or ascetic form of spirituality in which they must neglect their callings as spouses, parents, children, workers, and citizens to give themselves to a life of sheer contemplation. Rather, he must apply the doctrines of Scripture to show them how to fill the whole domain of their activity with the glory of Christ.

Alister McGrath writes that Reformation spirituality is "life in the world orientated towards God, rather than its classical association of life undertaken in withdrawal from the world."[34] Thomas Manton (1620–1677) says, "This is the difference between a Christian and others, he can make commerce worship . . . and whatever he doth to man, he doth it for God's sake, out of love to God, fear of God."[35]

What kind of spirituality does Reformed preaching aim to produce by the power of the Spirit? As we have already seen, it is spirituality rooted in faith in Christ as the only Mediator and fruitful in reverential love for the sovereign God. To draw out what this looks like in more detail, I will

---

33. Hughes Oliphant Old, "What Is Reformed Spirituality? Played Over Again Lightly," in *Calvin Studies VII*, ed. John H. Leith, Colloquium on Calvin Studies (Davidson, NC: Davidson College, 1994), 61. This article is a revised version of Hughes Oliphant Old, "What Is Reformed Spirituality," *Perspectives* 9, no. 1 (January 1994): 8–10.
34. Alister McGrath, *Roots That Refresh: A Celebration of Reformation Spirituality* (London: Hodder & Stoughton, 1991), 25.
35. Thomas Manton, "A Practical Commentary . . . on the Epistle of James," in *The Complete Works of Thomas Manton* (London: James Nisbet, 1871), 4:176 [James 1:27].

follow the outline that Old offers in his sketch of Reformed spirituality. These are the sorts of things that Reformed preaching cultivates in the life of the people of God.

1. *The Spirituality of the Word.* Christ himself is the Word (John 1:1). The Christian life consists of pious wisdom. This begins with preaching through books of the Bible, explaining and applying the meaning of one text at a time. It continues and deepens with reading through the Bible in our private devotions and family worship, as well as memorizing verses and passages of Scripture, and reading published sermons and doctrinal books.

In Reformed spirituality, however, such immersion in the Word is not just the job of a minister, but the calling of every Christian.[36] Therefore, when you preach the Word, call people to immerse themselves in it. Exhort them to become Psalm 1 Christians, who meditate on the Bible day and night, and walk in its ways with delight. Calvin said this kind of man counts "nothing more desirable or delicious" than growing in the Word; he is "always watered with the secret influences of divine grace."[37]

2. *The Spirituality of Praying the Psalms.* Old writes, "Reformed spirituality is a spirituality of the Psalter . . . praying the psalms, singing and meditating on them, not only at Church but at family prayers every day of the week." Christ, as a godly Jew, constantly prayed the Psalms. Calvin calls them the prayers of the Holy Spirit.[38] Old adds: "Any kind of Protestant spirituality is going to be a singing spirituality. For Reformed Protestantism a good part of that singing is going to be psalm singing."[39]

Preachers should constantly hold up before the church a lifestyle of continual prayer and praise (1 Thess. 5:17–18). The Spirit-filled life is a life of addressing each other with the Psalms (Eph. 5:18–19). Show the people how the Psalms open up the heart toward God in all our various experiences. Calvin says: "The varied and resplendent [shining] riches which are contained in this treasury it is no easy matter to express in words. . . . I have been accustomed to call this book, I think not inappropriately, 'An Anatomy of all the Parts of the Soul;' for there is not an emotion of which any one can be conscious that is not here represented as in a mirror."[40]

---

36. Old, "Reformed Spirituality," in *Calvin Studies VII*, 62–63.
37. *Commentary* [introduction to *Commentary on the Book of Psalms*].
38. *Commentary* [Ps. 20:1].
39. Old, "Reformed Spirituality," in *Calvin Studies VII*, 63–64.
40. *Commentary* [introduction to *Commentary on the Book of Psalms*].

3. *The Spirituality of the Lord's Day.* The sanctification of the Lord's Day is not Sabbatarian legalism; rather, it secures a day of peace, rest, refreshment, prayer, and love for God's people. Unlike the Lenten fasts rooted in the belief that asceticism and physical self-denial produce holiness (Col. 2:21, 23; 1 Tim. 4:1–5), the Lord's Day is a festive and joyous celebration of Christ's resurrection. It is a foretaste of heaven (Heb. 4:9). It is also a day for helping the poor with our voluntary gifts (1 Cor. 16:2).[41]

Teach people to "call the sabbath a delight" so that they can "delight [themselves] in the LORD" (Isa. 58:13–14). Help them to see that it is not an obsolete Jewish regulation, but truly "the Lord's Day" (Rev. 1:10), that is, a day to draw near to Christ, who is the Lord of the Sabbath (Mark 2:28). If a woman delights to have a date with the man she loves, how much more should a Christian delight to have a date with the living God? Watson says, "Rejoice at the approach of the day, as a day wherein we have a prize for our souls, and may enjoy much of God's presence."[42]

4. *The Spirituality of Works of Mercy.* The office of deacon is not a stepping-stone to pastoral leadership. In the Reformed tradition, the role of deacon is a distinct calling to lead the church in serving the poor and to care for the widow and the orphan (Acts 6:1–6). For example, in the seventeenth century, Christians in the Netherlands generously donated money and volunteered time for organizations serving the needy and disabled. Nineteenth-century believers in the United States saw a similar flowering of Christian benevolence.[43]

Apply the sweet and amazing love of God to our duty to love our fellow human beings at the point of physical suffering and spiritual misery. Build bridges between heavenly doctrine and earthly mercy. Those who think they seek God's grace while turning a blind eye and heart to the needs of men forget that the Savior says, "Blessed are the merciful: for they shall obtain mercy" (Matt. 5:7). Labor to convince your people that, as Jeremiah Burroughs (c. 1600–1646) says, "It's a more blessed thing to be merciful to others, than to be rich to themselves."[44]

5. *The Spirituality of the Lord's Supper.* Old says: "A Reformed spirituality finds in the celebration of the Lord's Supper a sign and seal of the covenant of grace. . . . It restores and strengthens that covenantal

---

41. Old, "Reformed Spirituality," in *Calvin Studies VII*, 64–65.
42. Watson, *The Ten Commandments*, 101 [Ex. 20:8–11].
43. Old, "Reformed Spirituality," in *Calvin Studies VII*, 65.
44. Jeremiah Burroughs, *The Saints' Happiness* (London: by M. S. for Nathaniel Brook, 1660), 381.

relationship." This rich piety of the Table is nurtured first of all through meditation leading up to the celebration of the Lord's Supper. It is no automatic conferral of grace, but an exercise of faith. Reformed Christians cherish the opportunity to experience the redeeming love of Jesus Christ more deeply and to pledge to him their faithful love.[45]

Let your preaching before the celebration of the Supper call believers to a rich feast in Jesus Christ. Help them to look through the bread and wine as through a window into heaven to see the love, forgiveness, and empowering grace of God for them. Matthew Henry (1662–1714) writes: "Though the sacrament directs us immediately to Christ, yet through Him it leads us to the Father. . . . Come, then, my soul, and see with joy and the highest satisfaction, the God that made thee entering into covenant with thee, and engaging to make thee happy."[46]

6. *The Spirituality of Stewardship.* Christ's parables often portray faithful servants entrusted with the master's resources. In the Reformation, this idea of stewardship transformed believers' views of money and work. Businessmen, housewives, farmers, bankers, those caring for the elderly, and craftsmen came to see themselves as entrusted with a sacred vocation or calling to serve the Lord. The so-called Protestant work ethic grounded hard work upon the gospel, resulting in the production of wealth to be used positively for the kingdom of God and the good of men. Thus, the questions of how one makes money and how one budgets one's spending are profoundly spiritual matters.[47]

Teach the congregation to rule their money, time, and talents for the Lord, and not to let their resources rule them (Matt. 6:24). As George Swinnock (c. 1627–1673) says, the righteous man "tradeth with his temporal stock for the true riches."[48] Swinnock proceeds to say that if the world smiles on him, the godly man does not trust it. It may give him its treasures, but he does not give it his heart. When his prosperity abounds, he abounds in thanksgiving to God and in a desire to use his wealth rightly, not just to get more. If the world frowns on him, he sees it as an opportunity to kill his love for the world, like putting out a fire by withdrawing its fuel.

---

45. Old, "Reformed Spirituality," in *Calvin Studies VII*, 65–66.
46. Matthew Henry, *The Communicant's Companion* (Philadelphia: Presbyterian Board of Publication, 1825), 211, quoted in Joel R. Beeke and Paul M. Smalley, eds., *Feasting with Christ: Meditations on the Lord's Supper* (Darlington, England: Evangelical Press, 2012), 106.
47. Old, "Reformed Spirituality," in *Calvin Studies VII*, 66–67.
48. George Swinnock, "The Christian Man's Calling, Part II," in *The Works of George Swinnock* (Edinburgh: Banner of Truth, 1992), 1:380.

7. *The Spirituality of Meditating on God's Ways.* This refers not just to meditating on Scripture, but to meditating on God's works in our lives through the lens of Scripture. The lives of Abraham, Joseph, David, Christ, and the apostles were shaped and directed by a secret providence. So, too, are our lives (Prov. 16:1, 4, 9, 33). Old says: "Each one of us has a purpose in life. The devout life is one dedicated to fulfilling that purpose."[49]

If you guide your flock to think often about God's gracious ways with them, they will find much comfort in trials. They will be like David, who, when he hid from Saul in the cave, prayed, "I will cry unto God most high; unto God that performeth all things for me" (Ps. 57:2). John Flavel (c. 1628–1691) says, "It is the duty of the saints, especially in times of straits [distress], to reflect upon the performances of Providence for them in all the states and through all the stages of their lives."[50]

8. *The Spirituality of Evangelism and Missions.* Old writes, "The spirituality of God's eternal purposes has often led to an evangelistic, missionary spirituality." The covenant blesses us to be a blessing to the world. The heroes of Reformed piety were often imbued with a missionary spirit, praying, sending, going—and suffering.[51]

A classic example is David Brainerd. He poured his life into pioneer missions among the Native Americans. Though tuberculosis cut short his life, his journal, published by Jonathan Edwards, is now counted as one of the treasures of Reformed experiential writing. Our Reformed ancestors gave their heart, soul, and strength to spreading the gospel, and today we reap the harvest they planted.[52] Therefore, the Reformed minister preaches with an eye on the Great Commission (Matt. 28:18–20). He encourages likeness to Christ, who sent his church into the world just as he was sent by the Father (John 17:18).

To Old's list, I would add two more qualities of Reformed spirituality.

9. *The Spirituality of Godly Fellowship.* Reformed spirituality encourages fellowship among the godly for mutual encouragement. It is relational, not individualistic. Puritanism was characterized by a "spiritual brotherhood," a supportive network of people with similar beliefs and experiences.[53] F. Ernest Stoeffler writes that Puritanism and similar move-

---

49. Old, "Reformed Spirituality," in *Calvin Studies VII*, 67–68.
50. John Flavel, *The Mystery of Providence* (Edinburgh: Banner of Truth, 1963), 20.
51. Old, "Reformed Spirituality," in *Calvin Studies VII*, 68.
52. Old, "Reformed Spirituality," in *Calvin Studies VII*, 68.
53. Tom Webster, *Godly Clergy in Early Stuart England: The Caroline Puritan Movement, c. 1620–1643* (Cambridge, UK: Cambridge University Press, 1997), 333. The term "spiritual brotherhood" originated from William Haller, *The Rise of Puritanism: Or, The Way to the New*

ments put "great emphasis on religious fellowship called the *koinonia*,"[54] a fellowship that provides "the human support" for our spiritual life and "transcends the boundaries of race or class, church or nation, space or time, life or death."[55]

Teach the people the privileges of being active members of the church of Christ (1 Corinthians 12). Warn them against isolating themselves or trying to go it alone. Encourage spiritual friendships and mutual accountability. One of the greatest joys of the godly is to find people of the same mind-set, talk with them about the Lord, pray with them, and worship with them (Ps. 16:3; 84:4). God gives special promises of his presence and grace to the gatherings of the people of God (Ps. 87:2; Matt. 18:20; Col. 2:2; 3:16). David Clarkson (1622–1686) says that God is present in public worship "more effectually, constantly, intimately" than in private devotions.[56]

10. *The Spirituality of Heavenly-Minded Obedience.* Reformed spirituality produces zeal for obeying God's laws and standing against worldliness. Preachers must show people that this is not legalism because it is rooted in love for God. Gerard Wisse (1873–1957) says, "Obedience to God is the panting of the soul who is enamored with God."[57] To obey God's laws is to follow Jesus in the pathway of rejoicing in and walking according to divine love (John 15:10–12). Preach obedience to the law by the grace of Christ. The law is no means for sinners to find justification before God, but it is also no enemy of grace.

Grace makes us citizens of a holy kingdom. The grace of God, the redeeming death of Christ, and the coming of the Lord in glory are "teaching us that, denying ungodliness and worldly lusts, we should live soberly, righteously, and godly, in this present world" (Titus 2:12). Obedience to Christ is the heavenly path. Calvin says, "This world is but a pilgrimage, and this life is but a journeying."[58] True spirituality frees us from the entanglements of the lust of the flesh, the lust of the eyes, and

Jerusalem as Set Forth in Pulpit and Press from Thomas Cartwright to John Lilburne and John Milton, 1570–1643 (New York: Columbia University Press, 1938), chap. 2.

54. F. Ernest Stoeffler, "Pietism—Its Message, Early Manifestation, and Significance," in *Contemporary Perspectives on Pietism: A Symposium* (Chicago: Covenant Press, 1976), 12. *Koinonia* is the Greek term for "fellowship, sharing, and communion."

55. Stoeffler, "Pietism," in *Contemporary Perspectives*, 10.

56. David Clarkson, "Public Worship to Be Preferred before Private," in *The Practical Works of David Clarkson* (Edinburgh: James Nichol, 1865), 3:190.

57. Gerard Wisse, *Christ's Ministry in the Christian*, trans. Bartel Elshout and William Van Voorst (Sioux Center, IA: Netherlands Reformed Book and Publishing, 1993), 90.

58. *Commentary* [Eph. 6:1–4].

the pride of life, with all the ways in which the world promotes them. It sets our minds on things above, and the glory of Christ becomes our grand pursuit.

Conclusion

Reformed preaching is the proclamation of Reformed truth for Reformed spirituality. We must preach the whole counsel of God revealed in Scripture and summarized in the great Reformed confessions and catechisms. Above all and in all, we must preach Christ as the Mediator of the gracious covenant of the sovereign God. Preachers, ask yourselves: "Is my preaching rooted in the glorious truths of Christ rediscovered in the Reformation? Do I know what those truths are? Do I faithfully make them known, even in the face of indifference and hostility?"

Furthermore, ask yourselves: "Do I design my preaching to be a sharp instrument by which the Lord shapes a holy people for his glory? Do I call unbelievers to repentance? Am I guiding the church to a robust and full-orbed spirituality as just described? Or is my preaching aiming at something else?" Too often preachers aim at false goals, such as:

- attracting and entertaining a crowd of people;
- educating big brains while neglecting withered hearts;
- seeking superficial decisions for Christ to count as "conversions";
- promoting a social or political agenda without a heavenly focus;
- generating warm feelings but not touching the heart with the truth; and
- advancing their own honor and influence.

Let us humble ourselves before the almighty God and seek by the blood of Jesus to have the sins of our preaching forgiven and our souls transformed. May God raise up an army of preachers who are Reformed by the Word and Spirit!

4

The Experiential Preacher

One of the major problems with preaching today is the stark contrast between the serious nature of the message that is proclaimed and the casual or "conversational" way in which it is delivered. Preachers who preach casually convey the impression that they do not have anything really important to say. They should not be surprised if they are not given serious attention. In the Puritan tradition, such preaching would have been anathema. This is far more than a matter of style.[1]

In the previous chapter, I touched on the great priority of holiness in the life of the preacher. In this chapter, I will focus more on the spirit in which the minister preaches. It is a mysterious thing, but some preachers bring with them into the pulpit a wondrous sense of the glory of God, the sweetness of grace, the weightiness of eternity, and the hatefulness of sin. One senses the fear of the Lord in them almost before they speak. It is not a show. It is the spiritual reality of Christ shining from their hearts out of their facial expressions, the tone of their voices, and the way they carry themselves.

What kind of heart does a man need to cultivate in order to be an experiential preacher? Let me highlight several characteristics.

A Passionate Preacher

Reformed experiential preaching is the earnest proclamation of a message that is both urgent and important. Such preaching strives to emulate

---

1. Portions of this chapter are adapted from Joel R. Beeke, "The Utter Necessity of a Godly Life," in *Reforming Pastoral Ministry: Challenges for Ministry in Postmodern Times*, ed. John H. Armstrong (Wheaton, IL: Crossway, 2001), 59–82, and "Applying the Word," in *Living for God's Glory: An Introduction to Calvinism* (Lake Mary, FL: Reformation Trust, 2008), 268–72. Used with permission.

Paul: "Therefore seeing we have this ministry, as we have received mercy, we faint not; but have renounced the hidden things of dishonesty, not walking in craftiness, nor handling the word of God deceitfully; but by manifestation of the truth commending ourselves to every man's conscience in the sight of God" (2 Cor. 4:1–2).

Earnest experiential preaching avoids all levity. By levity, I refer to treating divine matters without proper reverence by mixing them with jokes and frivolity. At its root, the word *levity* means treating weighty things as if they were light. Richard Baxter writes, "Of all the preaching in the world, I hate that preaching which tends to make the hearers laugh, or to move their minds with tickling levity and affect them as stage plays used to, instead of affecting them with a holy reverence for the name of God."[2]

Earnest preaching aims to please God rather than men. The minister speaks in the conviction that God is his witness. All masks are stripped away; all flattery is abhorred. Here is Baxter again:

> Oh sirs, how plainly, how closely, how earnestly should we deliver a message of such moment as ours. . . . In the name of God, brethren, labor to awaken your own hearts before you go into the pulpit that you may be fit to awaken the hearts of sinners. Remember, they must be awakened or damned. And a sleepy preacher will hardly awaken drowsy sinners. . . . Speak to your people as to men that must be awakened either here or in hell.[3]

Though an experiential preacher may also be a teacher, he knows that preaching is not lecturing. J. I. Packer says, "Preaching is essentially teaching plus application."[4] This implies that preaching cannot consist of the cold, dry communication of information. It is not merely pointing an arrow in a particular direction. Preaching is fitting the arrow to the bowstring, drawing it back with strength, and launching it straight at the heart. Packer writes, "Preaching mediates not only God's authority, but also His presence and His power."[5] No doubt, mindless Christianity is spineless Christianity. But the goal is more than to inform the mind;

---

2. Richard Baxter, *The Reformed Pastor* (Edinburgh: Banner of Truth, 1974), 119–20.

3. Baxter, *The Reformed Pastor*, 147–48.

4. J. I. Packer, "Introduction: Why Preach?" in *The Preacher and Preaching: Reviving the Art in the Twentieth Century*, ed. Samuel T. Logan Jr. (Phillipsburg, NJ: Presbyterian and Reformed, 1986), 3.

5. Packer, "Why Preach?" 13.

preaching aims to reach the heart through the mind, and thereby to change the whole person.

Preaching also differs from lecturing in terms of the simplicity of its content. This is especially true in our day, when people are not trained to think logically and critically. Most Puritans were educated in the method of Petrus Ramus (1515–1572), an influential French humanist and educational reformer who attempted to infuse order and simplicity into philosophical and scholastic education by providing a sense of dialectic as the overriding methodological basis for various disciplines. Ramus recommended the use of summaries, headings, subheadings, citations, and examples. Consequently, Puritans could listen well to a message with three points, each of which had several subpoints, and each of which had several sub-subpoints, and so on. Today, a well-trained congregation can follow a few main points and some subpoints. But if the preacher goes beyond that, he loses them in confusion. Some congregations that are not used to doctrinal preaching think even three or four points with a few subpoints make for a complicated sermon. In a world of thirty-second commercial advertisements, 280-character "tweets," and two-word text messages (mssng vwls!), most people need more training before they are prepared for complicated theological messages, as beneficial as those can be. That is not to say that sermon material should not be organized to its roots, even if the minister does not announce his subpoints. People today need to hear a single theme derived from the scriptural text and pressed home in a memorable, organized way with passion, energy, and application.

Therefore, the glory of God and the needs of our listeners compel us to preach with sincerity and holy energy. This is more than raising our voices and waving our arms. I speak here of the energy of the heart: zeal for Christ, fervency of spirit, and burning love for God and man.[6] Charles H. Spurgeon says:

> If I were asked—What in a Christian minister is the most essential quality for securing success in winning souls for Christ? I should reply, "earnestness" . . . an intense zeal, a consuming passion for souls, and an eager enthusiasm in the cause of God, and we believe

---

6. For a Puritan-based guide to cultivating true zeal for the Lord, see Joel R. Beeke and James A. La Belle, *Living Zealously* (Grand Rapids, MI: Reformation Heritage Books, 2012).

that in every case, other things being equal, men prosper in the divine service in proportion as their hearts are blazing with holy love.[7]

A Prayerful Preacher

Reformed experiential preaching is marked by prayerful dependence on the Holy Spirit. Where else can preachers get illumination in the truth and holy fire to preach it? Reformed experiential preachers keenly feel their inability to preach rightly, to bring anyone to Christ, and to mature Christ's saints. They know they are totally dependent on the work of the Spirit to effect regeneration and conversion when, how, and in whom he will. They believe that the Spirit alone persuades sinners to seek salvation, renews corrupt wills, and makes scriptural truths take root in stony hearts.

Packer writes of man-made soul winning, "All devices for exerting psychological pressure in order to precipitate 'decisions' must be eschewed, as being in truth presumptuous attempts to intrude into the province of the Holy Ghost." Such pressures may even be harmful, he goes on to say, for while they "may produce the outward form of 'decision,' they cannot bring about regeneration and a change of heart, and when the 'decisions' wear off those who registered them will be found 'gospel-hardened' and antagonistic." Packer concludes, "Evangelism must rather be conceived as a long-term enterprise of patient teaching and instruction, in which God's servants seek simply to be faithful in delivering the gospel message and applying it to human lives, and leave it to God's Spirit to draw men to faith through this message in his own way and at his own speed."[8]

This sense of dependence prompts experiential preachers to strive, albeit with many shortcomings, to bathe all their preaching in prayer. They aim to be "men of the closet" first of all. Baxter says: "Prayer must carry on our work as well as preaching; he preacheth not heartily to his people, that prayeth not earnestly for them. If we prevail not with God to give them faith and repentance, we shall never prevail with them to believe and repent."[9]

---

7. Charles H. Spurgeon, *Lectures to my Students*, Lecture VIII (Pasadena, TX: Pilgrim Publications, 1990), 11, quoted in David Eby, *Power Preaching for Church Growth* (Fearn, Ross-shire, Scotland: Christian Focus, 1996), 72.

8. J. I. Packer, *A Quest for Godliness: The Puritan Vision of the Christian Life* (Wheaton, IL: Crossway, 1990), 163–64.

9. Baxter, *The Reformed Pastor*, 122.

Thomas Boston (1676–1732) says that since we must follow Christ to become fishers of men (Matt. 4:19), then we must follow him in his example of much prayer. The preacher must seek true wisdom from God and not preach what is merely the product of his own mind. He must pray that the needs of his people would affect his soul. He must ask that God would inflame his heart with zeal for God's glory so that his preaching would flow from love for God and for souls. He must pray that the Lord would apply the message he is preparing to bring to his own heart, both in the study and the pulpit. He must obtain from the throne of grace the clarity of mind and boldness of spirit to speak the whole truth to men. He must cry for physical strength for the labor of preaching. And he must ask God to make the preached Word a "convincing and converting word" to the indifferent, an edifying and instructive word to the young Christian, a reconciling and restoring word to the disenchanted and disaffected church member, a word in season to the mature Christian who nonetheless struggles to bear life's burdens and fight against temptation, and a "healing word" to the brokenhearted believer.[10]

A story about Robert Murray M'Cheyne (1813–1843) illustrates this well. An old sexton in M'Cheyne's church noticed the awe on the face of a visitor and invited him into the minister's study. "Tell me," said the visitor, "having sat under this godly man's ministry, what is the secret of his success?" The sexton told the visitor to sit at M'Cheyne's desk. Then he asked the man to bow his head. Then he said to put his face in his hands and weep. Next the two men walked into the church sanctuary and ascended to the pulpit. "Lean over the pulpit," the sexton said. "Stretch out your hands and weep. Now you know the secret of M'Cheyne's ministry."

The church today desperately needs preachers whose private prayers season their pulpit messages, and who continually remind themselves that awakening, heart-engaging, life-transforming preaching does not depend on ministerial eloquence, self-generated passion, or powers of persuasion, but on the sovereign good pleasure of God operating through the ministry of the Holy Spirit. Let us pray unceasingly that God will provide seminaries and seminary teachers who model experiential religion and preaching, and that he will send forth into his white and ready fields thousands of such Spirit-dependent preachers to proclaim

---

10. Thomas Boston, *The Art of Manfishing: A Puritan's View of Evangelism* (Fearn, Ross-shire, Scotland: Christian Focus, 1998), 91–94.

the unsearchable riches of Jesus Christ to needy sinners and to hungry saints all over the globe (John 4:35).

An Authentic Preacher

Nobody admires a fake. The old divines stressed that ministers must seek to build the house of God with two hands, the hand of their doctrine (teaching and preaching) and the hand of their life. The Presbyterians used to say, "Truth is in order to goodness."[11] Doctrine must produce life, and life must adorn our doctrine. As Robert Murray M'Cheyne says, "A minister's life is the life of his ministry."[12]

M'Cheyne probably says it best of all: "In great measure, according to the purity and perfections of the instrument, will be the success. It is not great talents God blesses so much as great likeness to Jesus. A holy minister is an awful [awesome] weapon in the hand of God."[13]

We must be as holy in private as we are in the pulpit. We must be watchful, sincere, and earnest in our personal relationship with the Lord. Paul warns, "Take heed unto thyself, and unto the doctrine; continue in them: for in doing this thou shalt both save thyself, and them that hear thee" (1 Tim. 4:16).

The preacher must not only apply himself to his text, but he must also apply his text to himself. As the German pastor and scholar John Albert Bengel (1687–1752) famously says, "*Te totum applica ad textum: rem totam applica ad te*" ("Thyself wholly apply to the text; the substance of it wholly apply to thyself").[14] Gardiner Spring (1785–1872) writes, "His heart must be a transcript of his sermons."[15] After almost forty years of ministry, Spring observed that only piety makes an effective preacher. A man without godliness may do some good in society. He may not fall into scandalous sins. His education and conscience may produce some helpful truth in his teaching. He might even enjoy the ministry all his life if he

---

11. This is what the old Presbyterians actually said, though later it was often quoted as "Truth is in order to godliness." That, too, is true, of course, but there is such a thing as insincere and hypocritical godliness, or false religion; however, goodness is purely and simply goodness. S. G. Winchester, "The Importance of Doctrinal and Instructive Preaching," in *A Series of Tracts on the Doctrines, Order, and Polity of the Presbyterian Church in the United States of America* (Philadelphia: Presbyterian Board of Publication, 1840), 2:295.

12. Quoted in Charles Bridges, *The Christian Ministry* (London: Banner of Truth, 2006), 160.

13. Letter to Dan Edwards, Oct. 2, 1840, in *Memoir & Remains of Robert Murray M'Cheyne*, ed. Andrew Bonar (1892; repr., Edinburgh: Banner of Truth, 1966), 282.

14. From J. A. Bengel's 1734 edition of the Greek New Testament. Eberhard Nestle cites it as a superscription to the introduction to his critical edition of the Greek New Testament, *The Interlinear Greek-English New Testament* (Grand Rapids, MI: Zondervan, 1975).

15. Gardiner Spring, *The Power of the Pulpit* (1848; repr., Edinburgh: Banner of Truth, 1986), 154.

is a proud hypocrite or is deluded with false hopes. But he will die, and even while men praise him at his funeral, he may be in torment in hell.[16]

Lack of piety is as deadly as a spear thrust to the heart. Half-hearted piety slowly bleeds away the minister's strength. Spring writes: "It makes the preacher ashamed to look his people in the face; his conscience smites him; his heart trembles; and he may well feel that he can never more open his mouth, because of his shame. His energy is weak and pusillanimous [cowardly]; his holy daring is faint-hearted; his affectionate tenderness is fled and gone, because the words he utters do not find a distinct and full echo from his own heart."[17]

But piety or godliness enlivens a minister to seek God's kingdom. Spring says, "What is piety, but that state of mind and moral feeling which regards God as God: which loves him as God; which obeys him as God, and honors him as our Lawgiver and our Redeemer?"[18] Piety lifts a man's head and makes him as bold as a lion. Piety gives God's servants the inward power to live unto God with burning zeal. "What is piety but that great astounding principle, which, while it is the mainspring of action in the heart, has the vigor and efficacy to make itself felt in every artery, and vein, and muscle, and delicate nerve of the moral man?"[19]

It is too easy to wear a ministerial mask on the Lord's Day. It is too easy to pretend to be spiritual because people expect it instead of humbling ourselves before God and drawing strength from him and the power of his might. But playing the professional pastor cuts the nerves of ministry and paralyzes our preaching. John Piper writes: "Professionalism has nothing to do with the essence and heart of the Christian ministry. . . . For there is no professional childlikeness (Matt. 18:3); there is no professional tenderheartedness (Eph. 4:32); there is no professional panting after God (Ps. 42:1)."[20]

Authenticity demands that we face our weaknesses and cease proudly projecting a strong, always-in-control persona to the world. As Paul states so eloquently in his second epistle to the Corinthians, ministry is a

---

16. Spring, *The Power of the Pulpit*, 145–46.
17. Spring, *The Power of the Pulpit*, 153–54.
18. Spring, *The Power of the Pulpit*, 150.
19. Spring, *The Power of the Pulpit*, 151. A mainspring is a spring of coiled metal ribbon once commonly used in clocks, watches, and other wind-up machines or toys. It supplied the power and motion to the device.
20. John Piper, *Brothers, We Are Not Professionals: A Plea to Pastors for Radical Ministry* (Nashville: Broadman & Holman, 2002), 1–2.

kind of dying even as the life of Christ triumphs through us (2 Cor. 6:9). Piper says: "We are fools for Christ's sake, but professionals are wise. We are weak, but professionals are strong. Professionals are held in honor; we are in disrepute."[21]

In fact, professional clerics are exactly what the scribes and the Pharisees were, whom Jesus so despised. Jesus says, "The scribes and the Pharisees sit in Moses' seat: all therefore whatsoever they bid you observe, that observe and do; but do not ye after their works: for they say, and do not" (Matt. 23:2–3). Jesus hates the disjunction between a holy calling and unholy living, and between orthodox preaching and hypocritical practice.

Even in godly Christians, ministry too easily becomes a substitute for a daily, vital relationship with Christ. There are clear and present dangers facing preachers: temptations of laziness, sexual immorality, and so forth. But Spurgeon warns, "There are more secret snares than these, from which we can less easily escape; and of these the worst is the temptation to ministerialism—the tendency to read our Bibles as ministers, to pray as ministers, to get into doing the whole of our religion as not ourselves personally, but only relatively, concerned in it."[22] We must ever live as children of God, not only as ministers of his Word.

A Growing Preacher

The daily exercise of faith and repentance through the means of grace leads the preacher into a growing experience of Christ. It is essential that our experience be renewed if we would be fresh and powerful in our preaching. James Stalker says, "Power for work like ours is only to be acquired in secret; it is only the man who has a large, varied and original life with God who can go on speaking about the things of God with fresh interest."[23] Let's consider each of these three qualities that Stalker highlights.

A Large Life with God

Peter admonishes us to "grow in grace, and in the knowledge of the Lord and Saviour Jesus Christ" (2 Pet. 3:18). Paul describes being changed by the Holy Spirit from one degree of glory to another (2 Cor. 3:18).

---

21. Piper, *Brothers, We Are Not Professionals*, 2.
22. Spurgeon, *Lectures to My Students*, 1:10–11.
23. James Stalker, *The Preacher and His Models* (New York: A. C. Armstrong & Son, 1891), 55.

Spiritual life is a dynamic reality that begins in the heart and grows by grace and knowledge. If the heart of the preacher is increasingly sanctified toward God, his preaching gains new depths and nuances that reflect his spiritual growth.

We preach the same truths, the same God, and the same covenant of grace, but our preaching is enriched by our growing relationship with God. When a minister is walking with God and growing spiritually, a wise listener should be able to say, "He is preaching the same Christ as he did ten years ago, but his preaching is richer, deeper, and fuller now."

It's like a good marriage. As the years pass, the couple remains faithful and committed to each other: one man and one woman bound together until death separates them. But that does not mean the relationship stays the same. It is alive and dynamic. The husband and the wife grow in knowing, loving, and serving each other. Facing the heartaches and disappointments of life together while forbearing with each other and forgiving the sins they commit against each other, they develop a history of grace together. After ten years, their marriage is sweeter and more solid than during the honeymoon. With each passing decade, it grows richer still. If that's true for a merely human relationship, how much more can it be true of the relationship between a man of God and the infinite Lord?

Don't stagnate. When water ceases to flow, it forms a stagnant pond where bacteria multiply and mosquitoes breed. You can build a million-dollar house on its shores, but the water still stinks. Sadly, a big church can hide a stagnant preacher. We don't have to be like that. Jesus Christ says: "If any man thirst, let him come unto me, and drink. He that believeth on me, as the scripture hath said, out of his belly shall flow rivers of living water" (John 7:37–38). By God's grace, we live downstream from a vast source of life—the infinite love of God.

No matter how long you have served the Lord, you are just beginning to get to know him. Like Paul, we must press on: "Brethren, I count not myself to have apprehended: but this one thing I do, forgetting those things which are behind, and reaching forth unto those things which are before, I press toward the mark for the prize of the high calling of God in Christ Jesus" (Phil. 3:13–14). Pursue a large life with God.

A Varied Life with God

The book of Psalms eloquently testifies that walking with God is a varied experience. Some people view the Christian life as nothing but joy and victory. But such a view denies the messages in nearly half the psalms, in which the psalmists cry out in pain, sorrow, frustration, and loneliness. The Psalter gives us an authentic theology of Christian experience. As I noted in the previous chapter, John Calvin called the psalms "An Anatomy of all the Parts of the Soul" for their depiction of every human emotion toward God.[24] We ought, therefore, to look to the psalms to give us a better understanding of what we encounter in our walk with God. They serve us well as the songs of our earthly pilgrimage.

Walking with God leads us along a winding path with many ups and downs. A godly person may experience times of unspeakable joy and peace that passes understanding. He also has days of constant wrestling and groaning heaviness. There are times of clarity and times of confusion. There are seasons of power and seasons of weakness. Sometimes the Lord delivers his servant and honors him; sometimes God stands with his servant in trouble (Ps. 91:15).

As pastors, we need to make the psalms our language of prayer in every experience. At times, we can shout, "My soul shall be satisfied as with marrow and fatness; and my mouth shall praise thee with joyful lips" (Ps. 63:5). At other times, we can groan: "Will the Lord cast off for ever? and will he be favourable no more? Is his mercy clean gone for ever? doth his promise fail for evermore? Hath God forgotten to be gracious? hath he in anger shut up his tender mercies?" (Ps. 77:7–9).

Preachers above all others should appreciate the varied experiences of God's children because they serve as spiritual counselors to them. If a pastor thinks that true spirituality equals constant joy, he will wear out himself and his flock with unbiblical expectations. If a pastor tends to equate holiness with unmitigated grief over sin, then he will weaken the people, for the joy of the Lord is our strength. Biblical ministry flows out of experiencing both Christ's death and his life, "as sorrowful, yet alway rejoicing" (2 Cor. 6:10; 4:10). Truly Reformed ministry weaves together the great themes of experiencing our misery, deliverance, and gratitude.[25] Only then are we "able to comfort them which are in any trouble, by the comfort wherewith we ourselves are comforted of God" (2 Cor. 1:4).

---

24. John Calvin, *Commentaries of Calvin*, various translators and editors, 45 vols. (Edinburgh: Calvin Translation Society, 1846–1851; repr., 22 vols., Grand Rapids, MI: Baker, 1979) [introduction to *Commentary on the Book of Psalms*].

25. See the Heidelberg Catechism, Q. 2.

An Original Life with God

Scripture abounds with teaching about our union with Christ and the communion we share with all the saints. We are children in one family under the same Father. We are living stones in one spiritual temple sharing the same Spirit. We are members of one body, of which Christ is Head. And yet, the Scriptures also emphasize that each member of the body is different from the others, and very much needed in its distinct giftedness (1 Corinthians 12). We are "stewards of the manifold grace of God" (1 Pet. 4:10). There is goodness in our variety, the intentional goodness planned by sovereign grace. The Spirit distributes our multiplicity of talents "as he will" (1 Cor. 12:11).

We are all leaves on the same tree, but no two leaves are exactly alike. If you go to a flower show, you can see that God created an astonishing variety of shapes, colors, and sizes of roses, from tiny, red miniature roses to fluffy, white alba roses. He is the God of the snowflakes, which crystallize and fall by the millions each winter, with no two of them quite the same. The Lord delights in the details. Christ says in Matthew 10:30, "But the very hairs of your head are all numbered." The Good Shepherd "calleth his own sheep by name" (John 10:3). He knows you by name!

Therefore, no two believers and no two preachers are exactly alike. God knows this and designed it to be this way. He gave you your personality and shaped you through your experiences. He has sent you to a particular place and people at this particular time. He has prepared good works for you to do there (Eph. 2:10). He already knows whom he will save by your ministry (Acts 13:48; 18:10).

Walk with God in the path he has traced for you. Follow Christ along the road God has prepared uniquely for you. Christians are like ships crossing the ocean from New York to England. We all start in the same place (being born again) and end in the same place (heaven), but no ship carves a pathway others can follow. Each ship makes its own way through the sea.

You can learn from the lives of great men who have gone ahead of you, but you cannot walk their paths. Perhaps you like the story of John Newton's conversion. But you must have your own story. Maybe you find Martyn Lloyd-Jones's ministry an inspiration. But don't try to be Lloyd-Jones or fault yourself because you are not. Be your own man. Don't try to copy someone else. That doesn't mean, of course, that we don't need models that we should choose with great care; after all, we do learn by imitation. But as we mature, we must carve out our own paths with our own gifts. Follow worthy models only insofar as they follow Christ (1 Cor. 11:1), but do not make any of them into your Christ (1 Cor. 1:13). Fix your eyes on Jesus.

God has written all your days in his book (Ps. 139:16). Each day, turn a page to discover the wonderful story the Author of all good things has written for you. In the end, God will be far more glorified in the unified diversity of his servants than he would have been with cookie-cutter, look-alike preachers. He has chosen *you* for his glory. Therefore, don't envy others, but strive to be what God wants you to be.

Cultivate a large, varied, and original life with God. There is a mystery about ministry. It is not a mechanical work in which we get the right results by assembling the right parts. It is a relational work: "we are labourers together with God" (1 Cor. 3:9). When we walk closely with him, it is amazing how he blesses us in providence and grace. Sometimes the most effective parts of our ministry are the things we didn't plan or anticipate.

A Decreasing Preacher

It seems odd to talk about a decreasing preacher after urging you to have a vital and growing spiritual life. But there is a sense in which we grow only by shrinking. John the Baptist said, "He must increase, but I must decrease" (John 3:30). John's disciples had approached him with the dismaying news that his ministry was shrinking. All the attention was going to a new preacher named Jesus. John replied with a remarkable statement of God's sovereignty and Christ's supremacy:

> A man can receive nothing, except it be given him from heaven. Ye yourselves bear me witness, that I said, I am not the Christ, but that I am sent before him. He that hath the bride is the bridegroom: but the friend of the bridegroom, which standeth and heareth him, rejoiceth greatly because of the bridegroom's voice: this my joy therefore is fulfilled. *He must increase, but I must decrease.* (John 3:27–30)

We all enter ministry with mixed motives because we are imperfect men. Sadly, it is possible to preach Christ for our own glory (Phil. 1:15). We all need to die to our egos. God uses afflictions and disappointments to expedite this process; indeed, the absence of such chastening should be a disturbing sign (Heb. 12:5–7). Pain becomes the sandpaper by which he strips away the old layers of varnish to make way for a new finish. Sometimes he works in the midst of prosperity to bow down our souls through inward piercings. The Spirit of God is free and sovereign in his methods, but his aim is always the same: to put to death the old man, to crucify that god of self that once ruled us (Rom. 6:6; 8:13).

Our calling is to deny ourselves, take up our crosses, and follow Christ (Luke 9:23). Cultivating an original life with God does not mean self-fulfillment, but paradoxically finding life in self-abnegation for Christ (v. 24). The self denied is a self put into the right place to be sanctified, transformed, and eventually glorified. Only when you seek and submit to the Spirit's application of Christ's death to your self and your sins do you become what God designed you to be.

Spurgeon speaks of this in terms of "that sweet feeling of self-annihilation." We must not press this language too far, for Christ came to save sinners, not destroy them. But there is a piercing truth that we must hear in all the biblical language of mortification and crucifixion. Spurgeon says: "I have now concentrated all my prayers into one, that one prayer into this, that I may die to self, and live wholly to him. It seems to me to be the highest stage of man—to have no wish, no thought, no desire but Christ . . . to feel that it did not matter what became of one's self, so that one's Master was but exalted."[26]

To adapt one of Spurgeon's metaphors, we are like coal, pieces of carbon graphite in the earth—of little value in ourselves. We must be willing to be crushed under the pressure and heat of the earth so that we can become diamonds for the Lord. Yet even as diamonds, we are still in the rough, needing to be cut and polished, and our prayer should always be, "Lord, let me be cut ever so sharply, polished ever so thoroughly, that I may sparkle in the crown of my Savior!"

Spurgeon says: "We do not covet the life of self-will, but we sigh after the spirit of self-denial; yea, of self-annihilation, that Christ may live in us, and that the old *Ego*, the carnal *I*, may be altogether slain. I would be as obedient to my God as are those firstborn sons of light, his messengers of flaming fire."[27]

---

26. Charles H. Spurgeon, Sermon No. 101, "The Exaltation of Christ," Nov. 2, 1856, in *The New Park Street Pulpit* (1857; repr., Pasadena, TX: Pilgrim Publications, 1975), 2:380.
27. Charles H. Spurgeon, Sermon No. 597, "Preparation for Revival," Oct. 30, 1864, in *Metropolitan Tabernacle Pulpit* (1865; repr., Pasadena, TX: Pilgrim Publications, 1976), 10:610.

Make it your constant prayer: "May Christ increase; may I decrease. May all see that he is the Bridegroom and I am just a friend of the Bridegroom, introducing them to him."

A Prioritized Preacher

Ministers know that in the ministry you do a hundred things, and they are all important. When I was helping to start a seminary, at the same time I served full-time as the only minister for a church of eight hundred people. As you can imagine, I felt overwhelmed. I was working ninety to a hundred hours a week. I could have used another hundred hours. The consistory (church officers) became concerned and asked me to make a list of everything I was doing. I wrote a long list of every activity, every class, and every committee. We talked about it all evening, and in the end they decided I should delete only *one thing*—the half-hour of teaching I gave the consistory each meeting about being effective church officers!

The point is that ministers bear great burdens, and churches often have huge expectations of them. This is as true in small churches as in large ones, if not more so. I would not argue that most of these activities are not important. Who can measure the value of counseling a couple seeking help for a marriage in crisis? Who can put a price tag on catechizing young people in the basics of the faith? So we pour ourselves out for the sake of others. Yet people still wonder, "What does he do with all his time during the week?"

A pastor can be very godly and earnest about serving the Lord but still fail to discharge his primary calling to preach the Word if he does not hold himself to biblical priorities. The classic example of right priorities is found in Acts 6. A very significant ministry need had emerged. In a time without old-age pensions, social insurance, or government programs for the poor, a group of Christian widows was being neglected. They were not receiving food. They might have starved. The church in Jerusalem was led by the apostles at that time. They immediately took the initiative to address the problem. But they did not take the responsibility on themselves; they instead delegated it to seven godly men.

Why didn't the apostles personally oversee this precious ministry of mercy? Couldn't at least some of the Twelve have taken it on? Were they lazy and selfish? Were they too proud for such a lowly task? No, these men laid down their lives for the gospel in the face of dangerous persecution (Acts 5:29–33). Were they distant and aloof, and therefore not willing to be personally involved in people's lives? No, they constantly taught "in the temple, and in every house" (Acts 5:42). Why, then, did they delegate this work? They said, "It is not reason [right] that we should leave the word of God, and serve tables. . . . But we will give ourselves continually to prayer, and to the ministry of the word" (Acts 6:2, 4).

The apostolic pattern gives highest priority to the ministry of prayer and the Word. This priority has been passed down to today's ministers of the Word. Literally the text says, "But as for us, to the prayer and to the ministry of the word we will diligently devote ourselves." The use of the idiomatic "the prayer" implies that this was leading in prayer at set times in the public assemblies (Acts 1:14; 2:42; 3:1). So the highest priorities of the pastor are to prepare and lead the public worship of the church, and to devote himself to the ministry of the Word.

I am not advising you to neglect other aspects of ministry. But I am calling you to say, "No," or, "Wait," to anything that makes you neglect the core of your ministry: the preaching of the Word. You are a minister of the Word. Who does God count as a good minister? The Bible says a good minister is a man who feeds himself in the Word in order to feed others: "If thou put the brethren in remembrance of these things, thou shalt be a good minister of Jesus Christ, nourished up in the words of faith and of good doctrine, whereunto thou hast attained" (1 Tim. 4:6).

No matter how many legitimate tasks clamor for your attention or how many needy people cry out for your time, the ministry of the Word must dominate your life. Don't fool yourself into thinking you can put it off because other things are more pressing. A lack of discipline and courage in this area will undermine your ministry. Sometimes you just have to humble yourself, pick up the phone, and reschedule that appointment so that you will have time to devote yourself to prayer and the Word. You have to avoid wasting time online or reading frivolous books, and give yourself to disciplined study. Ministerial study can be wearisome to the flesh, and that fact is not appreciated by many in the church, but it is essential and life-giving to the soul, and therefore to your congregation.

If you faithfully give yourself to prayer and the Word while attending to other ministry tasks, you will be surprised how the Lord blesses your whole ministry. Our time management is like tithing our money. People who faithfully tithe regularly discover that they have more with 90 percent (or less) than they had with 100 percent of their income. God provides. Similarly, God blesses ministers when we obey the priorities commanded in his Word. We would have less need for personal counseling if we provided more application in the pulpit. We would have less problems in the church and face them with greater wisdom and power if we prayed more for the Word of Christ to dwell richly in us and our congregations. We don't have time *not* to pray.

Sometimes it is helpful to actually write down your ministry functions, as I mentioned earlier, and then to prioritize them. Everything that is before you can be categorized as either something you *must do*, *should do*, or *would like to do*. In reality, you rarely ever have time to do items in the third category. You often have to delay or delegate items in the second category. But you must do the first things. And one thing that a pastor must do is prayerfully and studiously prepare for preaching the Word.

At the core of prioritizing the ministry of the Word is our confidence in the power of the Bible. Kent Hughes says, "No one will give his life to biblical exposition who does not believe in Scripture's potency."[28] If you think that it's more important that you lead a meeting or attend a social function, and so sermon preparation must take a back seat, then what do you really believe about the Word of God? Perhaps you object, "I believe the Bible is the inerrant, inspired Word of God." Yes, but do you believe that the Bible is powerful?

Can you affirm these biblical assertions with all your heart?

- For I am not ashamed of the gospel of Christ: for it is the power of God unto salvation to every one that believeth; to the Jew first, and also to the Greek (Rom. 1:16).
- For the word of God is quick, and powerful, and sharper than any twoedged sword, piercing even to the dividing asunder of soul and spirit, and of the joints and marrow, and is a discerner of the thoughts and intents of the heart (Heb. 4:12).
- For as the rain cometh down, and the snow from heaven, and returneth not thither, but watereth the earth, and maketh it bring

---

28. R. Kent Hughes, "Restoring Biblical Exposition to Its Rightful Place," in *Reforming Pastoral Ministry*, 84.

forth and bud, that it may give seed to the sower, and bread to the eater: so shall my word be that goeth forth out of my mouth: it shall not return unto me void, but it shall accomplish that which I please, and it shall prosper in the thing whereto I sent it (Isa. 55:10–11).

- How then shall they call on him in whom they have not believed? and how shall they believe in him of whom they have not heard? and how shall they hear without a preacher? . . . So then faith cometh by hearing, and hearing by the word of God (Rom. 10:14, 17).

If you can say these things sincerely, then you can also say, "There are many things that would be good to do, but there is one thing that I must do: prayerfully preach the Word." Indeed, that is the very thing to which you have been called by God and his church.

The Reformers understood this priority and staked their lives on it. They consumed their time and energy with studying, preaching, and teaching the Holy Scriptures. They implemented it in their very architecture, placing the pulpit front and center in their places of worship instead of images and sacramental tables. They confessed it in their catechisms with words that would surprise many today, declaring that the Holy Spirit "works faith in our hearts by the preaching of the gospel."[29] What? What about small groups, personal devotions, mercy ministry to the poor, reading good books, and friendship evangelism? All those things have their place. But God's primary means of saving the lost and sanctifying the saved is the preaching of the Word.

If you are called to preach the Word, then give it the best hours of your life.

Conclusion

What kind of man gives an experiential sermon? A preacher who is:

- passionate in his love for God and men;
- prayerfully dependent on God for understanding and power;
- authentic in seeking to know God himself and not just talking about God;
- growing in his personal experience of his sin and Christ's grace;

---

29. Heidelberg Catechism, Q. 65, in Joel R. Beeke, ed., *Doctrinal Standards, Liturgy, and Church Order* (Grand Rapids, MI: Reformation Heritage Books, 2003), 53.

- decreasing in self-will, self-importance, self-sufficiency, and self-righteousness; and
- prioritized in his use of time and devoted to prayer and the ministry of the Word.

I urge you, brothers, by the grace of God, to become that kind of man.

To fill out this portrait of a preacher and his experiential preaching, we next will consider the lives and examples of great Reformed preachers through the centuries.

PART 2

———————— ◎ ————————

Reformed Experiential
Preaching Illustrated

5

Reformation Preachers: Zwingli, Bullinger, and Oecolampadius

Just as the gospel of salvation by faith in Christ alone was the central message of the Reformation, so the preaching of the Scriptures was the central means of the Reformation. T. H. L. Parker (1916–2016) contrasts the vast output of sermons by the Reformers to the meager offerings that preceded them, and observes: "In the Reformation, preaching occupied a position which it had not since the fifth century. The gospel is a return through Augustine to the New Testament; the form [of the sermon] is a return to the homily of the Fathers."[1]

Even factoring in the advantages of having the printing press at their disposal to preserve a record of their sermons, we can safely assert that the Reformers, far more than any group before them, preached the Word of God. Preaching came to be recognized early in the Reformation as the primary task of the ministry, dethroning the celebration of the Mass in the process.

Preaching was so central in the Reformed ministerial order that those who preached were often designated simply as "minister of the Word" or "preacher of the gospel." The entire office of the ministry became defined by the act of preaching. This renewed emphasis on preaching soon manifested itself in church architecture. The pulpit was placed front and

---

1. T. H. L Parker, *The Oracles of God: An Introduction to the Preaching of John Calvin* (London: Lutterworth, 1947), 20; cf. Edwin C. Dargan, *A History of Preaching* (Grand Rapids, MI: Baker, 1954), 1:366.

center in the sanctuary; it became the most important piece of furniture in the church. There could be preaching without the sacraments, but not the reverse. Reformed services came to be called "preachings" or "sermons." It was common to ask, "Did you go to sermon?" or "Did you go to the preaching?"

From the early days of the Reformation, the very being of the church was grounded in preaching. It was regarded as the primary means, nearly the exclusive means, whereby God's saving grace and love came home to the consciousness of the individual. To be genuinely Reformed meant to allot preaching a high and central place as the primary means both for calling the unconverted to flee to Christ and for edifying the saints in the faith. Preaching was the means to effect either the forgiveness or condemnation of its hearers.

The roots of Reformed experiential preaching are deeply embedded in the preaching of the Reformers. It was out of this emphasis on biblical exposition mingled with continual application that the Puritan style of preaching developed. Therefore, I will proceed to illustrate Reformed experiential preaching by inviting you to sit at the feet of great Reformed and Puritan preachers of previous centuries.

In Part 1, we considered what Reformed experiential preaching is, constructing a bare-bones explanation. Now, in Part 2, we will consider how it was fleshed out in the ministries of specific preachers of the past. We will start by looking at some Reformers from the sixteenth century.

Ulrich Zwingli and Heinrich Bullinger

Ulrich Zwingli (1484–1531) was born on New Year's Day, seven weeks after Martin Luther was born.[2] He studied at Bern and in Vienna before

---

2. On Zwingli, see Ulrich Zwingli and Heinrich Bullinger, *Zwingli and Bullinger*, ed. Geoffrey W. Bromiley, Library of Christian Classics, vol. 24 (Philadelphia: Westminster, 1953); Raget Christoffel, *Zwingli: Or, the Rise of the Reformation in Switzerland*, trans. John Cochran (Edinburgh: T&T Clark, 1858); Jaques Courvoisier, *Zwingli: A Reformed Theologian* (Richmond, VA: John Knox Press, 1963); Oskar Farner, *Zwingli the Reformer: His Life and Work*, trans. D. G. Sear (Hamden, CT: Archon, 1968); Edward J. Furcha and H. Wayne Pipkin, *Prophet, Pastor, Protestant: The Work of Huldrych Zwingli after Five Hundred Years* (Allison Park, PA: Pickwick, 1984); Ulrich Zwingli, *Selected Writings of Huldrych Zwingli*, ed. Edward J. Furcha and H. Wayne Pipkin (Allison Park, PA: Pickwick, 1984); Gottfried Wilhelm Locher, *Zwingli's Thought: New Perspectives* (Leiden: Brill, 1981); G. R. Potter, *Zwingli* (Cambridge, UK: Cambridge University Press, 1984); Jean Rilliet, *Zwingli, Third Man of the Reformation*, trans. Harold Knight (London: Lutterworth, 1964); W. P. Stephens, *The Theology of Huldrych Zwingli* (Oxford: Clarendon, 1986); *Zwingli: An Introduction to His Thought* (Oxford: Clarendon, 1992); "Zwingli on John 6:63: 'Spiritus Est Qui Vivificate, Caro Nihil Potest,'" in *Biblical Interpretation in the Era of the Reformation: Essays Presented to David C. Steinmetz in Honor of His Sixtieth Birthday*, ed. John L. Thompson

matriculating at the University of Basel, where he became enamored with humanistic studies. But he also came under the influence of Reformer Thomas Wittenbach (1472–1526).[3] H. H. Howorth writes: "Wittenbach was a strenuous upholder of the new [Reformation] views and not only denounced the sale of indulgences at Basle, but also openly taught that the death of Christ was the only way to salvation. He was also an opponent of the celibacy of the clergy."[4] Wittenbach encouraged Zwingli in the direction that would eventually lead him to embrace the basic Reformed tenet of *sola Scriptura*. Also, he directed him, at least in beginning steps, to the doctrine of justification by grace through faith alone.

From 1506 to 1516, Zwingli served as the parish priest of Glarus, a small Swiss canton. Then, from 1516 to 1518, he preached in Einsiedeln. Strasbourg Reformer Caspar Hedio (1494–1552) describes his preaching during this period as "elegant, learned, weighty, rich, penetrating, and evangelical, clearly such as to return us to the effect of the ancient theologians."[5]

Sometime around 1516, after studying Desiderius Erasmus's (1466–1536) Greek New Testament and wrestling for a considerable time (probably several months) with his sins and weaknesses, Zwingli experienced a kind of evangelical breakthrough. It was not quite as dramatic a breakthrough as Luther's, but it was of the same kind and, interestingly, happened about the same time as Luther came to spiritual liberty for himself. This breakthrough made Zwingli turn all the more to the Scriptures, and it also made him very hostile to the medieval system of penance and the veneration of relics. He began to attack this system from the pulpit in 1518.

Luther posted his Ninety-Five Theses in the autumn of 1517. When it comes to Zwinglian studies, there has been a great deal of debate about how much Luther influenced Zwingli. Zwingli himself said that he was not influenced very much by Luther because he was going through the same things at the same time and coming to the same conclusions independently. That might be a slight exaggeration. No doubt he was

---

and Richard A. Muller (Grand Rapids, MI: Eerdmans, 1996), 156–85; Sigmund Widmer, *Zwingli, 1484–1984: Reformation in Switzerland* (Zürich: Theologischer Verlag, 1983).

3. H. H. Howorth, "The Origin and Authority of the Biblical Canon According to the Continental Reformers: II. Luther, Zwingli, LeFevre, and Calvin," *The Journal of Theological Studies* 9 (1908): 198–99.

4. Howorth, "Origin and Authority of the Biblical Canon," 199.

5. Quoted in Lee Palmer Wandel, "Zwingli, Huldrych," *The Oxford Encyclopedia of the Reformation*, ed. Hans Joachim Hillerbrand (Oxford: Oxford University Press, 1996), 4:321.

influenced somewhat by Luther, but Luther's theology was not well developed at this point either. So the idea that Zwingli was just a follower of Luther is certainly an exaggeration on the other side.

One of the greatest moments of the Reformation happened in 1519, when Zwingli began his ministry as a preacher in the Grossmünster (great "minster" or "church building") of Zurich, which is a beautiful building still today. He announced to his congregation that he was going to preach exegetical sermons, starting with Matthew 1 and working his way through the Gospel and then the rest of the New Testament. In this regard, he followed John Chrysostom (c. 347–407). He popularized early on in the Reformation what is called *lectio continua*, which means "continual public reading," what we today would call the expository preaching of the text of Scripture in sequential order.[6]

Zwingli's style of preaching was a homily method that resembled the early preaching of the ancient fathers. The minister would ascend into the pulpit and start preaching at the place where he had left off the last time. He would not necessarily have a theme or points. He would continue preaching until his time was up, make an application or two, and pick up there next time. Generally, in one sermon, two to four verses were covered from the New Testament or four to seven verses from the Old Testament. Zwingli set that pattern, and John Calvin did the same, as we shall see.

Zwingli preached faithfully through a number of books of the Bible for twelve years, until he died in 1531 while serving as a chaplain to Zurich's troops at war with the Roman Catholic Swiss cantons. Zwingli's noble character, his firm commitment to scriptural authority, and his diligent propagation of evangelical reform in preaching and worship, even more than his writings, made him one of the Reformation's most appealing early leaders. He was a very popular preacher. People in Einsiedeln, where he served for a little while, and in Zurich would return from hearing one of his sermons and would discuss with others in the streets what they had heard. They basically would tell visitors: "We just heard a wonderful sermon. You have to go hear Ulrich Zwingli preach." So word got around, the locals and tourists went to hear him, and the church grew and flourished. You could say of

---

6. Hughes Oliphant Old, *The Reading and Preaching of the Scriptures in the Worship of the Christian Church, Volume 4: The Age of the Reformation* (Grand Rapids, MI: Eerdmans, 1998), 43.

Zwingli what was said of the Lord Jesus Christ: "The common people heard him gladly" (Mark 12:37).

The most amazing thing about Zwingli—and it is difficult for us to grasp the excitement of the people in this regard—is that, as the people would say to one another, "He preaches the Bible!" That was unusual if not unprecedented in their experience. He didn't preach mere traditions of men and he didn't preach mere theological polemics; rather, he preached Scripture. This method was powerful to them, because Zwingli would declare the message of the Word with authority, then apply it to their souls. The tone of "Thus saith the Lord" left a deep impression. This type of exegetical, applicatory preaching, which we almost take for granted in our churches, was revolutionary in Zwingli's day. So was the manner in which he restructured the worship service so as to center it on the Word of God. The preaching was the largest part of the service, taking perhaps fifty to sixty minutes.

Zwingli had a very able assistant named Heinrich Bullinger (1504–1575).[7] Converted to the Reformation faith while at the University of Cologne in 1522, he became head teacher in a monastery at Kappel. His lectures on the New Testament brought about the abolition of the Mass there. Bullinger replaced Zwingli when the latter died in 1531. When Bullinger preached his first sermon in the Grossmünster of Zurich after Zwingli's death, people were overwhelmed with excitement. As Oswald Myconius (1488–1552) tells us, "Bullinger thundered out such a sermon that many believed that Zwingli was not dead but, like the phoenix, has been raised again to life." As a result, Zurich quickly called Bullinger, who was only a visiting preacher, to be its minister.[8]

---

7. On Bullinger, see J. Wayne Baker, *Heinrich Bullinger and the Covenant: The Other Reformed Tradition* (Athens, OH: Ohio University Press, 1980); Zwingli and Bullinger, *Zwingli and Bullinger*; George Melvyn Ella, *Henry Bullinger (1504–1575): Shepherd of the Churches* (Eggleston, UK: Go Publications, 2007); Heinrich Bullinger, *The Decades*, ed. Thomas Harding, 2 vols. (Grand Rapids, MI: Reformation Heritage Books, 2004); Bruce Gordon and Emidio Campi, eds., *Architect of Reformation: An Introduction to Heinrich Bullinger, 1504–1575*, Texts and Studies in Reformation and Post-Reformation Thought (Grand Rapids, MI: Baker Academic, 2004); David John Keep, "Henry Bullinger and the Elizabethan Church: A Study of the Publication of His 'Decades,' His Letter on the Use of Vestments and His Reply to the Bull Which Excommunicated Elizabeth" (PhD diss., University of Sheffield, 1970); Charles S. McCoy, J. Wayne Baker, and Heinrich Bullinger, *Fountainhead of Federalism: Heinrich Bullinger and the Covenantal Tradition* (Louisville, KY: Westminster/John Knox Press, 1991); Cornelis P. Venema, *Heinrich Bullinger and the Doctrine of Predestination: Author of "the Other Reformed Tradition"?* Texts and Studies in Reformation and Post-Reformation Thought (Grand Rapids, MI: Baker Academic, 2002).

8. Walter Hollweg, *Heinrich Bullingers Hausbuch: Eine Untersuchung Über Die Anfänge Der Reformierten Predigtliteratur* (Neukirchen, Kreis Moers: Verlag der Buchhandlung des Erziehungsvereins, 1956), 18–19.

Bullinger's productivity in the pulpit was amazing. He preached through fifty-three of the sixty-six books of the Bible at least once. Some books he preached through twice (Isaiah, Daniel, Hosea, Amos, Nahum, Matthew, Mark, Paul's epistles, and 2 Peter), three times (Joel, Obadiah, Jonah, Habakkuk, Zephaniah, Haggai, Zechariah, Malachi, Luke, John, Acts, 1 Peter, and 1 John), or even four times (Hebrews).

Bullinger also wrote thirteen volumes of commentaries that covered the entire New Testament except for Revelation. Later, however, he published one hundred sermons on Revelation, so he actually did a lot of work on that book. He also published sermons on some books from the Old Testament. He wrote 170 sermons on Jeremiah, sixty-six sermons on Daniel, and 190 sermons on Isaiah. In all, he published 618 sermons, but none of them became as popular as those that were collected as *The Decades*, a collection of fifty sermons in which Bullinger moves through the whole field of Reformed systematic theology. These fifty sermons became one of the most famous books that he ever wrote. Bullinger used the word *decades* as the title for his book because it contains five "decades" or series of ten sermons each. He addresses one doctrine in each sermon, and together these sermons became more popular than Calvin's *Institutes of the Christian Religion* in their day. His messages are generally irenic and not polemic, making *The Decades* an edifying introduction to Reformed theology even today.

Contemporary scholarship now thinks that Bullinger was every bit as influential in the Reformation as Calvin. In fact, there are twelve thousand to thirteen thousand extant letters to and from Bullinger, compared to ninety-five hundred letters of Luther, Calvin, and Theodore Beza (1519–1605) combined. Bullinger was at the center of the entire European Reformation as much as Calvin was. Bullinger helped to stabilize the gains of the Reformation. His books were powerful and helpful, and were used throughout Europe, particularly in England. Until his death in 1575, he and Beza were considered patriarchs of the Reformation. (Bullinger outlived Calvin by eleven years, even though he had been born five years earlier.)

Bullinger also wrote 150 treatises. His writings can be divided into three categories: (1) his confessional writings, which resulted in some very significant statements of faith, such as the Second Helvetic Confession, almost exclusively his work; (2) some polemical writings—he wrote books against the Anabaptists, the Lutherans, and the Roman Catholics, as one might expect; but the large majority of his writings were (3) pastoral, taking the form of biblical commentaries, published lectures on theological doctrines, and printed sermons.

Though different in style, Zwingli and Bullinger were both great preachers who proclaimed the Scriptures faithfully and applied them to the heart. Zwingli probably preached seven days a week. Bullinger preached every Lord's Day for more than forty years, and probably an average of three times during the week. In 1532, it was determined in Zurich that every pastor in town had to preach twice on the Lord's Day and once during the week. Thus, every pastor had to prepare a minimum of 150 new sermons each year. It became commonplace for the Zurich Protestant pastors to be working their way through three different sections of Scripture at any given time. They might be working through the Psalms on Lord's Day mornings, through one of Paul's epistles on Lord's Day evenings, and through one of the four Gospels on a weeknight. But whatever book or order they chose, the important thing was that the people were being fed from the Word of God week by week, sermon by sermon, which affected them profoundly.

As different as their styles of preaching were, it appears that their actual sermon content was quite similar. We do not have many extant sermons of Zwingli, unfortunately, but we can categorize the features of their sermons that stand out.

The first is this: there was a strong, explicit accent on the Holy Spirit in the sermons of both Zwingli and Bullinger. Again and again we see references to dependence on the work of the Spirit. Luther was suspicious of this accent. He wrongly suspected that they were really mystics ("Spiritualists") at heart. This characterization grew out of Luther's famous debate with Zwingli at the University of Marburg, the Marburg Colloquy (Oct. 1–3, 1529). There they disagreed on the presence of Christ in the Lord's Supper. But even a cursory reading of both authors' sermons shows that there was not a trace of such "Spiritualism" in either Zwingli's or Bullinger's preaching.

Second, they emphasized the great Reformation principle of *sola Scriptura*. Both ministers were convinced that they should preach nothing but Scripture (remember how radical this was at that time). This preaching of Scripture was to be done preferably in a sequential manner, so that the whole counsel of God would be proclaimed in due course.

Hughes Oliphant Old describes Zwingli's preaching this way:

Zwingli was inspired by the *lectio continua* preaching of Chrysostom. He followed the system through his entire ministry, covering in succession Matthew, which took a whole year's worth of daily preaching, the Acts of the Apostles, 1 Timothy, the two epistles of Peter, and Hebrews. In 1524 he is known to have preached through the Gospel of John and then to have finished up the rest of the Pauline Epistles. After seven years of daily preaching he had treated most of the New Testament. He then turned to the Old Testament, preaching first the Psalms. Then he began the Pentateuch in the middle of July 1526. He seems to have continued through the Historical Books until March 1528, when he began Isaiah. Then he continued through the Prophets for some time—how long we do not know. This systematic interpretation of Scripture was received with considerable enthusiasm in Zurich, and his colleagues observed it with great interest. One by one the Christian humanist preachers of the Upper Rhineland began to follow his example. In southern Germany it was this kind of systematic biblical preaching which won the people to the Reformation.[9]

As Old notes, Zwingli at times broke from his *lectio continua* and delivered messages for special occasions. For example, he preached a sermon on the pastor's office at the second Zurich Disputation. He had an opportunity to preach to the Dominican sisters at Outenbach on the clarity and the certainty of the Word of God. He preached sermons on the major feast days of the Christian year and took time to address controversies when they arose.[10] So his was not a slavish system; he worked realistically with the situation at hand. But generally speaking, he moved through the books of the Bible one by one.

Zwingli believed that as God's Word, the Scriptures had clarity (perspicuity) and authority in themselves. He writes, "When the Word of God shines on the human understanding, it enlightens it in such a way that it understands and confesses the Word and knows the certainty of it."[11] He quoted Psalm 119:130: "The entrance of thy words giveth light; it giveth understanding unto the simple." Thus, when the Word of God came to a prophet, he "knew that it was from God and not from any other," Zwingli says.[12] The Bible is self-authenticating, for it is the voice

---

9. Old, *Reading and Preaching of the Scriptures*, 4:46.
10. Old, *Reading and Preaching of the Scriptures*, 4:46–47.
11. Ulrich Zwingli, "Of the Clarity and Certainty of the Word of God," in *Zwingli and Bullinger*, 75.
12. Zwingli, "Clarity and Certainty," 76.

of God. The Word of God "comes with such clarity and assurance that it is surely known and believed."[13] This belief gave him confidence to preach the Scriptures only, not the ideas of men. He says: "No matter who a man may be, if he teaches you in accordance with his own thought and mind his teaching is false. But if he teaches you in accordance with the Word of God, it is not he that teaches you, but God who teaches him."[14] This put the preacher in the position of a humble servant under the authority of the Lord. After a nearly fatal bout with the plague in 1519, Zwingli writes in prayer to God, "do what you will," for "I am your tool, to make whole or break."[15]

It is hard to determine how much Zwingli's preaching was shaped by his personal experience. But he was a man who grew to love the Scriptures; he came to drink them in, to study them continually. As a result, he knew his Bible well. This helped him immensely in his preaching; as he preached, he could appeal to texts from all over the Bible. And this is what gives his writings, still today, a ring of authority. The authority of Scripture always transcends the age and the culture in which we live. That is why, when we are scriptural men, our sermons have abiding value. The Word of God, as Peter tells us, "liveth and abideth for ever" (1 Pet. 1:23). Zwingli delighted in the life he found in Scripture—life that manifested itself in the free and sovereign power of God. He says: "The Word of God is so alive and strong and powerful that all things have necessarily to obey it, and that as often and at the time that God himself appoints. . . . If it is not fulfilled at the time when you desire, that is not due to any deficiency of power but to the freedom of his will."[16]

Zwingli and Bullinger felt so strongly about *sola Scriptura* that they were moved to establish what we might call the first theological seminary of Reformed Protestantism, to train other men in the authority and teachings of Scripture. The seminary was called the *Prophezei*, signaling the continuity between the Christian preacher and the ancient prophet. After it was established in 1525, Zwingli and Bullinger became two of the most important teachers there. Scholars debate the nature of the seminary education it offered. The exegetical works of Peter Martyr Vermigli (1500–1562), Theodor Bibliander (1509–1564), and other important theologians from that day became the textbooks

---

13. Zwingli, "Clarity and Certainty," 77.
14. Zwingli, "Clarity and Certainty," 90.
15. Quoted in Wandel, "Zwingli, Huldrych," 321.
16. Zwingli, "Clarity and Certainty," 72.

for this seminary. The students also were trained in the ancient languages. They also helped the teachers in their work and in publishing. In a way, it seems that the students served as teaching assistants even as they were learning. One interesting task the students performed was assisting the faculty with the translation of the Bible, resulting in the so-called Zurich Translation. This version was more accurate than Luther's translation, although its influence later faded. Luther translated as a skillful poet, but the Zurich scholars translated as knowledgeable students of the ancient languages.

Third, Zwingli's and Bullinger's preaching was Christ centered. Being grounded in *sola Scriptura*, they naturally preached *solus Christus*. Old says, "Zwingli above all preached Christ and the saving power of his death and resurrection."[17] He emphasized that Christ had made atonement by dying as our substitute to satisfy God's justice for our sins. In fact, that is how Zwingli came to be a famous preacher. People essentially said: "You not only go up to hear the Word of God, but he is preaching Jesus Christ without preaching Mary and the saints. Did you know that according to Zwingli, you can go straight to God through Jesus Christ?" Again, what is so commonplace for us today was revolutionary and radical for the people of that time. We owe a great deal to Zwingli for the clarity with which he taught the gospel and for establishing a Christological emphasis and focus for the Reformation preachers to follow.

It is interesting to look at the title pages of the writings of Zwingli and Bullinger. In those days, a title was usually long, essentially constituting a summary of the book, almost like what we find on the back cover of a book today. Underneath the author's name there would usually be a text, handpicked by the author, that summarized his main emphasis in the book. On the title pages of Zwingli's and Bullinger's works, these texts are almost always Christological. One of Zwingli's books has Matthew 11:28: "Come unto me, all ye that labour and are heavy laden." For one of his books, Bullinger chose Matthew 17:5: "This is my beloved Son, in whom I am well pleased; hear ye him."

Zwingli's writings are full of Christ-centered statements and principles. His sixty-seven theses are much more Christ centered than Luther's Ninety-Five Theses. Here is a typical statement, taken from the begin-

---

17. Old, *Reading and Preaching of the Scriptures*, 4:50.

ning of Zwingli's conclusions: "The summary of the gospel is that our Lord Jesus Christ, true Son of God, has made known to us the will of his Heavenly Father, and has redeemed us from death and reconciled us with God by his guiltlessness."[18] We find this emphasis on the righteousness of Jesus Christ and all our salvation lying in Jesus Christ, all received by faith in Christ, throughout Zwingli's theses.

Christ was also the core of Bullinger's preaching. His Christology was already found in a seminal form in his *Studiorum ratio*, written in 1528. He says: "I read that Christ was affixed to the Cross. I believe that Christ is the satisfaction of all believers. I read that Christ raised up the dead, etc. I teach that Christ alone should be invoked in all dangers. I read that Christ spurned worldly things, that he taught innocence and charity. I conclude, therefore, that the worship of God consists in purity of life and in innocence and charity and not at all on external sacrifices, feasts, vestures, etc."[19]

This Christological focus is all the more evident in Bullinger's *The Decades*. Since his goal in his sermons in *The Decades* is to lead his reader to Jesus Christ, the whole set of sermons is permeated with Christology.

Johannes Oecolampadius

Johannes Huszgen (1482–1531) was a brilliant scholar and a significant Reformer in Basel.[20] His surname was Latinized as Oecolampadius, or "house lamp." Old calls him "one of the anchormen of the Reformation."[21] Born in the Palatinate, he studied law and theology, coming under the influence of the humanist scholar Jakob Wimpfeling (1450–1528). After working as a tutor for the sons of Elector Philipp (1448–1508) of the Palatinate, he began preaching in his hometown

---

18. Quoted in James T. Dennison Jr., ed., *Reformed Confessions of the Sixteenth and Seventeenth Centuries in English Translation: Volume 1, 1523–1552* (Grand Rapids, MI: Reformation Heritage Books, 2008), 3.

19. Heinrich Bullinger, *Studiorum ratio—Studienanleitung*, ed. Peter Stotz (Zurich: LIT Verlag, 1987), 25.

20. On Oecolampadius, see Diane Poythress, *Reformer of Basel: The Life, Thought, and Influence of Johannes Oecolampadius* (Grand Rapids, MI: Reformation Heritage Books, 2011); "Johannes Oecolampadius' Exposition of Isaiah, Chapters 36–37" (PhD diss., Westminster Theological Seminary, 1992); Demura Akira, "Church Discipline According to Johannes Oecolampadius in the Setting of His Life and Thought" (PhD diss., Princeton Theological Seminary, 1964); E. Gordon Rupp, *Patterns of Reformation* (London: Epworth, 1969), 3–64; Thomas A. Fudge, "Icarus of Basel? Oecolampadius and the Early Swiss Reformation," *Journal of Religious History* 21, no. 3 (October 1997): 268–84; Ed L. Miller, "Oecolampadius: The Unsung Hero of the Basel Reformation," *Iliff Review* 39, no. 3 (Fall 1982): 5–25.

21. Old, *Reading and Preaching of the Scriptures*, 4:53.

of Weinsberg. Then he returned to school to study Greek and Hebrew, where he met Wolfgang Capito (c. 1478–1541), who would serve in Basel, Mainz, and Strasbourg. He mentored Philip Melanchthon (1497–1560), who later was influenced by his treatise on the symbolic significance of Christ's words, "This is my body." He helped Erasmus complete his annotations on the Greek New Testament. He also translated a number of the Greek fathers and published a Greek grammar.

Late in 1518, he went to the cathedral of Augsburg, one of the most important pulpits in all of Germany. This was just a few months after Luther had posted his theses, and Oecolampadius followed the development of the controversy over those theses with great interest. In 1520, he left Augsburg to become a confessor priest in the monastery of Altomünster. There he made use of his solitude to meditate on the church fathers and Luther's writings, finding Luther to be "closer to the evangelical truth than any of his opponents."[22] He corresponded with Luther and Melanchthon, and also developed a friendship with Zwingli.

Persecution of the Reformers soon began to heat up. In 1521, the Edict of Worms declared Luther a heretic, forcing him into temporary hiding. Oecolampadius, though a renowned scholar, found himself a refugee without a job. But in God's providence, he returned to Basel in 1522 and became a university lecturer on the Bible and a minister preaching at Saint Martin's Church. In 1523–1524, he lectured on Isaiah to an audience of four hundred people, publishing his lectures in a commentary (1525) that won the praise of Luther and Calvin. His comments on Isaiah 55:3 contain perhaps the earliest Reformed reference to a pact between the Father and the Son as the foundation of God's everlasting covenant of grace.[23] He also wrote commentaries on twenty other books of the Bible, none of which as yet have been translated into English.[24]

In 1528, he married Wibrandis, a twenty-six-year-old widow who, after his death, went on to marry Capito, and then, widowed again, later married Martin Bucer (1491–1551).

In 1529, Basel's government officially declared itself for the Reformation. The first article of the Reformation Act reads: "From now on nothing is to be preached but the holy Word of God, the Gospel of

---

22. Quoted in Robert C. Walton, "Oecolampadius, Johannes," *The Oxford Encyclopedia of the Reformation*, ed. Hans Joachim Hillerbrand (Oxford: Oxford University Press, 1996), 170.
23. Poythress, *Reformer of Basel*, 50.
24. Translations of his commentaries on Isaiah 36–37 are available in Poythress, *Reformer of Basel*, 171–201.

Jesus Christ. The glad tidings are to be preached to the faithful, pure, clear, and simple, to the glory of God and the building up of brotherly love."[25] Oecolampadius was promoted to cathedral preacher in Basel. He preached through the Gospel of Mark, a series of which we still have 131 sermons, and also Colossians, and preached other series of expositions that have been lost.[26]

His strong leadership, combined with a diplomatic avoidance of unnecessary controversy, helped to unify and further the Reformation in Basel. Also in 1529, he attended the Marburg Colloquy, standing with Zwingli against Luther's and Melanchton's belief in Christ's local or physical presence in the Lord's Supper. And he worked to reduce the government's control over the church and to give the church its rightful powers to discipline its members.

He continued to labor in Basel until his death in 1531. His writings and reforms had a profound impact on Calvin, who worked on the first edition of his *Institutes* in Basel just a few years after Oecolampadius's death and continued to meditate on his commentaries for years. Truly the German-Swiss Reformer proved to be a "lamp" whose light illuminated many in the house of God.

Diane Poythress, after a careful study of Oecolampadius's messages on Isaiah, has made the following observations about four experiential themes in his preaching:

1. "Oecolampadius excels in exposing evil."[27] He teaches a great deal about how to recognize the devices of Satan and how to reject him when he comes with his deceit. There is an experiential theme in his preaching: he expresses how the soul can battle against the forces of evil. He points out that Satan even uses God's holy things, mingling his lies with God's truth. He slanders the godly, perverts justice, and torments anxious people with doubts. Believers can expect to be attacked by the Devil. Oecolampadius queries, "Would he [Satan] spare us who did not even fear to attack Christ?" Satan especially aims to grieve believers by persuading them that God has rejected them. The Basel Reformer writes: "Behold among these sure trials how often the devil suggests that your faith is in vain and that you are among the number of the damned. . . . For just as when we are assured of God's grace we are gladdened in

---

25. Quoted in Old, *Reading and Preaching of the Scriptures*, 4:64.
26. Old, *Reading and Preaching of the Scriptures*, 4:63.
27. Poythress, "Johannes Oecolampadius' Exposition of Isaiah, Chapters 36–37," 405.

conscience, so when we believe that God is angry with us we are most greatly terrified. Indeed, this is Hell itself."[28] But the Devil's temptations cannot finally win, for Christ is Lord.

2. Oecolampadius says that "remembering the consummation" of history is a useful "spur" to "provoke a soul towards piety."[29] Doing so encourages the believer in a number of ways. It assures him that God's justice will prevail and severely punish the enemies of his people. It comforts him to know that God will one day completely crush the sin within us, overthrowing our inward "Babylon." And anticipating judgment day helps the Christian to see Christ's glory, which is "to follow God with heart and soul, wherever He may lead."[30]

3. Oecolampadius encourages believers to personal piety. He applies the law as a guide to a Christian life that is empowered by faith in Christ: "The commands of God are easy. . . . It appears to be an arduous mountain and a most difficult ascent, to lay down one's life for brothers, to do good to enemies, to renounce all worldly things; but nothing is difficult to him who believes."[31] He calls believers to find the power to obey by growing in their understanding of God's power and the trustworthiness of his promises. He applies the examples of biblical heroes to stimulate the godliness of his hearers. He opens up the comforting meaning of God's names, such as "the Lord Sabaoth" ("the Lord of hosts or armies"), writing, "All armies are His servants, the heavenly as much as the earthly, and He can send them for the aid of His own people." He exhorts believers to encourage one another by speaking the gospel to one another: "You have here what you ought to announce, namely the mercy and power and advent of Christ. . . . We who are the true announcers say, 'Behold your God.'"[32]

4. Above all, Oecolampadius views preaching as the personal proclamation of Christ. This arises from his view of the Scriptures. He says, "Because the Word of God is inspired by the Holy Spirit, I am unable not to affirm that in all places the Spirit of the Scriptures has regard for Christ Jesus in purpose, goal, and method." Therefore, the first

---

28. Quoted in Poythress, "Johannes Oecolampadius' Exposition of Isaiah, Chapters 36–37," 406.

29. Quoted in Poythress, "Johannes Oecolampadius' Exposition of Isaiah, Chapters 36–37," 407.

30. Quoted in Poythress, "Johannes Oecolampadius' Exposition of Isaiah, Chapters 36–37," 407–8.

31. Quoted in Poythress, "Johannes Oecolampadius' Exposition of Isaiah, Chapters 36–37," 409–10.

32. Quoted in Poythress, "Johannes Oecolampadius' Exposition of Isaiah, Chapters 36–37," 410–411.

and fundamental act of the student of Scripture is to come to the Bible seeking Christ: "The sense of Scripture does not come to any, except to those who also seek Christ and to whom Christ reveals Himself."[33] This goes hand in hand with humbling ourselves, for God reveals himself for his glory, and the more we know God, the more we are confronted by our "foulness."[34]

Conclusion

I hope that this brief survey of the lives and ministries of Zwingli, Bullinger, and Oecolampadius has given you a taste of the biblical and experiential preaching God stirred up in the sixteenth century. The Reformation is remembered by its heirs today for its theology, and rightly so. However, that theology spread and took hold of nations through the preaching of God's Word from heart to heart. Founded upon the exposition of Scripture, one book at a time, such preaching aimed not merely to inform the mind, but also to inflame the heart with grief for our sins and longing for the glory of the Savior. Though often forgotten, these three men were faithful to serve as burning and shining lights in the situations where God put them, and as a result, they still speak to the church five centuries later. May God give us grace to be faithful in our day as they were in theirs.

---

33. Quoted in Poythress, *Reformer of Basel*, 121.
34. Quoted in Poythress, *Reformer of Basel*, 121–22.

6

Reformation Preachers: Calvin

John Calvin embraced a high view of preaching.[1] He calls the preaching office "the most excellent of all things," commended by God that it might be held in the highest esteem. "There is nothing more notable or glorious in the church than the ministry of the gospel," he concludes.[2] In commenting on Isaiah 55:11, he says, "The Word goeth out of the mouth of God in such a manner that it likewise goeth out of the mouth of men; for God does not speak openly from heaven but employs men as his instruments."[3]

Calvin viewed preaching as God's ordinary or normal means of salvation and benediction. He says that the Holy Spirit is the "internal minister" who uses the "external minister" in preaching the Word. The external minister "holds forth the vocal word and it is received by the ears," but the internal minister "truly communicates the thing proclaimed [which] is Christ."[4] Thus, God himself speaks through the mouths of his servants by his Spirit. "Wherever the gospel is preached, it is as if God himself came into the midst of us," Calvin writes.[5] Preaching is the instrument and the

---

1. This chapter is adapted from Joel R. Beeke, "Calvin as an Experiential Preacher," *Puritan Reformed Journal* 1, no. 2 (July 2009): 131–54. Used with permission. See also the chapter on Calvin's preaching in Herman J. Selderhuis, *John Calvin: A Pilgrim's Life* (Downers Grove, IL: IVP Academic, 2009), 110–44.

2. John Calvin, *Institutes of the Christian Religion*, trans. Ford Lewis Battles, ed. John T. McNeill, Library of Christian Classics, vols. 20–21 (Philadelphia: Westminster, 1960), 4.3.3, hereafter, *Institutes*.

3. John Calvin, *Commentaries of Calvin*, various translators and editors, 45 vols. (Edinburgh: Calvin Translation Society, 1846–1851; repr., 22 vols., Grand Rapids, MI: Baker, 1979) [Isa. 55:11], hereafter, *Commentary*.

4. John Calvin, *Tracts and Treatises*, trans. Henry Beveridge (Grand Rapids, MI: Eerdmans, 1958), 1:173.

5. *Commentary* [Matt. 26:24].

authority that the Spirit uses in his saving work of illuminating, converting, and sealing sinners. "There is . . . an inward efficacy of the Holy Spirit when he sheds forth his power upon hearers, that they may embrace a discourse [sermon] by faith."[6]

Calvin taught that the preached Word and the inner testimony of the Spirit should be distinguished but cannot be separated. Word and Spirit are joined together organically; without the Spirit, hearing the preached Word only adds to the condemnation of unbelievers. On the other hand, Calvin admonished those who emphasized the Spirit apart from or at the expense of the Word, saying that only the spirit of Satan separates itself from the Word.[7]

This stress on preaching moved Calvin to be active on several fronts in Geneva, Switzerland, where he ministered for twenty-six years. First, he showed his convictions through his own example. Calvin preached from the New Testament on Lord's Day mornings, the Psalms on Lord's Day afternoons, and the Old Testament at 6 a.m. on one or two weekdays. Following this schedule during his last period of ministry in Geneva from 1541 to 1564, Calvin preached nearly four thousand sermons, more than 170 a year. On his deathbed, he spoke of his preaching as more significant than his writings.[8]

Second, Calvin often preached to his congregation about their responsibility to hear the Word of God aright. He taught his people the spirit in which they should come to the sermon, what to listen for in preaching, and how to respond. Since, for Calvin, all true preaching is biblical preaching and ministers are to open the Word so as to preach only what God commands, people are to test sermons by this criterion. Unscriptural sermons are to be rejected; scriptural sermons are to be accepted as the Word of God and obeyed. Calvin's goal was that the people would grasp the importance of preaching, learn to desire preaching as a supreme blessing, and participate as actively in the sermon as the preacher himself. Their basic attitude was to be one of "willingness to obey God completely and with no reserve."[9]

Calvin was motivated to stress profitable hearing of the Word because he believed that few people hear well. Here is a typical assessment

---

6. *Commentary* [Ezek. 1:3].

7. Willem Balke, "Het Pietisme in Oostfriesland," *Theologia Reformata* 21 (1978): 320–27.

8. William Bouwsma, *John Calvin: A Sixteenth-Century Portrait* (New York: Oxford University Press, 1988), 29.

9. Quoted in Leroy Nixon, *John Calvin: Expository Preacher* (Grand Rapids, MI: Eerdmans, 1950), 65.

of Calvin: "If the same sermon is preached, say, to a hundred people, twenty receive it with the ready obedience of faith, while the rest hold it valueless, or laugh, or hiss, or loathe it."[10] I found more than forty similar comments in Calvin's sermons (especially on Deuteronomy), commentaries (e.g., on Ps. 119:101 and Acts 11:23), and the *Institutes* (especially 3.21–24). If profitable hearing was a problem in Calvin's day, how much more so today, when ministers have to compete for their congregation's attention with all the mass media that bombard us on a daily basis?

Third, the Genevan system Calvin established emphasized preaching. The Genevan *Ordinances* stipulated that on the Lord's Day, sermons were to be preached in each of the three churches at daybreak and again at 9 a.m. After the children were catechized at noon, a third sermon was to be preached in each church at 3 p.m. Weekday sermons were also scheduled in the three churches on Mondays, Wednesdays, and Fridays at varying hours so that they could be heard one after the other. That way, people could take in three sermons in one day if they so desired. By the time Calvin died, at least one sermon was preached in every church every day of the week.

Calvin's gifts and high view of preaching, both theologically and in practice, motivate us to study his sermons. In this chapter, I want to give a broad overview of how Calvin preached before focusing more narrowly on the questions of how he preached experientially and how such preaching interfaced with related or consequent doctrines, such as assurance of faith, election, and self-examination.

Calvin's Preaching

Calvin preached serially from various books of the Bible, striving to show the meaning of a passage and how it should impact the lives of his hearers. Much like ancient church homilies in style, his sermons had no divisions or points other than what the text dictated. As Paul Fuhrmann writes, "They are properly homilies as in the ancient church: expositions of Bible passages [in] the light of grammar and history, [providing] application to the hearers' life situations."[11]

Calvin was a careful exegete, an able expositor, and a faithful applier of the Word. His goals in preaching were to glorify God, to cause be-

---

10. *Institutes*, 3.24.12.
11. Paul T. Fuhrmann, "Calvin, Expositor of Scripture," *Interpretation* 6, no. 2 (April 1952): 191.

lievers to grow in the grace and knowledge of Christ Jesus, and to unite sinners with Christ, so "that men [would] be reconciled to God by the free remission of sins."[12] This aim of saving sinners blended seamlessly with his emphasis on scriptural doctrines. He writes that ministers are "keepers of the truth of God; that is to say, of His precious image, of that which concerneth the majesty of the doctrine of our salvation, and the life of the world."[13] Calvin frequently admonished ministers to keep this treasure safe by handling the Word of God carefully, always striving for pure biblical teaching. That did not exclude bringing the Word to bear on contemporary events in people's lives, however. As current events related to the passage being expounded, Calvin felt free to apply his sermon to those events in practical, experiential, and moral ways.[14]

The image of the preacher as a teacher moved Calvin to emphasize the importance of careful sermon preparation. How he accomplished that goal for himself, with his frequency of preaching and heavy additional workload, remains a mystery, but he obviously studied the text to be expounded with great care and read widely what others had said about it. He preached extemporaneously, relying heavily on his remarkable memory. He often declared that the power of God could best be exhibited in extemporaneous delivery.

This is why there are no extant manuscripts of Calvin's sermons. As far as we know, he never wrote out any sermons. The only reason that we have more than two thousand of Calvin's sermons is that a certain Denis Raguenier took them down in shorthand from 1549 until the scribe's death in 1560. Apparently, Calvin never intended for them to be published.

The average length of the texts Calvin covered in his sermons was four or five verses in the Old Testament and two or three verses in the New Testament. His sermons were fairly short for his day (perhaps due in part to his asthmatic condition), probably averaging thirty-five to forty minutes. He is reported to have spoken "deliberately, often with long pauses to allow people to think," though others say that he must have spoken rapidly to complete his sermon on time.[15]

---

12. *Commentary* [John 20:23].

13. John Calvin, *The Mystery of Godliness* (Grand Rapids, MI: Eerdmans, 1950), 122.

14. A. Mitchell Hunter, "Calvin as a Preacher," *Expository Times* 30, no. 12 (September 1919): 563.

15. Philip Vollmer, *John Calvin: Theologian, Preacher, Educator, Statesman* (Richmond, VA: Presbyterian Committee of Publication, 1909), 124; George Johnson, "Calvinism and Preaching," *Evangelical Quarterly* 4, no. 3 (July 1932): 249.

Calvin's style of preaching was plain and clear. In a sermon titled "Pure Preaching of the Word," Calvin writes, "We must shun all unprofitable babbling, and stay ourselves upon plain teaching, which is forcible."[16] Rhetoric for its own sake must be avoided, though true eloquence, when subjected to the simplicity of the gospel, is to be coveted. When Joachim Westphal charged Calvin with "babbling" in his sermons, Calvin replied that he stuck to the main point of the text and practiced "cautious brevity."[17]

Calvin's sermons abound with application throughout. In some cases, application consumes more time than exposition. Short, pungent applications, sprinkled throughout his sermons, constantly urge, exhort, and invite sinners to act in obedience to God's Word. Calvin stresses that we do "not come to the preaching merely to hear what we do not know, but to be incited to do our duty."[18]

T. H. L. Parker suggests that Calvin's sermons follow a pattern:

1. Prayer
2. Recapitulation of previous sermon
3a. Exegesis and exposition of the first point
3b. Application of the first point and exhortation to obedience of duty
4a. Exegesis and exposition of the second point
4b. Application of the second point and exhortation to obedience of duty
5. Closing prayer, which contains a brief, implicit summary of the sermon[19]

John Gerstner (1914–1996) points out that, though this was the structural order that Calvin often followed and probably intended to follow, he frequently departed from it because "he was so eager to get at the application that he often introduced it in the midst of the exposition. In other words, application was the dominant element in the preaching of John Calvin to which all else was subordinated."[20]

---

16. Calvin, *Mystery of Godliness*, 55.
17. Quoted in John C. Bowman, "Calvin as a Preacher," *Reformed Church Review* 56 (1909): 251–52.
18. Quoted in Steven J. Lawson, *The Expository Genius of John Calvin* (Lake Mary, FL: Reformation Trust, 2015), 104.
19. As summarized in John H. Gerstner, "Calvin's Two-Voice Theory of Preaching," *Reformed Review* 13, no. 2 (1959): 21.
20. Gerstner, "Calvin's Two-Voice Theory of Preaching," 22. Interestingly, the same formlessness is present in Calvin's sacramental forms. Petrus Dathenus was careful to give them a much more definite outline for the Dutch versions of Reformed liturgy.

Calvin's Stress on Piety in Preaching

Calvin understood true religion as fellowship between God and man. The part of the fellowship that moves from God to man Calvin called *revelation*; the part of the fellowship that moves from man to God, which involves man's obedient response, he called *piety*. Piety functions through God's grace by faith, and involves such devout acts as childlike trust, humble adoration, godly fear, and undying love. Calvin's applications in preaching often aimed to excite these acts.

For Calvin, the goal of the preacher is to promote piety while remaining acutely aware that the listener cannot produce it himself. The listener is only a recipient of piety by the grace of the Holy Spirit, not the author of it. Nevertheless, the Spirit accompanies the Word with divine gifts of pious graces.

Calvin's piety, like his theology, is inseparable from the knowledge of God. The true knowledge of God results in pious activity that aims to go beyond personal salvation to embrace the glory of God. Where God's glory is not served, true piety cannot exist. This knowledge of God compels discipline, obedience, and love in every sphere of the believer's life. For Calvin, the law gives love its mandate and content for our thoughts, words, and actions, to obey God in a disciplined life, and so to live to his glory. Indeed, love is the fulfillment of the law. Thus, for Calvin, true piety is both a vertical (Godward) and horizontal (manward) relationship of love and law.

Grace and law, therefore, are both prominent in Calvin's theology and preaching. Keeping the law is especially important because of its supreme purpose to lead us to consecrate our entire lives to God. Lionel Greve writes, "Grace has priority in such a way that Calvin's piety may be considered as a quality of life and response to God's grace that transcended law but at the same time included it." He goes on to conclude: "Calvin's piety may be termed 'transcendent piety.' It transcends the creature because it is founded in grace but yet includes the creature as he is the subject of faithfulness. He is the subject in such a way that his piety is never primarily for his welfare. . . . The general movement of Calvin's piety is always Godward. The benefits of God's goodness are merely byproducts of the main purpose—glorifying God."[21]

---

21. Lionel Greve, "Freedom and Discipline in the Theology of John Calvin, William Perkins, and John Wesley: An Examination of the Origin and Nature of Pietism" (PhD diss., Hartford Seminary Foundation, 1976), 149.

Calvin's combined emphases on God's glory and the believer's Spirit-worked piety led him to a theology of Christian experience. Experience was a theological and spiritual necessity for him. That is quite understandable, given his accent on the Spirit's work in the life of the believer—an emphasis that earned him the title "the theologian of the Holy Spirit." So we ought not be surprised that his pneumatological, experiential emphasis of piety spilled over into his sermons. The question is not whether Calvin was an experiential preacher—that is obvious from his sermons, commentaries, and even his *Institutes*. The question is: What role did experience play in his theology and preaching?

Calvin and Experience

In his writings, Calvin values experience so long as it is rooted in Scripture and springs out of the living reality of faith. He repeatedly defines the experience of believers as beyond verbal expression. For example, he writes: "Such, then, is a conviction that requires no reasons, such a knowledge with which the best reason agrees—in which the mind truly reposes, more securely and constantly than in any reasons: such finally, a feeling that can be born only of heavenly revelation. I speak of nothing other than what each believer experiences within himself—though my words fall far beneath a just explanation of the matter."[22] Calvin goes on to say that believers' recognition of God "consists more in living experience than in vain and high-flown speculations." But then he hastens to add, "Indeed, with experience as our teacher, we find God just as he declares himself in his Word."[23]

False experience fabricates a god that does not square with the Scriptures, but true experience always flows out of the truths of Scripture and confirms them. Holy Scripture is consistent with sacred, Spirit-worked experience, since Calvin understood that the Bible is not a book of abstract or scholastic doctrines, but a book of doctrine that is rooted in reality, and that informs and transforms daily living. Thus, experience played an important role in Calvin's exegesis. Willem Balke writes: "Experience can serve as a hermeneutical key in the explanation of the Scriptures. The Bible places us in the center of the struggle of faith, *coram*

---

22. *Institutes*, 1.7.5.
23. *Institutes*, 1.10.2.

Deo, and therefore Calvin can recommend himself as an exegete as he does in the introduction to the Commentary on the Psalms (1557) since he has experienced what the Bible testifies."[24]

Calvin viewed his multifaceted experiences as a Reformer as an important qualification for exegeting and preaching God's Word. Though he related his experiential qualification particularly to the Psalms, since the Psalms relate best to the suffering people of God and are, as he calls them, "An Anatomy of all the Parts of the Soul," all of his sermons and commentaries reveal that he believed no book of Scripture can be reduced to mere doctrine.

Though Calvin ascribed a large place to experience in his exegesis and preaching, he understood that experience has significant limitations. When divorced from the Word, experience is altogether unreliable and always incomplete. Calvin concluded that the depths of the human heart, which always remain a focal point for the mystic, cannot reveal the way to God. Rather, he agreed with Martin Luther that the only way to God is by Word-centered faith. The believer does not learn to know God's will from "*nuda experientia*," Calvin says, but only through the testimony of Scripture.[25]

If Scripture is not the foundation of our experience of faith, Calvin said, we will be left with only vague feelings that have no anchor. True faith, however, anchors itself in the Word. We ought not measure the presence of God in our lives by our experience, for that would soon bring us to despair. "If we should measure out the help of God according to our feelings," Calvin writes, "our faith would soon waver and we would have no courage or hope."[26]

Thus, Calvin was careful not to be an experientialist—that is, one who frequently calls attention to his own experiences in a rather mystical or purely subjective manner. He well understood that experience is to be defined by the testimony of the written Word.

Calvin avoided both experientialism and dry scholasticism. He did not see the Bible as a collection of doctrines, but rather viewed biblical

---

24. Willem Balke, "The Word of God and *Experientia* according to Calvin," in *Calvinus Ecclesiae Doctor*, ed. Wilhelm H. Neuser (Kampen: Kok, 1978), 22. Much of what I write in this and the following subheading is a summary and fine-tuning of Balke's helpful effort to grapple with Calvin's understanding of experience in the life of the believer.

25. *Opera quae supersunt omnia*, ed. Guilielmus Baum, Eduardus Cunitz, and Eduardus Reuss, vols. 29–87 in *Corpus Reformatorum* (Brunsvigae: C. A. Schwetschke, 1863–1900), 31:424, hereafter, CO.

26. CO, 31:103.

doctrines as "embedded in the life and faith of the church and of the individual, in the natural habitat of the verification of faith in Christian and ecclesiastical existence."[27]

Experientia Fidei *or* Sensus Fidei

The experience or sense of faith (*experientia fidei* or *sensus fidei*), according to Calvin, is also inseparable from the ministry of the Holy Spirit. The Spirit renews the very core of man. That work involves illumination and sealing; the Spirit's illumination of the mind and his efficacious work in the heart coalesce. The Spirit's sealing work certifies the authority of the Word and the reality of the Spirit's saving work. It promotes confidence in God's promises of mercy and experience of them. This doctrine, Calvin says, is "not of the tongue, but of life. It is not apprehended by the understanding and memory alone, as other disciplines are, but it is received only when it possesses the whole soul, and finds a seat and resting place in the inmost affection of the heart."[28]

Such *experientia fidei* is thus not a part of the believer's own ability, but is the creative effect of the Spirit who uses the Word. It contains both objective and subjective truth. The Spirit testifies both in the Word of God and in the heart of the believer, and the believer hears and experiences the reality of this testimony. Through the Spirit's objective and subjective testimony, the believer is persuaded experientially of the absolute truth of God and of his Word. Being made willing by the powerful operations of the Spirit, the heart, will, and emotions all respond in faith and obedience to the triune God. Since the Spirit is the Spirit of the Son, and it is the Spirit's great task to lead the believer to Christ, and through him to the Father, the center of faith's experience is, as John calls it, having "fellowship . . . with the Father, and with his Son" (1 John 1:3). True experience always leads, then, to true communion and to *praxis pietatis*, the practice of piety.

This is not to say that true experience is always that easily dissected and understood. The experience of faith contains numerous paradoxes. For example, a paradox exists in the life of faith when we are called to believe that God is still with us when we feel that he has deserted us. Or, how can we believe that God is favorably inclined to us when he strips

---

27. Balke, "The Word of God and *Experientia* according to Calvin," 22.
28. *Institutes*, 3.6.4.

us at times of all consciousness of that favor and seems to providentially postpone fulfilling his merciful promises?[29] The believer can experience such apparent contradictions on a daily basis, Calvin says. He can feel forsaken of God, even when he knows deep within that he is not (Isa. 49:14–16). These conflicting experiences transpire within one heart and seem, like hope and fear, to cancel each other out. If fear gets the upper hand, Calvin writes, we ought to simply throw ourselves wholly on the promises of God.[30] Those promises give us courage to go on in spite of temptations to doubt. Moreover, it is especially when we acknowledge by faith that God is present, even though we cannot see him or feel his goodness and power, that we truly honor his lordship and his Word.[31] To believe in God when experience seems to annul his promises takes great faith, but it is precisely this experience of faith that enables believers to remain undisturbed when their entire world seems to be shaken.[32]

Experience and Assurance of Faith

Calvin's doctrine of assurance reaffirms the basic tenets of Luther and Ulrich Zwingli, and also discloses emphases of his own.[33] Like Luther and Zwingli, Calvin says faith is never merely assent (*assensus*), but involves both knowledge (*cognitio*) and trust (*fiducia*). Faith rests firmly upon God's Word; it always says amen to the Scriptures.[34] Hence, assurance must be sought *in* the Word and flows *out of* the Word.[35] Assurance is as inseparable from the Word as sunbeams are from the sun.

Faith and assurance are also inseparable from *Christ and the promise of Christ*, for the totality of the written Word is the living Word, Jesus Christ, in whom all God's promises are "yea, and . . . amen" (2 Cor. 1:20).[36] Calvin makes much of the promises of God as the ground of

---

29. *CO*, 31:344.

30. *CO*, 31:548.

31. *CO*, 31:525.

32. *CO*, 31:703; 32:194.

33. Portions of the remainder of this chapter have been condensed and adapted from Joel R. Beeke, *The Quest for Full Assurance: The Legacy of Calvin and His Successors* (Edinburgh: Banner of Truth, 1999), 37–65.

34. *Commentary* [John 3:33; Ps. 43:3]; cf. K. Exalto, *De Zekerheid des Geloofs bij Calvijn* (Apeldoorn: Willem de Zwijgerstichting, 1978), 24. Edward Dowey mistakenly dichotomizes the Scriptures and assurance when he asserts that the center of Calvin's doctrine of faith is assurance rather than the authority of the Scriptures. For Calvin, the separation of the Word of God from assurance is unthinkable. *The Knowledge of God in Calvin's Theology* (New York: Columbia University Press, 1965), 182.

35. *Commentary* [Matt. 8:13; John 4:22].

36. *Commentary* [Gen. 15:6; Luke 2:21].

assurance, for these promises are based on the very nature of God, who cannot lie. The promises are fulfilled by Christ; therefore, Calvin directs sinners to Christ and to the promises as if they were synonyms.[37] Since faith takes its character from the promise on which it rests, faith takes on the infallible stamp of God's own Word. Consequently, faith possesses assurance in its own nature. Assurance, certainty, trust: such is the essence of faith.

More specifically, Calvin argues that faith involves something more than objectively believing the promise of God; it involves personal, subjective assurance. In believing God's promise to sinners, the true believer recognizes and celebrates that God is gracious and benevolent to him in particular. Faith is an assured knowledge "of God's benevolence toward *us* . . . revealed to *our* minds . . . sealed upon *our* hearts."[38] Calvin writes, "Here, indeed, is the hinge on which faith turns: that we do not regard the promises of mercy that God offers as true only outside ourselves, but not at all in us; rather that we make them ours by inwardly embracing them."[39]

Thus, as Robert Kendall notes, Calvin repeatedly describes faith as "certainty (*certitudino*), a firm conviction (*solido persuasio*), assurance (*securitas*), firm assurance (*solida securitas*), and full assurance (*plena securitas*)."[40] While faith consists of knowledge, it is also marked by heartfelt assurance that is "a sure and secure possession of those things which God has promised us."[41]

Calvin also emphasizes throughout his commentaries that assurance is integral to faith.[42] In expounding 2 Corinthians 13:5, Calvin even states that those who doubt their union with Christ are reprobates: "[Paul] declares, that all are *reprobates*, who doubt whether they profess Christ and are a part of His body. Let us, therefore, reckon *that* alone to be right faith, which leads us to repose in safety in the favour of God, with no wavering opinion, but with a firm and steadfast assurance."[43]

Throughout his lofty exposition of the doctrine of faith, however, Calvin repeats these themes: unbelief dies hard; assurance is often con-

---

37. *Institutes*, 3.2.32; *Commentary* [Rom. 4:3, 18; Heb. 11:7, 11].
38. *Institutes*, 3.2.7, emphasis added.
39. *Institutes*, 3.2.16; cf. 3.2.42.
40. Robert T. Kendall, *Calvin and English Calvinism to 1649* (New York: Oxford University Press, 1979), 19; cf. *Institutes*, 3.2.6; 3.2.16; 3.2.22.
41. *Institutes*, 3.2.41; 3.2.14.
42. *Commentary* [Acts 2:29; 1 Cor. 2:12].
43. *Commentary* [2 Cor. 13:5].

tested by doubt; severe temptations, wrestlings, and strife are normative; Satan and the flesh assault faith; and trust in God is hedged with fear.[44] Calvin freely acknowledges that faith is not retained without a severe struggle against unbelief, and that it is not left untainted by doubt and anxiety. He writes: "Unbelief is, in all men, always mixed with faith. . . . For unbelief is so deeply rooted in our hearts, and we are so inclined to it, that not without hard struggle is each one able to persuade himself of what all confess with the mouth, namely, that God is faithful. Especially when it comes to reality itself, every man's wavering uncovers hidden weakness."[45]

In expounding John 20:3, Calvin seems to contradict his assertion that true believers know themselves to be such when he testifies that the disciples had faith without awareness of it as they approached the empty tomb: "There being so little faith, or rather almost no faith, both in the disciples and in the women, it is astonishing that they had so great zeal; and, indeed, it is not possible that religious feelings led them to seek Christ. *Some seed of faith, therefore, remained in their hearts, but quenched for a time, so that they were not aware of having what they had.* Thus the Spirit of God often works in the elect in a secret manner."[46]

This prompts us to ask how Calvin can say that faith is characterized by full assurance, yet still allow for the kind of faith that lacks assurance? The two statements appear antithetical. Assurance is free from doubt, yet not free. It does not hesitate, yet can hesitate. It contains security, but may be beset with anxiety. The faithful have assurance, yet waver and tremble.

Calvin uses at least four principles to address this complex issue. Each helps make sense of his apparent contradictions.

First, Calvin distinguishes between *the definition of faith* and *the reality of the believer's experience*. After explaining faith in the *Institutes* as embracing "great assurance," Calvin writes:

> Still, someone will say: "Believers *experience* something far different: In recognizing the grace of God toward themselves they are not only tried by disquiet, which often comes upon them, but they are repeatedly shaken by gravest terrors. For so violent are the temptations that trouble their minds as not to seem quite compatible with

---

44. *Institutes*, 3.2.7; *Commentary* [Matt. 8:25; Luke 2:40].
45. *Institutes*, 3.2.4; 3.2.15.
46. Commentary [John 20:3], emphasis added; cf. *Institutes*, 3.2.12.

that certainty of faith." Accordingly, we shall have to solve this difficulty if we wish the above-stated doctrine to stand. Surely, while we teach that faith *ought* to be certain and assured, we cannot imagine any certainty that is not tinged with doubt, or any assurance that is not assailed.[47]

In short, Calvin distinguishes between what faith *ought to* be and what faith often *is* in daily life. His definition of faith serves as a recommendation of how believers ought "habitually and properly to think of faith."[48] Faith should always aim at full assurance, even if it cannot reach that point in experience. In principle, faith gains the victory (1 John 5:4); in practice, it recognizes that it has not yet fully apprehended the promised victory (Phil. 3:12–13).

Nevertheless, the practice of faith validates faith that trusts in the Word. Calvin is not as interested in experiences as he is in validating Word-grounded faith. Experience confirms faith, Calvin says. Faith "requires full and fixed certainty, such as men are wont to have from things experienced and proved."[49]

Thus, bare experience (*nuda experientia*) is not Calvin's goal, but experience grounded in the Word, flowing out of the fulfillment of the Word. Experimental knowledge of the Word is essential.[50] For Calvin, two kinds of knowledge are needed: knowledge by faith (*scientia fidei*) that is received from the Word, "though it is not yet fully revealed," and the knowledge of experience (*scientia experientiae*) "springing from the fulfilling of the Word."[51] The Word of God is primary to both the former and the latter, for experience teaches us to know God as he declares himself to be in his Word.[52] Experience not consonant with Scripture is never an experience of true faith. In short, though the believer's experience of true faith is far weaker than he desires, there is an essential unity in the Word between faith's perception (the *ought-to* dimension of faith) and experience (the *is* dimension of faith).

The second principle that helps us understand Calvin's tension in assurance of faith is the principle of *flesh versus spirit*. Calvin writes:

---

47. *Institutes*, 3.2.16–17, emphasis added.
48. Paul Helm, *Calvin and the Calvinists* (Edinburgh: Banner of Truth, 1982), 26.
49. *Institutes*, 3.2.15.
50. *Institutes*, 1.7.5.
51. *Commentary* [Joel 3:17; Zech. 2:9]; cf. Charles Partee, "Calvin and Experience," *Scottish Journal of Theology* 26 (1973): 169–81, and Balke, "The Word of God and *Experientia* according to Calvin," 23ff.
52. *Institutes*, 1.10.2.

It is necessary to return to that division of flesh and spirit which we have mentioned elsewhere. It most clearly reveals itself at this point. Therefore the godly heart feels in itself a division because it is partly imbued with sweetness from its recognition of the divine goodness, partly grieves in bitterness from an awareness of its calamity; partly rests upon the promise of the gospel, partly trembles at the evidence of its own iniquity; partly rejoices at the expectation of life, partly shudders at death. This variation arises from imperfection of faith, since in the course of the present life it never goes so well with us that we are wholly cured of the disease of unbelief and entirely filled and possessed by faith. Hence arise those conflicts, when unbelief, which reposes in the remains of the flesh, rises up to attack the faith that has been inwardly conceived.[53]

Like Luther, Calvin sets the "ought to/is" dichotomy against the backdrop of spirit/flesh warfare.[54] Christians experience this spirit/flesh tension acutely because it is instigated by the Holy Spirit.[55] The paradoxes that permeate experiential faith (e.g., Rom. 7:14–25 in the classical Reformed interpretation) find resolution in this tension: "So then with the mind [spirit] I myself serve the law of God; but with the flesh the law of sin" (v. 25).

Calvin sets the sure consolation of the spirit side by side with the imperfection of the flesh, for these are what the believer finds within himself. Since the final victory of the spirit over the flesh will be fulfilled only in Christ, the Christian perpetually struggles in this life. His spirit fills him "with delight in recognizing the divine goodness" even as his flesh activates his natural proneness to unbelief.[56] He is beset with "daily struggles of conscience" as long as the vestiges of the flesh remain.[57] The believer's "present state is far short of the glory of God's children," Calvin writes. "Physically, we are dust and shadow, and death is always before our eyes. We are exposed to a thousand miseries . . . so that we always find a hell within us."[58] While still in the flesh, the believer may even be tempted to doubt the whole gospel.

---

53. *Institutes*, 3.2.18.
54. C. A. Hall, *With the Spirit's Sword: The Drama of Spiritual Warfare in the Theology of John Calvin* (Richmond, VA: John Knox Press, 1970).
55. Victor A. Shepherd, *The Nature and Function of Saving Faith in the Theology of John Calvin* (Macon, GA: Mercer University Press, 1983), 24–28.
56. *Institutes*, 3.2.18; 3.2.20.
57. *Commentary* [John 13:9].
58. *Commentary* [1 John 3:2].

Even as he is tormented with fleshly doubts, the believer's spirit trusts God's mercy by invoking him in prayer and by resting upon him through the sacraments. By these means, faith gains the upper hand over unbelief. "Faith ultimately triumphs over those difficulties which besiege and . . . imperil it. [Faith is like] a palm tree [that] strives against every burden and raises itself upward."[59]

In short, Calvin teaches that from *the spirit* of the believer rise hope, joy, and assurance; from *the flesh*, fear, doubt, and disillusionment. Though spirit and flesh operate simultaneously, imperfection and doubt are integral only to the flesh, not to faith; the works of the flesh often *attend* faith but do not *mix* with it. The believer may lose spiritual battles along the pathway of life, but he will not lose the ultimate war against the flesh.

Third, despite the tensions between definition and experience, spirit and flesh, Calvin maintains that faith and assurance are not so mixed with unbelief that the believer is left with probability rather than certainty.[60] The smallest germ of faith contains assurance in its very essence, even when the believer is not always able to grasp this assurance due to weakness. The Christian may be tossed about with doubt and perplexity, but the seed of faith, implanted by the Spirit, cannot perish. Precisely because it is the Spirit's seed, faith retains assurance. This assurance increases and decreases in proportion to the rise and decline of faith's exercises, but the seed of faith can never be destroyed. Calvin says: "The root of faith can never be torn from the godly breast, but clings so fast to the inmost parts that, however faith seems to be shaken or to bend this way or that, its light is never so extinguished or snuffed out that it does not at least lurk as it were beneath the ashes."[61]

Calvin thus explains "weak assurance in terms of weak faith without thereby weakening the link between faith and assurance."[62] Assurance is normative but varies in degree and constancy in the believer's consciousness of it. So, in responding to weak assurance, a pastor should not deny the organic tie between faith and assurance, but should

---

59. *Institutes*, 3.2.17.
60. Cornelis Graafland, *De Zekerheid van het geloof: Een onderzoek naar de geloof-beschouwing van enige vertegenwoordigers van reformatie en nadere reformatie* (Wageningen: H. Veenman & Zonen, 1961), 31n.
61. *Institutes*, 3.2.21.
62. A. N. S. Lane, "The Quest for the Historical Calvin," *Evangelical Quarterly* 55 (1983): 103.

urge the pursuit of stronger faith through the use of the means of grace in dependence upon the Spirit.

Experience, the Trinity, and Election

Through a fourth sweeping principle, namely, *a Trinitarian framework* for the doctrine of faith and assurance, Calvin spurs the doubt-prone believer onward. As surely as the election of the Father must prevail over the works of Satan, the righteousness of the Son over the sinfulness of the believer, and the assuring witness of the Spirit over the soul's infirmities, so certainly assured faith shall and must conquer unbelief.

Calvin's arrangement of Book III of the *Institutes* reveals the movement of the grace of faith from God to man and man to God. The grace of faith is from the Father, in the Son, and through the Spirit, by which, in turn, the believer is brought into fellowship with the Son by the Spirit, and consequently is reconciled to and walks in fellowship with the Father.

For Calvin, a complex set of factors establishes assurance, not the least of which is the Father's election and preservation of believers in Christ. Hence, Calvin writes that "predestination duly considered does not shake faith, but rather affords the best confirmation of it,"[63] especially when viewed in the context of calling: "The firmness of our election is joined to our calling [and] is another means of establishing our assurance. For all whom [Christ] receives, the Father is said to have entrusted and committed to Him to keep to eternal life."[64]

Decretal election is a sure foundation for preservation and assurance; it is not coldly causal. Gordon Keddie writes: "Election is never seen, in Calvin, in a purely deterministic light, in which God . . . is viewed as 'a frightening idol' of 'mechanistic deterministic causality' and Christian experience is reduced to either cowering passivity or frantic activism, while waiting some 'revelation' of God's hidden decree for one's self. For Calvin, as indeed in Scripture, election does not threaten, but rather undergirds, the certainty of salvation."[65]

Such a foundation is possible only in a Christ-centered context; hence Calvin's constant accent on Christ as the mirror of election, "wherein we

---

63. *Institutes*, 3.24.9.
64. *Institutes*, 3.24.6.
65. Gordon J. Keddie, "'Unfallible Certenty of the Pardon of Sinne and Life Everlasting': The Doctrine of Assurance in the Theology of William Perkins," *Evangelical Quarterly* 48 (1976): 231; cf. G. C. Berkouwer, *Divine Election*, trans. Hugo Bekker (Grand Rapids, MI: Eerdmans, 1960), 10ff.

must, and without self-deception may, contemplate our own election."[66] Election turns the believer's eyes from the hopelessness of his inability to meet any conditions of salvation to focus on the hope of Jesus Christ as God's pledge of undeserved love and mercy.[67]

Through union with Christ, "the assurance of salvation becomes real and effective as the assurance of election."[68] Christ becomes ours in fulfillment of God's determination to redeem and resurrect us. Consequently, we ought not to think of Christ as "standing afar off, and not dwelling in us."[69] Since Christ is for us, to contemplate him truly is to see him forming in us what he desires to give us, himself above all. God has made himself "little in Christ," Calvin states, so that we might comprehend and flee to Christ, who alone can pacify our consciences.[70] Faith must begin, rest, and end in Christ. "True faith is so contained in Christ, that it neither knows, nor desires to know, anything beyond Him," Calvin says.[71] Therefore, "we ought not to separate Christ from ourselves or ourselves from Him."[72]

In this Christological manner, Calvin reduces the distance between God's objective decree of election from the believer's subjective lack of assurance that he is elect. For Calvin, election answers, rather than raises, the question of assurance. In Christ, the believer sees his election; in the gospel, he hears of his election.

The question remains, however: How do the elect enjoy communion with Christ, and how does that communion produce assurance? Calvin's answer is pneumatological: the Holy Spirit applies Christ and his benefits to the hearts and lives of guilty, elect sinners, through which they are assured by saving faith that Christ belongs to them and they to him. The Holy Spirit especially confirms within them the reliability of God's promises in Christ. Thus, personal assurance is never divorced from the election of the Father, the redemption of the Son, the application of the Spirit, and the instrumental means of saving faith.

---

66. *Institutes*, 3.24.5; cf. John Calvin, *Sermons on the Epistle to the Ephesians* (repr., Edinburgh: Banner of Truth, 1973), 47; *Sermons from Job* (Grand Rapids, MI: Eerdmans, 1952), 41ff.; CO 8:318–321; 9:757.

67. *Institutes*, 3.24.6; cf. William H. Chalker, "Calvin and Some Seventeenth Century English Calvinists" (PhD diss., Duke University, 1961), 66.

68. Wilhelm Niesel, *The Theology of Calvin*, trans. Harold Knight (Grand Rapids, MI: Baker, 1980), 196; cf. *Institutes*, 3.1.1; Shepherd, *Faith in the Theology of John Calvin*, 51.

69. *Institutes*, 3.2.24.

70. *Commentary* [1 Pet. 1:20].

71. *Commentary* [Eph. 4:13].

72. *Institutes*, 3.2.24.

The Holy Spirit has an enormous role in the application of redemption, Calvin says. As personal Comforter and seal, the Holy Spirit assures the believer of his gracious adoption: "The Spirit of God gives us such a testimony, that when he is our guide and teacher our spirit is made sure of the adoption of God; for our mind of itself, without the preceding testimony of the Spirit, could not convey to us this assurance."[73] The Holy Spirit's work underlies all assurance of salvation without detracting from the role of Christ, for the Spirit is the Spirit *of Christ*, who assures the believer by leading him to Christ and his benefits, and by working out those benefits within him.[74]

Experience and Self-Examination

Nevertheless, Calvin is acutely aware that a person may think that the Father has entrusted him to Christ when such is not the case. It is one thing to underscore Christ's task in the Trinitarian, salvific economy as the recipient and guardian of the elect; the center, author, and foundation of election; and the guarantee, promise, and mirror of the believer's election and salvation. But it is quite another to inquire whether a person has been joined to Christ by a true faith. Many appear to be Christ's who are estranged from him. Says Calvin: "It daily happens that those who seemed to be Christ's fall away from him again. . . . Such persons never cleaved to Christ with the heartfelt trust in which certainty of salvation has, I say, been established for us."[75]

Calvin never preached so as to instill in his flock a false assurance of salvation.[76] Many scholars minimize Calvin's emphasis on the need for a subjective, experiential realization of faith and election by referring to Calvin's practice of approaching his congregation as people already saved. They misunderstand. Though Calvin practiced what he called "a judgment of charity" (i.e., addressing as saved those church members who maintain a commendable, external lifestyle), we have seen that he also frequently asserted that only a minority receive the preached Word with saving faith. He says: "For though all, without

---

73. *Commentary* [Rom. 8:16]; cf. *Commentary* [John 7:37–39; Acts 2:4; 3:8; 5:32; 13:48; 16:14; 23:11; Rom. 8:15–17; 1 Cor. 2:10–13; 2 Cor. 1:21–22; Gal. 3:2, 4:6; Eph. 1:13–14; 4:30]; *Institutes*, 3.2.11, 34, 41; *Tracts and Treatises*, 3:253ff.; J. K. Parratt, "The Witness of the Holy Spirit: Calvin, the Puritans and St. Paul," *Evangelical Quarterly* 41 (1969): 161–68.
74. *Institutes*, 3.2.34.
75. *Institutes*, 3.24.7.
76. Cornelis Graafland, "'Waarheid in het Binnenste': Geloofszekerheid bij Calvijn en de Nadere Reformatie," in *Een Vaste Burcht*, ed. K. Exalto (Kampen: Kok, 1989), 65–67.

exception, to whom God's Word is preached, are taught, yet scarce one in ten so much as tastes it; yea, scarce one in a hundred profits to the extent of being enabled, thereby, to proceed in a right course to the end."[77]

For Calvin, much that resembles faith lacks a saving character. He thus speaks of faith that is unformed, implicit, temporary, illusionary, false, a shadow-type, transitory, and under a cloak of hypocrisy.[78] Self-deception is a real possibility, Calvin says. Because the reprobate often feel something much like the faith of the elect,[79] self-examination is essential. He writes: "Let us learn to examine ourselves, and to search whether those interior marks by which God distinguishes his children from strangers belong to us, *viz.*, the living root of piety and faith."[80] Happily, the truly saved are delivered from self-deception through proper examination directed by the Holy Spirit. Calvin says: "In the meantime, the faithful are taught to examine themselves with solicitude and humility, lest carnal security insinuate itself, instead of the assurance of faith."[81]

Even in self-examination, Calvin emphasizes Christ. He says we must examine ourselves to see if we are placing our trust in *Christ alone*, for this is the fruit of biblical experience. Anthony Lane says that for Calvin, self-examination is not so much "Am I *trusting* in Christ?" as it is "Am I trusting in *Christ*?"[82] Self-examination must always direct us to Christ and his promise. It must never be done apart from the help of the Holy Spirit, who alone can shed light upon Christ's saving work in the believer's soul. Apart from Christ, the Word, and the Spirit, Calvin says, "if you contemplate yourself, that is sure damnation."[83]

---

77. *Commentary* [Ps. 119:101]. Calvin refers to the fewness of those who possess vital faith. Cf. *Institutes*, 3.21–24.

78. *Institutes*, 3.2.3, 5, 10–11. For Calvin on temporary faith, see David Foxgrover, "'Temporary Faith' and the Certainty of Salvation," *Calvin Theological Journal* 15 (1980): 220–32; A. N. S. Lane, "Calvin's Doctrine of Assurance," *Vox Evangelica* 11 (1979): 45–46; Exalto, *De Zekerheid des Geloofs bij Calvijn*, 15–20, 27–30.

79. *Institutes*, 3.2.11.

80. *Commentary* [Ezek. 13:9]. Foxgrover shows that Calvin related the need for self-examination to a great variety of topics: knowledge of God and ourselves, judgment, repentance, confession, affliction, the Lord's Supper, providence, duty, the kingdom of God, etc. "John Calvin's Understanding of Conscience" (PhD diss., Claremont, 1978), 312ff.; cf. J. P. Pelkonen, "The Teaching of John Calvin on the Nature and Function of the Conscience," *Lutheran Quarterly* 21 (1969): 24–88.

81. *Institutes*, 3.2.7.

82. Lane, "Calvin's Doctrine of Assurance," 47.

83. *Institutes*, 3.2.24.

Conclusion

Calvin was an experiential theologian and preacher who strove to balance how spiritual matters should go in the Christian life, how they do go, and what their end goal is. In his preaching and writing, he hedged himself in from excesses by confining himself to the limits of Scripture and by always tying the Spirit's experiential work to Scripture. At the same time, he used experiential preaching as a way to minister to the needs of believers and as a discriminatory tool for unbelievers. Above all, all of his experiential emphases strove to lead the believer to end in glorifying the Trinity through Jesus Christ.

7

Reformation Preachers: Beza

Theodore Beza, John Calvin's successor in Geneva, was born into the ranks of the lesser nobility.[1] Though he was only ten years younger than Calvin, he outlived Calvin by forty-one years. He became the old patriarch of the Reformation movement, preaching and teaching into his eighties.

---

1. On Beza, see Irena Dorota Backus, *The Reformed Roots of the English New Testament: The Influence of Theodore Beza on the English New Testament*, The Pittsburgh Theological Monograph Series 28 (Pittsburgh: Pickwick, 1980); Henry Martyn Baird, *Theodore Beza: The Counsellor of the French Reformation, 1519–1605*, Burt Franklin Research & Source Works Series 475 (Eugene, OR: Wipf & Stock, 2004); John S. Bray, *Theodore Beza's Doctrine of Predestination*, Bibliotheca Humanistica Et Reformatorica 12 (Nieuwkoop: De Graaf, 1975); Robert Letham, "Theodore Beza: A Reassessment," *Scottish Journal of Theology* 40, no. 1 (1987): 25–40; Jeffrey Mallinson, *Faith, Reason, and Revelation in Theodore Beza, 1519–1605*, Oxford Theological Monographs (Oxford: Oxford University Press, 2003); Scott M. Manetsch, *Theodore Beza and the Quest for Peace in France, 1572–1598* (Leiden: Brill, 2000); Tadataka Maruyama, *The Ecclesiology of Theodore Beza: The Reform of the True Church*, Travaux D'humanisme Et Renaissance no. 166 (Geneve: Droz, 1978); Ian McPhee, "Conserver or Transformer of Calvin's Theology? A Study of the Origins and Development of Theodore Beza's Thought, 1550–1570" (PhD diss., University of Cambridge, 1979); Richard A. Muller, *Christ and the Decree: Christology and Predestination in Reformed Theology from Calvin to Perkins* (Grand Rapids, MI: Baker, 1988); Jill Raitt, *The Eucharistic Theology of Theodore Beza: Development of the Reformed Doctrine*, AAR Studies in Religion no. 4 (Chambersburg, PA: American Academy of Religion, 1972); David Curtis Steinmetz, *Reformers in the Wings: From Geiler Von Kaysersberg to Theodore Beza*, 2nd ed. (Oxford: Oxford University Press, 2001); Kirk M. Summers, *Morality after Calvin: Theodore Beza's Christian Censor and Reformed Ethics* (New York: Oxford University Press, 2017); Shawn D. Wright, "The Pastoral Use of the Doctrine of God's Sovereignty in the Theology of Theodore Beza" (PhD diss., Southern Baptist Theological Seminary, 2001); *Our Sovereign Refuge: The Pastoral Theology of Theodore Beza*, Paternoster Biblical and Theological Monographs (Carlisle, UK: Paternoster, 2004); *Theodore Beza: The Man and the Myth* (Fearn, Ross-shire, Scotland: Christian Focus, 2015); Joel R. Beeke, "Theodore Beza's Supralapsarian Predestination," *Reformation and Revival Journal* 12, no. 2 (Spring 2003): 69–84; Theodore Beza, *The Christian Faith*, trans. James Clark (Lewes, UK: Focus Christian Ministries Trust, 1992); Théodore de Bèze, "The Potter and the Clay: The Main Predestination Writings of Theodore Beza," trans. Philip C. Holtrop (Grand Rapids, MI: Calvin College, 1982); Théodore de Bèze, *A Little Book of Christian Questions and Responses in Which the Principal Headings of the Christian Religion Are Briefly Set Forth*, trans. Kirk M. Summers, Princeton Theological Monograph Series 9 (Allison Park, PA: Pickwick, 1986).

Beza was born in France, but he left for Germany in 1534 to study law. This was his father's desire for him, just as Calvin's father had wanted him to do the same. Upon completion of his law degree in 1539, Beza returned to Paris to set up a legal practice. His heart, however, remained in humanism, that is, in classical studies, especially Latin poetry and literature.

Like Ulrich Zwingli's, Beza's conversion to Protestantism resulted from his suffering through a crisis of mind, heart, and body. It took place sometime between 1546 and 1548. When he was restored to health, the fruits of his internal struggle with sin and his subsequent joy at his deliverance in Christ became self-evident. He writes: "From the moment I could leave my bed, I broke all the bonds that until then had enchained me. I gathered all my belongings and left my country, my family and my friends in order to follow Christ, willingly retiring to Geneva with my wife." He abandoned literary fame and fortune. In short, he left his entire life behind when he came to know Christ, and he looked forward into the unknown future. Like Abraham, he went forth at God's command, but not knowing where he was going.

Beza arrived in Geneva in late October 1548 and was warmly welcomed by Calvin. Once he got there, French authorities banished Beza from France on three counts: heresy; the sale of two church benefices his family had secured for his financial support; and his flight to Geneva. Then, two years later, in 1550, the French government confiscated all his remaining possessions (he was fairly wealthy) and condemned him to be burned at the stake if he ever returned to France. After a brief stay in Geneva, Beza journeyed on to Lausanne and remained there as a Greek professor from 1549 to 1558. Throughout those ten years, he retained a close friendship with Calvin and seldom, if ever, published anything without getting Calvin's seal of approval.

In the fall of 1558, Beza returned to Geneva, having accepted the call to serve as professor of the newly established Genevan Academy. He remained in Geneva until his death, serving as professor of theology from 1559 to 1599, nearly forty-one years. He also was rector from 1559 to 1563. Meanwhile, he took a very active part among the preachers in Geneva. He moderated Geneva's Company of Pastors from 1564 to 1580.

Though he was not as prolific a writer as Calvin, few Reformers produced such a varied literary corpus as did Beza. In addition to theological writings, he composed some Latin poems, dramas, satires, and polemical treatises. He wrote Greek and French grammars. He wrote biographies and political treatises. And, most famously, he edited and annotated texts of the Greek New Testament. He bequeathed to Cambridge University one of the most valuable of the ancient New Testament manuscripts, subsequently called *Codex Bezae*.

Beza was a good polemicist who defended Reformed doctrine at various colloquies. He attended the Colloquy of Poissy (1561–1562), where he defended the evangelical cause before Roman Catholicism. He also sought unity between Lutherans and Reformers as late as 1586 at the Colloquy of Mumpelgart. Then, at the Colloquy of Bern (1587), Beza defended the doctrine of supralapsarian predestination.

The last years of Beza's life were spent rather quietly. He died in 1605, having outlived all the other Reformers by decades. While Calvin, Martin Luther, Martin Bucer, Heinrich Bullinger, Peter Martyr Vermigli, and William Farel lived on merely as names in the memory of Geneva, Beza continued to be very much an active figure until the beginning of the seventeenth century. Appropriately, his last words on his deathbed to a friend were, "The city, in full safety and quiet," reflecting his heart for Geneva and its well-being.

Preacher of Christ

Beza's preaching has been neglected by scholars, who tend to focus on his supralapsarian theology of predestination. However, Scott Manetsch has shown that preaching played a central role in Beza's ministry in Geneva. He writes, "From the time he arrived in Geneva in the fall of 1558, until poor health finally forced him to step down permanently from the pulpit in 1600, Beza may have preached as many as four thousand sermons to his congregation at St. Pierre's."[2]

Of these thousands of sermons, only eighty-seven are now extant. As Manetsch notes, these are "his sermons on the Song of Songs (1586), his sermons on the passion of Jesus Christ (1592), and his sermons on the

---

2. Scott M. Manetsch, *"Onus Praedicandi*: The Preaching Ministry of Theodore Beza" (unpublished paper, Calvin College and Seminary, n.d.), 1. In this section, I am indebted to Manetsch's research, much of which is included in his book *Calvin's Company of Pastors: Pastoral Care and the Emerging Reformed Church, 1536–1609* (Oxford: Oxford University Press, 2012).

resurrection of Jesus Christ (1593)."[3] Few of these have been translated from French into English.[4]

When Beza came to Geneva to be rector of and professor in the academy, he was also elected a minister of the gospel. He became the chief minister of the largest parish church in the city and the moderator of the Company of Pastors when Calvin died in 1564. So Beza preached from St. Pierre's for more than three decades. Though he was assisted by one or two other pastors, he played a central role in the proclamation of the Scriptures in Geneva.[5]

The Genevan churches practiced a rigorous schedule of regular preaching. In addition to regular Lord's Day services, special predawn services were often held on weekdays. During a given week near the end of Calvin's life, the Genevan pastors delivered twenty-seven sermons. Sermons normally lasted for sixty minutes—enforced by an hourglass—though, as noted earlier, Calvin himself preached considerably shorter sermons. Adults and children were required to attend at least the Lord's Day sermons, and people who did not do so were formally rebuked.[6]

Beza usually preached once or twice on the Lord's Day from the New Testament and regularly at weekday services from the Old Testament. We do not know Beza's whole preaching schedule in the kind of detail that we have for Calvin, but we do know that in 1574 he preached through the epistle of Hebrews and the epistle of James. In 1578, he preached through all of Isaiah. In 1583, he completed his series on the Song of Solomon, and then he preached on the death and resurrection of Christ for a year or two. He also preached on the Psalms (1579), Ecclesiastes (1588), and Job (1589).[7]

We may observe Beza's high regard for preaching in his understanding of how God gives his Son to elect sinners. He says that the Holy Spirit unites us to Christ "in creating in us, by His pure goodness and Divine mercy, that which we call 'faith.' . . . In order to create in us this instrument of faith, and also to feed and strengthen it more and more, the Holy Spirit uses two ordinary means (without however communicating

---

3. Manetsch, "*Onus Praedicandi*: The Preaching Ministry of Theodore Beza," 2.
4. An English translation of Beza's ninth sermon on the resurrection may be found in Wright, *Our Sovereign Refuge*, 243–58.
5. Manetsch, "*Onus Praedicandi*: The Preaching Ministry of Theodore Beza," 3.
6. Manetsch, "*Onus Praedicandi*: The Preaching Ministry of Theodore Beza," 3–4.
7. Manetsch, "*Onus Praedicandi*: The Preaching Ministry of Theodore Beza," 5–6.

to them His power, but working by them): the preaching of the Word of God, and His sacraments."[8] The sacraments do not function apart from the Word, but, Beza writes, "they are certain signs, visible marks . . . to represent to our outward senses what He tells us in His Word."[9] So the sacraments "belong to, and depend on, the Word . . . the Sacraments can never be legitimately administered without the Word."[10]

Therefore, Beza believed that the preaching of the Word is central to the life of faith. The preaching of the law wounds the soul with guilt and fear. The preaching of the gospel heals the wound with the grace of Christ. He says, "The Holy Spirit . . . uses this external preaching as a pipe or channel; He comes then to pierce to the depth of the soul."[11] Then the preaching of law comes to the believer in another mode than before his conversion, namely, "as a guide to teach us the good works" God plans for us to do.[12]

We must cast away the image of Beza as a cold theologian plumbing the depths of the divine decrees in a way that drew more from Greek philosophy than from the Bible. When lecturing on Job 1, he asserted God's predestination, yet he rejected "that iron disposition and unsensibleness [lack of feeling] of the Stoics," commending Job's grief as an appropriate sorrow that did not question God.[13] Beza gave these comments to the academy students while Geneva was besieged by the Duke of Savoy, thereby affirming both faith in God's sovereign purposes and grief over the losses experienced in this life.

As a preacher, he was warm, pastoral, simple, and evangelistic. People could follow him easily and enjoyed his sermons. We have a taste of that in books now available in English, such as *The Christian Faith*. It is a short, popular-level book that covers all the Christian doctrines in about one hundred pages. The caricature that men who preach predestination are cold, distant, and out-of-touch intellectuals is refuted by Beza's example, as it is also by William Perkins, as we will see.

After a thorough examination of Beza's writings, Shawn Wright concludes that his ministry was characterized by hope in spiritual warfare and

---

8. Beza, *The Christian Faith*, 16 [4.3–4].
9. Beza, *The Christian Faith*, 51 [4.31].
10. Beza, *The Christian Faith*, 54 [4.35].
11. Beza, *The Christian Faith*, 48 [4.28].
12. Beza, *The Christian Faith*, 49 [4.29].
13. Jill Raitt, "Lessons in Troubled Times: Beza's Lessons on Job," in *Calvin and the State*, ed. Peter De Klerk, Colloquia on Calvin and Calvin Studies (Grand Rapids, MI: Calvin Studies Society, 1993), 26, 38.

comfort by faith. Regarding hope in spiritual warfare, Wright says, "Beza's main concern in life was to make certain that he, his parishioners, and his students stood firm in the midst of the spiritual battle raging around them and arrived safely in their eternal bliss." He also says, "For Theodore Beza God's complete sovereignty was a comforting doctrine."[14]

That is not to deny that Beza taught predestination. His book *Tabula Praedestinationis* (1555) contains Beza's influential diagram of the order of salvation. It was probably written as a polemical tract to counter the arguments of Jerome Bolsec (c. 1524–1584), a French physician who strongly opposed Calvin. Beza's chart begins with God's decree. Flowing from it, he lists the two destinies of the elect and reprobate, including all the cardinal doctrines of salvation—calling, conversion, grace, faith, justification, sanctification, and glorification—culminating in heaven for believers and hell for the wicked.

On the basis of the *Tabula*, some modern scholars accuse Beza of losing Calvin's Bible-based, Christ-centered piety. But they fail to understand the *Tabula* according to its function. It was not a sermon for the church but a polemical treatise responding to attacks on the Reformed doctrine of predestination. Beza would have written differently if his intent had been pastoral.[15] Furthermore, Beza's critics sometimes fail to get past the chart to read the actual treatise, which is very much centered on Christ. Beza says in chapter 5 of the *Tabula*, "Christ is the second heavenly Adam, the foundation and very substance of the elect's salvation."[16] So even in an academic debate about predestination, Beza made Christ central.

Christ is central to predestination in part because salvation depends upon the atoning work of the Mediator. As Beza writes elsewhere, God does not save by a bare act of sovereignty, but "brings his sovereign righteousness and his sovereign mercy together" in Christ, for "in order to save those whom God had destined to salvation, the Savior had to be God" to bear and exhaust the wrath of God, and "he had to be still a true son of Adam" to stand as a surety for fallen men.[17] We know

---

14. Wright, *Our Sovereign Refuge*, 232, 233.

15. Richard A. Muller, "The Use and Abuse of a Document: Beza's *Tabula Praedestinationis*, the Bolsec Controversy, and the Origins of Reformed Orthodoxy," in *Protestant Scholasticism: Essays in Reassessment*, ed. Carl R. Trueman and R. Scott Clark (Carlisle, UK: Paternoster, 1999), 33–61.

16. Beza, *Tabula*, v. i., quoted in John B. Roney and Martin I. Klauber, eds., *The Identity of Geneva* (Westport, CT: Greenwood Press, 1998), 60.

17. Theodore Beza, "Sermons sur l'Histoire de la Resurrection: Sermon 9," in Wright, *Our Sovereign Refuge*, 254.

our predestination to eternal life by a living faith in Christ, evidenced through good works. He writes:

> This faith, I say, takes hold of Christ, through whom, being justified and sanctified, we have the enjoyment of the glory to which we have been predestined before the foundation of the world (Rom. 8:30; Eph. 1:3, 4). . . . Faith is nothing other than that by which we are sure of possessing eternal life; by it, we know that before the foundation of the world, God has predestined us to possess, through Christ, so great salvation and such excellent glory.[18]

Preacher to Human Experience

As Manetsch notes, Beza understood the calling of a pastor to be the imparting of knowledge, but not in the manner of a theological professor.[19] Beza did not see the preacher as someone merely explaining theological maxims, but as a shepherd caring for his sheep. Beza writes:

> At all times, the prophets, Jesus Christ and the Apostles spoke ever and only in the language of the common people, so that they were understood by every man in their nation . . . we say, and practice thus, that the pastors must feed their flock with the Word of Life, and that the sheep, on their side, should know and understand that which is proclaimed to them, in order to be nourished and consoled by it, and in order to be put on their guard against the wolves and false prophets.[20]

Preachers aim to apply truth to living souls whom they know by name.[21] Beza says: "But pastors must go further [than teaching doctrine]. For, in preaching, they apply the doctrine to the needs of the Church, to teach, to rebuke, to console and exhort in public and in private, according to the need . . . they also make public prayer. In brief, they watch day and night over their flock whom they feed in public and in private with the Word of life (Acts 20:20)."[22]

Beza believed that a minister must be a sincere disciple of Christ and a careful student of the Bible. The first qualification of a preacher is per-

---

18. Beza, *The Christian Faith*, 35 [4.19].
19. Manetsch, "*Onus Praedicandi*: The Preaching Ministry of Theodore Beza," 8.
20. Beza, *The Christian Faith*, iv.
21. Manetsch, "*Onus Praedicandi*: The Preaching Ministry of Theodore Beza," 8.
22. Beza, *The Christian Faith*, 93 [5.26].

sonal piety and an exemplary life. Then he must labor to draw out the meaning of the biblical text in the original languages, comparing Scripture to Scripture to make a proper interpretation.[23] "True humility of spirit" requires receiving all that Scripture teaches, not just what appeals to our fallen minds.[24] By such study, the preacher discovers "doctrine the Holy Spirit wants to engrave well on the heart of each one."[25] Then he must not allow the criticisms of men to confine him "simply to explain his text and settle some questions of doctrine"; rather, he must apply the medicine to his patients by "sweet consolations" and strong "reproofs," even if guilty men take the latter as "insults."[26]

Beza counsels a young minister to read regularly through the Bible in order to grow in spiritual discernment. He goes on to say that the minister should preach the Scriptures with simple truthfulness, avoiding his own speculations and opinions, and never try to impress his hearers with his skill or flowery words. He must carefully guard his tongue when he admonishes sinners, lest what he thinks to be his zeal for the Lord prove to be the harshness of his foolish passion. In all things, he should be diligent to apply the truth of Scripture to people's lives, both in the pulpit and in private. Beza concludes his counsel with a personal note: "Receive all this advice, from one who loves you."[27]

Faith receives the plain gospel. The simplicity of the gospel offends men, who expect to receive from Christ even worldly "magnificence" and visible "triumph" over enemies. Instead, Beza says, we should be "simply trusting what has been well attested to us by Scripture," the proclamation of which is "the very powerful instrument of God in the salvation of all who believe (Rom. 1:16)," even though the world considers it folly.[28]

He does not reject all use of rhetorical skill in preaching: "And what I say is not to criticize the elegance or grace of arranging one's words in an orderly manner, and of using proper and significant words and terms— whether it is in teaching, in exhorting, or in reproving or speaking."[29]

---

23. Manetsch, "*Onus Praedicandi*: The Preaching Ministry of Theodore Beza," 9.
24. Beza, "Sermon," in Wright, *Our Sovereign Refuge*, 251.
25. Beza, "Sermon," in Wright, *Our Sovereign Refuge*, 246.
26. Beza, "Sermon," in Wright, *Our Sovereign Refuge*, 246.
27. Quoted in Manetsch, "*Onus Praedicandi*: The Preaching Ministry of Theodore Beza," 10. He is quoting Beza's letter to Louis Courant, July 2, 1601, in Archives Tronchin, fonds. Bèze, vol. 5, fol. 296–97.
28. Beza, "Sermon," in Wright, *Our Sovereign Refuge*, 244.
29. Beza, "Sermon," in Wright, *Our Sovereign Refuge*, 245.

He calls for "sacred rhetoric" that avoids putting on a show but instead possesses a "gravity" and "vehemence" (or energetic forcefulness) fitting for divine things.[30]

Beza himself practiced a very direct and applied form of preaching. Manetsch writes: "In his pulpit ministry, therefore, we see Beza functioning as exegete, theologian, social commentator, personal counselor, and public information director. Far from being elegant or speculative, Beza's preaching is direct and passionate, intended to excite interest, instill conviction, and compel change in his audience."[31] In fact, his denunciation of the sins of Geneva and its spiritual apathy sometimes stirred the resentment of both church members and the civil magistrates.[32]

Beza also addressed what the Puritans would later call cases of conscience, questions about discerning righteousness versus sin. For example, when preaching from the resurrection accounts of Luke 24,[33] Beza paused to consider the distinction between lying (which is sinful) and not revealing all of one's mind (which is justifiable, even if it results in people making false assumptions). He used this distinction not only to illuminate texts about the Lord's ways with men, but also to address cases of war and espionage.[34] The treatment of such cases furnished the consciences of the congregation with a biblical system of practical ethics and moral wisdom.

Drawing lines between right and wrong and sounding the trumpet against sin requires courage and discernment. Beza describes the calling of a faithful preacher to stand against sin as follows:

> If he wants to please men, he is no longer a servant of God (Gal. 1:10). Therefore after knowledge he will ask God first for a spirit of discretion not to reprove anything lightly without knowing and understanding the fact that he is reproving. Next he will ask for the true use of the language of God, not just to speak, but to speak frankly as one must speak (Eph. 6:20). And closing his ear to threats and all respect for persons, he should listen to the Lord who is admonishing him in the manner of Isaiah, "Proclaim it with a full voice, do not spare

---

30. Beza, "Sermon," in Wright, *Our Sovereign Refuge*, 245.
31. Manetsch, "*Onus Praedicandi*: The Preaching Ministry of Theodore Beza," 12.
32. Manetsch, "*Onus Praedicandi*: The Preaching Ministry of Theodore Beza," 13–14.
33. Particularly Christ's conduct in Luke 24:28: "And they drew nigh unto the village, whither they went: and he made as though he would have gone further."
34. Beza, "Sermon," in Wright, *Our Sovereign Refuge*, 256–57.

yourself, raise up your voice like a horn and declare their trespasses to my people, and declare their sins to the house of Jacob." [Isa. 58:1][35]

At the same time, he understood that mere words, no matter how true, are insufficient to overcome man's natural blindness. Even believers need more grace to make their knowledge into a true knowing. He writes, "But we, my brothers, who are of the number of those to whom God gave the grace of calling them from darkness into so admirable a light (1 Pet. 2:9) . . . let us learn to ask our God for an increase of this true sense of his light."[36] He exhorts men to pray for inward spiritual light and heat: "We must ask the Lord that he change and correct [our reason], even as dead as it is with regard to that truth (Eph. 2:1); he gives us life, by giving us movement and affection from the beginning until the end." Even those who have "eyes of faith" see at best "bleary-eyed or completely one-eyed."[37]

With a true experiential balance, Beza calls for a Christianity that is real in both the heart and in conduct. He says: "The Lord does not want only that we believe, but he wants us to believe from the heart. . . . [N]ever will a man be recognized as a Christian before God, unless he believes inwardly and shows it clearly on the outside."[38]

Conclusion

Beza led Geneva and the international Reformed movement through a time of great transition and trial. His shoulders received the mantle of Calvin, one of the premier second-generation Reformers. He oversaw the academy where Reformed ministers trained and then went out to the world. As a pastor, he had to comfort and strengthen the people in 1572 when the horrific news arrived that Roman Catholics had murdered thousands of French Reformed Christians, and afterward, when thousands of Reformed refugees flooded Geneva.[39] Yet through it all, he sustained a remarkable ministry of preaching the Word of God week after week— a testimony to his steady conviction that the gospel is the power of God. Beza preached his last sermon on January 13, 1600, at St. Pierre's, and appropriately the text was, "Thy will be done on earth as it is in heaven."[40]

---

35. Beza, "Sermon," in Wright, *Our Sovereign Refuge*, 246–47.
36. Beza, "Sermon," in Wright, *Our Sovereign Refuge*, 249.
37. Beza, "Sermon," in Wright, *Our Sovereign Refuge*, 250–51.
38. Beza, "Sermon," in Wright, *Our Sovereign Refuge*, 251.
39. See Manetsch, *Theodore Beza and the Quest for Peace in France, 1572–1598*, 30ff.
40. Manetsch, "*Onus Praedicandi*: The Preaching Ministry of Theodore Beza," 17.

8

Introduction to
Puritan Preaching

The Puritan movement from the mid-sixteenth century to the late seventeenth century has been called the golden age of preaching.[1] Through preaching and the publication of sermons, the Puritans sought to reform the church and the everyday lives of the people.[2] Though they failed to reform the church, they succeeded in reforming everyday lives, ushering in, as Alexander F. Mitchell says, "a season of spiritual revival as deep and extensive as any that has since occurred in the history of the British Churches."[3]

With few exceptions, Puritan ministers were great preachers who lovingly and passionately proclaimed the whole counsel of God set forth in Holy Scripture. No group of ministers in church history has matched their biblical, doctrinal, experiential, and practical preaching.[4]

---

1. Tae-Hyeun Park, *The Sacred Rhetoric of the Holy Spirit: A Study of Puritan Preaching in a Pneumatological Perspective* (Apeldoorn: Theologische Unversiteit Apeldoorn, 2005), 4. This chapter is largely a condensed version of "Puritan Preaching I, II," chapters 41 and 42 in Joel R. Beeke and Mark Jones, *A Puritan Theology: Doctrine for Life* (Grand Rapids, MI: Reformation Heritage Books, 2012). Used with permission.

2. J. I. Packer, foreword to *Introduction to Puritan Theology: A Reader*, ed. Edward Hindson (Grand Rapids, MI: Baker, 1976).

3. Alexander F. Mitchell, introduction to *Minutes of the Sessions of the Westminster Assembly of Divines*, ed. Alexander F. Mitchell and John Struthers (Edmonton: Still Waters Revival Books, 1991), xv.

4. For additional books and articles on Puritan preaching, see R. Bruce Bickel, *Light and Heat: The Puritan View of the Pulpit* (Morgan, PA: Soli Deo Gloria, 1999); J. W. Blench, *Preaching in England in the Late Fifteenth and Sixteenth Centuries* (Oxford: Basil Blackwell, 1964); John Brown, *Puritan Preaching in England* (London: Hodder & Stoughton, 1900); J. A. Caiger, "Preaching—Puritan and Reformed," in *Puritan Papers, Volume 2, 1960–1962*, ed. J. I. Packer (Phillipsburg, NJ: P&R, 2001), 161–85; Murray A. Capill, *Preaching with Spiritual Vigour* (Fearn, Ross-shire,

The common people gladly heard Puritan preaching. Henry Smith (1560–1591), sometimes called "the golden-tongued Chrysostom of the Puritans," was so popular as a preacher that, as Thomas Fuller writes, "persons of good quality brought their own pews with them, I mean their legs, to stand upon in the aisles."[5] No wonder the Puritan minister was called "the hero of sixteenth-century Puritanism."[6]

Puritan preaching was—and still is—transforming. Brian Hedges says that Puritan preachers "lift our gaze to the greatness and gladness

Scotland: Mentor, 2003); Horton Davies, *The Worship of the English Puritans* (Morgan, PA: Soli Deo Gloria, 1997), 182–203; Eric Josef Carlson, "The Boring of the Ear: Shaping the Pastoral Vision of Preaching in England, 1540–1640," in *Preachers and People in the Reformations and Early Modern Period*, ed. Larissa Taylor (Leiden: Brill, 2003), 249–96; Mariano Di Gangi, *Great Themes in Puritan Preaching* (Guelph, ON: Joshua Press, 2007); Alan F. Herr, *The Elizabethan Sermon: A Survey and a Bibliography* (New York: Octagon, 1969); Babette May Levy, *Preaching in the First Half Century of New England History* (New York: Russell & Russell, 1967); Peter Lewis, *The Genius of Puritanism* (Grand Rapids, MI: Reformation Heritage Books, 2008); D. M. Lloyd-Jones, *The Puritans: Their Origins and Successors* (Edinburgh: Banner of Truth, 1987), 372–89; Irvonwy Morgan, *The Godly Preachers of the Elizabethan Church* (London: Epworth, 1965); Hughes Oliphant Old, *The Reading and Preaching of the Scriptures in the Worship of the Christian Church, Volume 4: The Age of the Reformation* (Grand Rapids, MI: Eerdmans, 2002), 251–79; *The Reading and Preaching of the Scriptures in the Worship of the Christian Church, Volume 5: Moderatism, Pietism, and Awakening* (Grand Rapids, MI: Eerdmans, 2004), 170–217; J. I. Packer, *A Quest for Godliness* (Wheaton, IL: Crossway, 1990), 163–76, 277–308; Park, *The Sacred Rhetoric of the Holy Spirit*; Joseph A. Pipa Jr., "Puritan Preaching," in *The Practical Calvinist*, ed. Peter A. Lillback (Fearn, Ross-shire, Scotland: Mentor, 2002), 163–82; John Piper, *The Supremacy of God in Preaching* (Grand Rapids, MI: Baker, 1990); Caroline F. Richardson, *English Preachers and Preaching 1640–1670* (New York: Macmillan, 1928); Michael F. Ross, *Preaching for Revitalization* (Fearn, Ross-shire, Scotland: Mentor, 2006); Leland Ryken, *Worldly Saints: The Puritans as They Really Were* (Grand Rapids, MI: Zondervan, 1986), 91–107; Harry S. Stout, *The New England Soul: Preaching and Religious Culture in Colonial New England* (Oxford: Oxford University Press, 1986).

Dissertations that deal with Puritan preaching include Ruth Beatrice Bozell, "English Preachers of the 17th Century on the Art of Preaching" (PhD diss., Cornell University, 1939); Ian Breward, "The Life and Theology of William Perkins, 1558–1602" (PhD diss., University of Manchester, 1963); Diane Marilyn Darrow, "Thomas Hooker and the Puritan Art of Preaching" (PhD diss., University of California, San Diego, 1968); Andrew Thomas Denholm, "Thomas Hooker: Puritan Preacher, 1568–1647" (PhD diss., Hartford Seminary, 1972); M. F. Evans, "Study in the Development of a Theory of Homiletics in England from 1537–1692" (PhD diss., University of Iowa, 1932); Frank E. Farrell, "Richard Sibbes: A Study in Early Seventeenth Century English Puritanism" (PhD diss., University of Edinburgh, 1955); Anders Robert Lunt, "The Reinvention of Preaching: A Study of Sixteenth and Seventeenth Century English Preaching Theories" (PhD diss., University of Maryland College Park, 1998); Kenneth Clifton Parks, "The Progress of Preaching in England during the Elizabethan Period" (PhD diss., Southern Baptist Theological Seminary, 1954); Joseph A. Pipa Jr., "William Perkins and the Development of Puritan Preaching" (PhD diss., Westminster Theological Seminary, 1985); Harold Patton Shelly, "Richard Sibbes: Early Stuart Preacher of Piety" (PhD diss., Temple University, 1972); David Mark Stevens, "John Cotton and Thomas Hooker: The Rhetoric of the Holy Spirit" (PhD diss., University of California, Berkeley, 1972); Lynn Baird Tipson Jr., "The Development of Puritan Understanding of Conversion" (PhD diss., Yale University, 1972); Cary Nelson Weisiger III, "The Doctrine of the Holy Spirit in the Preaching of Richard Sibbes" (PhD diss., Fuller Theological Seminary, 1984).

5. Quoted in Winthrop S. Hudson, "The Ministry in the Puritan Age," in *The Ministry in Historical Perspectives*, ed. H. Richard Niebuhr and Daniel D. Williams (New York: Harper and Brothers, 1956), 185.

6. Michael Walzer, *The Revolution of the Saints: A Study in the Origins of Radical Politics* (Cambridge, MA: Harvard University Press, 1965), 119.

of God. They open our eyes to the beauty and loveliness of Christ. They prick our consciences with the subtlety and sinfulness of sin. They ravish and delight the soul with the power and glory of grace. They plumb the depths of the soul with profound biblical, practical, and psychological insight. They sustain and strengthen the soul through suffering by expounding the doctrine of the sovereignty of God. They set our sights and focus our affections on eternal realities."[7]

Before we examine the preaching of specific Puritans, beginning in chapter 9, I will introduce Puritan preaching in general. I will limit this overview to five themes: their view of the primacy of preaching, their program for preaching, their passion for preaching, their power in preaching, and their plainness in preaching.

Primacy of Preaching

The Puritans had a profound sense that God builds his church primarily by the instrument of preaching. This understanding created an ethos under which preaching stood at the center of worship and devotion.

The substance of preaching is declaring God's Word to men. John Preston provides us with a simple, yet typically Puritan, working definition of preaching: "a public interpretation or dividing the Word, performed by an ambassador or minister who speaks to the people instead of God, in the name of Christ."[8]

Anthony Burgess (d. 1664) stresses that ministers "must dress every Sermon at the glass [mirror] of the Word; they must preach as they read in Scripture."[9] Ministers must preach the Word only, Burgess says, for three reasons: (1) for God's sake—because it is *his* Word that ministers are proclaiming, his honor that is at stake, and he does not think lightly of a minister's thoughts replacing his own; (2) for man's sake—because if the Word preached is not God's Word, it loses all its power and nourishment for men, and becomes only hay and stubble; and (3) for the minister's sake—because the preacher is given a ministry, not a "magistery"; that is, he is called to be a servant, not the

---

7. Brian G. Hedges, "Puritan Writers Enrich the Modern Church," *Banner of Truth* 529 (October 2007): 5–10.

8. Quoted in Everett H. Emerson, *English Puritanism from John Hooper to John Milton* (Durham, NC: Duke University Press, 1968), 45.

9. Anthony Burgess, *The Scripture Directory, for Church Officers and People* . . . (London: Abraham Miller for T. U., 1659), 141; see also John Mayer, Praxis Theologica: *or The Epistle of the Apostle St. James . . . Expounded* (London: R. Bostocke, 1629), 127.

Lord, so he must not endanger his soul by bringing his own words, but must remember that God, and not himself, can best determine what his hearers need.[10]

The Puritans viewed preaching as the minister's "principal work" and the hearers' "principal benefit."[11] Preaching is God's great "converting ordinance," they said. Seldom would anyone be converted apart from it. William Ames writes, "Preaching is the ordinance of God, sanctified for the begetting of faith, for the opening of the understanding, for the drawing of the will and affections to Christ."[12] Thomas Cartwright (1535–1603) says preaching is vitally necessary compared to merely reading the Bible. He writes, "As the fire stirred giveth more heat, so the Word, as it were blown by preaching, flameth more in the hearers, than when it is read."[13]

The Puritans were in awe that a mere man could be the mouthpiece and ambassador of the almighty, triune God. Richard Baxter writes, "It is no small matter to stand up in the face of a congregation, and deliver a message of salvation or damnation, as from the living God, in the name of our Redeemer."[14]

Other than the Holy Spirit, the ascended Christ bestows no higher gift on earth than the call to preach to his New Testament church, says Richard Sibbes (1577–1635): "It is a gift of all gifts, the ordinance of preaching. God esteems it so, Christ esteems it so, and so should we esteem it."[15] Therefore, the Puritans put the pulpit rather than the altar at the center of their churches, put preaching rather than the sacraments at the center of their worship, and regarded a personal call to the ministry as essential for the preacher.[16]

---

10. Burgess, *The Scripture Directory*, 142–44.

11. Robert Traill, "By What Means May Ministers Best Win Souls?" in *Select Practical Writings of Robert Traill* (Edinburgh: Printed for the Assembly's Committee, 1845), 120; Arthur Hildersham, *CLII Lectures Upon Psalm LI* (London: J. Raworth, for Edward Brewster, 1642), 732; Lewis, *Genius of Puritanism*, 37–43.

12. William Ames, *The Marrow of Theology*, trans. and ed. John D. Eusden (Boston: Pilgrim Press, 1968), 194.

13. Quoted in Davies, *The Worship of the English Puritans*, 186; see also John Owen, *An Exposition of the Epistle to the Hebrews*, ed. William H. Goold, 7 vols. (Edinburgh: Banner of Truth, 1991), 7:312–13; Nehemiah Rogers, *The True Convert* (London: George Miller for Edward Brewster, 1632), 71.

14. Richard Baxter, *The Reformed Pastor*, in *The Practical Works of Richard Baxter*, 4 vols. (Ligonier, PA: Soli Deo Gloria, 1990–1991), 4:383, hereafter, *Works*.

15. Richard Sibbes, "The Fountain Opened," in *The Complete Works of Richard Sibbes*, ed. Alexander B. Grosart (Edinburgh: Banner of Truth, 1977), 5:509, hereafter, *Works*.

16. Lloyd-Jones, *The Puritans*, 380. For the Puritan view of the calling to the ministry, see Owen C. Watkins, *The Puritan Experience* (London: Routledge & Kegan Paul, 1972), 61–63.

Such a perspective made each sermon a momentous occasion. "There is not a sermon which is heard, but it sets us nearer heaven or hell," writes Preston.[17] One of John Cotton's (1584–1652) listeners wrote in response to a sermon, "Mr. Cotton preaches with such authority, demonstration, and life that, methinks, when he preaches out of any Prophet or Apostle I hear not him; I hear that very Prophet and Apostle; yea, I hear the Lord Jesus Christ speaking in my heart."[18]

The Puritans were earnest preachers who made it their aim to please God rather than people. God was their witness. All masks were stripped away; all flattery was abhorred. Listen to Baxter: "In the name of God, brethren, labor to awaken your hearts before you come, and when you are in the work, that you may be fit to awaken the hearts of sinners. Remember, they must be awakened or damned. And a sleepy preacher will hardly awaken them. . . . Speak to your people as to men that must be awakened either here or in hell."[19]

Program for Preaching

The Puritans' sense of the priority of preaching moved them to establish an impressive program for comprehensive reform of the church. Their burning love for Christ motivated them to pour their lives into the proclamation of the Word in every form possible. Sibbes says, "Preaching is the chariot that carries Christ up and down the world."[20] Basically, the Puritans used a five-part approach to influence people and promote pastoral reform through preaching.

First was *reforming preaching* itself, primarily by frequently preaching wherever God opened a pulpit to them. We will later give attention to the Puritans' ideal or "plain" style of preaching.

The second aspect of the Puritan program for preaching was *lectureships*, which were not academic lectures but specially appointed times for preaching. Lecturers, in contrast to parish clergy, were usually hired by wealthy private supporters, by a town council, or by the Inns of Court (the law schools of London) to preach and teach in Puritan-minded

---

17. John Preston, *A Pattern of Wholesome Words*, quoted in Christopher Hill, *Society and Puritanism in Pre-Revolutionary England* (New York: Schocken, 1964), 46.
18. Roger Clap, *Memoirs of Captain Roger Clap*, quoted in Alden T. Vaughan and Francis J. Bremer, eds., *Puritan New England: Essays on Religion, Society, and Culture* (New York: St. Martin's, 1977), 70.
19. Baxter, *The Reformed Pastor*, in *Works* 4:412, 426.
20. Sibbes, "The Fountain Opened," in *Works*, 5:508.

churches or groups of churches to satisfy the spiritual appetite of the people who found the parish ministers dry and unedifying.[21] The lectureships became increasingly popular throughout the first century of Puritanism (1560–1662); they sprang up everywhere in England—in towns and villages, as well as in Cambridge and Oxford, and, of course, in London, where more than a hundred lectureships were maintained during the first three decades of the seventeenth century. Many of the greatest Puritans served as lecturers, such as Ames, Paul Baynes (c. 1573–1617), Cartwright, Laurence Chaderton (c. 1536–1640), John "Decalogue" Dod (c. 1549–1645), John Field (1545–1588), Richard Greenham (c. 1542–1594), Arthur Hildersham (1563–1632), William Perkins, Preston, and Sibbes.[22]

A third aspect of the Puritan program for preaching was *prophesyings*— also called "exercises" or "godly exercises." Prophesyings were a kind of Bible conference for the continuing education of ministers.[23] Three to six ministers would preach on the same text, moving from the youngest to the oldest. The last preacher would summarize the findings and emphasize the practical "uses" of the doctrines that were expounded. A senior moderator would then lead a session critiquing the sermons. In these "iron-sharpens-iron" sessions, ministers could hone their exegetical and preaching skills.

These prophesyings, which started in the 1520s in Zurich, were imported by the early Puritans in the 1550s, used extensively at Christ's College by Chaderton, and soon proliferated in several counties in England. They grew out of a need for Puritan ministers to improve their preaching, though they were sometimes initiated by bishops who felt the need to remedy "ignorant preaching." The prophesyings reached their peak in the mid-1570s, when the public was invited to join them. In 1577, against the advice of Archbishop of Canterbury Edmund Grindal, Queen Elizabeth I—who viewed the prophesyings as a threat to her control of

---

21. The origins and varieties of the lectureships are documented by Paul S. Seaver, *The Puritan Lectureships: The Politics of Religious Dissent, 1560–1662* (Stanford: Stanford University Press, 1970), 72–87; cf. Morgan, *The Godly Preachers of the Elizabethan Church*, 33–60; William Haller, *The Rise of Puritanism* (Philadelphia: University of Philadelphia Press, 1972), 53, 330; Lloyd-Jones, *The Puritans*, 378.

22. Seaver, *The Puritan Lectureships*, 30–31; cf. Marshall M. Knappen, *Tudor Puritanism: A Chapter in the History of Idealism* (Chicago: University of Chicago Press, 1939), 221–22; Hill, *Society and Puritanism in Pre-Revolutionary England*, 80; Lewis, *Genius of Puritanism*, 61–62.

23. See especially Patrick Collinson, *The Elizabethan Puritan Movement* (London: Jonathan Cape, 1967), 168–76; cf. Knappen, *Tudor Puritanism*, 253–54; Pipa, "William Perkins and the Development of Puritan Preaching," 25–26; Daniel Neal, *History of Puritans* (Stoke-on-Trent, UK: Tentmaker, 2006), 1:181–82; Davies, *The Worship of the English Puritans*, 188–89.

state and church—encouraged her bishops to prohibit them.[24] In this, she was only partially successful; some prophesyings continued into the reign of King James I, particularly where bishops tolerated them.[25]

Fourth, Puritan preaching was greatly augmented by *the printing and publishing of sermons.* The Puritans printed numerous sermons in the form of books, which became a major means of grace and communication. In the 1560s, nine volumes of Puritan sermons were published; in the 1570s, sixty-nine volumes; in the 1580s, 113 volumes; and in the 1590s, 140 volumes.[26] A. F. Herr writes, "The printing of sermons constituted a rather large business in Elizabethan England. It has been estimated that more than forty percent of all publications issued at that time were religious or philosophical in nature and it is evident that sermons account for a large part of those religious publications."[27] A number of Puritan sermon books went through scores of English editions, and hundreds of books were translated into various European languages, such as Dutch.[28] Such books were frequently and widely read, and God used them for many conversions and the growth in grace of thousands of believers.

Fifth, the Puritan program for preaching took the form of *ministerial training* that promoted good preaching. The Puritans demanded a college-trained clergy. To accomplish this, the Puritans were educated at universities such as Cambridge, Oxford, Trinity College in Dublin, and Harvard College. These schools were a mighty force in shaping young men with staunch Puritan convictions about preaching.[29]

Passion for Preaching

The extensive Puritan program for preaching was driven by an inward passion created by the Spirit of God. John F. H. New quips, "Preach-

---

24. S. E. Lehmberg, "Archbishop Grindal & the Prophesyings," *Historical Magazine of the Protestant Episcopal Church* 24 (1965): 87–145.

25. Collinson, *The Elizabethan Puritan Movement*, 168.

26. A. F. Herr, *The Elizabethan Sermon* (New York: Octagon, 1969), 27.

27. Herr, *The Elizabethan Sermon*, 67.

28. Fred A. van Lieburg, "From Pure Church to Pious Culture: The Further Reformation in the Seventeenth-Century Dutch Republic," in *Later Calvinism: International Perspectives*, ed. W. Fred Graham (Kirksville, MO: Sixteenth Century Journal Publishers, 1994), 423–25; cf. C. W. Schoneveld, *Intertraffic of the Mind* (Leiden: Brill, 1983); Willem Jan op 't Hof, *Engelse pietistische geschriften in het Nederlands, 1598–1622* (Rotterdam: Lindenberg, 1987).

29. Pipa, "William Perkins and the Development of Puritan Preaching," 24; Seaver, *The Puritan Lectureships*, 183; John Eliot, *New England's First Fruits*, quoted in Perry Miller and Thomas H. Johnson, eds., *The Puritans*, rev. ed. (New York: Harper, 1963), 2:701; Knappen, *Tudor Puritanism*, 195, 218–19, 466–80; H. C. Porter, *Puritanism in Tudor England* (New York: MacMillan, 1970), 180–203, 223–27.

ing, by mouth or by pen, was life for the Puritan."[30] The Puritans loved the gospel of Christ. They loved to proclaim the entire gospel, which included, as Packer points out, diagnosing the plight of man and the issue of sin; stressing the goal of grace and the sufficiency of Christ in his humiliation and exaltation; and offering grace together with proclaiming the demands of evangelical repentance and faith.[31]

Puritan preaching involved declaring redemption by focusing on the saving work of all three persons of the Trinity, while simultaneously calling sinners to a life of faith and commitment, and warning that the gospel will condemn forever those who persist in unbelief and impenitence. Thomas Manton puts it this way:

> The sum of the gospel is this, that all who, by true repentance and faith, do forsake the flesh, the world, and the devil, and give themselves up to God the Father, Son, and Holy Spirit, as their creator, redeemer, and sanctifier, shall find God as a father, taking them for his reconciled children, and for Christ's sake pardoning their sin, and by his Spirit giving them his grace; and, if they persevere in this course, will finally glorify them, and bestow upon them everlasting happiness; but will condemn the unbelievers, impenitent, and ungodly to everlasting punishment.[32]

The Puritans loved to preach Christ—biblically, doctrinally, and typologically.[33] Preaching Christ with winsomeness and grace was the most essential task of the Puritan preacher. Samuel Rutherford (1600–1661) said he had but "one joy" next to Christ, that is, "to preach Christ."[34]

The Puritan ministers loved *preparing for preaching*. They spent long hours poring over the meaning of the text of Scripture within its context. They were expository and didactic preachers. They often preached straight through passages.

Puritan preachers loved *preaching to themselves* first and foremost; they despised cold professionalism. The best sermons, they said, are

---

30. John F. H. New, *Anglican and Puritan: The Basis of Their Opposition, 1558–1640* (Stanford: Stanford University Press, 1965), 71.

31. Packer, *A Quest for Godliness*, 170–75.

32. Thomas Manton, "Wisdom is Justified of Her Children," in *The Complete Works of Thomas Manton*, ed. T. Smith (Worthington, PA: Maranatha, 1980), 2:102ff.

33. See Chad Van Dixhoorn, "Preaching Christ in Post-Reformation Britain," in *The Hope Fulfilled: Essays in Honor of O. Palmer Robertson*, ed. Robert L. Penny (Phillipsburg, NJ: P&R, 2008), 361–89.

34. *Letters of Samuel Rutherford*, ed. Andrew Bonar (London: Oliphants, [1904]), 420, 438 (letters of July 7 and 13, 1637).

those that the preacher first preaches to his own heart. "I preached what I felt, what I smartingly [painfully] did feel," writes John Bunyan. "Indeed I have been as one sent unto them from the dead. I went myself in chains to preach to them in chains; and carried that fire in my own conscience that I persuaded them to beware of."[35] Baxter puts it this way: "Preach to yourselves first, before you preach to the people, and with greater zeal. O Lord, save thy church from worldly pastors, that study and learn the art of Christianity, and ministry; but never had the Christian, divine nature, nor the vital principle which must difference them and their services from the dead."[36]

Then, too, they loved the *act of preaching*, not for its own sake, but because they believed that God uses preaching to save those who must believe, or, as Perkins puts it, "to collect the church and to accomplish the number of the elect."[37] No wonder, then, that many Puritans, like Bunyan, said that they would rather go to jail than give up preaching. When told that he could be released from jail if he agreed to stop preaching, Bunyan reputedly replied that if he were released, he would be preaching the next day.

Furthermore, the Puritans loved the people they preached to, and relentlessly sought their conversion and edification. Puritan preachers understood that the minister with great preaching gifts who fails to love his people will fail miserably in his calling. They knew that to fail in love is to fail in all.

They said a minister must strive to preach and shepherd his people with so much love that he mirrors the Father's love as pictured in the father's reception of the prodigal son and his response to his elder brother (Luke 15:11–32). They tenderly invited weak, doubting Christians to draw near to the Father through Christ.[38] Baxter writes, "The whole course of our ministry must be carried on in a tender love to our people. . . . When the people see that you unfeignedly [sincerely] love them, they will hear anything, and bear anything, and follow you the more easily."[39]

---

35. Quoted in Brown, *Puritan Preaching in England*, 146.
36. Baxter, "A Sermon Preached at the Funeral of Mr. Henry Stubbs" (1678), in *Works*, 4:974; cf. Murray A. Capill, *Preaching with Spiritual Vigour: Including Lessons from the Life and Practice of Richard Baxter* (Fearn, Ross-shire, Scotland: Christian Focus, 2003), 39–50.
37. Quoted in Lloyd-Jones, *The Puritans*, 381.
38. Manton, "Exposition of the Lord's Prayer," in *Works*, 1:35, 50–51 [Matt. 6:6–8]; cf. Simon Ford, *The Spirit of Bondage and Adoption* (London: T. Maxey, for Sa. Gellibrand, 1655), 200; Samuel Petto, *The Voice of the Spirit: or, An Essay towards a Discovery of the Witnessings of the Spirit* (London: Livewell Chapman, 1654), 56–62.
39. Baxter, *The Reformed Pastor*, in *Works*, 4:394.

Power in Preaching

The Anglicans, representing the established church in England, felt that the Puritans greatly exaggerated the role of the sermon in salvation while undermining other means of grace.[40] For Queen Elizabeth and other Anglicans, books of homilies (essentially sermons that were read out loud) were preferable to sermons preached extemporaneously because they were more carefully constructed and subject to control.

Conversely, the Puritans complained that Anglican sermons were too ornate, oratorical, metaphysical, and moralistic, and not sufficiently evangelical, experiential, and practical.[41] What a contrast there is between Baxter's urgent description of preaching as "a dying man [speaking] to dying men"[42] and Anglican sermons critically described as "orations of the excellent Constitution of their Church, or of Passive Obedience, or an Exclamation against Schism, or a Discourse of Morality, or only exclaiming against such vices as the very light of Nature condemns."[43] After describing the rhetorical flourishes of Anglican preaching, John Owen writes, "Such things become not the authority, majesty, greatness, and holiness, of him who speaks therein . . . the great possessor of heaven and earth!"[44]

Puritan preaching *addressed the mind with clarity*. This preaching was directed to people as rational beings. The Puritans viewed the mind as the palace of faith. They refused to set mind and heart against each other, teaching that knowledge is the soil in which the Spirit plants the seed of regeneration. Preston stressed that reason is elevated in conversion, and Cotton Mather added that ignorance is the mother of heresy rather than of devotion. Thus, they informed the mind with biblical knowledge and reasoned with the mind through biblical logic.[45] They understood that a mindless Christianity fosters a spineless Christianity.

Puritan preaching *confronted the conscience pointedly*. The Puritans regarded the consciences of sinners as the "light of nature." Plain preaching

---

40. Davies, *The Worship of the English Puritans*, 16.

41. See Pipa, "William Perkins and the Development of Puritan Preaching," 28–67, for a study of Anglican preaching in Elizabethan England; cf. Lloyd-Jones, *The Puritans*, 375, 381–83.

42. Richard Baxter, *The Dying Thoughts of the Reverend Learned and Holy Mr. Richard Baxter*, abridged by Benjamin Fawcett (Salop: J. Cotton and J. Eddowes, 1761), 167.

43. *Plain Reasons for Dissenting from the Church of England*, 3rd ed. (London, 1736), 6, quoted in Davies, *The Worship of the English Puritans*, 202. *Plain Reasons* was published anonymously, but it is now known that the author was Charles Owen.

44. John Owen, *An Exposition of Hebrews* (Marshalltown, DE: The National Foundation for Christian Education, 1960), 1:52.

45. For an example of Puritan reasoning with sinners, see Joseph Alleine, *A Sure Guide to Heaven* (Edinburgh: Banner of Truth, 1995), 30.

named specific sins, then asked questions to press home the guilt of those sins upon the consciences of men, women, and children. Puritan preachers used the law's convicting power to bring sinners before God in their nakedness (Heb. 4:12). Only then will they cry to be clothed in the righteousness of Christ. So the Puritans preached *urgently, directly, and specifically* to the conscience, taking seriously Christ's command "that repentance and remission of sins should be preached in his name" (Luke 24:47).

Puritan preaching *wooed the heart passionately*. Their preaching was affectionate, zealous, and optimistic. Walter Cradock (c. 1606–1659) said to his flock, "We are not sent to get galley-slaves to the oars, or a bear to the stake: but He sends us to woo you as spouses, to marry you to Christ."[46] The Puritans used compelling preaching, personal pleading, earnest praying, biblical reasoning, solemn warning, joyful living—any means they could—to turn sinners from the road of destruction and to God via the mind, the conscience, and the heart—in that order. Samuel Willard (1640–1707) puts it this way:

> The Truths of the Word are first applied to the Understanding, by which we may know the meaning, and discern the reasons of them; for here all human Actions begin; and being approved by the Judgment, it must be passed over to the will for its Election [decision]; whereby it embraceth the Truth commended, and is won over to it; and from thence it is imprinted on the Affections.[47]

The Puritans believed that God would use their powerful preaching as a weapon to conquer and convert sinners. So Ames writes, "Preaching, therefore, ought not to be dead, but alive and effective so that an unbeliever coming into the congregation of believers should be affected and, as it were, transfixed by the very hearing of the word so that he might give glory to God."[48]

Plainness in Preaching

In terms of style, the Puritans believed in plain preaching. This plainness did not mean anti-intellectualism. Rather, plainness referred to a

---

46. Quoted in I. D. E. Thomas, comp., *The Golden Treasury of Puritan Quotations* (Chicago: Moody Press, 1975), 222. Bears were tied to a stake and then forced to fight dogs in the cruel sport of bear-baiting, which the Puritans often opposed. What a contrast to a wedding!

47. Quoted in Perry Miller, *The New England Mind: The Seventeenth Century* (Boston: Beacon, 1961), 295; cf. Westminster Larger Catechism, Q. 68.

48. Quoted in Ryken, *Worldly Saints*, 107.

simple and clear communication from the Bible to the mind, then into the heart, and then outward to direct the conduct. Henry Smith says, "To preach simply, is not to preach unlearnedly, nor confusedly, but plainly and perspicuously [clearly], that the simplest which doth hear, may understand what is taught, as if he did hear his name."[49] Cotton Mather writes in his eulogy for John Eliot (1604–1690), a great Puritan missionary to the Indians, that his "way of preaching was very plain; so that the very *lambs* might wade into his discourses on those texts and themes, wherein *elephants* might swim."[50] Increase Mather (1639–1723) writes of the preaching of his father, Richard, "His way of preaching was plain, aiming to shoot his arrows not over his people's heads, but into their hearts and consciences."[51]

The first part of a Puritan sermon was exegetical and expositional; the second, doctrinal and didactic; and the third, applicatory.[52] First, Puritan preaching was *biblical*, that is, an exposition of the text of the Bible. "The faithful Minister, like unto Christ, [is] one that preacheth nothing but the word of God," says Puritan Edward Dering (c. 1540–1576).[53] Owen agrees: "The first and principal duty of a pastor is to feed the flock by diligent preaching of the word."[54] Millar Maclure notes that "for the Puritans, the sermon is not just hinged to Scripture; it quite literally exists inside the Word of God; the text is not in the sermon, but the sermon is in the text. . . . Put summarily, listening to a sermon is being in the Bible."[55]

Second, the exposition of Scripture led the Puritans to develop clear and well-defined *doctrines*. Perkins calls doctrine "the science of living well and blessedly for ever";[56] Ames refers to "the doctrine or teaching

---

49. Henry Smith, "The Art of Hearing," in *The Works of Henry Smith*, 2 vols. (Stoke-on-Trent, UK: Tentmaker, 2002), 1:337.

50. Cotton Mather, *The Great Works of Christ in America: Magnalia Christi Americana*, 3 vols. (London: Banner of Truth, 1979), 1:547–48. For a bibliography of Eliot's sermons and writings, see Frederick Harling, "A Biography of John Eliot" (PhD diss., Boston University, 1965), 259–61.

51. Increase Mather, *The Life and Death of that Reverend Man of God, Mr. Richard Mather* (Cambridge, MA: S. G. and M. J., 1670), 31–32.

52. Miller, *The New England Mind: The Seventeenth Century*, 332–33.

53. Edward Dering, "Certaine godly and comfortable Letters, full of Christian consolation," in *M. Derings Workes* (New York: Da Capo, 1972), 456.

54. John Owen, "The Especial Duty of Pastors of Churches," in *The Works of John Owen*, ed. William H. Goold (repr., Edinburgh: Banner of Truth, 1965), 16:74.

55. Millar Maclure, *The Paul's Cross Sermons, 1534–1642* (Toronto: University of Toronto Press, 1958), 165. On how the Puritans interpreted Scripture, see Thomas Lea, "The Hermeneutics of the Puritans," *Journal of the Evangelical Theological Society* 39, no. 2 (June 1996): 271–84.

56. William Perkins, "A Golden Chaine: or, the Description of Theologie," in *The Workes of that Famovs and VVorthy Minister of Christ in the Vniuersitie of Cambridge, Mr. William Perkins*, 3 vols. (London: John Legatt, 1612–1613), 1:10.

of living to God."[57] Sinclair Ferguson writes of the Puritans: "To them, systematic theology was to the pastor what a knowledge of anatomy is to the physician. Only in the light of the whole body of divinity (as they liked to call it) could a minister provide a diagnosis of, prescribe for, and ultimately cure spiritual disease in those who were plagued by the body of sin and death."[58]

Packer describes their convictions: "To the question, 'Should one preach doctrine?,' the Puritan answer would have been, 'Why, what else is there to preach?' Doctrinal preaching certainly bores the hypocrites; but it is only doctrinal preaching that will save Christ's sheep. The preacher's job is to proclaim the faith, not to provide entertainment for unbelievers."[59]

Puritan preaching recognized that all biblical doctrine centers on Christ.[60] According to Thomas Adams (1583–1652), "Christ is the sum of the whole Bible, prophesied, typified, prefigured, exhibited, demonstrated, to be found in every leaf, almost in every line; the Scriptures being but as it were the swaddling bands of the child Jesus."[61] "Think of Christ as the very substance, marrow, soul, and scope of the whole Scriptures," Isaac Ambrose (1604–1664) says.[62] Robert Bolton (1572–1631) agrees: "Jesus Christ is offered most freely, and without exception of any person, every Sabbath, every Sermon."[63] Preaching the doctrines of

---

57. Ames, *The Marrow of Theology*, 77.

58. Sinclair B. Ferguson, "Evangelical Ministry: The Puritan Contribution," in *The Compromised Church: The Present Evangelical Crisis*, ed. John H. Armstrong (Wheaton, IL: Crossway, 1998), 266.

59. Packer, *Quest for Godliness*, 284–85.

60. Thomas Taylor, *Christ Revealed: or The Old Testament Explained; A Treatise of the Types and Shadowes of our Saviour* (London: M. F. for R. Dawlman and L. Fawne, 1635) is the best Puritan work on Christ in the Old Testament. Thomas Goodwin, "*Christ Our Mediator*," vol. 5 of *The Works of Thomas Goodwin* (Eureka, CA: Tanski, 1996), ably expounds primary New Testament texts on the mediatorship of Christ. Alexander Grosse, *The Happiness of Enjoying and Making a True And Speedy Use of Christ* (London: Tho: Brudenell, for John Bartlet, 1647) and Isaac Ambrose, *Looking Unto Jesus* (Harrisonburg, VA: Sprinkle, 1988) are experiential Christology at its best. Ralph Robinson, *Christ All and In All: or Several Significant Similitudes by which the Lord Jesus Christ is Described in the Holy Scriptures* (1660; repr., Ligonier, PA: Soli Deo Gloria, 1992); Philip Henry, *Christ All in All, or What Christ is Made to Believers* (1676; repr., Swengel, PA: Reiner, 1976); and John Brown, *Christ: the Way, the Truth, and the Life* (1677; repr., Morgan, PA: Soli Deo Gloria, 1995) contain precious sermons extolling Christ in all his relations to believers. John Owen, *A Declaration of the Glorious Mystery of the Person of Christ* (reprinted in vol. 1 of *Works of Owen*), is superb on the relation of Christ's natures to his person. James Durham, *Christ Crucified; or The Marrow of the Gospel in 72 Sermons on Isaiah 53*, 2 vols. (Glasgow: Alex Adam, 1792) remains unrivaled as a scriptural exposition of Christ's passion.

61. Thomas Adams, "Meditations upon the Creed," in *The Works of Thomas Adams* (1862; repr., Eureka, CA: Tanski, 1998), 3:224.

62. Isaac Ambrose, "Media: The Middle Things," in *The Works of Isaac Ambrose* (London: for Thomas Tegg & Son, 1701), 201.

63. Robert Bolton, *A Treatise on Comforting Afflicted Consciences* (Ligonier, PA: Soli Deo Gloria, 1991), 185.

Christ naturally led them also to preach other doctrines in connection to Christ, such as the doctrines of the triune God, of sin, and of sanctification and self-denial.[64]

Third, the teaching of doctrine led to the *application*, often called the "uses" of the text, which could become lengthy as the minister applied Scripture to various listeners. The goal always was to drive the Word of God home or, as Baxter puts it, "to screw the truth into their minds, and work Christ into their affections."[65]

These applications must target the right people, or they might do more spiritual harm than good. Therefore, Puritan preaching was marked by a *discriminating application* of truth to the non-Christian and the Christian. Puritan preachers took great pains to identify the marks of grace that distinguish the church from the world, true believers from merely professing believers, and saving faith from temporary faith.[66] Thomas Shepard (1605–1649) in *The Ten Virgins*, Matthew Mead (1629–1699) in *The Almost Christian Discovered*, Jonathan Edwards in *Religious Affections*, and other Puritans wrote dozens of works to differentiate imposters from true believers.[67]

Puritan preaching aimed to be transforming. The applicatory part is "the life of preaching," writes James Durham (c. 1622–1658): "Hence, preaching is called persuading, testifying, beseeching, entreating, or requesting, exhorting."[68] The Puritans taught that when God's Word is preached experientially, the Holy Spirit uses it to transform individuals and nations.[69] Captain John Spilman provides us with an example of the transforming power of Puritan experiential preaching:

> Once in a carnal condition as I was, I did slight the Ministers of Christ, especially your long Preachers, and could not abide that any

---

64. For choice samples of Puritan preaching on God, sin, sanctification, and self-denial, see, respectively, Stephen Charnock, *Discourses on the Existence and Attributes of God*, 2 vols. (Grand Rapids, MI: Baker, 1996); Jeremiah Burroughs, *The Evil of Evils* (Morgan, PA: Soli Deo Gloria, 1995); Walter Marshall, *The Gospel Mystery of Sanctification* (Grand Rapids, MI: Zondervan, 1954); Thomas Watson, *The Duty of Self-Denial* (Morgan, PA: Soli Deo Gloria, 1995), 1–37.

65. Baxter, *The Reformed Pastor*, in *Works*, 4:370.

66. Thomas Watson, *The Godly Man's Picture* (Edinburgh: Banner of Truth, 1992), 20–188, sets forth twenty-four marks of grace for self-examination.

67. Thomas Shepard, *The Parable of the Ten Virgins* (Ligonier, PA: Soli Deo Gloria, 1990); Matthew Mead, *The Almost Christian Discovered; Or the False Professor Tried and Cast* (Ligonier, PA: Soli Deo Gloria, 1988); Jonathan Edwards, *Religious Affections* (New Haven, CT: Yale University Press, 1959).

68. James Durham, *A Commentary Upon the Book of the Revelation* (Amsterdam: John Frederickszoon Stam, 1660), 260–66 [Rev. 3:14–22].

69. Cf. Park, *The Sacred Rhetoric of the Holy Spirit*, 373–74.

should preach long; but at last I was catched [caught] by one, and he was [preaching] on Hebrews 8:8, 10 [on] the new covenant made in Christ, which was applied to me very home, and touched me to the heart.[70]

Toward the end of transforming the hearers for the glory of God alone, the Puritans called preachers to conduct themselves in the fear of the Lord. The preacher must walk in humility, not flaunting his abilities. "A crucified style best suits the preachers of a crucified Christ," writes John Flavel. "Words are but servants to matter. An iron key, fitted to the wards of the lock, is more useful than a golden one, which will not open the door to the treasure."[71]

Concluding Requisites for Preaching

Finally, Puritan preaching is inseparable from the Puritan minister's lifestyle. That lifestyle must display three requistes for preaching: dependence on the Holy Spirit, personal holiness, and a spirit of fervent prayer.

First, ministers must show a profound dependence on the Holy Spirit in everything they say and do. They must feel keenly their inability to bring anyone to Christ, as well as the magnitude of conversion. "God never laid it upon thee to convert those he sends thee to. No; to publish the gospel is thy duty," William Gurnall (1616–1679) says to ministers.[72] The Puritans were convinced that both preacher and listener are totally dependent on the work of the Spirit to effect regeneration and conversion in whom he will.[73] As Thomas Watson writes, "Ministers knock at the door of men's hearts, the Spirit comes with a key and opens the door."[74]

Second, dependence on the Holy Spirit requires the minister to pursue holiness in his own life. Baxter says, "We must study as hard how to live well as how to preach well. . . . If it be not your daily business to study your own hearts and to subdue corruptions, and live as [dependent] upon God; if you make not this your very work to which you constantly attend, all will go amiss, and you will starve your auditors [hearers]."[75]

70. John Spilman, *A Tabernacle for the Sun*, 4, quoted in Owen C. Watkins, *The Puritan Experience: Studies in Spiritual Autobiography* (New York: Schocken, 1972), 58.
71. John Flavel, "The Character of a True Evangelical Pastor," in *The Works of John Flavel*, 6 vols. (1820; repr., London: Banner of Truth, 1968), 6:572.
72. William Gurnall, *The Christian in Complete Armour*, 2 vols. in one (London: Banner of Truth, 1964), 2:574; see Baxter, "A Call to the Unconverted," in *Works*, 2:513.
73. Packer, *Quest for Godliness*, 296–99.
74. Thomas Watson, *A Body of Divinity* (1692; repr., Edinburgh: Banner of Truth, 2000), 221.
75. Baxter, *The Reformed Pastor*, in *Works*, 4:372, 425.

Owen writes, "If a man teach uprightly and walk crookedly, more will fall down in the night of his life than he built in the day of his doctrine."[76]

Finally, ministers must give themselves to prayer, both for themselves and for their ministries. Robert Traill writes, "Some ministers of meaner gifts and parts are more successful than some that are far above them in abilities; not because they preach better, so much as because they pray more. Many good sermons are lost for lack of much prayer in study."[77]

---

76. Owen, "Eschol, a Cluster of the Fruit of Canaan," in *Works*, 13:57.
77. Robert Traill, "Sermons Concerning the Throne of Grace," in *The Works of the Late Reverend Robert Traill*, 4 vols. (1810; repr., Edinburgh: Banner of Truth, 1975), 1:246.

9

Puritan Preachers: Perkins

Samuel Clarke provides a striking example of the evangelistic heart of William Perkins.[1] He says a condemned prisoner was climbing the gallows, looking "half-dead," when Perkins said to him: "What, man! What is the matter with thee? Art thou afraid of death?" The prisoner confessed that he was less afraid of death than of what would follow it. "Sayest thou so?" said Perkins. "Come down again man and thou shalt see what God's grace will do to strengthen thee." When the prisoner came down, they knelt together, hand in hand, and Perkins offered "such an effectual prayer in confession of sins . . . as made the poor prisoner burst out into abundance of tears." Convinced the prisoner was brought "low enough, even to Hell gates," Perkins showed him the freeness of the gospel in his prayer. Clarke writes that the prisoner's eyes were opened "to see how the black lines of all his sins were crossed, and cancelled with the red lines of his crucified Saviour's precious blood; so graciously applying it to his wounded conscience, as made him break out into new showers of tears for joy of the inward consolation which he found." The prisoner arose from his knees, went cheerfully up the ladder, testified of salvation in Christ's blood, and bore his death with patience, "as if he actually saw himself delivered from the Hell which he feared before, and heaven opened for the receiving of his soul, to the great rejoicing of the beholders."[2]

---

1. Portions of this chapter are condensed from Joel R. Beeke, "William Perkins on Predestination, Preaching, and Conversion," in *The Practical Calvinist: An Introduction to the Presbyterian and Reformed Heritage: In Honor of Dr. D. Clair Davis*, ed. Peter A. Lillback (Fearn, Ross-shire, Scotland: Christian Focus, 2002), 183–213. Used with permission. For a fulsome bibliography of books, dissertations, and theses on Perkins, see the notes of that chapter.
2. Samuel Clarke, *The Marrow of Ecclesiastical History* (London: W. B., 1675), 416–17.

Elizabethan England's premier Puritan preacher, William Perkins, has been called the "father of Puritanism." He was a bridge between the Genevan Reformed thought of John Calvin and Theodore Beza, and the English Puritans who followed him.

Born in Warwickshire in 1558, Perkins gave his youth to recklessness, profanity, and drunkenness.[3] In 1577, he entered Christ's College in Cambridge. He earned a bachelor's degree in 1581 and a master's degree in 1584. While a student, he experienced a powerful conversion, initiated when he overheard a woman in the street warn her naughty child against becoming like "drunken Perkins."[4] He turned from sin to Christ, and from a fascination with black magic and the occult to theology.[5] He soon joined the spiritual brotherhood of Puritans led by Laurence Chaderton at Cambridge, where he learned Reformed doctrine oriented toward practical application.[6]

From 1584 until his death from kidney stone complications in 1602, Perkins served as lecturer, or preacher, at Great St. Andrew's parish church, Cambridge, a most influential pulpit across the street from Christ's College. He also served as a fellow at Christ's College from 1584 to 1595. Fellows were required to preach, lecture, and tutor students, acting as "guides to learning as well as guardians of finances, morals, and manners."[7] On Lord's Day afternoons, he worked as an adviser, counseling the spiritually distressed. "The balm which he applied most commonly to the walking wounded who shared with him their spiritual insecurities was the doctrine of divine predestination," writes Mark Shaw.[8]

---

3. Thomas Fuller provided the basics of what is known about Perkins's life: *Abel Redevivus; or, The Dead Yet Speaking* (London: William Tegg, 1867), 2:145–54, and *The Holy and Profane State* (London: William Tegg, 1841); see Ian Breward, "The Life and Theology of William Perkins" (PhD diss., University of Manchester, 1963); Breward, introduction and ed., *The Work of William Perkins*, Courtenay Library of Reformation Classics, vol. 3 (Abingdon, England: Sutton Courtenay, 1970), hereafter, *Work of Perkins*; Charles Robert Munson, "William Perkins: Theologian of Transition" (PhD diss., Case Western Reserve, 1971); J. R. Tufft, "William Perkins, 1558–1602" (PhD diss., Edinburgh, 1952), for the best accounts to date.
4. Benjamin Brook, *The Lives of the Puritans* (Pittsburgh: Soli Deo Gloria, 1994), 2:129.
5. William Perkins, *The Workes of That Famovs and VVorthy Minister of Christ in the Vniuersitie of Cambridge, Mr. William Perkins*, 3 vols. (London: John Legatt, 1612–1613), 2:653, hereafter, *Works*.
6. Patrick Collinson, *The Elizabethan Puritan Movement* (Berkeley: University of California Press, 1967), 125; cf. Peter Lake, *Moderate Puritans and the Elizabethan Church* (Cambridge: Cambridge University Press, 1982); Munson, "William Perkins: Theologian of Transition," 18–25; William T. Costello, *The Scholastic Curriculum at Early Seventeenth-Century Cambridge* (Cambridge, MA: Harvard University Press, 1958), 146; James Bass Mullinger, *The University of Cambridge* (Cambridge: Cambridge University Press, 1884), 2:404.
7. Mark Curtis, *Oxford and Cambridge in Transition 1558–1642* (Oxford: Oxford University Press, 1965), 80.
8. Mark R. Shaw, "William Perkins and the New Pelagians: Another Look at the Cambridge Predestination Controversy of the 1590s," *Westminster Theological Journal* 58 (1996): 284.

In time, Perkins—a rhetorician, expositor, theologian, and pastor—became the principal architect of the young Puritan movement. Perkins had exceptional gifts for preaching and an uncanny ability to reach common people with plain preaching and theology. By the time of his death, Perkins's writings in England were outselling those of Calvin, Beza, and Heinrich Bullinger combined.[9] He "molded the piety of a whole nation," H. C. Porter says.[10] Eleven posthumous editions of Perkins's writings, containing nearly fifty treatises, were printed by 1635.[11] His writings were translated into Dutch, German, Spanish, French, Italian, Irish, Welsh, Hungarian, and Czech.[12] Perkins's influence continued through such theologians as William Ames, Richard Sibbes, John Cotton, and John Preston, and many preachers trained in Cambridge even after his death, including the Puritans who led the migration to New England to build a city on a hill for the world to see.[13]

Practical Predestination in Christ

Perkins was primarily concerned with the conversion of souls and their subsequent growth in godliness. He believed that a biblical understanding of God's sovereign grace in predestination is vital for spiritual comfort and assurance. It is the hope, expectation, and guarantee of salvation for the true believer.

Perkins articulates his doctrine of predestination in his *Armilla Aurea* (1590), translated from Latin as *A Golden Chaine* (1591).[14] The most

9. Louis B. Wright, *Middle-Class Culture in Elizabethan England* (Chapel Hill: University of North Carolina Press, 1935), 281–84; Ian Breward, "The Significance of William Perkins," *Journal of Religious History* 4 (1966): 116.

10. H. C. Porter, *Reformation and Reaction in Tudor Cambridge* (London: Cambridge University Press, 1958), 260. Porter claims that more than fifty of the 210 books printed in Cambridge between 1585 and 1618 were written by Perkins. *Reformation and Reaction in Tudor Cambridge*, 264.

11. For modern printings of Perkins's writings, in addition to Ian Breward, ed., *Work of Perkins*, see Thomas F. Merrill, ed., *William Perkins, 1558–1602, English Puritanist—His Pioneer Works on Casuistry: "A Discourse of Conscience" and "The Whole Treatise of Cases of Conscience"* (Nieuwkoop: B. DeGraaf, 1966); hereafter, *Works on Casuistry*; William Perkins, *A Commentary on Galatians*, ed. Gerald T. Sheppard (New York: Pilgrim Press, 1989); *A Commentary on Hebrews 11*, ed. John H. Augustine (New York: Pilgrim Press, 1991); and *The Art of Prophesying*, ed. Sinclair B. Ferguson (Edinburgh: Banner of Truth, 1996).

12. Munson, "William Perkins: Theologian of Transition," 56–59.

13. Louis B. Wright, "William Perkins: Elizabethan Apostle of 'Practical Divinity,'" *Huntington Library Quarterly* 3, no. 2 (1940): 194; Porter, *Reformation and Reaction in Tudor Cambridge*, 258–60; Samuel Morison, *The Intellectual Life of Colonial New England*, 2nd ed. (New York: New York University Press, 1956), 134; Perry Miller, *Errand into the Wilderness* (Cambridge, MA: Belknap Press, 1956), 57–59.

14. For a list of Perkins's writings, see Munson, "William Perkins: Theologian of Transition," 231–34; Donald Keith McKim, "Ramism in William Perkins" (PhD diss., University of Pittsburgh, 1980), 335–37.

notable feature of *A Golden Chaine* is Perkins's supralapsarian doctrine of double predestination. It is outlined in his famous chart entitled: "A Survey or Table declaring the order of the causes of salvation and damnation according to Gods word."[15] Like Beza's chart, though more detailed, it begins with God and his decree of predestination, and then is divided into two chains of causes for the execution of election and reprobation. It traces the orderly progression of those executions from the eternal decree of God to the final consummation, when all things end in God's glorification.

Perkins believed that predestination is the means by which God manifests the glory of the Godhead outside of himself to the human race. He returns glory to himself via mercy to the elect and justice to the reprobate. Both proceed from his sovereignty. Election is God's decree "whereby of his own free will, he hath ordained certain men to salvation, to the praise of the glory of his grace." Reprobation is "that part of predestination, whereby God, according to the most free and just purpose of his will, hath determined to reject certain men unto eternal destruction, and misery, and that to the praise of his justice."[16]

The doctrine of reprobation is not harmful, but is a helpful revelation of God's purposes. The reprobation of the divine Potter (Rom. 9:21–24) must be preached to warn the ungodly to flee from sin and seek grace to obey the revealed will of God, as well as for the benefit of the elect, Perkins says. Preaching reprobation involves showing how far a reprobate can go in the appearance of "actions of grace." It lovingly urges the elect to seek further exercises of grace and to make their calling and election sure in Christ (2 Pet. 1:10). It moves the godly to examine themselves for marks of election. And it provides an antidote to pride and a foundation for grateful humility before the Lord, who chose his own purely out of sovereign grace.[17]

Election to eternal life does not affect anyone apart from the work of Jesus Christ. Thus, Perkins states that, from God's viewpoint, a reprobate man has no possibility of salvation because he has absolutely no link with Christ in the golden chain. Without Christ, man is totally hopeless.

---

15. For an exposition of Perkins's chart, see Cornelis Graafland, *Van Calvijn tot Barth: Oorsprong en ontwikkeling van de leer der verkiezing in het Gereformeerd Protestantisme* ('s-Gravenhage: Boekencentrum, 1987), 72–84.

16. Perkins, "The Order of the Causes of Salvation & Damnation," in *Works*, 1:24, 106.

17. Perkins, "A Treatise of Predestination," in *Works*, 2:620ff; cf. William Haller, *The Rise of Puritanism* (New York: Columbia University Press, 1938), 130–31; R. T. Kendall, *Calvin and English Calvinism to 1649* (Carlisle, UK: Paternoster, 1997), 67–74.

Christ is the foundation of election. He is predestined to be the Mediator. He is promised to the elect. He is offered by grace to the elect. Finally, he is personally applied to their souls in all his benefits, natures, offices, and states.[18] The center of Perkins's table is the work of Christ as "mediator of the elect." Perkins draws lines connecting the work of Christ with the progress of the Christian life, showing how faith apprehends Christ and applies him to justification and sanctification. Perkins was well aware of the believer's sense of spiritual combat. Like election, Christian volition and faithful obedience are meaningful only in Christ. Christ is thus central to predestination.

God executes his decree in Christ through steps of love. Here we see the centrality of preaching in Perkins's teaching. Effectual calling, the first part of the process, represents the saving grace "whereby a sinner being severed from the world, is entertained into God's family."[19] The first part of effectual calling is a right hearing of the Word by those who were dead in sin; their minds are illuminated by the Spirit with irresistible truth. The preaching of the Word accomplishes two things: "the Law showing a man his sin and the punishment thereof, which is eternal death," and "the Gospel, showing salvation by Christ Jesus, to such as believe."[20]

The second part of this process is the breaking of the sinner's heart. It is "bruised in pieces, that it may be fit to receive God's saving grace offered unto it." God bruises sinners under the preaching of his law and the piercing of the heart with a sense of his wrath against sin.[21]

The product of effectual calling is saving faith, which Perkins defines as "a miraculous and supernatural faculty of the heart, apprehending Christ Jesus being applied by the operation of the Holy Ghost, and receiving him to itself."[22] As Charles Munson says: "Faith then saves the elect, not because it is a perfect virtue, but because it apprehends a perfect object, which is the obedience of Christ. Whether faith is weak or strong does not matter for salvation rests on God's mercy and promises."[23] According to Perkins, God "accepts the very seeds and rudiments of faith and repentance at the first, though they be but in measure, as a grain of mustard seed."[24]

---

18. Perkins, "A Treatise of Predestination," in *Works*, 2:608.
19. Perkins, "The Order of the Causes of Salvation & Damnation," in *Works*, 1:77.
20. Perkins, "The Order of the Causes of Salvation & Damnation," in *Works*, 1:78.
21. Perkins, "The Order of the Causes of Salvation & Damnation," in *Works*, 1:79; cf. 2:13.
22. Perkins, "The Order of the Causes of Salvation & Damnation," in *Works*, 1:79.
23. Munson, "William Perkins: Theologian of Transition," 100.
24. Perkins, "The Order of the Causes of Salvation & Damnation," in *Works*, 1:79–80.

For Perkins, faith is a supernatural gift given by God to enable the sinner to take hold of Christ with all the promises of salvation.[25] The object of faith is not the sinner, his experiences, or faith itself: it is Jesus Christ alone. Faith sees Christ, first, as the sacrifice on the cross for the remission of sins, then learns to experience him as strength to battle temptation, as comfort in a storm of affliction, and ultimately as everything needed in this life and in the life to come.[26] In sum, faith shows itself when "every several person doth particularly apply unto himself, Christ with his merits, by an inward persuasion of the heart which cometh none other way, but by the effectual certificate of the Holy Ghost concerning the mercy of God in Christ Jesus."[27] Faith has no meaning outside of Jesus Christ. "Faith is . . . a principal grace of God, whereby man is ingrafted into Christ and thereby becomes one with Christ, and Christ one with him," Perkins says.[28] Perkins outlines five steps in saving faith: knowing the gospel by the illumination of God's Spirit; hoping for pardon; hungering and thirsting after the grace offered in Christ Jesus; fleeing to the throne of grace to take hold of Christ; and applying, by the Spirit's persuasion, the promises of the gospel to oneself.[29]

Once a sinner has been effectually called to faith, he is justified by faith. According to Perkins, justification is God's loving declaration that those who believe are counted righteous before God through Christ's obedience. The foundation of justification is the obedience of Christ, expressed in "his Passion in life and death, and his fulfilling of the Law joined therewith." Christ frees the elect from the debt of fulfilling the law "every moment, from our first beginning, both in regard of purity of nature and purity of action," and of making "satisfaction for the breach of the law." Christ is our surety for this debt, and God accepts his obedience for us, "it being full satisfaction." Justification thus consists of "remission of sins, and imputation of Christ's righteousness."[30] It takes place when a sinner is brought before God's judgment seat, pleads guilty, and flees to Christ as his only refuge for acquittal.[31] Justification is clearly a judicial, sovereign act of God's eternal good pleasure.

---

25. Perkins, "An Exposition of the Creed," in *Works*, 1:124.
26. Perkins, "An Exposition of the Creed," in *Works*, 1:124.
27. Perkins, "The Order of the Causes of Salvation & Damnation," in *Works*, 1:79.
28. Perkins, "Cases of Conscience," in *Works*, 2:18.
29. Perkins, "The Order of the Causes of Salvation & Damnation," in *Works*, 1:79–80.
30. Perkins, "The Order of the Causes of Salvation & Damnation," in *Works*, 1:81–82.
31. Perkins, "A Commentary on the Epistle to the Galatians," in *Works*, 2:204 [Gal. 2:15–16].

Sanctification, the third part of this process, receives more attention from Perkins than any other part. It is an essential part of salvation; with faith comes repentance and new obedience in a true conversion.[32]

Perkins defines sanctification as that work "by which a Christian in his mind, in his will and in his affections is freed from the bondage and tyranny of sin and Satan and is little by little enabled through the Spirit of Christ to desire and approve that which is good and walk in it." Sanctification has two parts. "The first is mortification when the power of sin is continually weakened, consumed and diminished. The second is vivification by which inherent righteousness is really put into them and afterward is continually increased."[33] All of this depends on Christ. Victor Priebe writes: "Sanctification, then, is dependent upon a moment by moment renewal as the believer looks away from himself and his deeds to the person and work of Christ. Mortification and vivification are evidence of that most vital and definitive reality—union with Christ upon which all reception of grace depends. . . . It is unquestionably clear that sanctification is the result of the activity of divine grace in man."[34]

After sanctification comes the final step: glorification. This part of God's love is "the perfect transforming of the Saints into the image of the Son of God," Perkins says. Glorification awaits the fulfillment of the last judgment, when the elect shall enjoy "blessedness . . . whereby God himself is all in all his elect." By sovereign grace the elect will be ushered into perfect glory, a "wonderful excellency" that includes beholding the glory and majesty of God, fully conforming to Christ, and inheriting "the new heavens and the new earth."[35]

At every stage except for glorification, God saves his elect through means, primarily the means of the preaching of his Word.

Predestinarian Preaching

Perkins views preaching as the "mighty arm of God" to draw in the elect, or the chariot on which salvation comes riding into the hearts of men. He defines preaching as "prophesying in the name and room of Christ, whereby men are called to the state of grace and conserved in it."[36] In

---

32. *Works on Casuistry*, 106–7.
33. Perkins, "A Treatise of Conscience," in *Works*, 1:541.
34. Victor L. Priebe, "The Covenant Theology of William Perkins" (PhD diss., Drew University, 1967), 141.
35. Perkins, "The Order of the Causes of Salvation & Damnation," in *Works*, 1:92, 94.
36. Perkins, "The Art of Prophecying," in *Works*, 2:646.

essence, Perkins's goal is to help preachers realize their responsibility as God's instruments to explain election and the covenant. Biblically balanced preaching is paramount, for the Word preached is the power of God unto salvation, without which there can be no salvation.[37] With such a high view of preaching, Perkins does not hesitate to assert that the sermon is the climax of public worship.

Preaching is the most solemn task a human being could ever undertake. It is serious business for both the preacher and the listener. Eternal issues are at stake. Consequently, the true preacher may never neglect studious sermon preparation or the plain, effective delivery of a sermon.

Since the elect are known only to God, Perkins assumes that everyone who listens to a sermon could potentially be gathered into gospel grace. He thus presses every sinner to accept God's offer of salvation in Christ. The gospel promise must be offered freely to every hearer as a "precious jewel," Perkins says.[38] At the same time, he explains that there are two ways of regarding election: "One especially whereby God knows who are his. The other is more general, whereby we repute all men to be Elect that profess faith in Christ, leaving secret judgments to God. Thus Paul writes to the Ephesians, Philippians, etc. as Elect. And the ministers of the word are to speak to their congregations, as to the Elect people of God."[39]

This effectively eliminates any need for a preacher to determine who in his congregation might be elect and who might be reprobate. Rather, a preacher must so clearly preach the marks of saving grace that, with the help of the Holy Spirit, the sinner's heart may confirm God's judgment concerning his eternal welfare.

Perkins calls preaching the way to "lay hold of Christ," to "repair the image of God," and to "form Christ in the hearts of all believers."[40] The elect are not just called by preaching, then neglected; rather, preaching serves as a continual "converter" in repairing the image of God in a believer.

According to Perkins, the golden chain of salvation (effectual calling, justification, sanctification, and glorification) is applied to the elect via the preaching of God's covenant. Consequently, Perkins was interested

---

37. Perkins, "The Order of the Causes of Salvation & Damnation," in *Works*, 1:83.
38. Cited in *Work of Perkins*, 300.
39. Perkins, "The Art of Prophecying," in *Works*, 2:646ff.
40. Perkins, "A Commentary on the Epistle to the Galatians," in *Works*, 2:289, 294 [Gal. 4:16–17].

in preaching not only God's sovereign grace to his elect from eternity, but also God's covenant acts of salvation in history and personal experience, by which election is realized. He was deeply concerned about how this personal, redemptive process breaks into man's experience—how the elect respond to God's overtures and acts, as well as how the will of God is carried out in the hearts of the elect.[41]

The Art of Reformed Experiential Preaching

No Puritan was more concerned about preaching than Perkins. Detesting the substitution of eloquence for the "lost art" of preaching, Perkins led the Puritan movement to reform preaching. He did this in his instruction to theological students at Cambridge; in his manual on preaching, *The Arte of Prophecying* (Latin 1592, English 1606), which quickly became a classic among Puritans; in his advocacy of a method and plain style of preaching in his own pulpit exercises; and, above all, in his stress on the experiential application of predestinarian doctrines.

Joseph Pipa suggests three reasons why Perkins wrote his preaching manual. First, there was a "dearth of able preachers in Elizabethan England."[42] Despite calls for the training of preachers as early as the time of William Tyndale, by 1583 only a sixth of English clergy were licensed to preach, and even in 1603 there were only half as many preachers as parishes. Second, there were gaps in the university curriculum, with particular deficiencies in theology, preaching, and spiritual direction. Perkins wrote his textbook to help fill the gap in practical theology. Third, Perkins aimed to promote a "plain" style of preaching as opposed to the ornate style of high-church Anglicans.[43] The latter style heaped up quotations from ancient authorities, often in Greek or Latin, together with many puns, extravagant and surprising analogies, rhymes, and alliteration. Such "witty" preaching tended to seek to please the ear with art and to impress the mind with philosophy. This style went hand in hand with the belief that grace came primarily through the sacraments, in contrast to the Puritan emphasis on the Word as the central means of grace.[44]

---

41. See Donald K. McKim, "William Perkins and the Theology of the Covenant," in *Studies of the Church in History*, ed. Horton Davies (Allison Park, PA: Pickwick, 1983), 85–87; Priebe, "Covenant Theology of Perkins."

42. Joseph A. Pipa Jr., "William Perkins and the Development of Puritan Preaching" (PhD diss., Westminster Theological Seminary, 1985), 86.

43. Pipa, "William Perkins and the Development of Puritan Preaching," 87–88.

44. See Pipa, "William Perkins and the Development of Puritan Preaching," 37–42.

Perkins's model of preaching influenced generations to come. Ian Breward writes of Perkins, "His emphasis on simplicity in preaching and his advocacy of a sermon structured according to doctrine, reason and use was taken for granted as homiletic orthodoxy until the end of the seventeenth century and beyond."[45]

We see in Perkins's *The Arte of Prophecying* several themes that contributed to Reformed experiential preaching. I will illustrate these themes with examples of his preaching from his commentary on Galatians, which is sermonic material edited for publication.

First, Perkins sets forth a high view of the Word of God. It is sufficient: "so complete, that nothing may be either put to it, or taken from it, which appertaineth to the proper end thereof." It is pure: "void of deceit and error." It is authoritative: "the supreme and absolute determination of the controversies of the church ought to be given unto it." The Word is powerful, able to discern the spirit of man and to bind the conscience. The Bible is the Word: "The Scripture is the word of God written . . . by men immediately called to be the clerks or secretaries of the Holy Ghost." The sum of its message is the incarnate Christ and his saving work. Therefore, the preacher must confine himself to the Holy Scriptures for the matter of his sermons, and insofar as he does so, he is "the voice of God."[46]

Perkins's *Commentary on Galatians* repeatedly commends a very high view of Scripture. For example, he says, "It is a principle not to be called in question, that the apostles and prophets, in writing and preaching, could not err."[47] The apostolic teachings are "the immediate and mere word of God," with respect to both "matter and words."[48] Perkins says, therefore, that Paul's gospel "is not human, but divine, and preached not by human, but by divine authority."[49]

Second, Perkins calls preachers to study the Scriptures both accurately and wisely. Much of his preaching manual teaches principles of biblical interpretation. His method of interpretation is: (1) *theological*, built upon a fundamental knowledge of Christian doctrine found in the Apostles' Creed, the Ten Commandments, and other major teachings of theology; (2) *broadly biblical*, viewing any one text in the light of the

---

45. Breward, introduction, *Work of Perkins*, 112.
46. Perkins, "The Art of Prophecying," in *Works*, 2:731–32.
47. Perkins, *Galatians*, 139 [Gal. 3:1].
48. Perkins, *Galatians*, 4 [Gal. 1:1].
49. Perkins, *Galatians*, 32 [Gal. 1:12].

teaching of the whole Bible, especially in key books such as Genesis, Psalms, Isaiah, John, and Romans; (3) *historical*, rooting interpretation in the writings of the church through the ages, works that the preacher must be reading; (4) *prayerful*, asking God to open the preacher's eyes (Ps. 119:18), for "the principal interpreter of the Scripture is the Holy Ghost"; (5) *literal and grammatical*, seeking the natural sense of the words and sentences, and avoiding fanciful readings; (6) *contextual*, asking questions about the people and settings of the text; and (7) *rhetorical*, recognizing figures of speech, such as metaphors, irony, or examples of speaking of God by analogy to human qualities.[50] Such principles all aim at "the opening of the words and sentences of the Scripture, that one entire and natural sense may appear."[51]

Consider how Perkins applies these principles in his exposition of Galatians 5:24, "And they that are Christ's have crucified the flesh with the affections and lusts." He opens by identifying the scope of the text (its purpose) as showing why no law puts a spiritual man under condemnation or bondage, thereby immediately connecting the text with the verse before it, "against such there is no law" (Gal. 5:23). He then interprets the text to say that (1) "A Christian is one that is Christ's"; (2) the flesh "is the corruption of the whole nature of man," especially active in "inordinate and insatiable desires after the things of this world"; and (3) it "is the work of a Christian man to crucify the flesh."[52]

Third, Perkins instructs preachers to crystallize the meaning of the Scripture text into doctrine or distinct teaching. Some texts clearly express a doctrine. In other texts, the preacher may deduce doctrines through sound reasoning and logic. The examples of biblical people can point to principles applicable to someone in a similar position in the family, the government, or the church. Doctrines derived from the Bible "by just consequence" should be confirmed by a few testimonies from other Scripture passages, but merely human testimonies do not have the authority to prove a point.[53]

We have already seen how Perkins's interpretation of Galatians 5:24 led to three clear doctrines. He proceeds to develop these doctrines by drawing upon the broader teachings of Scripture. For example, he lists

---

50. Perkins, "The Art of Prophecying," in *Works*, 2:736–49.
51. Perkins, "The Art of Prophecying," in *Works*, 2:737.
52. Perkins, *Galatians*, 397–98 [Gal. 5:24].
53. Perkins, "The Art of Prophecying," in *Works*, 2:750–51. On Perkins's commendation at this point of Ramist methods of logic for the interpretation of Scripture, see Wilbur Samuel Howell, *Logic and Rhetoric in England, 1500–1700* (New York: Russell and Russell, 1961), 206–7.

five ways in which the Christian belongs to Christ: by right of creation, by right of redemption, by the Father's gift in election and effectual calling, by propagation from his blood, and by our giving ourselves to him in baptism.[54]

He also develops the biblical doctrine of sharing in Christ's crucifixion. This is first the act of Christ, in that Christ died in our place on the cross so that we were crucified with him (Gal. 2:20), and he then applies the power of his death to the hearts of those who are joined to him, and seals these spiritual realities upon believers through baptism. It is also our action in that we arrest our own souls, bring them to judgment, condemn our sins, apply Christ's work to ourselves by trusting that he died for us and we died with him, strike down our sinful desires with God's Word, flee from all temptations, and attack sin in its first stirrings.[55] In brief compass, Perkins presents an excellent summary of the doctrine of dying to sin in Christ.

Fourth, Perkins teaches preachers to make suitable application of the doctrine to people's lives. The foundational question for application is whether the text is law or gospel. Law defines righteousness, exposes sin, and pronounces God's curse on sin. Gospel reveals Christ and his benefits received by a fruitful faith.[56] One may also make a positive doctrinal application, teaching the truth; a negative doctrinal application, refuting error; a positive practical application, calling men to live well; and a negative practical application, calling men to turn from wickedness.[57]

Preaching on Galatians 5:24, Perkins gives three "uses" for his first point on belonging to Christ, one for his second point on the flesh, four for his third point on how to crucify the flesh by means of crucifixion with Christ, and then ends with three more brief points on how to make suitable applications—eleven points of application for a single verse of Scripture. Unlike some Puritan preaching, he wisely scatters his applications throughout his exposition rather than reserving them all for the end after lengthy doctrinal discussions.[58]

Listen to his first "use" on belonging to Christ, and observe how the gospel places practical and experiential demands upon professing Christians:

---

54. Perkins, *Galatians*, 397 [Gal. 5:24].
55. Perkins, *Galatians*, 399 [Gal. 5:24].
56. Perkins, "The Art of Prophecying," in *Works*, 2:752.
57. Perkins, "The Art of Prophecying," in *Works*, 2:756–58.
58. Perkins, *Galatians*, 397–400 [Gal. 5:24].

This must teach us to resign [or surrender] ourselves to Christ, and to suffer [or permit] him to reign in our hearts: and to take the yoke of the gospel upon us. But alas, it is far otherwise with many of us. For some live in the transgression of the very law of nature, so far are they from observing the gospel. Others think it sufficient to follow the teaching of nature. If they worship God in some general manner, if they live peaceably, and hurt no man, and mean well (as they say) then all is well: and the doing of further duties, is reputed curious preciseness [or perfectionistic legalism]. . . . These men are content that Christ shall be theirs: but they will not be Christ's, and suffer him to have lordship over them.[59]

Another key to unlocking application is to consider the spiritual condition of those who hear the sermon. Perkins schematizes listeners into seven categories.[60] His analysis reflects what we call discriminatory preaching, sermons that give distinct applications aimed at different spiritual conditions. The listeners may be:

1. *Ignorant and Unteachable Unbelievers.* These people need to hear the doctrine of the Word in clear, reasonable teaching, as well as by reproof and pricking of their consciences.

2. *Ignorant but Teachable Unbelievers.* These people must be taught the foundational doctrines of the Christian religion. Perkins recommends they learn from his book *Foundations of the Christian Religion*, which covers the subjects of repentance, faith, the sacraments, the application of the Word, the resurrection, and the last judgment.

3. *Those Who Have Some Knowledge but Are Not Humbled.* To them, the preacher must especially proclaim the law to stir up sorrow and repentance for sin, followed by the preaching of the gospel.

4. *The Humbled.* The preacher must not give comfort to such people too soon, but must first determine whether their humility results from God's saving work rooted in faith or from mere common conviction. To the partly humbled, who are not yet stripped of self-righteousness, the law must be propounded yet more, albeit tempered with the gospel, so that "being terrified with their sins, and with the meditation of God's judgment, they may together also at the same instant receive solace by the gospel." To the fully humbled, "the doctrine of faith and repentance,

---

59. Perkins, *Galatians*, 397 [Gal. 5:24].
60. Perkins, "The Art of Prophecying," *Works*, 2:752–56.

and the comforts of the gospel ought to be promulged [proclaimed] and tendered."[61]

5. *Those Who Believe*. Believers need to be taught the key doctrines of justification, sanctification, and perseverance, along with the law as the rule of conduct rather than its sting and curse. Before faith, the law with the curse is to be preached; after conversion, the law without the curse.

6. *Those Who Are Fallen, Either in Faith or in Practice*. These people have backslidden in faith, in knowledge, or in apprehending Christ. If they have fallen in knowledge, they are to be instructed in the particular doctrine from which they have erred. If they have failed to apprehend Christ, they should examine themselves by the marks of grace, then fly to Christ as the remedy of the gospel. Those who have fallen in practice have become involved in sinful behavior. They need to be brought to repentance by the preaching of the law and the gospel.

7. *A Mixed Group*. This may refer to the mixture of both believers and unbelievers in a church, or it may refer to individuals who contain within themselves a combination of the traits of the first six kinds of listeners. If the latter is what Perkins intends, much wisdom is needed to know how much law and how much gospel to bring to them.

Perkins tags his applications of Galatians 5:24 with discriminating phrases, such as "If thou be Christ's," "By this see what a carnal man is," or "This doctrine serves to condemn the drowsy Protestants of our time."[62] We saw earlier from Perkins's first application on belonging to Christ how he distinctly addresses different kinds of unbelievers: those whose gross sins violate even the laws of nature and those who mistakenly count their outward civility and general religion as saving faith. Yet we also see that he does not employ the exact sevenfold scheme of his preaching manual, reminding us that not every sermon need address every kind of application to every kind of listener. Rather, application is driven by the content of the specific Scripture text and by the needs of the congregation.

Fifth, Perkins advises preachers to deliver their sermons with Spirit-worked liberty, sincerity, and power. He recommends that the preacher memorize an outline of his sermon and not be concerned about specific words. The minister should modestly conceal his scholarship, but preach with the demonstration of the Spirit (1 Cor. 2:1–5). He explains, "The

---

61. Perkins, "The Art of Prophecying," *Works*, 2:754–55.
62. Perkins, *Galatians*, 398–99 [Gal. 5:24].

demonstration of the Spirit is, when as the minister of the Word doth in the time of preaching behave himself, that all, even ignorant persons and unbelievers may judge that it is not him that speaketh, as the Spirit of God in him and by him." The spiritual preacher speaks with simplicity, clarity, the fear of God's majesty, and love for the people. He avoids Greek and Latin words, entertaining stories, and jesting. Instead, he displays dignity, seriousness, teaching skill, authority as God's messenger, and "zeal, whereby being most desirous of God's glory he doth endeavor to fulfill and execute the decree of election concerning the salvation of men by his ministry."[63] In the hands of the Holy Spirit, the preacher is an instrument for the execution of the decree of divine election.

Perkins's written exposition of Galatians sets forth the Scriptures with sincerity, sobriety, simplicity, authority, and application. Thomas Goodwin (1600–1680) said that when he came to Cambridge ten years after Perkins's death, the university was still "filled with the discourse of the power of Mr. William Perkins' ministry."[64] Perkins certainly preached with the demonstration of the Spirit.

Lastly, Perkins calls ministers to preach Christ. He concludes by saying: "The sum of the sum. *Preach one Christ by Christ to the praise of Christ.*"[65] In expositing Galatians 5:24, he preaches Christ's lordship over the saved soul; his redeeming death for sins; his providential care for his people and our committing ourselves to him; and his conquering of our sins on the cross and in our hearts, and our imitation of Christ by faith in his finished work. Christ's centrality and supremacy pervade his preaching, and in that Perkins is a model for us all.

Conclusion

Perkins earned the titles "scholastic, high Calvinist" and "father of pietism."[66] His theology affirmed divine sovereignty in the predestinating decree of the Father, the satisfaction made by Christ for the elect, and the saving work of the Spirit. Yet Perkins never allowed himself to distort sovereignty so as to prevent a practical, evangelical emphasis on the individual believer working out his own salvation as hearer of the

---

63. Perkins, "The Art of Prophecying," in *Works*, 2:758–61.
64. Thomas Goodwin, *"Memoir of Thomas Goodwin,"* in *The Works of Thomas Goodwin, D.D.*, ed. John C. Miller (Edinburgh: James Nichol, 1862), 2:xiii–xiv.
65. Perkins, "The Art of Prophecying," in *Works*, 2:762.
66. Heinrich Heppe, *Geschichte des Pietismus und der Mystik in der reformierten Kirche namentlich in der Niederlande* (Leiden: Brill, 1879), 24–26.

Word, follower of Christ, and warrior of the conscience. He inseparably intertwined divine sovereignty, individual piety, and the gospel offer of salvation.

Perkins's emphasis on sound doctrine and the reform of souls influenced Puritanism for many years after his death.[67] J. I. Packer writes, "Puritanism, with its complex of biblical, devotional, ecclesiastical, reformational, polemical and cultural concerns, came of age, we might say, with Perkins, and began to display characteristically a wholeness of spiritual vision and a maturity of Christian patience that had not been seen in it before."[68]

Perkins's preaching, heard by the ear and printed in the press, had a remarkable influence over people of many nations. His sermons were of many "colours," writes Thomas Fuller. They seemed to be "all Law and all gospel, all cordials and all corrosives, as the different necessities of people apprehended" them.[69] He was able to reach many types of people in various classes, being "systematic, scholarly, solid and simple at the same time."[70] As Fuller says, "His church consisting of the university and town, the scholar could have no learneder [better educated], the townsmen [no] plainer, sermons." Most importantly, he lived his sermons: "As his preaching was a comment on his text, so his practice was a comment on his preaching."[71]

---

67. Richard Muller, "William Perkins and the Protestant Exegetical Tradition: Interpretation, Style, and Method," in Perkins, *Commentary on Hebrews 11*, 72.

68. J. I. Packer, *An Anglican to Remember: William Perkins, Puritan Popularizer* (London: St. Antholin's Lectureship Charity, 1996), 4.

69. Fuller, *Abel Redevivus*, 2:148.

70. Packer, *An Anglican to Remember*, 3.

71. Fuller, *Abel Redevivus*, 2:151.

10

Puritan Preachers: Rogers, Sibbes, and Preston

As we saw in the previous chapter on William Perkins, a "spiritual brotherhood" formed at Cambridge University in the late sixteenth century, united by a common concern for promoting Reformed doctrine and godliness.[1] Many of the men of this brotherhood shared a spiritual lineage, a family tree of influence upon each other.

Laurence Chaderton mentored Perkins. Paul Baynes succeeded Perkins—as Elisha succeeded Elijah with a double portion of the same spirit, William Ames said.[2] Baynes's preaching resulted in the conversion of Richard Sibbes. God used Sibbes's ministry to convert John Cotton. Cotton, convinced that he must use the plain style of preaching, did so with the glad consequence that John Preston was arrested by conviction and then rested his soul in Christ. The preaching of Sibbes and Preston influenced Thomas Goodwin, who came to Christ after a funeral sermon by another Cambridge man, Thomas Bainbridge (d. 1646). In 1622, Chaderton stepped down from his position as master of Emmanuel College so that Preston could take his place.

---

1. Paul R. Schaefer, *The Spiritual Brotherhood: Cambridge Puritans and the Nature of Christian Piety* (Grand Rapids, MI: Reformation Heritage Books, 2011), 6; William Haller, *The Rise of Puritanism: Or, The Way to the New Jerusalem as Set Forth in Pulpit and Press from Thomas Cartwright to John Lilburne and John Milton, 1570–1643* (New York: Columbia University Press, 1947), 49ff.

2. William Ames, preface to Paul Baynes, *The Diocesans Tryall: Wherein All the Sinnewes of Doctor Dovvnhams Defence Are Bought into Three Heads, and Orderly Dissolved* (London: n.p., 1621), (no pagination).

Having examined the preaching of Perkins, we now proceed to look at the ministries of two other members of this Cambridge brotherhood, Sibbes and Preston, along with an older minister, Richard Rogers (1551–1618), who had graduated from Cambridge before Perkins began to study there and helped to train Baynes for ministry.

Richard Rogers

Rogers was born in Essex and was educated at Christ's College, Cambridge, graduating with a BA in 1571 and an MA in 1574.[3] Chaderton had been serving as a fellow (a teacher) at Christ's College since 1567, and thus influenced Rogers through his instruction, as well as his preaching at St. Clement's Church in Cambridge. Rogers went on to labor faithfully in Essex for a couple of years as a curate and for forty years as a lecturer at Wethersfield. Baynes stayed in Rogers's home as his pupil at Wethersfield, which illustrates Rogers's impact in training up spiritually minded preachers of the Word.[4]

He was a man of great learning and great godliness, humble and peaceable in his conduct. Two of his sons and three of his stepsons became Puritan ministers. His grandson, William Jenkyn (1613–1685), compared him to Enoch, because he walked with God and looked to heaven.

Yet Rogers suffered for his Nonconformist views. When Archbishop of Canterbury John Whitgift (1530–1604) demanded strict conformity to the use of the Book of Common Prayer in 1583, Rogers and twenty-six other ministers petitioned for relief. They were all promptly suspended from the ministry until they were willing to subscribe and conform completely. Later, a nobleman by the name of Sir Robert Wroth intervened for Rogers, and he received permission to preach again.

In 1603, Rogers was again suspended from preaching and summoned to appear before the archbishop. He wrote in his diary, "It greatly troubles me that after laboring betwixt thirty and forty years in the ministry, I am now accounted unworthy to preach; while so many idle and scandalous people enjoy their ease and liberty."[5]

---

3. On Rogers, see Richard Rogers and Samuel Ward, *Two Elizabethan Puritan Diaries*, ed. M. M. Knappen, Studies in Church History Vol. II (Chicago: American Society of Church History, 1933); Haller, *The Rise of Puritanism*, 35–48; Irvonwy Morgan, *The Godly Preachers of the Elizabethan Church* (London: Epworth, 1965), 116–45, 150–52, 166–74.

4. Irvonwy Morgan, *Prince Charles's Puritan Chaplain* (London: Allen & Unwin, 1957), 40.

5. Quoted in Benjamin Brook, *Lives of the Puritans*, 3 vols. (1813; repr., Pittsburgh, PA: Soli Deo Gloria, 1994), 2:233.

Providentially, the archbishop died on the day of the appointment, and Rogers was released.

According to a well-known story, Rogers was once in the company of a gentleman who remarked to him, "Mr. Rogers, I like you and your company very well, only you are so precise." Rogers answered, "Oh, sir, I serve a precise God."[6] When Rogers died in 1618, Stephen Marshall (c. 1594–1655) succeeded him at the lectureship at Wethersfield.

Practical and Experiential Sermons in Judges

Rogers is best known today for his massive commentary on the book of Judges.[7] It is a collection of 103 practical and experiential sermons he preached at Wethersfield. For example, in Sermon 74 (on Judges 14:1–4), he describes the Holy Spirit's inward work of conversion upon the soul: "While we give heed to the doctrine of the Lord Jesus, which is plainly, soundly, and powerfully taught us, the Lord enlighteneth us with grace and power of the Holy Ghost, and giveth us another heart to serve him (as he saith in Ezek. 36), than we had before."[8]

Here again we see the Reformed doctrine of predestination applied to the personal experience of salvation. Referring, like Perkins, to "that golden chaine" of Romans 8:30, Rogers says, "There is no other way to seek out the certainty of our election" apart from "the gift of faith, and the Spirit of God sanctifying" in our effectual calling. He explains that "predestination itself is manifested in time, by the enlightening and opening of the heart to receive the glad tidings of the gospel," so that "Christ is embraced by faith" and "the Holy Ghost is given to the believer, who quickens the heart with spiritual grace." God gives different degrees of grace to different people, but the work of salvation is fundamentally the same.[9]

God works by means, and the experience of conversion comes in stages. With respect to the beginnings of saving faith, Rogers says, similarly to Perkins, that first God is "stirring up in them an earnest coveting of these graces, a special hunger and thirst after them," until he brings them to "the certainty and assurance of salvation." God preserves and

---

6. Quoted in Giles Firmin, *The Real Christian, or A Treatise of Effectual Calling* (London: for Dorman Newman, 1670), 67.

7. Richard Rogers, *A Commentary Vpon the Whole Booke of Ivdges* (London: by Felix Kyngston for Thomas Man, 1615); reprinted as Richard Rogers, *A Commentary on Judges* (Edinburgh: Banner of Truth, 1983).

8. Rogers, *A Commentary on Judges*, 655–56 [Judg. 14:1–4].

9. Rogers, *A Commentary on Judges*, 656 [Judg. 14:1–4].

nourishes these strong desires for his grace in believers so that they continue to grow and to serve him better.[10]

In the same sermon, Rogers gives very practical counsel for parents and children regarding finding a mate. He admonishes them not to marry an idolater (by which he means a Roman Catholic), arguing that it is not possible "that they who are so unequally yoked together, can enjoy the chief benefits of their marriage," which are that "they should consent and agree together in all good things, as in conferring, praying, and reading together, and be of one mind." This requires not only marrying someone of the same religion, but also marrying "in the Lord" (1 Cor. 7:39), that is, someone who is truly a godly Christian and not a "bad" or "lewd" professing Christian.[11]

Children should not allow their youthful inexperience to lead them into great sorrows, but instead should "seek their parents' consent." At the same time, parents should not "exercise such a tyrannical power over their children" as to compel them to marry someone against their will. Choosing a mate requires much wisdom, since people can put on appearances. One should "learn both the disposition, and behavior" of the other person, looking beyond outward beauty and emotional responses. Yet "seeing marriage is for a man's lifetime, it is meet that there should be a good liking the one of the other, to the well-bearing of all molestations [troubles], crosses, and adversities that may befall couples: yet with this liking, the one of the person of the other, there must also be good grace and qualities."[12]

This is just a small sample from one sermon of how Rogers worked through a book of the Bible, applying it in an experiential and practical manner to his hearers.

Practical Christianity

Roger's best-known book in his own era was his *Seven Treatises* (1603), which ran through five editions by 1630. An abridged version in 1618 (*The Practice of Christianity*) went to press as the fifth edition in 1635. Sadly, neither version has been reprinted since the seventeenth century.

This popular work laid the foundation for a great number of Puritan manuals on the Christian life. The full title (in modern spelling) is: *Seven*

---

10. Rogers, *A Commentary on Judges*, 656 [Judg. 14:1–4].
11. Rogers, *A Commentary on Judges*, 658–60 [Judg. 14:1–4].
12. Rogers, *A Commentary on Judges*, 660–61 [Judg. 14:1–4].

Treatises Containing Such Direction as Is Gathered out of the Holy Scriptures, Leading and Guiding to True Happiness, Both in This Life and in the Life to Come, and May be Called the Practice of Christianity.[13] In this book, we get another taste for how practical and experiential Rogers's preaching was. William Haller writes: "The *Seven Treatises* was the first important exposition of the code of behavior which expressed the English Calvinist, or more broadly speaking, the Puritan, conception of the spiritual and moral life. As such it inaugurated a literature the extent and influence of which in all departments of life can hardly be exaggerated."[14]

The *Seven Treatises* consists of a seven-part exposition of true saving faith. In the first treatise, Rogers delineates the marks of those who are the true children of God. He describes conversion and how to discern true saving faith. The second treatise presents the godly life, one marked by keeping God's commandments by faith in God's promises.

The third treatise teaches about the means of helping and growing true godliness. Rogers speaks of the public means of the preaching of the Word, the sacraments, and public prayers. There are also private means of grace. Irvonwy Morgan writes: "Rogers distinguishes seven private helps to godliness. First, those which are practiced alone, namely watchfulness, meditation, and what he calls 'the armour of a Christian'; then those which are practised with others, namely conference [godly conversation] and family-exercise [or family devotions]; lastly those which are common to both, namely prayer and reading."[15] There are also the extraordinary means of responding to God's providence: solemn times of thanksgiving for periods of unusual blessing, and solemn times of fasting for periods of unusual affliction.

The fourth treatise gives eight reasons why a Christian should practice the daily disciplines of godliness, and calls the reader to walk with God through nine daily duties. In the fifth treatise, Rogers examines the obstacles to walking with God, such as Satan, leaving our first love, and evil and worldly lusts. The sixth treatise offers a lovely view of the privileges of believers and how we may enjoy them. In the seventh treatise, he wraps up the book by answering objections.

---

13. Richard Rogers, *Seuen Treatises, Containing Such Direction as Is Gathered Out of the Holie Scriptures, Leading and Guiding to True Happines, Both in This Life, and in the Life to Come: And May Be Called the Practise of Christianitie* (London: by Felix Kyngston, for Thomas Man, 1603).
14. Haller, *The Rise of Puritanism*, 36.
15. Morgan, *The Godly Preachers of the Elizabethan Church*, 129.

Rogers's *Seven Treatises* commends to us a Christianity that is both Reformed and experiential, characterized by a disciplined, warfare mentality operating with spiritual discernment. It engages the Christian to live each day with an eternal perspective, seeking first the kingdom of God and his righteousness. Rogers emphasizes the heart as the central arena where battles are fought and won. Over the course of 663 folio pages, he explores these matters in great detail.

Here we see the balanced idealism of Reformed experiential preaching. It aims high; it sets heavenly goals. At the same time, it speaks about obstacles and inward warfare. Interestingly, Rogers's diary reveals that he did not always succeed in governing his own life according to these ideals. For example, on September 12, 1587, he writes: "But this afternoon I felt a strong desire to enjoy more liberty in thinking upon some vain things which I had lately weaned myself from. Me thought it [to be] great bondage to be tied from delighting in such things as I took pleasure in. . . . And thus I see how hard it is to keep our minds in awe and attending upon the Lord in some good duty or other, at least to be strongly settled against evil."[16] So he too had problems with a wandering mind and worldly thoughts. Yet he fought to keep his mind focused on Christ.

Rogers set a pattern for maintaining a careful walk of holiness. Such practical godliness leads in turn to pulpit proclamation that demands a high level of holiness from the people, and yet recognizes that we always fall short of the ideal. Today, people are prone to say, "That's legalism; it's too high; it's too hard." They want an easy Christianity with a Christ who meets all their immediate desires. They may tolerate some discipline in the outward life to attain their earthly goals. However, it is common that they use the banner of "grace alone" to claim that spiritual blessings come easily once you find the right key, without pain or wrestling against evil.

They forget that "the grace of God" teaches us to deny "ungodliness and worldly lusts," and instead "live soberly, righteously, and godly," with our eyes fixed on the "blessed hope" of Christ's appearing, all the while being "zealous of good works," as Paul taught us (Titus 2:11–14). The Puritans preached discipline by grace and self-control in hope as models of Reformed biblical and experiential preaching.

---

16. Rogers and Ward, *Two Elizabethan Puritan Diaries*, 59–60.

Richard Sibbes

Sibbes was one of the greatest Puritans of his age.[17] He greatly influenced the direction and content of Puritan preaching in England and in America. Sibbes was a native of Suffolk, a Puritan county that produced more of the illustrious immigrants to New England than any other county. As a boy, he loved to read and study. His father sought to draw him into his trade as a wheelwright, but the boy bought books with every reward he got.

Sibbes went to Cambridge, graduating with a BA in 1599 and an MA in 1602. In 1603, he was converted under Paul Baynes's preaching. He served as a fellow in the college, earned his bachelor of divinity degree in 1610, and served as a lecturer at Holy Trinity Church, Cambridge, from 1611 to 1616. As noted earlier, his preaching there influenced Cotton and Goodwin. From 1617 to 1635, he served as a lecturer at Gray's Inn in London. In 1626, he became the master of St. Catharine's Hall at Cambridge, which awarded him a doctor of divinity degree the following year. People referred to him as "the heavenly Doctor" due to his godly preaching and heavenly conversation. Izaac Walton (c. 1594–1683) wrote of Sibbes:

> Of this blest man, let this just praise be given,
> Heaven was in him before he was in heaven.[18]

Under his leadership, a number of Puritans received their training, including Westminster divines John Arrowsmith (1602–1659), William Spurstowe (c. 1605–1666), and William Strong (d. 1654).

---

17. On Sibbes, see Bert Affleck, "The Theology of Richard Sibbes, 1577–1635" (PhD diss., Drew University, 1968); Stephen Paul Beck, "The Doctrine of *Gratia Praeparans* in the Soteriology of Richard Sibbes" (PhD diss., Westminster Theological Seminary, 1994); Mark Dever, *Richard Sibbes: Puritanism and Calvinism in Late Elizabethan and Early Stuart England* (Macon, GA: Mercer University Press, 2000); Frank E. Farrell, "Richard Sibbes: A Study in Early Seventeenth Century English Puritanism" (PhD diss., University of Edinburgh, 1955); Tae-Hyeun Park, *The Sacred Rhetoric of the Holy Spirit: A Study of Puritan Preaching in a Pneumatological Perspective* (Apeldoorn: Theologische Universiteit Apeldoorn, 2005); Harry Lee Poe, "Evangelistic Fervency among the Puritans in Stuart England, 1603–1688" (PhD diss., Southern Baptist Theological Seminary, 1982); Sidney H. Rooy, *The Theology of Missions in the Puritan Tradition: A Study of Representative Puritans, Richard Sibbes, Richard Baxter, John Eliot, Cotton Mather, and Jonathan Edwards* (Grand Rapids, MI: Eerdmans, 1965); Schaefer, *The Spiritual Brotherhood*; Harold Patton Shelly, "Richard Sibbes: Early Stuart Preacher of Piety" (PhD diss., Temple University, 1972); Beth E. Tumbleson, "The Bride and Bridegroom in the Work of Richard Sibbes, English Puritan" (MA thesis, Trinity Evangelical Divinity School, 1984); Cary N. Weisiger, "The Doctrine of the Holy Spirit in the Preaching of Richard Sibbes" (PhD diss., Fuller Theological Seminary, 1984); Chong-ch'on Won, "Communion with Christ: An Exposition and Comparison of the Doctrine of Union and Communion with Christ in Calvin and the English Puritans" (PhD diss., Westminster Theological Seminary, 1989).

18. Walton wrote this in his copy of Sibbes's *The Returning Backslider*. Stephen Martin, *Izaak Walton and His Friends* (London: Chapman & Hall, 1903), 174.

Mark Dever writes, "For Sibbes, Christianity was a love story," beginning with God's love for his people.[19] Though Sibbes never married, he led a spiritual family by cultivating an astonishing network of friendships with both religious and political leaders. He was a gentle and warm man who disliked controversy, though he did not hesitate to oppose Roman Catholicism and Arminianism. Most of all, Sibbes delighted to draw people to Christ with cords of love.[20]

Dever explains the centrality of preaching in Sibbes's view of salvation:

Sibbes taught that the primary means Christ used to prepare his elect's hearts for salvation was "by the ministry of the gospel" [1:23–24; 2:63, 216; 7:404]. "Hearing begets seeing in religion. Death came in by the ear at the first. Adam hearing the serpent, that he should not have heard, death came in by the ear. So life comes in by the ear" [4:251–52; cf. 3:367, 377, 386; 6:353, 380, 409; 7:198, 404–405, 434, 476].[21]

Sibbes believed that the affectionate preaching of Christ in his saving work is the central means by which God begets and grows godly affections. Making Christ known in his states and offices is God's ordinance to open the mind and draw the will and heart to Christ. This makes preaching a precious gift from God that we should highly esteem.[22]

Sibbes excelled as a Christ-centered, experiential preacher. David Masson, biographer of John Milton, says, "From the year 1630, onwards for twenty years or so, no writings in practical theology seem to have been so much read among pious English middle classes as those of Sibbes."[23] Haller says that Sibbes's sermons "were among the most brilliant and popular of all the utterances of the Puritan church militant."[24]

Christ Preached among the Nations

One source in which Sibbes reveals his view of preaching is *The Fountain Opened*, a collection of his sermons on 1 Timothy 3:16, which

---

19. Dever, *Richard Sibbes*, 143.
20. Richard Sibbes, "The Fountain Opened," in *The Works of Richard Sibbes* (Edinburgh: Banner of Truth, 2001), 5:505–6, hereafter, *Works*.
21. Dever, *Richard Sibbes*, 129. I have inserted in brackets the references to Sibbes's *Works* found in Dever's footnotes.
22. Dever, *Richard Sibbes*, 155–56.
23. David Masson, *The Life of John Milton* (Cambridge: Macmillan and Co., 1859), 1:478.
24. Haller, *The Rise of Puritanism*, 152.

says, "And without controversy great is the mystery of godliness: God was manifest in the flesh, justified in the Spirit, seen of angels, preached unto the Gentiles, believed on in the world, received up into glory."[25] He addresses the office of the preacher particularly when he comes to the phrase "preached unto the Gentiles."[26]

When a king is enthroned, both his nobles and his common subjects must know it. Therefore, it is not enough for Christ to be "seen of angels," his heavenly nobility. His kingdom must also be proclaimed to the entire world, all men called to submit to him. He must be preached before he can be "believed on in the world," Sibbes writes, for "faith is the issue and fruit of preaching."[27] Sibbes says, "Preaching is the ordinance of God, sanctified for the begetting of faith, for the opening of the understanding, for the drawing of the will and affections to Christ." This is the ladder of heaven that we must ascend one step at a time: first preaching, then faith, then prayer (Rom. 10:14–17).[28]

Sibbes advocates world missions, even though English exploration of other continents was in its infancy in his day.[29] Taking up the words "preached unto the Gentiles," he boldly says, "Hence we have a ground likewise of enlarging the gospel to all people, because the Gentiles now have interest in Christ; that merchants, and those that give themselves to navigation, they may with good success carry the gospel to all people." The gospel, like the sun, is traveling from east to west until it shall illuminate all nations.[30] Though a people be "savages, ever so barbarous," Christians must "labor to gain them for Christ." Along these lines, Sibbes calls upon explorers and merchants not to compel people into Christianity by force: "There is nothing so voluntary as faith. It must be wrought by persuasions, not by violence."[31] Preaching, not the sword, is the means by which the nations find Christ, whether England or India.

---

25. Portions of this section have been adapted from Joel Beeke, "Puritan Preachers: Richard Sibbes," *Meet the Puritans*, June 9, 2017, http://www.meetthepuritans.com/blog/puritan-preachers-richard-sibbes. Used with permission.
26. Weisiger, "Doctrine of the Holy Spirit," 166–67.
27. Sibbes, "The Fountain Opened," in *Works*, 5:504.
28. Sibbes, "The Fountain Opened," in *Works*, 5:514.
29. The Spanish and Portuguese dominated world exploration in the fifteenth and sixteenth centuries. Francis Drake (c. 1540–1596) was the first Englishman to circumnavigate the world, doing so in 1577–1580. The abortive attempt of Walter Raleigh (c. 1554–1618) to establish the first English colony in North America began in 1584. Jamestown was settled by the Virginia Company in 1607. British merchants obtained trading rights with the rulers of India in 1617. The Pilgrims came to New England in 1620, and the Puritans to Massachusetts in 1630.
30. Sibbes, "The Fountain Opened," in *Works*, 5:512.
31. Sibbes, "The Fountain Opened," in *Works*, 5:513.

Preaching is the instrument for the application of redemption. Christ is medicine that must be taken, clothing that must be put on, a foundation on which we must build, a treasure to be dug up, a light to be set forth, and a food that must be eaten. Therefore, the preacher must "open the mystery of Christ" in his natures; his offices of Prophet, Priest, and King; his state of humiliation to work our salvation for us; his state of exaltation to apply our salvation to us; and his promises, which are "but Christ dished and parceled out."[32] Even when we listen to Sibbes preaching about preaching, we sense the centrality of Christ and the usefulness of imaginative and affectionate language.

He anticipates this question: "But must nothing be preached but Christ?" He replies, "Nothing but Christ, or that tends to Christ." The law serves Christ. The threats of the law bring men low so that Christ may lift them up. Moral duties show us what it means to walk worthy of Christ (Col. 1:10). Sibbes says, "The graces for these duties must be fetched from Christ; and the reasons and motives of a Christian's conversation [or conduct] must be from Christ, and from the state that Christ hath advanced us unto." With respect to the gospel, we must add nothing to Christ, lest we fall away from him by building on our own merit. This concern for *solus Christus* drove Sibbes's opposition to Romanism: "Why is the Church of Rome so erroneous, but because she leaves Christ and cleaves to other things?"[33]

Preaching is more than teaching; it is the language of divine love. Sibbes says that "it is not sufficient to preach Christ" merely by teaching people the doctrines of the Bible; rather, "there must be an alluring of them, for to preach is to woo."[34] He compares the preacher to a friend of the Bridegroom, who seeks to win the soul to marry Christ.[35] On the one hand, marriage must be entered with eyes wide open, based on a factual knowledge of the other person. So the friend of the Bridegroom makes known to the woman both her desperate need and her heavenly Suitor's riches and nobility.[36] On the other hand, this is not just an intellectual matter, so the preacher must "entreat for a marriage," employing all his abilities and powers to woo a bride for Christ.[37]

---

32. Sibbes, "The Fountain Opened," in *Works*, 5:505.
33. Sibbes, "The Fountain Opened," in *Works*, 5:509–10.
34. Sibbes, "The Fountain Opened," in *Works*, 5:505.
35. For the biblical background of this imagery, see John 3:29; 2 Cor. 11:2.
36. Sibbes, "The Fountain Opened," in *Works*, 5:514.
37. Sibbes, "The Fountain Opened," in *Works*, 5:506.

Sibbes's matrimonial language does not negate the necessity of preaching the law and its curses against sinners, but it does give a sweet purpose to severe preaching. Preaching of sin and misery is not an end to itself; it "makes way for the preaching of Christ." For even the sweetest foods are despised by a full stomach (Prov. 27:7). Sibbes queries, "Who cares for Christ, that sees not the necessity of Christ?" Yet preaching the terrors of divine judgment should arise from a tender and humble heart. Preachers must "beseech" or beg sinners to be reconciled with God (2 Cor. 5:20); indeed, "Christ, as it were, became a beggar himself, and the great God of heaven and earth begs our love, that we would so care for our own souls that we would be reconciled unto him." The fact that we should be the ones begging God for mercy makes God's sweet beseeching of us all the more poignant.[38] Like Paul, who wept over the enemies of the cross of Christ (Phil. 3:18), ministers must preach with "grief and compassion" for lost sinners, "because they are led by the Spirit of Christ, who was all made of compassion."[39]

Seeing preaching as divine wooing also highlights the power of the ministry of the Word above other means of grace. Sibbes commends the personal reading of the Bible to learn the truth, but "the truth unfolded hath more efficacy."[40] Preaching not only offers Christ, but through it, Christ is given to the heart: "Together with it goes a power—the Spirit clothing the ordinance of preaching—to do all." That is why Paul calls preaching of the gospel "the ministration of the spirit" (2 Cor. 3:8).[41]

Some people might object that they already know enough and do not need more teaching. Sibbes says, "The word of God preached, it is not altogether to teach us, but, the Spirit going with it, to work grace, necessary to 'strengthen us in the inward man' (2 Cor. 4:16)." It is hard enough to learn how to talk and think rightly about the things of God— far harder than learning a trade, for which men train for several years. But true religion is not just the ability to talk and think, but a mysterious knowledge in the heart. We do not really know God's grace until his grace is within us. This indwelling of grace is effected by preaching: "Preaching is the chariot that carries Christ up and down the world.

---

38. Sibbes, "The Fountain Opened," in *Works*, 5:506.
39. Sibbes, "Exposition of Philippians Chapter III," in *Works*, 5:126.
40. Sibbes, "The Fountain Opened," in *Works*, 5:507.
41. Sibbes, "The Fountain Opened," in *Works*, 5:514.

Christ doth not profit but as he is preached."⁴² Preaching does more than inform; by God's grace, it unites us to Christ.

Preaching is a profoundly relational act joining preacher and listener in Christ. This is part of the reason why God decided that mere men would preach his Word. That is not to say that the preacher wins his hearers by his personal charisma; he calls them to "obedience to the truth." Nevertheless, in preaching, God aims to "knit man to man by bonds of love." He does not terrify us by a cloud of fire or an angelic visitation, but magnifies his power by working through weak men like us. It helps "our weakness to have men that speak out of experience from themselves that preach the gospel, that they have felt the comfort of [it] themselves." When Paul and Peter preached, they did so as men humbled by their sins and astonished by the mercy of God. Such preaching by redeemed sinners gives much hope to fearful sinners.⁴³

Thus, Sibbes makes preaching a thoroughly experiential work, a vital triangle drawing together Christ, the preacher, and the hearers. It is a net thrown wide to catch the nations and a wooing of souls by the agent of a heavenly Lover. Preaching includes doctrinal teaching and goes beyond it, engaging the affections and most fundamental commitments of the will. In all this, the ministry of the Word is an instrument in the hands of the sovereign, electing God of grace.

John Preston

Preston was born in Northamptonshire.⁴⁴ His father, a farmer, died when he was twelve years old. He studied philosophy and medicine at Cambridge, receiving his BA in 1607 and his MA in 1611. While a student, he went with some friends to mock Cotton's plain style of preaching. Cotton had counted the cost of rejecting the ornate style craved by the aristocracy. Later that night, Preston knocked on Cotton's door, seeking answers for the salvation of his soul. The two became lifelong friends.

---

42. Sibbes, "The Fountain Opened," in *Works*, 5:508.
43. Sibbes, "The Fountain Opened," in *Works*, 5:507.
44. On Preston, see Thomas Ball, *The Life of the Renowned Doctor Preston*, ed. E. W. Harcourt (London: Parker and Co., 1885); Jonathan Moore, *English Hypothetical Universalism: John Preston and the Softening of Reformed Theology* (Grand Rapids, MI: Eerdmans, 2007); Irvonwy Morgan, *Puritan Spirituality: Illustrated from the Life and Times of the Rev. Dr. John Preston* (London: Epworth, 1973); Morgan, *Prince Charles's Puritan Chaplain*; Schaefer, *The Spiritual Brotherhood*; Young Jae Timothy Song, *Theology and Piety in the Reformed Federal Thought of William Perkins and John Preston* (Lewiston, NY: Edwin Mellen Press, 1998); James F. Veninga, "Covenant Theology and Ethics in the Thought of John Calvin and John Preston" (PhD diss., Rice University, 1974).

Preston redirected his studies to theology and graduated with his bachelor of divinity degree in 1620. By 1618, he had already begun to serve as dean and catechist at Queen's College, Cambridge. Around 1620, he became chaplain to Charles I, then a youthful prince of Wales. He used his influence at the court to improve the lot of Puritans. From 1622 to his death in 1628, he served as master of Emmanuel College at Cambridge. During that same period, he also preached at Lincoln's Inn, London, succeeding the poet John Donne (1573–1631). In 1624, Preston was confirmed as lecturer at Holy Trinity, thereby winning back for the Puritans the most influential preaching position in Cambridge, which had originated with Sibbes. It was one of the last victories of the Puritans at court.

Preston was instrumental in raising up other preachers, as well as influencing young preachers. Goodwin, Thomas Shepard, and Samuel Fairclough (1594–1677) were greatly impacted by his preaching.[45]

Though Preston died at a young age (almost forty-one), he left behind a rich legacy of preaching in his written sermons. When Bishop of Durham Richard Neile (1562–1640) heard him preach in 1627, he complained that Preston preached with great certainty, "as if he was familiar with God."[46] Above all, Preston was a preacher of Christ, and of faith in Christ. Preston says, "We must do as those stewards, that set bread and salt upon the table, whatsoever other dish there is: so we should always preach Christ, and persuade you to believe in him."[47] Christ is the staple, the basic ingredient, of preaching. After Preston's death, eleven volumes of his sermons were published, some of which went through ten or more editions. Surprisingly, no publisher has issued a multivolume set of his works.

Preaching Great Gospel Themes

Preston's preaching was more topical and organized by theological categories and questions than the verse-by-verse biblical expositions of John Calvin. Hughes Oliphant Old writes:

> The text is studied briefly in order to draw out of it a specific teaching or theme, and then this theme is developed in a number of points

---

45. Morgan, *Prince Charles's Puritan Chaplain*, 44–45.
46. Quoted in Morgan, *Prince Charles's Puritan Chaplain*, 39.
47. John Preston, *The Breast-Plate of Faith and Love* (Edinburgh: Banner of Truth, 1979), 1:70. This is a facsimile of the 1634 edition.

which are then supported by various arguments, drawn mostly from Scripture. They are illustrated by examples or illuminated by similes. Then, finally, they are applied to the lives of the congregation. In this respect Preston's sermons resemble those of medieval Scholasticism. . . . Preston usually takes one verse and develops from it a theme or a number of themes.[48]

We see an example of this method in *The Breast-Plate of Faith and Love* (1630), which is a classic statement of Puritan spirituality.[49] In the first section of the book, Preston preaches four sermons (117 pages) on a single text, Romans 1:17: "For therein is the righteousness of God revealed from faith to faith: as it is written, The just shall live by faith." He opens three doctrines: (1) that righteousness is revealed and offered in the gospel to as many as will take it, (2) that by faith we are made to partake of this righteousness, and (3) that faith has degrees, and every Christian should grow from one degree to another.[50] We can see that Preston derives these doctrines from the text, but he spends little time in his sermons studying the meaning of the text. Rather, he moves quickly to ask questions about each doctrine, which he answers from other Scripture passages. In his first point about the righteousness revealed in the gospel, he queries: (1) Why is this righteousness revealed? (2) How does this righteousness save? (3) How is it offered to us? (4) To whom is it offered? (5) Upon what qualifications is it offered? (6) How is it made ours? and (7) What is required of us when we have it?[51] These questions are followed by two warnings to those who reject Christ or put off receiving him, and then by three exhortations to receive Christ.[52]

The result is clear, applied preaching of the gospel. Old comments: "These sermons may properly be regarded as evangelistic sermons. Their aim is the conversion of those to whom they are addressed. Preston is fully aware that he is preaching to baptized Christians, but he is concerned that his congregation enter into the full reality of which their baptism is a sign and a promise."[53] Addressed to those inside the church, Preston's evangelistic teaching focuses on the

---

48. Hughes Oliphant Old, *The Reading and Preaching of the Scriptures in the Worship of the Christian Church, Volume 4: The Age of the Reformation* (Grand Rapids, MI: Eerdmans, 1998), 284.
49. Old, *Reading and Preaching of the Scriptures*, 4:280–86.
50. Preston, *The Breast-Plate of Faith and Love*, 1:1–117, esp. 2, 31, 99.
51. Preston, *The Breast-Plate of Faith and Love*, 1:2–22.
52. Preston, *The Breast-Plate of Faith and Love*, 1:22–30.
53. Old, *Reading and Preaching of the Scriptures*, 4:281.

meaning of conversion so as to distinguish between true believers and mere nominal Christians.

In a sermon series based on 2 Timothy 1:13, *A Pattern of Wholesome Words*, Preston lays out some of his views on the work of the preacher. Morgan observes that here too we see Preston starting with a doctrine and then developing it by answering questions and objections. He says that preachers should generally avoid quoting the church fathers, though some exceptions may be allowed for more recent writers, such as Calvin. But they should study broadly in human learning and digest the material well so that they can preach the same truths simply and usefully, much as livestock eat hay but produce wool and milk fit for men.[54]

The preacher is an ambassador who speaks for God to the people as his public representative. He must interpret the Word by raising a doctrine from the text, supporting it with confirming Scripture passages, then making application of it to particular kinds of people. The text must be understood according to proper grammar; rhetorical devices, such as metaphors; the "scope" or purpose of the text; and the analogy of faith. Each sermon must be applied by deriving its inherent uses. In these things, Preston sounds very much like Perkins in his *Arte of Prophecying.* One also senses his medical training in the background as he describes how the preacher must apply a different cure to the fever of lust, the swelling of pride, the palsy of anger, the lethargy of idleness, the humor of vainglory, the pleurisy of security, and the unsavory breath of evil speech.[55] General applications are not nearly as helpful as speaking to specific sins.

The minister must preach the Word. Preachers should feed their flocks, preaching the Scriptures at least twice on the Sabbath and also catechizing. Morgan says, "The Word must be presented in a spiritual manner, plain and unadorned, and easy to follow."[56] However, the sermon should not be just a running commentary on the Bible, but a structured discourse with distinct points. It is said that the stones of the walls of Byzantium were fitted so closely together that the wall appeared as one stone. Preston quipped that though this is "a commendation in a wall, it is not in a sermon."[57] Also, beware of filling your sermon with

---

54. Morgan, *Puritan Spirituality*, 12–14.

55. Morgan, *Puritan Spirituality*, 13–14. "Humor" here probably refers to an imbalance in bodily fluids, which in the medicine of that time were believed to produce the temperaments of melancholic, choleric, phlegmatic, and sanguine.

56. Morgan, *Puritan Spirituality*, 14.

57. John Preston, *Riches of Mercy to Men in Misery, or Certain Excellent Treatises Concerning the Dignity and Duty of God's Children* (London: J. T., 1658), 303.

material foreign to the Scriptures. Children may think that weeds in a cornfield are pretty, but the farmer knows they make the crop less fruitful. Even in making illustrations, the best material can be found in the Bible itself, though other illustrations are permissible so long as they do not merely please weak and flighty minds. We have already seen a number of Preston's own extrabiblical illustrations.[58]

In all things, the preacher operates as an instrument of the Spirit of Christ. He is totally dependent upon the Lord for any good results to come of his preaching. Preston says:

> When Christ showeth himself to a man, it is another thing than when the ministers shall show him, or the Scriptures nakedly read do show him: for when Christ shall show himself by his Spirit, that showing draweth a man's heart to long after him, otherwise we may preach long enough, and show you that these spiritual things, these privileges are prepared for you in Christ, but it is the Holy Ghost that must write them in your hearts; we can but write them in your heads.[59]

---

58. Morgan, *Puritan Spirituality*, 14–15.
59. Preston, *The Breast-Plate of Faith and Love*, 1:163.

11

The Westminster Directory and Preaching

Twice I've had the privilege of visiting the Jerusalem Chamber, the room in Westminster Abbey, London, where the Westminster Assembly met. It is a remarkably small room, and you can imagine the heated debates that took place with several dozen men packed into it. When the assembly members, known as divines, first gathered on July 1, 1643, they probably did not think that the assembly would last very long. Parliament had summoned them only to revise the Thirty-Nine Articles of the Church of England. They aimed to establish greater theological unity according to the treaty between the English and Scottish Parliaments known as the Solemn League and Covenant. But, in fact, the assembly would meet for nearly six years. When it met for its last plenary session on February 22, 1649, the assembly had held more than a thousand sessions and had produced an entirely new Confession of Faith, as well as the Larger Catechism, the Shorter Catechism, the Form of Presbyterial Church Government, and the Directory for the Public Worship of God, and had given its approval to a new metrical version of the Psalms.[1]

---

1. All of these documents may be found in *Westminster Confession of Faith* (Glasgow: Free Presbyterian Publications, 1994). This book also contains other documents related to the Westminster Assembly but not composed by it, such as the Scottish Directory for Family Worship. The latter was preceded by the anonymous *Familie Exercise, or The Service of God in Families* (Edinburgh: Robert Bryson, 1641), perhaps composed by Alexander Henderson. It was adopted by the Scottish church in 1647. Both the Directory for the Public Worship of God and the Directory for Family Worship laid the foundation for the American Presbyterian Directory for Worship (1788); see Stanley R.

These documents, collectively known as the Westminster Standards, have enjoyed an unusual divine blessing. The Westminster Assembly's work has directed an international movement of English-speaking Reformed Christianity for some 370 years. Benjamin Warfield said that the Westminster Standards are the "crystallization of the very essence of evangelical religion." In terms of theology, they are "the richest and most precise and best guarded statement possessed by man, of all that enters into evangelical religion and of all that must be safeguarded if evangelical religion is to persist in the world"; and in terms of godliness, they are "the very expressed essence of vital religion."[2]

In this chapter, we give our attention to one standard in particular: the Directory for the Public Worship of God.[3] The directory was drafted by a subcommittee of four Scottish commissioners and five English divines, one of whom was a Scot by birth. It was completed on December 27, 1644, making it the first document produced by the assembly. In early 1645, it was adopted successively by the English Parliament, the Scottish church's General Assembly, and the Scottish Parliament. On April 17, 1645, the English Parliament made the directory the official guide for public worship instead of the Book of Common Prayer.[4] This change was swept away by the restoration of the monarchy in 1660 and the Act of Uniformity in 1662. But in the 1690s, the directory again rose in influence among English Nonconformists as a guide to simple, biblical worship.[5]

Hall, "The American Presbyterian 'Directory for Worship': History of a Liturgical Strategy" (PhD diss., University of Notre Dame, 1990), 80–83.

2. Benjamin B. Warfield, *The Significance of the Westminster Standards as a Creed* (New York: Scribner, 1898), 36.

3. On the Directory for the Public Worship of God, see Ian Breward, ed., *The Westminster Directory: Being a Directory for the Publique Worship of God in the Three Kingdomes* (Bramcote, UK: Grove Books, 1980); J. A. Caiger, "Preaching—Puritan and Reformed," in *Puritan Papers: Volume Two, 1960–1962*, ed. J. I. Packer (Phillipsburg, NJ: P&R, 2001); Alan Clifford, "The Westminster Directory of Public Worship (1645)," in *The Reformation of Worship* (N.p.: Westminster Conference, 1989), 53–75; Mark Dever and Sinclair B. Ferguson, *The Westminster Directory of Public Worship* (Fearn, Ross-shire, Scotland: Christian Heritage, 2008); Hall, "The American Presbyterian 'Directory for Worship,'" 31–80; "The Westminster Directory and Reform of Worship," in *Calvin Studies VIII: The Westminster Confession in Current Thought*, ed. John H. Leith, Colloquium on Calvin Studies (Davidson, NC: Davidson College, 1996), 91–105; Thomas Leishman, *The Westminster Directory.* Edited, with an Introduction and Notes by T. Leishman (Edinburgh: Blackwood and Sons, 1901); Frederick W. McNally, "The Westminster Directory: Its Origin and Significance" (PhD diss., University of Edinburgh, 1958); Richard A. Muller and Rowland S. Ward, *Scripture and Worship: Biblical Interpretation and the Directory for Public Worship* (Phillipsburg, NJ: P&R, 2007); Iain H. Murray, "The Directory for Public Worship," in *To Glorify and Enjoy God: A Commemoration of the 350th Anniversary of the Westminster Assembly*, ed. John L. Carson and David W. Hall (Edinburgh: Banner of Truth, 1994), 169–91.

4. More importantly, in terms of subsequent history, it was adopted as the liturgical manual of the Church of Scotland, and from there it went out over the whole world.

5. Muller and Ward, *Scripture and Worship*, 90–92.

Zeal for Biblical, Spiritual Worship

It is striking that in the midst of civil war and great theological upheaval, the Westminster divines gave priority to the matter of worship before writing the confession and catechisms. They invested more than seventy sessions, plus many subcommittee meetings, in writing this short directory.[6] However, worship had always stood at the center of the Reformation. Iain Murray writes, "According to the Reformers and the Puritans, the message of Christianity is not simply about how man is to be saved, it is about how God is *glorified* in man's salvation. . . . 'The worship of God,' says Calvin, 'is to be preferred to the safety of men and angels.'"[7]

The foundational concern of the Reformers and Puritans was that worship be directed by Scripture alone—God's will and not the inventions of men (Matt. 15:9). The directory says in its preface, "Wherein our care hath been to hold forth such things as are of divine institution in every ordinance; and other things we have endeavoured to set forth according to the rules of Christian prudence, agreeable to the general rules of the word of God."[8] Thus, our worship is always a response to God's Word. We must bring to the holy God only those things that he has commanded, or we presume and trespass against his holiness. As the Westminster Confession (21.1) says, "The acceptable way of worshipping the true God is instituted by Himself, and so limited by His own revealed will, that He may not be worshipped according to the imaginations and devices of men, or the suggestions of Satan, under any visible representation, or any other way not prescribed in the holy Scripture."[9]

The centrality of the Word in worship also appears in the ample instructions the Directory for the Public Worship of God gives for preaching. Stanley Hall says that in this scheme, preaching is "the unifying center of worship."[10] Though the directory covers fifteen topics, more than a tenth of its substance is devoted to "the Preaching of the Word." Only the pastoral prayer before the sermon receives more attention, and that section consists of a lengthy sample prayer. In the order of worship, the directory places preaching after the call to worship, an opening

---

6. Hall, "The Westminster Directory and Reform of Worship," 91.
7. Murray, "The Directory for Public Worship," 172.
8. "The Directory for the Public Worship of God," in *Westminster Confession of Faith*, 374; see Murray, "The Directory for Public Worship," 176–78; Muller and Ward, "Scripture and Worship," 96–98.
9. "Confession of Faith," in *Westminster Confession of Faith*, 89–90. The confession cites Deut. 12:32; Matt. 15:9; Acts 17:25; Matt. 4:9; Deut. 4:15–20; Ex. 20:4–6; Col. 2:23.
10. Hall, "The Westminster Directory and Reform of Worship," 98.

prayer for God's help and blessing, consecutive Scripture readings from the Old and New Testaments,[11] the singing of a psalm, and the offering of a substantial prayer by the pastor. After the sermon comes another prayer, the singing of another psalm, and, as needed, the administration of the sacraments, concluding with the benediction. All these directions for public worship are rich in biblical truth and wisdom, but I will focus on preaching.

Still, I would be remiss if I passed by the long prayer before the sermon, for it reveals the assembly's profound sense of the preacher's dependence on the Lord. The sermon is wrapped in prayer. Preaching does not take place until the minister has publicly confessed sins against God and the sufficiency of Christ as sacrifice and intercessor. He asks God for the outpouring of the Holy Spirit. Indeed, he prays not just for his own congregation, but for the evangelization of all nations and for divine blessing on rulers and authorities. With longing and desire, he petitions the throne of grace for "fellowship with God" and "grace and effectual assistance for the sanctification of his holy sabbath, the Lord's day, in all the duties thereof."[12]

He then particularly seeks assistance for the preaching and hearing of the Word. Confessing that "we have been unprofitable hearers in times past, and now cannot of ourselves receive, as we should, the deep things of God," he asks that God would "pour out the Spirit of grace" so that they will know Christ, treasure him above all things, and long for the joys of being with him in heaven. He asks for God's special assistance to "his servant," that the preacher will give to each hearer his portion of the Word of life "with wisdom, fidelity, zeal . . . in evidence and demonstration of the Spirit and power." He intercedes for the hearers of the Word, that God will "circumcise" their ears and hearts, and make them good soil to receive the Word and to bear fruit in every good work.[13]

Clearly the Westminster divines saw preaching not merely as a human activity, but as a work of God through man, and therefore a work requiring preparation through humble, fervent prayer. Now we come to consider what kind of preaching they expected to follow such prayer.

---

11. Hall notes that the Scripture readings are disconnected from the text of the sermon, perhaps because the reading of Scripture was considered a distinct ordinance from its preaching. Hall, "The Westminster Directory and Reform of Worship," 98.

12. "The Directory for the Public Worship of God," in *Westminster Confession of Faith*, 376–78.

13. "The Directory for the Public Worship of God," in *Westminster Confession of Faith*, 378–79.

Westminster's Directions for Preaching

The divines begin their guidelines for preaching with an impressive statement drawn from the Scriptures: "Preaching of the word being the power of God unto salvation, one of the greatest and most excellent works belonging to the ministry of the gospel, should be so performed that the workman needs not be ashamed but may save himself and those that hear him."[14]

In short scope, the directory lays down a remarkable set of principles for the public proclamation of God's Word. We may classify what follows in the directory as (1) preparation for preaching, (2) introduction in preaching, (3) instruction in preaching, (4) application in preaching, (5) adaptation in preaching, (6) dedication of the preacher, and (7) cooperation among preachers and teachers.[15] Let us consider each of these aspects of preaching.

Preparation for Preaching

Before the sermon is prepared, the man must be prepared. The directory lists gifts that qualify a man for the weighty task of preaching, beginning with knowledge of Greek and Hebrew, of the arts and sciences as "handmaids unto divinity," and of "the whole body of theology," what today we would call systematic theology. J. A. Caiger comments on the last: "Notice this characteristically Puritan view of the counsel of God as a body of divinity, with all its parts properly fashioned, proportioned, and related. The minister of the Gospel must be able to see it whole."[16] "But most of all," the directory insists, the preacher must be knowledgeable "in the Holy Scriptures, having his senses and heart exercised in them above the common sort of believers." Such knowledge must come with "the illumination of God's Spirit, and other gifts of edification," that is, spiritual gifts to communicate God's truth in public ministry.

The Directory for the Public Worship of God here refers to "the rules for ordination." They were quite demanding of ministerial candidates. In the Form of Presbyterial Church Government, published the same year as the directory, we read that a candidate for ordination must be required by the presbytery to read from the Greek and Hebrew Scriptures, trans-

---

14. "The Directory for the Public Worship of God," in *Westminster Confession of Faith*, 379; see Rom. 1:16; 2 Tim. 2:15; 1 Tim. 4:16.

15. "The Directory for the Public Worship of God," in *Westminster Confession of Faith*, 379–81. All further quotes from the preaching section in the directory are from these three pages.

16. Caiger, "Preaching—Puritan and Reformed," 167.

late a portion into Latin, and perhaps show his proficiency in logic and philosophy. He must demonstrate a familiarity with the major writers in theology, be able to explain orthodox doctrine and to refute contemporary errors, exegete a text of Scripture, answer cases of conscience (questions about assurance and ethics), and know the chronology of biblical history and the history of Christianity. In addition to preaching before the people, he must also give a discourse in Latin to the presbytery on some doctrine assigned to him.[17] (In the seventeenth century, Latin was the international official language of the ministry, schools and universities, academic writing, the sciences, and government.[18])

Later, the candidate for ordination must be examined before the congregation about his faith in Christ, his Reformed beliefs according to the Scriptures, his sincerity and diligence for "praying, reading, meditation, preaching, ministering the sacraments, discipline, and doing all ministerial duties," his zeal and faithfulness for both truth and unity, his care that he and his family be examples to the flock, his humble submission to correction, and his resolve to fulfill his calling regardless of "trouble and persecution."[19] Academically and spiritually, these are rigorous demands for a disciplined, gifted man suitable for a high calling.

The directory says that the man of God must not rest on his training, however, but continue in "reading and studying of the word" and "seek by prayer, and an humble heart" further knowledge and illumination in his private preparations. A preacher must always be a student with the Bible as his textbook and the Spirit as his Teacher. The public prayers of the minister for the Spirit's assistance must be undergirded by his private prayers.

Each sermon must be the preaching of a text of Scripture. The preacher may select his Scripture text topically, to speak to some doctrine or special occasion, or by preaching through a chapter or book of the Bible. The directory does not mandate either method, but gives the preacher freedom to do "as he shall see fit." We note here that the minister has liberty about the subjects and series on which he preaches. Yet, as Caiger observes, "it is noteworthy that preaching for some special occasion still calls for an exposition of Scripture."[20]

This brings us now to consider the content of the sermon itself. The directory speaks to it in terms of introduction, instruction, and application.

---

17. "The Form of Presbyterial Church Government," in *Westminster Confession of Faith*, 413.
18. Latin was the official language of government documents in England from 1066 to 1733.
19. "The Form of Presbyterial Church Government," in *Westminster Confession of Faith*, 414.
20. Caiger, "Preaching—Puritan and Reformed," 168.

Introduction in Preaching

The directory does not approve of a long, complicated introduction, but calls for a short and clear introduction focused on the Scripture text. The minister can develop his introduction out of the text itself, its context, a parallel text, or the general teaching of Scripture. In other words, it must be a biblical introduction to a biblical text. I might add that it can also be helpful to lead the hearers to the text by starting with a contemporary problem or situation. But the assembly encourages the preacher to start immediately in the Bible even with the introduction.

The preacher should present the contents of the text to his hearers, either by a summary if it is long (e.g., a historical narrative or a parable) or a paraphrase if it is short. He should highlight the "scope" of the text, that is, its purpose in the context, or what end the writer has in view. Then he should tell the congregation the main points of doctrine found in it. Making too many divisions of the text or using "obscure terms" only makes it hard for the congregation to understand and remember all the divisions and terms. This introduction sets the stage for the minister to proclaim the teachings of that portion of Scripture.

Instruction in Preaching

The backbone of preaching is drawing out doctrines from the Bible. Each doctrine on which a minister preaches must pass three tests. First, it must be "the truth of God," that is, the teaching of Holy Scripture. Second, it must be "grounded on [a] text, that the hearers may discern how God teacheth it from thence." Even topical preaching must be expository in that every doctrine must stand upon a text that clearly teaches it. Third, it must be one of "those doctrines which are principally intended, and make most for the edification of the hearers." In other words, the preacher must let the text of Scripture and the needs of the people set the agenda for the sermon. This guideline stops the preacher from pro-claiming a doctrine that is only tangentially related to the Scripture text; he must preach the main thrust. It also guards him against preaching on speculative topics that might be discussed in academic circles but are ir-relevant to the spiritual needs of the congregation.

The directory says, "The doctrine is to be expressed in plain terms." The preacher should explain things that might not be clear. If the doc-trine is not obviously stated in the text but is deduced from it, then the preacher must convincingly show how it comes from the text. The goal is that the listeners may be sure that this doctrine is the point of the Scripture text and that their consciences may embrace it as God's authoritative message to them.

After stating the doctrine as rooted in the text, the preacher should then develop it so that it may both fill the mind and grasp the heart. The divines suggest a number of tools for doing this. It might involve opening up "parallel places of scripture" that are "plain and pertinent" in order to confirm the truth in view. The divines wisely say that it is better to have a few confirming texts that speak directly and clearly to the question than to have many texts that only dance around it. Opening up the doctrine may require making "arguments or reasons" that are "solid" and "convincing." The preacher can use "illustrations, of what kind soever" as are "full of light" and "convey the truth into the hearer's heart with spiritual delight." Illustrations should not merely entertain, but act as humble servants carrying delicious spiritual food to the table where the guests are seated. He may also find it helpful to address "any doubt" arising from an apparent contradiction in Scripture, a conflict with human reason, or anything obnoxious to human prejudice. Answering objections can be very helpful, but it can also turn into an endless list of arguments that does not edify. One must use moderation and discernment in addressing such matters.

The Puritans excelled in preaching doctrine, making each sermon an exploration in biblical truth. However, in developing a doctrine, one can lose sight of the Scripture text. It is safer to stick close to the text and develop the main points of the sermon out of the text itself. Again, this allows Scripture to set the agenda for preaching. At times, the Puritans did this well, as with William Perkins's *Commentary on Galatians* or Thomas Manton's sermons on James. But sometimes their preaching lost its tight connection to a text of Scripture, such as when Thomas Hooker preached a very long series on Acts 2:37, printed as several hundred pages in the tenth book of his *Application of Redemption*. For a theological treatise on a particular theme, that is fine, but such is often not the preaching of Scripture in a balanced way.

Application in Preaching

The directory advises, "He is not to rest in general doctrine, although never so much cleared and confirmed, but to bring it home to special use, by application to his hearers." This is a difficult work, "requiring much prudence, zeal, and meditation." The preacher's flesh shrinks from spiritual applications, and fallen men find applied preaching offensive. But the Holy Spirit has often used preaching with application to save sinners and glorify God. Therefore, "he is to endeavour to perform it in such a manner, that his auditors [listeners] may feel the word of God to be quick and powerful, and a discerner of the thoughts and intents of the heart."[21]

Application occupies 40 percent of the directory's treatment of preaching, so clearly it is a predominant concern in the Westminster method. The assembly offers six forms of application or "uses" of the text:

1. *Instruction or Information.* The preacher may deduce some logical "consequence from his doctrine" and "confirm it by a few firm arguments." This helps the congregation to see each doctrine as a part of the whole counsel of God. It reinforces one truth with another, and helps people to develop a unified and comprehensive perspective on all of life.

2. *Confutation of False Doctrines.* The divines warn against raising "an old heresy from the grave" or unnecessarily exposing people to evil. "But," they say, "if the people be in danger of an error, he is to confute it soundly, and endeavor to satisfy their judgments and conscience against all objections." Mark Dever writes, "Preachers are not only encouraged to take on controversial issues; they are required to do so in the Puritan conception of the pastorate."[22]

3. *Exhortation to Duties.* In addition to pressing God's commands upon his hearers, the preacher should explain "the means that help in the performance of them." In other words, he should command them what to do and teach them how to do it through Christ and the instruments by which Christ gives us grace. Sinclair Ferguson says: "'Duty' is a much misunderstood term in our modern culture and carries with it the aroma of legalism. In contrast the Puritan minister realised that grace always leads to and commands duties; he was a Paulinist in this sense—all his imperatives were rooted in the indicatives of grace; but every indicative of grace gave rise in his preaching to an imperative of grace-filled obedience."[23]

4. *Public Admonition.* The minister is to preach against specific sins, which requires "special wisdom." The minister should expose "the nature and greatness of the sin, with the misery attending it." He should

---

21. See Heb. 4:12.
22. Dever, "Preaching Like the Puritans," in *Westminster Directory of Public Worship*, 45.
23. Ferguson, "Puritans: Ministers of the World," in *Westminster Directory of Public Worship*, 29.

help people to see how this temptation captures people, and the danger it presents to them. And he should show them "the remedies and best way to avoid it."

5. *Application of Comfort.* He may give comfort in general "or particularly against some special troubles or terrors." Here the pastor must be a skillful physician of the soul, learning from Scripture and experience about the afflictions of the heart. He must not only match comfort to affliction, but also answer "such objections as a troubled heart and afflicted spirit may suggest to the contrary." Guilty sinners resist God's comforts and need help to embrace them.

6. *Trial, to Help People Examine Themselves.* This form of application leads people to ask themselves: Have I attained to this grace? Have I performed this duty? Am I guilty of that sin? Am I in danger of that judgment? Can I rightfully claim these consolations? This use of examination, in the hands of a wise preacher well-studied in the Scriptures, makes application profitable. It moves each listener from abstractly considering the truth to bringing it home to his own condition. As a result, by the Spirit's grace, the hearers are stirred to obedience, humbled for sin, distressed by their danger, or strengthened with comfort, as is appropriate for them.

These applications are linked by logic and inference to the doctrine. They are structured in the following manner. Since the doctrine drawn from the text is true, the preacher must urge his hearers to (1) be sure of additional truths that this truth implies; (2) abjure the following errors that this truth contradicts; (3) do whatever good things that this truth requires; (4) stop doing or avoid doing whatever bad things that this truth forbids; (5) take to themselves the encouragement that this truth offers; and (6) ask themselves where they stand spiritually in the light of this truth and how far they are resolved to live by it.

Clearly the Westminster Assembly had in mind a sermon in which a large chunk of time is given to application. Even in an hour-long sermon, such as the Puritans were accustomed to preach, developing two or three kinds of application as outlined above would occupy a significant portion of the message.

Adaptation in Preaching

The directory offers a detailed and demanding set of guidelines for preaching biblical doctrine and making spiritual application. But at this point, the assembly wisely inserts a note of flexibility. The preacher should not follow this method rigidly, but adapt it so as to best feed his flock.

If a minister derives three doctrines from a text, addresses each one to all of Perkins's seven categories of listeners (see pp. 170–71), and applies it all according to the six "uses" of the text (see pp. 198–99), then each sermon would have 126 applications. Therefore, the directory says, the preacher should not develop "every doctrine which lies in his text." He should also be selective in his applications based on personal knowledge of the congregation gained "by his residence and conversing with his flock." Here we see the essential connection between a preaching ministry and a relational ministry. How can the preacher know what is "most needful and seasonable" for the flock if he does not know them? Above all, he must major on those applications "such as may most draw their souls to Christ, the fountain of light, holiness, and comfort." Believing that Christ is the center of the Bible and the answer to our needs, the preacher must labor in his applications to offer men the Bread of Life.

The directory says, "This method is not prescribed as necessary for every man, or upon every text." The divines recognize the individuality of each servant of Christ and the freedom of Christians where God's Word does not lay down laws. As Ferguson writes, "Homiletical cloning was not their purpose any more than it should be ours."[24] But their method of instruction and application, the divines say, is "found by experience to be very much blessed of God, and very helpful for the people's understandings and memories." Therefore, they commend it.

Even more important than the method of preaching is the man who preaches. He is "the servant of Christ," and this fact leads the divines next to outline the qualities of a godly ministry.

Dedication of the Preacher

The Westminster divines state seven characteristics that should mark the "whole ministry" of a godly preacher. He must serve Christ:

1. *Painfully, Not Negligently.* In the divines' parlance, *painful* means "with labor, toil, and hard work." Today we might say *painstakingly.* They have no tolerance for a lazy minister or for one who neglects his true calling in the Word and prayer to attend to other pursuits. This work

---

24. Ferguson, "Puritans: Ministers of the World," in *Westminster Directory of Public Worship*, 27.

ethic is clear from the standards they set for a minister, which we saw earlier under "Preparation for Preaching" (see pp. 194–95).

2. *Plainly*. He must speak the truth with simplicity, clarity, and directness, so that even the uneducated will understand. The Puritans see this not merely as an educational goal but as a spiritual law exemplified by the apostle Paul, whose words they cite in support of this rule, "delivering the truth not in the enticing words of man's wisdom, but in demonstration of the Spirit and of power, lest the cross of Christ should be made of none effect."[25] This requires the preacher to avoid "unprofitable use" of foreign languages in the pulpit, though he must use Hebrew, Greek, and Latin in the study. He must not follow the style of preaching popular in aristocratic circles, displaying his cleverness by playing artistic games with words, meanings, and sounds. Quotations of other writers should be "sparingly" cited, whoever they may be.

Joseph Pipa notes that the directory takes a cautious and somewhat controversial step in allowing a limited use of foreign words and quotations in the sermon. Perkins had permitted some quotations but had forbidden foreign words. Some of the committee members working on the directory wanted to forbid quotations, arguing that listeners should base their faith on the Scriptures, not the authority of a man. Some also argued that there is nothing necessary or edifying about using Hebrew, Greek, or Latin words in the sermon. Samuel Rutherford reputedly said that just as we cook soup in a big pot but serve it in little bowls, so the preacher should study with human scholarship but preach with utter simplicity. Others supported a limited use of quotations and the ancient languages. They argued that quotations help people to see that the minister is not preaching a new idea or his own opinion. Foreign words and phrases may help the sermon to grasp the minds of the educated. The minister is not shackled by the requirement that every word of the sermon should be helpful to every hearer. In the end, the divines compromised by saying that the preacher should avoid "unprofitable use of foreign tongues" and should quote only "sparingly" from the works of mere men.[26]

3. *Faithfully*. The divines call on the minister to preach from pure motives. He should seek Christ's glory and the salvation and sanctification of men, not "his own gain or glory." He must preach the whole counsel

---

25. See 1 Cor. 1:17; 2:1–5.
26. Joseph A. Pipa Jr., "William Perkins and the Development of Puritan Preaching" (PhD diss., Westminster Theological Seminary, 1985), 203–5.

of God, "keeping nothing back which may promote these holy ends." He should not show partiality in the pulpit, but give each person "his own portion," neither ignoring the poor and weak nor sparing the great from his rebukes. In other words, he must preach as a servant of Christ and not as a man pleaser (Gal. 1:10).

4. *Wisely.* Preaching requires skill in crafting both doctrine and application so that it is "most likely to prevail." This skill or tact is especially crucial when reproving sin. Whether preparing to teach, to reprove, to correct, or to train in righteousness, the minister should not only study the Bible but also his audience. He constantly asks: "What will woo them? What will win them?"

Wisdom also shows a minister how to preach boldly but not disrespectfully, or in "passion or bitterness." So we see that on the one hand, the Puritan preacher should not be a man pleaser, and yet in the fear of God, he must still honor all men and especially all in authority. He must preach against sin, yet avoid preaching from his own sinful anger or frustration.

5. *Gravely.* In its older sense, the term *gravity* refers to seriousness or solemnity appropriate to the weightiness of a matter, as opposed to levity that treats matters as light or trifling. There is a divine authority to the biblical message, and so there should be a dignity to the messenger. He must not be a court jester, comedian, or entertainer, but should shun "all such gesture, voice, and expressions" as may provoke people to despise his authority. Later, the Westminster divines say in the Larger Catechism (Q. 112) that the Third Commandment requires all men to handle "the name of God, his titles, attributes, ordinances, the word, sacraments, prayer," and other means of knowing him "holily and reverently."[27] Certainly this commandment binds ministers to special reverence, for their constant trade, so to speak, is in the holy things of God.

6. *Affectionately.* The people should be able to see that everything their minister does comes from "his godly zeal, and hearty desire to do them good." It is a beautiful thing if the people of a church, though they may disagree with their minister over certain matters, still can say: "I know that my minister loves me. He really wants to do me good, especially eternal good." Such is the character of the Good Shepherd, and it is no accident that his sheep hear his voice and follow him (John 10).

---

27. "The Larger Catechism," in *Westminster Confession of Faith*, 198–99.

7. *Earnestly.* Both in public and in private, the preacher must serve with eager desire and a sincere spirit: "as taught of God, and persuaded in his own heart, that all that he teacheth is the truth of Christ; and walking before his flock, as an example to them."

The Westminster Assembly had high standards for preachers, but it also had great expectations of what the ministry of such men can accomplish: "So shall the doctrine of truth be preserved uncorrupt, many souls converted and built up, and himself receive manifold comforts of his labours even in this life, and afterward the crown of glory laid up for him in the world to come."

Cooperation among Preachers and Teachers

In a closing note, the directory encourages ministers serving in the same congregation to work out arrangements so that each can use his strengths to the utmost profit. It recognizes that some men are more gifted in "doctrine" and others in "exhortation." Where more than one preacher serves a church, they should come to an agreement as to how best to use their gifts.

The Form of Presbyterial Church Government expands on this concept:

> The Lord having given different gifts, and divers exercises according to these gifts, in the ministry of the word; though these different gifts may meet in, and accordingly be exercised by, one and the same minister; yet, where be several ministers in the same congregation, they may be designed to several employments, according to the different gifts in which each of them doth most excel. And he that doth more excel in exposition of scripture, in teaching sound doctrine, and in convincing gainsayers [polemics], than he doth in application, and is accordingly employed therein, may be called a teacher, or doctor. . . . Nevertheless, where is but one minister in a particular congregation, he is to perform, as far as he is able, the whole work of the ministry.[28]

With these words, the divines set up a partnership between "pastors and teachers" so that they might labor together "for the edifying of the body of Christ" (Eph. 4:11–12). While we should never separate teaching from exhortation (2 Tim. 4:2), it is wise to recognize the Spirit's

---

28. "The Form of Presbyterial Church Government," in *Westminster Confession of Faith*, 401–2.

will in gifting men in different ways (1 Cor. 12:11). Each must have his place to serve.

Conclusion

The Westminster Assembly is remembered for passing on to subsequent generations brilliant statements of biblical, Reformed Christianity. We have seen in this chapter that the divines also captured, in comparatively few words, much wisdom about Reformed experiential preaching. They had a high view of preaching because they had a high view of the Word of God. Through the Word, the Spirit applies Christ to the soul, thus building a living church of elect sinners called to salvation. And the divines recognized that in the mystery of God's will, preaching holds the preeminent place among the various ways God's Word comes to men.

They wrote in the Shorter Catechism (Q. 90), "The Spirit of God maketh the reading, *but especially the preaching of the word*, an effectual means of convincing and converting sinners, and of building them up in holiness and comfort, through faith, unto salvation."[29] For this reason, they also called upon men to cherish preaching. The Larger Catechism (Q. 160) says, "It is required of those that hear the word preached, that they attend upon it with diligence, preparation, and prayer; examine what they hear by the scriptures; receive the truth with faith, love, meekness, and readiness of mind, as the word of God; meditate, and confer of it; hide it in their hearts, and bring forth the fruit of it in their lives."[30]

May God grant us more preachers and more listeners like those described by the Westminster Assembly, that the church may flourish through the faithful preaching and the diligent hearing of the Word of God.

---

29. "The Shorter Catechism," in *Westminster Confession of Faith*, 312, emphasis added.
30. "The Larger Catechism," in *Westminster Confession of Faith*, 253.

12

Puritan Preachers:
Goodwin and Shepard

The Puritans preached doctrinal truth from the Scriptures, but they did more. They preached the truth with hearts aflame. John Rogers (c. 1572–1636) preached in Dedham with such zeal that people used to say, "Come, let us go to Dedham to get a little fire."[1] Sidrach Simpson (c. 1600–1655) wrote, "Some books are like a frosty day, clear, but dry and cold," but not Rogers—he "was a burning and shining light, having a heart inflamed with love to Christ, truth, and the souls of men; his words were as sparks of fire."[2] One day, Thomas Goodwin, then a young student at Cambridge, rode up to Dedham to hear Rogers preach. Later, Goodwin recounted his experience to John Howe (1630–1705), who wrote:

> And in that sermon he [Rogers] falls into an expostulation with the people about their neglect of the Bible: (I am afraid it is more neglected in our days): he personates God to the people, telling them, "Well, I have trusted you so long with my Bible: you have slighted it, it lies in such and such houses all covered with dust and cobwebs: you care not to look into it. Do you use my Bible so? Well, you shall have my Bible no longer." And he takes up the Bible from his cushion, and

1. Quoted in Oliver Heywood, "Life of Rev. J. Angier," in *The Whole Works of the Rev. Oliver Heywood* (Edinburgh: by John Vint for F. Westley, et al., 1827), 1:521.
2. Sidrach Simpson, "To the Reader," in John Rogers, *A Godly and Fruitful Exposition Upon All the First Epistle of Peter* (London: by John Field, 1650).

seemed as if he were going away with it and carrying it from them; but immediately turns again and personates the people to God, falls down on his knees, cries and pleads most earnestly, "Lord, whatsoever thou dost to us, take not thy Bible from us: kill our children, burn our houses, destroy our goods; only spare us thy Bible, only take not away thy Bible." And then he personates God again to the people; "Say you so? Well, I will try you a while longer; and here is my Bible for you, I will see how you will use it, whether you will love it more, whether you will value it more, whether you will observe it more, whether you will practice it more, and live more according to it." But by these actions (as the doctor [Goodwin] told me) he put all the congregation into so strange a posture that he never saw any congregation in his life; the place was a mere Bochim [Judg. 2:4–5], the people generally (as it were) deluged with their own tears: and he told me that he himself, when he got out and was to take horse again to be gone, he was fain to hang a quarter of an hour upon the neck of his horse weeping, before he had power to mount; so strange an impression was there upon him, and generally upon the people, upon having been thus expostulated with for the neglect of the Bible.[3]

That student who was overcome by weeping, Goodwin, would go on to become a mighty preacher of the Word himself. In this chapter, we will look at the ministries of Goodwin and Thomas Shepard, learn from their examples, and pray to "get a little fire" for our own preaching.

Thomas Goodwin

Goodwin was born on October 5, 1600, in Rollesby, near Yarmouth in Norfolk, an area known for Puritan resistance to government persecution.[4] This climate influenced Goodwin's God-fearing parents, Richard

---

3. John Howe, "The Principles of the Oracles of God," in *The Works of the Rev. John Howe* (New York: John P. Haven, 1838), 2:1085.

4. On Goodwin, see Paul Blackham, "The Pneumatology of Thomas Goodwin" (PhD diss., University of London, 1995); John Brown, *Puritan Preaching in England: A Study of Past and Present* (New York: C. Scribner's Sons, 1900); Paul E. Brown, "The Principle of the Covenant in the Theology of Thomas Goodwin" (PhD diss., Drew University, 1950); Choon-Gill Chae, "Thomas Goodwin's Doctrine of the Sealing of the Holy Spirit: Historical, Biblical, and Systematic-Theological Analysis" (ThM thesis, Toronto Baptist Seminary, 2010); Gordon D. Crompton, "The Life and Theology of Thomas Goodwin, D.D." (ThM thesis, Greenville Theological Seminary, 1997); Stanley Fienberg, "Thomas Goodwin: Puritan Pastor and Independent Divine" (PhD diss., University of Chicago, 1974); Michael Scott Horton, "Christ Set Forth: Thomas Goodwin and the Puritan Doctrine of Assurance, 1600–1680" (PhD diss., Wycliffe Hall, Oxford and Coventry College, 1996); Mark Jones, "Why Heaven Kissed Earth: The Christology of Thomas Goodwin (1600–1680)" (PhD diss., University of Leiden, 2009); Thomas M. Lawrence, *Transmission and*

and Catherine Goodwin. They did their best to train their son to become a minister through personal example, as well as by providing him with the best classical education offered by local schools. As a child, Goodwin experienced both convictions of sin and flashes of joy about the things of God.

By age thirteen, Goodwin was enrolled at Christ's College, Cambridge. The memory of William Perkins still permeated Cambridge, and Richard Sibbes regularly preached at Holy Trinity Church. But when Goodwin's tutor prevented him from receiving Communion, deeming him too young and immature to take the sacrament, he was offended and stopped attending Sibbes's sermons and lectures, ceased praying, and stopped reading the Scriptures and Puritan literature. He set his heart on becoming a popular preacher so as to be accepted by many in the Church of England who belittled Puritan preaching.

Goodwin graduated with a BA from Christ's College in 1617. In 1619, he continued his studies at St. Catherine's Hall in Cambridge, graduated with an MA in 1620, and was elected a fellow and lecturer there. Other fellows who served there were John Arrowsmith, William Spurstowe, and William Strong; all would one day work alongside Goodwin in the Westminster Assembly. These men, reinforced by the preaching of Sibbes and John Preston, pressed upon Goodwin's conscience his need to turn aside from empty displays of pulpit rhetoric and follow Christ. On October 2, 1620, just before his twentieth birthday, he was converted through the preaching of Thomas Bainbridge on repentance. In meditation after the sermon, the words of Ezekiel 16:6 carried spiritual life into his soul: "Live; yea, I said unto thee . . . Live." He wrestled with doubts from 1620 to 1627, but finally came to solid assurance through the counsel of a godly minister.

Shortly before this time, in 1625, Goodwin was licensed as a preacher. The following year, he helped bring Sibbes to St. Catherine's Hall as master. In 1628, Goodwin was appointed lecturer at Holy Trinity Church, succeeding Sibbes and Preston at age twenty-seven. From 1632 to 1634, Goodwin served as vicar of the church. Many people, including

Transformation: Thomas Goodwin and the Puritan Project, 1600–1704 (Cambridge: University of Cambridge, 2002); Alexander McNally, "Some Aspects of Thomas Goodwin's Doctrine of Assurance" (ThM thesis, Westminster Theological Seminary, 1972); Harry Lee Poe, "Evangelistic Fervency among the Puritans in Stuart England, 1603–1688" (PhD diss., Southern Baptist Theological Seminary, 1982); Alexander Whyte, *The Spiritual Life: The Teaching of Thomas Goodwin as Received and Reissued* (London: Oliphants, 1918); Chong-ch'on Won, "Communion with Christ: An Exposition and Comparison of the Doctrine of Union and Communion with Christ in Calvin and the English Puritans" (PhD diss., Westminster Theological Seminary, 1989).

several who later became influential Puritan pastors, were converted under Goodwin's preaching and lecturing at Cambridge. Then Goodwin was forced to resign his offices because he was unwilling to submit to Archbishop of Canterbury William Laud's articles of conformity. He left Cambridge.

During the mid-1630s, Goodwin adopted Independent principles of church government, largely under the influence of John Cotton. From 1634 to 1639, he was a Separatist preacher in London. In 1639, because of increasing restrictions against preaching, with threats of fines and imprisonment, Goodwin took refuge in the Netherlands. He worked in Arnhem with other well-known Independent ministers, serving a church of more than a hundred people who had fled from Laud's persecution.

In 1641, after Laud was impeached, Goodwin responded to Parliament's invitation to Nonconformists to return to England. Goodwin preached before Parliament on April 27, 1642. He was subsequently appointed a member of the Westminster Assembly, where he frequently spoke as a representative of Independency as distinct from Presbyterianism.

In 1650, Goodwin became president of Magdalen College, Oxford, and John Owen became dean of Christ Church. Even the Anglican Lord Clarendon had to admit that at the time the university "yielded a harvest of extraordinary good and sound knowledge in all parts of learning."[5] Philip Henry (1631–1696), father of Matthew Henry, the famous Bible commentator, looked back on his studies at Oxford in those days with memories of the serious godliness and devotion to prayer practiced at Magdalen College in Goodwin's time.[6]

The 1650s were busy and fruitful years for Goodwin. He started an Independent church; was awarded a doctorate in divinity from Oxford; sat on various boards examining men for ministry; helped to edit the Savoy Declaration of Faith (1658), a Congregationalist modification of the Westminster Confession; and ministered personally to Lord Protector Oliver Cromwell.

With the accession of Charles II in 1660 and the accompanying loss of Puritan power, Goodwin felt compelled to leave Oxford. He and most of his Independent congregation moved to London, where they started

---

5. Quoted in George C. Brodrick, *A History of the University of Oxford* (London: Longmans, Green, and Co., 1886), 150.
6. J. B Williams and Matthew Henry, *The Lives of Philip and Matthew Henry* (Edinburgh: Banner of Truth, 1974), 1:19.

another church. Despite assurances to the contrary, the new king gave his assent to strict acts of conformity. In 1662, about two thousand godly ministers were ejected from the national church. Since he was in an Independent church and held no government-appointed offices, Goodwin did not suffer from the "Great Ejection." He continued preaching through many years of persecution under Charles II. He also stayed with his London congregation through the dreaded plague, when most clergy of the established church abandoned the city. He devoted his last years to preaching, pastoral work, and writing.

Goodwin died in London at age eighty. His son wrote of his godly father: "He rejoiced in the thoughts that he was dying, and going to have a full and uninterrupted communion with God. 'I am going,' said he, 'to the three Persons, with whom I have had communion.'"[7]

Preaching the Compassionate Christ

Goodwin was a profoundly Christ-centered, affectionate preacher. A number of examples of his preaching have been preserved for us, including thirty-six sermons he preached from Ephesians 1.[8] Hughes Oliphant Old writes: "Goodwin's sermons are a hymn of praise to the love of God as it is manifested in Christ. They set forth the wonder of God's redemptive purposes. It is in this context that Goodwin sets the doctrine of predestination and develops it in doxological terms. . . . Goodwin is a marvelous exegete. His sermons are filled with tightly-stitched expositions of the Greek text."[9]

To afford the reader a taste of Goodwin's preaching, we will look at his sermon "The Heart of Christ in Heaven to Sinners on Earth."[10] John Brown (1830–1922) writes, "The purpose of his sermon was to make intensely real to the men to whom he spoke the Christ who had gone beyond the region of sight into the heavens—to make them feel that He was as closely one with them in sympathy, and personal relations of helpfulness as though they could look into His face."[11]

---

7. Thomas Goodwin, "Memoir of Thomas Goodwin, D.D.," in *The Works of Thomas Goodwin* (Grand Rapids, MI: Reformation Heritage Books, 2006), 2:lxxiv, hereafter, *Works*.
8. Goodwin, "Exposition of the First Chapter of the Epistle to the Ephesians," in *Works*, vol. 1.
9. Hughes Oliphant Old, *The Reading and Preaching of the Scriptures in the Worship of the Christian Church, Volume 4: The Age of the Reformation* (Grand Rapids, MI: Eerdmans, 1998), 288.
10. Goodwin, "The Heart of Christ in Heaven to Sinners on Earth," in *Works*, 4:93–150. This section is adapted from Joel R. Beeke, "Thomas Goodwin on Christ's Beautiful Heart," in *The Beauty and Glory of Christ* (Grand Rapids, MI: Reformation Heritage Books, 2011), 141–47.
11. Brown, *Puritan Preaching in England*, 107–8.

Goodwin centers his discussion of Christ's heavenly heart of compassion upon Hebrews 4:14–15: "Seeing then that we have a great high priest, that is passed into the heavens, Jesus the Son of God, let us hold fast our profession. For we have not an high priest which cannot be touched with the feeling of our infirmities; but was in all points tempted like as we are, yet without sin." This Scripture passage, as Goodwin sees it, contains both a problem for our faith in Christ and a solution.

Goodwin recognizes that sinful men might be put off by the words "a *great* high priest, that is passed into the *heavens*." He writes that we might think that even if Christ remembers us in heaven, "having cast off the frailties of his flesh which he had here, and having clothed his human nature with so great a glory, that he cannot now pity us, as he did when he dwelt among us here below, nor be so feelingly affected and touched with our miseries." Surely he has left behind all memories of weakness and pain.[12]

Goodwin sees this as a "great stone of stumbling which we meet with (and yet lieth unseen) in the thoughts of men in the way to faith." Christ is absent. Surely it would be better for us if we could talk with him as Mary and Peter did on earth. He was so gentle with them. "But now he is gone into a far country, and hath put on glory and immortality."[13] Christ sits as King at God's right hand in heaven. His human nature is aflame with glory. How can we approach such a King boldly? How can we expect him, in perfect power and holiness, to bear patiently with us when we are so weak, foolish, and, above all, sinful? But this same passage that speaks of Christ's exaltation also reveals his compassion.

Against this obstacle to faith, Goodwin wields the sword of the Spirit, the Word of God. Hebrews 4:15 tells us that "we have not an high priest which cannot be touched with the feeling of our infirmities." Christ's mercy is so certain that the Scriptures use a double negative to forcefully declare the positive truth: "We have *not* an high priest which *cannot* be touched."

Our infirmities stir his compassion. Goodwin argues from the context of Hebrews that "infirmities" include both our troubles and our sins. The epistle to the Hebrews addresses people facing pressure and persecution. So "infirmities" must be our earthly troubles. Yet they are also our sins. In Hebrews 5:2, we read that a high priest must be someone who "can

---

12. Goodwin, "The Heart of Christ in Heaven," in *Works*, 4:112.
13. Goodwin, "The Heart of Christ in Heaven," in *Works*, 4:95.

have compassion on the ignorant, and on them that are out of the way." Even our foolishness and sinful choices awaken Christ's compassion.[14]

Goodwin makes a comparison to drive the point home. He writes to believers, "Your very sins move him to pity more than to anger . . . even as the heart of a father is to a child that hath some loathsome disease, or as one is to a member of his body that hath the leprosy, he hates not the member, for it is his flesh, but the disease, and that provokes him to pity the part affected the more."[15] If your child becomes very sick, you don't scold him and push him away. You weep with that child and tend to his needs. So Christ responds to us with compassion despite his hatred of our sins.

Christ's compassion grows out of his personal human experience. Hebrews 4:15 says that he "was in all points tempted like as we are, yet without sin." Earlier, Hebrews 2:18 tells us, "For in that he himself hath suffered being tempted, he is able to succour [help] them that are tempted." Goodwin explains that in his days on earth, "Christ took to heart all that befell him as deeply as might be; he slighted no cross, either from God or men, but had and felt the utmost load of it. Yea, his heart was made more tender in all sorts of affections than any of ours, even as it was in love and pity; and this made him 'a man of sorrows,' and that more than any other man was or shall be."[16]

Today in heaven, Jesus in his human nature knows everything that happens to his members on earth. Jesus says to his church on earth, "I know thy works, and thy labour, and thy patience" (Rev. 2:2). This is possible because Christ's human nature has been filled with the Holy Spirit beyond measure, and the Spirit serves as Christ's eyes in all the earth (Rev. 5:6). Knowing our distress, he remembers how he felt when he faced similar miseries.[17] As the crucified Christ, he even knows the experience of the guilt of sin and the horror of facing God's wrath against sin. Although personally sinless, he bore all the sins of all his people.[18] His knowledge of our pain, along with his memory of his own pain, moves his heart to overflow with compassion.

The glorified Christ possesses glorious human tenderness. Christ sympathizes with us. That is not to say that Christ is still suffering in heaven.

---

14. Goodwin, "The Heart of Christ in Heaven," in *Works*, 4:111–12.
15. Goodwin, "The Heart of Christ in Heaven," in *Works*, 4:149.
16. Goodwin, "The Heart of Christ in Heaven," in *Works*, 4:141.
17. Goodwin, "The Heart of Christ in Heaven," in *Works*, 4:141–42.
18. Goodwin, "The Heart of Christ in Heaven," in *Works*, 4:149.

Goodwin was a very careful theologian. He understood that Christ's humiliation was completed at the cross and tomb. His exaltation has placed him far above all earthly powers. His human nature is glorified and free from all pain. How then can Christ be said to be "touched with the feeling of our infirmities"?

Goodwin insists that this is an act not of weakness but of the power of heavenly love. He writes: "And whereas it may be objected, that this were a weakness. The apostle affirms that this is his power, and a perfection and strength of love surely, in him, as the word [*able*] importeth; that is, that makes him thus able and powerful to take our miseries into his heart, though glorified, and so to be affected with them, as if he suffered with us."[19]

On the one hand, we should not think of Jesus suffering in heaven as he did on earth. Yes, he remains a man with human emotions and a human body. He is not a spirit or a ghost. However, he is no longer subject to any frailty, mortality, weariness, weeping, exhaustion, or fear as he was on this earth. His frailty has been replaced with a vastly expanded capacity and energy for the affections of love, for Christ's humanity is now an exalted humanity. Christ is God and man. As God, Christ is infinite, eternal, and unchanging. But as a man, he has been lifted up to a new level of glory in every way. Goodwin says: "For it is certain that as his knowledge was enlarged upon his entering into glory, so his human affections of love and pity are enlarged in solidity, strength, and reality. . . . 'The love of Christ,' God-man, 'passeth knowledge' (Eph. 3:19)."[20] So Christ is not being hurt by our sufferings, but his human soul responds to our sufferings with a glorious, beautiful tenderness.

Gordon Crompton summarizes Goodwin's teaching this way: "Christ, as our High Priest was not just touched with the feelings of our infirmities during His time on earth, taking only the memory of it to heaven. But now in heaven, in a glorified state, He is touched in His very feelings for us. This is by no means a weakness of any sort. Rather, this ability to feel for us is part of His power. It is a perfection and strength of love and grace."[21]

Goodwin proceeds to look at various promises of Christ's merciful heart. First he looks at promises of compassion that the Lord Jesus gave

---

19. Goodwin, "The Heart of Christ in Heaven," in *Works*, 4:112–13.
20. Goodwin, "The Heart of Christ in Heaven," in *Works*, 4:143–46.
21. Crompton, "The Life and Theology of Thomas Goodwin, D.D.," 299.

before his death. Here Goodwin dwells on John 13–17. He reminds us that this Scripture passage opens with these words: "Now before the feast of the passover, when Jesus knew that his hour was come that he should depart out of this world unto the Father, having loved his own which were in the world, he loved them unto the end" (John 13:1). When Jesus's mind was set upon his imminent exaltation to supreme glory, Goodwin observes, "his heart ran out in love towards, and was set upon, 'his own:' . . . his own, a word denoting the greatest nearness, dearness, and intimacy founded upon propriety [or ownership]."[22] It was precisely then that Jesus washed the feet of his disciples. All of this demonstrates that Christ's glorification did not diminish, but rather increased, the expressions of his love and grace for his people.

Jesus said in John 14–16 that he would ascend into heaven to secure our happiness as believers. He went to prepare a place for us. He will return like a bridegroom to bring his beloved bride to her final home. In the meantime, Christ will not leave his bride alone in the world as an orphan. He has committed her to the care of his "dearest friend," the Comforter. In Goodwin's words, Jesus told us that the Holy Spirit would comfort us with "nothing but stories of my love," for he would not speak of himself but as one sent from Christ. Meanwhile, Christ himself promised to pray for us in heaven. And he demonstrated his commitment to pray for us by interceding even then, as seen in John 17.[23]

Christ also gave assurances of his compassion *after his resurrection.* Goodwin asks, "Now when Christ came first out of the other world, from the dead, clothed with that heart and body which he was to wear in heaven, what message sends he first to them?" The answer is in John 20:17, where we read that Jesus called his disciples "my brethren" and said, "I ascend unto my Father, and your Father." What sweet words of grace to the men who had denied him and abandoned him in his darkest hour! He promised to intercede for us as a brother intercedes with his father for the rest of the family. Later, when Jesus appeared to the disciples, his first words were, "Peace be unto you" (John 20:19, 21). Even after his resurrection, Christ's heart remained full of mercy and concern for sinners.[24]

---

22. Goodwin, "The Heart of Christ in Heaven," in *Works*, 4:96–97.
23. Goodwin, "The Heart of Christ in Heaven," in *Works*, 4:98–103.
24. Goodwin, "The Heart of Christ in Heaven," in *Works*, 4:104–5.

To be sure, Christ rebuked his disciples. But for what? Luke 24:25 says, "Then he said unto them, O fools, and slow of heart to believe all that the prophets have spoken." Goodwin writes, "Only because they would not believe on him . . . he desires nothing more than to have men believe in him; and this now when glorified." When Jesus restored Peter after his fall, he commanded him, "Feed my lambs" (John 21:15). Christ demanded this of Peter as the way to show his love for Christ. Goodwin comments, "His heart runs altogether upon his lambs, upon souls to be converted."[25] Christ's glorified heart still beats for sinners.

Goodwin next presents the pledges of Christ's compassion that came *with his ascension.* When Jesus ascended into heaven, Goodwin points out, his last act on earth was to pronounce a blessing on his disciples (Luke 24:50–51). Then his first official act as the enthroned King was to pour out the Holy Spirit upon his church (Acts 2:33). Therefore, all the works of the Holy Spirit testify of Christ's present love for his church. Does a minister preach the gospel by the Holy Spirit? It is because of Christ's heart for sinners. Does the Spirit move you to pray? It is because Christ is praying for you. Does the New Testament express Christ's love for sinners? It was all written "since Christ's being in heaven, by his Spirit."[26]

Goodwin offers yet another pledge to sinners in Christ's glorious appearance to Paul on the road to Damascus. Paul explains why Jesus saved him in 1 Timothy 1:15–16: "This is a faithful saying, and worthy of all acceptation, that Christ Jesus came into the world to save sinners; of whom I am chief. Howbeit for this cause I obtained mercy, that in me first Jesus Christ might shew forth all longsuffering, for a pattern to them which should hereafter believe on him to life everlasting." Goodwin comments, "It is express, you see, to assure all sinners, unto the end of the world, of Christ's heart towards them."[27]

Goodwin's final pledge comes from Christ's last recorded words at the end of the Bible. The Spirit and the bride call out for Christ to come back to earth. Then Jesus answers: "And let him that is athirst come. And whosoever will, let him take the water of life freely" (Rev. 22:17). Goodwin writes, "They cannot desire his coming to them, so much as he desires their coming to him . . . hereby expressing how much his heart now longs after them."[28]

---

25. Goodwin, "The Heart of Christ in Heaven," in *Works*, 4:106.
26. Goodwin, "The Heart of Christ in Heaven," in *Works*, 4:107–8.
27. Goodwin, "The Heart of Christ in Heaven," in *Works*, 4:108.
28. Goodwin, "The Heart of Christ in Heaven," in *Works*, 4:109.

It should be evident from this sample of Goodwin's preaching that his sermons were exegetical and theological in content and method. Yet what is most striking is how full of feeling and experience they are, even in discussing the heavenly ministry of the exalted Christ. In this regard, they are a model for the experiential preaching of God's Word, leading the church to exclaim, "How sweet are thy words unto my taste! yea, sweeter than honey to my mouth!" (Ps. 119:103).

Thomas Shepard

Shepard was born on November 5, 1605, in Northamptonshire.[29] On that same day, British authorities foiled the "Gunpowder Plot" to blow up the House of Lords, kill King James I, and open the way for a Roman Catholic monarch to ascend the throne. Shepard's father was a grocer. His mother died when he was four years old, and his father died when he was ten. Sadly, his stepmother was harsh to him, and his first school-teacher was extremely cruel. But his older brother took care of him.

Shepard went to Emmanuel College, Cambridge. For a time, he neglected religion and fell in with students given to lust, pride, gambling, and drinking. But the preaching of Preston arrested his conscience, and hearing of the fullness of God's grace from 1 Corinthians 1:30, Shepard embraced Christ. He also had great respect for Goodwin, who was serving as a fellow of the university at the time, writing, "Dr. Preston and Mr. Goodwin were the most able men for preaching Christ in this later age."[30] He graduated with a BA in 1624 and an MA in 1627. For a few years, he served in pastoral ministry and as a lecturer, but was repeatedly summoned by Archbishop Laud to answer charges of Nonconformity. Having been influenced by Thomas Hooker, Shepard

---

29. On Shepard, see John A. Albro, *The Life of Thomas Shepard* (Boston: Massachusetts Sabbath School Society, 1847); Richard A. Hasler, "Thomas Shepard, Pastor-Evangelist (1605–1649): A Study in the New England Puritan Ministry" (PhD diss., Hartford Seminary, 1964); Richard A. Humphrey, "The Concept of Conversion in the Theology of Thomas Shepard (1605–1649)" (PhD diss., Drew University, 1967); James William Jones, "The Beginnings of American Theology: John Cotton, Thomas Hooker, Thomas Shepard and Peter Bulkeley" (PhD diss., Brown University, 1970); Doris G. Marquit, "Thomas Shepard: The Formation of a Puritan Identity" (PhD diss., University of Minnesota, 1978); Michael McGiffert, ed., *God's Plot: Puritan Spirituality in Thomas Shepard's Cambridge*, rev. ed. (Amherst: University of Massachusetts Press, 1994); Urian Oakes, *An Elegie Upon the Death of the Reverend Mr. Thomas Shepard* (Aiken, SC: W. L. Washburn, 1902); William K. B. Stoever, *A Faire and Easie Way to Heaven: Covenant Theology and Antinomianism in Early Massachusetts* (Middletown, CT: Wesleyan University Press, 1978); Alexander Whyte, *Thomas Shepard, Pilgrim Father and Founder of Harvard: His Spiritual Experience and Experimental Preaching* (Grand Rapids, MI: Reformation Heritage Books, 2007).
30. Shepard, "Autobiography," in McGiffert, *God's Plot*, 49.

followed him across the Atlantic Ocean to New England in 1635. His wife died four months later from tuberculosis. Shepard then married Hooker's daughter, Joanna, in 1637. He himself suffered from chronic ill health.

Settling in Newtown, Massachusetts (renamed Cambridge in 1638), Shepard helped to start Harvard College in 1636. At his instigation, the colony began raising funds for scholarships for students. He played a central role in the debates over antinomianism that were sparked by some members of Cotton's church, most significantly Anne Hutchinson. He also encouraged John Eliot's nearby missionary efforts to the Native Americans. Though he died young (August 25, 1649) at age forty-three, his influence lived on through his writings. Jonathan Edwards later quoted from Shepard's writings more than seventy-five times in his masterpiece on true conversion, *A Treatise on the Religious Affections*.[31]

Shepard's works are collected in three volumes.[32] His most famous works are *The Sincere Convert* (1640), *The Sound Believer* (1645), and *The Parable of the Ten Virgins* (1660).[33] We also have in published form his autobiography, part of his diary, and public professions of conversion made by those seeking membership in his church.[34] Shepard gave himself to uncovering the deceitful ways of sin and Satan so people could fight them. Alluding to the historic significance of his birthday, he said, "When a powder plot is discovered, the danger is almost past."[35]

With respect to his writings, a few notes of caution are in order. First, some of his books are notes someone took of his sermons and published without his review. Therefore, one must ask whether the printed words accurately reflects his spoken words. Second, Shepard's books can be overwhelming in their scrupulous demands upon the soul. Tender consciences may fall into unnecessary self-condemnation by reading them. Third, Shepard's books contain a doctrine that most Puritans vigorously rejected: the idea that before a person can be saved, he must submit contentedly to God's judgment, even if God should send him to hell. The Puritans in general taught that in order to trust in Christ alone for salvation, a person must recognize that God would be entirely just to damn

31. Introduction to Jonathan Edwards, *The Works of Jonathan Edwards*, vol. 2, *Religious Affections*, ed. John E. Smith (New Haven, CT: Yale University Press, 1959), 54.
32. Thomas Shepard, *The Works of Thomas Shepard*, 3 vols. (New York: AMS Press, 1967).
33. All three of these treatises have been reprinted by Soli Deo Gloria.
34. McGiffert, *God's Plot*, 149–225.
35. Shepard, "The Sincere Convert," in *Works*, 1:68.

him to hell for his sins. But they thought it a contradiction to expect anyone to be content to go to hell.

Such caveats notwithstanding, there is much that is valuable in Shepard's preaching, as Edwards himself believed, and therefore we turn now to consider his evangelistic preaching.

Sincere and Sound Conversion

The books *The Sincere Convert* and *The Sound Believer* appear to stand together as two parts of a whole series on personal salvation. Shepard organized *The Sincere Convert* according to six principles intended not merely "to enlarge the understanding" but to "work chiefly upon the affections." They are:

1. There is one most glorious God.
2. This God made all mankind at first in Adam in a most glorious estate.
3. All mankind is now fallen from that estate into a bottomless gulf of sin and misery.
4. The Lord Jesus Christ is the only means of redemption out of this estate.
5. Those who are saved out of this woeful estate by Christ are very few, and these few are saved with much difficulty.
6. The greatest cause why so many die and perish in this estate is from themselves.[36]

Shepard was especially intent to strip away men's excuses for not coming to Christ. Phyllis and Nicholas Jones write, "The sermons so fully emphasize the countless ways one frustrates one's own salvation that the last two principles take up half the volume."[37] More precisely, the sixth principle occupies 40 percent of the book, developing in four points the idea that "every man that perisheth is his own butcherer or murderer," namely, through "black ignorance" of his spiritual estate, "carnal security" in his slavery to sin, "carnal confidence" in his power to save himself by good works, and "bold presumption" through a false faith.[38]

---

36. Shepard, "The Sincere Convert," in *Works*, 1:8.
37. Phyllis M. Jones and Nicholas R. Jones, eds., *Salvation in New England: Selections from the Sermons of the First Preachers* (Austin: University of Texas Press, 1977), 61.
38. Shepard, "The Sincere Convert," in *Works*, 1:68.

To these six principles, Shepard then adds three more, expounded in *The Sound Believer*:

1. Christ's saving acts of power include conviction, compunction, humiliation, and faith. Each of these answers to one of the four means by which men cause their own damnation.
2. The blessed estate of believers consists in their justification, reconciliation, adoption, sanctification, access in prayer, and glorification.
3. It is a necessity for all believers to live in love and obedience.[39]

Almost half of the book (44 percent) consists of his discussion of conviction, compunction, and humiliation, the divine preparations for saving faith.

We can see that in these two books, Shepard outlines the gospel in its necessity, essence, method of reception, and benefits. This outline demonstrates the gracious, Christ-centered quality of Shepard's preaching. At the same time, we note his emphasis on bringing unconverted sinners to an experience of their sins, so that they might see themselves entirely to blame for their damnation yet utterly unable to save themselves. Pressing upon the unconverted both their culpability and inability is a mark of classic Reformed experiential preaching. Such preaching drives men to despair of self and to look to Christ alone. It is here that men such as Hooker and Shepard excelled. Yet it is precisely here that they tended to go too far, demanding such total submission to God's will as a mere preparation for conversion that even mature believers might question their own sincerity. For this, other Puritans, such as Giles Firmin (1614–1697), would later take them to task.[40]

Let's consider how Shepard exposes the ways in which perishing sinners perpetuate their "carnal security" even when they know something about their lost estate. These are ways in which people's hearts remain "hard or sleepy" even though their minds understand their misery, and so their souls do not "greatly care to come out of it." As you consider these ten devices of carnal security, imagine what it would be like to be a complacent hypocrite in the congregation while Shepard peels away the wicked rationalizations of your heart, exposing you to judgment.

---

39. Shepard, "The Sound Believer," in *Works*, 1:115–284.
40. Giles Firmin, *The Real Christian, or A Treatise of Effectual Calling* (London: for Dorman Newman, 1670).

1. God's wrath does not seem real to perishing sinners. The full measure of divine wrath is reserved for the day of judgment. Smaller judgments and the warnings of the Word do not strike them with horror over the coming fire. "Until God's arrows stick in men's hearts, they will never seek out of themselves unto Jesus Christ (Eccl. 8:11)." As with Pharaoh, God's plagues may temporarily induce them to cry out, but as soon as the plague is lifted, their hearts are hardened again.[41]

2. They put the evil day far from them. They tell themselves they have plenty of time, so they can repent later. "Therefore they say, Soul, eat, drink, follow thy sports, cups, queens [girlfriends]; thou hast a treasure of time which shall not be spent in many years (Isa. 22:12–13)." Just as wax does not melt unless the fire is near, hearts do not soften unless God's wrath seems near to them.[42]

3. "They think they can bear God's wrath." The provoked God of justice is not seen "so terrible as indeed he is." Sinners fail to believe the prophetic warnings that "present God's wrath as a thing intolerable" (e.g., Nah. 1:6). So they foolishly say "they will have their swing in sin," and if God damns them, it is but a little thing.[43]

4. They have no experiential knowledge of a better estate. A wife who knows her husband's love and character mourns when he must be gone on a journey, but sinners do not shed a tear that God is absent from them. Why? Shepard explains:

> They have never tasted the sweetness of his presence. It is strange to see men take more content [satisfaction] in their cups and cards, pots and pipes, dogs and hawks, than in the fellowship of God and Christ, in word, in prayer, in meditation; which ordinances are burdens and prison unto them. What is the reason of it? Is there no more sweetness in the presence of God's smiling in Christ than in a filthy whore? Yes; but they know not the worth, sweetness, satisfying goodness of a God.[44]

5. The pleasures of sin bewitch them and their lazy souls detest the difficulty of conversion. Like Israel, they prefer the onions and garlic of slavery in Egypt to fighting their way into the Promised Land of Canaan. Perhaps they have tried to pray or hear the Scriptures, but they found it

---

41. Shepard, "The Sincere Convert," in *Works*, 1:89.
42. Shepard, "The Sincere Convert," in *Works*, 1:89–90.
43. Shepard, "The Sincere Convert," in *Works*, 1:90.
44. Shepard, "The Sincere Convert," in *Works*, 1:91.

hard, and now, with a "testy, sullen spirit," they go back to their pleasant lusts. "Therefore men walk in the broad way, because the other way to life is strait [difficult] and narrow; it is a plague, a burden, a prison, to be so strict; men had rather sit almost an hour in the stocks than be an hour at prayer."[45]

6. "The strange, strong power of sin" rules over their souls. They must serve it, like prisoners who have come to submit to their jailers. They are the soldiers of sin who have taken their pay (the pleasures of sin), and so must follow their captain even to "eternal ruin." They "must and will serve their lusts," even "though doomsday should be tomorrow." They are like the Sodomites who, even after the angels struck them blind, still groped for the door of Lot.[46]

7. Perishing sinners despair of God's mercy. Like Cain, they are "renegades from the face of God." Though God promises life upon submission, they convince themselves it cannot be true. They cast away their lives in spiritual suicide. Strangely, their very despair confirms them in their sinful course until the end.[47]

8. They "nourish a blind, false, flattering hope of God's mercy." They know that their case is bad, but they still cherish some hope that God will save them, even though "they lie down securely" in sin. Such people use a hope of God's mercy not to spur themselves on to repentance but to cultivate a wicked passivity. "They hope God will be merciful unto them; if not, they cannot help it."[48] Here we see an example of how a preacher of predestination does not excuse passivity, but blames the passive for not doing all they can to find mercy.

9. They approach the Word arrogantly. They do not listen to it to hear God speak. "Men bring not their hearts under the hammer of God's word to be broken, they never bring their consciences to be cut. . . . Men put themselves above the word, and their hearts above the hammer; they come not to have the minister to humble them, but to judge of him, or to pick some pretty fine thing out of the word, and so remain secure sots all their days." As a path repeatedly trodden grows hard, so their hearts, repeatedly exposed to sermons, "grow hard by the word."[49]

45. Shepard, "The Sincere Convert," in *Works*, 1:91–92.
46. Shepard, "The Sincere Convert," in *Works*, 1:92.
47. Shepard, "The Sincere Convert," in *Works*, 1:92.
48. Shepard, "The Sincere Convert," in *Works*, 1:92.
49. Shepard, "The Sincere Convert," in *Works*, 1:92–93.

10. Such perishing sinners do not daily meditate on God's wrath or the horrible nature of sin. They do not chew and digest the medicine, so it never affects them. They deal superficially with the Word, and it quickly leaves their minds.[50]

Shepard then sounds the trumpet call of warning:

> Awaken, therefore, all you secure creatures; feel your misery, that so you may get out of it. Dost thou know thine estate is naught [bad], and that thy condemnation will be fearful, if ever thou dost perish? And is thine heart secretly secure, so damnably dead, so desperately hard, that thou hast no heart to come out of it? What! No sigh, no tears? Canst thou carry all thy sins upon thy back, like Samson the gates of the city, and make a light matter of them? Canst thou see hell fire before thee, and yet wilt venture? Art thou worse than a beast which we cannot beat nor drive into the fire if there be any way to escape? O, get thy heart to lament and mourn under thy miseries; who knows then but the Lord may pity thee? But O, hard heart! Thou canst mourn for losses and crosses, of burning of goods and houses, yet though God be lost, and his image burnt down, and all is gone, thou canst not mourn.[51]

Such plain and earnest dealings with sinners affected many. The bitterness of sin makes Christ sweet indeed, and it is said that many found Christ under Shepard's preaching.

Conclusion

Our brief dip into the sermons of Goodwin and Shepard confirms the assertion that the Puritans did not merely teach a doctrinal system, but tried to help their hearers to feel the terrifying darkness of sin and be drawn to the radiant beauty of Christ. Neither should we think that Goodwin only preached Christ and Shepard only preached sin. Shepard preached about the glory of God, the redemption of Christ, the free offer of the gospel to all people, faith in Christ, and the benefits of union with Christ.[52] Goodwin published a 550-page treatise on the guilt and evil of sin.[53] Both men declared the whole counsel of God, though each sermon and series had a different emphasis.

---

50. Shepard, "The Sincere Convert," in *Works*, 1:93.
51. Shepard, "The Sincere Convert," in *Works*, 1:93.
52. Shepard, "The Sincere Convert," in *Works*, 1:9–17, 46–52; "The Sound Believer," in *Works*, 1:190–274.
53. Goodwin, "An Unregenerate Man's Guiltiness before God," in *Works*, vol. 10.

As preachers, Goodwin and Shepard had this trait in common: both preached doctrine in a very affectionate manner. Goodwin's sermons on Christ's heart in heaven are filled with pathos as he describes the glorious compassion of the Lord for his suffering people. His sermons helped people to go beyond head knowledge to sense the overwhelming reality of Christ's love for them. Similarly, in Shepard's dealing with the excuses of sinners, we feel that the preacher has somehow looked into our hearts by the insight of Scripture. There he wages war against the deceitfulness of sin and everything that stands against the knowledge of God and the obedience of Christ (2 Cor. 10:4–5). While the effectiveness of preaching always depends on the Holy Spirit, experiential preaching is the means by which the heart of God revealed in Scripture grasps the heart of the preacher and speaks to the hearts of the listeners.

13

Puritan Preachers: Bunyan

John Bunyan preached with a heart humbled by God's glory and refreshed by God's grace.[1] On the one hand, Bunyan was keenly aware that God is "that incomprehensible Majesty, in comparison of whom, all nations are less than the drop of a bucket."[2] Yet Bunyan also marveled at the mercy of this great God, writing, "To see a prince entreat a beggar to receive an alms would be a strange sight; to see a king entreat a traitor to accept of mercy would be a stranger sight than that; but to see God entreat a sinner, to hear Christ say, 'I stand at the door and knock,' with a heart full and a heaven full of grace to bestow upon him that opens, this is such a sight as dazzles the eyes of angels."[3]

This combination of fear toward God and hope in his love is crucial for preaching. Today we are witnessing an erosion of biblical preaching.[4] In his biography of George Whitefield (1714–1770), Arnold Dallimore (1911–1998) called for biblical preachers:

[We need] men mighty in the Scriptures, their lives dominated by a sense of the greatness, the majesty and holiness of God, and their

---

1. This chapter is adapted from chap. 43 in Joel R. Beeke and Mark Jones, *A Puritan Theology: Doctrine for Life* (Grand Rapids, MI: Reformation Heritage Books, 2012), 711–24. Used with permission. I am indebted to John Harris's 1988 Westminster Conference paper "Moving the Heart: the Preaching of John Bunyan," in *Not by Might nor by Power* (London: Westminster Conference, 1989), 32–51, for several useful thoughts and quotations. I also wish to thank Kyle Borg for research assistance.
2. John Bunyan, *A Treatise of the Fear of God*, in *The Works of John Bunyan*, ed. George Offor (1854; repr., Edinburgh: Banner of Truth, 1991), 1:437–38, hereafter, *Works*.
3. John Bunyan, *Saved by Grace*, in *Works*, 1:350.
4. T. David Gordon has stated that in his opinion less than 30 percent of those ordained to the ministry in Reformed churches can preach even a mediocre sermon. *Why Johnny Can't Preach* (Phillipsburg, NJ: P&R, 2009), 11.

minds and hearts aglow with the great truths of the doctrines of grace ... men who are willing to be fools for Christ's sake, who will bear reproach and falsehood, who will labour and suffer, and whose supreme desire will be, not to gain earth's accolades, but to win the Master's approbation when they appear before His awesome judgment seat. They will be men who preach with broken hearts and tear-filled eyes.[5]

We need such ministers today. Yet even if the church falters and the pulpit grows cold, the history of Christianity shows us that the Lord has never abandoned his church. In every generation, he has raised up men who stormed the gates of hell with the simplicity of heaven's wisdom. For us, the past is a beacon of hope in which we find encouragement for our own times.

In the midst of sound Puritan preachers, Bunyan stands among the highest beams in the beacon of hope from the past, for he had the God-given ability to engage not only the mind but also the heart through his preaching. Let us focus on Bunyan as a preacher—especially as a preacher to the heart.

Bunyan the Preacher

King Charles II once asked John Owen, "the prince of Puritans," why he went to hear the preaching of Bunyan, the unlearned tinker of Bedford. Owen responded, "May it please your majesty, could I possess the tinker's abilities for preaching, I would willingly relinquish all my learning."[6]

In 1655, at the request of several brethren in his local church, the twenty-seven-year-old Bunyan began preaching to various Bedford congregations while he was still afflicted sorely by doubts about his eternal state. Of that early preaching, he writes: "The terrors of the law, and guilt for my transgressions, lay heavily on my conscience. I preached what I felt, what I smartingly did feel, even that under which my poor soul did groan and tremble to astonishment. . . . I went myself in chains to preach to them in chains; and carried that fire in my own conscience that I persuaded them to beware of."[7]

---

5. Arnold Dallimore, *George Whitefield: The Life and Times of the Great Evangelist of the 18th Century Revival* (Edinburgh: Banner of Truth, 2009), 1:16.

6. Andrew Thomson, "Life of Dr. Owen," in *The Works of John Owen*, ed. William H. Goold (1850–1853; repr., Edinburgh: Banner of Truth, 1965–1968), 1:xcii.

7. Bunyan, *Grace Abounding to the Chief of Sinners*, in *Works*, 1:42. Cf. Christopher Hill, *A Tinker and a Poor Man: John Bunyan and His Church, 1628–1688* (New York: Knopf, 1989), 103–4.

Hundreds came to hear Bunyan, which genuinely astonished him. Ola Winslow writes, "Incredulous at first that God would speak through him 'to the heart of any man,' he presently concluded it might be so, and his success became a reassurance."[8] Anne Arnott says that Bunyan "was a sinner saved by grace, who preached to other sinners from his own dark experience. 'I have been as one sent to them from the dead,' he said. 'I had not preached long before some began to be touched by the Word, and to be greatly afflicted in their minds at the apprehension of the greatness of their sin and of their need for Jesus Christ.'"[9]

Within two years, Bunyan began preaching less about sin and much more about Christ. As Gordon Wakefield puts it:

[Bunyan lifted up Christ] in his "offices," that is, in the whole range of what he could do for the human soul and for the world; Christ as the saving alternative to the bogus securities of getting and spending or of the philosophies of godless self-interest. And in consequence of this, "God led me into something of the mystery of union with Christ" [Bunyan said,] and this he came to preach also, the union, which was the heart of Calvinist spirituality.[10]

Bunyan's preaching no longer brought only "a word of admonition," but also edification and comfort to believers. This greatly strengthened his sense of internal calling, powerfully assisting in persuading him that he was proclaiming truth.

Thus, God matured Bunyan's preaching with a more evangelical balance of law and gospel. Bunyan had found that in Christ's church, there is "music in the house, music in the heart, and music also in heaven, for joy that we are here."[11] This was no shift from legalism to antinomianism. Gospel-induced joy only increased Bunyan's sense of God's majestic glory, for his grace is glorious grace. Bunyan said, "There is nothing in heaven or earth that can so *awe* the heart as the grace of God."[12] Faith in Christ does not relax the believer's stance toward sin, but renews the Christian's determination to fight sin to the end. Bunyan said, "Faith is a principle of

---

8. Ola Winslow, *John Bunyan* (New York: MacMillan, 1961), 75.
9. Anne Arnott, *He Shall with Giants Fight* (Eastbourne, UK: Kingsway, 1985), 67.
10. Gordon Wakefield, *Bunyan the Christian* (London: HarperCollins, 1992), 32.
11. Bunyan, *The Pilgrim's Progress . . . The Second Part*, in *Works*, 3:198.
12. Bunyan, *The Water of Life*, in *Works*, 3:546, emphasis original.

life . . . a principle of strength, by which the soul opposeth its lust, the devil, and this world, and overcomes them."[13]

While preaching in a farmhouse in 1660, five years after he began proclaiming God's Word, Bunyan was arrested on the charge of preaching without a license from the king. Though Bunyan was certainly no rebel and no politician, the Bedfordshire gentry appear to have regarded his preaching as "dangerous rabble-rousing" that "fanned the discontent that many felt with the restored regime and church."[14] Sir Henry Chester, a local justice, put his case against Bunyan even more strongly: "He is a pestilential fellow, there is not [another] such a fellow in the country."[15] So Bunyan was thrown into prison, where he made shoelaces and wrote prolifically for twelve and a half years (1660–1672).

Bunyan had been married for several years to a woman whose name is unknown, and they had had four children (including one who was blind). Bunyan's wife died in 1658, but prior to his arrest, he had married a godly young woman named Elizabeth. She pleaded repeatedly for his release, based on her care of the four small children and a recent miscarriage. The presiding judge told her to convince Bunyan to stop preaching. She replied, "My lord, he dares not leave off preaching as long as he can speak."[16] Bunyan did offer to hand over the notes of all his sermons to the judicial authorities to assure them that he was not preaching seditiously in any way. But that, too, was to no avail. So Bunyan remained in prison for violating the statute that required adult participation in Church of England worship services at least monthly ("occasional conformity") and forbade religious meetings ("conventicles") not authorized by that church.[17]

Throughout his imprisonment, Bunyan maintained a zealous love for preaching. He writes: "When, by the good hand of my God, I had for five or six years together, without any interruption, freely preached the blessed gospel of our Lord Jesus Christ . . . the devil, that old enemy of man's salvation, took his opportunity to inflame the hearts of his vassals . . . that at last I was laid out for by the warrant of a justice, and was taken and committed to prison."[18] When asked what he would do if he were released from prison, he responded, "If I was out of prison today

---

13. Bunyan, *Christian Behaviour*, in *Works*, 2:551.
14. Hill, *A Tinker and a Poor Man*, 106–7.
15. Quoted in Hill, *A Tinker and a Poor Man*, 108.
16. Quoted in Bunyan, "A Relation of the Imprisonment of Mr. John Bunyan," in *Works*, 1:61.
17. Bunyan, "A Relation of the Imprisonment of Mr. John Bunyan," in *Works*, 1:57, 59.
18. Bunyan, "A Relation of the Imprisonment of Mr. John Bunyan," in *Works*, 1:50.

I would preach the gospel again tomorrow, by the help of God."[19] On another occasion, he said, "Neither guilt or hell could take me off my work";[20] he went so far as to state that he "could not be content, unless I was found in the exercise of my gift."[21]

In all his adversity, the Word was like a burning fire in Bunyan's heart. In fact, he anticipated dying for that Word. He writes: "It was for the Word and way of God that I was in this condition, [and] I was engaged not to flinch a hair's breadth from it. . . . It was my duty to stand to his Word, whether he would ever look upon me or no, or save me at the last; wherefore, thought I, I will leap off the ladder even blindfold into eternity, sink or swim, come heaven come hell, Lord Jesus, if thou wilt catch me, do; if not I will venture for thy name."[22]

In 1661 and from 1668 to 1672, certain jailers permitted Bunyan to leave prison at times to preach. George Offor (1787–1864) notes, "It is said that many of the Baptist congregations in Bedfordshire owe their origins to his midnight preaching."[23] Prison years were times of difficult trials, however. Bunyan experienced what his *Pilgrim's Progress* characters Christian and Faithful would suffer at the hands of Giant Despair, who thrust pilgrims "into a very dark dungeon, nasty and stinking."[24] Bunyan especially felt the pain of separation from his wife and children, particularly Mary, "my poor blind child," describing it as "pulling the flesh from my bones."[25]

Bunyan's popularity as a preacher did not wane in his later years. He often visited London, "where," Robert Southey (1774–1843) says, "his reputation was so great, that if a day's notice was given, the meeting-house at Southwark at which he generally preached, would not hold half the people that attended. Three thousand persons have been gathered together there; and not less than twelve hundred on week days, and dark winter's mornings at seven o'clock."[26]

Bunyan preached to men's hearts as well as to their minds. No doubt this was possible because he was personally acquainted with temptations,

---

19. Bunyan, "A Relation of the Imprisonment of Mr. John Bunyan," in *Works*, 1:57.
20. Bunyan, *Grace Abounding*, in *Works*, 1:42.
21. Bunyan, *Grace Abounding*, in *Works*, 1:41.
22. Quoted in Hill, *A Tinker and a Poor Man*, 109.
23. George Offor, "Memoir of John Bunyan," in Bunyan, *Works*, 1:lix.
24. Bunyan, *Pilgrim's Progress*, in *Works*, 3:140.
25. Bunyan, *Grace Abounding*, in *Works*, 1:48.
26. Robert Southey, "A Life of John Bunyan," in John Bunyan, *Pilgrim's Progress* (London: John Murray and John Major, 1830), lxxiii.

sins, and fears, and had experienced the grace of God in Jesus Christ in a remarkably powerful way. In his introduction to Bunyan's *Some Gospel Truths Opened*, John Burton writes of its author, "He hath, through grace taken these three heavenly degrees, to wit, union with Christ, the anointing of the Spirit, and experience of the temptations of Satan, which do more fit a man for that mighty work of preaching the gospel, than all university learning and degrees that can be had."[27]

Bunyan had a high regard for the office of preacher. When Christian of *Pilgrim's Progress* journeys to the Interpreter's house, he is shown a picture of a preacher, "a very grave person," whose eyes are "lifted up to heaven, the best of books in his hand." Bunyan writes: "The law of truth was written upon his lips, the world was behind his back, and a golden crown on his head. He stood as if pleading with men." The Interpreter tells Christian what this picture represents: "It is to show thee, that his work is to know and unfold dark things to sinners . . . to show thee that slighting and despising the things that are present, for the love that he hath to his Master's service, he is sure in the world that comes next to have glory for his reward."[28] This, for Bunyan, is the ideal of what a preacher should be. For Bunyan, the preacher is God's authorized spiritual guide. Wakefield writes:

> The Interpreter explains, in New Testament metaphors, that this man begets (spiritual) children, travails in bringing them to birth, and then is their nurse. His posture and his biblical resource and the truth written upon his lips make plain "that his work is to know and unfold dark things to sinners." He opens the divine secrets of mercy and judgment. And he must do this from a renunciation of this world and a belief that his reward is in the world to come, for here he may well receive obloquy, scorn and persecution, as Bunyan and many others did under the Stuarts.[29]

Bunyan's love for preaching was not confined to words; he also had a passionate zeal for the souls of his hearers. He loved preaching *and* he loved people's souls. He says, "In my preaching I have really been in pain and have as it were travailed to bring forth children unto God; neither could I be satisfied unless fruits did appear in my work."[30] Else-

---

27. Bunyan, "Some Gospel Truths Opened," in *Works*, 2:141.
28. Bunyan, *Pilgrim's Progress*, in *Works*, 3:98.
29. Wakefield, *Bunyan the Christian*, 34. *Obloquy* is contemptuous and reproachful speech.
30. Bunyan, *Grace Abounding*, in *Works*, 1:43.

where, he writes, "If any of those who were awakened by my ministry did after that fall back, as sometimes too many did, I can truly say their loss hath been more to me than if one of my own children, begotten of my body, had been going to its grave."[31] Bunyan was also overwhelmed with the greatness of the soul: "Because the soul, and the salvation of it, are such great, such wonderful great things; nothing is a matter of that concern as is, and should be, the soul of each one of you. House and land, trades and honours, places and preferments, what are they to salvation, to the salvation of the soul?"[32]

If ever a man was called for gospel ministry, it was Bunyan. The Holy Spirit granted him divine benediction, and he could not, without a serious breach of conscience, lay aside those gifts. Even when he was imprisoned, he spent the bulk of his time turning his preached sermons into books. Christopher Hill concludes, "It would appear that all his writings published before *Grace Abounding* derived from sermons, and probably most of what he published later." Hill speculates that Bunyan's spoken sermons were likely much more personal and demonstrative than his published works. He adds, "We may also suppose that the colloquialisms, the homely touches which survive in the dignity of print, may have played a larger part in his spoken words."[33]

A Heart That Reverences God's Word

The rock-solid foundation of Bunyan's preaching was his conviction that the Bible is not the word of men, but the Word of God.[34] The prophets and apostles "have spoken by divine inspiration."[35] Bunyan wrote, "All the Holy Scriptures are the words of God" (2 Tim. 3:16; 2 Pet. 1:21).[36] Bunyan said the Scriptures "are the truth as really as if God should speak to you from heaven through the clouds."[37]

Bunyan reverenced the Bible in part because he understood that, as God's Word, it is the inerrant truth. He said, "It is to be called a fearful

---

31. Bunyan, *Grace Abounding*, in *Works*, 1:43.
32. Bunyan, "The Greatness of the Soul and Unspeakable of the Loss Thereof," in *Works*, 1:105.
33. Hill, *A Tinker and a Poor Man*, 104–5.
34. This section is abridged and adapted from Joel R. Beeke and Paul M. Smalley, *John Bunyan and the Grace of Fearing God* (Phillipsburg, NJ: P&R, 2016), ISBN 978-1-62995-204-8, pp. 102–115, with permission from P&R Publishing Co., P.O. Box 817, Phillipsburg, N J 08865, www.prp books.com.
35. Bunyan, "A Few Sighs from Hell, Or, The Groans of a Damned Soul," in *Works*, 3:707.
36. Bunyan, "A Confession of My Faith," in *Works*, 2:601.
37. Bunyan, "A Few Sighs from Hell," in *Works*, 3:720.

Word, because of the truth and faithfulness of it." Christ taught that the Scriptures cannot be broken (John 10:35). They are "the scripture of truth" and "the true sayings of God" (Dan. 10:21; Rev. 19:9).[38] The apostles were "endued with the Holy Ghost" so that "they, as to their doctrine, were infallible, it was impossible they should err; he that despises their doctrine, despised God himself."[39]

Therefore, God's own majesty thunders in his Word. Bunyan wrote in a mighty rush of biblical texts, "The word of a king is as the roaring of a lion; where the word of a king is, there is power; what is it then when God, the great God shall roar out of Zion, and utter his voice from Jerusalem, whose voice shakes not only earth, but also heaven. . . . The voice of the Lord is powerful, the voice of the Lord is full of majesty" (Prov. 19:12; Eccl. 8:4; Joel 3:16; Ps. 29:4).[40]

To believe God's Word is an act of worship toward God (Acts 24:14).[41] Bunyan counseled, "Keep always close to your conscience the authority of the Word; fear the commandment as the commandment of a God both mighty and glorious, and as the commandment of a father both loving and pitiful [full of compassion]."[42]

Only on the authority of God's Word can we know how to serve God. Bunyan said, "Zeal without knowledge is like a mettled [high-spirited] horse without eyes, like a sword in a madman's hand." Without the Word, we have no wisdom (Isa. 8:20).[43] It is the Devil's work to give men a low view of the Scriptures and encourage them to depend on what is in their own minds and hearts.[44] Neither can people determine what is right based only on circumstances and opportunities that providence presents them. The only safe road is to follow the Word of God.[45]

Bunyan stood upon the sufficiency of the Scriptures to guide mankind in spiritual things. Regarding one's salvation, he said, "Christian, you are not in this thing to follow your sense and feeling: but the very Word of God. . . . You must give more credit to one syllable of the written Word of the gospel, than you must give to all the saints and angels in heaven

---

38. Bunyan, *Treatise on the Fear of God*, in *Works*, 1:443.
39. Bunyan, "The Holy City," in *Works*, 3:417.
40. Bunyan, *Treatise on the Fear of God*, in *Works*, 1:443.
41. Bunyan, "Instruction for the Ignorant," in *Works*, 2:683
42. Bunyan, *Treatise on the Fear of God*, in *Works*, 1:485.
43. Bunyan, "Christian Behaviour," in *Works*, 2:554.
44. Bunyan, "Some Gospel Truths Opened," in *Works*, 2:136; "A Few Sighs from Hell," in *Works*, 3:710.
45. Bunyan, "Exposition on . . . Genesis," in *Works*, 2:482.

and earth."[46] Thus, the Word is "the rule of worship," and to substitute human traditions to direct our worship is a great backsliding from God.[47] Bunyan said, "The Holy Scriptures, of themselves, without the addition of human inventions, are able" to fully equip God's servants, to make the lost "wise unto salvation through faith in Jesus Christ," and to teach people how to worship God and walk righteously toward men (2 Tim. 3:14, 17).[48]

Bunyan believed that a lack of reverence for the Word of God is the cause of "all disorders" of heart, life, conduct, and church. All sin begins with "wandering from the Word of God." He quoted Proverbs 13:13, "Whoso despiseth the word shall be destroyed: but he that feareth the commandment shall be rewarded." The Word is our life and safety (Ps. 17:4; Prov. 4:20–22). In every age, the wicked reject the Word and follow their lusts and pride, but they will perish and be counted as fools (Jer. 8:9; 44:16).[49]

If we really believe that the Bible is God's Word, then we must be willing to obey it and proclaim it when men oppose it. Bunyan wrote, "This rebukes them that esteem the words and things of men more than the words of God, as those who are drawn from their respect of, and obedience to the Word of God by the pleasures or threats of men." Acknowledging the divine authority of the Bible is not enough; one must be willing to stand against the world in following it. Otherwise, the dread words of Christ will apply: "Whosoever therefore shall be ashamed of me and of my words in this adulterous and sinful generation; of him also shall the Son of man be ashamed, when he cometh in the glory of his Father with the holy angels" (Mark 8:38).[50]

Reverence for God's Word puts the preacher in his place. The preacher is only a conduit of God's truth. He is like a "cloud" that draws its water "out of the sea" and pours rain down on the earth: "ministers should fetch their doctrine from God" and "should give out what they know of God to the world."[51] Like the shepherds on the Delectable Mountains, faithful preachers must bear the names "Knowledge, Experience, Watchful, and Sincere," and give their flocks a balanced perspective so that they

---

46. Bunyan, *The Doctrine of the Law and Grace Unfolded*, in *Works*, 1:562.
47. Bunyan, "The Jerusalem Sinner Saved: Or, Good News for the Vilest of Men," in *Works*, 1:69.
48. Bunyan, "A Confession of My Faith," in *Works*, 2:601.
49. Bunyan, *Treatise on the Fear of God*, in *Works*, 1:444.
50. Bunyan, *Treatise on the Fear of God*, in *Works*, 1:444.
51. Bunyan, *The Pilgrim's Progress . . . The Second Part*, in *Works*, 3:203.

see both the terrible dangers of false doctrine and worldliness, as well as the glorious hope of heaven.[52]

When preaching, Bunyan was "often tempted to pride and liftings up of heart." The Lord mercifully countered such temptations in a number of ways. Bunyan wrote that God daily showed him something of "the evil of my own heart" and the "multitude of corruptions and infirmities" in it. God also used the Scriptures to remind him that gifts and abilities are nothing without love (1 Cor. 13:1–2). Bunyan learned to see his preaching as a "fiddle" that Christ played to make music for the church. Shall a mere fiddle be proud? He also remembered that spiritual gifts will pass away, but love will last forever (1 Cor. 13:8). People may be able to preach well but in the end still go to hell. People with little gifts in knowledge or speech may have a thousand times more grace than those who can preach like angels, and so be much the more pleasing to God. Bunyan concluded, "A little grace, a little love, a little of the true fear of God is better than all these gifts."[53]

Bunyan also learned to regard his preaching in the light of the needs of the church and the approaching judgment day. It helps the preacher to "be little in his own eyes" when he remembers "that his gifts are not his own, but the church's, and that by them he is made a servant of the church, and he must also give at last an account of his stewardship unto the Lord Jesus, and to give a good account will be a blessed thing." Therefore, Bunyan wrote, "let all men . . . prize a little with the fear of the Lord; gifts indeed are desirable, but yet great grace and small gifts are better than great gifts and no grace." Only grace leads to glory.[54]

Understanding the Heart

Oratorical skill or passion did not make Bunyan such a powerful preacher, though he certainly had the gifts needed for preaching the Word. Neither did degrees from Cambridge or any other university, for he had none. Bunyan had a lively, experiential faith, which acquainted him with the full scope of religious troubles and affections. He experienced things that cannot be learned from a schoolbook, but only as a student of living faith. This is what made Bunyan such a powerful weapon in God's hand for tearing down strongholds; by his own admission, he preached

---

52. Bunyan, *The Pilgrim's Progress*, in *Works*, 3:143–45.
53. Bunyan, *Grace Abounding*, in *Works*, 1:44–45.
54. Bunyan, *Grace Abounding*, in *Works*, 1:45.

what he felt.[55] While much more could be said about Bunyan's spiritual history, I will restrict myself to a few areas and suggest further reading about Bunyan in his autobiography, *Grace Abounding to the Chief of Sinners*, where he opens his mind and heart.

Terror

Assessing his spiritual condition, Bunyan remarks that even from childhood his unrighteousness had "but few equals."[56] At the age of nine, Bunyan recalls, he was "greatly afflicted, while asleep, with the apprehensions of devils and wicked spirits."[57] But despite these disturbing dreams, he continued to delight in sin and ungodly companionship. As a young married man, Bunyan came under conviction of sin, particularly regarding how lightly he had treated the Sabbath. Yet this conviction did not result in true reformation; rather, it hardened his heart to grace. He says, "I was persuaded I could never attain to other comfort than what I should get in sin."[58]

The chastisement of an ungodly woman and an encounter with a professing Christian brought Bunyan to an outward change. By the measure of some men, he was made anew as he put away some of his besetting sins. Yet, even in this, he says, he "knew not Christ, nor grace, nor faith, nor hope."[59] Despite external praise, Bunyan knew his own hypocrisy and was overwhelmed with fear, particularly of death. In his autobiography, he tells about a time he wanted to see a church bell rung. As he stood below the tower, however, he began to fear the bell might fall and crush him, so he positioned himself under the main beam. Then he began to worry that the main beam might fall, so he removed himself to the steeple door. Then he became persuaded that the whole steeple could fall upon him, so he fled from the building altogether.[60]

Bunyan also tells of a day prior to his conversion when he heard four women in Bedford speaking about the temptations of Satan and the hope of the new birth. Eavesdropping on this conversation, Bunyan experienced a deep affliction in his soul: "I saw that in all my thoughts about religion and salvation, the new birth did never enter into my mind,

---

55. Bunyan, *Grace Abounding*, in *Works*, 1:42.
56. Bunyan, *Grace Abounding*, in *Works*, 1:6.
57. Bunyan, *Grace Abounding*, in *Works*, 1:6.
58. Bunyan, *Grace Abounding*, in *Works*, 1:8–9.
59. Bunyan, *Grace Abounding*, in *Works*, 1:9.
60. Bunyan, *Grace Abounding*, in *Works*, 1:10.

neither knew I the comfort of the Word and promise, nor the deceitfulness and treachery of my own wicked heart."[61] Bunyan frequently visited Bedford to listen to Christians engaged in mutual conference about Scripture and spiritual experience, resulting in "a very great softness and tenderness of heart, which caused me to fall under the conviction of what by Scripture they asserted."[62] Yet, even then, the terrors of the law and guilt for his transgressions lay heavy on Bunyan's conscience.[63]

Doubt

In the midst of many temptations, Bunyan experienced the Lord's protecting hand. The Bible gradually became precious to him, but the more he read, the more he recognized his ignorance. In this unbelieving state, Bunyan realized he was afraid to acknowledge his lack of faith. Yet he could not be content until he came to the certain knowledge of faith. "This was always running in my mind," he says.[64] As Bunyan wrestled on, he was overcome with concerns about his eternal state: "I began to find my soul to be assaulted with fresh doubts about my future happiness, especially with concerns as whether I was elected? But how could I be, if the day of grace was now past and gone?"[65]

Even while grace was at work in his soul, doubt continued to assail Bunyan: "I should cry with pangs after God that he would be merciful unto me; but then I should be daunted again with such conceits as these; I should think God did mock at these, my prayers, saying . . . 'This poor simple wretch doth hanker after me as if I had nothing to do with my mercy but bestow it on such as he,'" he writes. "Alas, poor fool! How art thou deceived!"[66]

Grace

Despite times of terror and doubt, Bunyan gradually experienced God's grace. He writes, "The Lord did more fully and graciously discover himself unto me; and indeed, did quite, not only deliver me from the guilt that, by these things, was laid upon my conscience, but also from the very filth thereof; for the temptation was removed, and I was put into my

---

61. Bunyan, *Grace Abounding*, in *Works*, 1:10.
62. Bunyan, *Grace Abounding*, in *Works*, 1:11.
63. Bunyan, *Grace Abounding*, in *Works*, 1:42.
64. Bunyan, *Grace Abounding*, in *Works*, 1:12.
65. Bunyan, *Grace Abounding*, in *Works*, 1:13.
66. Bunyan, *Grace Abounding*, in *Works*, 1:19.

right mind again."[67] From this time on, the wickedness and blasphemy of his heart prompted Bunyan to fly to the blood of Christ that made God his friend in the pact of reconciliation.

In 1651, a group of God-fearing women introduced Bunyan to John Gifford, their Bedford pastor. Bunyan particularly found help in a sermon that Gifford preached on Song of Solomon 4:1, "Behold, thou art fair, my love; behold, thou art fair." He also discovered blessing in reading Martin Luther's commentary on Galatians, in which he found his own experience "largely and profoundly handled, as if [Luther's] book had been written out of my heart."[68] Then, while Bunyan was walking through a field one day, Christ's righteousness was revealed to his soul and he was set forever free. Bunyan writes of that unforgettable experience:

> One day, as I was passing in the field, and that too with some dashes on my conscience, fearing lest yet all was not right, suddenly this sentence fell upon my soul, Thy righteousness is in heaven; and methought withal, I saw, with the eyes of my soul, Jesus Christ at God's right hand; there, I say, as my righteousness; so that wherever I was, or whatever I was adoing, God could not say of me, He wants my righteousness, for that was just before Him. I also saw, moreover, that it was not my good frame of heart that made my righteousness better, nor yet my bad frame that made my righteousness worse; for my righteousness was Jesus Christ Himself, the same yesterday, and to-day, and forever.
>
> Now did my chains fall off my legs indeed, I was loosed from my afflictions and irons, my temptations also fled away; so that, from that time, those dreadful scriptures of God left off to trouble me; now I went home rejoicing, for the grace and love of God. . . .
>
> I lived for some time very sweetly at peace with God through Christ; Oh methought, Christ! Christ! There was nothing but Christ that was before my eyes. I was now not for only looking upon this and the other benefits of Christ apart, as of his blood, burial, and resurrection, but considered him as a whole Christ! . . .
>
> It was glorious to me to see his exaltation, and the worth and prevalency of all his benefits, and that because of this: now I could look from myself to him, and should reckon that all those graces

---

67. Bunyan, *Grace Abounding*, in *Works*, 1:19.
68. Bunyan, *Grace Abounding*, in *Works*, 1:22.

of God that now were green in me, were yet but like those cracked groats and fourpence-halfpennies that rich men carry in their purses, when their gold is in their trunks at home! Oh, I saw that my gold was in my trunk at home! In Christ my Lord and Saviour! Now Christ was all.[69]

So, as a matter of personal experience, Bunyan knew sin, conviction, temptation, doubt, fear, Satan, forgiveness, and grace. He writes, "When God shows a man the sin he has committed, the hell he has deserved, the heaven he has lost; and yet that Christ, and grace, and pardon may be had; this will make him serious, this will make him melt, this will break his heart . . . and this is the man, whose heart, whose life, whose conversation and all, will be engaged in the matters of the eternal salvation of his precious and immortal soul."[70] Bunyan's personal experience was the life of his preaching. His words were not merely a rhetorical exercise, but the words of one who had seen the exceeding sinfulness of sin and the glorious truth of the gospel of grace. Bunyan preached as a man touched by God. By grace, he had discovered Jesus Christ, who "is such a one for beauty and glory, that whoso sees him must both love and fear him."[71]

Preaching to the Heart

Experiential knowledge led Bunyan to aim the arrow of his preaching at people's hearts. Because it is by the heart that a person "understands, wills, affects, reasons, and judges,"[72] Bunyan purposefully sought in his preaching to deliver an "awakening word" to the understanding, the will, the affections, the reason, and the judgment.[73] Winslow writes, "Bunyan had the gift of being able to put emotional compulsion behind his words, and he also knew how to bring the here and now of the urgency home to his hearers."[74]

Preparing primarily with a Bible and a concordance, deeply rooting his sermons in the Scriptures, Bunyan preached what he felt and longed for in his hearers. He writes, "O that they who have heard me speak this

---

69. Bunyan, *Grace Abounding*, in *Works*, 1:36.
70. Bunyan, "The Acceptable Sacrifice," in *Works*, 1:719.
71. Bunyan, *The Holy War*, in *Works*, 3:299.
72. Bunyan, "The Greatness of the Soul," in *Works*, 1:108.
73. While only one treatise in Bunyan's works is labeled as a sermon, many of his other writings were either reworked sermons or at least mirrored the way he preached. Consequently, I have taken the liberty to draw from many of his writings to make conclusions about the way he preached.
74. Winslow, *John Bunyan*, 75.

day did but see as I do what sin, death, hell, and the curse of God is; and also what the grace, and love, and mercy of God is, through Jesus Christ."[75] To better grasp how he preached to the heart, let us examine three particulars of Bunyan's preaching: it was participatory, pleading, and Christ-exalting.

Participatory Preaching

Bunyan believed that those listening to preaching should be participants, not spectators. To that end, he usually addressed his hearers very personally, commonly using the second person. He was direct, often describing various cases of conscience. He was also illustrative and simple, so that even the common people heard him gladly.[76] Wakefield says, "He was folksy and colloquial as he confronted his hearers with the issues of life and death, heaven and hell," often using sanctified imaginative enlargements of Scripture. For example, when he preached on John 6:37, which affirms that those whom the Father gave to Christ "shall come to Him, Bunyan turns the words 'shall come' into a character by that name. He answers the objections of trembling doubters by assuring them that they need not worry, for '*Shall-come* answered all this.'"[77] In all of these ways and many more, Bunyan drew his hearers into the sermon so that they became participants.

Examples of Bunyan's directness in preaching abound. In his sermon to "Jerusalem sinners" (i.e., great sinners, comparable to those in Jerusalem who rejected and then crucified Christ), Bunyan depicts Peter preaching:

> *Peter.* Repent, every one of you; be baptized, every one of you, in his name, for the remission of sins, and you shall, every one of you, receive the gift of the Holy Ghost.

> *Objector.* "But I was one of them that plotted to take away his life. May I be saved by him?"

> *Peter.* Every one of you.

> *Objector.* "But I was one of them that bare false witness against him. Is there grace for me?"

---

75. Bunyan, *Grace Abounding*, in *Works*, 1:42.
76. John Brown, *Puritan Preaching in England* (London: Hodder & Stoughton, 1900), 149.
77. Wakefield, *Bunyan the Christian*, 38–39.

Peter. For every one of you.

Objector. "But I was one of them that cried out, Crucify him, crucify him; and desired that Barabbas, the murderer, might live, rather than him. What will become of me, think you?"

Peter. I am to preach repentance and remission of sins to every one of you, says Peter.

Objector. "But I was one of them that did spit in his face when he stood before his accusers. I also was one that mocked him, when in anguish he hanged bleeding on the tree. Is there room for me?"

Peter. For every one of you, says Peter.

Objector. "But I was one of them that, in his extremity, said, Give him gall and vinegar to drink. Why may not I expect the same when anguish and guilt is upon me?"

Peter. Repent of these your wickednesses, and here is remission of sins for every one of you.

Objector. "But I railed on him, I reviled him, I hated him, I rejoiced to see him mocked at by others. Can there be hopes for me?"

Peter. There is, for every one of you. "Repent, and be baptized every one of you in the name of Jesus Christ, for the remission of sins, and ye shall receive the gift of the Holy Ghost."[78]

Bunyan's writings suggest that he preached by laying before his hearers powerful evidence of both sin and grace, then calling upon them to render a verdict. It is not that Bunyan viewed the preaching of the Word as subservient to the hearers' judgment; rather, he sought to disarm his hearers by plainly showing them their sin and misery, then revealing the glories of grace. In this way, Bunyan forged an intimate connection with his hearers. He writes, "I thank God he gave unto me some measure of bowels and pity for their souls, which also did put me forward to labor with great diligence and earnestness, to find out such a word as might, if God would bless it, lay hold of and awaken the conscience."[79]

---

78. Bunyan, "The Jerusalem Sinner Saved," in *Works*, 1:71–72.
79. Bunyan, *Grace Abounding*, in *Works*, 1:41.

Bunyan passionately reasoned with his listeners to respond to the truth of sin and judgment, as well as the promises of forgiveness and grace. He says: "Poor sinner, awake; eternity is coming. God and his Son, they are both coming to judge the world; awake, art thou yet asleep, poor sinner? Let me set the trumpet to thine ear once again! The heavens will be shortly on a burning flame; the earth, and the works thereof, shall be burned up, and then wicked men shall go into perdition; does thou hear this, sinner?"[80] Bunyan was not satisfied with simply asserting the truth; he "set the trumpet" to the ear of his listeners, compelling them to respond. He preaches: "Sinner, be advised; ask thy heart again, saying, 'Am I come to Jesus Christ?' For upon this one question, 'Am I come, or, am I not?' hangs heaven and hell as to thee. If thou canst say, 'I am come,' and God shall approve that saying, happy, happy, happy man art thou! But if thou are not come, what can make thee happy? Yea, why can a man be happy that, for his not coming to Jesus Christ for life, must be damned in hell?"[81]

Bunyan encouraged heart-searching self-examination. He would not let listeners be content only to hear good words, but prodded them to seek truth in the heart. So he warns: "Ah, friends, consider there is now hopes of mercy, but then there will not; now Christ holds forth mercy unto you, but then he will not. Now there are his servants that do beseech you to accept of his grace, but if thou lose the opportunity that is put into thine hand, thou thyself mayest beseech hereafter, and no mercy be given thee."[82]

In all of his preaching, Bunyan urged his hearers to respond to the preached Word. A sermon was not a classroom lecture. Rather, it drew in the sinner to engage the faculties of his heart and to force a response. There was urgency and earnestness in Bunyan's preaching. It was not enough for him merely to declare the truth and hope it would yield a response in the future. As the blacksmith knows he must strike the steel while it is hot, so Bunyan demanded an immediate response. He could not rest content until each person to whom he preached had responded to the message; he could not afford to see his congregants go home, putting off what should be done at that moment. His command was, "To day if ye will hear his voice, harden not your hearts" (Heb. 4:7).

---

80. Bunyan, "The Strait Gate," in *Works*, 1:386.
81. Bunyan, "Come and Welcome to Jesus Christ," in *Works*, 1:296.
82. Bunyan, "A Few Sighs from Hell," in *Works*, 3:702.

Pleading Preaching

Aware of the power of Satan's temptations, Bunyan writes: "Oh! The rage and the roaring of this lion, and the hatred that he manifests against the Lord Jesus, and against them that are purchased with his blood!"[83] In one sense, pastors have something to learn from Satan's devices. Satan lives to torment the soul, to induce men's hearts to forsake Christ, and to entice them to embrace sin and temptation. The best way to respond to Satan's pleading, Bunyan says, is for preachers to "outshoot the devil in his own bow."[84] So Bunyan did not merely set life and death before the eyes of people, but by all means possible implored them to forsake sin and embrace life in Christ.

In his pleading, Bunyan painted terrible word pictures of eternal condemnation. He says, "In my preaching of the Word I took special notice of this one thing, namely, that the Lord did lead me to begin where his Word begins with sinners; that is, to condemn all flesh, and to open and allege that the curse of God, by the law, doth belong to, and lay hold on all men as they come into the world, because of sin."[85] Again: "The soul that is lost will never be found again, never be recovered again, never be redeemed again. Its banishment from God is everlasting; the fire in which it burns, and by which it must be tormented, is a fire that is everlasting fire, everlasting burning. That is fearful." Bunyan continues, "Now tell the stars, now tell the drops of water, now tell the blades of grass that are spread upon the face of all the earth, if thou canst; and yet sooner mayest thou do this than count the thousands of millions of thousands of years that a damned soul shall lie in hell."[86]

Bunyan often impersonated God, Christ, and a hell-bound sinner as he pleaded with sinners to turn to Christ and live. This is particularly true in his sermon that compares a person who claims to be a Christian but bears no fruit to a barren fig tree. Listen to Bunyan plead:

> Death, come smite me this fig-tree. And withal the Lord shakes this sinner, and whirls him upon a sick-bed, saying, Take him, death, he hath abused my patience and forbearance, not remembering that it should have led him to repentance, and to the fruits thereof. Death,

---

83. Bunyan, "The Jerusalem Sinner Saved," in *Works*, 1:96.
84. Bunyan, "The Law and Grace Unfolded," in *Works*, 1:572.
85. Bunyan, *Grace Abounding*, in *Works*, 1:42.
86. Bunyan, "The Greatness of the Soul," in *Works*, 1:124.

fetch away this fig-tree to the fire, fetch this barren professor to hell! At this death comes with grim looks into the chamber; yea, and hell follows with him to the bedside, and both stare this professor in the face, yea, begin to lay hands upon him; one smiting him with pains in his body, with headache, heart-ache, back-ache, shortness of breath, fainting, qualms, trembling of joints, stopping at the chest, and almost all the symptoms of a man past all recovery. Now, while death is thus tormenting the body, hell is doing with the mind and conscience, striking them with its pains, casting sparks of fire in thither, wounding with sorrows, and fears of everlasting damnation, the spirit of this poor creature. And now he begins to bethink himself, and to cry to God for mercy; Lord, spare me! Lord, spare me! Nay, saith God, you have been a provocation to me these three years. How many times have you disappointed me? How many seasons have you spent in vain? How many sermons and other mercies did I, of my patience, afford you? But to no purpose at all. Take him, death![87]

Bunyan describes the fruitless professor's death so powerfully that you feel that you are standing at the bedside. As Erroll Hulse (1931–2017) said, "Bunyan carries forward the illustration of the tree being felled so well, that you are left at the end with both the echoes of the chopper and the ghastly death rattles and chokings of the unrepentant one."[88]

While Bunyan pleaded with people to see the severity of sin and hell, he also pleaded the mercies of God. He urges, "Cast but up thine eyes a little higher, and behold, there is the mercy-seat and throne of grace to which thou wouldest come, and by which thou must be saved."[89] He adds, "Coming sinner, what promise thou findest in the word of Christ, strain it whither thou canst, so thou dost not corrupt it, and his blood and merits will answer all; what the word saith, or any true consequence that is drawn there from, that we may boldly venture upon . . . take it then for granted, that thou, whoever thou art, if coming, may come."[90]

If Satan will not rest for a moment in pleading with men's souls, so preachers must not rest from their great duty to plead with men's souls.

---

87. Bunyan, "The Barren Fig Tree," in *Works*, 3:579–80.
88. Erroll Hulse, *The Believer's Experience* (Haywards Heath, Sussex, UK: Carey, 1977), 64.
89. Bunyan, "The Saint's Privilege and Profit," in *Works*, 1:647.
90. Bunyan, "Come and Welcome," in *Works*, 1:263.

And in all of our pleading, we must labor to reveal sin as ugly and hateful, and to make Christ altogether lovely (Song 5:16), for our enemy labors to do the opposite. Bunyan's ability to plead with the heart was largely due to his own spiritual journey. Because of his experience with the weight of sin and guilt, Bunyan could plead with those under conviction; because he had tasted divine grace, he could equally plead the mercies of God in Christ. In sum, Bunyan writes:

> I went for the space of two years, crying out against men's sins, and their fearful state because of them. After which the Lord came in upon my own soul with some staid peace and comfort through Christ; for he did give me many sweet discoveries of his blessed grace through him. . . . I still preached what I saw and felt; now therefore I did much labour to hold forth Jesus Christ in all his offices, relations, and benefits unto the world.[91]

Listen to one example. Bunyan impersonated a great sinner, saying: "Say, when thou art upon thy knees, Lord, here is a Jerusalem sinner! A sinner of the biggest size! One whose burden is of the greatest bulk and heaviest weight! One that cannot stand long without sinking into hell, without thy supporting hand. . . . I say, put in thy name with Magdalene, with Manasseh, that thou mayest fare as the Magdalene and the Manasseh sinners do!"[92]

Christ-Exalting Preaching

The singular aim of a heart mastered by grace is to lift up and magnify Jesus Christ, both as the Christ of the revealed Word and as the Christ of personal experience based on that Word. Bunyan excelled in both.[93] He particularly focused on Christ and the riches of his grace, moving his listeners to exalt their Savior. He preaches: "O Son of God! Grace was in all the tears, grace came bubbling out of thy side with thy blood, grace came forth with every word of thy sweet mouth. Grace came out where the whip smote thee, where the thorns pricked thee, where the nails and spear pierced thee. O blessed Son of God! Here is grace indeed! Unsearchable riches of grace! Grace enough to make angels wonder,

---

91. Bunyan, *Grace Abounding*, in *Works*, 1:42.
92. Bunyan, "The Jerusalem Sinner Saved," in *Works*, 1:89.
93. Austin Kennedy DeBlois, "England's Greatest Protestant Preacher," in *John Bunyan, the Man* (Philadelphia: Judson, 1928), 156–57.

grace to make sinners happy, grace to astonish devils."[94] For Bunyan, this is persevering grace, for it will never perish.[95]

Bunyan's first love was to exalt Christ through preaching him doctrinally with passion and theological grandeur:

> For I have known my preaching, especially when I have been engaged in the doctrine of life by Christ, without works, as if an angel of God had stood at my back to encourage me. Oh! it hath been with such power and heavenly evidence upon my own soul, while I have been laboring to unfold it, to demonstrate it, and to hasten it upon the consciences of others, that I could not be contented with saying, "I believe and am sure"; methought I was more than sure (if it be lawful so to express myself) that those things which I then asserted were true.[96]

Bunyan's preaching was not only doctrinal, dealing with the weighty matters of the faith, but it was also doxological, praising God and calling forth praise from awakened hearts. This doxological emphasis must also be characteristic of preaching today. In the words of William Perkins, "Preach one Christ, by Christ, to the praise of Christ."[97]

For Bunyan, exalting Christ meant much more than praising him just because he converts us. Ultimately, Bunyan had in mind that the saved will exalt Jesus Christ in glory forever:

> Then shall we have perfect and everlasting visions of God and that blessed one his Son, Jesus Christ. . . . Then shall our will and affections be ever in a burning flame of love to God and his Son Jesus Christ. . . . Then will our conscience have that peace and joy that neither tongue nor pen of men or angels can express. . . . Then will our memory be so enlarged to retain all things that happened to us in this world . . . and how God made all work together for his glory and our good, to the everlasting ravishing of our hearts.[98]

Bunyan taught that such exaltation is possible only by the indwelling Spirit's gracious ministry in believers' souls:

---

94. Bunyan, "Saved by Grace," in *Works*, 1:346.
95. See Robert Alan Richey, "The Puritan Doctrine of Sanctification: Constructions of the Saints' Final and Complete Perseverance as Mirrored in Bunyan's *The Pilgrim's Progress*" (ThD diss., Mid-America Baptist Theological Seminary, 1990).
96. Bunyan, *Grace Abounding*, in *Works*, 1:42, quoted in DeBlois, "England's Greatest Protestant Preacher," 158.
97. William Perkins, *The Art of Prophesying* (Edinburgh: Banner of Truth, 2002), 79.
98. Bunyan, "Saved by Grace," in *Works*, 1:341–42.

By this Spirit we come to see the beauty of Christ, without a sight of which we should never desire him, but should certainly live in the neglect of him, and perish. By this Spirit we are helped to praise God acceptably, but without it, it is impossible to be heard unto salvation. By this blessed Spirit the love of God is shed abroad in our hearts, and our hearts are directed into the love of God.[99]

Finally, Bunyan repeatedly stressed that this glorious, Christ-exalting salvation ought to move us with longing and eager anticipation toward God. This should be especially true as we catch a vision of the warmth and sincerity of his invitation to come to him and partake of such a glorious Savior. Bunyan preaches:

O sinner! what sayest thou? How dost thou like being saved? Doth not thy mouth water? Doth not thy heart twitter at being saved? Why, *come* then: "The Spirit and the bride say, come. And let him that heareth say, Come. And let him that is athirst come. And whosoever will, let him take the water of life freely" (Rev. 22:17).[100]

Conclusion

Bunyan experienced the failures and victories of the Christian life. His soul had been weighed down by sin, but he also drank deeply of the riches of Jesus Christ's grace. His spiritual journey enabled him to meet sinners and saints where they were. We can learn much from this famed Puritan preacher. Though the church in America weakens as pulpits become showcases for humorists, storytellers, and pop psychologists, the tinker from Bedford remains a remarkable memorial to the Spirit's mighty power in days of laxity and spiritual deadness. It is amazing to see how God uses the weak and foolish things of this world to shame the wise: Bunyan's college was a dungeon; his library, the Bible. Clad in the armor of Ephesians 6, he came forth with power to grapple with the prince of darkness.

God blessed Bunyan with extraordinary abilities, even on the purely human and natural level. There were many other tinkers in England in those days, no doubt some very devout Christians among them, but only one Bunyan. His verbal gifts, powers of imagination, and remarkable achievements as an autodidact point to the providential hand of God

---

99. Bunyan, "Saved by Grace," in *Works*, 1:346.
100. Bunyan, "Saved by Grace," in *Works*, 1:342.

that enriched him far above the average preacher to reach the minds and hearts of sinners and saints. This divine gifting does not wholly explain his success and usefulness as a preacher, but neither does it count for nothing at all.

Bunyan's pointed preaching had a plain but colorful style, which made him appealing to average people, yet powerfully eloquent, shaming the finest orator. He was an evangelistic fisher of men and experiential preacher par excellence, warmly inviting sinners to come to Christ, proclaiming emphatically both what Christians should experience and what they actually do experience in their spiritual pilgrimage. The three elements of preaching that we studied—participating, pleading, and Christ-exalting—are just a few of the mighty weapons that Bunyan wielded to reach the hearts of men. They are, in part, what gave Bunyan's preaching such heavenly force and, under the Spirit's blessing, brought forth great fruit.

Stories abound about the fruitfulness of Bunyan's preaching. Remarkable conversions took place under his ministry. Arnott provides an example: "Bunyan was going to preach in a certain village church. Rather the worse for drink, a Cambridge scholar said he was resolved 'to hear the tinker prate.' So he went into the church to laugh, but stayed to listen, and as a result was himself converted and became a preacher."[101]

Though Bunyan was an unusually gifted preacher, the same Spirit upon whom he depended is still at work in the church of Jesus Christ today. Bunyan's life and ministry remind us that in God's hands, the preaching of the Word is a powerful weapon. As John Harris says, for Bunyan "the battle is for the hearts of men—their minds are in darkness because their hearts are in captivity. The reality of that dreadful condition led Bunyan to use every weapon in his armory to assail the fortress and to break through to the inner being"[102] as he preached to the heart. As Charles H. Spurgeon says, if we wish to "cause a burning which will set the forests of error on fire, and warm the very soul of this cold earth,"[103] we must preach with the fire of hell behind us and the glory of heaven before us. We must strive by all means to invite listeners to participate in the divine drama of loving their souls and plead with them

101. Arnott, *He Shall with Giants Fight*, 69.
102. Harris, "Moving the Heart: the Preaching of John Bunyan," 50.
103. Charles H. Spurgeon, *Lectures to My Students* (Pasadena, TX: Pilgrim Publications, 1990), 1:83.

to close with Christ in order to exalt King Jesus forever. May the Spirit be pleased to give us men like Bunyan who, being mastered by free and sovereign grace, are aglow with divine truth and are made willing to be counted as fools, to endure prison bonds, and to defy the power of death itself for the sake of Christ.

14

Introduction to the Dutch Further Reformation

The Reformation initially penetrated the Netherlands through Lutheran influences (1517) and then Anabaptist influences (1531). But from 1545 onward, the Reformation in the Netherlands generally followed the Reformed or Calvinist trajectory.[1] The Heidelberg Catechism, a strong statement of Reformed experiential beliefs, was written in German in 1563, translated into Dutch that same year, and published in Dutch with a metrical Psalter in 1566. Just months later, it was being regularly preached in the churches. In 1568, the catechism received the blessing of the Synod of Wesel.

However, the Dutch Reformed movement did not come to full fruition until it was cultivated by the *Nadere Reformatie* ("Further Reformation"), a primarily seventeenth- and early eighteenth-century movement that paralleled English Puritanism[2] and was fortified by the Synod of Dort (1618–1619). Before we look at some Dutch Reformed experiential preachers, we will introduce the Dutch *Nadere Reformatie* and the Synod of Dort.

The Dutch Further Reformation

The *Nadere Reformatie* dates from Willem Teellinck (1579–1629), often called the father of the movement, to its last brilliant contributors,

---

1. For a more detailed treatment of the Dutch Further Reformation, see the appendix in Joel R. Beeke, *The Quest for Full Assurance: The Legacy of Calvin and His Successors* (Edinburgh: Banner of Truth, 1999), 286–309.

2. Parts of this section are adapted from "Introduction to the Dutch Further Reformation," in Joel R. Beeke and Randall J. Pederson, *Meet the Puritans: With a Guide to Modern Reprints* (Grand Rapids, MI: Reformation Heritage Books, 2006), 741–44.

Alexander Comrie (1706–1774) and Theodorus van der Groe (1705–1784). Scholars offer the following definition of the *Nadere Reformatie:*

> The *Nadere Reformatie* is that movement within the Nederduits Gereformeerde Kerk (Dutch Reformed Church) during the seventeenth and eighteenth centuries, which, as a reaction to the declension or absence of a living faith, made both the personal experience of faith and godliness matters of central importance. From that perspective the movement formulated substantial and procedural reformation initiatives, submitting them to the proper ecclesiastical, political, and social agencies, and pursued those initiatives through a further reformation of the church, society, and state in both word and deed.[3]

The term *Nadere Reformatie* is a problem for English speakers because the Dutch word *nadere* allows for no precise English translation. Literally, *Nadere Reformatie* means a nearer, more intimate, or more precise Reformation. Its emphasis was the working out of the Reformation more intensely in people's lives, in the church's worship, and in society at large. Although some sources speak of the Dutch "Second Reformation," it is best to speak in English of the Dutch "Further Reformation." The latter term captures the very profound continuity that this movement felt and stressed with the prior history of the Reformation in the Netherlands.

The Dutch Further Reformation has also been called "Dutch Puritanism." At first glance, this description seems helpful, since the *Nadere Reformatie* is the Dutch counterpart to English Puritanism. The link between those movements is strong, historically and theologically. Keith Sprunger has shown that during the seventeenth century, tens of thousands of Anglo-Scottish believers of Puritan persuasion lived in the Netherlands. Those believers represented about forty congregations and 350 ministers.[4]

The divines of English Puritanism and the Dutch Further Reformation respected each other. They enriched each other through personal contacts and their writings, both their Latin treatises and

---

3. C. Graafland, W. J. op 't Hof, and F. A. van Lieberg, "Nadere Reformatie: opnieuw een poging tot begripsbepaling," in *Documentatieblad Nadere Reformatie* 19 (1995): 108. The English translation of this paragraph is from Bartel Elshout, *The Pastoral and Practical Theology of Wilhelmus à Brakel* (Grand Rapids, MI: Reformation Heritage Books, 1997), 9.
4. Keith L. Sprunger, *Dutch Puritanism: A History of English and Scottish Churches of the Netherlands in the Sixteenth and Seventeenth Centuries* (Leiden: Brill, 1982).

the many books translated from English into Dutch. Willem Jan op't Hof says that from 1598 to 1622, sixty English Puritan works were translated into Dutch and printed in a total of 114 editions. William Perkins eclipsed all other English writers (seventy-one editions of twenty-nine works in translation). One Dutch theologian, Gisbertus Voetius (1589–1676), possessed thirty Puritan works in Latin and 270 in English. Op't Hof estimates that 260 new translations in 580 editions appeared from 1623 to 1699.[5] More Reformed theological books were printed in the seventeenth century in the Netherlands than in all other countries combined. English Puritan and Dutch Further Reformation divines also had similar aims: to foster God-glorifying experiential piety and ethical precision in individuals, churches, and nations.

Despite similar outlooks, however, English Puritanism and the *Nadere Reformatie* developed historically and theologically distinct identities. Though English Puritanism was a primary influence on the Further Reformation—particularly in its stress on the need for a personal and congregational life of practical godliness—it was not an exclusive influence. Non-English factors also contributed.

In some respects, the Dutch movement was more Puritan than English Puritanism itself. Jonathan Gerstner says: "In England from an orthodox Reformed perspective, for all but a short period under Cromwell, there were always grossly unbiblical things to fight: the presence of bishops, superstitious rites in the Book of Common Prayer, vestments, etc. In the Netherlands none of these were present, and the task was all the more subtle. Defenders of the *status quo* were not so clearly unreformed as in England. In this context the true spirit of Puritanism came to the fore."[6]

Divines of the Dutch Further Reformation were less interested in reforming the government and church than were their English brethren. Then, too, the Dutch were more inclined to emphasize theology as a science, whereas the English emphasized the practical aspects of theology. Nevertheless, the essence of the Dutch Further Reformation does match the emphasis of English Puritanism on the practice of authentic Reformed spirituality.

---

5. Willem Jan op't Hof, *Engelse pietistische geschriften in het Nederlands* (Rotterdam: Lindenberg, 1993), 636–37, 640, 645.
6. Jonathan N. Gerstner, *The Thousand Generation Covenant: Dutch Reformed Covenant Theology and Group Identity in Colonial South Africa* (Leiden: Brill, 1991), 77–78.

Thankfully, several Dutch Further Reformation books have recently been translated into English as the Classics of Reformed Spirituality series.[7] So has the "crème de la crème" of the movement's literature, *The Christian's Reasonable Service* by Wilhelmus à Brakel.[8]

Experiential Ministry in the Netherlands

The Further Reformation called for orthodox, biblical beliefs and warm, personal spirituality producing vital, practical obedience. One can see the experiential emphasis of this movement in the definitions of faith and good works given by Wilhelmus Schortinghuis (1700–1750):

Q. What does genuine faith consist of?

A. (1) Of a literal, and, especially, an experiential knowledge of the truths of the gospel, God, oneself, Christ, and the way of grace (Isa. 53:11); (2) of a warm-hearted and willing assent (John 3:33); and (3) of a trust that finds refuge with God in Christ (Isa. 27:5; Prov. 18:10; Ps. 2:12).[9]

Q. What are the marks of good works?

A. Good works that truly please God are not those that are done to serve our own will and pleasure (Matt. 15:9), but those done from faith through union with Christ (Rom. 14:23; John 15:1–3), according to God's law (Ps. 119:4–5; Isa. 8:20; Gal. 6:16), and to God's honor (1 Cor. 10:31).[10]

Jean Taffin (c. 1529–1602), a forerunner of the Further Reformation, highlighted the centrality of preaching in God's work among the faithful.

---

7. Godefridus Udemans, *The Practice of Faith, Hope, and Love*, ed. Joel R. Beeke, trans. Annemie Godbehere (Grand Rapids, MI: Reformation Heritage Books, 2012); Guilelmus Saldenus and Wilhelmus à Brakel, *In Remembrance of Him: Profiting from the Lord's Supper*, ed. James A. De Jong, trans. Bartel Elshout (Grand Rapids, MI: Reformation Heritage Books, 2012); Jodocus van Lodensteyn, *A Spiritual Appeal to Christ's Bride*, ed. Joel R. Beeke, trans. Bartel Elshout (Grand Rapids, MI: Reformation Heritage Books, 2010); Wilhelmus Schortinghuis, *Essential Truths in the Heart of a Christian*, ed. James A. De Jong, trans. Harry Boonstra and Gerrit W. Sheeres (Grand Rapids, MI: Reformation Heritage Books, 2009); Jean Taffin, *The Marks of God's Children*, ed. James A. De Jong, trans. Peter Y. De Jong (Grand Rapids, MI: Baker Academic, 2003); Willem Teellinck, *The Path of True Godliness* (Grand Rapids, MI: Baker Academic, 2003); Gisbertus Voetius and Johannes Hoornbeeck, *Spiritual Desertion*, ed. M. Eugene Osterhaven, trans. John Vriend and Harry Boonstra (Grand Rapids, MI: Baker Academic, 2003); Jacobus Koelman, *The Duties of Parents*, ed. M. Eugene Osterhaven, trans. John Vriend (Grand Rapids, MI: Baker Academic, 2003).

8. Wilhelmus à Brakel, *The Christian's Reasonable Service*, 4 vols., ed. Joel R. Beeke, trans. Bartel Elshout (Grand Rapids, MI: Reformation Heritage Books, 1995–1999).

9. Schortinghuis, *Essential Truths in the Heart of a Christian*, 89.

10. Schortinghuis, *Essential Truths in the Heart of a Christian*, 98.

The preeminent mark of a true church, he says, is "the pure preaching of God's Word." Through biblical preaching, the sheep hear the voice of their Shepherd (John 10:27). Taffin says, "By the administration of his Word undoubtedly God offers peace, grace, salvation, and life."[11] God speaks with a living voice through the preacher, revealing his will to save sinners: "God who is Truth itself reveals his counsel and will concerning our adoption and salvation in the preaching of the gospel."[12]

Schortinghuis says that "a righteous minister" is one gifted and called by the Lord, "who seeks to win souls for the King, and who oversees them in the power of Christ by serving compassionately, seriously, and faithfully in all areas of his service (John 21:15–17; 1 Tim. 3:1–7)." This engages him to "pray earnestly" for himself and the church, and to preach the Scriptures with faithful discernment and the demonstration of "the Spirit and power."[13]

Herman Witsius (1636–1708) spoke of every seminary student and minister as a "theologian" in the broadest and truest sense of the word— one who discourses on God. He writes: "A true theologian is a humble disciple of the Scriptures. But as the Word of God is the only rule of faith, so it is also necessary that our theologian, in order to understand it in a spiritual and saving manner, give himself up to the internal teaching of the Holy Spirit. Thus, he who is a disciple of the Scriptures must also be a disciple of the Spirit."[14] This equips him to teach others as a man taught by God, not "by mere speculation but by real experience," so that he can open the deep underground streams of God's Word "that an overflowing fountain of water, springing up to everlasting life, bursts forth to allay the thirst of his brethren."[15]

Preachers are not just teachers but evangelical comforters. Voetius says that "the ministers of the Word" should be the best friends of those suffering from afflictions of conscience, for "these ought above all to be equipped with the gift and art of consolation."[16] His student Johannes Hoornbeeck (1617–1666) writes that defeated souls need someone "to speak to the heart."[17] Those experiencing darkness of the soul find great

---

11. Taffin, *The Marks of God's Children*, 36.
12. Taffin, *The Marks of God's Children*, 42.
13. Schortinghuis, *Essential Truths in the Heart of a Christian*, 128.
14. Herman Witsius, *On the Character of a True Theologian*, ed. J. Ligon Duncan III (Greenville, SC: Reformed Academic Press, 1994), 35.
15. Witsius, *On the Character of a True Theologian*, 38.
16. Voetius and Hoornbeeck, *Spiritual Desertion*, 47.
17. Voetius and Hoornbeeck, *Spiritual Desertion*, 79.

help in the companionship of godly people, especially a minister who is both "able to comfort" and "mighty in the Scriptures."[18] The training of ministers must be, as Voetius says, "piety joined with knowledge." When serving as a theological professor at Utrecht, he regarded his vocation as to "practically treat of the solid and orthodox science of theology, which is by its nature practical."[19] Thus, these divines wedded careful study and spiritual piety, rejecting both heartless theology and mindless activity. As Hoornbeeck says, "There is no practice without theory."[20]

In modern times, the term *theology* often connotes abstract, philosophical, and irrelevant debates. But these divines saw theology as a vibrant way of life. Witsius writes, "By a theologian, I mean one who, imbued with a substantial knowledge of divine things derived from the teaching of God Himself, declares and extols, not in words only, but by the whole course of his life, the wonderful excellencies of God and thus lives entirely for His glory." Such a man does not concern himself with drawn-out "subtleties of curious questions," but "the devout contemplation of God and His Christ." Ministers of this stamp preached such that, "impressing upon the mind an exact representation of sacred things, [they] inflamed the soul with their love."[21]

Such teaching requires men who know God experientially. Witsius writes, "And how, I ask, is it possible that he who knows the truth as it is in Jesus, should not be inflamed with His love and sanctified by His truth?" The minister must have a "true relish" for heavenly things and a heavenly conduct in the image of Christ. He must be "panting after the things which are above and eternal," but viewing the riches, honors, and pleasures of this world with contempt. Every preacher should be humbled by the holy calling God has extended to him. But he should with Witsius neither "lose courage" nor "lower the exact standard of duty," but instead, "through the grace of God," he should "spare no efforts" to be a faithful servant of the Lord.[22]

The preaching of the gospel is the hand of God extending to sinners the saving work of Christ. The Dutch Further Reformation preachers

---

18. Voetius and Hoornbeeck, *Spiritual Desertion*, 153.
19. Gisbertus Voetius, *Ta asketika sive Exercitia Pietatis* (Gorinchem: Vink, 1654), 3, quoted in Joel R. Beeke, *Gisbertus Voetius: Toward a Reformed Marriage of Knowledge and Piety* (Grand Rapids, MI: Reformation Heritage Books, 1999), 14.
20. Johannes Hoornbeeck, *Theologiae Practicae* (Utrecht: Versteegh, 1663), 1:85, quoted in Beeke, *Gisbertus Voetius*, 20.
21. Witsius, *On the Character of a True Theologian*, 27.
22. Witsius, *On the Character of a True Theologian*, 44–48.

reveled in the thought that God's sovereign mercy reaches out from Christ through the preached Word. Taffin prays:

> But O gracious God, while we were children of wrath, Thy enemies and surrendered to all evil, Thou hadst compassion on us poor and wretched sinners. Thou didst turn Thy eyes of mercy and favor toward us. Thou gavest Thy dear and beloved Son Jesus Christ to the shameful and accursed death of the cross for us. Thou didst send Thy holy gospel, that blessed and joyful message of our salvation. Thou didst accompany that gospel with Thy Holy Spirit to enlighten us, to draw us to Thyself, and to give us a share in the treasures of Thy kingdom and everlasting life. Thou didst stretch out Thy hand from heaven into the very depths of hell to rescue and make us Thy blessed children. All this Thou didst according to the good pleasure of Thy will, showing mercy to those to whom Thou wast pleased to be merciful.[23]

Having surveyed the Dutch Further Reformation and its experiential emphasis, we turn next to the major doctrinal statement issued during this period in the Netherlands and its implications for the ministry of the Word.

The Canons of Dort

The Synod of Dort (or Dordrecht, a city in South Holland) was called to settle a controversy raging in the Dutch churches. A professor at Leiden named Jacob Arminius (1560–1609) had departed from the Reformed faith on a number of points. His ideas found a wide reception and received the support of some key government leaders, who put pressure on local churches to adopt Arminius's views. After his death, his followers, "the Remonstrants," drew up their "Remonstrance," summing up their objections to the teachings of the Reformed faith in five points. They presented it to the government in 1610, seeking to revise the Belgic Confession and Heidelberg Catechism. This controversy took on political overtones, and soon civil war threatened the peace of the nation. In 1617, the States General (the Dutch parliament) called a national synod to address the challenge of the Remonstrants.

---

23. Taffin, *The Marks of God's Children*, 141–42. This translation has been adjusted to coincide with Taffin's addressing God as *Gij* ("Thou").

The Synod of Dort met in 154 sessions from November 1618 to May 1619. Though it was a national synod with sixty-two delegates from Dutch churches, it also drew twenty-seven foreign delegates representing Reformed churches in eight countries. It produced the Canons of Dort; *canon* refers to an authoritative ruling in a matter of church doctrine or discipline.

These canons are popularly called the five points of Calvinism, but this is a misnomer in a number of ways. First, the delegates would not have called themselves "Calvinists" but Reformed Christians, viewing John Calvin as one among many good teachers in the Reformation. Second, the synod organized the canons under four headings, not five, since they believed that human sinfulness and regenerating grace must be addressed together, and so canons ("Heads of Doctrine ") III and IV were combined as one. Third, the canons do not offer a full-orbed presentation of Reformed theology, but only the response of orthodoxy to the errors of the Remonstrants. Thus, the Canons of Dort are the Reformed answer to the five points of Arminianism, and they are confined to soteriology, or the doctrine of salvation.

The Arminians declared in the Remonstrance and clarified at the Synod of Dort:

1. That God eternally decreed to save believers in Christ who persevere to the end, and to damn unbelievers. He did not elect anyone to eternal life without foresight of their future faith, obedience, and perseverance. There is no hidden will in God to save only some men, but only that will, proclaimed in the gospel, to save all men.

2. That Christ died for every man so that he obtained salvation for them all, but only believers actually enjoy this salvation. His death reconciled the entire human race to God. As a result, the Father can righteously make a covenant of grace with sinners on the condition that they believe that Christ died for them.

3. That man cannot produce faith or any saving grace of his free will. He must be born again by the Holy Spirit. But the sinner may obtain faith and regeneration by hearing God's Word, grieving over his sins, and desiring grace. As Cornelis Venema observes, the Remonstrants taught that "sinful man must predispose himself to receive and cooperate with the grace of God in order to be saved."[24]

---

24. Cornelis P. Venema, *But for the Grace of God: An Exposition of the Canons of Dort* (Grandville, MI: Reformed Fellowship, 2011), 61.

4. That man cannot do any good apart from God's grace, but that grace is not irresistible. God by his Word and Spirit gives the power to believe, but man is able to despise this grace and to reject faith, and so to perish. Everyone who hears God's Word receives sufficient grace to believe unto salvation, if he so chooses.

5. That believers have in Christ all that they need to persevere, but if they are negligent, they can lose God's grace and fall away into the world. It is not uncommon for believers to fall into such sin that they lose faith and justification, though they may be converted and saved again. Therefore, no believer can have certain assurance that he will never fall away and ultimately be damned.[25]

The Synod of Dort responded to these assertions with remarkable pastoral wisdom and theological balance. The canons reflect biblical depth, evangelistic zeal, and warm gratitude. They merit our reading and meditation. In summary, against the Arminians, the synod declared:

1. That God out of his mercy sent his Son to save sinners, and sent preachers to proclaim that all who repent and trust in Christ will be saved. But only those whom God chose will repent and believe because their conversion is a gift of God. God did not choose them because they believe; they believe because he chose them.

2. That God gave his Son to make satisfaction to God's justice for the sins of God's chosen ones. Christ's death is of infinite value, so the promise of the gospel should be preached to all. But it was God's will that his death redeem only the elect, who will be certainly and completely saved despite sin and Satan.

3/4. That although men still retain their minds and wills, the soul is so utterly dead in sin that they are neither able nor willing to come to God, or to dispose themselves to do so. God does not give men the power to believe if they so choose; rather, he raises them from the deadness of sin and renews their hearts and wills so that they willingly choose to believe.

5. That believers have many remaining weaknesses and may sadly fall into sin. God remains merciful, however, according to his eternal purpose of love. He preserves them so that they do not fall away but persevere in faith. Though they may experience doubts about their salvation,

---

25. See the Remonstrance in Philip Schaff, *The Creeds of Christendom: With a History and Critical Notes* (New York: Harper, 1877), 3:545–49; and "The Opinions of the Remonstrants," in Homer C. Hoeksema, *The Voice of Our Fathers: An Exposition of the Canons of Dordrecht* (Grand Rapids, MI: Reformed Free Publishing Association, 1980), 103–9.

it is possible for them to enjoy solid comfort and assurance of salvation and eternal life.

As a result of the rulings of the synod, Arminian ministers were removed from their pulpits. Led by Simon Episcopius (1583–1643), they continued outside the national church and were granted tolerance in the Netherlands in 1625. Over time, many of them fell into the grosser errors of Socinianism and Unitarianism, denying the doctrines of the Trinity and substitutionary atonement by Christ's blood.

It is not the purpose of this book to explain and defend the teachings of Dort. But I highly commend them to the reader for further study. Begin by reading the canons themselves. They are full of scriptural truth and wisdom. Then read good study materials on the canons.[26] As the purpose of this chapter is to illustrate Reformed experiential preaching, we now move on to consider what the synod taught about the ministry of the Word.

The Canons of Dort and Preaching the Word

While the Canons of Dort are famous for their doctrinal pronouncements about God's sovereign grace to sinners, Peter De Jong observes that it is "a glaring misrepresentation" to limit the synod's work to theology. Both before and after addressing Arminianism, the synod dealt with a number of other questions raised by the churches, and "preaching in the churches constituted one of its chief concerns."[27]

First, the synod reaffirmed the custom of preaching on the Heidelberg Catechism. Catechism preaching had been introduced in 1566 by Pieter Gabriël (d. 1573) and made mandatory for the churches in 1586. The catechism itself had been apportioned for weekly exposition when it was divided into fifty-two Lord's Days. However, congregational neglect and pastoral overwork threatened the survival of this practice. The synod stated, "The Ministers everywhere shall briefly explain on Sunday, ordinarily in the afternoon sermon, the sum of Christian doctrine compre-

---

26. On the Canons of Dort, see Peter Y. De Jong, ed., *Crisis in the Reformed Churches: Essays in Commemoration of the Great Synod of Dort, 1618–1619* (Grand Rapids, MI: Reformed Fellowship, 1968); Hoeksema, *Voice of Our Fathers*; P. G. Feenstra, *Unspeakable Comfort: A Commentary on the Canons of Dort* (Winnipeg: Premier Printing, 1997); Cornelis Pronk, *Expository Sermons on the Canons of Dort* (St. Thomas, ON: Free Reformed Publications, 1999); William Twisse, *The Doctrine of the Synod of Dort and Arles, Reduced to the Practise* (Amsterdam: Successors of G. Thorp, 1631); Venema, *But for the Grace of God*; Joel R. Beeke, *Living for God's Glory: An Introduction to Calvinism* (Lake Mary, FL: Reformation Trust, 2008), 24–26, 48–131.

27. Peter Y. De Jong, "Preaching and the Synod of Dort," in *Crisis in the Reformed Churches*, 120–21.

hended in the Catechism which at present is accepted in the Netherland Churches, so that it may be completed every year in accordance with the division of the Catechism itself made for that purpose."[28] The synod did add that the sermons should be "brief and easy to comprehend for the sake of the uneducated."[29] So the Canons of Dort express a concern that the people receive instruction in the doctrinal standards of the church through regular catechism preaching. As we saw in an earlier chapter, the Heidelberg Catechism expresses Reformed experiential Christianity with great warmth and depth.

Second, the Synod of Dort commended the preaching of predestination. The divines rejected the idea that predestination is an irrelevant or abstract notion, or, worse, a harmful idea best left alone. It was preached by the Old Testament prophets, the New Testament apostles, and Christ himself. Therefore, the canons say, the doctrine of election should be preached, "provided it be done with reverence, in the spirit of discretion and piety, for the glory of God's most holy Name, and for enlivening and comforting His people, without vainly attempting to investigate the secret ways of the Most High" (1.14).[30] Preachers must stick closely to the Word, and preach the Word to the heart. The doctrines of election and reprobation do not encourage sin, fatalism, or despair, but instead they can and should be preached "to the glory of the divine Name, to holiness of life, and to the consolation of afflicted souls," as the canons say in their concluding remarks.

Venema says: "God has been pleased, for the edification and salvation of His people, to reveal the truth concerning His electing grace in Christ in the Scriptures. It would be unfaithfulness and ingratitude on our part, not to preach what the Word teaches on this subject." Yet he cautions, "The preaching of election must be carefully disciplined by the Word of God, declaring neither more nor less than God has been pleased to reveal to us in the Word."[31]

Third, the synod declared that the doctrines of grace, which the canons expound in five heads, have massive implications for preaching. The canons present a biblical perspective on God's saving grace that shapes

---

28. "Church Order," 3.68, in Joel R. Beeke, ed., *Doctrinal Standards, Liturgy, and Church Order* (Grand Rapids, MI: Reformation Heritage Books, 2003), 187.
29. Quoted in De Jong, "Preaching and the Synod of Dort," 121.
30. "The Canons of Dort," head 1, article 1, in *Doctrinal Standards*, 97. Further references to the canons are noted in the text by the head and article number. Note that heads 3 and 4 are combined, resulting in a reference like 3/4.1.
31. Venema, *But for the Grace of God*, 32–33.

why and how we preach the Word. In what follows, under three points, I offer some of the canons' lessons for preaching.

Preaching Is a Means of Sovereign Grace

The canons say, "As all men have sinned in Adam, lie under the curse, and are deserving of eternal death, God would have done no injustice by leaving them all to perish, and delivering them over to condemnation on account of sin" (1.1). But God's heart overflowed with mercy, and he sent his Son to save sinners (1.2). Furthermore, the canons say, "And that men may be brought to believe, God mercifully sends the messengers of these most joyful tidings to whom He will and at what times He pleaseth; by whose ministry men are called to repentance and faith in Christ crucified" (1.3). So from their opening, the Canons of Dort lift up preaching as the means through which God's mercy in Christ meets the needs of lost men. Cornelis Pronk says, "When we talk about election we should start with the fact that Christ is preached, and is freely offered to lost sinners."[32]

God's elect are not distinguished by any superiority rooted in their nature or nurture, but rather by the effect of the Word upon them. God has decreed to give his elect to Christ and "effectually to call and draw them to His communion by His Word and Spirit" (1.7). So the Spirit-filled preaching of the Bible plays a central role in effectual calling unto Christ. It also is a means by which God preserves his grace in believers so that they persevere (5.14). When they fall into sin, he, "by His Word and Spirit, certainly and effectually renews them to repentance" (5.7). The pairing of Word and Spirit reminds ministers that preaching requires the blessing of the Holy Spirit to be effective in evangelism and edification.

We have seen already that God is sovereign over the sending of a preacher to a particular people (1.3). The Synod of Dort emphatically denies that God has ever sent the ministry of the Word to a people because they were "better and worthier than another to whom the gospel was not communicated." On the contrary, it is "merely and solely the good pleasure of God" that rules over the sending of the preacher to a particular people (1.r9).[33] Therefore, when a preacher goes forth to serve a community, he may trust that he is there by God's sovereign will.

---

32. Pronk, *Expository Sermons on the Canons of Dort*, 19.
33. The notation 1.r9 means head 1, rejection 9.

Unless God sends a preacher of the gospel, there is no hope of salvation. Neither "the light of nature" nor the moral "law" can save a sinner. God saves the sinner "by the operation of the Holy Spirit through the word or ministry of reconciliation" (3/4.6). This last phrase is a reference to evangelistic preaching as described in 2 Corinthians 5:18–21:

> And all things are of God, who hath reconciled us to himself by Jesus Christ, and hath given to us the ministry of reconciliation; to wit, that God was in Christ, reconciling the world unto himself, not imputing their trespasses unto them; and hath committed unto us the word of reconciliation. Now then we are ambassadors for Christ, as though God did beseech you by us: we pray you in Christ's stead, be ye reconciled to God. For he hath made him to be sin for us, who knew no sin; that we might be made the righteousness of God in him.

In the midst of a confessional statement about sovereign, predestining grace, we are reminded that preachers are to plead with sinners to come to Christ.

When God sends a preacher, it is an immense grace to the people who hear him. They should not try to pry into God's reasons for passing by others and giving the gospel to them. Neither should they think they were "superior" or "making a better use of the light of nature." Rather, they must acknowledge God's mercies to them "with humble and grateful hearts" (3/4.7).

Preaching Makes a Sincere Offer of Christ to All Men

God's election remains a secret until it bears fruit in conversion. Therefore, the preacher must proclaim the gospel to all who hear him. The canons read: "Moreover, the promise of the gospel is, that whosoever believeth in Christ crucified, shall not perish, but have everlasting life. This promise, together with the command to repent and believe, ought to be declared and published to all nations, and to all persons promiscuously and without distinction, to whom God out of his good pleasure sends the gospel" (2.5). The phrase "promiscuously and without distinction" is a pleonasm, meaning the gospel is to be proclaimed to any person and to all alike, and applies to both the promise and the command of the gospel. It implies that the minister has no business trying to guess which unconverted people may or may not be elect, but must press upon all his hearers their *duty* to turn from sin and trust in Christ.

The canons make this statement in the midst of teaching the doctrine of "limited atonement" or definite redemption. Some people think that preaching the gospel requires us to tell people: "Christ died for you. Believe that and you are saved." On this basis, they accuse those who believe that Christ redeemed his elect of not being able to preach the gospel freely to all men. But here the canons teach both the redemption of a particular people and the gospel invitation for all to come to Christ. As Pronk points out, the apostles "did not call sinners to believe that Christ died for them, but they called sinners to believe in Christ."[34] Acts 16:31 says, "Believe on the Lord Jesus Christ, and thou shalt be saved." Nowhere in the New Testament do we see Christ or his disciples telling people that "Christ died for you." Rather, biblical evangelism declares that Christ died for sinners and promises to save all who believe in him.

The gospel call expresses God's sincere invitation for all sinners to come to Christ. The canons say: "As many as are called by the gospel, are unfeignedly called. For God hath most earnestly and truly shown in his Word, what will be acceptable to Him, namely, that those who are called should comply with the invitation. He, moreover, seriously promises eternal life, and rest to as many as shall come to Him, and believe on Him" (3/4.8). Christ is truly "offered" in the gospel, though many men who are "called by the ministry of the Word" nevertheless reject him (3/4.9). Thus, the preacher proclaims a sincere call from God that all men should repent, offering Christ to them as the only Savior of sinners.

Some Reformed Christians mistakenly reject the doctrine of a free offer of the gospel. They dispute our understanding of the Canons of Dort, and even their translation.[35] For example, Homer Hoeksema objects to what he calls the "corruption of the call of the gospel into a general, well-meant offer of salvation."[36] Instead, he insists that the gospel call is "a demand,

---

34. Pronk, *Expository Sermons on the Canons of Dort*, 128.
35. Homer Hoeksema raises questions about the translation and interpretation of canons 3/4.8 in *Voice of Our Fathers*, 485–86. The words *unfeignedly*, *earnestly*, and *seriously* all translate the same Latin word (*serio*). Hoeksema especially objects to *earnestly*, but Latin lexicons allow for either *seriously* or *earnestly* as correct translations. See Ethan Allen Andrews, *A Copious and Critical Latin-English Lexicon* (New York: Harper & Brothers, 1851), 1401; Leo F. Stelten, *Dictionary of Ecclesiastical Latin: With an Appendix of Latin Expressions Defined and Clarified* (Peabody, MA: Hendrickson, 1995), 245. He is right, however, in asserting that the translation "comply with the invitation" is a loose rendering of the Latin (*ad se veniant*), better translated "come unto Him." For the Latin text of canons 3/4.8, see *Acta Synodi Nationalis, In nomine Domini nostri Iesv Christi, Autoritate Illvstr. et Praepotentvm DD. Ordinvm Generalevm Foederati Belgii Provinciarvm, Dordrechti Habitae Anno MDCXVIII et MDCXIX* (Lvgdvni Batavorvm: Isaaci Elzeviri, 1620), 257.
36. Hoeksema, *Voice of Our Fathers*, 489.

or a command."[37] Indeed, it is a command "to repent and believe" (2.5). As Scripture says, God "commandeth all men every where to repent" (Acts 17:30). But the canons also rightly say that Christ is "offered" through the gospel (3/4.9). Hoeksema says that the word translated "offered" (Latin *offero*) does not denote "a well-meant invitation," but means "presented or set forth."[38] But *to offer* often means to put something before someone for his acceptance or rejection, as in offering food or a gift. "Well-meant" is another way of saying "sincere" or "unfeigned"—which is how the canons describe the gospel call. And an *invitation* is a call to come. The Bible represents the gospel as an invitation to the banquet of God (Prov. 9:1–5; Luke 14:16–24). God personally, earnestly, sincerely, and seriously calls all men to come unto him and find salvation by trusting in his Son.

Faithfulness to the Bible at this point, as at many points, brings the charge of contradiction or incoherence. Arminians charge the Reformed with undermining evangelism. On the other side, even after his revision of the translation, Hoeksema complains that the divines at Dort "were not at their best" and suffered "a lack of clarity" in these articles.[39] On the contrary, I believe they were very clear. They grasped two biblical truths and refused to let either of them go: God has predestined some and God sincerely calls all. De Jong writes: "Indeed, the Reformed did not attempt to resolve what seemed also to them quite incomprehensible. But they emphasized man's responsibility as taught in Scripture fully as much as God's sovereignty."[40]

This has huge implications for preaching, for ministers speak as God's representatives. A Reformed preacher of predestination should offer Christ to everyone who hears the gospel, giving heartfelt calls for them to come to Christ and be saved. G. H. Kersten writes: "The Word must be preached to all without exception; the Gospel must be offered to converted and unconverted. Some object to this as if it would make the offer of grace too general. But the Lord Jesus has commanded it. 'Many are called, but few are chosen' (Matt. 22:14)."[41]

Peter Feenstra says: "The Canons of Dort stress that God is serious when He calls us to come to Him. The Lord has no pleasure in the death

37. Hoeksema, *Voice of Our Fathers*, 492.
38. Hoeksema, *Voice of Our Fathers*, 499–500.
39. Hoeksema, *Voice of Our Fathers*, 487.
40. De Jong, "Preaching and the Synod of Dort," 130.
41. G. H. Kersten, *Reformed Dogmatics: A Systematic Treatment of Reformed Doctrine*, trans. Joel R Beeke and J. C. Weststrate, 2 vols. (Grand Rapids, MI: Netherlands Reformed Book and Publishing Committee, 1980), 369.

of any one but that the sinner should turn from his way and live (Ezekiel 18:23, 30–32)."[42] Though God, for the larger purpose of his glory, has decreed that only his elect will turn to him, it remains true that he does not delight in destruction in itself, but has pleasure in the repentance of sinners, no matter who they may be. If we deny this, we run the risk of denying the very goodness of God.

However, this truth does not require us to preach like an Arminian. The canons say that God does not merely offer saving grace for men to take by "their own free will, which joins itself to the grace that is offered" to make it effective (2.r6). God does not offer "faith" to sinners, to be embraced or rejected. Instead, he offers Christ to all, commands faith as the duty of all, and works faith in some—he "produces both the will to believe and the act of believing also" (3/4.14). The rest reject Christ as a choice determined by their own corrupt wills.

Man is to be blamed for damnation; God is to be praised for salvation. God "calls men by the gospel," and it is not his fault that men "refuse to come and be converted." On the contrary, they themselves are culpable for rejecting the Word and for refusing to allow it to make "a lasting impression on their heart" (3/4.9). When men do repent and believe, it is not because of "the proper exercise of free will," but the gift of the electing God who "rescues them from the power of darkness, and translates them into the kingdom of His own Son" (3/4.10).

The Arminians embraced the biblical doctrine of the gospel call to all men, but then, through twisted human reasoning, misapplied it to deny the equally biblical doctrines of man's total inability and God's sovereignty. The canons embrace both biblical teachings: the free offer of the gospel and the effectual calling of God upon helpless sinners. Venema says:

> It is interesting to note that the language of the Canons, describing the serious and genuine call that God issues through the gospel to all, is virtually identical with that employed by the Remonstrants in their fourth article. However the Reformed authors of the Canons refused to follow the "logic" of the Remonstrants or Arminians, who drew the conclusion that all sinners must then be able of themselves to comply with the gospel's demands.[43]

---

42. Feenstra, *Unspeakable Comfort*, 115.
43. Venema, *But for the Grace of God*, 66n1.

Preaching Is the Channel of Supernatural Power

The doctrines of total human depravity and omnipotent divine grace imply that effective preaching is not merely an exercise in human communication and persuasion. Effective preaching is a supernatural event. God "not only causes the gospel to be externally preached to them and powerfully illuminates their minds by His Holy Spirit . . . but by the efficacy of the same regenerating Spirit, pervades the inmost recesses of the man; He opens the closed, and softens the hardened heart . . . infuses new qualities into the will, which though heretofore dead, He quickens" (3/4.11). God does not merely offer options to the will "by the external preaching of the gospel, by moral suasion [persuasion]," which man may accept or reject. He works a supernatural miracle in the heart so that without fail "man himself is rightly said to believe and repent" (3/4.12).

Here we come to another objection people make against irresistible grace. Pronk explains: "The charge is that Calvinists believe that the elect are saved against their will and man is like a puppet being dragged by his hair to Christ." However, as Pronk goes on to say, in reality all men resist God's grace until that grace overcomes this resistance in his elect.[44] The canons state "that where carnal rebellion and resistance formerly prevailed, a ready and sincere spiritual obedience begins to reign, in which the true and spiritual restoration and freedom of our will consist" (3/4.16). God does not save sinners against their wills; rather, he saves their wills, indeed their whole souls, from the reigning power of sin. We should not think that God hinders the freedom of our wills. God sets the enslaved will free with true freedom in Christ. The canons rightly point out that to deny that God can overcome the resistance in man's will is to deny that God is all powerful (3/4.r8). On the contrary, we exercise faith or believe "according to the working of his mighty power" (Eph. 1:19), and our very life and godliness are gifts of his power (2 Pet. 1:3).

Preaching remains instrumental in conversion because man remains a rational and volitional being, as God created him. The supernatural work of regeneration "does not treat men as senseless stocks and blocks" (3/4.16). God's almighty influence operates through "the use of means," especially "the use of the gospel," which is "the seed of regeneration." Therefore, ministers must faithfully perform "the exercise of the Word, sacraments, and discipline," not tempting God by trying to separate his

---

44. Pronk, *Expository Sermons on the Canons of Dort*, 264.

grace from his means. From our perspective, the more earnestly and fervently we preach the whole counsel of God in Jesus Christ, the more likely God's blessing will rest upon it and his saving work in sinners be advanced: "For grace is conferred by means of admonitions; and the more readily we perform our duty, the more eminent usually is this blessing of God working in us, and the more directly is His work advanced; to whom alone all the glory both of means, and of their saving fruit and efficacy is forever due. Amen" (3/4.17).

Venema says, "The wonderful confidence of gospel preaching, according to the Canons, is that God is pleased through these means to draw all His people without fail to Himself."[45] Therefore, let preachers be encouraged. The work of evangelism is not first and foremost our work, but the work of the triune God.[46] As De Jong points out, preaching should never be reduced "to an effort on the preacher's part which may well prove fruitless." God sent his Son to do his saving will. God sends the preacher wherever he wills. God sends the Spirit to make the preaching effective to save whomever he wills.[47] *Sola gratia! Soli Deo gloria!*

Having opened with Christ crucified, who is the One we preach, the Canons of Dort close by calling upon the Lord, who gives the gifts of preaching, preaches in our preaching, and presses our preaching home into the heart:

> May Jesus Christ, the Son of God, who, seated at the Father's right hand, gives gifts to men, sanctify us in the truth, bring to the truth those who err, shut the mouths of the calumniators [false accusers] of sound doctrine, and endue the faithful minister of His Word with the spirit of wisdom and discretion, that all their discourses may tend to the glory of God and the edification of those who hear them. Amen.[48]

---

45. Venema, *But for the Grace of God*, 75.
46. Venema, *But for the Grace of God*, 92–95.
47. De Jong, "Preaching and the Synod of Dort," 127.
48. *Doctrinal Standards*, 117.

15

Dutch Preachers: Teellinck, van Lodenstein, and à Brakel

In the previous chapter, I introduced the Dutch Further Reformation. In this chapter, I will briefly examine three of its many great preachers, beginning with a founding father of the movement and then proceeding to two men who served during its golden years.

Willem Teellinck

Willem Teellinck, often called "the father of the Dutch Further Reformation," was born January 4, 1579, in Zeeland.[1] He was the youngest of eight children in a godly, prominent family. His father, Joost Teellinck, died when Willem was fifteen years old. His mother, Johanna de Jonge, survived her husband by fifteen years but was often sick when Willem was young. Willem was well educated in his youth; he studied law at

---

1. This brief section on Teellinck's life is a condensed adaptation from Joel R. Beeke, "Introduction to Willem Teellinck," in Willem Teellinck, *The Path of True Godliness*, ed. Joel R. Beeke, trans. Annemie Godbehere (Grand Rapids, MI: Baker Academic, 2003), 11–29, and Joel R. Beeke and Randall J. Pederson, *Meet the Puritans: With a Guide to Modern Reprints* (Grand Rapids, MI: Reformation Heritage Books, 2006), 782–86. For other works on Teellinck in English, see Arie De Reuver, *Sweet Communion: Trajectories of Spirituality from the Middle Ages through the Further Reformation*, trans. James A. De Jong (Grand Rapids, MI: Baker Academic, 2007), 105–60; Fred Ernest Stoeffler, *The Rise of Evangelical Pietism* (Leiden: Brill, 1965), 127–33. In Dutch, see W. J. Op't Hof, *Willem Teellinck (1579–1629): Leven, Geschriften En Invloed* (Kampen: De Groot Goudriaan, 2008); W. J. Op't Hof, C. A. De Niet, and H. Uil, *Eeuwout Teellinck in Handschriften* (Kampen: De Groot Goudriaan i.s.m. Stichting Studie der Nadere Reformatie, 1989); M. Golverdingen, *Avonden Met Teellinck: Actuele Thema's Uit Zijn Werk* (Houten: Den Hertog, 1993); Willem Jodocus Matthias Engelberts, *Willem Teellinck* (Amsterdam: Ton Bolland, 1973); Harm Bouwman, *Willem Teellinck En De Practijk Der Godzaligheid* (Kampen: Kok, 1928).

St. Andrews University in Scotland and at the University of Poitiers in France, where he earned a law degree in 1603.

The following year, Teellinck spent nine months with the Puritan community in England, lodging with a godly family in Banbury. He was profoundly impressed by his exposure to Puritan godliness lived out through extensive family worship, private prayer, sermon discussions, Sabbath observance, fasting, spiritual fellowship, self-examination, heartfelt piety, and good works. This led to his conversion. A zeal for God's truth and for Puritan piety was born in his heart, never to be quenched.

While in England, Teellinck met Martha Greendon, a young Puritan woman from Derby who became his wife and returned to the Netherlands with him. She shared his life goal of living out the Puritan *praxis pietatis* ("practice of piety") in family life as well as in parish work—and beyond. Together they determined to bring the Puritan way of thinking and living to the Netherlands. Their impact was extensive. Three of their sons became Reformed ministers, and one daughter married a minister.

Teellinck edified his family by his godly example. He was hospitable and philanthropic, yet he stressed simplicity in household furnishings, clothing, and food. He generally steered conversation at mealtimes in a spiritual direction. Family worship was scrupulously practiced in the Puritan way. Once or twice a year, the Teellincks observed a family day of prayer and fasting. He regarded this practice as helpful for moving himself and his family to dedicate themselves entirely to God.

Teellinck studied for two more years at Leiden. He was ordained to the pastoral ministry in 1606 and served the Burgh-Haamstede parish on the island of Duiveland for seven fruitful years. There were several conversions, but, much like his predecessor, Godefridus Udemans (c. 1581–1649), he struggled with village life, which was rough and undisciplined. The classis minutes of that time frequently address the problems of alcohol abuse, Sabbath desecration, fighting, carnival attendance, and a general disorderly spirit.

In 1610, Teellinck visited England to renew ties with his Puritan colleagues Thomas Taylor (1576–1632), John Dod, and Arthur Hildersham. During that stay, he preached to the Dutch congregation in London. From 1613 until his death in 1629, he served as pastor in Middelburg, a flourishing city that had six Reformed churches—four Dutch, one English, and one French. People were drawn to his ministry by his sincere conversation and preaching, faithful visiting and catechizing, godly walk and selfless demeanor, and simple and practical writings. He demonstrated his conviction that a pastor ought to be the godliest person in the congregation—and his godliness involved self-denial. When a plague swept through Middelburg in 1624, for example, he not only called people to public and private repentance, but also visited numerous infected homes, even though he urged others not to put themselves at risk by doing so.

Teellinck's hard work in Middelburg bore fruit. Five years after his arrival, he wrote to his congregation in his *Noodwendig Vertoogh* ("Urgent Discourse"): "We have every reason to thank the Lord. You come to church in large numbers each Sunday; our four church buildings cannot contain all the people. Many of your families may be called 'little churches.' There is good order according to good rules. Many of you use the means of grace diligently and you gladly listen to our admonitions to exercise godliness." Yet he remained burdened by the indifference in and beyond his flock. The "constant hurt and pain" that he carried in his heart because of the spiritual laxity and carnality that prevailed in church and society moved him to use his prodigious energies and gifts in speaking and writing to bring about a comprehensive reformation in every sphere of life. Arie De Reuver writes: "His conviction was that this spiritual practice should simply cover all of life: hearth and home, church and civil government, education and medical care, vocation and spare time. . . . [T]he fullness of life had one, single center, namely personal communion with God."[2]

Teellinck died at the relatively young age of fifty on April 8, 1629, after a long battle with ill health. Though he never taught theology at a university or preached with eloquent words, he shaped the piety of the entire Dutch Further Reformation. His ministry exemplified his words: "Truly, the Word of God is the sword of the Spirit and the means to pull down the kingdom of darkness and strengthen the kingdom of grace (Eph. 6:17)."[3]

Plain, Practical Preaching

In his preaching, Teellinck infiltrated the Dutch scene with English Puritan earnestness. His sermons focused on the practice of godliness, and

---

2. De Reuver, *Sweet Communion*, 110.
3. Teellinck, *The Path of True Godliness*, 163.

he preached often on the necessity of repentance. He had the gift of rebuking sin and pronouncing God's impending judgments while simultaneously drawing people to the love of God and wooing them to Christ. He despised dealing in trivialities from the pulpit, which included flowery expressions and petty illustrations. He was blunt and forthright in expressing himself, even to the point of coarseness.

Teellinck believed that sound doctrine can produce real fruit when it is applied with appropriate logic. All doctrine contains material for chastisement, refutation, warning, and consolation. These must be applied rhetorically to pierce the conscience. For instance, in a sermon on the love of Christ (2 Cor. 5:14), he moves quickly from exegesis to a detailed development of the doctrine, presenting it with great warmth and love for God. Then he gives thorough, detailed applications, sometimes in the form of questions and answers. He preached with great seriousness and rebuked sin with earnestness. He was not afraid to name specific sins of his community or to complain of people's neglect of the Lord's Day. Neither did he allow sinners to cling to their excuses unchallenged. When he rebuked a drunkard, the man told him to mind his own business and joked, "Beer is not brewed for geese." The minister gravely answered, "That's true, my friend, but hell has also not been made for geese."[4]

His sermons probed human experience. Preaching about sin dwelling in believers (Rom. 7:24), he says that the difference between the unbeliever and the believer is like that between midnight and dawn. The unbeliever has no spiritual light, but the believer has a mixture, as light breaks into the darkness. Indeed, every part of his being contains both light and darkness.[5] Teellinck stirs the imagination and affections by comparing sin to a monstrosity with eyes where the ears should be and the mouth in the forehead, to maggots consuming a decaying corpse, and to a bear tearing open a man.[6] The saints "see the hatefulness of this Monster," he says, and would rather die than satisfy its lusts, though the world lives to feed it.[7] Paul's example shows us that this horrific beast "is even in the best and most holy of all."[8] Nevertheless, in the children

---

4. Quoted in Engelberts, *Willem Teellinck*, chap. 5.
5. Willem Teellinck, *Pauls Complaint Against His Naturall Corruption: With the Meanes How to Bee Deliuered from the Power of the Same: Set Forth in Two Sermons Vpon the 24 Verse of the 7 Chapter of His Epistle to the Romanes*, trans. Christopher Harmar (London: by Iohn Dawson for Iohn Bellamie, 1621), 3–4.
6. Teellinck, *Pauls Complaint*, 4–7.
7. Teellinck, *Pauls Complaint*, 11–12, 36–37.
8. Teellinck, *Pauls Complaint*, 18.

of God, this natural corruption does not sit "upon a throne, ruling, and commanding as a king, but lieth, as it were, stretched out upon a rack," where the Spirit works to weaken it daily unto death.[9] The presence of this "deadly and deceitful monster" with us constantly requires believers "to walk warily and circumspectly," as a city keeps watch over both a besieging army and traitors inside its walls.[10]

However, he offers this comfort: those who sincerely grieve over sin and fight to kill it by the Holy Spirit are the true children of God.[11] They have "a feeling, and experiential knowledge of the misery that ariseth from sin," which drives them "to seek our deliverance out of sin by Jesus Christ."[12] They have a true faith in Christ, not just mere words, but a faith that draws them to the Physician to be healed by "his blood, being the medicine of our souls." Saving faith consists of denying their own wisdom, will, and sinful desires, giving themselves to Christ to be ruled by him and his Word, and believing that he will save them as he promises.[13]

God calls the Christian to seek him in biblical devotion, which Teellinck calls "the practice of divine blessedness."[14] True believers must daily resolve to exalt the Lord in every aspect of life, at home, work, or church. God is "simply the very best," a "spring," a "full ocean," a "sun," "the holy fountain of everything that we desire," and "better than life itself."[15] Teellinck says, "When the preachers preach, that men should die to the world, and crucify the old man, etc., their meaning is not, to make men wretched, and miserable thereby (as some imagine) but their purpose therein is only to bring men to the true happiness, which all of us seek."[16] The believer presses forward in a constant "movement toward God," just as a fire by nature ascends heavenward with intense heat. He does this by "the stirrings and movements of the good Spirit of God."[17] Yet this Spirit is not to be found apart from the written Word. Here we see the centrality of Scripture and the priority of preaching in Teellinck's spirituality.

---

9. Teellinck, *Pauls Complaint*, 20.
10. Teellinck, *Pauls Complaint*, 23.
11. Teellinck, *Pauls Complaint*, 29, 43–44.
12. Teellinck, *Pauls Complaint*, 46.
13. Teellinck, *Pauls Complaint*, 57–64.
14. Quoted in De Reuver, *Sweet Communion*, 114.
15. Quoted in De Reuver, *Sweet Communion*, 117, 126–28.
16. Willem Teellinck, *The Resting Place of the Minde: That Is, A Propovnding of the Wonderfull Prouidence of God, Whereupon a Christian Man Ought to Rest and Repose Himself, Euen When All Outward Meanes of Helpe Are Cut Off from Him* (London: by Iohn Haviland for Edward Brewster, 1622), 35.
17. Quoted in De Reuver, *Sweet Communion*, 122.

De Reuver writes: "The Holy Bible is the point of contact with the Holy Spirit. . . . The breath of the Spirit is poured over it and has 'permeated it.' Every page and every verse as a result breathes out the sacred movements of the Spirit."[18] Thus, the life of hearing the Word, reading the Word, and meditating on the Word is a life of vibrant spirituality. The preacher serves as a Spirit-empowered stimulus for the saints to God-centered devotion.

In addition to speaking to inward experience, Teellinck was a practical preacher who addressed current events. For example, when the Dutch rejoiced over the capture of Spanish treasure ships by Admiral Piet Hein, he preached that the riches of this world are false and only the riches of Christ are real (1 Tim. 6:17–19). He also drew criticism by preaching against luxury in dress, reading of amorous literature, excessive drinking, dancing, traveling on the Sabbath, overindulgence in feasting, and the neglect of fasting. Most of all, he deplored spiritual deadness in the church and sought to build up believers in their most holy faith and the new life in Christ.

Homiletically, Teellinck was influenced by William Perkins, who advocated the Puritan "plain method" of preaching. After exegeting a text, Teellinck drew out various doctrines, explained how these doctrines should benefit the hearer by means of comfort and admonition, and then applied wisdom gleaned from the text to saved and unsaved hearers. Though not an eloquent orator, he was an effective preacher. After hearing him preach on a few occasions, Gisbertus Voetius said that he wished that he and all Dutch preachers could duplicate Teellinck's powerful way of preaching.

The Netherlands was not as ready for Teellinck as England had been for Perkins, however. His preaching against dead orthodoxy brought him under suspicion by some of the Reformed. On the other hand, Arminians censored him for his devotion to Reformed orthodoxy and resented his popularity with laypeople. Despite such opposition, he was mourned by thousands when he died.

Jodocus van Lodenstein

Jodocus van Lodenstein (1620–1677) was both a preacher and poet in the golden age of Dutch history.[19] He was born February 6, 1620, in

---

18. De Reuver, *Sweet Communion*, 123.
19. This brief section on van Lodenstein's life is a condensed adaptation from Joel R. Beeke, "Introduction to Jodocus van Lodenstein," in van Lodenstein, *A Spiritual Appeal to Christ's Bride*,

Delft, in the province of South Holland, in western Netherlands. Delft was situated along the Schie River between Rotterdam and The Hague.[20] His parents were both from prominent, aristocratic families.

Van Lodenstein was sensitive, caring, and musical. Godliness was his goal from early boyhood. He even took a vow of chastity in his preadolescent years so that he could serve the Lord single-mindedly all his life.[21] Jodocus suffered from chronic infections; he also had a severe speech impediment, which God later graciously healed.[22] His parents raised him to live a life of holiness.[23] While a young man, he heard the preaching of the great English Puritan Thomas Hooker. He developed a love for the Puritans, which led to his being called to the ministry and informed his preaching on repentance.[24]

At age sixteen, van Lodenstein entered Utrecht Academy, where he studied under Voetius.[25] After graduating from Utrecht, he returned home because there were no empty parishes. His father arranged for him to study Eastern languages in Franeker under the German pietist scholar Johannes Cocceius (1603–1669), with whom he boarded and studied for two years. Meanwhile, he increasingly felt the weight of his call to the ministry.[26]

From 1644 to 1650, he pastored a congregation in the small town of Zoetermeer. There, he wrestled against factions in the church, slack Sabbath observance, materialism, resistance to his preaching of repentance, and accusations of legalism and Arminianism.[27] In 1650, he accepted a

---

ed. Joel R. Beeke, trans. Bartel Elshout (Grand Rapids, MI: Reformation Heritage Books, 2010), 11–31. For other works on van Lodenstein in English, see Carl J. Schroeder, *In Quest of Pentecost: Jodocus Van Lodenstein and the Dutch Second Reformation* (Lanham, MD: University Press of America, 2001); Iain S. Maclean, "The First Pietist: An Introduction and Translation of a Communion Sermon by Jodocus Van Lodenstein," in *Calvin Studies VI*, ed. John H. Leith (Davidson, NC: Davidson College, 1992), 15–34; Stoeffler, *The Rise of Evangelical Pietism*, 141–48. In Dutch, see Pieter Proost, *Jodocus van Lodenstein* (Amsterdam: J. Brandt, 1880); Marinus J. A. de Vrijer, *Lodenstein* (Baarn: Ten Have, 1947); D. Slagboorn, *Jodocus van Lodenstein* (Utrecht: De Banier, 1966); J. C. Trimp, *Jodocus van Lodenstein: Predikant en Dichter* (Kampen: De Groot Goudriaan, 1987). A primary source of information on van Lodenstein is Evardus vander Hooght's biography (1696). In the section below, I lean much upon Schroeder.

20. "Delft," in *Encyclopædia Britannica*, http://www.britannica.com/EBchecked/topic/156478 /Delft.

21. Schroeder, *In Quest of Pentecost*, 17; see also Cornelis Graafland, "Jodocus van Lodenstein (1620–1676)," in *De Nadere Reformatie: Beschrijving van haar voornaamste vertegenwoordigers*, ed. Willem van't Spijker ('s–Gravenhage: Uitgeverij Boekencentrum, 1986), 86.

22. Schroeder, *In Quest of Pentecost*, 80.

23. Schroeder, *In Quest of Pentecost*, 24.

24. Schroeder, *In Quest of Pentecost*, 19.

25. Schroeder, *In Quest of Pentecost*, 20.

26. Schroeder, *In Quest of Pentecost*, 22.

27. Schroeder, *In Quest of Pentecost*, 24–28.

call to a congregation of about 1,200 people in Sluis, Flanders, in the province of Zeeland. People there were sympathetic to his pietist leanings, due to the prior preaching of Teellinck and Udemans. He formed a close bond with the congregation.[28]

But his time there was cut short by another call, this time from Utrecht, where he served from 1653 until his death in 1677. He served with Voetius as one of the ministers of the *Domkerk* (the Tower Church), a massive church building that could hold several thousand worshipers.[29] He stayed very busy preaching on the Lord's Day and during the week; teaching classes on the Heidelberg Catechism and Belgic Confession of Faith; giving lectures on spirituality based on the writings of Teellinck and William Ames; encouraging the congregation to read and memorize the Bible; and visiting thousands of members, especially the poor, orphans, and ill.[30] While in Utrecht, van Lodenstein joined the famous "Utrecht Circle," including Johannes Teellinck (c. 1623–1694), son of Willem Teellinck, and Theodorus à Brakel (1608–1669), author of several edifying works and father of the better known Wilhelmus à Brakel.

He experienced severe trials in the 1670s. First, the French conquered Utrecht in June 1672, making the *Domkerk* the site of a daily celebration of the Roman Mass. When forced to withdraw, the French seized van Lodenstein and thirteen other Dutch leaders as hostages on November 16, 1673, carried them in carts through three days of snowy weather, and imprisoned them for three months until a large ransom was paid.[31] Second, in July 1674, a horrendous storm swept through the Netherlands, causing a large portion of the roof of the *Domkerk* to collapse and leaving many people homeless. Third, in June 1675, a fellow laborer for the Further Reformation, Jacobus Koelman (1631–1695), was removed from his pulpit and banished from the region of Flanders.[32] Van Lodenstein did what he could to support him.

On November 1, 1676, his mentor, colleague, and friend Voetius passed away. Van Lodenstein himself fell ill in the spring of 1677 and died on August 10. In his last days, he said: "It is enough for me that I know and believe that in God is the fullness and all-sufficiency of every-

---

28. Schroeder, *In Quest of Pentecost*, 33–37.
29. Schroeder, *In Quest of Pentecost*, viii.
30. Schroeder, *In Quest of Pentecost*, 41–42, 84–86.
31. Schroeder, *In Quest of Pentecost*, 60–62; Teunis Brienen, "Jodocus van Lodenstein," in *De Prediking van de Nadere Reformatie* (Amsterdam: Ton Bolland, 1974), 1.4.2.a.
32. Schroeder, *In Quest of Pentecost*, 65–66.

thing. . . . In the Lord Jesus is the fullness of grace, and I lay myself down on that covenant that is unchangeable."[33] His influence lived on in his sermons and poetry, as was evident a century later in the personal writings of Eilardus Westerlo (1738–1790), a Dutch Reformed minister in North America.[34]

Preacher of Vital Holiness in Union with Christ

Van Lodenstein was a captivating preacher. Voetius once said, "Our colleague van Lodenstein can do it like none of the rest of us can say or do."[35] His preaching was simple and direct. He avoided lengthy introductions on the historical details of a text. M. Eugene Osterhaven (1915–2004) says, "His messages were built around Christ, the gift of the Holy Spirit, and the need for and reality of renewal."[36] His main focus was application, particularly the need for conversion and sanctification.[37]

Van Lodenstein viewed the Reformation as doctrinally sound but incomplete in terms of practice.[38] He equated the Reformation to Ezekiel in the valley of dry bones (Ezekiel 37). The Reformation renewed good doctrines, but these doctrines were only the bare bones of a skeleton on which flesh was yet needed.[39] Thus, the Reformation of doctrine needed the practical, applicatory work of the Spirit producing godly living. The church was not yet as purified as she should be.[40] The result was a cold and dead orthodoxy adhered to by nominal Christians who did not experience truth and did not cultivate holiness. The Reformation fell so far short in this area, he believed, that the church was even worse off in some ways under the Reformed faith than when she suffered under Rome. Indeed, he said that "a Reformation without Spirit has led to worse deformation as lives have not been transformed."[41] We might paraphrase him by saying that reformation without transformation is deformation.

---

33. Quoted in Schroeder, *In Quest of Pentecost*, 109.
34. Robert A. Naborn, "Eilardus Westerlo (1738–1790): From Colonial Dominee to American Pastor" (PhD diss., Vrije Universiteit Amsterdam, 2011), 1:101; 2:158.
35. Quoted in Schroeder, *In Quest of Pentecost*, viii.
36. Quoted in Schroeder, *In Quest of Pentecost*, viii.
37. Graafland, "Jodocus van Lodenstein," 110; see also A. J. Onstenk, "Lodenstein, Jodocus van," in *Biografisch Lexicon voor de Geschiedenis van het Nederlandse Protestantisme*, ed. D. Nauta, et al. (Kampen: Kok, 1988), 3:253.
38. Graafland, "Jodocus van Lodenstein," 91.
39. Graafland, "Jodocus van Lodenstein," 89.
40. Graafland, "Jodocus van Lodenstein," 113.
41. Quoted in Maclean, "The First Pietist," 16.

Christ taught, "This is life eternal, that they might know thee the only true God, and Jesus Christ, whom thou hast sent" (John 17:3). So van Lodenstein preaches: "This knowledge that is referred to in our text comes by enlightenment from above. One cannot bring it about himself any more than he can the rising of the sun." It is experiential knowledge: "Even as food is experienced by the eating, so the Lord shares Himself and permits us to sense who He is." It is transforming knowledge: "From this it follows necessarily that one lives for God. Show me a person who knows God and I will show you one who does and is all for the Lord."[42] How can such things be? Christ "sends us the Holy Spirit, who works such grace in our souls that He renews us: else we could not see the Kingdom of God [John 3:5]. . . . He works faith in our souls, uniting us more and more with our Savior. . . . He also makes us fruitful."[43]

He urged people not to rest in Reformed doctrine and worship, but to strive for perpetual reformation in the soul. In fact, he appears to have been the first author to employ the language of ever being reformed, saying that a wise man "would not have called the Reformed church *reformata*, or reformed, but *reformanda*, or being reformed," for to be "always thus occupied" would produce "a pure church," "precise in truth" and "holy in practice."[44] Michael Bush says that by this he did not advocate changing the theology of the church to match the times: "Rather, the problem for them was that it was impossible to maintain the church's purity of faith and holiness in practice without constant vigilance."[45] The consequence of failing to continue the Reformation was spiritual apathy, which was already prevalent in the Netherlands. Thus, van Lodenstein's preaching continually emphasized the need for further reformation.[46] However, though he was critical of the shortcomings of the Reformation, he was still deeply Reformed. He never divorced his pietistic and mystical preaching from Reformation truth; rather, his

---

42. Jodocus van Lodenstein, "Eternal Life," quoted in Schroeder, *In Quest of Pentecost*, 163.
43. Jodocus van Lodenstein, "Fifteenth Sermon," quoted in Schroeder, *In Quest of Pentecost*, 179.
44. Quoted in Michael Bush, "Calvin and the Reformanda Sayings," in *Calvinus sacrarum literarum interpres: Papers of the International Congress on Calvin Research*, ed. Herman J. Selderhuis (Göttingen: Vandenhoeck and Ruprecht, 2008), 286. Bush also shows that Jacobus Koelman cited his teacher, Johannes Hornbeeck, as saying that "we must come to be called Reforming, and not only Reformed, so that we always must be Reforming if we want to be Reformed and be worthy of that name." "Calvin and the Reformanda Sayings," 287. Thus, the idea was shared among some early Voetians.
45. Bush, "Calvin and the Reformanda Sayings," 299.
46. Graafland, "Jodocus van Lodenstein," 88.

pietistic and mystical tendencies served to further the cause of the early Reformers.

Carl Schroeder notes six characteristics of van Lodenstein's preaching: (1) he was scriptural, (2) he was faithful to the Reformed confessions, (3) he spoke with great authority, (4) he preached prophetically, (5) he emphasized repentance, and (6) he discouraged the observation of church feast days.[47] He preached both the law and gospel, using the law to convict nominal Christians of hypocrisy, sloth, worldliness, and self-seeking—and then called them to Christ.[48] For those who were converted, he offered the promises of God. With this double-edged sword, he preached in a discriminatory manner, classifying his congregation into a variety of categories, as was typical of Voetian preachers and other proponents of the *Nadere Reformatie*.[49]

Van Lodenstein called men to take up the cross, deny themselves, and follow Christ. This transformation of life was the fruit of Christ's death (2 Cor. 5:14–15). He preaches: "Once man has been translated into the kingdom of the Son, the kingdom of the Father's love (Col. 1:13), through Christ, who as Mediator was the Father's servant (Isa. 53:11), he then becomes God's possession. For this glorious reality the redeemed must live and work continually. . . . If, therefore, Jesus died for us, we also died to ourselves in order to live to God."[50]

With his strong views on sanctification, van Lodenstein put his imprint on the *Nadere Reformatie*. He and others called for a more profound commitment to Christ, for only such a commitment could deliver the church from shallowness and unholiness. By preaching repentance sermons each month, he hoped his congregation would not just embrace the truth with their minds, but experience it in every aspect of their lives. Schroeder writes of van Lodenstein: "He both modeled and taught a strong commitment to a process of growth in devotion to Christ that spells out what sanctification as taught in the New Testament is all about. Few who heard him regularly in Sunday morning worship could fail to feel his sense of urgency in these matters."[51]

---

47. Schroeder, *In Quest of Pentecost*, 71–76.
48. Brienen, "Jodocus van Lodenstein," 1.4.2.b.
49. For a summary of the classification method of preaching, see Joel R. Beeke, ed., *Forerunner of the Great Awakening: Sermons by Theodorus Jacobus Frelinghuysen (1691–1747)*, The Historical Series of the Reformed Church in America, no. 36 (Grand Rapids, MI: Eerdmans, 2000), xxx–xxxiv.
50. Van Lodenstein, *A Spiritual Appeal to Christ's Bride*, 42.
51. Schroeder, *In Quest of Pentecost*, 44.

In 1659, the stresses of life (a lack of sanctification in his congregants, difficulties with the magistrates, and lack of renewal throughout the Netherlands) threw van Lodenstein into a profound personal crisis. Spiritual dejection moved him to look inward and see that the only thing he could control was his personal devotion to Christ. This led him to embrace more individualism. At this time, he also learned more about what he called "the language of love."[52]

For consolation, van Lodenstein turned to the Song of Solomon. He feasted on these songs of love. He was also influenced by the medieval writings of Bernard of Clairvaux (1090–1153) and Thomas à Kempis (c. 1380–1471). In these writings and the Song of Solomon, van Lodenstein learned how to develop and cultivate personal devotion to Jesus.[53] He viewed the Song of Solomon as portraying the inner chamber where God and a believer's soul are united. This union is not one of a king to his people so much as a king to his bride. In bonding to Christ in love as the perfect Bridegroom, the spiritual bride is brought to self-denial, acknowledging that God is all-sufficient and that man in himself is nothing.[54]

For van Lodenstein, the beautiful language of the Song of Solomon expresses Christ's precious benefits for his bride and the bride's spiritual longings for her Bridegroom. He particularly emphasized the royal aspects of the believer's Bridegroom. By calling the Bridegroom *King*, he underscored Christ's immense attractiveness, majesty, and glory, as well as the bride's need to render him honor, service, and subjection.[55]

He equated what happens in the King's inner chambers with Christ's sympathetic love and the believer's intimate fellowship with him. Through spiritual communion with Christ, the believing bride tastes the first fruits of heavenly communion. When the bride sees the glory of God in the face of Christ Jesus in the King's inner chambers, she no longer sees herself, but is increasingly conformed to Christ's image and is more fully assured of the King's unchangeable faithfulness and love for her. She then loves God with her entire mind, soul, and being, and desires him for his own sake, viewing him as wholly delightful.[56]

---

52. Schroeder, *In Quest of Pentecost*, 79.

53. Schroeder, *In Quest of Pentecost*, 81–86; cf. Trimp, *Jodocus van Lodenstein*, 194–200.

54. Izaäk Boot, *De Allegorische Uitlegging van het Hooglied voornamelijk in Nederland: Een Onderzoek naar de Verhouding tussen Bernard van Clairvaux en de Nadere Reformatie* (Woerden: Zuijderduijn, 1971), 179–80.

55. Van Lodenstein, *A Spiritual Appeal to Christ's Bride*, 147.

56. Boot, *De Allegorische Uitlegging*, 182–83.

Van Lodenstein's preaching exemplified Reformed doctrine, the call to repentance, renewal by the Holy Spirit, the pursuit of piety, and mystical communion with Christ. In him, we see the beating pulse of the Dutch Further Reformation.

Next, we proceed to the son of one of van Lodenstein's colleagues, whose works greatly influenced generations of pious Dutch families.

Wilhelmus à Brakel

Wilhelmus à Brakel, the son of Reformed pastor Theodorus à Brakel, was born on January 2, 1635.[57] He and his five sisters were reared in a remarkably God-fearing home. Wilhelmus was converted as a boy, probably under his father's preaching and through his mother's prayers and pleading. He attended the Latin school in Leeuwarden, then entered the Franeker Academy at the age of nineteen in 1654. Upon completion of his studies in 1659, Classis Leeuwarden admitted him into the ministry. Due to a lack of vacancies at the time, à Brakel continued his theological training for a few years in Utrecht under Voetius and Andreas Essenius (1618–1677).

À Brakel served five congregations in the national church of the Netherlands during a ministry of nearly fifty years. His first charge was in Exmorra, Friesland (1662–1665), a difficult congregation because of widespread spiritual indifference. During his ministry there, he married Sara Nevius, widow of Henricus Veegen, who had been a Reformed pastor at Benthuizen. À Brakel's second congregation at Stavoren (1665–1670) was larger, and this proved to be a more fruitful pastorate. Next,

---

57. For sources in English on Wilhelmus à Brakel, see W. Fieret, biographical introduction to Wilhelmus à Brakel, in à Brakel, *The Christian's Reasonable Service: In Which Divine Truths Concerning the Covenant of Grace Are Expounded, Defended Against Opposing Parties, and Their Practice Advocated, as Well as the Administration of This Covenant in the Old and New Testaments* (Ligonier, PA: Soli Deo Gloria, 1992), 1:xxxi–lxxxi; Bartel Elshout, *The Pastoral and Practical Theology of Wilhelmus à Brakel: A Brief Evaluation of* The Christian's Reasonable Service (Grand Rapids, MI: Reformation Heritage Books, 1997); De Reuver, *Sweet Communion*, 231–58; Richard A. Muller, *After Calvin: Studies in the Development of a Theological Tradition*, Oxford Studies in Historical Theology (Oxford; New York: Oxford University Press, 2003), 175–89; Stoeffler, *The Rise of Evangelical Pietism*, 153–56; Lydia Kim-Van Daalen, "Wilhelmus à Brakel's Spirituality of Virtues and Its Implications for Soul Care," *Puritan Reformed Journal* 3, no. 1 (January 2011): 279–303; Jonathan Holdt, "Wilhelmus a Brakel's Use of Doctrine in Calling Sinners to Repentance and Faith," *Puritan Reformed Journal* 3, no. 2 (July 2011): 267–90; Paul M. Smalley, "Satisfied with the Lord's All-Sufficiency: Wilhelmus à Brakel on Joy," *Puritan Reformed Journal* 3, no. 2 (July 2011): 235–66. In Dutch, see F. J. Los, *Wilhelmus à Brakel* (Leiden: Groen en Zoon, 1991); W. Fieret, *Theodorus à Brakel, Wilhelmus à Brakel En Sara Nevius* (Houten: Den Hertog, 1988); H. F. Sorge, "Genadeverbond En Genaldeleven: Een Onderzoek Naar De Inhoud En Betekenis Van Het Genadeverbond Volgens De 'Redilijke Godsdienst' Van Wilhelmus à Brakel (1635–1711)" (n.p., 1998).

à Brakel went to the flourishing port city of Harlingen (1670–1673), where his ministry and those of his three colleagues were signally blessed with numerous conversions. From 1673 to 1683, à Brakel served the large Reformed congregation at Leeuwarden, which met in three different church buildings and had six ministers and thousands of members.

During this time, he was involved in some controversy. He was admonished by the classis for promoting conventicles, that is, gatherings of the godly for conference (sharing experiences) and mutual exhortation. He took a stand against the civil authorities, asserting that the government had no right to remove a minister from his pulpit. For this courageous act, he won the respect of many people. He also disputed with a Cocceian minister about the covenant of grace and the correct interpretation of Psalm 8.

After twenty-one years of ministry in Friesland, à Brakel accepted a call in 1683 to Rotterdam, where he remained for the rest of his life. Rotterdam, one of the republic's largest cities with a population of fifty-five thousand, provided a major field of labor. Here, too, à Brakel's work was greatly blessed in the building up of the godly in their faith and the conversion of the unsaved. He also entered into further controversies, opposing the teachings of Jean de Labadie (1610–1674) and his followers that promoted separation from the national church to form a pure church. However, although Brakel urged Dutch Christians to stay within the national Reformed church, he repeatedly had to stand against attempts by the civil government to interfere in the church's internal affairs.

À Brakel devoted his tranquil years in the 1690s to producing his *magnum opus*, entitled *De Redelijke Godsdienst* (1700), translated as *The Christian's Reasonable Service*. It became nearly as popular in Dutch circles as Bunyan's *Pilgrim's Progress* did in English circles. For family worship, a typical eighteenth-century Dutch farmer would read "een stukje van Vader Brakel" ["a little bit from Father Brakel"] every night to his family after the reading of Scripture. When he completed the whole, he would return to the beginning and read it through again. The book combines systematic theology on a lay level with practical ethics and personal devotion.

In the summer of 1711, à Brakel became very ill. When asked on his deathbed how his soul fared, he responded: "Very well; I may rest in my Jesus. I am united to Him and I am awaiting His coming for me; meanwhile, I submit myself quietly to Him." He died on October 30, 1711, at the age of seventy-six.

À Brakel was a leading popular representative of the Puritan-minded Dutch Further Reformation. He was so loved among his people for his fatherly ministry, both from the pulpit and in pastoral work, that many fondly called him "Father Brakel." That honorary title has stuck until today in the homes of many Dutch people in the Netherlands, who still read his classic work and appreciate the Puritan, experiential, and pietistic tradition that he so ably represented.

The Lively Preacher of the Living Truth

À Brakel was known in his day as a powerful and effective preacher who could hold people by the thousands spellbound with eloquence and intense delivery. His method of preaching was always Christ centered, applied, and experiential. He promoted Bible-based and Christ-centered self-examination, and warned frequently against sins of debauchery and worldliness.

In *The Christian's Reasonable Service*, he offers the following guidelines for the preacher regarding the preparation and delivery of sermons:

1. "He must seek to remind himself in a lively manner that God has sent him, that he ascends the pulpit as an ambassador of God, speaks in the name of God, and is as the mouth of the Lord unto the congregation. This ought to cause him to fear and tremble."

2. He must remind himself that the ministry of the Word is the "power of God unto salvation and the means whereby God translates souls out of the kingdom of the devil and from the power of darkness into His marvelous light, and thus into the kingdom of the Lord Jesus." He should carefully shape his content and manner toward that goal.

3. "He must have the heart of a preacher," that is, fear of the Lord, love for people, and a profound sense of his inability despite all his studies. He should "pray much beforehand" for a "sanctified heart," freedom from man pleasing, God's presence, wise words, and "the conversion, comfort, and edification of souls."

4. "He must first seek to impress upon his own heart the matters to be preached, seeking to be brought into the frame in which he wishes to bring others, and thus speak from heart to heart."

5. "He ought to use all his scholarship to formulate the matters to be presented, in order that he might express them in the clearest and most

powerful manner. While using his scholarship, however, he must conceal his scholarship in the pulpit." However, à Brakel allowed for explaining the meaning of Hebrew and Greek words in the Bible.

6. "He must select subject matter for consideration (preceded by prayer) which he deems to be most suitable for his congregation, as well as for the circumstances and events of the moment. If he deals with a chapter, book, or epistle sequentially, there ought nevertheless to be occasion for the preaching of free texts."

7. "In all his preaching his objective ought to be to touch hearts, and thus while aiming for the heart, to apply this, to comfort, and to stir up."

8. "Having performed his task, he ought to descend from the pulpit as Moses descended from the mountain, so that his awe for God and the weightiness of that great task may as yet be manifested upon his countenance, and that, after having descended from the pulpit, he would not immediately begin a discussion about other matters or ask about what is new." À Brakel did not commend being cold or unfriendly, but warned here against a descent into levity and worldliness after the sermon; the fear of God and sense of the eternal implications of the Word should permeate the Lord's Day.

9. "Upon arrival at home, he immediately ought to go to his room and consider in what frame he has preached. There he ought to humble himself before God concerning that which was lacking, to thank the Lord for His assistance, and to pray for a blessing upon the Word for himself and for the congregation."[58]

We do not have many of à Brakel's sermons; some fifteen are extant.[59] His normal method was to study carefully and then preach without notes. His preaching centered upon Christ's dealings with the soul in the covenant of grace. He made powerful use of biblical metaphors, such as being "dead in sins" (Eph. 2:5). He also presented his sermons in a well-structured outline. When preaching on Ephesians 4:30, "And grieve not the holy Spirit of God, whereby ye are sealed unto the day of redemption," he followed an outline like this:

I. The Command (v. 30a)
   A. The Holy Person: the Spirit who applies salvation and gives holiness.
   B. The Evil Deed: do not grieve the Holy Spirit.

---

58. à Brakel, *The Christian's Reasonable Service*, 2:138–39.
59. The following description of à Brakel's sermons is based on the analysis of Brienen, *De Prediking Van De Nadere Reformatie*, 118–25.

C. The Explanation: what it means to grieve the Spirit.
II. The Reason (v. 30b)
   A. Sealing: the confirmation that we belong to God (Eph. 1:13; 2 Cor. 1:22).
   B. Permanence: sealed until the day of redemption.
III. The Applications

He applied his sermons in such a way as to distinguish the different spiritual conditions of his hearers. In some sermons, this was done in a simple manner, but in others it was quite thorough. In his sermon on grieving the Spirit, he classifies his hearers into five categories of unconverted people and four categories of God's children. He categorizes unbelievers as either ignorant; indifferent; casual Christians; causing others to stumble; or seeking to be saved. He categorizes believers as discouraged by a lack of experiencing God; encouraged yet tempted; fearful from an overactive conscience; or doubting their salvation. To each category of people, he speaks directly and seeks to make a fitting application.

Ultimately, à Brakel's zeal for applied preaching arose from his confidence in the power of God's Word. He could speak with authority because he preached the Word of God. He writes that "wherever the gospel is preached, hearts are conquered and brought into subjection to Scripture. The more those who confess the truth of Scripture are suppressed and persecuted, the more the Word will exert its power." The Bible's divine power shows itself by "the wondrous light with which the Word illuminates the soul, the internal and external change it engenders, and the manner in which it fills believers with sweet comfort and inexpressible joy. It enables them to endure all persecution in love and with joy as well as to surrender themselves willingly to death."[60] Faith in the God of the Bible made him a bold preacher and an effective one.

---

60. à Brakel, *The Christian's Reasonable Service*, 1:32.

16

Dutch Reformed Preaching in America: Frelinghuysen

In the previous two chapters, we examined the Dutch Further Reformation and some of its outstanding preachers. Now we begin to transition out of that era into the time of the Great Awakening in Britain and America. In this chapter, we consider an eighteenth-century preacher in the American colonies.

Theodorus Jacobus Frelinghuysen (1691–1747) has been described as a forerunner or catalyst of the Great Awakening.[1] Though less known than figures such as Jonathan Edwards, George Whitefield, and John (1703–1791) and Charles Wesley (1707–1788), Frelinghuysen's manner of preaching and experience of smaller revivals paved the way for the great works that would follow in the colonies. Edwards knew of his ministry, referring to him as a "very pious," "eminent and successful" Dutch minister through whom God had sent showers of divine blessing.[2]

---

1. This chapter is adapted from Joel R. Beeke and Cornelis Pronk, "Biographical Introduction," in *Forerunner of the Great Awakening: Sermons by Theodorus Jacobus Frelinghuysen (1691–1747)*, ed. Joel R. Beeke (Grand Rapids, MI: Eerdmans, 2000), vii–xxxviii. Used with permission. For further resources on Frelinghuysen, see Scott Maze, *Theodore Frelinghuysen's Evangelism: Catalyst to the First Great Awakening* (Grand Rapids, MI: Reformation Heritage Books, 2011); F. J. Schrag, "Theodorus Jacobus Frelinghuysen, the Father of American Pietism," *Church History* 14 (1945): 201–216; James Tanis, *Dutch Calvinistic Pietism in the Middle Colonies: A Study in the Life and Theology of Theodorus Jacobus Frelinghuysen* (The Hague: Martinus Nijhoff, 1967). For an annotated bibliography of many other sources, see *Forerunner of the Great Awakening*, 335–39.

2. Jonathan Edwards, "A Faithful Narrative," in *The Works of Jonathan Edwards*, vol. 4, *The Great Awakening*, ed. C. C. Goen (New Haven, CT: Yale University Press, 1972), 156; "To the Reverend John Erskine," letter of June 28, 1751, in *The Works of Jonathan Edwards*, vol. 16, *Letters and Personal Writings*, ed. George S. Claghorn (New Haven, CT: Yale University Press, 1998), 376.

When Whitefield met him in 1739, the Englishman wrote in his journal the following about Frelinghuysen:

> He is a worthy old soldier of Jesus Christ, and was the beginner of the great work which I trust the Lord is carrying on in these parts. He has been strongly opposed by his carnal brethren, but God has appeared before him, in a surprising manner, and made him more than conqueror, through His love. He has long since learnt to fear Him only, who can destroy both body and soul in hell.[3]

At the same time, Frelinghuysen was so severely criticized that he defiantly wrote on the back of his sleigh the following poem for all to see as he rode along:

> No one's tongue, and no one's pen
> Can make me other than I am.
> Speak slanderer! Speak without end
> In vain you all your slanders send.[4]

Who was this man who provoked such admiration and such opposition? The son of a German Reformed pastor and a minister's daughter in Westphalia, Frelinghuysen was baptized on November 6, 1692. He was admitted to communicant membership in the church at age seventeen, studied philosophy and theology at the Reformed *gymnasium* in Hamm, and completed his theological education at the University of Lingen. There he embraced the Voetian blend of Reformed theology and vital experience. He also mastered the Dutch language so that he might preach among the Dutch people.

His first pastorate lasted only fourteen months, ending after a terrible flood so impoverished the people that they could no longer support a minister. After a short stint as the coregent of a Latin school in North Holland, he was invited by Classis Amsterdam to take a pastoral post in Rarethans (Raritan, New Jersey). He accepted, thinking it was a nearby province in the Netherlands. When he learned that it was across the ocean, he felt convicted by Psalm 15:4 to keep his word of acceptance, believing that God blesses the man who "sweareth to his own hurt, and changeth not." He was also influenced by a providential meeting with a godly minister who encouraged him to spread vital religion in America. Dutch

---

3. *George Whitefield's Journals* (London: Banner of Truth, 1960), 352 [Tues., Nov. 20, 1739].
4. Quoted in Beeke and Pronk, "Biographical Introduction," xix.

settlers had arrived in the New World in the early seventeenth century, but few ministers had come along to serve them. The classis did not permit pastors to be trained in the colonies, and not many ministers were willing to cross the Atlantic. Therefore, the spiritual life of the colony was very low. Abraham Messler (1800–1882), who translated several of Frelinghuysen's sermons and eventually became one of his successors, says: "We must remember that the necessity of a new heart had almost entirely been lost sight of, and that formalism and self-righteousness almost universally prevailed. Christians were not ashamed to ridicule Christian experience, and many had become very resolute in opposing it."[5]

After bidding farewell to relatives and friends, Frelinghuysen set sail for the New World in September 1719, arriving in January 1720. Immediately, his heavy stress on regeneration as well as his criticism of indulging in material luxuries alienated two prominent ministers, Gualtherus DuBois (1671–1751) and Henricus Boel (1692–1754).

Frelinghuysen proceeded to take up his responsibilities, caring for four small congregations along the Raritan River, which emptied into a bay just south of New York City. He preached a searching call to repentance and applied strict standards to exclude the unconverted from the Lord's Table. During one Communion service, when Frelinghuysen saw some approach the table even though he had admonished them not to partake, he exclaimed: "See! See! Even the people of the world and the impenitent are coming, that they may eat and drink judgment to themselves!"[6] Several other people who were approaching the table thought the minister meant them and returned to their seats.

Predictably, the disciplinary actions of Frelinghuysen and his consistories (the officers of his churches) upset many in the congregation, particularly the wealthy. They complained to influential Reformed ministers in New York, whose views differed from those of Frelinghuysen. Some of the ministers sided with the complainants—most notably, DuBois and Boel, who had had negative impressions of Frelinghuysen from the outset. They levied serious accusations at Frelinghuysen, who responded in kind. Matters became extremely tense when Frelinghuysen openly referred to colleagues who opposed him, including

---

5. Abraham Messler, *Forty Years at Raritan: Eight Memorial Sermons* (New York: A. Lloyd, 1873), 30.
6. Quoted in Beeke and Pronk, "Biographical Introduction," xvi–xvii.

DuBois and Boel, as unconverted ministers. Other pastors, such as Guiliam Bartholf (1656–1726), Bernardus Freeman (1660–1743), and Cornelius Van Santvoord (1687–1752), supported him, though they cautioned him not to be so harsh and judgmental. They felt that his manner lacked tact and his standards for the Lord's Supper were too demanding.

The conflict created factions within the colonial Dutch Reformed churches. A large group of church members accused Frelinghuysen of heresy. The *Klagers* ("Complainers"), as they came to be called, turned to Dominie[7] Boel and his brother Tobias, an attorney, for aid and advice. Instead of advising the *Klagers* to follow the principles of Matthew 18:15–17 and the Reformed Church Order in dealing with their grievances, the Boel brothers sided with the *Klagers*, which provoked the anger of Frelinghuysen's consistories. The consistories drew up a summons (*daagbrief*), which they sent to the *Klagers*. In this summons, the *Dagers* ("Summoners"), as they became known, listed the errors of their opponents and warned that if they did not withdraw their accusations, they would be excommunicated. Later, in the spring of 1723, Frelinghuysen's consistories issued two additional summonses to the agitators. Each summons threatened to excommunicate those who did not repent and return to the church. When no replies were received by September, the consistories controlled by the *Dagers* unanimously excommunicated four ringleaders of the opposition. This action sent shock waves throughout the entire Dutch Reformed community. Classis Amsterdam, which had to tread cautiously as arbitrator, was thousands of miles away.

In 1725, the *Klagers* finally responded to the summons in a *klagte* ("complaint")—a document of 146 pages addressed to Classis Amsterdam. The *klagte*, presumably written by the Boel brothers, was signed by sixty-four heads of households, which represented close to one fourth of the membership in Frelinghuysen's four congregations. The *klagte* detailed every conceivable criticism of Frelinghuysen, presenting him as a tyrant with homosexual tendencies, a false teacher, and a schismatic. To add fuel to the fire, the *Klagers* decided to frustrate Frelinghuysen's efforts by locking him out of two church buildings.

---

7. In America for many years, a Dutch Reformed minister was called "dominie" (Dutch, *dominee*), a title of respect meaning "master" (Latin *dominus*), but carrying more of the connotation of "teacher" or "minister."

He responded by calling the *Klagers* "impious" and "the scum of these four congregations."[8] He and his supporters maintained that they were only trying to keep the church pure by exercising the keys of discipline—both the key of preaching and the key of excommunication—as Lord's Day 31 of the Heidelberg Catechism directed them to do. They said that more than half of the signatories of the *klagte* had never made a profession of faith and warned them that "the wrath of God and eternal damnation abide on them."[9] Consequently, even though Article 76 of the Church Order stated that "no one shall be excommunicated without the previous advice of Classis,"[10] Frelinghuysen defended his actions by appealing to Article 86, which declared that changes could be made in the Church Order if the well-being of the church required it—the classis being across the sea.

The controversy raged on for several more years, severely impacting Frelinghuysen's mental and emotional health. Finally, on November 18, 1733, the churches served by Frelinghuysen adopted eleven "Peace Articles," which were read from the pulpits on the first three Lord's Days of 1734, then forwarded to Amsterdam for final approval. The articles, to which the *Klagers* subscribed, stated that the consistories should forgive the shortcomings of the *Klagers* and rescind their excommunications, provided the *Klagers* accepted Frelinghuysen as an orthodox Reformed minister and returned to the church. Though Boel's opposition to Frelinghuysen and the revivals continued, DuBois made peace.

Despite relentless criticism, Frelinghuysen faithfully carried on his labors. He not only preached, but also trained lay preachers. Most notable among them was the first translator of Frelinghuysen's sermons, Hendrik Visscher, whose own sermons were published and cherished for years by Reformed pietists in Raritan Valley. Frelinghuysen also trained several men for ordained ministry (including Samuel Verbryck, John Goetachius, and Thomas Romeyn) and advocated the establishment of a colonial theological seminary. After much striving by Frelinghuysen and his allies, the classis finally granted their petitions for preaching in English, local self-government, and the training of ministers in America. Furthermore, he connected with Anglican and Presbyterian ministers of like mind, fostering revival and experiential preaching throughout the region.

---

8. Quoted in Beeke and Pronk, "Biographical Introduction," xxii.
9. Quoted in Beeke and Pronk, "Biographical Introduction," xxii.
10. "Church Order of Dordrecht (1618–1619)," in *The Psalter* (Grand Rapids, MI: Eerdmans, 1991), 188.

While his searching preaching offended some people, God used it to convict others and to bring them to a saving knowledge of Christ. It appears that more than three hundred people in his congregations were converted under Frelinghuysen's ministry in New Jersey, not to mention those outside his churches. Those numbers become more significant when one considers that the total number of communicants in 1726 was approximately twenty. There were several mini-revivals under Freling-huysen's ministry that paved the way for the Great Awakening.

Frelinghuysen's preaching was richly biblical, containing a steady flow of numerous Scripture quotations. At times, his heart overflowed in declaring the wondrous mercies of God in his covenant with the elect. At other times, he pressed upon the unconverted their horrifying state and terrifying future. In what follows, we will focus on two aspects of his preaching: his calling of nominal Christians to Christ and his method of classifying his hearers.

Calling the Complacent to Conversion

The Raritan Valley area in New Jersey was settled mostly by Dutch Reformed farmers, who were attracted to its rich soil. Though most of them showed more interest in improving their economic condition than in pursuing spiritual growth, the farmers still looked forward to the arrival of their new preacher. But they soon realized that they had received no ordinary Reformed minister. Frelinghuysen preached his inaugural sermon on January 31, 1720, from 2 Corinthians 5:20: "Now then we are ambassadors for Christ, as though God did beseech you by us: we pray you in Christ's stead, be ye reconciled to God." The sermon caused quite a stir, as the new minister made it abundantly clear that he intended to labor among them "in Christ's stead"—that is, with ear-nestness and an emphasis on personal examination, as if Christ himself stood among them.

If the Dutch Reformed parishioners of the Raritan Valley were sur-prised by their minister's probing sermons and intense pastoral work, Frelinghuysen was no less surprised by his worldly parishioners. Though he had anticipated their low level of spirituality because of rumors he had heard in the Netherlands, he soon discovered that the situation was far worse than he had expected. William Demarest notes that "he found that great laxity of manners prevailed throughout his charge . . . that while horse-racing, gambling, dissipation, and rudeness of various kinds were common, the [church] was attended at convenience, and religion consisted of the mere formal pursuit of the routine of duty."[11] Bluntly put, Frelinghuysen realized that many of his parishioners showed no fruits of conversion. Practical spirituality—"the life of God in the soul of man"[12]—was largely absent. General ignorance and blatant godlessness abounded.

Consequently, Frelinghuysen's preaching focused on the conversion of sinners rather than the nurture of believers. He taught that an outward profession and an upright life are not sufficient for salvation. The Holy Spirit must reveal to a sinner his sinful state and lost condition before God, which, in turn, drives the convicted sinner to Christ for mercy and salvation. In a sermon on Isaiah 66:2, "The Poor and Contrite God's Temple," he says:

> In a contrite spirit are found: a deep sense and clear perception of sin. . . . Heart-felt disquietude [anxiety] and sadness. . . . An open and free confession of sin. Because of the greatness of his sins, the sinner does not know where to look or turn. Nevertheless, he places his dependence upon the grace that God can exercise through His Son. The contrite in spirit thus flees from the curse of the law to the gospel. . . . Thus the sinner is driven out of himself to the sovereign grace of God in Christ for reconciliation, pardon, sanctification, and salvation.[13]

Frelinghuysen taught that only those who have *experienced* the fruits of conversion are truly saved. Those fruits include, according to the Heidelberg Catechism, not only the knowledge of sin and misery, but also the experience of deliverance in Christ, resulting in a lifestyle of gratitude and sanctification to God. In his sermon "The Way of God with His People in the Sanctuary," Frelinghuysen invites sinners to come to Christ as earnestly as he warns them against sin: "If you are weary of sin and sincerely desire to draw near to God through Christ, then come."[14] Later in the same sermon, he presents God as running to meet those who have repented, just as the father of the prodigal ran to meet his returning son.

---

11. William Demarest, "Biographical Sketch," in Theodorus Jacobus Frelinghuysen, *Sermons* (New York: Board of Publication of the Reformed Protestant Dutch Church, 1856), 7.

12. This memorable description is the title of the best-known work by Scottish theologian Henry Scougal (1650–1678).

13. Frelinghuysen, "The Poor and Contrite God's Temple," in *Forerunner of the Great Awakening*, 14–16.

14. Frelinghuysen, "The Way of God with His People in the Sanctuary," in *Forerunner of the Great Awakening*, 131.

In another sermon, he says: "Jesus stands before us with extended arms, inviting sinners and the ungodly to repentance. Oh let him who senses his sins and his state of condemnation before God surrender himself to the Lord Jesus!"[15]

He says that a true experience of joyous salvation in Christ will necessarily result in a life of Christian sanctification, a life of total submission to God's Word, "marked by a new and hearty service."[16] Progress in grateful sanctification is possible only when the believer continually flees to Christ for strength in his war against indwelling sin and in his striving to regulate his life by God's Word. The Voetian themes of the narrow gate and the "strait" or hard way, the life of precision, the scarcity of those who are saved, the priority of internal motives that effect external observance, and others consistently reappear in Frelinghuysen's sermons.

Though members in Frelinghuysen's churches did not object to such scriptural and Reformed doctrines in themselves, many resented the pastor's forceful application of this experiential theology to their souls. Had he referred to people outside of the churches as unregenerate, self-righteous hypocrites, church members might have concurred. But Frelinghuysen made it clear that he was speaking to his own parishioners. For instance, in one sermon, he applies the lesson of an earthquake in no uncertain terms:

> Come here, you careless ones at ease in sin; you carnal and earthly-minded ones, you unchaste whoremongers and adulterers; you proud, haughty men and women; you seekers after pleasure; you drunkards, gamblers, disobedient and wicked rejectors of the gospel; you hypocrites and dissemblers. How do you think the Lord will deal with you? . . . Be filled with terror, you impure swine, adulterers, and whoremongers. Without true repentance you will live with the impure devils. All who burn in their vile lusts will be cast into a fire that is hotter than that of Sodom and Gomorrah.[17]

Frelinghuysen clearly viewed most of his members as unregenerate and hell bound. This was a bitter pill for them to swallow, especially

---

15. Frelinghuysen, "The Miserable End of the Ungodly," in *Forerunner of the Great Awakening*, 104.

16. Frelinghuysen, "The Believer's Well-Founded Expectation of Future Glory," in *Forerunner of the Great Awakening*, 185.

17. Frelinghuysen, "The Great Earthquake: Emblem of Judgment upon Enemies of the Church," in *Forerunner of the Great Awakening*, 226–28.

when he warned against their casual way of coming to the Lord's Supper. In his sermon "The Acceptable Communicant" he says:

> Much loved hearers who have so often been at the Lord's Table, do you know that the unconverted may not approach? Have you then with the utmost care examined whether you be born again? . . . Therefore reflect upon and bear in mind this truth. Remember, that though moral and outwardly religious, if you are still unregenerate and destitute of spiritual life, you have no warrant to approach the Table of grace.[18]

Classification Preaching for Direct Application

In 1726, one year after the publication of the *klagte*, Gilbert Tennent (1703–1764), a young Presbyterian minister, came to New Brunswick, New Jersey, to labor among the English-speaking colonists. The young preacher soon won the admiration and friendship of his neighbor, Dominie Frelinghuysen. Tennent was impressed by the soundness of the numerous conversions that were taking place under his Dutch colleague's preaching and felt discouraged by his own, seemingly unfruitful labors. In his journal, he wrote:

> When I came there which was about seven years after [Frelinghuysen] I had the privilege of seeing much of the fruits of his ministry. . . . This together with a kind letter which he sent me respecting the necessity of dividing the Word aright, and giving to every man his portion in due season, through the divine blessing, excited me to greater earnestness in ministerial labours.[19]

What was it in Frelinghuysen's style of preaching that led, with the Spirit's blessing, to so many conversions? Visscher, Frelinghuysen's friend and assistant, described it as "his exceeding talent, of drawing one matter out of another, thereby discovering the state and condition of his auditors to themselves."[20] Frelinghuysen, in other words, excelled in *discriminatory preaching*. As he states in "Duties of Watchmen on the Walls of Zion," an ordination sermon for a colleague, "Though I would

---

18. Frelinghuysen, "The Acceptable Communicant," in *Forerunner of the Great Awakening*, 40–41.

19. Quoted in Milton J. Coalter Jr., *Gilbert Tennent, Son of Thunder: Case Study of Continental Pietism's Impact on the First Great Awakening in the Middle Colonies* (New York: Greenwood, 1986), 16–17.

20. Quoted in Tanis, *Dutch Calvinistic Pietism*, 69.

not prescribe a method of preaching to anyone, yet I believe that the application should be discriminating, adapted to the various states of all hearers (Jude 20–21; Jer. 15)."[21]

Tennent was a fast learner and soon excelled in discriminatory preaching. Emphasizing the necessity of regeneration, he challenged his hearers to examine whether they possessed the scriptural evidence of the new birth.

Tennent's ministry became increasingly bound up with Frelinghuysen's. On occasion, they held combined worship services in the Dutch and English languages. The *Klagers* charged that by allowing "this English Dissenter"[22] (i.e., Tennent, a Presbyterian) to preach and administer the sacraments in his church, Frelinghuysen was violating the Dutch Reformed Church Order and liturgy, and thereby undermining the authority of Classis Amsterdam. Viewing themselves as the guardians of Dutch orthodoxy, they deplored his ecumenicity as inimical to the true Dutch Reformed religion. As orthodox traditionalists, they appealed to Classis Amsterdam, saying, "We must be careful to keep things in a Dutch way in our churches."[23]

Frelinghuysen's goal, on the other hand, was the conversion of sinners. Whoever shared this vision was his friend, regardless of denominational attachments, ethnic and linguistic backgrounds, parish boundaries, and social distinctions. Ironically, his refusal to discriminate between national or ethnic groups arose directly from his commitment to discriminate between true believers and the wicked in his preaching.

Frelinghuysen excelled in distinguishing between true and false religion. He developed this skill with the assistance of Dutch pietistic mentors who divided a congregation into various states and conditions of soul, and then made personal applications in preaching to each group. Pioneers of this classification method in Dutch pietism were Jean Taffin, Godefridus Udemans, and Willem Teellinck. This practice of classification expanded and developed under the Voetian circle of preachers, such as Jodocus van Lodenstein, Wilhelmus à Brakel, and Bernardus Smytegelt (1665–1739). Those *Nadere Reformatie* divines represented the cream of Dutch pietism.

Frelinghuysen's foremost mentor, Johannes Verschuir (1680–1737), belonged to this Voetian circle of preachers. Verschuir distinguished

---

21. Frelinghuysen, "Duties of Watchmen on the Walls of Zion," in *Forerunner of the Great Awakening*, 280.
22. Quoted in Beeke and Pronk, "Biographical Introduction," xxvi.
23. Quoted in Beeke and Pronk, "Biographical Introduction," xxvii.

between several categories of churchgoers, all of whom need to be addressed by the preacher: (1) the strong Christian (*sterk Christen*), who is converted and has reached a degree of maturity in spiritual life; (2) the concerned Christian (*bekommerde Christen*), who also is converted but struggles with many doubts and lacks assurance of faith; (3) the "letter-learned" (*letterwyse*), who are unconverted but instructed and conversant in truth, though not knowing its experience or power; and (4) the ignorant (*onkunde*), who are unconverted and unlearned, but who may still be persuaded to learn because they have native intelligence.[24]

Frelinghuysen's sermons show that he usually followed Verschuir's method of classification. He devoted more preaching to counselling the concerned Christian than the strong Christian. We may conclude that Frelinghuysen believed that most of the true believers in his congregation belonged to this category. Most of his warnings were directed to the "letter-learned." He saw them as being in great danger because they were "almost Christians," not far from the kingdom of God. They walked with Christians and talked like Christians, but they did not possess the new birth. Despite their outward morality and profession of the truth, they would perish if death overtook them.

At the heart of Frelinghuysen's theology—and that of the Dutch Further Reformation—stood the conviction that the one thing needful is regeneration. In a typical sermon, he exhorted his hearers to examine whether they possessed the evidences of the new birth. Closely related to this was the call to conversion, by which Frelinghuysen usually did not mean the daily conversion of the believer but the initial conversion of the unsaved. He used the word *conversion* in that sense interchangeably with *regeneration* or *the new birth*.

Frelinghuysen preached that the new birth must be experiential. That is to say, a convert had to know how he had passed from death to life and was expected to be able to relate what God had done for his soul. These two emphases in Frelinghuysen's ministry—the necessity of the new birth and the various classifications of churchgoers—impressed Tennent, Whitefield, and other revival preachers.

All of this was consistent with Frelinghuysen's theology of preaching. In the application to the sermon "Duties of Watchmen," he reflects upon his duty as a preacher:

---

24. Beeke and Pronk, "Biographical Introduction," xxxi.

The church includes all kinds of people: wicked and unconverted persons, moral persons, and Christians in appearance and profession. This last group is the largest, for "many are called but few are chosen." There are also converted people in the church. These include babes in grace as well as those who are more advanced. Each has desires and needs. Each must therefore be preached to and dealt with according to his condition, as Jeremiah 15:19 says. Many zealous divines have shown how dangerous general applications can be (Ezek. 13:19–20).[25]

According to Teunis Brienen, who wrote his doctoral dissertation on the classification method used by preachers of the *Nadere Reformatie*, this approach varied from the method of John Calvin and other early Reformers, who simply divided church members into two categories: believers and unbelievers.[26] Calvin was not unaware of differences between strong and weak believers or that there are various kinds and degrees of unbelief, but he did not draw such detailed distinctions as did the later representatives of the *Nadere Reformatie*.

The difference between early Reformers such as Calvin and post-Reformation divines such as Frelinghuysen is due in part to the different settings in which they preached. The Reformers preached, as John Macleod has pointed out, to "a generation of believers on which the Gospel of the free grace of God in Justification burst in all its wonder as something altogether new."[27] Post-Reformers such as Frelinghuysen preached several generations later in a time when many regarded mere assent to the truths of Scripture as sufficient for salvation. Against this background, it became essential to distinguish clearly between saving faith and historical faith by placing a heavier emphasis on self-examination, the marks of grace, and the classification of hearers into various groups.

Brienen said that the English Puritans did not go as far as their Dutch counterparts in making distinctions among various hearers.[28] That may explain why Tennent and Whitefield were impressed by Frelinghuysen's

25. Frelinghuysen, "Duties of Watchmen on the Walls of Zion," in *Forerunner of the Great Awakening*, 280–81.

26. Teunis Brienen, *De Prediking Van De Nadere Reformatie* (Amsterdam: Ton Bolland, 1974), 5–25.

27. John Macleod, *Scottish Theology in Relation to Church History since the Reformation* (Edinburgh: Banner of Truth, 1974), 28.

28. Brienen, *De Prediking Van De Nadere Reformatie*, 331.

preaching. His method of classifying hearers and his soul-searching applications went beyond what they were accustomed to hearing. James Tanis concludes: "Tennent's preaching was Frelinghuysen's method perfected. . . . Whitefield's own method of preaching was greatly affected by this instruction, and so the torch which Frelinghuysen had borne from East Friesland passed to Tennent, on to Whitefield."[29]

Conclusion

Was Frelinghuysen's classification method of preaching biblical in every respect? Brienen goes too far in rejecting the classification method, but he is correct in pointing out the danger of its going beyond Scripture. The Bible *generally* draws only one distinction between hearers; it says people respond to the Word either with faith or in unbelief. While the Scriptures do recognize different stages in the life of faith, as well as varying degrees of unbelief, they do not support a system so detailed that everyone is *habitually* placed in a separate category. On the other hand, we should not forget that the positive, scriptural purposes of such categorizing were to focus on the necessity of the new birth; to foster growth in grace through specific instruction, encouragement, and warning; and to point out the danger of deceiving oneself for eternity. The classification method has its place, providing that it is not overdone by being forced out of the text that is being expounded. If the preacher is properly controlled by his text, the classification method yields a rich harvest of specific and diverse applications. When applications in preaching are not controlled by the text, the classification method tends to produce repetition or, even worse, to promote the preacher's own criteria for self-examination rather than the criteria of Scripture.

Despite his weaknesses and shortcomings, Frelinghuysen was used powerfully by the Lord in building his church in America. Heinrich Melchior Mühlenberg (1711–1787), a Lutheran pietist who toured the Middle Colonies in 1759, refers to Frelinghuysen as "a converted Dutch preacher who was the first in these parts to insist upon true repentance, living faith, and sanctification, and who had much success."[30] God is sovereign, and he accomplishes his purposes through a great variety of instruments, even flawed ones.

---

29. Tanis, *Dutch Calvinistic Pietism*, 80–81.
30. Quoted in Randall H. Balmer, *A Perfect Babel of Confusion: Dutch Religion and English Culture in the Middle Colonies* (Oxford: Oxford University Press, 1989), 122.

Though Frelinghuysen did not have an irenic character, he was a man of profound spiritual conviction and tremendous courage. He personified the concluding words of the preface to a collection of his sermons, *Laudem non quæro; culpam non timeo* ("I seek not praise; I fear not blame").[31] In matters concerning the truth, he would not waver: "I would sooner die a thousand deaths," he declared to his flock, "than not preach the truth."[32] He was an eloquent speaker, a vigorous writer, an able theologian, and a zealous experiential preacher. "By the fervor of his preaching," Leonard Bacon writes, "he was to win the signal glory of bringing in the Great Awakening."[33] Throughout his long tenure in New Jersey, he served as God's man of the hour to herald a number of bountiful harvests that promoted Reformed, spiritual piety.

Tanis concludes: "His influence in the developing structures of American theology was enormous. His role was that of a transmitter between the Old World and the New; his great contribution was his infusing into the Middle Colonies that Dutch evangelical pietism which he carried within himself."[34]

Age often mellows, matures, and sanctifies people. In his later years, Frelinghuysen became more aware of his character flaws. He became less judgmental of others and realized that he had at times made life unnecessarily difficult for himself and others. It troubled him increasingly that he had treated some of his colleagues with disdain, and he apologized for calling some of them unconverted. Reconciliation efforts between Frelinghuysen and DuBois were successful; at a revival meeting in 1741 at which Whitefield preached, both ministers sat on the platform. May we experience in our divisive day more spiritual unity with all who love the Lord Jesus Christ in sincerity and who long for revivals such as those God gave in the days of Frelinghuysen, Tennent, and Whitefield.

Few could remain neutral toward Frelinghuysen. His searching theology of regeneration, his demand that the converted live in a holy and precise manner, and his zeal to keep the church pure produced many friends and many foes. In the end, however, Frelinghuysen's indefatigable

---

31. Quoted in Demarest, "Biographical Sketch," 8.
32. Frelinghuysen, "The Acceptable Communicant," in *Forerunner of the Great Awakening*, 40.
33. Leonard W. Bacon, *A History of American Christianity* (New York: Christian Literature Co., 1897), 81.
34. Tanis, *Dutch Calvinistic Pietism*, 97.

work, zeal, and piety won the day; even many of his former enemies came to accept him, for they could not deny the fruits of his ministry. His ministry underscores for us the importance of enduring hardship as good soldiers of Jesus Christ and of keeping our hand on the plow in doing kingdom work.

17

Eighteenth-Century Preachers: Halyburton, Edwards, and Davies

In order to illustrate Reformed experiential preaching in a way that moves the heart, we have looked at shining examples of preachers from the Reformation, English Puritanism, and the Dutch Further Reformation. We have traversed two centuries and touched upon numerous particular preachers. But before we leave this section of the book, we must give attention to English-speaking preachers in the eighteenth, nineteenth, and twentieth centuries. Though we cannot possibly give these faithful servants of God their due credit—that must wait until judgment day—we will benefit from seeing how the torch continues to be passed down from generation to generation.

In this chapter, we will focus on three preachers of the eighteenth century. We begin with a man who died in the early part of that century, and then move on to consider two preachers who served God around the time of the Great Awakening.

Thomas Halyburton

Thomas Halyburton (1674–1712) was born on December 25 in Dupplin, Perthshire, in Scotland.[1] His father died when he was seven; his

---

1. On Halyburton, see the introductions to each volume in Thomas Halyburton, *The Works of Thomas Halyburton*, 4 vols. (Aberdeen: James Begg Society, 2000–2005). This freshly retypeset edition contains the following: *Volume 1: Faith and Justification*, which includes a treatise on the nature of faith, another on the order of regeneration and justification, and a third on God's act of

mother raised him for a time in the Netherlands to escape persecution. While studying at Edinburgh University and then at the University of St. Andrews, he began to suffer from a disabling immobility of the limbs, but graduated from the latter school with an MA in theology in 1696. During his studies, he went through a profound struggle with the skeptical rationalism of Deism. He finally came to Christ in 1698. He served a church in Fife near St. Andrews for ten years, but his health declined. He became professor of divinity at St. Andrews in 1710, but died at the age of thirty-seven on September 23, 1712. At his request, he was buried next to Samuel Rutherford because he wanted to see Rutherford's joy when they both arose from the dead upon Christ's second advent.

Halyburton is known for three major works. The first is his *Memoirs*, which in spiritual depth matches John Bunyan's *Grace Abounding to the Chief of Sinners* and Augustine's *Confessions*. In it, he describes his deliverance in terms of a transforming sight of God through the Scriptures, "the light of the knowledge of the glory of God in the face of Jesus Christ" (2 Cor. 4:6), that created faith and made him a new man.[2] John Macleod says that while Jonathan Edwards gives us one of the classic statements in Reformed theology on "the reality of spiritual light," Halyburton's description of the "character of this light" is worthy to stand alongside Edwards's treatment.[3] He goes on to say that Halyburton was regarded as one of the greatest theologians of Scotland, a man on par with the Dutch divine Herman Witsius, and one who drew from the same well as the English theologian John Owen.[4]

The second major book that Halyburton wrote is a classic intellectual defense of Christianity against Deism, titled *Natural Religion Insuf-*

---

justification; *Volume 2: Faith and Salvation*, which contains his classic work, *The Great Concern of Salvation*, which is a remarkable experiential treatment of how the Holy Spirit works salvation in sinners; *Volume 3: Faith and Revelation*, which contains his magnum opus against Deism; and *Volume 4: Faith and Experience*, which contains his famous autobiography. Halyburton's autobiography was earlier reprinted as *Memoirs of Thomas Halyburton*, ed. Joel R. Beeke, intro. Sinclair B. Ferguson (Grand Rapids, MI: Reformation Heritage Books, 1996). See also John D. Nicholls, "Thomas Halyburton, 1674–1712," in *Faith and Ferment* (London: Westminster Conference, 1982), 32–49; Hugh Cartwright, "Faith and Assurance in the Teaching and Experience of Thomas Halyburton (1674–1712)," *Scottish Bulletin of Evangelical Theology* 11, no. 2 (Autumn 1993): 109–28; Edgar Primrose Dickie, "Thomas Halyburton," *Scottish Journal of Theology* 5, no. 1 (March 1952): 1–13.

2. Halyburton, *Memoirs*, 94–112.

3. John Macleod, *Scottish Theology in Relation to Church History since the Reformation* (Edinburgh: Banner of Truth, 1974), 119.

4. Macleod, *Scottish Theology in Relation to Church History since the Reformation*, 117–18, 124.

ficient. It critiques the efforts of Lord Edward Herbert (d. 1648) to set aside divine revelation and to build religion on the natural principles of belief in a deity, reverence, morality, repentance of sin, and expectation of future judgment. John Nicholls writes of Halyburton's book:

> Its argument is straightforward: Natural religion, as championed by Herbert, is insufficient because it does not give us clear knowledge of God, of the way of happiness, or of the nature of sin. . . . Natural religion is insufficient to give effective motives to duty, to reveal the means of obtaining pardon and to eradicate or subdue our innate inclinations to sin. . . . [N]o rational evidences or arguments can replace the self-authenticating power of the Scriptures applied by the Holy Spirit.[5]

We see Halyburton's experiential preaching especially in his third major book, *The Great Concern of Salvation.* It is a wonderful experiential volume that outlines the work of the Spirit in the soul with respect to misery, deliverance, and gratitude. Halyburton says, "Whoever considers his present condition, will soon see that his great business and chief concern lies in three important inquiries: 'What have I done?' (Jer. 8:6); 'What shall I do to be saved?' (Acts 16:30); 'What shall I render to the Lord?' (Ps. 116:12)."[6] Frederick Leahy writes of this book: "It is striking to see how plainly and directly he speaks in these sermons. There is a warmth and passion in every line and his treatment of Scripture is exhaustive. . . . He speaks from the heart."[7]

In declaring the misery of fallen men, Halyburton's method begins with God. He wisely sets the doctrine of sin in its God-centered context by elaborating the following principles:

- God is the absolute and independent Sovereign of the world.
- God has prescribed laws to all his creatures, by which he governs them.
- The great Lawgiver of the world has annexed rewards and punishments to those laws.
- These laws are holy, just, good, and spiritual.[8]

---

5. Nicholls, "Thomas Halyburton, 1674–1712," 42.
6. Halyburton, *The Great Concern of Salvation*, in *Works, Volume 2, Faith and Salvation*, 29.
7. Frederick S. Leahy, review of Halyburton, *Faith and Salvation*, in *Banner of Truth* 475 (April 2003): 26.
8. Halyburton, "The Great Concern of Salvation," in *Works*, 2:31–34.

He then explains that sin is any lack of conformity to the laws of God in thought, word, deed, or condition of heart. All transgressions of the law arise from contempt of God's authority. Sin always brings with it defilement of the soul with moral filth, and guilt or obligation to suffer the penalty of the curse of God's law. All people are involved in sin, regardless of their age, religion, rank in society, or generation or era in history.[9]

To give his readers a view of sin's ugliness, Halyburton urges them to consider:

- *God's law*: "See the holy, the high and exalted God, exhibiting his mind and will in two tables, tables containing safe, good, holy, just, spiritual, and very advantageous rules. . . . See sin breaking, nay, dashing to pieces these two tables, in a worse sense than Moses did. . . . Is it a small thing to you to trample upon, to tread under foot, the holy, the righteous law of God, that is the perfect image of all his holiness and spotless purity?"
- *God's nature*: "Take a view of it in the nature of the great God, the seat of all majesty, glory, beauty, and excellency. . . . The meanest, most apparently deformed creature in the world, the toad, the crawling insect, carries in its nature nothing really opposite to the nature of God; sin, only sin, stands in opposition to him."
- *God's threats*: See sin in its true light, "in the threatening of the law, and see there what estimate God puts on it, and what a thing it is. All the power of heaven, the anger, the fury, the vengeance of God, all are levelled [aimed] at the head of sin."
- *God's judgments*: "What think you of all these lamentable evils, miseries, and woes? . . . Who brought all these sons of pride, who not long ago were strangely ruffling it out in the light of warlike glory, down to the sides of the pit? Who filled your churchyards [cemeteries] with heaps upon heaps, fathers and sons, high and low, rich and poor, of all sexes, ranks, ages, and degrees? Surely sin hath done this."
- *God's damnation*: "See the poor wretches lying in bundles, boiling eternally in that stream of brimstone, roaring under the intolerable, and yet eternal anguish of their spirits . . . every faculty of their soul, every joint of their body, brim full of the fury of the

---

9. Halyburton, "The Great Concern of Salvation," in *Works*, 2:34–38.

eternal God: behold, and wonder at this terrible and astonishing sight; and in this take a view of sin."

- *God's crucified Son*: See "what God's thoughts of sin are. So highly opposite to his nature is it, that the bowels of affection he had to the Son of his love, whom he so highly honoured, when the voice came from the excellent glory, saying, 'This is my beloved Son, in whom I am well-pleased,' were not able to hold up the hand of inexorable [uncompromising] justice from striking at him, nay, striking him dead, for the sin of the elect world."[10]

To people convinced of their sin and misery, Halyburton says, "'Believe on the Lord Jesus Christ, and thou shalt be saved, and thy house' (Acts 16:31). This Lord Jesus Christ is God and man in one person, and so He is approachable. He can identify with both God and men, for He is touched with a feeling of our infirmities."[11]

Halyburton says that Christ is everything the sinner needs. He is the Prophet called by God, granted God's Word, and commissioned to speak to convinced sinners to satisfy their desires, and that not in a terrifying manner, but as a man like them. He is the holy, merciful, and faithful Priest ordained by God's oath to offer the atoning sacrifice to God for sins and to intercede with God for sinners. He is the King set up by God with power and authority to decree the laws of his kingdom, to bring his people to willing obedience, to protect his subjects from all attacks, to conquer all his enemies, and to subdue the entire universe to himself.[12]

Christ therefore can give the sinner relief from the threefold evil that oppresses him. First, Halyburton writes, man "finds himself extremely ignorant, perfectly in the dark, as to the mind and will of God." Christ the Prophet brings the sinner "into his marvelous light," revealing God and his grace. Second, "man is pressed down with guilt, and it is only in Christ's priestly office that the awakened sinner can find relief against this," for only the blood of Christ can purge our consciences from the guilt of dead works. Third, man is "enslaved by sin" and is therefore not only "weak" but "unwilling to become willing." Christ the King can transform disobedient sinners into willing, wise, and righteous servants of God.[13]

10. Halyburton, "The Great Concern of Salvation," in *Works*, 2:44–48.
11. Halyburton, "The Great Concern of Salvation," in *Works*, 2:188; cf. 189–90.
12. Halyburton, "The Great Concern of Salvation," in *Works*, 2:191–95.
13. Halyburton, "The Great Concern of Salvation," in *Works*, 2:196.

Here is a Christ both able and willing to save sinners, for he was sent by the Father to do this very work. Sinners look upon God and question how they can ever draw near to such majesty. Justice demands their deaths; holiness excludes all that is impure; and God's very voice would destroy them. But the Priest satisfied justice for sinners, the King has the power to purge our filth by the Spirit, and the Prophet brings the message of good news in human gentleness.[14]

Satan and his forces of darkness threaten the sinner with overwhelming attacks on his soul, Halyburton writes: "They charge him with things that he cannot deny. They lay deep contrivances against him that he cannot discover. They fall upon him with a force that he is not able to resist." But as Priest, Christ gives the believer an answer to all Satan's accusations. As Prophet, Christ "gives him wisdom to escape his snares." And as King, Christ gives him power "whereby he is made more than conqueror."[15]

Indeed, Christ in his offices satisfies every aspect of human need. He opens the blinded mind and fills it with light. He quiets the guilty conscience and fills it with peace. He captivates the will and fills it with contentment in himself. In every way, Halyburton preaches that Christ is an all-sufficient Savior.[16]

After calling sinners to trust in this great Savior, Halyburton spends the last quarter (some one hundred pages) of *The Great Concern of Salvation* calling believers to serve their Savior. He observes that a believer (1) must serve God "deliberately, resolutely, and willingly," (2) must first serve God himself before he can engage others to serve him, and (3) "will endeavour to have his family engaged too."[17]

True service to God consists in doing his will, not following our imaginations: "The master's precept is the measure of the servant's obedience. We never find the Lord approving any for doing what he did not command them."[18] Such service must be done with an eye always upon the authority of the law and Lawgiver. It also must be done "in the name of the Lord Jesus" (Col. 3:17), which means at his command, by his strength, through his acceptance with the Father, and to his glory.[19]

---

14. Halyburton, "The Great Concern of Salvation," in *Works*, 2:197–98.
15. Halyburton, "The Great Concern of Salvation," in *Works*, 2:198.
16. Halyburton, "The Great Concern of Salvation," in *Works*, 2:198–99.
17. Halyburton, "The Great Concern of Salvation," in *Works*, 2:312.
18. Halyburton, "The Great Concern of Salvation," in *Works*, 2:315.
19. Halyburton, "The Great Concern of Salvation," in *Works*, 2:316.

If someone asks, "Who is the Lord, that we should serve him?" Halyburton replies that he is "a great King," infinitely nobler than the kings of the earth, most of whom are "slaves to the basest of lusts." Also, he is "a good Master," who assigns his servants work that is "suitable and reasonable," blesses the faithful with "bounty," and "is indulgent, compassionate, and merciful to the failings of his servants," if they do not "obstinately persist in them."[20]

Thus, the sincere Christian will ask himself: Am I really a servant of the Lord? Do I have a sound heart that fears the Lord? Is my eye single in seeking "God's glory, and the enjoyment of him, which is heavenly treasure indeed," or corrupted by worldly aims? Do I follow a safe rule, that is, Scripture alone, neither adding to it nor subtracting from it? Is my hand diligent, serving God with all my might? Does my service please God?[21]

So we see that Halyburton preached a rich message of misery, deliverance, and gratitude. His preaching was highly structured and organized, but he was no theorist; he preached as one who had passed through the depths of testing and temptation, and yet persevered in holy combat.

Next, we pass on to perhaps the most famous preacher in North American history.

Jonathan Edwards

The literature on Edwards is colossal.[22] We can only scratch the surface of this great man's ministry here. He was born on October 5, 1703, in East Windsor, Connecticut,[23] the son of Puritan pastor Timothy Edwards. His mother, Esther, was the daughter of the great New England preacher Solomon Stoddard. Jonathan graduated with two theological degrees that included the study of classical languages, logic, and natural philosophy: a BA from Yale in 1720 and an MA in 1722. During this period, New England Congregationalism was suffering notable apostasies to Arminian Anglicanism. Edwards early positioned himself as a champion of

---

20. Halyburton, "The Great Concern of Salvation," in *Works*, 2:328–29.
21. Halyburton, "The Great Concern of Salvation," in *Works*, 2:341–44.
22. For an annotated bibliography of thousands of published sources on Edwards, see M. X. Lesser, *Reading Jonathan Edwards: An Annotated Bibliography in Three Parts, 1729–2005* (Grand Rapids, MI: Eerdmans, 2008).
23. On Edwards's biography, see George M. Marsden, *Jonathan Edwards: A Life* (New Haven, CT: Yale University Press, 2003); Iain H. Murray, *Jonathan Edwards: A New Biography* (Edinburgh: Banner of Truth, 1987).

Reformed doctrine. He had resisted the doctrines of divine sovereignty until, in 1721, he was transformed by a sweet sense of the loveliness of God as "the King eternal, immortal, invisible" (1 Tim. 1:17).

Edwards took up the minister's mantle as an assistant to his grandfather at Northampton, in the Connecticut River valley of central Massachusetts. Stoddard died in 1729, leaving Edwards as the sole minister in the church. During his service there, he saw remarkable movements of God's Spirit in 1734–1735 and again in 1740–1743, local manifestations of the widespread revival known as the Great Awakening. Edwards preached in many places during this outpouring of the Spirit and welcomed the evangelical Anglican George Whitefield into his pulpit. He wrote both to defend the revival and to discern true Spirit-worked religion from its nonsaving counterfeits. His *Treatise Concerning Religious Affections* (1746) remains one of the greatest books ever written on the distinguishing marks of true godliness. He also edited and published the *Diary of David Brainerd* (1749), the work of a man whose sacrificial efforts to reach the Native Americans inspired people for centuries afterward to give themselves to evangelizing the world.

Sadly, the revivals did not prevent the church from removing Edwards from his office in 1750. A controversy erupted because he had come to believe, contrary to his late grandfather, that the Lord's Supper is not a "converting ordinance," and therefore only those who profess to be regenerate should partake of the sacrament. In 1751, he became pastor to English settlers and missionary to Native Americans in Stockbridge, on the western frontier of Massachusetts. Edwards was already an accomplished theological writer, but his years there produced some of his greatest books, including his treatises *Freedom of the Will* (1754) and *Original Sin* (1758). In 1758, the College of New Jersey (later renamed Princeton University) invited him to become its president. Shortly after he arrived, a smallpox inoculation turned deadly, and the great theologian passed into glory on March 22, 1758.

His works have been gathered into several forms over the years. The two sets most commonly used today are the two-volume edition, edited by Edward Hickman in 1834 and reprinted by the Banner of Truth Trust,[24] and the Yale edition, published in twenty-six volumes

---

24. Jonathan Edwards, *The Works of Jonathan Edwards*, ed. Edward Hickman, 2 vols. (Edinburgh: Banner of Truth, 1974), hereafter, *Works (Banner of Truth)*.

over five decades (1957–2008) and now available with other sources online.[25]

Though Edwards's theological treatises have often been studied, increasing attention is being given to his sermons.[26] Wilson Kimnach says that Edwards's sermons were "the hub" on which his other interests and activities centered, "like so many spokes of a wheel."[27] Though he was perhaps not the most moving orator, Edwards's sermons excelled in their doctrinal and spiritual content. John Gerstner (1914–1996) says of his preaching, "From the standpoint of deep and solid exegesis, clear and profound articulation of doctrine, searching, thorough, and fervent evangelistic application, I have never found Edwards' equal."[28]

Edwards is best known for his sermon "Sinners in the Hands of an Angry God," in which he verbally dangles his hearers over the pit of hell to impress upon them the fearful danger of resisting God's call to repent and trust in Christ. However, he also preached "Heaven Is a World of Love," a glorious discourse in which he labors to describe the indescribable love of God that floods the spirits who dwell in Christ's heavenly presence. Michael McClymond and Gerald McDermott observe: "Edwards is best known for his 'terror' preaching. This is unfortunate because he was obsessed with God's beauty, not his wrath."[29]

In this section, we will touch upon one theme from Edwards's Reformed experiential preaching: the free offer of the gospel.

---

25. See The Jonathan Edwards Center at Yale University online, http://edwards.yale.edu/.
26. On Edwards and preaching, see *The Salvation of Souls: Nine Previously Unpublished Sermons on the Call of Ministry and the Gospel by Jonathan Edwards*, ed. Richard A. Bailey and Gregory A. Wills (Wheaton, IL: Crossway, 2002); *The Sermons of Jonathan Edwards: A Reader*, ed. Wilson H. Kimnach, Kenneth P. Minkema, and Douglas A. Sweeney (New Haven, CT: Yale University Press, 1999); John H. Gerstner, *The Rational Biblical Theology of Jonathan Edwards*, 3 vols. (Powhatan, VA; Lake Mary, FL: Berea Publications; Ligonier Ministries, 1991), 1:480–540; 3:1–49; Charles L. Geschiere, "Taste and See That the Lord Is Good: The Aesthetic-Affectional Preaching of Jonathan Edwards" (ThM thesis, Calvin Theological Seminary, 2008); Wilson H. Kimnach, introduction to *The Works of Jonathan Edwards*, vol. 10, *Sermons and Discourses, 1720–1723*, ed. Wilson H. Kimnach (New Haven, CT: Yale University Press, 1992), 1–258; Samuel T. Logan, "Jonathan Edwards and the 1734–35 Northampton Revival," in *Preaching and Revival* (London: Westminster Conference, 1984), 57–85; Glenn T. Miller, "The Rise of Evangelical Calvinism: A Study in Jonathan Edwards and the Puritan Tradition" (ThD diss., Union Theological Seminary, 1971), 227–383; Michael J. McClymond and Gerald R. McDermott, *The Theology of Jonathan Edwards* (Oxford: Oxford University Press, 2012), 494–512; Patrick Pang, "A Study of Jonathan Edwards as a Pastor-Preacher" (DMin thesis, Fuller Theological Seminary, 1990); Douglas A. Sweeney, *Jonathan Edwards and the Ministry of the Word: A Model of Faith and Thought* (Downers Grove, IL: IVP Academic, 2009).
27. Kimnach, introduction to *The Works of Jonathan Edwards*, vol. 10, 3.
28. Gerstner, *The Rational Biblical Theology of Jonathan Edwards*, 1:480.
29. McClymond and McDermott, *The Theology of Jonathan Edwards*, 497.

Great Guilt No Obstacle

Perhaps sometime early in his ministry at Northampton,[30] Edwards preached on Psalm 25:11, "For thy name's sake, O LORD, pardon mine iniquity; for it is great." He titled the sermon, "Great Guilt No Obstacle to the Pardon of the Returning Sinner."[31] After briefly examining the text and its context, Edwards draws out this doctrine: "If we truly come to God for mercy, the greatness of our sin will be no impediment to pardon." The sinner has no hope of pardon based on his own righteousness or worthiness, but only God's glory and grace. Indeed, he makes the greatness of his iniquity the basis of his plea for salvation, because it shows how much he needs God's grace.[32]

Edwards starts with an explanation of what it means to "truly come to God for mercy." It requires, first, that we "see our misery, and be sensible of our need of mercy." Otherwise, the notion of God's mercy is mere nonsense. Therefore, the seeker of mercy must have a sense that God's law curses him and God's wrath abides on him because of the guilt of his sins. He needs to realize that it is a dreadful and awful thing to have God as his enemy. He must see that God must save him, or else his situation is truly hopeless.[33] Second, he must sense that he is not worthy of God's mercy. He comes as a beggar, not demanding what he deserves—for he deserves wrath and misery—but "lying in the dust at the foot of mercy." Third, he must come "in and through Jesus Christ alone." He must hope in Christ, trusting in "what he is, what he hath done, and what he hath suffered." He must trust that Christ is the only Savior, and that Christ's blood "cleanses from all sin."[34] If a sinner comes to God seeking mercy in this manner, the greatness of his sins is no obstacle to God forgiving him completely.

Edwards then produces five arguments to convince sinners that the way is truly wide open for them to find mercy if they come in this manner:

1. God's mercy is "sufficient for the pardon of the greatest sins" because "his mercy is infinite." Infinity is just as far above great things as it is above small. Edwards uses illustrations to drive the point home. The

---

30. Sereno Edwards Dwight (1786–1850), Edwards's great-grandson and editor of his works, dated the sermon sometime before 1733 (Miller, "The Rise of Evangelical Calvinism," 276).

31. "Great Guilt No Obstacle to the Pardon of the Returning Sinner," in *Works of Jonathan Edwards Online*, vol. 47, *Sermons, Series II, 1731–1732* (Jonathan Edwards Center at Yale University, 2008), 422–28, http://edwards.yale.edu/archive?path=aHR0cDovL2Vkd2FyZHMueWFsZS5lZHUvY2dpLWJpbi9uZXdwaGlsby9nZXRvYmplY3Gw/Yy40NTozOS53amVVv, hereafter, *WJE Online*, 47. The sermon may also be found in Edwards, *Works (Banner of Truth)*, 2:110–13.

32. Edwards, "Great Guilt No Obstacle," in *WJE Online*, 47:422.

33. Edwards, "Great Guilt No Obstacle," in *WJE Online*, 47:422–23.

34. Edwards, "Great Guilt No Obstacle," in *WJE Online*, 47:423.

infinite God is as much above angels and kings as he is above beggars and the lowest worm on earth. God's infinite mercy can pardon the greatest sins or ten thousand sins as much as it can the least sin.

2. Christ's satisfaction is "sufficient for the removal of the greatest guilt." His blood "cleanseth us from all sin" (1 John 1:7). Those who believe in him "are justified from all things" (Acts 13:39). The honor of God's majesty and holiness requires satisfaction for sin, but Christ has suffered and paid the full debt to satisfy justice so that it is fully consistent with God's attributes for him to pardon those who come through Christ seeking mercy. Christ is the "propitiation" so that God "might be just, and the justifier of him which believeth in Jesus" (Rom. 3:25–26). Christ was "cursed" for sinners, so he "hath redeemed us from the curse of the law" (Gal. 3:13).

3. "Christ will not refuse to save the greatest sinners" who come rightly seeking mercy, because it is his "business to be a Savior of sinners." He came to be the physician of sin-infected souls (Matt. 9:12–13), and no "physician of compassion" refuses to treat the people who most need his healing if he has the ability to help them.

4. God glorifies his grace by the salvation of great sinners. Edwards says: "The greatness of divine grace appears very much in this, that God by Christ saves the greatest offenders. The greater the guilt of any sinner is, the more glorious and wonderful is the grace manifested in his pardon." Thus, where "sin abounded," it is glorious for grace to abound all the more (Rom. 5:20). Christ saved Paul for this purpose, to glorify himself as the Savior of great sinners (1 Tim. 1:13).

5. Edwards concludes: "Pardon is as much offered and promised to the greatest sinners as any, if they will come aright to God for mercy. The invitations of the gospel are always in universal terms: as, Ho, every one that thirsteth; Come unto me, all ye that labor and are heavy laden; and, Whosoever will, let him come. And the voice of Wisdom is to men in general: Prov. viii. 4, 'Unto you, O men, I call, and my voice is to the sons of men.' Not to moral men, or religious men, but to you, O *men*. So Christ promises, John iv. 37. 'Him that cometh to me, I will in no wise cast out.'"[35]

Then Edwards urges sinners to make "proper use of this subject," namely, if one's conscience is burdened with guilt, "immediately go to

---

35. Edwards, "Great Guilt No Obstacle," in *WJE Online*, 47:423–25.

God through Christ for mercy." Sinners who come to God in the manner prescribed in the gospel may rest assured, "the arms of mercy are open wide to embrace you." Edwards says, "If you are but willing, you may freely come and unload yourselves, and cast all your burdens on Christ, and rest in him."[36]

He ends by answering objections that sinners might raise against this free offer. In these objections, we see the classification method by which Edwards divides his hearers into categories and addresses each. First, someone might object that he has wasted his life in sin and now has only his old age to offer God. Edwards replies by asking, Where does God say anywhere in the Bible that all may come except the old? We fool ourselves if we think that God accepts young sinners because they can offer their lives to serve the Lord. He warns, "A self-righteous spirit is at the bottom of such objections." We have nothing to offer God to make us more worthy; therefore, we may come when we are most unworthy.[37]

Second, someone might object that he has sinned as a reprobate by rejecting the truth and resisting the convictions of the Holy Spirit, perhaps with an arrogant and hateful spirit. Edwards replies, "There is no sin peculiar to reprobates but the sin against the Holy Ghost." No other is taught in the Scriptures, and we dare not go beyond Scripture. If a sinner thinks that God's mercy is not sufficient to pardon his sins or the blood of Christ not sufficient to cleanse him, then he has not yet seen the glory of the Savior. While persistence in sin and hardness of heart make it less likely that a sinner will come to Christ, Edwards says, "if you can find it in your hearts to come to Christ, and close with him, you will be accepted not at all the less readily because you have committed such sins."[38]

Third, someone might object that he had "better stay till I shall make myself better," for he dares not "presume to come to Christ" until he mends his ways. Edwards replies with a rebuke: "Consider how unreasonably you act. You are striving to set up yourselves for your own saviors. . . . And is not this to rob Christ of the glory of being your only Savior?" If a sinner would ever come to Christ, Edwards says, he must see that he can never make himself more worthy. He must see that there

---

36. Edwards, "Great Guilt No Obstacle," in *WJE Online*, 47:425–26.
37. Edwards, "Great Guilt No Obstacle," in *WJE Online*, 47:426.
38. Edwards, "Great Guilt No Obstacle," in *WJE Online*, 47:426–27.

is enough in Christ to save him. He must come as a patient to the physician so that Christ can make him better. Edwards says, "Say, as the psalmist in the text, not Pardon mine iniquity, for it is not so great as it was, but, 'Pardon my iniquity, for it is great.'"[39]

God was pleased to use this kind of preaching to bless many hearers. Edwards did not merely call sinners to Christ. He showed them what it means to come to Christ. He gave them reasons to believe that Christ would not cast them out if they came. And he spoke to their doubts and objections, clearing their minds of excuses so that they might feel the full force of the free offer of the gospel.

Next, we consider a younger contemporary of Edwards who ministered largely in Virginia and later became Edwards's successor at Princeton.

Samuel Davies

Samuel Davies (1723–1761) was a vibrant Presbyterian preacher in colonial Virginia.[40] He was born on November 3, 1723, into a Welsh family residing in Delaware. In 1732, his mother left the Baptist church and joined the Presbyterian church. He received his early education from that church's minister. At age twelve, he experienced conviction, and at age fifteen, he joined the church by profession of faith. He studied for the ministry in Pennsylvania under Samuel Blair (1712–1751), a Latin scholar and mighty preacher trained at William Tennent's (1673–1746) "log college," the forerunner of Princeton Theological Seminary. During his time as a student, the Great Awakening flowered in America. Blair saw a season of awakening in his town, and Whitefield also visited and

---

39. Edwards, "Great Guilt No Obstacle," in *WJE Online*, 47:427–28.

40. On Davies, see Samuel Davies, *The Reverend Samuel Davies Abroad: The Diary of a Journey to England and Scotland, 1753–55*, ed. George William Pilcher (Urbana: University of Illinois Press, 1967); William Henry Foote, *Sketches of Virginia: Historical and Biographical, First Series* (Richmond, VA: John Knox Press, 1966), 157–307; Barbara Ann Larson, "A Rhetorical Study of the Preaching of the Reverend Samuel Davies in the Colony of Virginia from 1747–1759" (PhD diss., University of Minnesota, 1969); Iain H. Murray, *Revival and Revivalism: The Making and Marring of American Evangelicalism 1750–1858* (Edinburgh: Banner of Truth, 1994), 1–31; George W. Pilcher, *Samuel Davies: Apostle of Dissent in Colonial Virginia*, 1st ed. (Knoxville: University of Tennessee Press, 1971); James H. Smylie, "Samuel Davies: Preacher, Teacher, and Pastor," in *Colonial Presbyterianism: Old Faith in a New Land: Commemorating the 300th Anniversary of the First Presbytery in America*, ed. S. Donald Fortson (Eugene, OR: Pickwick, 2007), 181–97; William B. Sprague, "Memoir," in Samuel Davies, *Sermons of Samuel Davies*, 3 vols. (Pittsburgh: Soli Deo Gloria, 1993), 1:11–29; Geoffrey Thomas, "Samuel Davies and the God of Wonders," in *Triumph through Tribulation* (London: Westminster Conference, 1998), 119–34; Ernest Trice Thompson, *Presbyterians in the South* (Richmond, VA: John Knox Press, 1963), 1:53–61. For a brief introduction to Davies, see Thomas Talbot Ellis, "Samuel Davies: Apostle of Virginia," and "Samuel Davies: Characteristics of His Life and Message," http://www.puritansermons.com/pdf /sdavies2.pdf, both of which are reprinted from *Banner of Truth* nos. 235–236 (April–May 1983).

preached there. Davies was licensed to preach in 1746 by the "New Side" (prorevival) Presbytery of New Castle, Delaware. He married, but within a year, his wife experienced complications in childbirth such that both she and their infant son died. Davies himself was slender and frail in health.

In 1747, he was ordained as an evangelist to Virginia, particularly to Hanover County. The Church of England was the established religion of the colony, and there were tensions between Anglicans and dissenters. The dissenters were required by law to obtain government approval for their ministers and meeting houses, and to pay tithes to the Church of England. But despite this lack of religious liberty, Davies carefully avoided criticizing the Anglicans in his public preaching, choosing to focus instead upon the glory of God, the gospel of grace, the life of Spirit-worked godliness, and the great realities of heaven and hell. This kind of preaching drew many people out of Anglicanism, which in the eighteenth century had become largely marked by a lukewarm spirit, rationalism, and the preaching of mere morality.

Poor health and depression over his wife's and child's deaths forced Davies to retire to Pennsylvania after a few months of ministry. But he continued to preach, and after a year away, he received a letter from a hundred heads of households scattered across Hanover County, calling him to be their minister. He returned to Virginia in 1748 to begin a twelve-year ministry there. He married again, this time to a lady from a prominent Anglican family in Williamsburg. He delighted in his wife, Jane, whom he nicknamed "Chara" (Greek for "joy").

Davies had little money and a large "parish," yet he was quite content with his life of studying and preaching in several meeting places distributed across the countryside. He influenced rich and poor, Anglican and Presbyterian alike. His labors included educating and providing books for black slaves, hundreds of whom attended his meetings. Patrick Henry, the great Republican orator and a founding father of the United States, sat under Davies's preaching while in his teens and was impressed by his ability in public speaking.

Davies enjoyed his ministry. He wrote to his brother-in-law and friend, "I can tell you I am as happy as perhaps the creation can make me: I enjoy all the necessaries and most of the conveniences of life; I have a peaceful study, as a refuge from the hurries and noise of the world around me; the venerable dead are waiting in my library to entertain me, and relieve me from the nonsense of surviving mortals."[41] He also wrote poetry, including the beautiful hymn "Great God of Wonders," and was perhaps the first American hymn writer.[42]

In 1753, his studies with "the venerable dead" won him an MA in theology from the College of New Jersey. Later that same year, he and William Tennent's son, Gilbert, were sent by the college to Britain in order to preach and raise funds for the institution. The mission was very successful, collecting a large amount of money and obtaining from King George II confirmation that the Act of Toleration applied to dissenters in the colony of Virginia. Upon his return, Davies and his fellow British colonists became caught up in the traumatic French and Indian War, in which a young colonel named George Washington distinguished himself in battle.[43]

In 1758, he received a call to replace the recently deceased Edwards as president of the College of New Jersey. His presbytery refused to release him, and he felt that his colleague Samuel Finley (1715–1766) was more qualified for the job. Nevertheless, in 1759, the Synod of New York and Philadelphia released him from his pastorate, and he accepted the call to the college presidency. Sadly, his poor health, combined with the dangerous medical practice of bloodletting, resulted in his death on February 4, 1761, a mere eighteen months after his arrival. Finley preached his funeral sermon and succeeded him as the college president. Davies himself had selected the text for the funeral, Romans 14:7–8: "For none of us liveth to himself, and no man dieth to himself. For whether we live, we live unto the Lord; and whether we die, we die unto the Lord: whether we live therefore, or die, we are the Lord's."

Davies lived only thirty-seven years, of which only fourteen or fifteen were spent in public ministry. But his short life had a profound influence for lasting good. His poetry was widely appreciated and his hymns have been sung for centuries since his death. He advocated religious toleration in Virginia and laid the groundwork for liberty of conscience in the New World. Above all, his preaching affected many in his day, and his sermons were reprinted and studied for generations by laypeople and pastors. D. Martyn Lloyd-Jones went so far as to say that Davies was the "greatest preacher" that America has ever produced—and

---

41. Quoted in Pilcher, *Samuel Davies: Apostle of Dissent in Colonial Virginia*, 37.
42. Samuel Davies, *Collected Poems of Samuel Davies, 1723–1761*, ed. Richard Beale Davis (Gainesville, FL: Scholars' Facsimiles & Reprints, 1968).
43. Davies, *Sermons*, 3:101.

Lloyd-Jones had tremendous respect for Edwards.[44] It is regrettable that this man is so little known today, even among Reformed and Presbyterian ministers.

Let us sample some of his great themes in proclaiming the Word of the Lord.

Convincing the World of Sin, Righteousness, and Judgment

Barbara Larson has shown that Davies's preaching of reconciliation with God began with preaching for conviction. He believed that sinners must be awakened to their sinful condition, alarmed over their danger in it, and convinced of their inability to save themselves.[45] This requires the preacher to speak against both actual sins and against sin as an inherent deformation of the soul. Davies says:

> We must alarm them with an impartial view of the state in which they now enter the world; that they were shapen in iniquity, and conceived in sin: that as they are born of the flesh, they are but flesh; that is (as the term generally signified in the language of the New Testament) degenerate and corrupt; and that in their flesh there dwelleth no good thing: that they are all by nature children of wrath; and as by the disobedience of Adam, their common father and federal representative, they were all judiciously constituted sinners; and by his offense, judgment came upon them all to condemnation.[46]

The preacher must "ring that shocking thunder of Sinai in their ears" and warn of God's wrath flaming in "the burning gulf below, yawning to swallow them." He must "pursue" the sinner with "the insufficiency of his best endeavors to make atonement for his sin."[47] In this regard, Davies stood in the same Reformed and Puritan tradition as Halyburton and Edwards.

Davies also preached the classic Reformation doctrine of justification by faith. He explains that the "righteousness of God" (Rom. 1:17) is the gift of "a complete, perfect, divine, and God-like righteousness, and not the mean, imperfect, scanty righteousness of sinful, guilty men." He says, "It is frequently called the righteousness of Christ; and it is said to

---

44. David Martyn Lloyd-Jones, *Knowing the Times: Addresses Delivered on Various Occasions, 1942–1977* (Edinburgh: Banner of Truth, 1989), 263.
45. Larson, "Preaching of the Reverend Samuel Davies," 139–40.
46. Quoted in Larson, "Preaching of the Reverend Samuel Davies," 140.
47. Quoted in Larson, "Preaching of the Reverend Samuel Davies," 141–43.

consist in his obedience; 'by the obedience of one shall many be made righteous' (Rom. 5:19)."[48] Thus, he preaches that "the scheme of salvation . . . represents the Lord Jesus as substituting himself in the place of the guilty, bearing the punishment due to their sin, and obeying the law of God in their stead; and it represents our injured Sovereign as willing to be reconciled to such of his guilty creatures, on this account."[49]

In order to be justified before God through Christ's atoning work, each person must exercise "justifying faith in Christ," for such faith is the instrument by which God imputes to sinners the righteousness of Christ. Such justifying faith, according to Davies, has two components: first, "a full persuasion of the truth" of the gospel based upon "the testimony of God"; and second, "a hearty approbation of the way of salvation through Christ; a willing, delightful dependence of the whole soul upon his righteousness; a free, vigorous choice of it, and a cheerful consent to all the terms of the gospel."[50] Davies emphasizes that saving faith engages the mind, the will, and the affections—it is an act of believing, choosing, and rejoicing. The justified believer no longer exercises himself in religion "from the painful compulsion of fear, horror, and necessity," but because "I see thy glory, O thou lovely Savior" (cf. 2 Cor. 4:6).[51]

But in leaving behind the terrors of divine wrath, the believer never gets beyond the fear of the Lord. Preaching on Isaiah 66:2, Davies reminds his hearers that the Lord looks with favor upon "him that . . . trembleth at my word." He says that the people under God's saving grace hear in the Word of God "the most tremendous realities." The godly man trembles at the "power" of the Word, not just "at the terror, but at the authority of the word." It is the Word of the living God. He is not like the many people "who regard the word of God no more than (with horror I express it) the word of a child or a fool." On the contrary, Davies says, "he considers it as his voice who spake all things into being, and whose glory is such that a deep solemnity must seize those that are admitted to hear him speak."[52] Such a prostration of heart before the Word of the great King is most becoming to both the preacher and the people.

---

48. Davies, *Sermons*, 2:646.
49. Davies, *Sermons*, 2:653.
50. Davies, *Sermons*, 2:652, 654.
51. Davies, *Sermons*, 2:655.
52. Davies, *Sermons*, 1:224–25.

Conclusion

Halyburton, Edwards, and Davies labored as good and faithful servants of the Lord. They preached the Scriptures, taught the doctrines of grace, and applied truth to the heart—first to their own and then to the hearts of their hearers. While we admire the contents of their sermons in printed form, we also recognize that there was more to their preaching than can be captured by paper and ink. These men preached the Word as standing "before God, and the Lord Jesus Christ, who shall judge the quick and the dead at his appearing and his kingdom" (2 Tim. 4:1). The Spirit of the fear of the Lord (Isa. 11:2) moved them to speak. This gave them great authority and power. Yet it humbled them even as they spoke. May God teach us today to preach "in demonstration of the Spirit and of power" (1 Cor. 2:4).

18

Nineteenth-Century Preachers: Alexander, M'Cheyne, and Ryle

The nineteenth century was a time of great change in the churches of Britain and the United States. This period witnessed an explosion of worldwide missions, as William Carey (1761–1834), Henry Martyn (1781–1812), Adoniram Judson (1788–1850), Hudson Taylor (1832–1905), and many others led waves of Protestant missionaries to fields around the world. At the same time, churches came under attack both from the challenge of new cults and sects, and from the philosophical acids of Darwinism and German Higher Criticism. In the midst of these remarkable events, God raised up a stream of faithful men who preached Reformed doctrine to the heart. In this chapter, we will examine three great figures of the nineteenth century: an American pastor-theologian, a Scottish minister, and an Anglican bishop.

Archibald Alexander

Archibald Alexander was born on April 17, 1772, near Lexington, Virginia.[1] He grew up as a member of a Scotch-Irish Presbyterian family on

---

1. On Archibald Alexander, see James W. Alexander, *Life of Archibald Alexander* (New York: Scribner, 1854); David B. Calhoun, *Princeton Seminary*, 2 vols. (Edinburgh: Banner of Truth, 1994); Stephen Clark, "Archibald Alexander: The Shakespeare of the Christian Heart," in *The Voice of God* (London: Westminster Conference, 2003), 103–20; James M. Garretson, *Princeton and Preaching: Archibald Alexander and the Christian Ministry* (Edinburgh: Banner of Truth, 2005); James M. Garretson, ed., *Princeton and the Work of the Christian Ministry*, 2 vols. (Edinburgh: Banner of Truth, 2012); Lefferts A. Loetscher, *Facing the Enlightenment and Pietism: Archibald Alexander and the Founding of Princeton Theological Seminary* (Westport, CT: Green-

the American frontier, living in a log cabin and memorizing the Westminster Shorter Catechism. He was also influenced by the writings of the English Puritan John Flavel. After a prolonged struggle with doubt and conviction of sin, he was converted at age seventeen.

He had already begun studying under William Graham (1745–1799) at Liberty Hall Academy (now Washington and Lee University). He continued those studies after his conversion with an eye to becoming a minister. Graham passed on to him the theology he had learned from John Witherspoon (1723–1794), president of the College of New Jersey (today's Princeton University) and the only minister to sign the American Declaration of Independence. Alexander continued to study renowned writers such as John Owen, William Bates (1625–1699), Thomas Boston, and Jonathan Edwards. After serving as an itinerant evangelist in Virginia and North Carolina, he was ordained as a settled pastor in 1794. In 1796, he became president of Hampden-Sydney College in Virginia while continuing to preach in various churches. He was called to serve as the pastor of the large Pine Street Presbyterian Church in Philadelphia in 1807. There he founded a society for street preaching and evangelistic visitation.

In 1808, he began to call for the founding of a seminary to train Presbyterian ministers. Two years later, he was awarded the doctor of divinity degree by the College of New Jersey. In 1812, the General Assembly of the Presbyterian Church appointed him the first professor of the newly instituted Princeton Theological Seminary. He served there for thirty-nine years, mostly as professor of didactic and polemical theology.

The small school blossomed and bore much fruit. W. J. Grier (1902–1983) writes, "His classes at Princeton grew from nine in the first year until by the time of his death 1,837 young men had sat at his feet."[2] His colleagues Charles Hodge and Samuel Miller (1769–1850) held him in the highest regard. There was a beautiful unity at Princeton, arising from the faculty's Christlike spirit and common devotion to the truth of the Scriptures. Hodge's son, Archibald Alexander Hodge (1823–1886; whose very name testifies of his father's love for Professor Alexander), writes:

---

wood, 1983). For a brief introduction to Alexander and his writings on godliness, see Archibald Alexander, *"A Scribe Well-Trained": Archibald Alexander and the Life of Piety*, ed. James M. Garretson (Grand Rapids, MI: Reformation Heritage Books, 2011).

2. W. J. Grier, "Biographical Introduction," in Archibald Alexander, *Thoughts on Religious Experience* (London: Banner of Truth, 1967), xiv.

I have had a wide experience of professors and of pastors, and I am certain, I have never seen any three who together approached these three in absolute singleness of mind, in simplicity and godly sincerity, in utter unselfishness and devotion to the common cause, each in honor preferring one another. Truth and candor was the atmosphere they breathed, loyalty, brave and sweet, was the spirit of their lives.[3]

Alexander established a pattern for the seminary that combined rigorous biblical studies in the original languages, vibrant preaching in hopes of seeing spiritual revival, faithful adherence to the Reformed theology of the Westminster Standards and Francis Turretin (1623–1687), defense of the truth of the faith with the tools of Scottish Common Sense Realism, and promotion of fervent piety and Christian experience. The original "Design of the Seminary" stated that the school aimed "to unite . . . piety of the heart . . . with solid learning; believing that religion without learning, or learning without religion, in the ministers of the gospel, must ultimately prove injurious to the church."[4]

Alexander and his colleagues at Princeton Theological Seminary trained men in Reformed theology and engaged in the theological controversies of the day, such as the debate over the "New Divinity" advocated by Charles Finney (1792–1875).[5] However, Alexander also wrote books to teach basic Bible truths, to call children to conversion, to provide readings for family devotions, and to illuminate the Christian's experience of sin and grace—some of which are still being reprinted, read, and cherished today.[6] James Garretson writes, "Alexander labored relentlessly to impress the importance of the presence and practice of piety on the generation in which he lived."[7]

In the promotion of piety in the church, Alexander plowed, planted, cultivated, and harvested the fields of God with the tool of preaching. He was known for the priority he gave to sermon preparation and for

---

3. Archibald Alexander Hodge, *The Life of Charles Hodge: Professor in the Theological Seminary, Princeton, N.J.* (New York: C. Scribner's Sons, 1880), 378.
4. "History of the Seminary," Princeton Theological Seminary website (Princeton, NJ), http://www.ptsem.edu/about/history.
5. See the articles by Archibald Alexander, Charles Hodge, et al. in *Princeton Versus the New Divinity: The Meaning of Sin, Grace, Salvation, Revival: Articles from the Princeton Review* (Edinburgh: Banner of Truth, 2001).
6. Archibald Alexander, *A Brief Compendium of Bible Truth*, ed. Joel R. Beeke (Grand Rapids, MI: Reformation Heritage Books, 2005); *The Way of Salvation: Familiarly Explained in a Conversation Between a Father and His Children* (Philadelphia: Presbyterian Board of Publication, 1839); *Evangelical Truth: Practical Sermons for the Christian Home* (Birmingham, AL: Solid Ground, 2004); *Thoughts on Religious Experience.*
7. Garretson, introduction to Alexander, *"A Scribe Well-Trained,"* 25.

his effective simplicity of style. He taught his seminary students to avoid "historical, philosophical, or political discussions," and instead to preach through the "whole system of theology," especially the "greatest truths," our moral "duties," "Christian experience, afflictions and temptations," and answers for "awakened souls."[8]

To get a taste of his experiential preaching, we will look at a sermon that Alexander delivered in April 1791 before the Presbytery of Lexington, Virginia, to obtain his license to preach.[9] Though it was preached very early in his career, later in life he recalled, "The view taken of the subject is not materially different from that which I should now take."[10]

Preaching Living Faith versus Dead Faith

Alexander opens his sermon by recognizing that the Scriptures teach that many people in professing Christian nations possess a kind of faith "which it is evident is not that faith which works by love (Gal. 5:6) and purifies the heart (Acts 15:9)." Therefore, he aims "to distinguish clearly between a living and a dead faith." This he does by showing the difference between the *causes* of these two kinds of faith, the *natures* they possess, and the *effects* they produce.[11]

First, the *cause* of a living faith is the Holy Spirit: "A living faith is produced by the Spirit of God, for in Scripture it is called 'the faith of the operations of God's Spirit' (Col. 2:12).[12] It is also said to be the gift of God (Eph. 2:8), and Christ is expressly declared to be the author of it (Heb. 12:2). But a dead faith is produced merely by the exertions of human nature without the assistance of the Spirit of God."[13] The true believer knows that he cannot produce saving faith in himself, for the Holy Spirit convinces him of his sin and unbelief (John 16:8). Nothing short of the power of the Creator of the universe can cause the light of the knowledge of the glory of God in the face of Jesus Christ to shine in the sinner's heart (2 Cor. 4:6). But the man with a dead faith thinks he

---

8. Loetscher, *Facing the Enlightenment and Pietism*, 237–38.
9. The manuscript of the sermon is in the collections at Princeton Theological Seminary. It has been published as Archibald Alexander, "A Treatise in Which the Difference Between a Living and a Dead Faith Is Explained, 1791," *Banner of Truth* 335–36 (September 1991): 39–54. It also appeared in the *Banner of Sovereign Grace Truth* 2, no. 6 (July/August 1994): 145; 2, no. 7 (September 1994): 181–82; 2, no. 8 (October 1994): 204–6.
10. Alexander, *Life of Archibald Alexander*, 110.
11. Alexander, "A Living and a Dead Faith," 40.
12. Colossians 2:12 refers to "the faith of the operation of God, who hath raised him from the dead."
13. Alexander, "A Living and a Dead Faith," 40–41.

has the power to believe in Christ. Indeed, he may think he has always believed in Christ because he was raised in the church and has always assented to the truths he was taught.

Second, the *nature* of a living faith is "a firm and realizing belief of the truths of revelation" that "is firmly seated in the heart and influences the will and affections in such a manner as to become a ruling principle of action." By contrast, a dead faith is "nothing more than an empty notion or speculative opinion" that "only swims in the brain and produces no real effect upon the heart." A living faith is a spiritual sight by which the believer "views eternal and invisible things as solemn realities," but a dead faith is a mere idea.[14]

A living faith embraces Christ, the whole man receiving the whole Christ: "Living faith always appropriates him, chooses him as a Savior suitable to itself, receives him as its portion, trusts and depends on him alone for salvation, resigns itself up to him to be governed and directed agreeable to his will, and is pleased and delighted with him above all other things."[15] But "natural men are unable to discern the beauty and excellency of Jesus Christ and the way of salvation through him," and therefore, "they never can choose and rest upon him as their Savior."[16] A dead faith always leads a soul to trust in something in itself.

Third, the *effect* of faith "is by far the most important and necessary part of the distinction between a living and a dead faith, for it is by the fruits alone we can determine our faith to be of the operation of the Spirit of God, or that it is in its nature saving."[17] Alexander, recognizing that he could write an entire book listing every Christian grace as a mark distinguishing a living faith from a dead one, selects some central fruit on which to focus: love, humility, and holiness. In this section, we hear echoes of Edwards's *Religious Affections*. Let's consider what Alexander teaches about love as a fruit of a living faith.

A living faith produces love for God: "Faith works by love and purifies the heart" (see Gal. 5:6; Acts 15:9). Love "is the very essence of religion, and without which the Apostle says, the exercise of all gifts, and the performance of all duties would profit nothing (1 Cor. 13:1–3)." A dead faith may prompt men to love God because they believe he will be good to them, but this is no better a love than wicked men have for their

---

14. Alexander, "A Living and a Dead Faith," 42.
15. Alexander, "A Living and a Dead Faith," 43.
16. Alexander, "A Living and a Dead Faith," 44.
17. Alexander, "A Living and a Dead Faith," 46.

friends (Matt. 5:46). They love a god of their own imagination, as when men think that God is all mercy and no justice. Such a love is "nothing more than self-love."[18]

Only a living faith comes with a "perception" of "the excellency of the nature of God" and "the beauty of holiness." This perception enables men to exercise "true love to God," that is, to "love him for his excellence." The love-awakening sight of God's loveliness comes through the gospel: "the moral character of God as it is seen in the face of Jesus Christ is the proper object and end of this affection." Evidences of such love appear in love for all that bears God's moral image. The believer has a special love for the people "begotten" of God (1 John 5:1), his brothers and sisters in Christ, "because they are holy and have the image of God." He also loves the law of God, "which is holy, just, and good, and is a transcript of [God's] moral character." He delights in God's law in his heart (Rom. 7:22) and keeps God's commandments out of love for him (John 14:21; 1 John 5:3).[19]

A living faith also produces benevolent love for one's neighbor (Mark 12:31). This includes "that important and self-denying duty of loving our enemies, of bearing injuries, of doing good to them that hate us and blessing and praying for them that curse us." The true believer especially desires mankind to "obtain the favor and friendship of God," because he knows that the "happiness of this world" is a tiny thing compared to eternity. He is willing to sacrifice himself like Christ (2 Cor. 8:9) and Paul (Rom. 9:3), not just for his friends but also for his enemies.[20]

The person with a dead faith "confines his love and good wishes to his own party" and bitterly rejects "all who differ from him." Though virtually all men pretend to love mankind, their "hearts are so contracted that they will not even put forth their hands to assist them when they are in want in this life." But pure religion that is undefiled before God consists in visiting the fatherless and the widow in their affliction (James 1:27).[21]

Here we see discriminating preaching done with biblical wisdom, helping people to examine themselves to see whether Christ is in them. We also see how Alexander sketched a portrait of experiential, practical Christianity consisting of faith and love. A theologian by vocation, he

---

18. Alexander, "A Living and a Dead Faith," 47–48.
19. Alexander, "A Living and a Dead Faith," 47–48.
20. Alexander, "A Living and a Dead Faith," 49–50.
21. Alexander, "A Living and a Dead Faith," 49–50.

never lost his passion for preaching Christ, and he imparted that passion to generations of men who graduated from Princeton Seminary.

Robert Murray M'Cheyne

Today you can visit St. Peter's Church in Dundee, Scotland, where Robert Murray M'Cheyne once preached. It is a remarkable building, designed to seat nearly a thousand people, and yet the acoustics make it possible to hear an unamplified preacher speaking with a conversational voice even in the back of the balcony.

M'Cheyne was born in Edinburgh, Scotland, on May 21, 1813.[22] His father was a lawyer for the prestigious Society of Writers to His Majesty's Signet. He attended the University of Edinburgh beginning in 1827, winning prizes in every class he took. He also showed much ability in poetry and gymnastics. The death of his godly older brother David in July 1831, along with the reading of David Dickson's (1583–1663) *Sum of Saving Knowledge*, led to his conversion. He studied under Thomas Chalmers (1780–1847) at Edinburgh. On July 1, 1835, he was licensed to preach and began to serve as an assistant to John Bonar. He then went to St. Peter's Church, Dundee, being ordained on November 24, 1836. Dundee's urban setting and his unrelenting devotion to the ministry further impaired his frail health.

M'Cheyne had a great evangelistic heart, grieving over the perishing souls all around him. He also had a passion for the doctrines of the Westminster Confession of Faith, viewing with concern the growing movement of "Moderatism" in the Church of Scotland. His poor health led him to take a sabbatical from ministry in Dundee in 1838. At the encouragement of Robert S. Candlish (1806–1873), he went with Andrew Bonar (1810–1892) and Alexander Keith (1781–1880) on a mission trip to Palestine to inquire into potential ministry among the Jews. On the return trip, he fell very ill, but he rejoiced to hear that God had visited his congregation in Dundee with revival through the ministry of William

---

22. On M'Cheyne, see *Memoir and Remains of Robert Murray M'Cheyne*, ed. Andrew A. Bonar (Edinburgh: Banner of Truth, 1966); William Lamb, *M'Cheyne from the Pew: Being Extracts from the Diary of William Lamb*, ed. Kirkwood Hewat (Belfast: Ambassador, 1987); David Robertson, *Awakening: The Life and Ministry of Robert Murray McCheyne* (Milton Keynes, UK: Authentic Media, 2004); Alexander Smellie, *Robert Murray McCheyne* (London: National Council of Evangelical Free Churches, 1913); John C. Smith, *Robert Murray M'Cheyne* (London: E. Stock, 1910); L. J. van Valen, *Constrained by His Love: A New Biography on Robert Murray McCheyne* (Fearn, Ross-shire, Scotland: Christian Focus, 2002). For a brief and well-illustrated introduction to M'Cheyne, see Derek Prime, *Robert Murray McCheyne: In the Footsteps of a Godly Scottish Pastor*, Travel With series (Leominster, UK: Day One, 2007).

Chalmers Burns (1815–1868). It was a mark of his humility that he was as glad that revival had come to his church through another minister as he would have been had it come through him.

Returning to St. Peter's in Dundee, he continued his vibrant ministry there and ministered in the surrounding region. God's reviving work went on. M'Cheyne wrote: "There have been evident tokens of the presence of the Spirit of God among my dear people many nights—more I think, upon the Thursday nights than on the Sabbaths. Some I have met with seemingly awakened without any very direct means. A good number of young mill-girls are still weeping after the Lord Jesus."[23] However, he was growing weaker. Alongside the busyness of ministering in the ongoing revival came the pressures of growing controversy in the Church of Scotland. His health suffered a further blow when a bar broke on some gymnastics equipment, causing him to fall several feet onto his back.

In February 1843, he was sent by the Church of Scotland to preach the gospel in the poorly evangelized regions of Deer and Ellon. In three weeks, he preached in twenty-four locations, sometimes more than once in the same place. Returning home exhausted, he found typhus fever ravaging the homes of many. He persisted in visiting the homes of the infected while maintaining the rigor of his other ministerial duties. Worn out and weakened, he too became infected. On March 25, 1843, aged twenty-nine, he entered into the immediate experience of which he had written in his hymn, "When This Passing World Is Done":

> When I stand before the throne,
> Dressed in beauty not my own,
> When I see Thee as Thou art,
> Love Thee with unsinning heart,
> Then Lord, shall I fully know—
> Not till then—how much I owe.

Unfolding the Believer's Experience

M'Cheyne's sermons infused Spirit-wrought fire into carefully crafted structures of thought and words. For example, consider his sermon on Romans 7:22–25: "For I delight in the law of God after the inward man: but I see another law in my members, warring against the law of

---

23. Letter to W. C. Burns (Sept. 1840), in M'Cheyne, *Memoir and Remains of Robert Murray M'Cheyne*, 288.

my mind, and bringing me into captivity to the law of sin which is in my members. O wretched man that I am! Who shall deliver me from the body of this death? I thank God through Jesus Christ our Lord. So then with the mind I myself serve the law of God; but with the flesh the law of sin."

This sermon is marked by a strong experiential emphasis and clear outline. M'Cheyne observes, "A believer is known not only by his peace and joy, but by his warfare and distress." Thus, he chooses to preach a discriminating sermon on "the Christian's warfare, that you may know thereby whether you are a soldier of Christ."[24] He structures his message in three main points, each with subpoints.

We may outline his message as follows:

I. A believer delights in the law of God: "I delight in the law of God after the inward man" (v. 22).
   A. Before a man comes to Christ, he hates the law of God: "The carnal mind is enmity against God: for it is not subject to the law of God, neither indeed can be" (Rom. 8:7).
      1. Unconverted men hate the law of God on account of its purity: "Thy word is very pure: therefore thy servant loveth it" (Ps. 119:140).
      2. They hate it for its breadth: "Thy commandment is exceeding broad" (Ps. 119:96). It extends to all their outward actions, seen and unseen; it extends to every idle word that men speak; and it dives into the deepest caves of their hearts.
      3. They hate it for its unchangeableness: "Till heaven and earth pass, one jot or one tittle shall in no wise pass from the law, till all be fulfilled" (Matt. 5:18). If the law would change, let down its requirements, or die, then ungodly men would be well pleased.
   B. When a man comes to Christ, all this changes: "O how love I thy law! It is my meditation all the day" (Ps. 119:97). This has two causes:
      1. The law is no longer an enemy. The man is able to say, "Christ hath redeemed [me] from the curse of the law, being made a curse for [me]" (Gal. 3:13).

---

24. M'Cheyne, *Memoir and Remains of Robert Murray M'Cheyne*, 428.

2. The Spirit of God writes the law on the heart. This is the promise: "After those days, saith the LORD, I will put my law in their inward parts, and write it in their hearts; and will be their God, and they shall be my people" (Jer. 31:33). Coming to Christ takes away a man's fear of the law, but it is the Holy Spirit coming into his heart that makes him love the law.

M'Cheyne then applies his first main point evangelistically. He exhorts, "Oh, come, sinners, and give up your hearts to Christ, that He may write on them His holy law!" And he warns, "If you die with your heart as it is, it will be stamped a wicked heart to all eternity."[25]

II. A believer feels an opposing law in his members: "I see another law in my members, warring against the law of my mind, and bringing me into captivity to the law of sin which is in my members" (Rom. 7:23).
   A. It is "another law," quite a different law from the law of God. It is a "law of sin" (v. 25), a law that commands the believer to commit sin. It is the same law that, in Galatians, is called "the flesh": "the flesh lusteth against the Spirit" (Gal. 5:17).
   B This law is "warring." This law in the members is not resting quiet, but is always fighting. There can never be peace in the bosom of a believer. There is peace with God, but constant war with sin. M'Cheyne compares indwelling sin to an army that lies quiet only when it is preparing an ambush and to an active volcano that may erupt at any time.

M'Cheyne then applies the second point experientially. He calls for self-examination: "Have you experienced this warfare? It is a clear mark of God's children." To anyone who is "groaning under this warfare," he gives the following directions: be humbled that even after receiving forgiveness and the Holy Spirit, your heart remains a fountain of sin; be dependent on Jesus, learning from this warfare that you need the blood of Christ every day to the end; and do not be discouraged, for everyone whom Christ saves has a heart like this. Therefore, keep up the good fight of the faith despite all setbacks.[26]

---

25. Point I appears in M'Cheyne, *Memoir and Remains of Robert Murray M'Cheyne*, 428–30.
26. Point II appears in M'Cheyne, *Memoir and Remains of Robert Murray M'Cheyne*, 430–32.

III. A believer engaged in this warfare takes certain actions.
   A. He feels wretched: "O wretched man that I am!" (Rom.
      7:24). Here M`Cheyne deals with the paradox of Christian
      experience. On the one hand: "There is nobody in this world
      so happy as a believer. He has come to Jesus, and found rest."
      On the other hand, "he feels the plague of his own heart"
      and "the loathsomeness of sin," like "a viper in the heart."
   B. He seeks deliverance: "Who shall deliver me?" (v. 24). The
      believer feels like a prisoner in ancient times, condemned to
      be chained to a carcass. Here again M`Cheyne sounds the
      discriminating note: "How is it with you, dear souls? Does
      corruption felt within drive you to the throne of grace?
      Does it make you call on the name of the Lord? . . . Ah,
      remember, if lust can work in your heart, and you lie down
      contented with it, you are none of Christ's."
   C. He gives thanks for victory: "I thank God through Jesus
      Christ our Lord" (v. 25). Despite the corruption and war
      within, "we are more than conquerors through him that
      loved us" (Rom. 8:37).

M`Cheyne ends on a beautiful note of exulting in Jesus Christ. He says:

Yes, even in the thickest of the battle we can look up to Jesus and
cry, "Thanks to God." The moment a soul groaning under corruption rests the eye on Jesus, that moment his groans are changed into
songs of praise. In Jesus you discover a fountain to wash away the
guilt of all your sin. In Jesus you discover grace sufficient for you,
grace to hold you up to the end, and a sure promise that sin shall soon
be rooted out altogether. "Fear not: for I have redeemed thee, I have
called thee by thy name, thou art mine." Ah, this turns our groans
into songs of praise! How often a psalm begins with groans and ends
with praises! This is the daily experience of all the Lord's people. Is it
yours? Try yourselves by this. Oh, if you know not the believer's song
of praise, you will never cast your crowns with them at the feet of
Jesus. Dear believers, be content to glory in your infirmities, that the
power of Christ may rest upon you. Glory, glory, glory to the Lamb![27]

M`Cheyne's preaching was founded upon his passionate pursuit of
holiness in Christ. Here he was a shining example for ministers. He says:

---

27. Point III appears in M`Cheyne, *Memoir and Remains of Robert Murray M`Cheyne*, 432–34.

"How diligently the cavalry officer keeps his saber clean and sharp; every stain he rubs off with the greatest care. Remember that you are God's sword—His instrument. . . . It is not great talents God blesses so much as great likeness to Jesus. A holy minister is an awful weapon in the hand of God."[28] He wrote to a fellow minister:

> I am also deepened in my conviction, that if we are to be instruments in such a work, we must be purified from all filthiness of the flesh and spirit [2 Cor. 7:1]. Oh, cry for personal holiness, constant nearness to God by the blood of the Lamb! Bask in His beams—lie back in the arms of love—be filled with the Spirit. . . . Do not think any sin trivial; remember it will have everlasting consequences. Oh to have [David] Brainerd's heart for perfect holiness—to be holy as God is holy—pure as Christ is pure. . . . How much more useful might we be, if we were only more free from pride, self-conceit, personal vanity, or some secret sin that our heart knows![29]

Having discussed the preaching ministries of an American and a Scot, we turn now to consider the preaching of an Englishman who was a bishop of the Church of England.

John Charles Ryle

When I first came to Grand Rapids, Michigan, only a few of the more than one thousand people in our church were reading spiritual classics. One evening, I held up a volume of *Expository Thoughts on the Gospels* by J. C. Ryle (1816–1900).[30] I said that I wanted everyone to read these books. More than 150 families signed up. Soon, many in the church were talking about these books. Sixteen years later, a woman told me that she was still reading them and that every time she reaches the end of the Gospel of John, she starts again in the Gospel of Matthew. Ryle has that kind of popular readability and spiritual appeal in his writings.

Ryle was born on May 10, 1816, at Macclesfield in northwest England.[31] The son of a wealthy banker, he went on to become a good

---

28. Letter to Daniel Edwards (Oct. 2, 1840), in M'Cheyne, *Memoir and Remains of Robert Murray M'Cheyne*, 282.
29. Letter to Burns, in M'Cheyne, *Memoir and Remains of Robert Murray M'Cheyne*, 289.
30. J. C. Ryle, *Expository Thoughts on the Gospels*, 7 vols. (1856–1869; repr., Edinburgh: Banner of Truth, 2009).
31. On Ryle, see M. Guthrie Clark, *John Charles Ryle, 1816–1900: First Bishop of Liverpool* (London: Church Book Room Press, n.d.); Ian D. Farley, *J. C. Ryle, First Bishop of Liverpool: A Study in Mission amongst the Masses* (Carlisle, UK: Paternoster, 2000); Marcus L. Loane, *John*

scholar and athlete at Oxford University, and appeared destined for greatness in the financial or political world. But God had a different calling for his life. His father's wealth disappeared in 1841 when his bank failed. Overnight, the family lost their money, their home, and property valued at a half-million pounds. For the next twenty years, Ryle assisted his father in paying off their massive debt.

Ryle might have utterly despaired had not God already introduced him to more enduring riches. In the summer of 1837, while shooting, he swore out loud and was rebuked by a friend, who told him to "think, repent, and pray." He began to do so, particularly when he fell ill later that year. One Lord's Day afternoon, he attended public worship and passed from death to life while hearing the Scripture lesson slowly and distinctly read from Ephesians 2: "by grace—are ye saved—through faith—and that not of yourselves—it is the gift of God."[32] Later in life, he said that the truths of the sinfulness of sin, Christ's perfect substitution for sinners, the necessity of the new birth by the Holy Spirit, the indispensability of a life of holiness, the need to come out of the world, and the supremacy of the Bible "seemed to flash on me like a sunbeam in the winter of 1837. . . . Nothing to my mind can account for it, but the free sovereign grace of God."[33]

Enriched in Christ and impoverished among men, Ryle found a new vocation. In 1842, he was ordained to the ministry of the Church of England and served country parishes in Suffolk. From 1844 to 1861, he was rector of Helmingham (pop. 300), and from 1861 to 1880, vicar of Stradbroke (pop. 1,300). His first wife, Matilda, died in 1848 after only three years of marriage; his second wife, Jessie, was in nearly constant poor health and died in 1860 after ten years of marriage. He married a third time in 1861 to Henrietta, who died in 1889, eleven years before Ryle passed away. Ryle also suffered from frequent ill health and, as noted earlier, prolonged financial troubles. Nevertheless, in 1880, at age sixty-four, he was appointed the first bishop of Liverpool through the intervention of none other than Prime Minister Benjamin Disraeli. He served there as bishop for twenty years.

Charles Ryle, 1816–1900 (London: Hodder & Stoughton, 1983); J. I. Packer, *Faithfulness and Holiness: The Witness of J. C. Ryle* (Wheaton, IL: Crossway, 2002); Eric Russell, *J. C. Ryle: That Man of Granite with the Heart of a Child* (Fearn, Ross-shire, Scotland: Christian Focus, 2008); J. C. Ryle, *J. C. Ryle, a Self-Portrait: A Partial Autobiography*, ed. Peter Toon (Swengel, PA: Reiner, 1975); Peter Toon and Michael Smout, *John Charles Ryle: Evangelical Bishop* (Cambridge: J. Clarke, 1976).

32. Toon and Smout, *John Charles Ryle*, 26–27.
33. Quoted in Packer, *Faithfulness and Holiness*, 28.

Ryle was a devoted shepherd, a gifted writer, and a very effective administrator. As a bishop, he focused on raising the pay scale and pensions of pastors rather than building a cathedral. He promoted the reading of the Puritans and similar eighteenth-century preachers. He became a leader of evangelical Anglicanism. Today, Ryle is best known for the more than two hundred tracts and twenty books he authored (many tracts at that time were booklets of fifteen to thirty pages). Perhaps most popular today, in addition to his *Expository Thoughts*, is his book *Holiness*, which consists of papers he wrote to advocate the biblical doctrines of sin and sanctification.[34]

When Ryle began his vocation as a preacher, his sermons, by his own admission, were too ornate and florid in style. However, by ministering to farmers, he learned to speak more simply and directly. He divided his thoughts into short sentences and his sermon material into small sections. He made applications in every sermon. He also preached with spiritual urgency, repeated key words, and illustrated abstract concepts with stories of shipwrecks, wars, and compassionate queens in order to personally engage his hearers.[35]

In a lecture to ministers, published as *Simplicity in Preaching*, Ryle encouraged preachers to read good models of the English language. The best model is the Bible itself, but he also told preachers to read other models both sacred and profane, from John Bunyan to William Shakespeare, and from John Flavel to Patrick Henry. Yet he cautioned that "language alters with years."[36] Therefore, we must also learn how our people talk by talking with them. He advised: "Do not be above talking to the poor, and visiting your people from house to house. Sit down with your people by the fireside, and exchange thoughts with them on all subjects. Find out how they think and how they express themselves, if you want them to understand your sermons."[37]

Preaching True Christianity

To get a sense of Ryle's preaching, let's look briefly at the collection of sermons *The True Christian*, originally published as *The Christian Race*

---

34. This classic book is reprinted in many formats, including J. C. Ryle, *Holiness* (Darlington, England: Evangelical Press, 2011). The shorter first edition is contained in Packer, *Faithfulness and Holiness*, 89–246.

35. Farley, *J. C. Ryle, First Bishop of Liverpool*, 6–7, 34–37.

36. J. C. Ryle, *Simplicity in Preaching: A Few Short Hints on a Great Subject* (London: William Hunt, 1882), 43–44.

37. Ryle, *Simplicity in Preaching*, 45.

(1900). There we find "The Character of the True Christian," a sermon on John 10:27: "My sheep hear my voice, and I know them, and they follow me." Ryle unfolds his text phrase by phrase in a simple and clear manner.

His first point is that the Lord Jesus Christ compares true Christians to sheep. Ryle spends significant time developing this comparison. He says, "Sheep are the most harmless, quiet, inoffensive creatures God has made." So Christians should be humble, gentle, and loving. He warns that if we see people "biting and devouring one another" like wolves, we have every right to rebuke them for not acting like members of Christ's flock and to tell them that they must be born again. Sheep are also "the most useful" animals to man. Christians likewise are marked by doing good and speaking "a quiet word on the Lord's side" when they can. He adds, "Sheep love to be together; they do not like being alone." Thus, Christians should delight to be with like-minded believers to whom they can open their feelings and experiences. Additionally, sheep are "of all animals most helpless" and "most ready to stray." Christians aim at perfection but fall far short of it. Also, sheep are "easily frightened." True believers have a "godly fear" that "proves that they feel their own helplessness," but "presumptuous confidence" raises questions as to whether a man is a sheep of Christ's at all. Lastly, sheep do not wallow in the mud like hogs. Christians distinguish themselves from the world by trying to avoid the filth of sin.[38] Here we see Ryle's down-to-earth preaching, which uses homey metaphors to distinguish between true Christians and hypocrites and worldlings.

His second point is that our Lord calls them "My sheep." His people are "His property." This offers great comfort to believers, for "even as men are careful and tender about their earthly belongings, and will not willingly allow them to be lost and damaged, so is our Lord and Saviour careful of the souls that belong to Him." Why are these sheep his? Ryle explains that they belong to Christ by "election," because the Father chose us and gave us to Christ before the foundation of the world. Though men may "abuse" this doctrine, it is still "a glorious, a soul-comforting doctrine . . . full of sweet, pleasant, and unspeakable consolation" to those who "really feel in themselves the working of Christ's Spirit." The sheep are also Christ's by "purchase." Christ

---

38. J. C. Ryle, *The True Christian* (Grand Rapids, MI: Baker, 1978), 111–18.

redeemed them from death and hell at the high price of his own blood. And they are Christ's by "adoption." He has put his Spirit in them and made them part of his family. Again Ryle applies this point for comfort: "Oh, believe: you may sometimes be cast down and faint-hearted, but . . . if you are really in the number of Christ's sheep, you have indeed good reason to rejoice."[39]

His time is passing and he has not addressed much of his text yet, so he says he "must hasten on" to his third point. Christ says, "My sheep hear my voice." He explains that this is not "the mere hearing of the ears," but "the hearing with the heart, the listening with attention; the believing what is heard, the acting manfully on what is believed." Though Christ's voice may speak in warnings of conscience or afflictions of providence, his voice may be heard "plain and distinct" in "the reading of Scripture or the preaching of the Gospel." True sheep of Christ once were "foolish and disobedient," but at last they heard Christ's voice, listened, and believed his promises. His Word is now "their rule of life" and "the meat and drink of their souls." Thus, "no music is so sweet to their ears" as the voice of Jesus in the written or preached Word.[40]

Ryle's fourth point is that Christ says his sheep "follow me." Ryle says, "To follow Christ, that is the grand mark of Christians." But what does this mean? "To follow Christ is to place implicit trust in Him as our Redeemer, Saviour, Prophet, Priest, King, Leader, Commander and Shepherd, and to walk in His ways, straightforward. It is to take up our cross and subscribe our name among His people, to look to the Lamb as our Guide and follow Him wheresoever He goes." The best of Christians may sometimes be slack in following Christ, distracted and drawn aside by the trifles of the world. But compared to the world, they are following Christ, and "they are determined to follow on to the end, and to say, 'None but Christ, in life and in death, in time and in eternity.'"[41]

Ryle closes by pressing upon his hearers the necessity of "self-inquiry," charging them to ask: "Am I a sheep of Christ's flock, or am I not? Do I hear His voice or do I not? Do I follow Him or do I not?" He disarms them of the excuses that they are doing no worse than the rest of the world and that God couldn't be so strict as to demand affirmative answers to such personal questions or else or few would be saved. Then

---

39. Ryle, *The True Christian*, 118–19.
40. Ryle, *The True Christian*, 119–21.
41. Ryle, *The True Christian*, 121–22.

he openly appeals to them to repent: "Remember, then, this day, I tell thee, that God is willing to receive thee if thou wilt only turn to Him: if thou wilt only resolve to think for thyself and never mind the world, if thou wilt only hear the voice of the Lord Jesus Christ and follow Him, if thou wilt only be in earnest and come unto Him for forgiveness and His Holy Spirit, He shall grant thee thy heart's desire, and thou shalt never perish but have eternal life."[42]

In Ryle, we see simple, straightforward, understandable preaching that offered Christ to all and demonstrated the difference between saved people and the lost world. His preaching was not perfect. Even in this sermon, he went on too long with his comparison of Christians to sheep (about half the sermon) and had to rush a bit through the more explicit teachings of John 10:27. There was some overlap between his third and fourth points. Nevertheless, his preaching was biblical and bold, daring to tell people who did not live like the sheep of Christ that they were not saved. There was tenderness to his words, compassion for both the saved and the lost. He honored God and his Word, and God honored Ryle's preaching.

A journalist who visited the church in Helmingham in March 1858, observed the congregation of about 160 people and their forty-one-year-old minister, and wrote, "The sermon was one of the longest we have met with, but the earnestness of the preacher's manner and ever ready flow of ideas, the simple yet forceful language and the wonderfully apt and forceful illustrations made the time pass very pleasantly, and we, who for that time at least had no pudding to be spoiled, were almost sorry when he concluded."[43] While we must not preach so long as to weary our people, may God grant us such simplicity, clarity, boldness, and imagination in preaching the Word that people are indeed "almost sorry" when we end.

---

42. Ryle, *The True Christian*, 123–25.
43. Quoted in Russell, *J. C. Ryle*, 58, 63.

19

Twentieth-Century Preachers: Wisse and Lloyd-Jones

The twentieth century witnessed staggering changes. Perhaps most obvious were the technological changes, running the gamut from the Model T automobile to the space shuttle and from the manual typewriter to laptop computers. During this period, the world was transformed from a collection of relatively isolated communities into a global economy, with information and images flashing through the Internet at phenomenal speeds. We can cure more diseases than ever before, and we can destroy an entire city in a single thermonuclear blast.

This century also was the stage for remarkable developments, both good and bad, in the life of the visible church. It saw the disastrous decline of mainline Protestant denominations into something not much more than baptized paganism; the rise of the Pentecostal movement; the fundamentalist and evangelical resurgence; the coming of age of the African and Asian churches; the doctrinal blurring and moral watering down of evangelicalism; and the heartening rediscovery of Reformed and Puritan theology.

In the midst of all these changes, however, Christians saw that both God and human nature remain the same. We face the same fundamental problems. The preaching of Christ's work for us and his work in us continues to offer the only real answer to our deepest needs. Thanks be to God, the Holy Spirit raised up a number of faithful ministers in the twentieth century to carry the torch of their forefathers in Reformed experiential preaching.

In this chapter, we will examine two such preachers, one of whom is little known among English speakers but cherished in conservative Dutch Reformed circles, while the other is perhaps the most widely recognized evangelical preacher of the twentieth century.

Gerard Wisse

Recently, I was reading a book, freshly translated from Dutch into English, as I was sitting on a lawn chair outside while on vacation with my family. I found myself convicted, yet comforted. I became oblivious to all around me and began weeping with joy. What was I reading? I held in my hands *Christ's Ministry in the Christian* by Gerard Wisse.

Born in 1873, Wisse was reared in the Netherlands by parents devoted to the old Reformed doctrines of grace.[1] Even as a boy, he experienced longings for salvation and delight in prayer and reading of the Word of God. He read John Bunyan and Wilhelmus à Brakel. In 1892, he began theological studies at Kampen under orthodox Reformed professors such as Herman Bavinck. He was ordained in 1898 as a minister in the *Gereformeerde Kerken in Nederland* (GKN). This denomination had been formed by Christians who separated from the established Dutch Reformed Church in two secessions, in 1834 and 1886, the latter under the leadership of Abraham Kuyper (1837–1920).

In 1920, Wisse left the GKN out of concern over the doctrine of presumptive regeneration[2] and an increasing bent toward cold intellectualism. He joined the *Christelijke Gereformeerde Kerk in Nederland* (CGK), a body also rooted in the Secession of 1834.[3] In 1926, he published a richly experiential book that was translated into English under the title *Godly Sorrow*.[4] From 1928 to 1936, he served as a professor of

---

1. For English sources on Wisse, see H. van der Ham, "Biographical Sketch," in Gerard Wisse, *Christ's Ministry in the Christian: The Administration of His Offices in the Believer*, trans. Bartel Elshout and William Van Voorst (Sioux Center, IA: Netherlands Reformed Book and Publishing, 1993), ix–xii; David H. Kranendonk, "Vital Balance: The Pursuit of Professors J. J. Van Der Schuit, G. Wisse, and L. H. Van Der Meiden" (MDiv thesis, Puritan Reformed Theological Seminary, 2004). For Dutch sources, see H. van der Ham, *Professor Wisse: Aspecten Van Leven En Werk* (Kampen: De Groot Goudriaan, 1993); Gerard Wisse, *Memoires: Onvergetelijke Bladzijden Uit Mijn Levensboek* (Houten/Utrecht: Den Hertog, 1982).
2. This is the belief that all children of believers baptized in infancy are regenerated by the Holy Spirit unless in subsequent development they show signs to the contrary.
3. Immigrants to the United States formed the Christian Reformed Church (from the GKN) and the Free Reformed Churches of North America (from the CGK). In 2004, the Dutch Reformed Church, the GKN, and the Evangelical Lutheran Church united to form the Protestant Church in the Netherlands.
4. Gerard Wisse, *Godly Sorrow* (St. Thomas, ON: Free Reformed Publications, 1998).

apologetics, philosophy, and homiletics at the CGK seminary in Apeldoorn. He then returned to pastoral ministry while continuing to lecture and write. In his lifetime, he produced about 140 published works. He issued strong warnings against both Fascism and Soviet Communism. Retiring in 1946, he remained active as an author and speaker until his death on November 19, 1957. Just twelve days prior to his death, he lectured on the significance of the launch of Sputnik 1 into orbit by the Soviet Union.

In his book *Godly Sorrow*, Wisse explains the importance of experiential religion:

> The central matter for us all is the experience of spiritual regeneration by the love of God. God's children are all partakers of the experiential knowledge of misery, deliverance, and thankfulness. There may be variance in degree and measure, but by the grace of the Spirit they learn to understand that there is nothing of themselves, and all of Him—thus they can appear before the God in Zion (Ps. 84:7).[5]

Wisse says, "Knowledge and experience are to be distinguished, though never separated." Knowledge of God, sin, and salvation is "the means" we need in order to enter into genuine spiritual experience. But "without the inward workings of the Spirit we are lost despite all our knowledge." On the other hand, all experience must be tested by the Word of God.[6]

Knowing Christ Experientially in His Offices

Wisse centers his experiential description of godliness upon Jesus Christ. We see this in his *Christ's Ministry in the Christian*, subtitled *The Administration of His Offices in the Believer*.[7] The book explores how Christ's threefold office brings us to the triple knowledge taught in the Heidelberg Catechism.[8] It gives us both an example of experiential preaching and a paradigm for experiential Christianity.

To understand the book, imagine a three-by-three grid or matrix. Next to the three rows, write the three offices of Christ: Prophet, Priest,

---

5. Wisse, *Godly Sorrow*, 9.
6. Wisse, *Godly Sorrow*, 10.
7. The subtitle reflects the original Dutch title, *De Ambetelijke Bediening van den Christus in de Geloovigen* (*The Administration of the Offices of Christ in the Believer*). It was first written as a series of articles, starting in February 1936, in the periodical *De Wekker*, and then published as a book around 1937.
8. "First, how great my sins and miseries are; . . . second, how I may be delivered from all my sins and miseries; . . . third, how I shall express my gratitude to God for such deliverance." Heidelberg Catechism, Q. 2.

and King. Over the three columns, write the triple knowledge of the Heidelberg Catechism: misery, deliverance, and thankfulness. Each part of the matrix represents one facet of how Christ's mediation interfaces with our experience.

	Misery	Deliverance	Thankfulness
Prophet	1. Christ our Prophet works an experience of our misery.	2. Christ our Prophet works an experience of our deliverance.	3. Christ our Prophet works an experience of our thankfulness.
Priest	4. Christ our Priest works an experience of our misery.	5. Christ our Priest works an experience of our deliverance.	6. Christ our Priest works an experience of our thankfulness.
King	7. Christ our King works an experience of our misery.	8. Christ our King works an experience of our deliverance.	9. Christ our King works an experience of our thankfulness.

This matrix is essentially the table of contents of the book, except that Wisse refers in his chapter titles to deliverance as "redemption" and to thankfulness as "sanctification." It's important to note, however, that for Wisse, "redemption" does not refer to Christ's objective work for us, but to its subjective application to us. Christ acts as Mediator both "objectively on our behalf before His Father" and "subjectively within us."[9] The latter work is the subject of *Christ's Ministry in the Christian*.

I cannot explore Wisse's doctrine systematically in this short treatment, but I want to introduce his experiential perspective. My purpose is to encourage you also to preach as Wisse did, in a Christ-centered and experiential manner.

Wisse's method addresses the whole Christian life. It is possible to view the triple knowledge as stages of Christian experience (conviction of misery, conversion by deliverance, and increasing consecration in thankfulness). Wisse acknowledges that in each stage, one of Christ's offices is more "preeminent" than the others. At the beginning, "the lost sinner will be subject in a more direct sense to the prophetic ministry." Then Christ "as Surety and Priest" is felt to be more and more necessary. His "royal

---

9. Wisse, *Christ's Ministry in the Christian*, 4.

ministry" is "the crowning piece of experiential life," as believers move ahead as warriors and pilgrims who need the King "to lead them through the midst of all their enemies to the gates of that splendid city of God."[10]

However, the experiences of misery and deliverance continue and deepen as a believer walks with God in gratitude.[11] Similarly, Christ's offices, Wisse says, are "intertwined," and the matrix represents "an economic order rather than a chronological order."[12] We never move beyond our need for the Prophet and the Priest. All nine categories in the matrix represent dimensions of the believer's normal experience of Christ's work to the end.

Wisse thereby makes Christian spirituality richly Christ centered from first to last. He writes: "Christ's administration of His offices is one of those matters which must be esteemed as being of the utmost significance for the subjective life of grace. . . . The Holy Spirit, who establishes the church and dwells in her, administers all salvation by way of this functioning of the three offices of Christ."[13]

By tying experience to the mediation of Christ, Wisse protects the church from legalistic introspection and morbidity. Though the law afflicts us with misery by showing us the worthiness of God and the loathsomeness of our sin, it is *Christ* who uses the law to work this sensibility of sin in us. Therefore, we know that God does not aim to destroy us with despair but to wound us like a surgeon so that he may heal and save us.[14] Indeed, it is a function of Christ's priestly ministry that this "uncovering" of the sinner's soul does not condemn and consume him, but humbles him for his good.[15] When the sinner rises up with self-justifications and hostility to the holy Lawgiver, the King "breaks the inner resistance in him against this uncovering work" with the sweet and irresistible power of his grace.[16] Wisse writes: "Christ acts with such inexpressible and loving power, that the soul is conquered in the most glorious fashion. At this point the great loss for Satan is not only the soul itself, but the fact that it becomes willing to be conquered and desirous for all that it first opposed."[17] Joining the experience of misery

10. Wisse, *Christ's Ministry in the Christian*, 70.
11. Wisse, *Christ's Ministry in the Christian*, 27.
12. Wisse, *Christ's Ministry in the Christian*, 70–71.
13. Wisse, *Christ's Ministry in the Christian*, 4.
14. Wisse, *Christ's Ministry in the Christian*, 9–10.
15. Wisse, *Christ's Ministry in the Christian*, 43.
16. Wisse, *Christ's Ministry in the Christian*, 71.
17. Wisse, *Christ's Ministry in the Christian*, 75.

to the mediation of Christ sprinkles bitter sorrows with a sweet intent to save from all sorrow.

Furthermore, this joining of our experiences to Christ's offices reminds us that we cannot build our lives on our experience of deliverance, but only upon Christ. Our Prophet reveals that he alone is our true foundation. As Wisse says: "We need to be taught time and again that we can neither live from our conversion nor from the fact that we are converted. The fountain of the spiritual life of redemption is ultimately not in any of our experiences, however true, genuine, and divinely wrought such experiences may be. . . . Only God in Christ is the fountain."[18] Yet the experiences are real. Christ brings "His heavenly milk and wine to the lips of our soul" so that in tasting his delicacies we "long all the more for Him who is [our] altogether lovely One."[19]

Desire for Christ distinguishes the "common workings of the Holy Spirit" from his saving work: "The person who has truly been uncovered will find himself drawn to the Lord Jesus." Only "Christ as Priest" can bring us deliverance in "a rightful manner."[20] Our deliverance comes from no "root principle" in ourselves, but only by the work of "the Intercessor, the substitutionary and priestly Christ who stands alongside God's throne of justice." By his Spirit, Christ works in his people a desire and delight to be delivered in "a way that is fully compatible with God's justice."[21] Ultimately, "this fleeing to Christ does not proceed from seeing our misery, but rather from seeing Christ" in "His adorable beauty" in an alluring and "stirring manner."[22]

Faith draws near, and love seeks union. These holy desires find consummation in the "full application of this deliverance" when "the Holy Spirit, as the Spirit of grace, brings Christ to the soul and unites the soul to Christ."[23] Here Wisse seems to speak of union with Christ not precisely as the gift of the Spirit in regeneration, for that has already been known by the sacred desires it produces. He writes experientially of the beginning of "blessed fellowship with God" in Christ our Priest, "a knowing, possessing, enjoying, and glorifying of God through God."[24]

---

18. Wisse, *Christ's Ministry in the Christian*, 23.
19. Wisse, *Christ's Ministry in the Christian*, 24.
20. Wisse, *Christ's Ministry in the Christian*, 45–46.
21. Wisse, *Christ's Ministry in the Christian*, 47–48.
22. Wisse, *Christ's Ministry in the Christian*, 51.
23. Wisse, *Christ's Ministry in the Christian*, 49.
24. Wisse, *Christ's Ministry in the Christian*, 52.

However, the attraction of the reconciling Priest meets intense opposition. Wisse points out that sinners not only resist being uncovered in their sin, but also resist being delivered from it. Men prefer to torment themselves with absurd religious disciplines than to be saved by grace. Here, Christ comes as the "resurrected King" to conquer us, the Lord "fully and entirely authorized to demand and bring about the deliverance of His redeemed one."[25] He especially shows himself to be our King when "Christ casts out unbelief and causes faith to triumph."[26]

Deliverance produces gratitude. Christ our Prophet continues his ministry under the rubric of thankfulness by teaching his people more about sin, afflictions, the gospel, and the law.[27] He points them to the triune God as the focus of life. He instructs them in the loathsomeness of their indwelling corruption so that they increasingly look to God in prayer. He illuminates them to see the goodness of God hidden in their afflictions. As a result, they do not falsely think that God is condemning them, and they do not murmur against him, but instead receive his training so as to become entirely his. Their heavenly Teacher leads them deeper into the gospel mysteries of salvation. Thus, they see how the riches of grace translate into practical godliness. Christ opens their eyes to the loveliness of God's law and what it means to keep his commandments, insulating them from antinomianism. Our Prophet directs his people not into Christomonism (as if God were nothing but Christ), but rather helps them to orient their lives to the triune God: Father, Son, and Holy Spirit.[28] Through the priesthood of Christ, we thus become holy temples and living sacrifices to God.[29]

As King, Christ exercises his authority over us to bring us to the essence of the "Godward" life: obedience. In a way that bridges from the experiential into the practical, Wisse asserts that the "essence of religion" is not "mysticism" but "to serve God . . . the triune God." Obedience was the work of Adam in Paradise, and obedience was the work of Christ on the cross. But Wisse does not divide duty from delight: "Obedience to God is the panting of the soul who is enamored with God." He says, "Obedience is not only a *must*, but also a *privilege*; consequently, it comprehends the mysticism of the new life."[30] Therefore, our King "will

---

25. Wisse, *Christ's Ministry in the Christian*, 80.
26. Wisse, *Christ's Ministry in the Christian*, 81.
27. See Heidelberg Catechism, Q. 114, 115.
28. Wisse, *Christ's Ministry in the Christian*, 25–37. On Christomonism, see also p. 90.
29. Wisse, *Christ's Ministry in the Christian*, 57, 65.
30. Wisse, *Christ's Ministry in the Christian*, 89–90.

render captive all thoughts . . . break the back of sinful lust and placate and regulate our passions." He stirs our "loyalty to Him as our King." He clothes us with "spiritual armor." He leads us into the fight. He woos us to desire no one but him as our Bridegroom. He keeps us faithful in persecution. He rewards our service.[31]

Ultimately, he will make his people into prophets, priests, and kings with him so that they are "fully, exclusively, and entirely of God, for God, and unto God." Wisse says that office bearing is "the great, essential, most magnificent, and central aspect of the covenant," for "God Himself will function through them."[32] He writes of believers' office bearing with Christ in a similar manner as we might think of mankind as being joint bearers of the image of God.

We have touched lightly upon the ninefold matrix of Wisse's theology of Christian experience. But the reader can already see the richness of his approach to Reformed experiential Christianity. The threefold scheme of Christ's offices enables us to see how Christ's total ministry addresses all our needs. The triple knowledge of misery, deliverance, and thankfulness illuminates our experience in a very realistic manner. Interwoven into a matrix, these nine points of knowledge help us to glorify Christ in all our experience. As with William Perkins's classification grid of listeners, this approach to Christian experience should not control our preaching, but it is richly suggestive of how we may make a wide array of applications.

D. Martyn Lloyd-Jones

David Martyn Lloyd-Jones was born in Cardiff, South Wales, on December 20, 1899.[33] He was raised within the Welsh Calvinistic Methodist Connexion,[34] the Presbyterian descendants of Great Awakening preachers such as Daniel Rowland (1711–1790), Howell Harris (1714–1773),

---

31. Wisse, *Christ's Ministry in the Christian*, 91–92.
32. Wisse, *Christ's Ministry in the Christian*, 94–95.
33. On Lloyd-Jones, see Iain H. Murray, *David Martyn Lloyd-Jones: The First Forty Years, 1899–1939* (Edinburgh: Banner of Truth, 1982); Iain H. Murray, *David Martyn Lloyd-Jones: The Fight of Faith, 1939–1981* (Edinburgh: Banner of Truth, 1990); John Brencher, *Martyn Lloyd-Jones (1899–1981) and Twentieth-Century Evangelicalism* (Carlisle, UK: Paternoster, 2002); Christopher Catherwood, ed., *Martyn Lloyd-Jones: Chosen by God* (Westchester, IL: Crossway, 1986); Christopher Catherwood, *Martyn Lloyd-Jones: A Family Portrait* (Eastbourne, UK: Kingsway, 1995); Bethan Lloyd-Jones, *Memories of Sandfields: 1927–1938* (Edinburgh: Banner of Truth, 1983). For brief introductions to Lloyd-Jones, see Philip H. Eveson, *Martyn Lloyd-Jones: In the Footsteps of the Distinguished Welsh Evangelist, Pastor and Theologian*, Travel With series (Leominster, UK: DayOne, 2004); J. I. Packer, "David Martyn Lloyd-Jones," in *Collected Shorter Writings of J. I. Packer*, vol. 4 (Carlisle, UK: Paternoster, 1998), 4:61–87.
34. Known today as the Presbyterian Church of Wales.

and William Williams (1717–1791).[35] Sadly, the preaching of that church had generally degenerated into recounting sentimental stories, almost a form of religious entertainment, on the assumption that every person in the church was already a Christian.

After completing his medical studies at St. Bartholomew's Hospital in London, he began a promising career assisting Thomas Horder, a physician to prominent English people, including the royal family. During 1924 and 1925, God illuminated the young physician's soul with an awareness of sin that culminated in his conversion to Christ. Diagnosing medical issues led him to realize that people, including the aristocratic elite, had far deeper problems than could be remedied by modern medicine. The problem was far worse than biological or behavioral; he saw that he himself was dead in sin. When God made him alive in Christ, he began to speak against sin with the boldness of a prophet.

He felt a sacred compulsion to preach. In 1926, Lloyd-Jones decided to leave medicine. Bypassing the typical denominational path of seminary training leading to ministry in an established church, he presented himself immediately as a candidate for mission work in South Wales. His passion was evangelism. From 1927 to 1938, he served as an ordained Calvinistic Methodist pastor of the mission church at Sandfields, Aberavon, a poor area near Swansea. The church grew from ninety-three members to 530, with an attendance of around 850.

Lloyd-Jones was next called as a copastor and, in 1943, successor to G. Campbell Morgan (1863–1945) at Westminster Chapel, London. There, Lloyd-Jones preached to a large congregation, but one that had been devastated by the long years and trials of World War II, so that he had to rebuild the church; it numbered more than fifteen hundred people at the time of his retirement in 1968. Once, during the war, a German bomb fell nearby while Lloyd Jones was preaching, badly damaging the church's roof. He had to intervene with the authorities to save the building from demolition. He was known to many simply as "the Doctor," both for his medical background and his authority as a "teacher" (which is the old Latin meaning of *doctor*).

He preached virtually every Lord's Day morning and evening except during long vacations in July and August, and also gave lectures on Friday nights. He also traveled extensively in Britain during the week to

---

35. See John Morgan Jones and William Morgan, *The Calvinistic Methodist Fathers of Wales*, trans. John Aaron (Edinburgh: Banner of Truth, 2008).

keep preaching appointments in many places. He provided direction and support to Inter-Varsity Christian Fellowship, the International Fellowship of Evangelical Students, the Evangelical Library, the Westminster Fellowship (a ministers' fraternal), the Banner of Truth Trust in its work of reprinting Puritan literature, the Puritan/Westminster conferences, the British Evangelical Council, and the Evangelical Movement of Wales.

In 1968, he retired from Westminster Chapel after undergoing successful surgery for cancer. He spent more time with his grandchildren, continued to travel and preach, and worked on the publication of his sermons, such as those on Paul's epistles to the Ephesians and the Romans.[36] In 1969, he visited the United States, giving the lectures at Westminster Seminary that were published as *Preaching and Preachers*.[37] Until 1976, he remained almost as active in the pulpit as he had been during his years as the minister of Westminster Chapel. He died of cancer on March 1, 1981.

Many people consider Lloyd-Jones to be the greatest preacher of the twentieth century. Let's consider some of the characteristics of his preaching and counsel with respect to the ministry of the Word.

Preaching the Glory of God

A defining characteristic of Lloyd-Jones's preaching was that his hearers came away feeling greatly reduced in their own eyes before the immense majesty of God in Christ. J. I. Packer remembers the Doctor as like "a lion, fierce on matters of principle, austere in his gravity, able in his prime both to growl and to roar as his argument required." Yet personally he was "delightfully relaxed . . . twinkling and witty to the last degree." His public arguments were "severe to the point of crushing, but always with transparent patience and good humour," even when people foolishly provoked him. He preached with all his energy, and with "the God-given liveliness and authority that in past eras was called *unction*."[38]

Packer recalls hearing him preach in the winter of 1948-1949, noting that "I felt and saw as never before the glory of Christ and of his gospel as modern man's only lifeline and learned by experience why historic Protestantism looks on preaching as the supreme means of grace and

---

36. David Martyn Lloyd-Jones, *An Exposition of Ephesians*, 8 vols. (Grand Rapids, MI: Baker, 1972); David Martyn Lloyd-Jones, *Romans*, 14 vols. (Grand Rapids, MI: Zondervan, 1970–2003).
37. David Martyn Lloyd-Jones, *Preaching and Preachers* (Grand Rapids, MI: Zondervan, 1971).
38. Packer, "David Martyn Lloyd-Jones," 4:82–84.

of communion with God." Lloyd-Jones "never put on any sort of act," but always "spoke as a debater making a case" or "as a physician making a diagnosis." Like Isaiah, his preaching seized men who thought themselves great and God small, and lifted their eyes to see that they were small and God is great. He always aimed at preaching the crucified Christ. Packer says, "I have never known anyone whose speech communicated such a sense of the reality of God."[39]

Iain Murray repeats some counsel that Lloyd-Jones gave him over the phone when Murray had to prepare to speak on "Is Calvinistic Evangelistic Preaching Necessary?" The Doctor told him:

> The superficiality of modern evangelism is not the result of an over-emphasis on justification, it was because it did not preach the law, the depth of sin and the holiness of God. The gospel was being preached in terms of the offer of a friend and a helper. The characteristic of Calvinistic evangelism is that the majesty and glory of God is put first, instead of some benefit provided for man.[40]

Lecturing to students at Westminster Seminary, Lloyd-Jones asked: "What is preaching? Logic on fire . . . theology on fire. . . . Preaching is theology coming through a man on fire." He queried, "What is the chief end of preaching?" and answered, "It is to give men and women a sense of God and His presence."[41] He explained:

> I can forgive a man for a bad sermon, I can forgive the preacher almost anything if he gives me a sense of God, if he gives me something for my soul, if he gives me the sense that, though he is inadequate himself, he is handling something which is very great and very glorious, if he gives me some dim glimpse of the majesty and glory of God, the love of Christ my Saviour, and the magnificence of the Gospel.[42]

Preaching the Truth of Holy Scripture

Lloyd-Jones was well aware of the scientific advances of the modern age. He was a brilliant medical doctor. Even after his calling into ministry, he continued to follow developments in the medical world. In a sermon on 1 Thessalonians 1, he says that he hears the constant clamor

---

39. Packer, "David Martyn Lloyd-Jones," 4:84–85.
40. Murray, *David Martyn Lloyd-Jones: The Fight of Faith, 1939–1981*, 732.
41. Lloyd-Jones, *Preaching and Preachers*, 97.
42. Lloyd-Jones, *Preaching and Preachers*, 98.

of voices saying that "owing to the advance of knowledge, and particularly science, we are confronted by a situation such as never confronted the Christian church before in her whole great and long history." He goes on to explain that we are told that modern people don't understand theological words, such as *justification* and *sanctification,* so we must learn how to communicate with them. As a result, even in the 1960s, the church was pressed to "learn the methods of big business advertizing" and to "modernize everything."[43]

Against this tendency and its imperative of so-called relevance, Lloyd-Jones asserts, "The problem confronting us is precisely the problem that has always confronted the Christian Church"—the world "never varies," but always "hates God." It uses different terminology, but the differences are only on the surface. What varies, sadly, is the state of the church. But the indifference and hostility of the world are not "new or novel or unique." The apostle Paul arrived in Thessalonica with his little missionary team and faced a pagan society immersed in immorality and ignorant of biblical truth—very much like the modern world.[44] The apostle responded with the ministry of Word and Spirit: "For our gospel came not unto you in word only, but also in power, and in the Holy Ghost, and in much assurance" (1 Thess. 1:5). In the same way, in order to evangelize the lost today, the church needs "the message and the power of the Spirit upon it."[45] The apostles did not come with antiwar protests, political agendas, or vague talk about inexpressible experiences of God. They came with doctrine. So must the church today, despite the sad reality that we live in an age when people dislike doctrine, theology, definitions, and clear and careful thinking.[46] But when have men ever liked the truth?

The message that pagans need to hear begins with God, as we see in 1 Thessalonians 1:9–10: "For they themselves shew of us what manner of entering in we had unto you, and how ye turned to God from idols to serve the living and true God; and to wait for his Son from heaven, whom he raised from the dead, even Jesus, which delivered us from the wrath to come." Even before we tell them about Christ and salvation, people need to hear about the true God. Lloyd-Jones warns: "We start

---

43. David Martyn Lloyd-Jones, "Not in Word Only," in Tony Sargent, *The Sacred Anointing: The Preaching of Dr. Martyn Lloyd-Jones* (Wheaton, IL: Crossway, 1994), 260.
44. Lloyd-Jones, "Not in Word Only," 261.
45. Lloyd-Jones, "Not in Word Only," 263.
46. Lloyd-Jones, "Not in Word Only," 264–65.

with ourselves, our needs, and then we always want something to satisfy us. Christianity never starts with man. It always starts with God."[47] Then it moves on to Christ, his death and resurrection, and salvation.

He preaches: "We are in such a hurry, we say, come to Jesus and the people do not come to Jesus. Do you know why? I can tell you. They have never seen any need of Jesus." They may look for emotional happiness, the healing of their bodies, guidance, or solutions to earthly problems, but without seeing the glory of God and his holy law, they will not come to Christ.[48]

The way to preach doctrine that centers on God in Christ is to preach the Holy Scriptures. Lloyd-Jones sees a place for lectures, but preaching is not lecturing with Scripture verses attached. Preaching is "always expository." That is, it always derives its message and main points from a passage of the Bible.[49]

The "golden rule" of sermon preparation is that the preacher must deal honestly with the meaning of the text. He cannot seize an idea or a phrase from the Bible and then say whatever he wants. Neither may he give a scholarly report about the text while neglecting the "main thrust" of its "spiritual meaning." It is remarkable how men can avoid preaching Christ and his cross, and end up in a sideshow that neglects the real message of the passage in its context. A text such as 2 Timothy 2:8, "Remember that Jesus Christ of the seed of David was raised from the dead according to my gospel," is twisted into an assertion of bare experientiality ("my gospel" is taken to mean that the only gospel that counts is the one that you have made your own). Meanwhile, the resurrection of Jesus Christ is neglected, if not denied outright. Preaching the true message of Scripture requires "spiritual perception" or "unction" from the Holy Spirit (1 John 2:20, 27).[50]

Lloyd-Jones became known for his expository series of sermons on books of the Bible, such as Romans, Ephesians, and 1 John, or on long passages such as the Sermon on the Mount. There is great wisdom in preaching through the Scriptures in a continuous fashion for the edification of the saints. However, it is less often appreciated that Lloyd-Jones always preached evangelistic sermons on Lord's Day nights. Generally,

---

47. Lloyd-Jones, "Not in Word Only," 268.
48. Lloyd-Jones, "Not in Word Only," 270.
49. Lloyd-Jones, *Preaching and Preachers*, 196.
50. Lloyd-Jones, *Preaching and Preachers*, 199–204.

each of these evangelistic messages expounded a Scripture text selected for the occasion without being part of a series.[51]

He advocates quite a bit of liberty in selecting a text for a sermon, whether for evangelism or for edification. He warns preachers against mapping out in advance exactly what they will preach for the next six months and sticking rigidly to the plan. At times, a text will speak powerfully to the preacher's soul. When this happens, he advises, the preacher should write down an outline and a few thoughts, and save them for a future occasion. Sometimes a number of texts will coalesce into a theme that the preacher can turn into a series, as Lloyd-Jones did with his sermons that became his book *Spiritual Depression*. The calendar, current world crises, or catastrophic events may provide opportunities to bring the Word of God directly to bear on what people are thinking about.

The preacher must be sensitive to the needs of his people. That includes not preaching a series that is too deep and too long for the congregation to follow. But whatever one preaches, it must be the Word of God.[52] It is worth noting that Lloyd-Jones began his work in serial exposition with a relatively short and simple series of sermons later published as *Expository Sermons on 2 Peter*.[53] He was content to begin that way, and so train his people for the more advanced kind of preaching found in his sermons on Romans and Ephesians.

Preaching with the Unction of the Holy Spirit

It is not enough to bring the Word; there must be the Spirit too. Lloyd-Jones says that when Paul wrote of the Word going out "in power, and in the Holy Ghost, and in much assurance" (1 Thess. 1:5), he was referring not merely to the experience of the listeners but also to the preacher. Paul preached "in the power of the Holy Ghost."[54]

Lloyd-Jones long stressed the necessity of preaching truth for doctrinal understanding. As he says, "When I came to England evangelicalism was non-theological, pietistic, and sentimental."[55] However, in the 1960s, he also began to emphasize that those who embraced orthodoxy must not rest in it; they need the work of the Holy Spirit in personal

---

51. Iain H. Murray, introduction to David Martyn Lloyd-Jones, *Old Testament Evangelistic Sermons* (Edinburgh: Banner of Truth, 1995), vii–viii, xi; see Lloyd-Jones, *Preaching and Preachers*, 63, 151–52.

52. Lloyd-Jones, *Preaching and Preachers*, 187–97.

53. D. M. Lloyd-Jones, *Expository Sermons on 2 Peter* (Edinburgh: Banner of Truth, 1983).

54. Lloyd-Jones, "Not in Word Only," 273.

55. Quoted in Carl Henry, "An Interview," in Catherwood, *Martyn Lloyd-Jones*, 102.

experience, especially for assurance of salvation.[56] The church needs both a clear understanding of biblical truth and a warm embrace of spiritual experience.

Experiential Christianity is not just a result of preaching; it is an essential qualification for the preacher. As Paul explained to the Thessalonians, he preached with purity of heart, not seeking to please men (1 Thess. 2:3–5). Lloyd-Jones enjoyed humor, but he says, "I cannot imagine the Apostle Paul bouncing up on to a platform, cracking a few jokes to put the congregation at ease, and then entertaining them with flippancies in order just to play upon their feelings." On the contrary, he quotes 1 Corinthians 2:4: "And my speech and my preaching was not with enticing words of man's wisdom, but in demonstration of the Spirit and of power."[57]

The same Spirit worked in Paul's listeners, so that they received the message not as the words of men but as the Word of God (1 Thess. 2:13). As a result, they turned from idols to serve the living God with faith, hope, and love, even in persecution (1 Thess. 1:3, 6, 9). Only the Holy Spirit can produce such a change; only he can convict of sin, illuminate the soul, and give life to the dead. This apostolic kind of gospel proclamation is preaching in the Holy Spirit, and it is an instrument of regeneration by the Spirit.[58]

We must both preach the sovereign grace of regeneration and preach with faith, believing it ourselves. Lloyd-Jones once told Murray: "Modern evangelism pays lip service to regeneration but it does not really believe in it. True Calvinistic preaching shows the complete helplessness of man and regards the humbling of man as the main part of its work. If that is left out, the true glory of salvation cannot begin to be measured."[59]

Lloyd-Jones knew that preaching involves us in a mysterious partnership or cooperation with almighty God. For this reason, despite all his experience in writing and delivering sermons, he confessed in 1967 that "to me preaching is a great mystery." At times, God grants a freedom and power that has little to do with our preparations and abilities. Yet preaching always feels like "an impossible task." It comes with "the element of dread, of terrible responsibility"; there is "the sense of fear, the

56. Iain H. Murray, *Lloyd-Jones: Messenger of Grace* (Edinburgh: Banner of Truth, 2008), 230.
57. Lloyd-Jones, "Not in Word Only," 274.
58. Lloyd-Jones, "Not in Word Only," 275–76.
59. Quoted in Murray, *David Martyn Lloyd-Jones: The Fight of Faith, 1939–1981*, 733.

sense of awe." The preacher cannot be sent by himself. He is sent by God by means of the call of the church (Rom. 10:15). The Spirit-empowered preacher speaks, as Paul confessed in 1 Corinthians 2:3, "in weakness, and in fear, and in much trembling." Great preachers, such as Paul or George Whitefield, did not slip easily into preaching. They were alarmed by their unworthiness and the solemn majesty of Christ.[60]

Preaching is also a personal interaction between the preacher and the congregation. It is not at all true that the preacher disappears and only God is seen. Lloyd-Jones agrees with Phillips Brooks (1835–1891) that preaching is "truth mediated through personality." He says:

> The whole man is involved in preaching. . . . It is not merely what the man says, it is the way in which he says it—this total involvement of the man; his body is involved, every part of him, every faculty is involved if it is true preaching, the whole personality of the individual; and, at the same time, as I said, the congregation is also making its contribution. Here are spiritually minded people, they have come prepared and they are under the influence of the Spirit, and so these two things blend together. There is a unity between preacher and hearers and there is a transaction backwards and forwards. That, to me, is true preaching.[61]

Preaching is a spiritual triangle whereby God draws the preacher and the hearers closer to himself and to each other. The Holy Spirit is at work, the preacher feels a holy "compulsion," and the people are "gripped and fixed" by the truth. This is a far cry from preaching only because it is the Lord's Day and it's your job. It is a labor of love. Love moves us to study and to organize our thoughts. But Lloyd-Jones says that to dress up our sermons simply "to attract people" is not love, but "prostitution."[62]

Preaching is delivering a "word from God," not in the sense of direct revelation, but as the result of studying Scripture and then speaking the truth of Scripture "in demonstration of the Spirit and of power" (1 Cor. 2:4). The preacher is an agent of God, and he himself is "taken up" by God into "this realm of the Spirit and God is giving a message through this man to the people." He is not tied to his notes or to following some perfect form, but speaks with a holy "freedom," often leaving "loose

---

60. David Martyn Lloyd-Jones, *Knowing the Times: Addresses Delivered on Various Occasions, 1942–1977* (Edinburgh: Banner of Truth, 1989), 258–62.
61. Lloyd-Jones, *Knowing the Times*, 273.
62. Lloyd-Jones, *Knowing the Times*, 273–74.

ends" or even interrupting himself in ways one would not expect in a polished theological treatise. God gives him insights and fire even in the act of preaching that he did not have before.[63] As a result, the preacher may say: "I am preaching, yet not I, but I am being used of God; I am being taken up, I am being employed, and God is using even me to speak to these people. I am an ambassador for God, I am a sent one, I am aware of this great responsibility—but it is all right, I am enabled to do it because of His grace and the power that He is gracious enough to give me."[64]

This is the divine mystery of preaching as Lloyd-Jones described it and as he experienced it through a lifetime of ministry in the pulpit.

---

63. Lloyd-Jones, *Knowing the Times*, 276–77.
64. Lloyd-Jones, *Knowing the Times*, 277.

PART 3

───────◎───────

Preaching Experientially Today

20

Preaching with Balance

In 1982, Lech Walesa was released by the Polish government after eleven months of imprisonment. He said: "I am released on a tightrope, under which there is a prison yard, and this tightrope has been greased. I do not intend to fall."[1] Walesa led the Polish Solidarity movement across the tightrope, and eight years later took office as the president of Poland when it transitioned from a satellite state of the Soviet Union to freedom and democracy.

In many ways, the Reformed experiential preacher also walks a greased tightrope. He may feel that in order to secure his grip on one aspect of Christianity, he needs to loosen his hold on another aspect. In trying not to fall into semi-Pelagianism, he may slip into hyper-Calvinism. In seeking to avoid emotionalism without substance, he must beware of falling into cold intellectualism. Sin and Satan do not make it easy to walk the line. But the preacher must embrace the whole counsel of God as it impacts the whole man.

We have explained the basic principles of Reformed experiential preaching. We have also illustrated Reformed experiential preaching by studying examples of faithful servants of God from the last five hundred years. Now we aim to apply these principles and illustrations to the work of actually practicing Reformed experiential preaching. That is not to say that we will consider the mechanics of sermon preparation; many other books address that subject. Rather, in this last section, we will consider some practical lessons on how to preach experientially today.

---

1. Ruth E. Gruber, "Walesa: Playing It Cool, Cautious, Cagey," UPI, Nov. 15, 1982, https://www.upi.com/Archives/1982/11/15/Walesa-playing-it-cool-cautious-cagey/5818406184400/.

In this chapter, I will discuss how to preach with balance. Four areas particularly require a careful and watchful balance to sustain a wholesome kind of experiential preaching. In some of these areas, preachers must embrace two seeming opposites. If we let go of either, we will fall short.

Embracing Both the Objective and the Subjective Elements in Christianity

Our Lord Jesus Christ prayed, "And this is life eternal, that they might know thee the only true God, and Jesus Christ, whom thou hast sent" (John 17:3). Here is objective truth: the reality of "the only true God." In a world where people worship a multitude of gods and idols, the Lord affirms that regardless of what we think, there is only one God. Furthermore, this God has sent his Revealer into the world to make himself known—"Jesus Christ," who could say, "I have manifested thy name" (vv. 3, 6). God gave Christ a people to save, and Christ was able to say in the darkest night of his life, "I have finished the work which thou gavest me to do" (v. 4). Thus, Christian preaching must revolve around the objective focus of the truth about God in Christ and his saving work accomplished for his people.

At the same time, there is subjective experience: the knowing of this God by the human soul. This knowledge is not merely an intellectual exercise; it is life-giving, life-transforming knowledge, even "eternal life." Christ's people not only know about his work *for them*, but they have Christ *in them* (John 17:23, 26). This knowledge of God in Christ so vivifies the soul that true believers become obedient to God's Word (v. 6), are separated from the world (v. 14), are sanctified unto holiness (v. 17), are sent out bearing Christ's Word to the world (vv. 18, 20), and are solidified together as one body with fellow believers in Christ (vv. 22–23). So preaching must also revolve around the subjective focus of the experience of God in Christ.

The Twin Foci around Which Experiential Preaching Revolves

The subjective must be kept rooted in the objective. Truth must lead to experience. Charles Bridges writes, "Christian experience is the influence of doctrinal truth upon the affections."[2] Experience detached from

---

2. Charles Bridges, *The Christian Ministry* (London: Banner of Truth, 1967), 259.

objective truth is delusion. If we lose the objective focus of our faith, then we make ourselves into gods in our own eyes and worship our experiences. Eternal life is not just feelings and actions; it is to "know thee the only true God, and Jesus Christ, whom thou hast sent." Faith looks outside of the soul to receive the Christ who is what we are not and who has done for us what we could not do.

Yet, in Christianity, the objective always aims at the subjective. It was an axiom of the Old Princeton theologians that "Truth is in order to goodness" (see p. 82, note 11). Bridges says that the life of Christianity "consists not in the exposition, but in the application of doctrine to the heart for the sanctification and comfort of the sincere Christian."[3] Truth without vital experience is vanity and can easily result in hypocrisy. If we lose the subjective focus of Christianity, then we have no more religion than the natural man. Yes, we might be able to accurately describe the objective reality of God and Christ. But we have no personal involvement or union with that reality. The death of Christ must become our death, and his life our life. That is the aim of redemption: that he should be our God and we should be his people.

Therefore, preaching must remain in close orbit around these two foci, the objective and the subjective. For example, when preaching on assurance, we must teach our people to rest upon the objective promises about Christ (2 Cor. 1:19–20), and we must guide them to examine themselves subjectively to see if Christ is in them (2 Cor. 13:5). By the subjective evidences of regeneration, the Spirit witnesses to us and makes the promises of Christ real to us in our experience. Without such self-examination, the promises can be twisted into pretexts for carnal presumption and self-deceit. On the other hand, if people are not directed away from their own righteousness to trust in what Christ has done, self-examination degenerates into the bondage of legalistic introspection, and assurance is made to stand on the shifting sands of experience. True assurance of salvation requires both the objective and the subjective.

Staying Balanced in an Unbalanced World

We presently live in a climate awash in subjectivism and relativism. Christians face a grave danger of accepting a self-centered mysticism in the place of the historic Christian faith. Imagination and sentimental

---

3. Bridges, *The Christian Ministry*, 260.

devotional readings drive private experiences of God; music, visual stimulation, and emotional stories drive corporate worship experiences. Sometimes the theme of "Christ in us" (as distinct from "Christ for us") becomes so prominent that churches follow so-called modern prophets, celebrity preachers, and personal "revelations" rather than the Holy Scriptures.

In such an atmosphere, it would be easy for us, especially as Reformed Christians, to retreat into an intellectual fortress of doctrinal knowledge about what Christ has done for us. We could glory in the fact that we have the truth, teach the truth, and defend the truth. But do we glory in knowing Christ? It is one thing to glory self-righteously in our knowledge about Christ. It is another to glory humbly in Christ as our only wisdom and righteousness. We may confess the truth, but can it be said of us as Jesus said, "And ye shall know the truth, and the truth shall make you free" (John 8:32)? Are we wise in the ways of spiritual combat against the world, the flesh, and the Devil? Let us beware of a merely historical faith that assents to truth but no real roots in Christ. We must preach in a way that exalts both Christ for us and Christ in us.

We must not separate the objective and the subjective. Such a separation is unacceptable because of the nature of God. God is the great objective reality, being infinite truth itself. Yet God is also the great personal reality, infinite love, involved in our lives from day to day. The temptation to focus exclusively on either the objective or the subjective to the neglect of the other is one way the deceptiveness of sin seeks to stupefy our hearts to reality. In Scripture, God never presents us with truth in a cold, detached manner. His light always blazes with heat—the fire of holy love. When we preach the Scriptures faithfully, we discover that the objective and subjective elements blend with each other, and the latter always flows from the former.

Examples of Preaching with Objective-Subjective Balance

For example, consider Titus 3:1–8. The passage opens with Paul's exhortation to Titus to remind believers to submit to governing authorities, engage in good works, and relate to all men with gentleness, not slandering and fighting (vv. 1–2). This is very practical. It invites us to consider the experiential difficulties of submitting to unjust leaders and loving wicked men.

Immediately afterward, Paul launches into a classic statement of human corruption (v. 3) and regeneration by the Spirit poured out through the Son because of God's unmerited love (vv. 4–7). This part of the passage is thoroughly doctrinal. Yet it is also experiential. It gives us the foundation for the conduct commanded in the beginning of the chapter. Knowing God's grace to us despite our sin motivates us to relate to others with humility and patience. It also raises questions about what is "the washing of regeneration, and renewing of the Holy Ghost" (v. 5)? How does one know if he has experienced it?

Then Paul says: "This is a faithful saying, and these things I will that thou affirm constantly, that they which have believed in God might be careful to maintain good works. These things are good and profitable unto men" (v. 8). In other words, the doctrine of salvation, when experientially realized, produces a life focused on zealously doing good to others. If we want to be faithful in our preaching of such a text, we will find ourselves constantly addressing both doctrinal and experiential questions.

When preaching objective truth in an experiential manner, we do more than present abstract propositions. Called to the ministry of the Word, we represent God. So, when preaching Titus 3:4 on "the kindness and love of God our Saviour," we should speak to believers with the same affection God has for them (Phil. 1:8). When people are frightened, downcast, or weak, they need more than ideas. They need solid comfort. They need to see God's steadfast, faithful love for them. We communicate this not merely by the objective truths that we proclaim, but by the subjective manner in which we proclaim them. We must speak with the tenderness of a nursing mother and the earnest love of a father, sharing with them not only the truth but opening our very souls to them (1 Thess. 2:7–8, 11–12).

The Objective and Subjective in Evangelistic Preaching

Consider how the preaching of the gospel must embrace both the objective truths of Scripture and the subjective experiences of the heart. To preach faithfully, we must teach the truths about God, sin, Christ, and salvation, and also exhort men to repent and believe. If, in the absence of any substantial doctrinal instruction, we merely call men to come to Christ, then they will not know why they must come or who Christ is. They will come to an idol of their own imagination to meet the felt needs of their sinful natures. If we merely teach people the truths of the gospel but never press them to respond, we fail to follow the example of Christ and the apostles, who commanded "all men every where" (Acts 17:30) to repent and believe (Mark 1:15; Acts 20:21; 26:20). We also give them the false impression either that they are all saved already (whether by their own goodness or by participating in the means of grace) or that they are saved simply by understanding the truth instead of by receiving Christ as Savior.

It is always a mistake to think that preaching the truth of the gospel is merely objective, whereas preaching the call of the gospel is merely subjective. Both are objective and both are subjective. When we preach about God, we must magnify his majesty in a way that stirs the affections of awe and reverence. Preaching about sin should not merely inform, but also pierce consciences and shatter guilty souls. Preaching Christ cannot be faithful unless it allures and woos sinners with his beautiful person and all-sufficient work. Furthermore, in preaching the gospel call, we cannot simply assume that people already know who God is, what Christ has done to save us, or what faith and repentance are. In a world full of spiritual counterfeits, they need eyes to discern between making a saving reception of Christ and taking refuge in soul-damning false religion. Likewise, if we only describe faith and repentance but never commend and command them, we cut off the hands and feet of the gospel. Real experiential preaching pursues men and strives to grasp their hearts.

In all likelihood, you will find yourself in danger of falling off the horse on one side or the other. Know yourself. If you read seventeenth-century Reformed scholastic theological treatises by William Ames or Francis Turretin for your devotions, then you probably need to push yourself to emphasize the experiential more. Don't go for more than ten minutes in a sermon without making some application or you will lose people's attention. On the other hand, if your books gather dust while you spend so much time talking to unbelievers at the coffee shop that they think you work there, then you may be tempted to neglect the study and proclamation of objective truth. Whatever your strengths and weaknesses, labor to overcome them and to embrace both elements in your preaching and in your life. It's helpful in this regard to have friends in the ministry who are different from you—iron sharpens iron. Your brothers may be able to show you where you fall short, such that you may have much to learn from their abilities and experience.

Embracing Both God's Sovereignty and Man's Responsibility

Let's suppose that you are preaching through Matthew 11. You come to the woes and warnings of verses 20–24, where the Son of Man denounces the cities of Galilee for not repenting of their sins despite hearing him preach the gospel and seeing him work miracles. Christ says that it will be "more tolerable" for wicked, pagan cities such as Tyre and Sidon on the day of judgment than it will be for these unrepentant cities so privileged with the means of grace. Christ strongly affirms man's obligation to repent upon hearing the gospel and his culpability for refusing to do so.

Then, in verses 25–27, Christ praises the Father because he hid these truths from the wise and revealed them to the foolish as it pleased him. Christ also says that no one knows the Father except the Son and anyone to whom the Son wills to reveal him. The Lord denies to men all ability truly to know God and to spiritually perceive the truth of the gospel. If anyone does know God through the gospel, Christ attributes it all to God's will and Christ's work, and the work of the Spirit with the Word.

Next, in verses 28–30, the Lord Jesus calls all the burdened to come to him and find rest. He commands men to take his yoke upon them, that is, to submit to his authority. He offers himself as a "meek and lowly" Master who gives rest to the souls of all who come under his lordship. Here we have the free offer of the gospel.

How will you preach these texts? Perhaps a better question is, do you feel free to preach the whole message of Matthew 11:20–30 with your whole heart? Can you preach man's responsibility for his sin, God's sovereignty in determining whom he will save, and Christ's free offer of the gospel to weary sinners, all with equal enthusiasm and sincerity? They are all biblical truths.

Wholehearted Proclamation of Sovereignty and Responsibility

One mark of the old Reformed preachers was that they preached man's responsibility with one hundred percent conviction and God's sovereignty with one hundred percent conviction. They clung to all that the Scriptures teach. They did not believe that to preach responsibility is to undermine sovereignty, or that to preach sovereignty is to nullify responsibility. We must preach both, as they did, with full conviction.

Too often people think that God's sovereignty and human responsibility are polar opposites, like hot and cold—more of one means less of the other. Even talk of balancing these two doctrines can mislead us, as if when one side of the balance beam goes up, the other must go down, and so we must not emphasize either side too much. In reality, they are not opposites or enemies. In response to the question, "How do you reconcile these two doctrines?" Charles H. Spurgeon said, "I never reconcile two friends."[4] Both aspects of gospel truth are the teaching of Scripture.

Both sovereignty and responsibility are rooted in the nature of God and his relation to his creatures. As the King, God reigns over men in all their activities. He is always in control, directing all events to accomplish his good and wise purposes. As the Judge, God holds men accountable for their actions. He is always measuring people by the standard of his righteous law.

Divine sovereignty and human responsibility are resented and resisted by fallen men. The sinner aspires to throw off God's reign and to be the master of his destiny and the captain of his fate. He would prefer to go to hell by his own choice than go to heaven as one whose choices are subject to the will of heaven's King. The sinner abhors the Judge, and his heart shouts at the heavens, "Who do you think you are?" If given the liberty to do so, we all would cast aside both the doctrines of sovereignty and responsibility, and would proclaim ourselves the kings and judges of all things, and free to live as we like.

Therefore, in order to preach to the glory of God, we must preach both God's sovereignty over man and man's responsibility under God. We will be tempted to use one doctrine as an excuse to deny the other. One's preaching can shift in a subtle manner. The heart is unsettled with one or the other of these doctrines. As a result, whenever it appears in our preaching, we hedge it about with numerous qualifications. Preaching ceases to be one's "Yea and Amen" to the Word, and instead becomes merely "Yes, but . . ." Though we may not acknowledge it openly, our listeners get the point: we really believe only part of what the Bible teaches. That is a tragedy.

Letting Scripture Set the Agenda

We must preach the whole counsel of God without apology and without regret or reservation. Remember, we are merely the messengers of God and ministers of his Word. Allow the text of Scripture to set the agenda.

---

4. Charles H. Spurgeon, Sermon No. 239, "Jacob and Esau" (Rom. 9:13), in *The New Park Street Pulpit* (1859; repr., Pasadena, TX: Pilgrim Press, 1975), 5:120.

Some texts reveal a remarkable conjunction of divine sovereignty and human responsibility, and so this is what we should preach. For example, consider the account of the plagues of hail and locusts sent against Egypt (Ex. 9:13–10:20). The text opens with an amazing declaration of God's sovereignty. God says that his plagues fall not only upon the Egyptians' bodies and possessions, but also upon Pharaoh's "heart" (9:14).[5] In other words, the worst plague is the hardening of Pharaoh's heart (9:12), which God had said he would perform before Moses ever went to Pharaoh (4:21). God is not frustrated by Pharaoh's stubbornness, but has raised up Pharaoh to demonstrate God's power by crushing the enemies of God (9:16). Therefore, we must preach that God hardens some of his enemies to glorify himself in destroying them.

Yet this is no excuse for Pharaoh's sin. The Egyptian king confesses, "I have sinned" (9:27), but after the plague is lifted, the text says, "he sinned yet more, and hardened his heart" (9:34). Moses brings the word of the Lord: "How long wilt thou refuse to humble thyself before me? Let my people go, that they may serve me" (10:3). When the locusts come, Pharaoh again confesses: "I have sinned against the LORD your God. . . . Now therefore forgive, I pray thee, my sin" (10:16–17). We must preach that sinners are responsible for their sins against God. We must tell them that God hates their sin and confront them with the folly of it. We must call them to confess, seek forgiveness for, and (unlike Pharaoh) truly forsake their sin.

Does this mean the text has backpedaled from God's sovereignty? Not a bit. In the midst of these confessions and exhortations, the Lord says to Moses, "Go in unto Pharaoh: for I have hardened his heart, and the heart of his servants, that I might shew these my signs before him" (10:1). Behind the stubborn sin of the wicked is the sovereign hand of God, who orders such things for his glory. This doctrine serves to encourage the saints and confront the wicked with the claims of God, for it reminds us that God's purposes cannot be thwarted. Even if we resist him to the end, he will manifest his glory through us. We will lose this precious application of comfort if we are afraid to preach God's absolute sovereignty over sinners.

It is legitimate to guard your sermons from misunderstanding. For example, when preaching a text that strongly asserts God's sovereignty,

---

5. The word *heart* tends to get lost in modern translations, but it is present in the Hebrew and accurately rendered in the Authorized Version.

it is wise to explain that God is not the author of sin. God never delights in sin, nor does he cause people to sin. As Pharaoh acknowledged, "the LORD is righteous" (9:27). But beware of so watering down the idea of God hardening sinners in their sin that you lose the sense of intentional and purposeful control present in the text. God does give people over to the master of sin as a judicial punishment (Rom. 1:24, 26, 28; 2 Thess. 2:10–11).

Never Be Ashamed of the Word of God

Other texts emphasize one doctrine but scarcely mention the other. Again, you must allow the particular text of Scripture to control the emphasis of your sermon. Never be embarrassed by or for the Word of God, as if some verses contradicted other verses. Let the whole Bible speak as with one voice, for it is the voice of God, and God is truth itself.

Consider Ezekiel 18:30–32:

> Therefore I will judge you, O house of Israel, every one according to his ways, saith the Lord GOD. Repent, and turn yourselves from all your transgressions; so iniquity shall not be your ruin. Cast away from you all your transgressions, whereby ye have transgressed; and make you a new heart and a new spirit: for why will ye die, O house of Israel? For I have no pleasure in the death of him that dieth, saith the Lord GOD: wherefore turn yourselves, and live ye.

How would you preach this text in a Reformed experiential manner? First, you should resist the temptation to take the easy way out and avoid the text. Jonathan Edwards preached it to the native tribes in Stockbridge, Massachusetts, in 1754.[6] Instead, let the text loose on the listener. Preach that (1) the Lord God will judge each man according to his ways, (2) the Lord God commands each man to repent of all his sins, and (3) the Lord God has no delight in the death of sinners. None of these truths contradicts the doctrines of unconditional divine election or total human depravity.

Even the exhortation "make you a new heart" is profitable for Reformed preaching. It does not teach human ability but human responsibility, particularly the absolute obligation to turn from the sins of our

---

6. Manuscript Sermon No. 1120, Ezekiel 18:30–32, preached June 1754 to the Stockbridge Indians, listed (but not published) at http://edwards.yale.edu/research/sermon-index/canonical ?chapter=18&book=26.

hearts and to embrace God and his righteousness with true love. We must root out sin from the core of our being. Ezekiel had said that sinners have "whorish heart[s]" (Ezek. 6:9). The law incessantly demands that we love God with all our hearts. John Calvin says, "He requires, therefore, from them a thorough renewal, so that they should not only conform their life to the rule of the law, but should fear God sincerely, since no one can produce good fruit but from a living root."[7] We should press this requirement upon sinners to show them both their guilt for not repenting and their helplessness to save themselves. Popular preaching makes conversion seem easy, a mere decision or act of the will. Biblical preaching makes clear that conversion is impossible for man but possible with God, for it requires a radical reorientation of the deepest motives and desires of the heart.

As Calvin says, God commands men to get new hearts "that men convicted of sin may cease to throw the blame on any one else," and, "as it concerns the elect, when God shows them their duty, and they acknowledge that they cannot discharge it, they fly to the aid of the Holy Spirit, so that the outward exhortation becomes a kind of instrument which God uses to confer the grace of his Spirit."[8] At first a sinner may dread and hate God's sovereignty. But when convinced of his responsibility to repent and his inability to do so, God's sovereignty becomes the sweetest of attributes, for only a sovereign Savior can help us.

Another trap to avoid is to preach the text and then to add so many qualifications that it loses its force. Preach the main thrust of each text. After the Dutch *Nadere Reformatie* subsided in the eighteenth century, it became too common for a preacher to give a brief exposition of a text, but then spend most of his time filling in everything it did not say. Preachers who fall into this trap end up trying to preach the whole counsel of God in every sermon. Effectively, this general approach can nullify the impact of a particular Scripture text.

Imagine a man preaching Isaiah 55:6–7, "Seek ye the LORD while he may be found, call ye upon him while he is near: Let the wicked forsake his way, and the unrighteous man his thoughts: and let him return unto the LORD, and he will have mercy upon him; and to our God, for he will abundantly pardon." He speaks a few words about repentance and our

---

7. John Calvin, *Commentaries of Calvin*, various translators and editors, 45 vols. (Edinburgh: Calvin Translation Society, 1846–1851; repr., 22 vols., Grand Rapids, MI: Baker, 1979) [Ezek. 20:31–32], hereafter, *Commentary*.

8. *Commentary* [Ezek. 20:31–32].

obligation to repent. But then, uncomfortable with human responsibility, he places his real stress on the fact that it is impossible to repent and that God is sovereign in giving the grace of repentance. What has he done? He has forced upon the text a tension that it does not contain. He has diminished the thrust of the text in its call for repentance, giving his hearers an apparently good excuse for their lack of repentance.

Therefore, in order to preach experientially, never sacrifice God's sovereignty or man's responsibility. Emphasize what your particular text emphasizes. It is permissible in some sermons to focus entirely on the glory of the sovereign God, in others to put the weight on human responsibility, and in others to expound both. Preaching through a book of the Bible will give you the opportunity to present both doctrines according to the balance of divine wisdom. If you are not preaching through a book of the Bible, be careful not to select your sermon texts so as to neglect either of these doctrines. Let your preaching over the weeks include ample references to both. Even if your congregation is imbalanced in the direction of hyper-Calvinism or Arminianism, they need to hear the biblical presentation and affirmation of both truths. Imbalanced preaching produces discord and divisions, as some people will agree with you while others will try to correct your imbalance with imbalances of their own.

The Power and Freedom of Balanced Reformed Preaching

Embracing divine sovereignty and human responsibility empowers effective preaching. Jean-Daniel Benoit, in his study of Calvin's pastoral ministry, addresses the question of why Reformed theology did not lead to a paralyzing fatalism. He asks, "Why has Calvinism, on the contrary, been such a school of energy and manifested itself in history as a tremendous dynamic power?" He answers, "No one has affirmed the sovereignty of God as firmly as Calvin; no one has affirmed more than he the responsibility of man."[9]

Taking responsibility for our ministry of the Word in submission to God's sovereignty will also enliven us as preachers. Though only God can make the gospel seed fruitful, there is a mysterious way in which preachers enter into the process as "labourers together with God" (1 Cor. 3:9).

---

9. Jean-Daniel Benoit, *Calvin in His Letters: A Study of Calvin's Pastoral Counseling Mainly from His Letters* (Appleford, England: Sutton Courtenay, 1986), 83, cited in Jean-Marc Berthoud, "John Calvin and the Spread of the Gospel in France," in *Fulfilling the Great Commission* (London: Westminster Conference, 1992), 44.

We do not preach impassionately, as did the Stoic philosophers. Rather, we follow the example of Paul, who preached passionately, often with tears in his eyes (Acts 20:31). One of the greatest evangelists of all time was George Whitefield. His soul was soaked in the Reformed experiential writings of the Puritans. God used Whitefield's preaching to revive the church and to save thousands of sinners. One mark of his preaching was his tears. He said, "You blame me for weeping, but how can I help it, when you will not weep for yourselves, although your immortal souls are on the verge of destruction."[10]

Only the Holy Spirit produces the new birth, and that with sovereign freedom (John 3:8). Yet Paul goes so far as to say to the Galatians, "My little children, of whom I travail in birth again until Christ be formed in you . . ." (Gal. 4:19). The words "travail in birth again" imply that when Paul first evangelized them, he labored as a mother does in childbirth. What more intense degree of pain could there be? We, too, must take up our responsibility to labor in our preaching—not just in studying and writing sermons, but in striving with sinners for their conversion with an energy that exhausts us while God works mightily (Col. 1:29). We can strive both humbly and hopefully when we are confident that God's sovereign Word will not return to him void (Isa. 55:10–11).

Embracing Biblical, Doctrinal, Experiential, and Practical Elements in Reformed Preaching

Preaching has many dimensions. Christian experience is but one of them. If we neglect it, then, to that extent at least, our sermons will be impoverished. But if we try to make Christian experience into the all-in-all of preaching, then our sermons will be woefully imbalanced and incomplete presentations of what the Scriptures teach.

Consider the dimensions of Peter's sermon at Pentecost (Acts 2:14–40). His preaching is *biblical*, quoting Joel 2, Psalm 16, and Psalm 110, and alluding to other Old Testament texts. At points, he explains a text he has quoted. For example, he shows how David's words that God will not "suffer thine Holy One to see corruption" (Acts 2:27) cannot apply to David (who had died, and whose body had decayed), but prophetically pointed to the resurrection of Christ (vv. 27–31). He does this through

---

10. Quoted in Joseph Belcher, *George Whitefield: A Biography* (New York: American Tract Society, [1857]), 507.

biblical theology, appealing to the promises of God's covenant with David.

Peter's preaching is also *doctrinal*, affirming and declaring "the determinate counsel and foreknowledge of God" (v. 23), his sovereign decree, by which God used the hands of wicked men to put his Son to death for our salvation (vv. 22–23). He teaches Christ's resurrection and exaltation to God's right hand (vv. 32–33), both as historical facts and as the demonstration that, by the will of God, Jesus is "both Lord and Christ," endowed with the full measure of the Holy Spirit (vv. 33, 36). So his sermon addresses the doctrines of the eternal decree, its execution in providence, God's covenant promise, Christ's incarnation, his ministry on earth, his humiliation in death as an offering for sin, and his exaltation in his resurrection and ascension to the throne of heaven, as well as the person and work of the Holy Spirit in relation to the person and work of Christ.

The Pentecost sermon is also *experiential* in its content, explaining and justifying from the Holy Scriptures the disciples' experience of the outpouring of the Holy Spirit (v. 16). It is experiential in its spiritual discrimination, declaring the wickedness of those who killed Jesus as the enemies of God and of his Christ, but comforting and commending those who repented and identified with Christ as the recipients of the Spirit (v. 38). It is also experiential in its effect, piercing the hearts of many hearers so that they cry out, "What shall we do [to be saved]?" (v. 37).

Peter's sermon is also *practical*, commanding his hearers, "Repent, and be baptized every one of you in the name of Jesus Christ for the remission of sins" (v. 38). The application is far longer than the message recorded in Acts, for the text says that Peter exhorts them with "many other words" to save themselves "from this untoward [wicked] generation" (v. 40).

Think of how incomplete Peter's sermon would be without all of these elements. What if the whole sermon were nothing but experiential in its emphasis? Without the appeal to the witness of Scripture, he would have no authority with his fellow Jews. They would regard him as a false prophet speaking his own opinions and words. Without the practical dimension, he would give no answers to the burning question, "What shall we do to be saved?" Without the doctrinal dimension, his hearers would not see that the spiritual phenomena of Pentecost indicates that

God's sovereign plan has culminated in Jesus, who, as the risen Christ, is enthroned as Lord of all. The sermon would not center on Christ, but on mere phenomena or abstract concepts.

We need to preach sermons enriched by all of these elements: biblical, doctrinal, experiential, and practical. There may be people in your congregation who think real preaching consists in only one or two of these matters. You may take some heat for "wasting time" by bringing in the other elements. But stick to your guns and patiently bear with such complaints. There is something about all four of these elements working together that resonates with true believers over time.

Be patient with people who criticize you for giving them balanced Reformed experiential preaching. Love them. Remember that they may not have had the benefits of the books you have read or the teaching you have heard. How long did it take you to get to the understanding of preaching that you have now? Give them time. Over the years, the preaching will bring more balance to their lives, and they will hunger for and value preaching that is biblical, doctrinal, experiential, and practical.

Embracing Diversity in Application

In 1 Thessalonians 5:14, Paul commands, "Now we exhort you, brethren, warn them that are unruly, comfort the feebleminded [faint-hearted], support the weak, be patient toward all men." Here Scripture calls us to apply God's truth differently to people in different spiritual conditions, yet always with love. We saw in previous chapters how William Perkins and the Dutch divines employed various classification schemes to rightly divide the Word and to give each hearer his proper portion. These schemes placed people in categories of spiritual condition so that the preacher could make specific application to each one. Such methods have the strength of such application, but also involve the dangers of rigidity and repetition in application.

John Jennings (c. 1687–1723), a nonconforming minister and tutor of Philip Doddridge (1702–1751), wrote a tract addressing "particular preaching" that is quite helpful in this regard.[11] Jennings does not lock people into categories, but he does classify their spiritual situations and reminds us that we should address them specifically. In

---

11. John Jennings, "Of Particular and Experimental Preaching," in *The Christian Pastor's Manual*, ed. John Brown (1826; repr., Ligonier, PA: Soli Deo Gloria, 1991), 47–62.

each sermon, he says, "there might properly arise in the application of most subjects, thoughts distinctly proper" to a great "variety of characters and persons," and "particular" and "lively" applications to each case "are the closest, most weighty, and most useful parts of the application."[12] He gives several examples. According to Jennings, ministers must at times:

1. Reprove "scoffers and confute gainsayers," as Scripture does with words such as: "Behold, ye despisers, and wonder, and perish" (Acts 13:41); or, "Thou fool, that which thou sowest is not quickened, except it die" (1 Cor. 15:36).

2. Address worldly, ignorant sinners in a way intended to make them fearful of what may happen if they do not repent: "Woe to them that are at ease" (Amos 6:1); or, "Ye stiffnecked and uncircumcised in heart" (Acts 7:51).

3. Point convicted sinners to Christ: "If ye will enquire, enquire ye: return, come" (Isa. 21:12); or, "Repent, and be baptized every one of you in the name of Jesus Christ for the remission of sins, and ye shall receive the gift of the Holy Ghost" (Acts 2:38).

4. "Reason with the moralist" who trusts in his own righteousness, showing that "we are all as an unclean thing, and all our righteousnesses are as filthy rags" (Isa. 64:6); or, "Therefore by the deeds of the law there shall no flesh be justified in his sight: for by the law is the knowledge of sin" (Rom. 3:20).

5. "Rebuke and expose presumptuous hypocrites": "Shew me thy faith without thy works. . . . The devils also believe, and tremble" (James 2:18–19).

6. "Rouse and encourage Christians who have but little strength": "Ye are dull of hearing. For when for the time ye ought to be teachers, ye have need that one teach you again which be the first principles of the oracles of God; and are become such as have need of milk, and not of strong meat" (Heb. 5:11–12).

7. Stir up backsliding Christians who are awakened, exhorting them to "be watchful, and strengthen the things which remain, that are ready to die" (Rev. 3:2).

8. Encourage "persecuted and afflicted" believers by invoking God's promise: "When thou passest through the waters, I will be with thee;

---

12. Jennings, "Of Particular and Experimental Preaching," 52–53.

and through the rivers, they shall not overflow thee: when thou walkest through the fire, thou shalt not be burned; neither shall the flame kindle upon thee" (Isa. 43:2).

9. Teach the mature and assured Christians, exhorting them "to be tender to the weak": "Him that is weak in the faith receive ye. . . . Let not him that eateth despise him that eateth not" (Rom. 14:1, 3).

10. Point those "groaning" under a sense of their own sinfulness to Christ: "All we like sheep have gone astray; we have turned every one to his own way; and the LORD hath laid on him the iniquity of us all" (Isa. 53:6); or, "If any man sin, we have an advocate with the Father, Jesus Christ the righteous" (1 John 2:1).

11. Comfort the broken and humbled "penitent," reminding them that God has said, "To this man will I look, even to him that is poor and of a contrite spirit, and trembleth at my word" (Isa. 66:2).

12. Guide those who lack "direction," exhorting them to pray, "O that my ways were directed to keep thy statutes!" (Ps. 119:5), and reminding them that "if any of you lack wisdom, let him ask of God, that giveth to all men liberally, and upbraideth not; and it shall be given him" (James 1:5).

13. Help those suffering spiritual desertion, exhorting them to go on trusting God in their distress: "Who is among you that feareth the LORD, that obeyeth the voice of his servant, that walketh in darkness, and hath no light? Let him trust in the name of the LORD, and stay upon his God" (Isa. 50:10).[13]

This is not to say that each sermon should address thirteen different spiritual cases. Studying each text of Scripture and knowing those to whom you preach will indicate some appropriate possibilities for application in each sermon. However, lists such as these are helpful because they enable us to step back and examine our sermons to see if our applications address a wide range of spiritual cases. It's easy to get stuck in a rut in making applications, always addressing the same cases or the same spiritual problems. Cultivate diversity.

Isaac Watts (1674–1748) commended Jennings's tract by observing: "With how much more efficacy does the Word of God impress the conscience, when every hearer finds himself described without the preacher's personal knowledge of him? When a word of conviction, advice, or

---

13. Jennings, "Of Particular and Experimental Preaching," 53–58.

comfort, is spoken so pertinently to his own case, that he takes it as directed to himself?"[14] It is a great blessing to preach in such a manner that each person in the congregation believes that God has specifically addressed him or her.

Conclusion

I opened this chapter with a call to seek balance in preaching and ended with a call to pursue richness and diversity. That's because balance arises from embracing the wealth of Scripture in its entirety. Whether we are dealing with objective truth and subjective experience; divine sovereignty and human responsibility; biblical, doctrinal, experiential, and practical preaching; or applications addressed to the various spiritual conditions of believers and unbelievers, the solution is not "either/or" but "both/and." As a result, as we preach through various portions of Scripture, we furnish the congregation a nutritious feast with many dishes. The congregation is not in danger of becoming sickly or dying because their spiritual diet lacks an important element or nutrient. Instead, the church grows into wholistic maturity, "unto the measure of the stature of the fulness of Christ" (Eph. 4:13).

---

14. Isaac Watts, preface (1723) to John Jennings, *Two Discourses: The First, Of Preaching Christ; The Second, of Particular and Experimental Preaching* (Boston: n.p., 1740), x.

21

Application Starts
with the Preacher

You cannot become an experiential preacher by mere head knowledge or book knowledge. The question then arises, how did the men of the past become effective experiential preachers? And how can we do so today? As I have shown in this book, a large part of becoming a better experiential preacher lies in becoming a better applier of God's Word. So we have a great need for personal application of the Word to our own hearts and lives.

John Broadus (1827–1895) says that application is "not merely an appendage" tacked onto the teaching, but "is the main thing to be done"—the goal of all preaching.[1] What, then, is application? Broadus says that it is showing "how the subject applies to the persons addressed, what practical instructions it offers them, what practical demands it makes upon them." Notice the emphasis on being practical, by which he means "bearing down on the feelings and the will" with a focused thrust to move the hearer in a particular direction.[2]

How does a preacher grow in his ability to make spiritual application to his hearers? To answer this question, we need to ask and answer more questions, such as:

---

1. John A. Broadus, *A Treatise on the Preparation and Delivery of Sermons*, ed. Edwin C. Dargan (New York: A. C. Armstrong & Son, 1898), 245.
2. Broadus, *The Preparation and Delivery of Sermons*, 246.

- What kind of ministry leads to effective application (chap. 21)?
- How do we apply specific areas of doctrine (chap. 22)?
- How should we preach Christ and the gospel to the heart (chap. 23)?
- How can we preach so as to promote holiness in our listeners' lives (chap. 24)?

Over the next few chapters, we will discuss these questions. In this chapter, we take up the first: What kind of ministry leads to effective application? To answer, we need to take a step back from the sermon itself and consider how your whole ministry can equip (or hinder) you to apply the Scriptures experientially.

Effective application of God's truth to human experience requires a lifestyle of walking with God, continuing study, learning about human nature, praying continually for the anointing of the Holy Spirit, speaking naturally from the heart, and cultivating pure motivation. Let's examine each of these elements in turn.

Walk Closely with God

Life and ministry are intertwined. Holy Scripture describes the character of Barnabas by saying that "he was a good man, and full of the Holy Ghost and of faith," and then it says that "much people" were "added unto the Lord" (Acts 11:24). This man's Spirit-filled life overflowed into a fruitful, Spirit-empowered ministry. So how can we expect to deliver spiritual preaching if we are not spiritual men? James Braga writes, "Preaching which warms the heart and stirs the experience is not born in the cold atmosphere of intellectualism but in intimate and continual fellowship with the Lord."[3] If our sermons are to be radiant with light and heat, then our lives first must glow. That is not just mysticism, but a call for the cultivation of biblically informed warmth that comes from a close life with God.

Thomas Brooks (1608–1680) says: "A preacher's life should be a commentary upon his doctrine; his practice should be the counterpane [counterpart] of his sermons. Heavenly doctrines should always be adorned with a heavenly life."[4]

---

3. James Braga, *How to Prepare Bible Messages*, rev. ed. (Portland, OR: Multnomah, 1981), 207. I am indebted to Braga for several thoughts in this chapter.
4. Thomas Brooks, "Epistle Dedicatory," in "The Crown and Glory of Christianity: Or, Holiness, the Only Way to Happiness," in *The Works of Thomas Brooks*, ed. Alexander B. Grosart (Edinburgh: Banner of Truth, 2001), 4:24.

You cannot be an effective experiential preacher if you live at a distance from God. It is simply impossible; you can't fake a close, personal relationship with God for very long. Perhaps you can be a visiting minister at another church for a Lord's Day or two and come across very well, but people will see through you after a while. The truth will come out.

We know this as pastors. You might visit someone's home and be very impressed. But then, a few weeks later, a young man from the family seeks counseling, and you discover that the family's home life is a disaster. Likewise, the people of the church will come to know you. This is especially true of those with whom you work closely, such as staff members and fellow office bearers.

After you have served in the church for several years, the people will have heard your best sermons (and some of your worst). The novelty and excitement will have worn off long ago. However, if you live close to God and your people feel it, that will cover a multitude of your infirmities or weaknesses. They will still be able to say, "At least we have a man of God in the pulpit." When they have a fundamental respect for you, they will be willing to listen to what you have to say, or rather, what God's Word has to say through you.

John Owen says that a minister needs an "experience of the power of the things we preach to others." He continues: "No man preaches that sermon so well to others who does not preach it first to his own heart. . . . Unless he finds the power of it in his own heart, he cannot have any ground of confidence that it will have power in the hearts of others. It is an easier thing to bring our heads to preach than our hearts to preach."[5]

Do you radiate genuine and authentic Christianity? That is a fundamental question for a Christian pastor. When authenticity is missing, nothing can compensate for it—no amount of giftedness or exegetical skill. A sincere walk with God is not sufficient for pastoral ministry, but it is absolutely essential and foundational for all else.

To live close to God, we must make habitual use of the means of grace ourselves. There are many disciplines to cultivate in the Christian life, and I would highlight one in particular: *meditation on the Scriptures*. To be an experiential preacher, you must be in the Scriptures and the Scriptures must be in you. This is the path to effectual prayer and a productive life. Our Lord said: "If ye abide in me, and my words abide

---

5. John Owen, "The Duty of a Pastor," in *The Works of John Owen*, ed. William H. Goold (New York: Robert Carter & Bros., 1851), 9:455.

in you, ye shall ask what ye will, and it shall be done unto you. Herein is my Father glorified, that ye bear much fruit; so shall ye be my disciples" (John 15:7–8). Meditation on the Word is the only alternative to following the world and the only way to drink from streams of living water—the blessed life (Ps. 1:1–3).

Therefore, be diligent in reading the Bible so that you feed your soul every day. Be systematic in reading the Bible, so that you regularly and continually read through all the Scriptures. They are all inspired of God and profitable for the man of God. The Word of God is the heartbeat of our sanctification, the lifeline of our souls, and the foundation of our ministries. Jesus warned the people of his day, "Ye do err, not knowing the scriptures" (Matt. 22:29). What a tragedy if our people have to say that of us as ministers. Rather, we should be able to say with the prophet, "Thy words were found, and I did eat them; and thy word was unto me the joy and rejoicing of mine heart" (Jer. 15:16). Would your wife, children, and best friends say that you are a man who loves the Word of God as men love their favorite foods?

Eating is an apt metaphor for meditation. We must do more than look at what is on our plates. We must ingest it, chew it, digest it, and assimilate it. We feed our souls with the Word in much the same way. Thomas Manton writes, "Faith is lean and ready to starve unless it be fed with continual meditation on the promises."[6]

Let me give you some Puritan directions for meditation.[7] Pray for the Holy Spirit to help you. You might use Psalm 119:18: "Open thou mine eyes, that I may behold wondrous things out of thy law." Read a portion of the Scriptures. Focus on one verse or a doctrine derived from a particular verse or passage, something applicable to your life. Repeat the verse or doctrine to yourself several times to get it into your memory. Think about what it means and how you might illustrate it. Preach the truth to yourself to stir up your affections toward God. Direct your will toward God's will. Turn your meditations into prayers and songs to the Lord. It also helps to write out your thoughts and prayers in a journal. Journaling focuses and clarifies your thoughts. It also creates a valuable record of God's dealings with your soul that can encourage you or your children later.

---

6. Thomas Manton, "Sermon 1 on Genesis 24:63," in *The Complete Works of Thomas Manton* (London: James Nisbet, 1874), 17:270.

7. Condensed from "The Puritan Practice of Meditation," in Joel R. Beeke, *Puritan Reformed Spirituality* (Darlington, England: Evangelical Press, 2006), 73–100.

Meditation weaves the Bible into the texture of our souls. It imparts true wisdom for the spiritual battle. Psalm 119:97–99 says: "O how love I thy law! It is my meditation all the day. Thou through thy commandments hast made me wiser than mine enemies: for they are ever with me. I have more understanding than all my teachers: for thy testimonies are my meditation." Meditation also primes the pump of our prayers. It enables us to pray God's Word back to him, and God loves to hear his own voice.

Study Books

Reading and meditating on Scripture to feed your mind and soul is necessary, but reading and studying helpful books to sharpen, inform, and expand your mind and soul is also very important. Ezra 7:9 says of Ezra that "the good hand of his God" was "upon him." God did mighty things through Ezra. Why? Verse 10 explains: "For Ezra had prepared his heart to seek the law of the LORD, and to do it, and to teach in Israel statutes and judgments." Even though Ezra was already "a ready scribe in the law of Moses" (v. 6), he was still determined to search and study the Word of God. Like him, we should never stop studying.

As a man called to give himself to doctrine, the preacher must engage in theological study with greater thoroughness than the average Christian. Just as a carpenter or a mechanic buys tools, so the preacher should buy books and build a library. Allow the great teachers of the past to become your mentors. Select a master, such as John Calvin, Richard Sibbes, or John Bunyan, and read his writings for a year or more, soaking in his theology and especially his sermons. Read his biography to learn about his life. In seminary, you invest a large amount of time and money to sit at the feet of your professors. After seminary, why not continue your education under the Reformers and Puritans?

I would especially encourage you to give your life to studying old Reformed experiential books. These will both inform your mind and enrich your heart. It is not a coincidence that the heart of this book consists in the examination of the preaching of Reformers, Puritans, and Dutch Further Reformation divines. We live in an era of unparalleled access to great old writings in English. Make full use of this opportunity. So many books that pastors read might win short-term popularity contests, but they have little biblical substance or spiritual depth. While solid Reformed books are being written now, few breathe the atmosphere of heaven like those of the old writers. That's not being nostalgic. Many of these men wrote in times when the Holy Spirit was poured out in a high degree upon the church for its reformation and revival.

The best way to make your reading profitable is to mingle it with prayer. In other words, read for a while and then pray about what you have read, then read some more, and pray again. This approach to reading helps you think about what you have read, and it engages the power of God to bring your study to fruition in your life and the lives of others. You also would benefit from underlining or writing in the margins or by making an outline as you read. (If you are writing in an old book, use a mechanical pencil so that the ink does not bleed through in years to come and obscure the text.) If you don't stop to pray or take notes to keep yourself engaged mentally and spiritually, you may find that your eyes have passed over the pages but you have profited little from them.

In order to diversify your studies, think of yourself as operating on three levels of ministry. The first level aims at people significantly below you intellectually. Studies for this level of ministry include preparation to catechize children in the basics of the faith or to evangelize people at a jail or mission. Studying and teaching the most basic expressions of the faith, such as the Heidelberg Catechism or the Westminster Shorter Catechism, or preparing elementary gospel messages will sharpen your ability to express biblical truth in concise and simple terms. This is a great gift. Some brilliant theologians would have been much more useful if they could have communicated with more simplicity.

The second level includes your regular ministry functions, such as preparing a sermon or teaching an adult class. Never assume that you know enough already to write your message. Broaden and deepen your understanding with the thoughts of wise men. Read commentaries and sermons on the text and portions of theological and experiential works that address specific topics touched on in your message. Reading Christian biographies will also enrich your preaching with illustrations, as well as give you a deeper knowledge of the human heart and the problems of life.

The third level (the one where most ministers fail) engages those on a level beyond you. Preparation for ministry on this level might mean reading books or listening to lectures about a subject of which you know little. It might involve reading books or articles written on an academic level that challenges you. This is hard, but if you don't do anything to stretch yourself, you will stagnate. The irony is that reading challenging books will stimulate you. The mind that is not being challenged is like a body that is not being exercised; the result is stagnation and deterioration.

Study People

One great locus of theological study is human nature. However, we learn about human nature not merely by studying books, but also by observing people through the spiritual eyeglasses of the Book. God's wisdom gives us insight to draw out men's deep things. Proverbs 20:5 says, "Counsel in the heart of man is like deep water; but a man of understanding will draw it out."

Knowing people begins with self-awareness. Here the saying applies: "Know thyself." If we would help others, then we must study our own hearts. To speak wisely to the experience of others, we must understand how our own souls act and react. By entering into combat with our pride, self-centeredness, worldly lusts, and unbelief, we discover the twistings and windings of the heart. By seeking comfort in our sorrows, we learn what sweetens the bitter. People exist in great variety, but are fundamentally the same. Knowing yourself makes you perceptive toward other people as well. When we refuse to grapple with our own sins but hypocritically ignore them, then the logs in our eyes prevent us from seeing what others need (Matt. 7:3–5).

This is not easy. The Scriptures warn, "The heart is deceitful above all things, and desperately wicked: who can know it?" (Jer. 17:9). On this point, we can agree with Benjamin Franklin, who writes, "There are three things extremely hard: steel, a diamond and to know one's self."[8] We do not naturally want to know ourselves as we really are. We cherish our illusions. But Holy Scripture penetrates and exposes the heart. Hebrews 4:12 says, "For the word of God is quick, and powerful, and sharper than any twoedged sword, piercing even to the dividing asunder of soul and spirit, and of the joints and marrow, and is a discerner of the thoughts and intents of the heart."

The wise preacher also carefully observes the conduct and needs of various groups in the church: the old and the young, the men and the

---

8. Benjamin Franklin, *Autobiography, Poor Richard, Letters*, ed. Ainsworth D. Spofford (New York: D. Appleton, 1904), 295.

women, and various ethnic and social clusters. We all relate to certain categories of people more easily than others. Here again, we must stretch ourselves beyond the ordinary pleasantries of conversation. Take a genuine interest in people. Ask intelligent questions and listen to the answers you receive. Play with the children. Visit the elderly. Find out what is important to them. Learn what hurts them and what tempts them. Earn their trust and keep their confidences. Love them all, and they will open up to you increasingly over time.

Phillips Brooks says: "These three rules seem to have in them the practical sum of the whole matter. I beg you to remember them and apply them with all the wisdom that God gives you. First, have as few congregations as you can [that is, stay in one place for a long time]. Second, know your congregation as thoroughly as you can. Third, know your congregation so largely and deeply that in knowing it you shall know humanity."[9]

Though you should never target a sermon application toward a specific person in the church, understanding the people will immeasurably enrich your preaching. What is it like to be a young adult and receive lewd or harassing comments from peers? What happens to a man's soul when he loses his job in his forties and is still out of work two years later? How does a grandfather feel when his grandchildren are suffering from their parents' divorce? How does an adult woman find comfort when she is exhausted from being the primary caregiver for an elderly parent? You must learn these things by watching, listening, and loving.

Remember, a sermon is not a performance. It is a gift to someone. To whom are you giving this sermon? I often look over the congregation before I preach and let a sense of their needs wash over me as a wave. Paul writes to the Philippians, "I have you in my heart" (Phil. 1:7). He also says, "I thank my God upon every remembrance of you" (v. 3). One test of how much you know and love your people is your private prayers for them. You should pray regularly through the membership list, mentioning each person's needs by name. Then you will rise from your knees and enter the pulpit with the power of love and compassion.

Pray in Continual Dependence upon the Spirit

Our Lord taught us that the Spirit gives life; the flesh profits nothing (John 6:63). Unless a person is born of the Spirit, he cannot even see the spiritual

---

9. Phillips Brooks, *Lectures on Preaching* (New York: E. P. Dutton, 1891), 190.

realities of the kingdom (John 3:3, 5). No one can be saved without a heartfelt confession that Jesus is Lord, but no one can make such a confession apart from the Holy Spirit (Rom. 10:9; 1 Cor. 12:3). Braga says, "In the last analysis persuasion is entirely the work of the Holy Spirit."[10]

The church needs Spirit-filled preachers. Only when we are filled with the Spirit do we speak the Word of God with boldness (Acts 4:31). Micah exclaims, "But truly I am full of power by the Spirit of the Lord, and of judgment, and of might, to declare unto Jacob his transgression, and to Israel his sin" (Mic. 3:8). A tall ship might be loaded with treasure, but it will go nowhere unless the wind fills its sails. Only the wind of the Spirit can blow the treasures of Scripture into the harbors of men's hearts. Thomas Watson says, "Ministers knock at the door of men's hearts, the Spirit comes with a key and opens the door."[11]

Therefore, we must pray. Paul writes, "Finally, brethren, pray for us, that the word of the Lord may have free course, and be glorified, even as it is with you" (2 Thess. 3:1). Robert Traill observes that some ministers of lesser ability may be more successful than others with more gifts, "not because they preach better, so much as because they pray more." He comments, "Many good sermons are lost for lack of much prayer in study."[12]

Let us plead with God before we plead with men. The story is told of how Gryffyth of Caernarvon came to preach at a place in Wales. The congregation had gathered, but the preacher was absent, so they sent a girl to get him from the room where he was staying. She returned and said that she did not think Mr. Gryffyth would be coming soon because through the door she had overheard him saying to someone, "I will not go unless you come with me." "Yes," replied the man who had sent her, "he will come, and I warrant the Other will come too." And when Gryffyth came, the Spirit indeed came with him and granted extraordinary power to transform lives.[13]

J. C. Weststrate, my first instructor in theology, used to say that we need prayer in the study and in the pulpit. He was not referring to the public pastoral prayer in the worship service. Even while we are

---

10. Braga, *How to Prepare Bible Messages*, 211.

11. Thomas Watson, *Body of Practical Divinity*, in *The Select Works of the Rev. Thomas Watson* (New York: Robert Carter, 1855), 148.

12. Robert Traill, "By What Means May Ministers Best Win Souls?" in *The Works of the Late Reverend Robert Traill* (Edinburgh: J. Ogle, M. Ogle, J. Steven, R. Ogle, T. Hamilton, and T. Johnson, 1810), 1:246.

13. Paxton Hood, *Christmas Evans: The Preacher of Wild Wales* (London: Hodder and Stoughton, 1881), 9–10.

preaching, we should continue in a posture of prayerful dependence upon the Lord. If Nehemiah sent short, pungent prayers to heaven even while publicly attending upon the king (Neh. 2:4), should not we launch short, secret prayers during the service, such as, "Help me, Lord," or, "Grant freedom and power, Lord"? Whenever we sense our inadequacy or the congregation's inattentiveness—or, conversely, whenever we have an unusual liberty from the Spirit—let us seek the Lord's blessing on our preaching.

Only God can make the harvest ripe, but we can pray for rain. Isaac Watts says: "Water the seed sown, not only with public, but secret prayer. Plead with God importunately [with pressing urgency], that He would not suffer you to labour in vain."[14]

Ephesians 6:18 says we should pray "always with all prayer and supplication in the Spirit, and watching thereunto with all perseverance and supplication for all saints." Perhaps the hardest part of that verse to implement is "with all perseverance." It is one thing to launch a ministry with fervent prayer. It is another to maintain fervent prayer after you have asked for a dozen fish but feel as if you have gotten a dozen stones instead—or a dozen snakes. Christ understands this temptation, and teaches us through the contrast of the unjust judge that "men ought always to pray, and not to faint" (Luke 18:1). Our Father is not a cruel or uncaring deity, but a true Father to his children, who hears their cries and gives them what they need (Luke 11:11).

It is striking that immediately after the parable of the unjust judge, we find another parable about prayer: the Pharisee and the tax collector (Luke 18:9–14). Could it be that our temptation to give up on praying with all our heart arises from our pride and self-righteousness? Don't we sometimes think, "How could God not give me what I've asked for after all that I've done for him and all that I've prayed?" Christ says to us, "Every one that exalteth himself shall be abased; and he that humbleth himself shall be exalted" (Luke 18:14). If we will let the burden of unanswered prayers drive us lower in humility before God, he will honor us in due time. Often God's delays drive us to pray less for visible and measurable goods, and more for the Holy Spirit. Such prayers he will surely answer at the right time, for he is pleased to give us the kingdom (Luke 11:13; 12:32). Don't give up, brethren. Persevere in prayer.

---

14. Isaac Watts, "Rules for the Preacher's Conduct," in *The Christian Pastor's Manual*, ed. John Brown (1826; repr., Ligonier, PA: Soli Deo Gloria, 1991), 232.

Speak Naturally from the Heart

After the spiritual topics we have covered so far in this chapter, talking about one's voice may seem pedantic. But we are not angels. We cannot communicate by telepathy. We have bodies, our listeners have bodies, and the voice and the ear play a crucial role in communication. At all costs, avoid anything fake or artificial, but rather communicate the godly affections of your heart through the tones of your voice.

Some teachers of homiletics would tell you to preach in an ordinary, conversational tone, even a casual tone. There may be points in a sermon where this would be appropriate. But preaching is far different from having a casual chat with a friend in a restaurant. We speak of eternal matters as the messengers of Christ. We are not just *sharing*. We are *proclaiming* the message given to us as authorized heralds of the King. Therefore, we should speak in a tone that carries a sense of earnestness, humility, and love mingled with authority. Braga says, "There is no eloquence greater than the natural and gracious speech that flows from a warm and loving heart."[15]

Paul writes, "Knowing therefore the terror of the Lord, we persuade men" (2 Cor. 5:11). Gravity and seriousness in our voices are not things we simply produce upon demand as an actor might. These qualities must come from having our hearts gripped by fear of the Lord and an awareness of the inevitable judgment of all men by the Lord Christ (v. 10). Such sacred reverence moves preachers to "beseech" and "pray," that is, to earnestly beg and plead with men to be "reconciled to God" (v. 20). This is not pitiful, whiny begging. It is the authoritative and loving pleading of "ambassadors for Christ," through whom the Lord speaks (v. 20). The "day of salvation" is here (6:2), and the day of judgment is coming.

Albert Martin says, "Genuine urgency is the mother of true eloquence."[16] He compares the preacher to a man trying to wake people up so that they can escape from a burning building. It is an apt metaphor. If we are confusing and incoherent, no one will understand our warning. But if we are casual and always quiet or even apologetic, no listeners will seriously believe they are in terrible danger—no matter how clear our explanations of the nature of fire may be.

---

15. Braga, *How to Prepare Bible Messages*, 211.
16. Albert N. Martin, *What's Wrong with Preaching Today?* (Edinburgh: Banner of Truth, 1967), 26.

I hesitate to criticize any man for the sound of his voice. But if we love the people to whom we preach, we should seek to speak in a way that grasps their attention and holds it. Some of us, by personality or tradition, tend to preach with voices that are annoying or hard to hear— speaking too quietly, whining, yelling, or droning in a tedious monotone. Generally, you should not be self-conscious about your voice when you preach; let it naturally express your heart. But if you discover that you habitually speak in a manner that is an obstacle to people listening to the Word, then make an effort to change.

Your goal should be to sound like yourself in the pulpit, not an imitation of someone else. Because speaking is your vocation from the Master, tune your vocal instrument to serve the Composer well. Develop a strong, serious tone of voice that you can sustain, a tone that engages the attention of the listener. Be sensitive to the people and what they are used to hearing. Also be sensitive to your limits so that you do not strain your voice. Remember that preaching is not a sprint. You are a marathon runner who needs to pace his voice to go the distance of several decades of preaching.

Cultivate Pure Motivation

I will address personal holiness of character in a later chapter, but here, as we enter the last part of our consideration of an all-round ministry that promotes experiential application, I want to address the matter of the purity of our motivation in the ministry. The preacher must be a God-centered visionary, and Christ teaches us, "Blessed are the pure in heart: for they shall see God" (Matt. 5:8). Without purity of heart, our ministries aim at pleasing men, not God, and we already have our reward (Matt. 6:5). On judgment day, what a disappointment that would be!

Martin identifies three key areas of motivation for the preacher: the fear of the Lord, the love of God's truth, and the love of people.[17] First, we must fear God. Do we study and preach the true character of God? John Brown writes, "Everything about God is fitted to fill the mind with awe."[18] Do we preach Christ crucified? Brown says, "Nothing is so well fitted to put the fear of God, which will preserve men from offending

---

17. Martin, *What's Wrong with Preaching Today?* 16–19.
18. John Brown, *Expository Discourses on the First Epistle of the Apostle Peter* (New York: Robert Carter and Brothers, 1855), 321 [1 Pet. 2:17].

him, into the heart, as an enlightened view of the cross of Christ."[19] Nowhere do we see the attributes of divine glory, especially his justice in punishing sin and his grace shown to sinners, shining more brightly than in Christ's death for our sins.

The fear of God is a mighty engine to drive our ministries forward: "Knowing therefore the terror of the Lord, we persuade men" (2 Cor. 5:11). It is our wisdom, for, "The fear of the LORD is the beginning of wisdom" (Ps. 111:10). Though, like Jeremiah, we may feel like children, the Lord says to us, "Be not afraid of their faces," and promises, "They shall fight against thee; but they shall not prevail against thee; for I am with thee . . . to deliver thee" (Jer. 1:6, 8, 17, 19). Like Ezekiel, though we face men who are "impudent and hardhearted," the Lord can give us foreheads like flint to preach to them (Ezek. 3:7–9).

On the other hand, "The fear of man bringeth a snare" (Prov. 29:25). Martin writes: "One of the elements of powerful preaching is preaching as a man that has been liberated. Liberated from what? From the ensnaring effects of the fear of man."[20] Effective preachers may feel like a bundle of fears at times, but by the grace of God they stand against their fears and come out as more than conquerors. Their eyes are fixed on Christ. Brown says, "It matters little to them that the world frowns on them, if he smiles; and it matters little to them that the world smiles, if he frowns."[21] When John Knox was buried after a life full of boldness in the face of opposition and danger, the Earl of Morton said, "Here lies a man who, in his life, never feared the face of man."[22] May God grant that the same commendation might be true of us.

Second, we must love the truth of Scripture. Most of us love peace, but the Lord says, "Love the truth *and* peace" (Zech. 8:19). Those who sacrifice truth for the sake of peace lose both, but the Bible says, "Great peace have they which love thy law" (Ps. 119:165).

We live in an age when people are perishing because they have "received not the love of the truth, that they might be saved" (2 Thess. 2:10). We are no different than our forebears. God said through Hosea millennia ago, "My people are destroyed for lack of knowledge: because thou hast rejected knowledge, I will also reject thee" (Hos. 4:6):

19. Brown, *The First Epistle of Peter*, 325 [1 Pet. 2:17].
20. Martin, *What's Wrong with Preaching Today?* 17.
21. Brown, *The First Epistle of Peter*, 103 [1 Pet. 1:17].
22. Quoted in David Calderwood, *The History of the Kirk of Scotland*, ed. Thomas Thomson (Edinburgh: Wodrow Society, 1843), 3:242.

Jeremiah recorded the words of the Lord: "They refuse to know me" (Jer. 9:6).

But the wise preacher knows that the only thing worth boasting about is not money, intelligence, or power, but that we know the Lord (Jer. 9:23–24). The godly preacher loves truth not because teaching it is his job, not out of intellectual pride, and not to promote his particular theological party. He loves truth because he loves God, and by the truth of Christ, God brings men near to himself. Though to some that truth is the fragrance of life and to others the stench of death, the ministry of preaching spreads the knowledge of Christ everywhere it can (2 Cor. 2:14–16).

Third, we must love people. Our hearts must go out to people in a longing to see them glorify God and enjoy him forever. We must genuinely care for them, and not see them as pawns to be moved about on the board so that we can win the modern ministerial game of "success" through numbers. If you do not love people, I seriously appeal to you to leave the ministry—or never go into it. How can you be an ambassador for Christ if you do not share in the love of Christ? Without love, all our knowledge is nothing; indeed, we are nothing (1 Cor. 13:2).

Charles Bridges writes: "Love is the grand distinctive mark of our office. It exhibits salvation flowing from the bosom of Divine mercy. It sets forth a most tender Father, a bleeding Saviour, and a faithful Comforter; so that the spirit of every discourse should be—'God is love.'"[23] Even when we pronounce divine judgment against sin, let us do it with a trembling, compassionate, broken heart. Do we not deserve the same judgment? Then let us speak with humility and sympathy, not with arrogance, as if we ourselves were the holy Judge.

Love is the essence of divine life, and love makes our preaching more lively. Bridges says, "Love is the life, power, soul, and spirit of pulpit eloquence."[24] Love gives us the tender affection of a mother and the tough benevolence of a father (1 Thess. 2:7, 11). Love especially empowers preaching when it sees people through eternal eyes, as sheep without a shepherd, harassed and helpless—in desperate need, yet without God and Christ in the world. Martin says, "We must have such a love that it will drive us to a sense of responsibility to do all within our power to

---

23. Charles Bridges, *The Christian Ministry* (London: Banner of Truth, 1967), 333.
24. Bridges, *The Christian Ministry*, 337.

make the truth of God live to them."[25] We cannot make them alive, but we can pour out our lives in a lively ministry.

It is true that your love for a flock grows as you spend years caring for them. The disappointments and disagreements can actually deepen the bond when you persevere and see them through together. It is rather like the deepening love between a father and his children through the years. So a seminary student or a young minister rarely has the depth of affection for people that a veteran should have. But the root of the matter must be there.

Only love motivates us to persevere in calling people to be reconciled to God and to walk closely with him. It is not an easy calling. Philip Doddridge says, "It is my desire, not to entertain an auditory [audience] with pretty lively things, which is comparatively easy, but to come close to their consciences, to awaken them to a real sense of their spiritual concerns, to bring them to God, and keep them continually near to him; which, to me at least, is an exceeding hard thing."[26]

But love is the most rewarding sacrifice in the world. In the end, we will think nothing of our sacrifices, only of Christ's sacrifice for our reward. David Livingstone (1813–1873), a renowned missionary to Africa, says:

> For my own part, I have never ceased to rejoice that God has ap-
> pointed me to such an office. People talk of the sacrifice I have made
> in spending so much of my life in Africa. Can that be called a sacrifice
> which is simply paid back as a small part of a great debt owing to
> our God, which we can never repay? Is that a sacrifice which brings
> its own blest reward in healthful activity, the consciousness of doing
> good, peace of mind, and a bright hope of a glorious destiny here-
> after? Away with the word in such a view and with such a thought!
> It is emphatically no sacrifice. Say rather it is a privilege. Anxiety,
> sickness, suffering, or danger now and then with a foregoing of the
> common conveniences and charities of this life, may make us pause
> and cause the spirit to waver and the soul to sink; but let this only be
> for a moment. All these are nothing when compared with the glory
> which shall be revealed in and for us. I never made a sacrifice.[27]

---

25. Martin, *What's Wrong with Preaching Today?* 18.

26. Quoted in Job Orton, *Memoirs of the Life, Character, and Writings, of the Late Rev. Philip Doddridge* (Edinburgh: Waugh and Innes, M. Ogle, R. M. Tims, and James Duncan, 1825), 80.

27. Quoted in W. Garden Blaikie, *The Personal Life of David Livingstone* (New York: Fleming H. Revell, 1880), 243.

Conclusion

Do you desire to be a shepherd whose sermons connect with your flock, enabling you to preach from your heart to their hearts? Walk closely with God, study books and people, pray in dependence on the Spirit, speak from your heart, and cultivate pure motivation.

22

Effective Preaching
about God and Man

The doctrine of God and the doctrine of man stand as two pillars of evangelical preaching. John Calvin famously opens his *Institutes of the Christian Religion* by saying, "Nearly all the wisdom we possess, that is to say, true and sound wisdom, consists of two parts: the knowledge of God and of ourselves."[1] The Westminster Shorter Catechism (Q. 3) says that "the scriptures principally teach what man is to believe concerning God, and what duty God requires of man."[2] In a sense, knowing God and knowing ourselves encompasses all of theology. Augustine says: "I desire to know God and the soul. Nothing more? Nothing whatever."[3]

The knowledge of God and of man is the heartbeat of Christian experience. For Calvin, real knowledge does not consist merely in the passive acceptance of truth in the mind, but in an experiential knowledge in the heart. He says, "Indeed, we shall not say that, properly speaking, God is known where there is no religion or piety." By "piety," he means "that reverence joined with love of God which the knowledge of his benefits induces."[4] In knowing God, we feel "dread and wonder," and know ourselves in our "lowly state"; our self-conceit dissipates like

---

1. John Calvin, *Institutes of the Christian Religion*, trans. Ford Lewis Battles, ed. John T. McNeill, Library of Christian Classics, vols. 20–21 (Philadelphia: Westminster, 1960), 1.1.1, hereafter, *Institutes*.
2. *Westminster Confession of Faith* (Glasgow: Free Presbyterian Publications, 1994), 287.
3. Augustine, "Soliloquies," 1.2.7, in *Earlier Writings*, ed. John H. S. Burleigh, Library of Christian Classics, vol. 6 (Philadelphia: Westminster, 1953), 26.
4. *Institutes*, 1.2.1.

fog in the sunshine and we begin to see our "stupidity, impotence, and corruption."[5] Without a biblical vision of God and man, we think little of him and far too much of ourselves.

Preaching the truth about God and man is a defining characteristic of Reformed experiential ministry. It is also a central aspect of proper application of the biblical text, for the covenant aims to produce a people who "all know me, from the least of them unto the greatest of them, saith the LORD" (Jer. 31:34). If our preaching leaves our people knowledgeable in principles for living but ignorant of the triune God, then we have failed.

In the last chapter, I introduced the question of how can we become more effective in application in our sermons. While the power of application flows from the Spirit, we can shape our lives and ministries in a manner that, rather than grieving the Spirit, aligns us with his purposes and invites his sovereign support (2 Chron. 16:9). In this chapter, I will take up another question: "How should you apply specific areas of doctrine?" We will focus specifically upon the doctrines of God and man.

Experiential Preaching of the Doctrine of God

Who is the most important person in the Old Testament? Is it Adam? Abraham? Moses? David? It is none of them. The most important person in the Old Testament—and in the New—is God. If the Bible were a stage play, God would be the main character and the spotlight would always be on him. Wayne Grudem wisely says: "The whole Bible is about God! Therefore we should always ask, 'What does this text teach us about God?'"[6]

In his commentary on Genesis 1, Derek Kidner says: "It is no accident that *God* is the subject of the first sentence of the Bible, for this word dominates the whole chapter and catches the eye at every point of the page: it is used some thirty-five times in as many verses of the story. The passage, indeed the Book, is about Him first of all; to read it with any other primary interest (which is all too possible) is to misread it."[7]

---

5. *Institutes*, 1.1.3.
6. Wayne Grudem, "Right and Wrong Interpretation of the Bible: Some Suggestions for Pastors and Bible Teachers," in *Preach the Word: Essays on Expository Preaching in Honor of R. Kent Hughes*, ed. Leland Ryken and Todd Wilson (Wheaton, IL: Crossway, 2007), 68.
7. Derek Kidner, *Genesis* (Downers Grove, IL: InterVarsity Press, 1967), 43.

God told Moses nine times that the purpose for his great works in bringing Israel out of Egypt was so that people would "know that I am the LORD" (Ex. 6:7; 7:5, 17; 8:22; 10:2; 14:4, 18; 16:12; 29:46). The knowledge of God is the only thing worth boasting in (Jer. 9:24). Knowing God is wisdom (Prov. 9:10). Knowing God gives courage (Dan. 11:32). Knowing God evokes faithful love (Hos. 6:6; cf. 1 John 4:19). Knowing God is eternal life (John 17:3). Knowing God is the key to grace, peace, godliness, and life (2 Pet. 1:2–3). All this is because he is the living God, the Holy One, the glory, riches, strength, and inheritance of his people.

The story is told about a boy who went to hear George Whitefield preach. Later, he fell ill, and his father attended upon him as he lay dying. The boy told his father he was not afraid to die. When his father asked why not, the child replied, "I want to go to Mr. Whitefield's big God."[8] Nothing can comfort and strengthen people like a grand vision of the big God. "Comfort ye, comfort ye my people, saith your God" (Isa. 40:1). How? Remind them that their God is so great that all the nations are "as a drop of a bucket" before him (Isa. 40:15). Tell them that "the everlasting God, the LORD, the Creator of the ends of the earth, fainteth not, neither is weary," indeed, "there is no searching of his understanding" (Isa. 40:28). He is our strength.

Therefore, when we preach the Bible, if we would do so in a manner faithful both to the Bible and to the needs of our listeners, we must constantly proclaim the glory of God. That is not to deny that sometimes other doctrines take the foreground, such as sanctification, atonement, baptism, or the end of the age. But all doctrine serves to set forth the sparkling brilliance of our glorious God. This is not to sideline the gospel of Christ, but to recognize that the gospel especially serves to magnify the triune God. The gospel calls to us, "Behold your God" (Isa. 40:9), and announces, "Thy God reigneth!" (Isa. 52:7). Evangelical preaching is an instrument in God's hand to produce in the heart "the light of the knowledge of the glory of God in the face of Jesus Christ" (2 Cor. 4:6). Sanctification takes place as we, "beholding as in a glass the glory of the Lord, are changed into the same image from glory to glory" (2 Cor. 3:18). Whatever we preach, it must shine with the glory of God or we have preached neither rightly nor effectively.

---

8. A. S. Billingsley, *The Life of the Great Preacher, Reverend George Whitefield, "prince of Pulpit Orators": With the Secret of His Success, and Specimens of His Sermons* (Philadelphia, New York: P. W. Ziegler & Company, 1878), 167–68.

The experiential preaching of the glory of God reaches to the affections of the heart. Effective preaching does not merely inform people about God; it glorifies God. Thomas Watson explains that glorifying God means:

- *Appreciation*: to set God highest in our thoughts. He says, "There is in God all that may draw forth both wonder and delight . . . there is in him a constellation of all beauties." We glorify God when we are "God-admirers."
- *Adoration*: to worship God "according to the pattern prescribed in his Word."
- *Affection*: to love God with "a love of delight . . . as a man's heart is set upon his treasure." Watson writes that such love is "exuberant" in its streaming forth, "superlative" in giving God our best, and "intense and ardent" like a fire.
- *Subjection*: to dedicate ourselves to God and his service with "golden obedience."[9]

To preach so as to glorify God, we must glory in God while we preach. John Piper says that preaching is "expository exultation."[10] To exult is to rejoice greatly at triumph or success. We might add that it is expository admiration for God, expository adoration of God, expository affection toward God, and expository subjection unto God. Indeed, sometimes it is expository lamentation over our sins against this beautiful and holy God. But real preaching is always a flame of worship arising from the wick of the preacher's soul immersed in the oil of the Spirit in the lamp of Scripture.

Phillips Brooks observes that the truth must engage our whole person if we would truly preach it. He writes: "Truth through personality is our description of real preaching. The truth must come really through the person, not merely over his lips, not merely into his understanding and out through his pen. It must come through his character, his affections, his whole intellectual and moral being."[11] There must be truth:

---

9. Thomas Watson, "Man's Chief End to Glorifie God," in *A Body of Practical Divinity, Consisting of Above One Hundred Seventy Six Sermons on the Lesser Catechism Composed by The Reverend Assembly of Divines at Westminster: With a Supplement of Some Sermons on Several Texts of Scripture* (London: Thomas Parkhurst, 1692), 1–2.

10. John Piper, "Preaching as Expository Exultation for the Glory of God," in Mark Dever, et al., *Preaching the Cross* (Wheaton, IL: Crossway, 2007), 113; see also John Piper, *Expository Exultation: Christian Preaching as Worship* (Wheaton, IL: Crossway, 2018).

11. Phillips Brooks, *Lectures on Preaching* (New York: E. P. Dutton, 1891), 8.

"No preaching ever had any strong power that was not the preaching of doctrine."[12] But there must also be a personality gripped by the truth: "Whatever is in the sermon must be in the preacher first."[13] Therefore, the truths about God must fill our souls. We must burn with God's flame if we would ignite others.

Preaching God's Attributes

A very profitable way of applying the doctrine of God to Christian experience is by meditating on the attributes of God. God is simple Being in himself, the "I Am." God's attributes are not parts of God; they are God. He exists in such simplicity that the Scriptures can say not only that God is spiritual, shines with light, and loves people, but, "God *is* a Spirit" (John 4:24), "God *is* light" (1 John 1:5), and "God *is* love" (1 John 4:8). Since we are mere creatures with finite minds, we cannot comprehend God in his essence, so he has revealed himself facet by facet, in distinct yet inseparable attributes.[14]

Just as the light of the sun may be refracted into the distinct colors of the rainbow through a prism, so also we may consider God's beauty as refracted through the prism of his Word into the distinct attributes of his nature. As the Puritans understood, contemplating God's attributes is a sweet delight, not merely in the exercise of our minds, but in the holy pleasures of seeing the perfections of the God who is ours to enjoy even now in the covenant and will be ours to enjoy in a much fuller manner forever.[15]

There is a tendency today to downgrade the value of knowing God's attributes. Why is this the case even in the church? First, people may *lack self-knowledge*. If we knew ourselves, our desperate need, and our poverty, then we would eagerly seek God's riches. Too often our eyes are dazzled by human abilities and material goods. Christ found the church in Laodicea as useless as lukewarm water "because thou sayest, I am rich, and increased with goods, and have need of nothing; and knowest not that thou art wretched, and miserable, and poor, and blind, and naked" (Rev. 3:17). We are full of ourselves, so we do not hunger to

---

12. Brooks, *Lectures on Preaching*, 129.
13. Brooks, *Lectures on Preaching*, 109.
14. Wilhelmus à Brakel, *The Christian's Reasonable Service* (Ligonier, PA: Soli Deo Gloria, 1992), 1:89.
15. See the prefatory epistle to Stephen Charnock, *The Existence and Attributes of God*, in *The Complete Works of Stephen Charnock* (Edinburgh: James Nichol, 1854), 1:123.

know God. Proverbs 27:7 says, "The full soul loatheth an honeycomb; but to the hungry soul every bitter thing is sweet." In our hearts, we know that God's glory exposes our emptiness and corruption, and so, to some degree, we (like the world) prefer the darkness to the light (John 3:19–20).

Second, people may suffer from *willful ignorance of God*. Sin creates a strong bias against knowing God. Unbelievers do not regard the knowledge of God as worth having and suppress what knowledge they do possess (Rom. 1:18, 28). Even some believers fail to make diligent use of the means of grace to know God better. Though they have had time to become as wise as teachers, they still need milk because they cannot take in the strong meat of the Word (Heb. 5:12).

Third, people may allow *unbelieving fear* to hold them back. They allow Satan to dull their desire to know God with the suggestion that his perfections are still against us. They fail to embrace and exercise the "boldness and access with confidence" to God that is ours through faith in Christ (Eph. 3:12). Sometimes when believers say that they find the doctrine of God boring, they secretly find God's glory unsettling and disturbing—their guilty consciences need to be washed in the blood of Christ again.

Fourth, people may wallow in *spiritual laziness*. They think that conversion is the end, failing to see that conversion is only the beginning of a great journey into the glory of God. People often settle for too little and end up in complacent mediocrity. They fail to press on in the knowledge of Christ (Phil. 3:8–14). Though rich in Christ, they live in experiential poverty. Such people are spiritual sloths, too lazy to pick up the food set before them and put it in their mouths (Prov. 19:24; 26:15).

Fifth, people may fall into *experientialism*. They turn Christian experience into an idol, grieving the Spirit over their failure to live out their experience to the glory of God. They seek to grasp emotional highs while neglecting the biblical, doctrinal, and practical dimensions of the faith. Ironically, they may despise ordinary, authentic Christian experience because they are captivated by false and extreme experiences.

Despite all these obstacles, knowing God in Christ is the life of the believer (John 17:3). As the windows of heaven open to reveal God's glory, the wind of heaven blows upon our souls, refreshing and renewing us. Knowing our Redeemer, we discover that he has come to dwell among us in the intimacy of the Holy Spirit (Ex. 29:46; Eph. 2:22). We become his living temple, and we cry out with the psalmist: "My soul longeth, yea, even fainteth for the courts of the LORD: my heart and my flesh crieth out for the living God. . . . For a day in thy courts is better than a thousand. I had rather be a doorkeeper in the house of my God, than to dwell in the tents of wickedness" (Ps. 84:2, 10). The soul of the believer pants after the living God (Ps. 42:1–2).

Preaching the text of Scripture naturally leads us to reflect upon the attributes of God. For example, one might be preaching on Psalm 23:6, "Surely goodness and mercy shall follow me all the days of my life." The words *surely* and *all the days of my life* cause the believer to reflect on the unchangeableness of his God. We might say to the congregation:

> David could not, and does not affirm that he himself shall never fail in faith, nor falter in obedience; but he does avow his conviction that the lovingkindness of the Lord shall never be taken away from him. His assured expectations are not directed to temporal happiness, earthly grandeur, or the glory of Israel's royal diadem, but the chief desire and strong confidence of his heart are fixed on the attainment of spiritual happiness, eternal riches, and a heavenly kingdom.
>
> David trusted implicitly upon a covenant-keeping God for the unfailing supply of indispensable spiritual and eternal blessings; nor was he disappointed in this Spirit-wrought trust. A covenant-decreeing Father through sovereign pleasure, a covenant-ratifying Mediator through substitutionary blood, and a covenant-sealing Spirit through heavenly application, was the irrevocable foundation upon which David's "surely" was grounded. Indeed, God's covenant was more than his desire; it had also been his experience. David had been personally led by the redeeming Messiah to the waterbrooks of God's eternal favor, where the Father revealed himself as reconciled and appeased in the righteousness of Christ.
>
> The grounds of inviolable security guaranteeing David's "surely," and each true believer's eternal bliss, lie solely in the Triune Being who sets His seal to His own proclamation, "I give unto them eternal life: and they shall never perish" (Jn. 10:28).[16]

Then we might speak to them of the "two precious, inescapable, heavenly escorts" that "will follow me all the days of my life—namely,

---

16. Joel R. Beeke, *Jehovah Shepherding His Sheep: Sermons on the Twenty-Third Psalm* (Sioux Center, IA: Netherlands Reformed Book and Publishing, 1982), 348–49.

goodness and mercy."[17] Here again, the text of Scripture draws us into a consideration of the attributes of God. We might talk to the church about God's goodness and mercy as characteristics of his essence, as blessings poured in common upon all his creatures, and as the special saving goodness and mercy shown to the elect:

(1) God is Goodness (Mark 10:18). The original Saxon meaning of our English word "God" is "The Good." God is perfect. His goodness is one with His absolute perfection. He is not goodness relatively, as compared to badness, for He cannot be compared to anything or anyone. He is pure Good, essential Good, absolute Good, infinite Good, perfect Good. He does not need to become anything, for whatever He is He is eternally, and within Himself. His goodness is sufficient, all-sufficient, self-sufficient (Is. 40:28–31). As Thomas Manton aptly writes:

> He is originally good, good of Himself, which nothing else is; for all creatures are good only by participation and communication from God. He is essentially good; not only good, but goodness itself; the creature's good is a superadded quality, in God it is His essence. He is infinitely good; the creature's good is but a drop, but in God there is an infinite ocean or gathering together of good. He is eternally and immutably good, for He cannot be less good than He is; as there can be no addition made to Him, so no subtraction.

(2) God reveals His common goodness and common mercy over all His creation and creatures, even reprobate men (Ps. 33:5; 136:25). "The Lord is good to all; and his tender mercies are over all his works" (Ps. 145:9).

(3) It is God's saving goodness and saving mercy, flowing out of Himself as Goodness and Mercy, that David has in mind when he confesses that these two benefits of Jehovah's shepherding shall be his heavenly escorts to pursue him all his lifelong journey until the very gates of heavenly bliss. In this special sense, goodness and mercy are inseparable (Ps. 136). Goodness supplies in spiritual want; mercy has compassion in spiritual misery, and forgives transgression. Goodness follows to provide; mercy follows to pardon. Richly does Thomas Watson write of divine mercy:

---

17. Beeke, *Jehovah Shepherding His Sheep*, 351.

It is the great design of the Scripture to represent God as merciful. The Scripture represents God in white robes of mercy more often than with garments rolled in blood; with His golden scepter more often than His iron rod. Mercy is His darling attribute which He most delights in. The bee naturally gives honey, it stings only when it is provoked; so God does not punish till He can bear no longer. As God's mercy makes the saints happy, so it should make them humble. Mercy is not the fruit of our goodness, but the fruit of God's goodness, Mercy is an alms [charity to the poor] that God bestows. They have no cause to be proud that live upon the alms of God's mercy.[18]

I trust you can see how the text naturally leads us to meditate on the attributes of God in an experiential manner. Perhaps the quotes from Manton and Watson are too long to be read in full from the pulpit, but the excerpts cited above give you two examples of preaching God's attributes.

Brothers, preach the attributes of God! Teach people that God not only shows mercy, "he delighteth in mercy" (Mic. 7:18). Mercy is his very heart. This may very well set at liberty some dear soul oppressed by a sense of divine wrath against sins, oppressed even though he does trust in the Mediator with a weak faith.

Teach them about God's infinity, eternity, immutability, and incomprehensibility. Let their hearts be humbled and their bent for sin weakened in the light of his unspeakable majesty. John Owen says: "Be much in thoughtfulness of the excellency of the majesty of God and thine infinite, inconceivable distance from him. Many thoughts of it cannot but fill thee with a sense of thine own vileness, which strikes deep at the root of any indwelling sin. . . . Be much in thoughts of this nature, to abase the pride of thy heart, and to keep thy soul humble within thee."[19]

To those who think that the doctrine of God has no practical relevance to life, we stress that the opposite is true. This is particularly the case when we view God through his self-revelation in Jesus Christ. A

---

18. Beeke, *Jehovah Shepherding His Sheep*, 351–52, 354–55. Note that the quotes from the Puritans have been abridged; see Thomas Manton, Sermon 2 upon Mark 10:17–27 in *The Complete Works of Thomas Manton* (London: James Nisbet, 1874), 16:428–31; Watson, "The Mercy of God," in *Body of Practical Divinity*, 53–54.

19. John Owen, "Mortification of Sin in Believers," in *The Works of John Owen*, ed. William H. Goold (New York: Robert Carter & Brothers, 1851), 6:63.

sight of the glory of God in Christ empowers sanctification. Owen rightly says, "He that hath slight thoughts of sin had never great thoughts of God."[20] Conversely, he also says, "No man can by faith take a real view of this glory, but virtue will proceed from it in a transforming power to change him 'into the same image' (2 Cor. 3:18)."[21]

We have considered the first pillar of evangelical preaching: the doctrine of God. Now we proceed to consider the second pillar, the doctrine of man.

Experiential Preaching of the Truth about Man

We live in an age of remarkable assaults upon the biblical doctrine of man. The theory of macro-evolution denies man's origin as a special creation in God's image. It also implicitly supports the elimination of people whom we deem undesirable or inferior, as is evident in both Nazi anti-Semitism and the abortion industry. Radical environmentalism blurs the distinction between men and beasts, treating animals as if they are our equals. Sometimes its adherents regard mankind as a plague on a pristine planet instead of stewards entrusted both to rule and to care for the earth. Feminism and homosexual activism treat sexuality and marriage as mere social constructs that we can alter at will without regard to the Creator's design or fear of his righteous judgments.

Popular Arminianism (which leans more to Pelagius than Arminius) asserts that people are able to choose God by their free will, as if the fall of man did not significantly impair the soul, much less render it dead in sin. Open Theism goes even further in confusing the sovereign Creator with his dependent creatures, insisting that men are cocreators with a God (or god) who must wait to discover what future man will create. Protestant liberal theology and its younger offspring in some parts of the amorphous Emergent Church movement reject the ideas that sinners stand under the wrath of God and that Christ propitiated divine wrath by standing in their place. What is especially striking is the widespread presence of these errors inside the visible church.

In the midst of all this confusion, Western culture manifests an increasing instability, lack of identity, and rootlessness. Many hearts cry out: "Who am I? Why am I here? And why is my life like this?" Sadly,

---

20. Owen, "An Exposition upon Psalm CXXX," in *Works*, 6:394.
21. Owen, "The Glory of Christ," in *Works*, 1:292.

postmodernism and rampant skepticism have led some to believe there simply are no answers to such questions. People are harassed and helpless, like sheep without a shepherd (Matt. 9:36), and do what is right in their own eyes (Judg. 17:6; 21:25).

In this mess we have made, the Bible declares a clear message about mankind. We must preach not only about God, but also about man. The biblical doctrine of man is rich in content, but here I will focus on two key aspects: our creation as God's masterpiece and our ruin in the fall.

Preaching to God's Masterpieces

It may surprise some people to learn that conservative Reformed preachers have something positive to say about the human race. Aren't we the ministers who preach depravity and damnation? Yes, but the Reformed tradition also honors man as unique among God's works. After introducing our misery in sin, the Heidelberg Catechism (Q. 6) asks, "Did God then create man so wicked and perverse?" It answers, "By no means; but God created man good, and after His own image, in true righteousness and holiness, that he might rightly know God his Creator, heartily love Him, and live with Him in eternal happiness to glorify and praise Him."[22] Even after the fall, there remain some sparks of the natural image of God, though the supernatural image of his righteousness is utterly effaced. Calvin recognized that fallen man retains many excellent gifts from God, including skill in civil law, science, logic, medicine, mathematics, and the visual arts. Wherever we encounter such abilities, we should give thanks to God's Spirit, who works in all creation.[23]

Let me suggest several reasons why Reformed experiential preaching should include the doctrine of man's noble origin. These reasons also imply how we can apply this doctrine.

1. *To Foster Trust and Gratitude toward God.* Genesis 1 repeatedly tells us that what God made was good, and after making mankind, God saw that creation was "very good" (Gen. 1:31). Man's created constitution, which is capable of both knowing God and ourselves, glorifies God and helps us to know him. Calvin says, "We must now speak of the creation of man: not only because among all God's works here is the

---

22. Joel R. Beeke, ed., *Doctrinal Standards, Liturgy, and Church Order* (Grand Rapids, MI: Reformation Heritage Books, 2003), 29.
23. *Institutes*, 2.2.15–16.

noblest and most remarkable example of his justice, wisdom, and goodness; but because, as we said at the beginning, we cannot have a clear and complete knowledge of God unless it is accompanied by a knowledge of ourselves."[24]

Though the fall robbed us of the greater glory of our created state, still "we ought to ascribe what is left in us to God's kindness."[25] This calls us to depend upon God for the natural abilities we need for daily life. It also rebukes men's ungrateful self-conceit: "They have within themselves a workshop graced with God's unnumbered works and, at the same time, a storehouse overflowing with inestimable riches. They ought, then, to break forth into praises of him but are actually puffed up and swollen with all the more pride."[26]

2. *To Encourage Excellence in Earthly Vocations.* Christianity does not denigrate the labors of the scientist, the legislator, the accountant, the housewife, and the farmer; it elevates them. Calvin writes that "the knowledge of all that is most excellent in life" comes to us "through the Spirit of God," and therefore God wills that we make use of the natural sciences and all other academic disciplines, even if the truth is discovered by ungodly men.[27] God conferred a dignity upon man at his creation that makes our work a noble calling to rule over the world, not a drudgery (Ps. 8:6). This should motivate us to do our work with hearts full of praise (Ps. 8:1, 9), because "God himself has shown by the order of Creation that he created all things for man's sake."[28]

3. *To Condemn the Injustice of Mistreating People.* Abuse and atrocities committed against people are often rooted in a false view of human origins. If we are on the same level as chickens, then why not slaughter each other? But Genesis 9:6 forbids murder precisely because men are made in God's image. James 3:9 similarly exposes the hypocrisy of worshiping God and cursing men "made after the similitude of God." Calvin says in regard to the sixth commandment, "Now, if we do not wish to violate the image of God, we ought to hold our neighbor sacred."[29] We should realize that it is a great thing to be human, and therefore "honour all men" (1 Pet. 2:17).

---

24. *Institutes*, 1.15.1.
25. *Institutes*, 2.2.17.
26. *Institutes*, 1.5.4.
27. *Institutes*, 2.2.16.
28. *Institutes*, 1.14.22.
29. *Institutes*, 2.8.40.

4. *To Grieve Sinners over the Depth of Their Fall into Sin.* Graffiti spray-painted on a blank wall is sad to see, but the same paint splashed over a treasured work of art provokes horror and outrage. People cannot feel the shock of our fall into sin until they have some sense of how high we were before we fell. Calvin says, "Since it is a great honor for us that God displayed his power and wisdom in a special way when it pleased him to create our father Adam, it is also to our great shame that we fell from the honor and dignity in which God established us."[30] Sin ruined the crowning work of creation: God's image and vice-regent on earth. God put us in Paradise to reign as holy kings; our sin cast us out of Paradise to suffer as fugitive criminals.

5. *To Disarm Excuses for Our Depravity.* Ever since the Lord God questioned Adam, we have had a tendency to blame God for our misdeeds (Gen. 3:12). Ecclesiastes 7:29 says, "God hath made man upright; but they have sought out many inventions." The doctrine of man's creation clears God of all charges and shuts the mouths of those who say, "God made me this way."

Furthermore, the account of Genesis 2–3 demonstrates that God created man with responsibility for his actions. God gave a law with warnings of punishment, and then executed that punishment when man willfully rebelled. Man is not the helpless victim of fate. He is a rational creature under a covenant of accountability for his works.

Calvin exclaims: "Now away with those persons who dare write God's name upon their faults, because we declare that men are vicious by nature! They perversely search out God's handiwork in their own pollution, when they ought rather to have sought it in that unimpaired and uncorrupted nature of Adam. . . . We have degenerated from our original condition."[31] This truth justifies God in his judgments and helps to foster a heart that willingly confesses its sin.

6. *To Awaken Desire for Restoration to What God Meant Us to Be.* If a peasant child knows nothing but poverty, illiteracy, and unsanitary conditions, he may consider these conditions normal. If an orphan discovers that he was once the heir of a noble lineage and estate before his father committed treason against the king, it may stir him to profound shame, a longing to regain his title, and efforts to find royal pardon and

---

30. John Calvin, *Sermons on Genesis, Chapters 1:1–11:4: Forty-Nine Sermons Delivered in Geneva Between 4 September 1559 and 23 January 1560* (Edinburgh: Banner of Truth, 2009), 91 [Gen. 1:26–28].

31. *Institutes*, 2.1.10; cf. 1.15.1.

restoration for his family. Calvin says: "Nothing was more desirable than Adam's first state. . . . It was like a mirror of ultimate happiness."[32]

7. *To Point Men toward the Last Adam, God's Exact and Complete Image, Jesus Christ.* The apostle Paul teaches us that Adam was a type of the One who was to come (Rom. 5:14). Christ is all that Adam was created to be, and "much more," for his obedience redeemed us from death unto an abundance of life (Rom. 5:17). In him, God restores the divine image among men (Rom. 8:29). He will bring his own back to paradise (Luke 23:43; Rev. 2:7), indeed, paradise infinitely enriched by the presence of the incarnate Lamb of God (Revelation 21–22). In fact, Calvin says that it is only in Christ that we can truly see what the image of God means.[33] Thus, seen through the lens of the gospel, the creation account can stir faith and hope in Christ.

For all these reasons (and no doubt there are more), we must faithfully preach the doctrine of man's noble creation in righteousness, holiness, and knowledge in order to subdue and have dominion over the earth.

Preaching the Ruin of Sin

The other side of preaching the truth about man is declaring the sad reality of human depravity. The word *depravity* in English and in its Latin root means "corruption, the badness of something once good, or the distortion of the straight into the crooked." Churches may err in a number of ways with respect to depravity. Some pulpits openly deny the corruption of mankind. Others subtly neglect it, resulting in a practical semi-Pelagianism. Still other churches hold to the doctrine of depravity only as a traditional emphasis, and thus it is only a homiletical cliché rather than a doctrine with power to pierce, humble, and incite us to glory in Christ.

We must do more than hold to total depravity as a doctrinal tenet and defend it in controversy. We must apply the holistic doctrine of depravity to the heart.

1. People need to see the *lawlessness* of our depravity: that they have sinned against God's holy and good law (1 John 3:4). They fail to conform in action, attitude, and nature to God's commandments and prohibitions. Every one of us has transgressed the lines drawn by God's prohibitions and refused to follow his voice in obedience. We cannot

---

32. Calvin, *Sermons on Genesis*, 105 [Gen. 1:26–28].
33. *Institutes*, 1.15.4; Calvin, *Sermons on Genesis*, 97 [Gen. 1:26–28].

submit to God's law because we hate God (Rom. 8:6–7). This reveals the ugliness of sin, its horrifying evil. Use this truth to call men to turn in horror from their sin as a gross contempt of God's goodness, worthiness, and rightful authority.

2. People need to see the *inwardness* of our depravity: its deep roots of corruption in the heart (Mark 7:21–23), lest we wash the outside of the cup but ignore the filth and defilement within (Matt. 23:25–27). They must reckon depravity as a fundamental refusal to love God with all our soul and to love our neighbor as ourselves (22:37–40). This leads the sinner to acknowledge not only that he has done evil, but that he himself is evil. Press upon people the need to acknowledge, "I am the problem."

3. People need to see the *inability* that results from our depravity: the impossibility of man's fleshly nature producing anything good apart from the supernatural influence of the Holy Spirit (John 3:6; 6:63; Rom. 8:8–9). This humbles the sinner, stripping him of his pretenses to save himself by his works. It makes sovereign grace no longer look like an obstacle, but our only hope. Apply this truth to the sinner to imprison him in a cage with only one door of escape, a door to which only God holds the key. Exhort sinners to cry out to God as utterly helpless, blind beggars.

4. People need to see the *persistence* of our depravity: sin permanently engraved on a heart of stone by an iron pen with a diamond point (Jer. 17:1). Martin Luther said that original sin is like a man's beard. He shaves it today and looks clean, but tomorrow it appears again. Our corruption never ceases to be active until we go to glory. This convinces men of the futility of self-reformation to save them. Tell people that they need more than new habits; they need new hearts. They need more than to turn over a new leaf; they need a new birth.

5. People need to see the *deceitfulness* of our depravity: our hearts lie to us and naturally grow harder with every sin (Jer. 17:9; Heb. 3:13). We are darkened in our understanding and alienated from the life of God (Eph. 4:17–18). Warn sinners to cease trusting in their own minds. Call them to submit to God's judgment of them, rather than judging God. Invite them to rest upon the Lord Jesus as the only Prophet who can illuminate their darkness with his Spirit.

6. People need to see the *totality* of our depravity: every inclination and every thought of the heart has been corrupted and stained by sin

(Gen. 6:5). True, men can do much civic good and are not as corrupt as they could be. But every faculty of our souls and every action we take is twisted by sin; apart from regenerating grace, no one does good (Rom. 3:12). Understanding this releases the sinner from the delusion that he can make amends for sin by doing good works. All his works cry out for atonement.

7. People need to see the *captivity* of our depravity: we are slaves bound by the chains of our corrupt minds and wills to follow Satan (John 8:34, 44; Rom. 6:17; Eph. 2:1–3). Sin is our master until the Lord Christ comes to set us free. Call people on this basis to treasure Christ as King and rejoice to be ruled by him instead of viewing sin as liberty.

8. People need to see the *futility* of our depravity: having forsaken the fountain of living waters, we are as stupid as birds sitting on eggs that do not belong to us; we set ourselves to rebel against a glorious high throne, and God's eyes pierce to our very hearts (Jer. 17:10–13). Knowing this brings down the sinner's pride by showing him how foolish he has been. Help people to see how their sinful pursuits will never satisfy them. They are fighting a battle they cannot win.

9. People need to see the *culpability* of our depravity: the horrendous weight of guilt we have incurred before God. God will judge and damn every sinner outside of Jesus Christ for his rebellion against the light he had (Romans 2). "The wages of sin is death" (Rom. 6:23). The wrath of God already flames from heaven against all unrighteousness of men (Rom. 1:18). We must drive sinners to flee to Christ from the wrath to come and to live in eternal gratitude for the atonement by his blood.

Conclusion

The human race, created in God's image but fallen into misery through sin, is like a king's castle ruined by an earthquake, abandoned by the king, and inhabited by bats and rodents. On the one hand, there remains a beauty and majesty about the ruins that can inspire awe. The remains of great towers, pillared halls, and high walls suggest its noble past. Its structures remain somewhat useful. But the earthquake has left the castle broken, empty, full of rubbish, dangerous in its instability and tendency to further collapse, and facing the threat of demolition. So it is with the human race. But, praise God, the great King is reclaiming his ancestral home. How to preach that good news is the subject of the next chapter.

23

Preaching the Gospel
to the Heart

When Charles H. Spurgeon preached his first sermon in the Metropolitan Tabernacle (March 25, 1861), he chose as his text Acts 5:42: "And daily in the temple, and in every house, they ceased not to teach and preach Jesus Christ." Spurgeon said: "It appears that the one subject upon which men preached in the apostolic age was *Jesus Christ*. . . . I would propose that the subject of the ministry of this house, as long as this platform shall stand, and as long as this house shall be frequented by worshippers, shall be the person of Jesus Christ."[1] Would this stricture limit preachers? No, Spurgeon said, for Christ is the most comprehensive of subjects: "If a man be found a preacher of Christ, he is doctrinal, experimental [experiential], and practical."[2]

Those called to "preach the word" must faithfully "do the work of an evangelist"—they must preach the gospel (2 Tim. 4:2, 5). If the preacher speaks to people about God and man, yet does not speak of Christ, he has not fulfilled his calling as an ambassador for Christ (2 Cor. 5:20). Indeed, a ministry that neglects Christ has not truly preached the Scriptures, for the aim of the whole Bible is "to make thee wise unto salvation through faith which is in Christ Jesus" (2 Tim. 3:15). If we love God and we love people, our passion as ministers will be to preach the gospel of Jesus Christ.

---

1. Charles H. Spurgeon, Sermon #369, "The First Sermon in the Tabernacle," March 25, 1861, in *The New Park Street and Metropolitan Tabernacle Pulpit* (Pasadena, TX: Pilgrim Publications, 1969), 7:169.
2. Spurgeon, "The First Sermon in the Tabernacle," 7:173.

The great thrust of the Bible is to declare the glory of the triune God as revealed in the grace of the only Mediator, Jesus Christ, for the obedience of faith in all nations (Rom. 1:5). I hinted at this in the last chapter when I said we must preach the glory of God *in Christ*. Now I must elaborate on this subject. Christ is the overarching theme of every topic and every branch of theology. Take away Christology and you mar and mangle the branches of theology left behind, such as the doctrine of God or eschatology. In fact, take away Christ and you have *no* theology. Christ is the center, the circumference, and the substance of Christianity.

I do not mean to set the gospel of Christ as an alternative to or a competitor alongside the doctrine of God. God's glory remains central. As Jonathan Edwards observes, the central purpose behind all of God's great acts is his own glorification among his creatures.[3] Cotton Mather says that the great aim of preaching is "to restore the throne and dominion of God in the souls of men."[4] The mission of Christ is the great means by which the Lord glorifies himself before men and angels, and establishes his kingdom among mankind.

This may be stated in various ways. Bruce Waltke says that the Bible centers on the theme of God's kingdom, and that God glorifies himself by bringing his kingdom through Christ and his covenant people.[5] James Hamilton has made an intriguing case that the center of biblical theology is "God's glory in salvation through judgment."[6] However we frame it, God's glory has been manifested in Christ. Not only redemption but creation itself is accomplished through Christ (John 1:3; Col. 1:16; Heb. 1:2). So our very commitment to preach the glory of God demands that we preach Christ, for Christ is "the brightness of his glory" (Heb. 1:3). For all eternity, the glory of God will be our light, and the glory of the Lamb will be the light of that light (Rev. 21:23).

Furthermore, although in systematic theology we may consider Christology as a separate *locus* for the sake of analysis, in preaching we cannot

---

3. See Jonathan Edwards, "The End for Which God Created the World," in *The Works of Jonathan Edwards*, vol. 8, *Ethical Writings*, ed. Paul Ramsey (New Haven, CT: Yale University Press, 1989), 403–536.
4. Quoted in John Piper, *The Supremacy of God in Preaching* (Grand Rapids, MI: Baker, 1990), 22.
5. Bruce K. Waltke, *An Old Testament Theology: A Canonical and Thematic Approach* (Grand Rapids, MI: Zondervan, 2006), 144.
6. James M. Hamilton, *God's Glory in Salvation through Judgment: A Biblical Theology* (Wheaton, IL: Crossway, 2010).

speak to men about God apart from the Mediator, who is the God-man, our Prophet, Priest, and King. And we must not speak of Christ without also speaking to the obligations and experience of faith and repentance.

Preaching Christ in the Power of the Spirit

It is the purpose of the Holy Spirit to glorify Christ. Our Lord Jesus said, "When the Comforter is come, whom I will send unto you from the Father, even the Spirit of truth, which proceedeth from the Father, he shall testify of me" (John 15:26). He linked this to the apostolic witness (v. 27; cf. Acts 1:8). Again, he said, "Howbeit when he, the Spirit of truth, is come . . . he shall glorify me" (John 16:13–14). The Comforter comes in Christ's "name," that is, representing him and his interests, and continuing his work in the believer (John 14:26).

If we want the Spirit to draw sinners to Christ, we must preach Christ. He is the magnet of lost souls (John 12:32). Thomas Brooks says, "There is a strange and strong energy or forcibleness in hearing Christ and his beauties and excellencies displayed and discovered."[7] Yes, to unbelievers, Jew and Gentile alike, Christ crucified is a stumbling block and foolishness, but to the called of God, he is the very wisdom and power of God (1 Cor. 1:22–24).

The Centrality of Christ to Biblical Preaching

The apostle Paul repeatedly testifies that his preaching centered on Jesus Christ. He describes himself as "Paul, a servant of Jesus Christ, called to be an apostle, separated unto the gospel of God, (which he had promised afore by his prophets in the holy scriptures,) concerning his Son Jesus Christ our Lord" (Rom. 1:1–3). Paul also describes his purpose in preaching, saying: "We preach Christ crucified. . . . For I determined not to know any thing among you, save Jesus Christ, and him crucified" (1 Cor. 1:23; 2:2).

The matter of "first" importance in Paul's preaching was "that Christ died for our sins according to the scriptures; and that he was buried, and that he rose again the third day according to the scriptures: and that he was seen" (1 Cor. 15:3–5). He writes, "For we preach not ourselves, but Christ Jesus the Lord; and ourselves your servants for Jesus' sake"

---

7. Thomas Brooks, "The Unsearchable Riches of Christ," in *The Works of Thomas Brooks*, ed. Alexander B. Grosart (Edinburgh: Banner of Truth, 2001), 3:208.

(2 Cor. 4:5). He binds himself with a solemn oath, saying, "God forbid that I should glory, save in the cross of our Lord Jesus Christ, by whom the world is crucified unto me, and I unto the world" (Gal. 6:14).

Luke tells us this characterized Paul's ministry from the very first, immediately after his conversion: "straightway he preached Christ" (Acts 9:20). Many years later, Paul reflects on his ministry, saying that he has testified to all men of "repentance toward God, and faith toward our Lord Jesus Christ" (20:21).

In this regard, Paul followed the mandate laid down by Christ himself. Luke reports of the risen Lord:

> He said unto them, These are the words which I spake unto you, while I was yet with you, that all things must be fulfilled, which were written in the law of Moses, and in the prophets, and in the psalms, concerning me. Then opened he their understanding, that they might understand the scriptures, and said unto them, Thus it is written, and thus it behooved Christ to suffer, and to rise from the dead the third day: and that repentance and remission of sins should be preached in his name among all nations, beginning at Jerusalem. (Luke 24:44–47)

The whole Bible revolves around this grand theme: Christ died and rose, and he saves sinners through the preaching of the gospel and its call to faith and repentance. Preaching the Old and New Testaments in a Christ-centered manner does not require us to force an alien theology on the text of Scripture. On the contrary, Christ-centered preaching is fidelity to the Bible and its message.

Tools for Crafting a Christ-Centered Sermon

Preaching Christ from all of Scripture is a rewarding but sometimes difficult task, demanding great effort and discernment from us. There are many texts in which the glory of Christ leaps off the page at us, but others in which we may struggle to see him. Let me offer you some helpful tools for this task.

1. *Prayer for the Holy Spirit's Illumination.* No one can say "Jesus is Lord" apart from the Holy Spirit (1 Cor. 12:3), much less preach a Christ-centered sermon. The greatest obstacle to seeing Christ in the Bible is that we remain "fools, and slow of heart to believe," as Jesus said to two of his followers on the road to Emmaus (Luke 24:25–27). We need Christ to teach us by the Spirit.

God has given us intellectual gifts, and we must develop and use them diligently, but Proverbs 3:5 says, "Trust in the LORD with all thine heart; and lean not unto thine own understanding." If we rely on our gifts, then we may have some insight into the words of the text, but we will fail to see through the text as looking through a heavenly window into the awesome spiritual realities to which it bears witness. Let us humble ourselves for our foolish intellectual pride! "Seest thou a man wise in his own conceit? There is more hope of a fool than of him" (Prov. 26:12).

2. *Broad Knowledge of Scripture.* If you desire to see and explain how a particular text bears witness to Christ, you need to stay fresh and extensive in your reading of the Bible. There simply is no substitute for reading through the Bible regularly in order to interpret each text properly. The Westminster Confession of Faith (1.9) says, "The infallible rule of interpretation of Scripture is Scripture itself."[8] If you know the breadth of the Word, when you are preparing to preach on the dedication of the temple (1 Kings 8), you will remember that Christ said that his body is the temple (John 2:21), and that Paul taught that believers are the temple by union with Christ (1 Cor. 3:16–17; 6:19).

3. *Biblical Theology of a Progressive yet Unified Revelation.* Due to the influence of dispensationalism, many Americans are somewhat blinded to the interconnectedness of Scripture. By chopping up redemptive history into pieces, dispensationalists sever the organic links that unify the Bible as the grand story of the gospel of Christ. The result is a collection of disconnected Bible stories with various moral lessons that are at best only a secondary aspect of the text.

A biblical and covenantal theology discerns how all the lines of the Bible converge in Christ. Edmund Clowney says, "Biblical theology serves to center preaching on its essential message: Jesus Christ."[9] Likewise, Graeme Goldsworthy writes, "Jesus Christ is the link between every part of the Bible and ourselves."[10]

Biblical theology offers some very helpful tools for interpreting the text of Scripture in a Christ-centered manner. These tools come from

---

8. *Westminster Confession of Faith* (Glasgow: Free Presbyterian Publications, 1994), 24.

9. Edmund P. Clowney, *Preaching and Biblical Theology* (Phillipsburg, NJ: Presbyterian and Reformed, 1979), 74. See also Michael P. V. Barrett, *Beginning at Moses: A Guide to Finding Christ in the Old Testament* (Grand Rapids, MI: Reformation Heritage Books, 2018); David Murray, *Jesus on Every Page: Ten Simple Ways to Seek and Find Christ in the Old Testament* (Nashville: Thomas Nelson, 2013).

10. Graeme Goldsworthy, *According to Plan: The Unfolding Revelation of God in the Bible* (Downers Grove, IL: InterVarsity Press, 2002), 72.

the New Testament itself, which is our divinely given, authoritative guide for interpreting the Old Testament. Let me present them briefly for you.[11]

a. *Gracious Promises.* Promises (God's words binding himself to bless his people) find their ultimate fulfillment in Christ: "For all the promises of God in him are yea, and in him Amen, unto the glory of God by us" (2 Cor. 1:20).

b. *Historical Types.* A type (Greek *typos*) is a person, event, or institution designed by God to foreshadow the spiritual realities of Christ and his kingdom. The epistle to the Hebrews uses Melchizedek and the priesthood in this manner. Likewise, Adam was a type of Christ (Rom. 5:14), and Israel's experiences were types of the temptations of the visible church under Christ (1 Cor. 10:6).

c. *God-Centered Themes.* There are many great themes that span the Bible and repeatedly point us to Christ as the glory of God, such as the creative word of God, man as made in God's image, covenant, redemption, God's dwelling with his people, sacrifices for sin, prophet and judgment, priest and sanctuary, king and kingdom, adoption, salvation through judgment, the suffering servant, and the exaltation of the stone that the builders rejected. For example, the Bible uses the theme of redemption to describe the deliverance of the godly from evil (Gen. 48:16; Ps. 69:18), the exodus from Egypt (Ex. 6:6; Deut. 7:8), the restoration of lost property or enslaved people (Leviticus 25; Ruth 4), the return from the exile (Isa. 48:20), the saving death of Jesus Christ (Titus 2:14), and the future resurrection of the righteous (Rom 8:23).

d. *Covenantal Contexts.* Ordinarily, one is able to locate the position of a text of Scripture with respect to the covenants with Adam (Genesis 2), Noah (Genesis 9), Abraham (Genesis 12–22), the children of Israel (Exodus–Deuteronomy), and David (2 Samuel 7). One can then relate that text to the relevant covenants, and see how it finds fulfillment in the new covenant in Christ.

e. *Progressive Fulfillments.* The promises, types, and themes of Scripture find fulfillment in multiple ways across redemptive history, cul-

---

11. For a detailed study, see Sidney Greidanus, *Preaching Christ from the Old Testament: A Contemporary Hermeneutical Method* (Grand Rapids, MI: Eerdmans, 1999).

minating in the full shining of the glory of God in the eternal kingdom of Christ. We find seeds that germinate, sprout, develop into saplings, grow into young trees, mature, and bear fruit in eternal glory. For example, God's promise of offspring to Abraham refers to Isaac and the nation of Israel (Gen. 21:12), yet Paul says that ultimately the "seed" is Christ and in him believers of all nations (Gal. 3:16, 29).

Consider how biblical theology can help us to preach the narrative of David and Goliath (1 Samuel 17). It is commonly preached as a moral tale about courage and faith against the "giants" of our lives. But by studying the text in context, we learn that David had been recently anointed by Samuel as the king of Israel and filled with the Spirit (1 Sam. 16:1–13). We see here the God-centered theme of God providing a savior to deliver his people from their enemies, as he did through the judges and King Saul. We also recognize the theme of God doing mighty works through what seems weak and despicable (e.g., Gideon) or rejected by men (Moses). In the covenantal context, we discover that God later promised David that his offspring would reign perpetually under God's love, described by Isaiah as "the sure mercies of David" (2 Sam. 7:12–16; 23:5; Isa. 55:3). We perceive that David was a type of Christ, who is called "David" by the prophets (Jer. 30:9; Ezek. 34:23–24; 37:24; Hos. 3:5).

David's battle with Goliath was not a personal duel but a contest of champions representing two peoples. Goliath was the champion of the wicked, the power that threatened the people of God with enslavement and death. We hear echoes of the battle between the seed of the woman and the seed of the Serpent (Gen. 3:15). The story reaches a theological high point in David's words in 1 Samuel 17:45–47, his proclamation that he would kill Goliath by God's power for the glory of God's name. His words contain a promise for God's people: "The battle is the LORD's" (v. 47). David's victory became the victory of all God's people, who celebrated him in their songs of praise.

All these factors converge to transform a tale of courage into a revelation of God's plan of salvation for his people through his King, for his glory. God's people face a terrifying enemy. Christ, though seemingly insignificant and weak (Isa. 53:1–3), has won the decisive victory over the champion of evil. Now we, his army, can press on while clinging to the promise that "the battle is the LORD's." Seated at the right hand of

God and present with us in his Spirit, he will lead us to victory over the Devil and all his hosts. Fear not, people of God! Our David, Christ the Son of David, has won the contest and reigns forever!

This example shows the potential of biblical theology to produce Christ-centered sermons. While we should not carry all our biblical theology into the pulpit, it equips us to preach Christ to weak and frightened sinners.

4. *Robust and Systematic Christology.* Preaching Christ does not lead to repetitive and predictable sermons—if we grasp the riches of Christ revealed in Scripture. Here Reformed systematic theology aids us by developing the biblical categories of Christ's work. It traces Christ's mission through his humiliation to his exaltation. It shows us how Christ is the Prophet who speaks truth and illuminates hearts, the Priest who offered himself as an atoning sacrifice and now intercedes with God, and the King who conquers all enemies and rules in righteousness. With two states, three offices, and at least two functions per office, we have multiple dimensions to Christ's work. Not only does this enable us to preach Christ from many different passages of Scripture, it also helps us to see that whenever Scripture exposes and addresses the needs of humanity, Christ is the answer.

If we have Christ in view only as a sacrifice-offering Priest (as crucial as that is), how can we preach about the mighty conquests of the King (as in the contest between David and Goliath) or the authoritative wisdom of the Prophet (as expressed in Proverbs and Ecclesiastes)? Indeed, if we cannot see how a part of God's Word points to Christ, then perhaps our view of Christ is too small. But a rich Christology embedded in our minds releases and equips us to preach Christ from all the Scriptures. We are equipped to help people see that Christ is everything to the believer.

5. *Ethical Dependence on Christ.* All Christians know that they must depend on Christ for their salvation. Sadly, many seem to forget that we also depend on Christ for living the Christian life. We must cultivate in ourselves as preachers a sense that no matter what moral, ethical, relational, or vocational demand we may face, we cannot fulfill it without Christ. He is our wisdom, righteousness, sanctification, and redemption (1 Cor. 1:30); in short, our all in all (Col. 3:11).

Paul's epistles exemplify ethical dependence on Christ. Are there divisions in the church? Paul runs to Christ: "Is Christ divided?" (1 Cor.

1:13). Is there an immoral man in the church? He runs to Christ again: "Purge out therefore the old leaven, that ye may be a new lump, as ye are unleavened. For even Christ our passover is sacrificed for us" (1 Cor. 5:7). Are Christians tempted to sexual sin? Christ is the answer: "And such were some of you: but ye are washed, but ye are sanctified, but ye are justified in the name of the Lord Jesus, and by the Spirit of our God. . . . For ye are bought with a price: therefore glorify God in your body" (1 Cor. 6:11, 20). Are husbands harsh with their wives? Paul directs them to Christ: "Husbands, love your wives, even as Christ also loved the church, and gave himself for it" (Eph. 5:25). His writings are a continual discourse on what it means to "live by the faith of the Son of God" (Gal. 2:20).

6. *Exposure to Christ-Exalting Literature.* Feed your soul with books written by men full of the Word of Christ and breathing the Spirit of Christ. Get such books as Thomas Goodwin's *Christ Our Mediator, Christ Set Forth,* and *The Heart of Christ in Heaven;* Isaac Ambrose's *Looking to Jesus;* John Brown's *Christ the Way, the Truth, and the Life;* John Owen's *The Glory of Christ* and *Communion with God;* John Flavel's *The Fountain of Life;* and Friedrich Krummacher's *The Suffering Savior.* Take up these books, read them, meditate on them, write in their margins, quote them in your sermons, turn their words into prayers, and, above all, commune with Christ in them. See how faithfully these men preached Christ, and learn how much they loved him.

One of the benefits of reading such books is that they will show you how to preach Christ to the heart in an experiential and practical manner. Flavel says, "That is the best sermon, that is most full of Christ." He believes that "the excellency of a sermon lies . . . in the plainest discoveries and liveliest applications of Jesus Christ."[12]

Richard Sibbes says, "To preach is to open the mystery of Christ, to open whatsoever is in Christ; to break open the box that the savor may be perceived of all." Sibbes then says, "But it is not sufficient to preach Christ . . . there must be an alluring of them, for to preach is to woo."[13] This leads us to consider how we must be wooing men to faith and repentance in Christ.

---

12. John Flavel, "The Fountain of Life," in *The Works of John Flavel* (London: Banner of Truth, 1968), 1:39.
13. Richard Sibbes, "The Fountain Opened," in *The Works of Richard Sibbes* (Edinburgh: Banner of Truth, 2001), 5:505.

Calling Sinners to Faith in Christ

The gospel does not merely announce what Christ has done; it says: "He was in the world, and the world was made by him, and the world knew him not. He came unto his own, and his own received him not. But as many as received him, to them gave he power to become the sons of God, even to them that believe on his name: which were born, not of blood, nor of the will of the flesh, nor of the will of man, but of God" (John 1:10–13). Christ must be received and believed, or his benefits will pass us by, just as they passed by most of those in the world around him.

Some Reformed Christians are afraid to call sinners to receive Christ because of the way in which these words have been abused by modern evangelists. Ironically, Reformed Christians can fall into Arminian logic by assuming that God's sovereignty and human responsibility are at odds with each other (we discussed that matter in chap. 20, pp. 357–63.) We rightly desire to avoid the "altar call" for a decision, because men need more than a decision; they need a Spirit-worked regeneration of the heart. But in avoiding the altar call, we must not neglect the gospel call.

To summon men to faith in Christ is not to deny *sola gratia* in favor of free-will theology; it is to declare *sola fide* as the fruit of grace. Faith has no merit in itself, but only in taking hold of the Mediator, for God justifies the ungodly by crediting them with the unmerited righteousness of Christ (Rom. 4:4–5). Faith does not arise from the power of the sinner's will, but from the power of God who raises the dead (Eph. 2:1–5). Nevertheless, the Bible clearly asserts that faith is absolutely necessary for salvation (Eph. 2:8–9). We are justified by faith in Christ (Gal. 2:16). If we do not receive Christ by the empty hand of faith, then God's wrath abides on us (John 3:18, 36).

The Reformed, Experiential Shape of Faith

We see the shape of faith in the contours of the Holy Spirit's work to glorify Christ. This is a corollary to our Reformed belief that the Spirit produces faith (1 Cor. 12:3). First, faith is *assenting to Christ as our truth*, as confirmed by the Spirit's inward witness. The Father bore witness to Christ by the Scriptures and by Christ's miracles (John 5:36–39). The Spirit confirms and seals that divine testimony by his inward testimony in the heart. Our Lord Jesus said, "The Spirit of truth, which proceedeth from the Father, he shall testify of me" (John 15:26). Thus, faith is a Spirit-worked assent to the truth of God's testimony to Christ. The

Westminster Confession (14.2) says, "By this faith, a Christian believeth to be true whatsoever is revealed in the Word, for the authority of God Himself speaking therein."[14]

The preacher must call people to believe the gospel as a trustworthy divine testimony: "He that hath received his testimony hath set to his seal that God is true" (John 3:33). We must challenge our hearers, saying: "Will you continue to treat God like a liar? That is what your unbelief does. Or will you take him at his word and build your life upon 'Thus saith the Lord'? It is not mere hearing the Word that saves, but making it the practical foundation of your life."

Second, faith is *hungering for Christ as our need*. Faith is rooted in the conviction of the poverty of our souls and a deeply felt thirst for righteousness (Matt. 5:3, 6). Christ taught us that the Holy Spirit would "reprove the world of sin . . . because they believe not on me" (John 16:8–9). The Christ-centered focus of this conviction shows that it is not the mere work of conscience in all mankind generally, but a special work of the Spirit through the preaching of the gospel to expose our pollution, guilt, and misery apart from Christ.

Faith is spiritual hunger. Faith is not a gift we bring to God in our hands to win his favor; faith is the empty hand of the beggar reaching out for divine charity. Faith regards man as dead in sin and glorifies God alone as the sovereign life giver (Rom. 4:19–20). Paul defines the true covenant people of God as those who "worship God in the spirit, and rejoice in Christ Jesus, and have no confidence in the flesh" (Phil. 3:3). The Puritans said that faith is a "self-emptying grace" and a "soul-emptying grace."[15] The one whom God justifies by faith does not put confidence in his good works, but cries out, "God be merciful to me a sinner" (Luke 18:9–14). Therefore, the preacher promotes faith by demoting self-confidence, self-righteousness, and self-sufficiency.

Third, faith is more than intellectual assent to the truth, or even a conviction of our need. Faith is *the act of coming to Christ to receive him as our life*, a motion not of the body but of a heart drawn by the Spirit. In words that echoed his teaching about the new birth, Jesus said, "It

---

14. Joel R. Beeke and Sinclair B. Ferguson, eds., *Reformed Confessions Harmonized* (Grand Rapids, MI: Baker, 1999), 95.

15. Thomas Parson, "Of Saving Faith," in *Puritan Sermons, 1659–1689* (repr., Wheaton, IL: Richard Owen Roberts, 1981), 5:361; William Gurnall, *The Christian in Complete Armour: A Treatise of the Saints' War Against the Devil* (London: Banner of Truth, 1964), 2:15; Walter Marshall, *The Gospel-Mystery of Sanctification Opened, in Sundry Practical Directions* (New York: Southwick and Pelsue, 1811), 76.

is the spirit that quickeneth; the flesh profiteth nothing" (John 6:63; cf. John 3:6). In the context, he was teaching "that no man can come unto me, except it were given unto him of my Father" (John 6:65). The Father draws men by the Spirit to come to Christ.

Faith is willingly receiving him into our hearts, just as the mouth receives bread to nourish the body (John 6:35, 51). The Westminster Confession (14.2) says that "the principal acts of saving faith are accepting, receiving, and resting upon Christ alone for justification, sanctification, and eternal life, by virtue of the covenant of grace."[16] The Belgic Confession (Art. 22) says that faith "embraces Jesus Christ with all His merits, appropriates Him, and seeks nothing more besides Him."[17]

Therefore, the preacher must offer Christ to people and command them to respond to God's invitation to the feast: "Ho, every one that thirsteth, come ye to the waters, and he that hath no money; come ye, buy, and eat; yea, come, buy wine and milk without money and without price" (Isa. 55:1). He must press upon people the reality that without faith they have no life, but with faith they have life forever in Christ. Flavel says, "The soul is the life of the body, faith is the life of the soul, and Christ is the life of faith."[18]

Fourth, faith is *trusting in and resting upon Christ as our righteousness*. Christ said that the Spirit of truth would testify to men's souls "of righteousness, because I go to my Father, and ye see me no more" (John 16:10). Christ was about to glorify God by dying for sinners, rising from the dead, and ascending to heaven to intercede for his people (John 13:31–32; 14:16; 16:5). Though Christ would no longer remain visibly on earth, the Spirit works in people a spiritual sight of Christ's righteousness—his perfect obedience to save sinners from condemnation (John 3:16–18).

John Calvin says: "We are justified by faith alone. . . . Indeed, it justifies in no other way but in that it leads us into fellowship with the righteousness of Christ."[19] William Gurnall says, "Faith hath two hands; with one it pulls off its own righteousness and throws it away . . . with the other it puts on Christ's righteousness over the soul's shame, as that

16. *Reformed Confessions Harmonized*, 95.
17. *Reformed Confessions Harmonized*, 94.
18. Flavel, "Method of Grace," in *Works*, 2:104.
19. John Calvin, *Institutes of the Christian Religion*, trans. Ford Lewis Battles, ed. John T. McNeill, Library of Christian Classics, vols. 20–21 (Philadelphia: Westminster, 1960), 3.11.20.

in which it dares alone see God or be seen of him."[20] Therefore, the preacher must urge men to flee to Christ and rest their guilty souls upon him alone for their righteousness.

Fifth, faith is *surrendering to Christ as our victorious King.* Christ said that the Spirit would testify to men "of judgment, because the prince of this world is judged" (John 16:11). The Spirit opens men's eyes to see past the shame, weakness, and apparent defeat of the cross in order to perceive that Christ conquered Satan on Calvary and reigned on the cross as King (John 12:27–33; Col. 2:14–15). It was no accident that "This is the King of the Jews" was written above Christ's head on the cross in Greek, Latin, and Hebrew (Luke 23:38). Turning from our prior allegiance to the world, the flesh, and the Devil (Eph. 2:1–3), we entrust ourselves to him who died and rose again to be Lord of all.

Faith is so much more than asking Christ to forgive us of our sins. We begin a new life, a life from Christ, by Christ, and for Christ (2 Cor. 5:14–15). In submission to our King, we begin to live as kings in the earth, fighting against sin and Satan in this life as "more than conquerors through him that loved us" (Rom. 8:37). "For whatsoever is born of God overcometh the world: and this is the victory that overcometh the world, even our faith" (1 John 5:4). Therefore, the preacher must summon men and women to submit to the King, join his heavenly army, take up arms against their former master in sin, and look to their King's sovereign grace for victory every step of the way to glory.

Conclusion: A Consistent Yet Diverse Call to Faith

In summary, Reformed experiential preaching of faith authoritatively calls people to believe the trustworthiness of God's testimony about Christ, rebukes and warns sinners about their utter inability to escape damnation apart from Christ, invites and urges men to come to Christ as their life, summons them to trust and rest in Christ alone as their only righteousness before a holy God, and commands them to bow in glad surrender to Christ as the conquering King.

Here again we see how rich Reformed experiential preaching can be, allowing us to call men to faith in a variety of ways according to the specific emphasis and teaching of each part of Scripture. Recognizing the

---

20. Gurnall, *The Christian in Complete Armour,* 2:15.

many dimensions of saving faith liberates the preacher to consistently call people to faith in Christ, and yet preach with diversity in application.[21]

This leads us to consider the next topic, repentance.

The Universal Call to Repent

Just as popular preaching avoids sin and judgment, so popular evangelism neglects the topic of repentance. Much Western culture is influenced by the error of a two-level Christianity, in which so-called converts known as "carnal Christians" live like the world while the "spiritual" elites claim to walk in the fullness of the Spirit. Against this unbiblical, God-dishonoring dichotomy, we must assert the biblical call to repentance. There is no salvation without repentance, and neither is there any spiritual growth. The faith that does not change our lives is a dead faith (James 2:26).

Repentance has been God's message in every age. The prophets called sinners to repentance, saying, "Let the wicked forsake his way, and the unrighteous man his thoughts: and let him return unto the LORD, and he will have mercy upon him; and to our God, for he will abundantly pardon" (Isa. 55:7). The Lord Jesus preached, "The time is fulfilled, and the kingdom of God is at hand: repent ye, and believe the gospel" (Mark 1:15). Christ showed us that preaching repentance is not an act of hatred or issuing a sentence of condemnation against sinners, but the loving work of a physician laboring to heal souls (Luke 5:31–32). Repentance is not morbidity, depression, or a lack of self-esteem. It is not harmful to the soul. Repentance is divine therapy.

The apostle Peter preached, saying, "Repent ye therefore, and be converted, that your sins may be blotted out" (Acts 3:19). He emphasized that the call to repentance reflects the patience and mercy of God, writing, "The Lord is not slack concerning his promise, as some men count slackness; but is longsuffering to us-ward, not willing that any should perish, but that all should come to repentance" (2 Pet. 3:9).

The apostle Paul challenged the unbeliever, saying: "Despisest thou the riches of his goodness and forbearance and longsuffering; not knowing that the goodness of God leadeth thee to repentance? But after thy hardness and impenitent heart treasurest up unto thyself wrath against the day of wrath and revelation of the righteous judgment of God"

---

21. For an explanation of the experiential role of faith in salvation, see Joel R. Beeke, "Justification *by* Faith Alone," in *Justification by Faith Alone*, ed. Don Kistler, 2nd ed. (Morgan, PA: Soli Deo Gloria, 2003), 53–105.

(Rom. 2:4–5). Paul's message to Jews and Gentiles alike was "that they should repent and turn to God, and do works meet for repentance" (Acts 26:20). He preached that God "commandeth all men every where to repent" (Acts 17:30).

If we are not calling men to repentance, then we have forsaken the heritage of the prophets, Christ, and his apostles. Whatever else we may say, we are not preaching the biblical gospel.

Summoning Sinners to the ABCs of Repentance

When the modern preacher confronts the sinner with God's call to repentance, he must explain what repentance is. Most people today have no idea what the word *repent* means, so preachers must start with the basics. Furthermore, the human heart is so deceitful that people generate many counterfeit forms of repentance. It is a fact of human nature that men would rather do penance (to try to atone for sin by doing good works) than repent (to hate and forsake sin). We need to know the real thing. Most dangerously, the deceitfulness of sin lulls sinners into a comfortable, drowsy state in which they do not feel their desperate need to repent.

It is every sinner's duty to repent immediately. The Reformed evangelist Asahel Nettleton (1783–1844) strenuously opposed the methods of Charles Finney, which have become so popular today in mass evangelism. Yet Nettleton preached repentance and saw thousands converted, who then persevered in the faith. In one sermon he queried: "Whose duty is it to repent? The text answers. All men, every where. . . . When is it their duty to repent? . . . God *now* commandeth all men every where to repent."[22] People's inability to repent does not excuse them, nor does it put off their obligation until they experience some work of the Spirit. Their inability consists of a settled hatred toward God and their obstinacy in sin.[23] Their inability itself is culpable, and they *must* repent. Therefore, we must press their duty upon them.

The preacher's responsibility, however, consists of more than shouting "Repent!" repeatedly. We must unfold the meaning of repentance, call sinners to do each part, and urge them onward with strong, biblical motives. Who knows but that God might use our preaching of repentance to work this grace in perishing hearts?

---

22. "The Nature and Reasonableness of Evangelical Repentance," in *Remains of the Late Rev. Asahel Nettleton*, ed. Bennet Tyler (Hartford, CT: Robins and Smith, 1845), 356, emphasis added.
23. Nettleton, "True Repentance Not Antecedent to Regeneration," in *Remains*, 70.

The Westminster Shorter Catechism (Q. 87) gives us an excellent definition: "Repentance unto life is a saving grace, whereby a sinner out of a true sense of his sin, and apprehension of the mercy of God in Christ, doth, with grief and hatred of his sin, turn from it unto God, with full purpose of, and endeavor after, new obedience."[24] On the one hand, we see here that repentance is a "saving grace" given by God.[25] On the other hand, it is the sinner who must repent by turning from sin to God and to new obedience.

The catechism describes the sinner's repentance in terms of its perception, its affection, its redirection, and its action. First, repentance has a twofold *perception*. There is "a true sense of . . . sin" and a sense of "the mercy of God in Christ." Consider David's words of penitence in Psalm 51, which is subtitled, "A Psalm of David, when Nathan the prophet came unto him, after he had gone in to Bathsheba." Verse 14 says, "Deliver me from bloodguiltiness, O God." David was confessing to God the specific ways in which he had broken God's laws by his acts of adultery and murder (2 Samuel 11). This was no vague admission with weasel words to avoid accountability. David saw the particular commands he had broken, and he named them.

David also saw the superabundant grace of God: "Have mercy upon me, O God, according to thy lovingkindness: according unto the multitude of thy tender mercies blot out my transgressions. Wash me thoroughly from mine iniquity, and cleanse me from my sin" (Ps. 51:1–2). Without this motivation, there can be no repentance. The prodigal son returned home when he saw his wretched state and remembered his father's goodness (Luke 15:17–19).

Therefore, we must preach sermons that help people to see the evils of specific sins and the mercies of God in Christ in glorious detail. We must teach people not to be satisfied with vague views of the law and the gospel. We must call them to confess specific sins they have actually committed, not just admit to the guilt that all mankind shares. There is a world of difference between saying, "Nobody's perfect," and confessing, "I have sinned against God."

Second, repentance engages a potent *affection*: "grief and hatred of . . . sin." David wrote, "The sacrifices of God are a broken spirit: a broken and a contrite heart, O God, thou wilt not despise" (Ps. 51:17). His

24. *Reformed Confessions Harmonized*, 109.
25. Zech. 12:10; Acts 5:31; 11:18; 26:18; 2 Tim. 2:25.

grief was an inward brokenness, as painful as broken bones (v. 8). He did not grieve merely because of the consequences of his sins, the way a thief is sad because the police have caught him in the act. He hated his sin because his sin was against God and was evil in God's sight (v. 4). Furthermore, he not only grieved over his behavior, but was brokenhearted that his nature had been corrupt from his mother's womb (v. 5). He moved from "I did an evil deed" to "I have an evil heart." Conviction of sin may produce terror of God's wrath, but the most important element of evangelical repentance is horror over the rottenness and rebellion of one's soul against a good and loving God.

Experiential preaching must portray the evil and ugliness of sin, and warn men that until they feel the horror of sinning against God, they cannot claim to love him. Contemporary evangelicalism has tended to relegate the affections to the caboose of the train. But the older evangelicalism recognized that our lives flow out of the affections of our hearts. It is true that different people express the feelings of their hearts differently. We must not teach people a rigid scheme of experience. But if we believe the Beatitudes, how can we call ourselves "blessed" by God if we do not "mourn" over our sins (Matt. 5:4)?

Third, repentance at its core consists of an inward *redirection* of the heart that shifts the whole course of one's life. The sinner turns "from" sin "unto God." Here is the essence of repentance as an act: turning from wickedness to God and obedience. The great Old Testament word for repentance is *shub* or "turn," sometimes translated "be converted" (Ps. 51:13; cf. Ps. 19:7).

The Heidelberg Catechism (Q. 88–90) reminds us of these two sides to true conversion: "the mortification of the old, and the quickening of the new man." Mortification, or putting to death the old man, is "a sincere sorrow of heart that we have provoked God by our sins, and more and more to hate and flee from them." It corresponds to turning away from sin. Quickening, or the bringing to life of the new man, is "a sincere joy of heart in God, through Christ, and with love and delight to live according to the will of God in all good works." It corresponds to turning to God.[26]

We must preach both sides of repentance. Some ministries may tend to focus on rebuking sin, proclaiming man's misery, and calling sinners

---

26. *Reformed Confessions Harmonized*, 110, 112.

to forsake their ways while they neglect turning toward God in love and delight. Other ministries may make so much of rejoicing in the Lord that they seem to have little place for the profound and painful struggles required to put off entrenched habits of sin. People need to hear both. We should help them to see the ugliness of sin, but remember that they will never really feel the evil of sin until they see the beauty of the Lord against whom they have sinned. It is God's love in Christ that breaks the sinner's heart.

Psalm 2:10–11 combines both when the psalmist exhorts the rebels conspiring against Christ, saying: "Be wise now therefore, O ye kings: be instructed, ye judges of the earth. Serve the LORD with fear, and rejoice with trembling." Therefore, let us preach with fear and trembling, and with joyful adoration.

Fourth, repentance leads to *action:* "with full purpose of, and endeavor after, new obedience." John the Baptist warned people against presuming they were saved because of their covenant heritage, and commanded them, "Bring forth therefore fruits worthy of repentance," for "every tree therefore which bringeth not forth good fruit is hewn down, and cast into the fire" (Luke 3:8–9). Paul explains in 2 Corinthians 7:10–11 that repentance is more than just a change in our thinking, but a turning unto God rooted in grief over sin and resulting in energetic action:

> For godly sorrow worketh repentance to salvation not to be repented of: but the sorrow of the world worketh death. For behold this self-same thing, that ye sorrowed after a godly sort, what carefulness it wrought in you, yea, what clearing of yourselves, yea, what indignation, yea, what fear, yea, what vehement desire, yea, what zeal, yea, what revenge! In all things ye have approved yourselves to be clear in this matter.

This is not justification by works, but works flowing out of the redemption purchased by Christ and applied by the Spirit to make us new creatures (Titus 2:14; 3:3–5; Eph. 2:10; 1 Cor. 6:9–11).

We must warn people that if they continue to live in sin as they used to, then they cannot claim to be born again (1 John 3:9). The Heidelberg Catechism (Q. 64) says, "It is impossible that those, who are implanted into Christ by a true faith, should not bring forth fruits of thankfulness."[27] Preaching the gospel of Christ does not undermine the preaching of our duty to do good works, for the gospel is the only living root from which truly good works spring. Good works are "the fruits and evidences of a true and lively faith" (Westminster Confession of Faith, 16.2).[28]

Conclusion: Preaching Christ to the Conscience

Reformed experiential preaching of the gospel brings the truth of Christ to bear upon the hearts of men. As Charles Bridges says, we must preach *to* the people, not just *before* them. Our sermons should communicate to each listener, "I have a message from God unto thee."[29] Matthew Henry says of his father, Philip Henry, "He did not shoot the arrow of the Word over their heads . . . but to their hearts in close and lively applications."[30]

We must address the conscience. We must speak to people as standing before the throne of God, whose eyes penetrate into all their secrets, and whose Word pierces and sifts the thoughts and intents of their hearts (Heb. 4:12–13). We must proclaim to them the Priest who is both glorious above the heavens and tenderly sympathetic to sinners who trust in him (Heb. 4:14–16).

Gospel preaching is applied preaching. As much as possible, we should make applications throughout the sermon so that people will learn constantly to connect the doctrine of Christ to their lives. Bridges says, "The method of perpetual application, therefore, where the subject will admit of it, is probably best calculated for effect—applying each head distinctly; and addressing separated classes at the close with suitable exhortation, warning, or encouragement."[31] If those applications are centered upon Christ as he is revealed in our particular text of Scripture, then they will not be scattered thoughts but steps moving the hearers along the line of the main thrust of that text, the line aimed at the glory of God in Christ.

We must regularly preach the gospel with unbelievers in our sights. The gospel call must go forth again and again. We never know which adults, young people, and children might yet need regeneration. In this

---

27. *Reformed Confessions Harmonized*, 114.
28. *Reformed Confessions Harmonized*, 115.
29. Charles Bridges, *The Christian Ministry* (London: Banner of Truth, 1967), 272–73.
30. Matthew Henry, *An Account of the Life and Death of Mr. Philip Henry* (London: for J. Lawrence, J. Nicholson, J. and B. Sprint, N. Cliffe, and D. Jackson, 1712), 51–52.
31. Bridges, *The Christian Ministry*, 275.

day of the Internet, our sermons may very well reach perishing sinners on the other side of the globe. We must also preach the gospel to believers. Paul referred to the Roman church as "called," "beloved of God," and "saints" (Rom. 1:6–7), yet he also said, "So, as much as in me is, I am ready to preach the gospel to you that are at Rome also" (v. 15). He understood that nothing deepens the love of the Christian for his Savior, and moves him to walk in holiness and humility, more than the gospel of Christ. To have been forgiven much is to love much (Luke 7:47), and love is the fulfilling of the law (Rom. 13:10).

24

Preaching for Holiness

In the last part of this book, I have sought to help the preacher apply the principles of Reformed experiential preaching that were explained in Part 1 and illustrated from history in Part 2. In Part 3, I first addressed preaching with balance that embraces objective and subjective; sovereignty and responsibility; the fourfold richness of biblical, doctrinal, experiential, and practical preaching; and variety in application by addressing specific cases.

Then I considered what kind of ministry leads to effective application. We saw that one's ministry must be characterized by walking closely with God, studying books, studying the people of your church with a wise and compassionate heart, speaking in a natural tone that expresses your heart's concerns, praying constantly for the Spirit's help, and cultivating pure motivation.

These general concerns led to another question: How do you apply specific areas of doctrine to your hearers? I talked about preaching the doctrines of God, man, Christ, faith, and repentance, with application to the experience of both the unbeliever and the believer.

In this final chapter, I will address preaching for holiness. How does a Reformed experiential preacher apply his sermons to the body of Christ so as to build them up in holiness of life? We will examine justification, union with Christ, the Holy Spirit, spiritual warfare, the moral law, love, affliction, Bible stories, heaven, and the preacher's humility as aspects of preaching holiness in the church of Christ.

Preach Justification as the Ground of Holiness

It is impossible to make progress in holiness until one has peace with God, for holiness consists of walking with God by faith as the fruit of his grace at work in us. Theologians speak of the *duplex gratia*, the "double grace" of justification and sanctification that flows from Christ to us. John Calvin says: "Christ was given to us by God's generosity, to be grasped and possessed by us in faith. By partaking of him, we principally receive a double grace: namely, that being reconciled to God through Christ's blamelessness, we may have in heaven instead of a Judge a gracious Father; and secondly, that sanctified by Christ's spirit we may cultivate blamelessness and purity of life."[1]

Justification and sanctification are distinct benefits, but we can never separate them; likewise, we must keep them in that order, moving from justification as the root that we must have to sanctification as the fruits that we must bear. Calvin says, "For unless you first grasp what your relationship to God is, and the nature of his judgment concerning you, you have neither a foundation on which to establish your salvation nor one on which to build piety toward God."[2] John Owen writes that we must not confuse the foundation with the building we construct upon it: "The foundation is to be laid, as was said, in mere grace, mercy, pardon in the blood of Christ."[3] He says, "First, to take up mercy, pardon, and forgiveness absolutely on the account of Christ, and then to yield all obedience in the strength of Christ and for the love of Christ, is the life of a believer (Eph. 2:8–10)."[4]

Therefore, when you call men to progressive sanctification, periodically place your call in the context of their perfect status as sinners justified wholly and freely by the grace of God. Preaching through the Scriptures naturally lends itself to this. For example, before one comes to preach on Romans 8:13, "For if ye live after the flesh, ye shall die: but if ye through the Spirit do mortify the deeds of the body, ye shall live," you will preach on Romans 8:1, "There is therefore now no condemnation to them which are in Christ Jesus." First, one preaches salvation by grace

---

1. John Calvin, *Institutes of the Christian Religion*, trans. Ford Lewis Battles, ed. John T. McNeill, Library of Christian Classics, vols. 20–21 (Philadelphia: Westminster, 1960), 3.11.1, hereafter, *Institutes*.
2. *Institutes*, 3.11.1.
3. John Owen, "Exposition of Psalm 130," in *The Works of John Owen*, ed. William H. Goold (repr., Edinburgh: Banner of Truth, 1965), 6:565 [Ps. 130:4].
4. Owen, "Exposition of Psalm 130," in *Works*, 6:566 [Ps. 130:4].

alone through faith alone from Ephesians 2:8–9, and then, salvation as being a new creation unto good works from Ephesians 2:10.

Psalm 130:3–4 says: "If thou, LORD, shouldest mark iniquities, O Lord, who shall stand? But there is forgiveness with thee, that thou mayest be feared." Forgiveness empowers piety. Owen says that conviction of sin and guilt may move men to spurts of religious endeavor, such as churchgoing and the like, but justification by the blood of Christ is "the only way and means to enable you unto obedience" with "stability or constancy in your course." Without justification, all our efforts are not "accepted with God." Without peace with God, we serve him "with heaviness, fear, and in bondage," but forgiveness enables obedience with "life, alacrity, and delight."[5]

Far from encouraging the Christian to sin, the doctrine of justification fills the believer's heart with gratitude and encourages him with the prospect that, in Christ, his flawed works can please his loving Father in heaven. As the Westminster Confession of Faith (16.6) tells us, "Yet notwithstanding [the remaining corruption and many shortcomings of our good works], the persons of believers being accepted through Christ, their good works also are accepted in Him, not as though they were in this life wholly unblameable and unreprovable in God's sight; but that He, looking upon them in His Son, is pleased to accept and reward that which is sincere, although accompanied with many weaknesses and imperfections."[6] People are helped immeasurably in their efforts to obey God if we teach them to view God in Christ as a forgiving and forbearing Father who delights in his children's works.

Preach Union with Christ as the Vital Root of Holiness

The Lord created and cultivated Israel to be a vineyard bearing the fruits of righteousness. As Isaiah said in his parable (Isa. 5:1–7), what more could God have done to make the inhabitants of Jerusalem and the men of Judah a fruitful vine? But they bore the rotten fruits of injustice and oppression. Fallen human nature can produce nothing good, no matter what external assistance it is granted. Isaiah foresaw, however, that one day "the branch of the LORD" would be "beautiful and glorious" (4:2), and Israel would "fill the face of the world with fruit" (27:6).

---

5. Owen, "Exposition of Psalm 130," in *Works*, 6:533–34 [Ps. 130:4].
6. *Westminster Confession of Faith* (Glasgow: Free Presbyterian Publications, 1994), 71.

Then Christ came, saying, "I am the vine, ye are the branches: He that abideth in me, and I in him, the same bringeth forth much fruit: for without me ye can do nothing" (John 15:5). Christ was teaching that he alone fulfills the promise of Isaiah and enables the people of God to bear the fruits of holiness, and if we would bear such fruit, we can do so only by a lasting, life-giving union with him, mediated through his Word and the Holy Spirit.

Preach to people that they can live in practical holiness only by the exercise of faith in Christ. Warn them that we never leave Christ behind. He is not just the door but the way, the road we must travel, and the life we must live. Colossians 2:6–7 says, "As ye have therefore received Christ Jesus the Lord, so walk ye in him: rooted and built up in him, and stablished in the faith, as ye have been taught, abounding therein with thanksgiving." Unless we want our holiness to degenerate into external religious acts, we must always walk in "faith which worketh by love" (Gal. 5:6).

We must preach this regularly because it is a mystery hidden from the eyes of natural man and contrary to our independent spirits. Everyone understands the rudiments of morality and programs of self-reformation. They also buy into a passive religious mysticism that simply waits for experiences. But it is a strange idea that we must work, labor, and love while at the same time looking to Christ as our life. Many Christians can identify with what Walter Marshall (1628–1680) says: "They account, that though they be justified by a righteousness wrought out by Christ, yet they must be sanctified by a holiness wrought out by themselves." We must teach them, Marshall says, "that the holy frame and disposition whereby our souls are furnished and enabled for immediate practice of the law, must be obtained by receiving it out of Christ's fullness, as a thing already prepared and brought to an existence for us in Christ, and treasured up in him."[7]

We do not obtain this treasure of holiness in Christ by mere imitation, though Scripture does call us to be followers or imitators of God in Christ (Eph. 4:32–5:2). Christ grants this holiness into the believing soul through his union with us as our head (Eph. 4:15–16). Marshall says: "Another great mystery in the way of sanctification, is, the glorious manner of our fellowship with Christ in receiving a holy frame of heart

---

7. Walter Marshall, *The Gospel-Mystery of Sanctification Opened, in Sundry Practical Directions* (New York: Southwick and Pelsue, 1811), 53.

from him. It is by our being in Christ, and having Christ himself in us; and that not merely by this universal presence as he is God, but by such a close union, as that we are one spirit and one flesh with him."[8]

Teach believers that we must exercise faith to benefit practically from our union with Christ, for Christ dwells in our hearts by faith (Eph. 3:17). Show them that while sin no longer reigns in us, it still remains in us. We cannot mortify sin and walk as sons of God apart from the Spirit of Christ (Rom. 8:9–14). Reasons and arguments that demonstrate our obligation to obey cannot give us the inward life to fulfill our obligations. The law is weak by reason of the flesh; only the Spirit can make us holy, by applying the power of Christ's death and resurrection (Rom. 8:2–4).

This leads us to our next point, for union with Christ is the channel through which the living waters of the Spirit flow.

Preach the Spirit as the Power of Holiness

The holy temple of the Lord is built "not by might, nor by power, but by my spirit, saith the LORD of hosts" (Zech. 4:6). In Christ, the church of God "groweth unto an holy temple in the Lord: in whom ye also are builded together for an habitation of God through the Spirit" (Eph. 2:21–22). God's call to each believer to separate from sin and walk in holiness is effective because "he that is joined unto the Lord is one spirit," and his "body is the temple of the Holy Ghost which is in you" (1 Cor. 6:17, 19).

There is much talk about the Holy Spirit in this age, but little preaching of him as "the spirit of holiness" (Rom. 1:4), by whom the resurrection life of Christ is applied to believers so that "we also should walk in newness of life" (Rom. 6:4). We must teach believers that because they are united to Christ in his death and resurrection, they "have crucified the flesh with the affections and lusts" and now bear "the fruit of the Spirit," which is "love, joy, peace, longsuffering, gentleness, goodness, faith, meekness, temperance" (Gal. 5:22–24).

Our contemporary discussions of the Spirit are largely severed from Christ and holiness, tending to focus on emotions, outward effects, continuing revelation, and ministry success. There are legitimate questions to be asked about the Spirit's empowerment for ministry, but our

---

8. Marshall, *Gospel-Mystery of Sanctification*, 54.

preaching should follow the great emphasis of the Scriptures: the Spirit applies what Christ purchased, namely, the redemption and reformation of believers into a new creation where righteousness dwells, God's law is obeyed, and God is glorified.

The Spirit plays the central role in working true holiness in our souls, though what he brings to us is the finished work of Christ done in obedience to the Father's will. Owen says, "It is the Holy Ghost who is the immediate peculiar sanctifier of all believers, and the author of all holiness in them."[9] He explains:

> Sanctification is an immediate work of the Spirit of God on the souls of believers, purifying and cleansing of their natures from the pollution and uncleanness of sin, renewing in them the image of God, and thereby enabling them, from a spiritual and habitual principle of grace, to yield obedience unto God, according unto the tenor and terms of the new covenant, by virtue of the life and death of Jesus Christ. Or more briefly: It is the universal renovation of our natures by the Holy Spirit into the image of God, through Jesus Christ.[10]

Therefore, we must teach Christians that when they look to Christ for holiness, they must seek from him the greatest gift that he has purchased for us: the Spirit of God (Gal. 3:13–14). They must come to him thirsting for those streams of living water that alone satisfy: the Spirit poured out from the hand of the exalted Christ (John 7:37–39). The call to be holy is a call to "walk in the Spirit, and ye shall not fulfil the lust of the flesh" (Gal. 5:16). Owen says, "To walk in the Spirit is to walk in obedience unto God, according to the supplies of grace which the Holy Ghost administers unto us."[11] The Holy Spirit causes God's covenant people to keep his commandments (Ezek. 36:27), even as he directs their hearts into the love of God (2 Thess. 3:5).

Preach holiness shaped by the work of each person of the Trinity. Call people to walk as obedient sons of the Father, who trust in the finished work of his Son as our Mediator, whose benefits flow to us in life-giving streams of the Holy Spirit. Neglecting any person in the Trinity impoverishes our holiness.

---

9. Owen, *Pneumatologia, Or, A Discourse Concerning the Holy Spirit*, in *Works*, 3:385.
10. Owen, "Discourse Concerning the Holy Spirit," in *Works*, 3:386.
11. Owen, "Discourse Concerning the Holy Spirit," in *Works*, 3:533.

Preach Spiritual Warfare as the Way of Holiness

One might think that since Christ is our life, and since he has ascended in total victory and we walk by his Spirit, then we should walk in total victory as well. But we are not in heaven yet. Though we are united to Christ in his triumph (Eph. 2:6), we still live in a mixed condition.

Galatians 5:17 says, "For the flesh lusteth against the Spirit, and the Spirit against the flesh: and these are contrary the one to the other: so that ye cannot do the things that ye would." The way of the Spirit of Christ is the way of wrestling against sin and Satan. Ephesians 6:12 says, "For we wrestle not against flesh and blood, but against principalities, against powers, against the rulers of the darkness of this world, against spiritual wickedness in high places."

The Christian life is spiritual warfare. Christians understand this, and yet they are surprised at how difficult and painful is the struggle to forsake sin and embrace godly attitudes and habits. Therefore, it is our duty as ministers to hold up before them the call to do battle for holiness.

Following Christ is costly. Self-denial is the first step in true discipleship (Matt. 16:24). This is a kind of death, or personal crucifixion, for us. Our Lord Jesus said, "And whosoever doth not bear his cross, and come after me, cannot be my disciple" (Luke 14:27). Christ told us we must count the cost or we will be ill-prepared for the work ahead of us (v. 28). He asked, "What king, going to make war against another king, sitteth not down first, and consulteth whether he be able with ten thousand to meet him that cometh against him with twenty thousand?" (v. 31).

William Gurnall writes that our warring with the Devil is called wrestling to reveal "the sharpness of the combat," in that "it is a single combat" and "a close combat." We do not encounter the spiritual powers of evil from a safe distance, but man to man, in hand-to-hand combat of such an intensity "as makes the body shake."[12] In a wrestling match, there may be many feints, grips, throws, and falls before the victor pins his opponent. Even the winner emerges tired, sore, and bathed in sweat.

We live in a culture that demands immediate results, a way of life shaped by microwave ovens, name-it-and-claim-it theology, high-speed Internet service, and many false expectations of the Holy Spirit. The biblical preacher must show his congregation that struggling and wrestling

---

12. William Gurnall, *The Christian in Complete Armour: A Treatise of the Saints' War Against the Devil* (London: Banner of Truth, 1964), 1:113.

against evil do not indicate that one is living in defeat or in second-class spirituality. The apostle Paul did not coast into heaven in a self-propelled La-Z-Boy recliner on wheels, but ran the race, contended, boxed, and even fought with beasts, and so he fought the good fight (1 Cor. 9:24–27; 15:32; 2 Tim. 4:7). Equip the saints to do the same.

And promise them that, strong in Christ's strength and clad in the armor of God, they are able to stand and, in the end, to overcome (Eph. 6:10, 11, 13, 16). William Gouge (1575–1653) says, "It is not sufficient to begin the fight well."[13] But he also says that in Christ we are "conquerors," and he counsels: "In all conflicts have an eye to this end, though your enemies be many and fierce, yet fear not, ye shall stand when they shall fly. Patiently wait, and faint not."[14]

Preach the Moral Law as the Rule of Holiness

The Bible exudes delight in the law of God. Paul writes: "Wherefore the law is holy, and the commandment holy, and just, and good. . . . For I delight in the law of God after the inward man" (Rom. 7:12, 22). David sings, "The statutes of the LORD are right, rejoicing the heart: the commandment of the LORD is pure, enlightening the eyes" (Ps. 19:8).

The godly value all parts of the law of God, rejoicing in his testimonies as in all riches (Ps. 119:14), delighting in his statutes (v. 16), longing for his precepts (v. 40), loving his commandments (v. 47), finding comfort in his Word during affliction (v. 50), believing the commandments (v. 66), treasuring God's law more than thousands of gold and silver coins (v. 72), meditating on it (v. 97), tasting the sweetness of his words (v. 103), following the light of his Word (v. 105), and choosing his precepts as their guide (v. 173).

Christ writes God's law upon the hearts of his people with the ink of the Spirit (2 Cor. 3:3; Jer. 31:33). Christ makes them like himself, a people who have the law in their hearts and who delight to do God's will (Ps. 40:8; Heb. 10:7). Yet even the people of God can become confused about the law of God, swamped with a flood of the church's antinomianism and the world's antiauthoritarianism. Even the words *law, judge,* and *legal* have a bad taste to us today. But this is not a great surprise.

---

13. William Gouge, *Panoplia Tou Theou: The Whole-Armor of God, or, The Spiritvall Fvrnitvre Which God Hath Prouided to Keepe Safe euery Christian Sovldier from All the Assaults of Satan* (London: Printed by Iohn Beale, 1616), 112.
14. Gouge, *The Whole-Armor of God,* 114–15.

Paul says in Romans 8:6–7 that the mind of fallen, carnal man is death, "because the carnal mind is enmity against God: for it is not subject to the law of God, neither indeed can be." Insofar as sin reigns or remains in people, they hate God and so also hate the law of God.

In such a hostile milieu, the preacher must not shrink from proclaiming the demands of the law of God. He must preach the law as a convicting and condemning revelation of sin (Rom. 3:19–20). The law is a divine weapon against legalism, for it shows that no sinner can be justified by his own works or sanctified by his own power. The law, rightly preached, exposes the hypocrisy of those who replace God's Word with man's traditions (Matt. 15:1–9). It drives men to Christ (Gal. 3:24) as the only Savior from the condemnation of the law.

The law also serves the justified people of Christ by guiding them in the good way. With respect to their conduct, nothing matters to them except "the keeping of the commandments of God" (1 Cor. 7:19). Though they are free from the old covenant ceremonies, they are "not without law to God, but under the law to Christ" (1 Cor. 9:21). Therefore, the Reformed experiential minister must preach the law to the saints of God, not as their judge but as their servant and guide to living in Christ.

Preach the Ten Commandments as a rule of life to all who are in Christ. God elevated these laws above all his other legislation by speaking them directly to the people from Mount Sinai, writing them with his own finger on the tablets of stone, assigning them a special place in the ark of the covenant, and referring to these "ten words" as his covenant.[15] It is astonishing how many professing Christians cannot list all ten of these precious commandments. Surely this ignorance is to be laid at the feet of the pastors of the churches, who have neglected the preaching of the moral law.

The Ten Commandments offer us a brief and helpful summary of God's law for all of life. Make good use of the wisdom compiled in the rich expositions of the Ten Commandments in the Heidelberg Catechism and the Westminster Shorter and Larger Catechisms. Dive into classic expositions of the moral law by Thomas Watson, James Durham, and other Reformed and Puritan preachers.[16] Preaching the law enables you to address people's lives with specific, pointed applications rather

---

15. Ex. 20:1; 25:16; 31:18; 32:16; 34:1, 28; Deut. 4:12–13; 10:1–5; 2 Chron. 5:10; Heb. 9:4.
16. Thomas Watson, *The Ten Commandments* (Edinburgh: Banner of Truth, 2000); James Durham, *A Practical Exposition of the Ten Commandments*, ed. Christopher Coldwell (Dallas: Naphtali, 2002).

than vague applications that grasp no one's conscience and fail to direct people in a practical way.

Also preach the various presentations of the law throughout the Bible. Preach Christ's Sermon on the Mount. It contains a remarkable exposition of the law, affirming that the moral law revealed in the Old Testament abides forever (Matt. 5:17–48). Our Lord said, "For verily I say unto you, Till heaven and earth pass, one jot or one tittle shall in no wise pass from the law, till all be fulfilled" (v. 18). William Perkins, commenting on this text, says that the moral law "remains forever a rule of obedience to every child of God, though he be not bound to bring the same obedience for his justification before God."[17] The Sermon on the Mount also highlights that the law is spiritual and addresses not merely external acts, but the anger, enmity, lust, hypocrisy, and hardness of our hearts.

Be careful, as you preach the law, to remember the points I made earlier about preaching justification and union with Christ. The law is given to a redeemed people by their covenant God (Ex. 20:2). But do not shrink back from preaching the law. There is nothing legalistic about pressing upon the saints their sacred obligation to live according to all of God's commandments. Though they are not judged by the rigor of the law, only full compliance to the law attains to the complete image of God, as seen in the blameless life of Christ. The law strengthens us. Many questions about God's will would be resolved if God's people would meditate deeply on his law. The holy law of God gives us a moral backbone by which to stand against the shifting tides of moral relativism around us.

Preach Love as the Soul of Holiness

When our Lord condensed the law down into a briefer summary than the Ten Commandments, he selected two Old Testament commands that center on one word: *love*. All the laws of God hang on our all-consuming love for God and our extension of proper self-love to embrace our neighbors (Matt. 22:37–40). Paul says, "Love is the fulfilling of the law" (Rom. 13:10; cf. Gal. 5:14; James 2:8). Thomas Watson says, by way of introducing the Ten Commandments, "Love is the soul of religion, and

---

17. Quoted in J. Stephen Yuille, *Living Blessedly Forever: The Sermon on the Mount and the Puritan Piety of William Perkins* (Grand Rapids, MI: Reformation Heritage Books, 2012), 59.

that which goes to the right constituting a Christian; love is the queen of the graces."[18]

If our preaching does not major on love, then we have missed the point of the Bible. We obscure the doctrine of God: "He that loveth not knoweth not God; for God is love" (1 John 4:8). Jonathan Edwards writes in lyrical, Trinitarian exultation:

> God is the fountain of love, as the sun is the fountain of light. . . . And therefore seeing he is an infinite Being, it follows that he is an infinite fountain of love. Seeing he is an all-sufficient Being, it follows that he is a full and overflowing and an inexhaustible fountain of love. Seeing he is an unchangeable and eternal Being, he is an unchangeable and eternal source of love. . . . There dwells God the Father, and so the Son, who are united in infinitely dear and incomprehensible mutual love. . . . There is the Holy Spirit, the spirit of divine love, in whom the very essence of God, as it were, all flows out or is breathed forth in love.[19]

Furthermore, if we neglect love, we confuse the gospel: "Herein is love, not that we loved God, but that he loved us, and sent his Son to be the propitiation for our sins" (1 John 4:10). We cover up the marks of true conversion: "Beloved, let us love one another: for love is of God; and every one that loveth is born of God, and knoweth God" (v. 7). People might do everything we preach to them, but if we do not preach love as the Christian's basic motivation, then their lives will still be spiritually empty in God's sight (1 Cor. 13:1–3).

Much of people's bias against holiness consists of a caricature in their minds of religious zeal without love. They rightly see that religion has no reality without love. Therefore, calling the church to love one another serves a vital evangelistic purpose. Jesus said, "By this shall all men know that ye are my disciples, if ye have love one to another" (John 13:35).

Preaching love also dispels much ethical mythology that enslaves people. *Love* is one of the most abused words in our language, misconstrued and perverted to justify all manner of evil. By preaching true love for God and one another as the most fundamental requirement of God's law, you can clarify for the people the meanings of both *love* and *law*.

---

18. Thomas Watson, *A Body of Practical Divinity in a Series of Sermons on the Shorter Catechism* (London: A Fullarton and Co., 1845), 215.

19. Jonathan Edwards, "Charity and Its Fruits," in *The Works of Jonathan Edwards*, vol. 8, *Ethical Writings*, ed. Paul Ramsey (New Haven, CT: Yale University Press, 1989), 369.

By linking the specific commandments of God to the grand mandate of love, you guard your church from an empty, ugly legalism and fill their ethical duties with a most attractive sweetness.

You also can be an instrument to put self-love in its place. Stripped of divine love, natural self-love has become a tyrant that destroys us by turning us inward into ourselves. Modern self-esteem theology tries to appease this tyrant by giving him his due. Edwards writes that in fallen man, human love is "shrunk into a little point, circumscribed and closely shut up within itself to the exclusion of others." Self-love, once a servant to God, now usurps God's place as the soul's "absolute master."[20] But true love for God and neighbor restores self-love to its position of a good and useful servant.

Proclaiming the law of love stirs your people toward holy activity, for love is an active grace. Watson writes, "Love to God must be active in its sphere; love is an industrious affection, it sets the head a-studying for God, hands a-working, feet a-running in the ways of his commandments, it is called 'the labour of love' (1 Thess. 1:3)."[21]

You also help to expand their souls into true greatness, in possession of fuller and more authentic humanity, for when they understand the biblical idea of love, they become like God in the way that matters most.

Preach Affliction as the Training Camp of Holiness

One of the most mysterious statements about Christ in the Bible appears in Hebrews 5:8: "Though he were a Son, yet learned he obedience by the things which he suffered." The Holy Spirit had just asserted that Christ, though tempted as we are, was "yet without sin" (Heb. 4:15). How then did he learn obedience through suffering? He did not have to cleanse his soul from evil, for he was "holy, harmless, undefiled" (Heb. 7:26). His human body and soul were holy from conception (Luke 1:35), and yet his human holiness had to grow through exercise, just as muscles grow stronger by exercise even to the point of pain. And what suffering Christ endured to learn obedience! It wrenched from him "prayers and supplications with strong crying and tears" (Heb. 5:7).

If righteous Jesus had to suffer so much to learn obedience, how much more do we need to suffer in order to purge away our sins and

---

20. Edwards, "Charity and Its Fruits," in *Works*, 8:253.
21. Watson, *A Body of Practical Divinity*, 215

grow in his likeness? Sin clings to our souls more stubbornly than stains to our clothes, but God will get it out. Gurnall says: "God would not rub so hard if it were not to fetch out the dirt that is ingrained in our natures. God loves purity so well that he had rather see a hole than a spot in his child's garments."[22]

Materialism and psychology fool us into thinking that our greatest goods in life are our physical, financial, and emotional well-being. Therefore, when afflictions come, we may question the truth of Romans 8:28: "All things work together for good to them that love God, to them who are the called according to his purpose." We cry out, "How can this affliction be working good for me?" But we need to read the next verse to discover what God decrees as our good: "to be conformed to the image of his Son" (v. 29). The Father elected us to holiness (Eph. 1:4). Christ died to make his church holy (5:25–27). God will stop at nothing to make his people holy, after the image of his Son.

Therefore, preach to your people a theology of suffering that places all our trials in the hands and will of a loving Father. Hebrews 12 teaches us to view our sorrows, even the persecutions of wicked men, as part of God's fatherly discipline: "Ye have not yet resisted unto blood, striving against sin. And ye have forgotten the exhortation which speaketh unto you as unto children, My son, despise not thou the chastening of the Lord, nor faint when thou art rebuked of him: for whom the Lord loveth he chasteneth, and scourgeth every son whom he receiveth" (vv. 4–6). Why would a loving God discipline his children so severely? He does it so "that we might be partakers of his holiness," for without that holiness, "no man shall see the Lord" (vv. 10, 14). He is drawing us into his fatherly presence by engraving his image upon us, even through the strokes of a rod.

Teach your congregation to view their sufferings as their training for holiness. Encourage them to submit to the rod of their Father, trusting in his goodness and love revealed at the cross (Rom. 8:32). Show them the many benefits of submitting to God's sanctifying trials with meekness. Thomas Brooks says that Christians should be "mute" or quiet under the smiting of God's rod so that they can (1) learn from God's correction and repent of sin, (2) distinguish themselves from the world, which murmurs against and curses God, (3) become like Christ, who suffered

---

22. Gurnall, *The Christian in Complete Armour*, 1:417–18.

quietly as a lamb led to slaughter, (4) escape the curse of a fretful spirit, which is a thousand times worse than any outward affliction, (5) enjoy the comfort of inward peace, (6) avoid a futile striving against almighty God, (7) frustrate Satan's design to tempt them to blaspheme God, and (8) follow in the footsteps of other saints who patiently endured suffering before us.[23]

Preach the Bible Stories as the Human Shape of Holiness

Reformed preaching is sometimes identified with the teaching of doctrine. We may contribute to this caricature if we are perpetually preaching on the Pauline Epistles. We are accused of building theological cathedrals, massive edifices of abstract thought, while the world suffers and perishes around us. Throughout this book, I have made the case for preaching that is biblical, doctrinal, experiential, and practical. There is no reason why a series, for example, on the epistle to the Hebrews cannot speak profoundly to the hearts of the people. In fact, though people sometimes view Hebrews as a lofty theological treatise, it is a written sermon that addressed people hurting so much they were tempted to walk away from the faith.

At the same time, there is much more to the Bible than the didactic epistles. There are the stirring apocalyptic visions of Daniel and Revelation. There are the pithy aphorisms of Proverbs and Ecclesiastes. There are soaring songs and prayers in the Psalms that help us to pour out our hearts before the Lord. And there are the narratives, the historical accounts of events and people who knew the Lord and saw his works.

Paul, after reciting some of the events in the history of Israel's exodus from Egypt, says: "Now these things were our examples. . . . All these things happened unto them for examples: and they are written for our admonition, upon whom the ends of the world are come" (1 Cor. 10:6, 11). The Spirit inspired the recording of these stories to warn and encourage us today. Romans 15:4 says, "Whatsoever things were written aforetime were written for our learning, that we through patience and comfort of the scriptures might have hope." The Scriptures give us the examples of a great cloud of witnesses, who are urging us to persevere in the race set before us (Heb. 12:1).

---

23. Thomas Brooks, "The Mute Christian under the Smarting Rod," in *The Works of Thomas Brooks*, ed. Alexander B. Grosart (Edinburgh: Banner of Truth, 2001), 1:312–19.

Don't neglect the Bible stories. Preach them. Perkins observes that "howsoever believers be greatly cheered in their spiritual travel, by the gracious promises which God in Christ hath made unto them; yet this their joy is much increased, by the view of those that have gone before them in the way of faith." He says that although "the truth of God be the only ground of sound consolation," yet because of our weakness, we like Thomas find much help and joy when godly examples are added to the promises of God.[24]

Preach the Bible stories as stories. Avoid turning them into doctrinal treatises. While each sermon should contain sound doctrine (clear statements of truth about God and man), it should be shaped by the literary genre of the text. Enter into the account and view the characters not merely as props for theological propositions but as real people. Sympathize with them. Do not rush through the narrative to get to the theological point. Pay attention to the details. Ask questions of the text: Why did he do that? What does that show us about him? Research the historical, geographical, and cultural backgrounds. Then, along the way, pause to draw valuable doctrinal, experiential, and practical lessons for your hearers. You will discover that the Bible stories add human flesh to the bones of theological principles, helping those principles to come alive in the understanding and experience of the hearers.[25]

Preach Heaven as the Aspiration of Holiness

The Lord Jesus said, "Blessed are the pure in heart: for they shall see God" (Matt. 5:8). The apostle John echoes this truth when he writes, "Beloved, now are we the sons of God, and it doth not yet appear what we shall be: but we know that, when he shall appear, we shall be like him; for we shall see him as he is. And every man that hath this hope in him purifieth himself, even as he is pure" (1 John 3:2–3). There is an inseparable relation between sanctification and the hope that we "shall see the king in his beauty" (Isa. 33:17). The same Christ who intercedes for his people, saying, "Sanctify them through thy truth: thy word is truth," also prays, "Father, I will that they also, whom thou hast given me, be with me where

---

24. William Perkins, "Epistle Dedicatorie," in *A Commentary on Hebrews 11, 1609 Edition*, ed. John H. Augustine (New York: Pilgrim Press, 1991), no pagination.

25. Some attempts on my part to preach biblical narratives may be found in Joel R. Beeke, *Portraits of Faith* (Bridgend, Wales: Bryntirion, 2004); *Walking as He Walked* (Grand Rapids, MI/ Bridgend, Wales: Reformation Heritage Books/Bryntirion, 2007).

I am; that they may behold my glory, which thou hast given me: for thou lovedst me before the foundation of the world" (John 17:17, 24). "Christ in you" is "the hope of glory" (Col. 1:27). Christ-centered preaching must be heavenly minded preaching, for Christ is enthroned in heaven.

The pursuit of holiness is a pilgrimage to heaven. Every iota of our growth in holiness is a step closer to the city of God. Christ our living head has gone ahead of us, we are raised up with him, and presently we shall follow him to glory. Therefore, to fix our eyes on holiness, we must "seek those things which are above, where Christ sitteth on the right hand of God" (Col. 3:1).

While our minds cannot fully comprehend the beauties of heaven, do not fall into the trap of assuming that heaven is to be hidden in a cloud of unknowing. Too many Christians say, "We just can't understand what heaven is like" and stop there. Preach what the Scriptures reveal. Show people what their inheritance with the saints in light is (Col. 1:12). What you will discover after careful study is that the Bible presents a fulsome doctrine of heaven revolving around the glory of God, the enthronement of Christ our Mediator, and the perfected holiness of his people (Heb. 12:22–24). Rather than speculations about the times and seasons of the end of the age, people need solid, biblical eschatology that makes them watchful, faithful, and hopeful (Matt. 24:36–51).

Holiness is the only highway to heaven; without it no one will see the Lord (Isa. 35:8–10; Heb. 12:14). The unclean and wicked shall never enter the holy city, but only those who keep God's commandments (Rev. 21:27; 22:14–15), for heaven is full of the glory of God. Owen warns:

> There is no imagination wherewith mankind is besotted more foolish, none so pernicious, as this, that persons not purified, not sanctified, not made holy, in this life, should afterward be taken into that state of blessedness which consists in the enjoyment of God. There can be no thought more reproachful to his glory, nor more inconsistent with the nature of the things themselves; for neither can such persons enjoy him, nor would God himself be a reward unto them. . . . Holiness, indeed, is perfected in heaven, but the beginning of it is invariably and unalterably confined to this world.[26]

Call your people to seek the kingdom of God and his righteousness. Preaching a heavenly mind-set releases people from the evil lusts of this

---

26. Owen, "Discourse Concerning the Holy Spirit," in *Works*, 3:574–75.

present world. You must exhort people, "Set your affection on things above, not on things on the earth" (Col. 3:2). Their pursuit of holiness will be greatly helped if you show them how fleeting, corrupt, and unsubstantial this world is (1 John 2:15–17), and how enduring, pure, and solid their inheritance is in heaven (1 Pet. 1:4). They will fear the frowns of this world much less, and trample its sordid pleasures underfoot, if they keep their crown in view. Calvin says, "We ought to apply our minds to meditation upon a future life, so that this world may become cheap to us, and we may be prepared when necessary to pour forth our blood in testimony to the truth."[27]

You can strengthen believers as soldiers of Jesus Christ to endure hardship and remain free from the entanglements of this life if you remind them that we who suffer with Christ will also reign with him (2 Tim. 2:3–4, 12). Therefore, engage your church with the "blessed hope" of seeing "the glorious appearing of the great God and our Saviour Jesus Christ," so that "denying ungodliness and worldly lusts, we should live soberly, righteously, and godly, in this present world" (Titus 2:12–13).

Preach Humbly as a Man of Holiness

Few comments about preachers are as devastating as Christ's words in Matthew 23:3: "They say, and do not." What a contrast to this is the example of Ezra: "For Ezra had prepared his heart to seek the law of the LORD, and to do it, and to teach in Israel statutes and judgments" (Ezra 7:10). The preacher must preach holiness as a man who practices holiness. Paul exhorted Timothy, "Let no man despise thy youth; but be thou an example of the believers, in word, in conversation, in charity, in spirit, in faith, in purity. . . . Take heed unto thyself, and unto the doctrine; continue in them: for in doing this thou shalt both save thyself, and them that hear thee" (1 Tim. 4:12, 16).

We all have much cause to humble ourselves in this regard. Horatius Bonar (1808–1889) tells us that in 1651, the ministers of Scotland gathered to confess their sins. Their confession was extensive, piercing, and grievous. Here is just part of it:

- Ignorance of God; want of nearness with him, and taking up little of God in reading, meditating, and speaking of him.

---

27. John Calvin, *Commentaries of Calvin*, various translators and editors, 45 vols. (Edinburgh: Calvin Translation Society, 1846–1851; repr., 22 vols., Grand Rapids, MI: Baker, 1979) [Dan. 3:19–20].

- Exceeding great selfishness in all that we do; acting from ourselves, for ourselves, and to ourselves.
- Not caring how unfaithful and negligent others were, so being it might contribute a testimony to our faithfulness and diligence, but being rather content, if not rejoicing at their faults.
- Least delight in those things wherein lieth our nearest communion with God; great inconstancy in our walk with God, and neglect of acknowledging him in all our ways.
- In going about duties, least careful of those things which are most remote from the eyes of men. Seldom in secret prayer with God, except to fit for public performances; and even that much neglected, or gone about very superficially.
- Glad to find excuses for the neglect of duties. Neglecting the reading of Scriptures in secret, for edifying ourselves as Christians; only reading them in so far as may fit us for our duty as ministers, and ofttimes neglecting that.
- Not given to reflect upon our own ways, nor suffering conviction to have a thorough work upon us . . . carelessness in self-searching; which makes much unacquaintedness with ourselves, and estrangedness from God.
- Not guarding nor wrestling against seen and known evils, especially our predominants.
- A facility to be drawn away with the temptations of the time, and other particular temptations, according to our inclinations and fellowship.
- Instability and wavering in the ways of God, through the fears of persecutions, hazard, or loss of esteem; and declining duties because of the fear of jealousies and reproaches.
- Not esteeming the cross of Christ, and sufferings for his name, honorable, but rather shifting sufferings, from self-love.
- Not laying to heart the sad and heavy sufferings of the people of God abroad, and the not thriving of the kingdom of Jesus Christ, and the power of godliness among them.
- Refined hypocrisy desiring to appear what, indeed, we are not.[28]

O brothers! Let us cast ourselves down before the throne of grace. We as ministers and teachers of the Word, who shall incur a stricter judgment (James 3:1), must more than all other Christians lean entirely

---

28. Horatius Bonar, *Words to Winners of Souls* (Boston: American Tract Society, n.d.), 47–50.

upon the blood of Christ and his priestly intercession for our justification, preservation, and perseverance in the way of holiness. Let us abide humbly in Christ as the vine who alone can make us fruitful. Let us walk in the Spirit with all humility, knowing that in our flesh dwells no good thing. We need the Spirit to illuminate us, or all our education and gifts for ministry will not keep us from wandering into heresy and immorality. We need the Spirit to subjugate us and keep us walking according to the will of God, or we will not be faithful.

Let us view with abhorrence all spiritual pride and arrogance. Though our pulpits and platforms may elevate us physically above the congregation, we know that many saints before us are our superiors in the Lord—and judgment day will show it in their greater rewards: "the last shall be first" (Matt. 19:30). Let us preach with personal meekness even as we boldly declare the Word of God. Let us renounce all temptations to woo the hearts of people to and for ourselves. Instead, may John the Baptist's dictum be our rule:

> A man can receive nothing, except it be given him from heaven. Ye yourselves bear me witness, that I said, I am not the Christ, but that I am sent before him. He that hath the bride is the bridegroom: but the friend of the bridegroom, which standeth and heareth him, rejoiceth greatly because of the bridegroom's voice: this my joy therefore is fulfilled. *He must increase, but I must decrease.* (John 3:27–30)

The true Reformed experiential preacher is a humble preacher, precisely because he is a true lover of Christ in pursuit of holiness, content to be nothing, if in that way Christ may be all in all.

Bibliography

Works Referenced in This Book[1]

Acta Synodi Nationalis, In nomine Domini nostri Iesv Christi, Autoritate Illvstr. et Praepotentvm DD. Ordinvm Generalivm Foederati Belgii Provinciarvm, Dordrechti Habitae Anno MDCXVIII et MDCXIX. Lvgdvni Batavorvm: Isaaci Elzeviri, 1620.

Adams, Thomas. The Works of Thomas Adams. 3 vols. 1862. Reprint, Eureka, CA: Tanski, 1998.

Affleck, Bert. "The Theology of Richard Sibbes, 1577–1635." PhD diss., Drew University, 1968.

Akira, Demura. "Church Discipline According to Johannes Oecolampadius in the Setting of His Life and Thought." PhD diss., Princeton Theological Seminary, 1964.

Albro, John A. *The Life of Thomas Shepard.* Boston: Massachusetts Sabbath School Society, 1847.

Alexander, Archibald. *A Brief Compendium of Bible Truth.* Edited by Joel R. Beeke. Grand Rapids, MI: Reformation Heritage Books, 2005.

———. "A Treatise in Which the Difference Between a Living and a Dead Faith Is Explained, 1791." In *Banner of Sovereign Grace Truth* 2, no. 6 (July/August 1994): 145.

———. "A Treatise in Which the Difference Between a Living and a Dead Faith Is Explained, 1791." In *Banner of Sovereign Grace Truth* 2, no. 7 (September 1994): 181–82.

---

1. As a general rule, when more than one printing of a title was referenced in this work, only one of those printings was listed in this bibliography.

————. "A Treatise in Which the Difference Between a Living and a Dead Faith Is Explained, 1791." In *Banner of Sovereign Grace Truth* 2, no. 8 (October 1994): 204–6.

————. "A Treatise in Which the Difference Between a Living and a Dead Faith Is Explained, 1791." In *Banner of Truth*, 335–36 (September 1991): 39–54.

————. *Evangelical Truth: Practical Sermons for the Christian Home.* Birmingham, AL: Solid Ground, 2004.

————. "Rightly Dividing the Word of Truth." In *The Princeton Pulpit.* Edited by John T. Duffield. New York: Charles Scribner, 1852.

————. *The Way of Salvation: Familiarly Explained in a Conversation Between a Father and His Children.* Philadelphia: Presbyterian Board of Publication, 1839.

————. *Thoughts on Religious Experience.* Philadelphia: Presbyterian Board of Publication, 1844.

Alexander, Archibald, Charles Hodge, et al. *Princeton Versus the New Divinity: The Meaning of Sin, Grace, Salvation, Revival: Articles from the Princeton Review.* Edinburgh: Banner of Truth, 2001.

Alexander, James W. *Life of Archibald Alexander.* New York: Scribner, 1854.

Alexander, Joseph A. *The Later Prophecies of Isaiah.* New York: Wiley and Putnam, 1847.

Alleine, Joseph. *A Sure Guide to Heaven.* Edinburgh: Banner of Truth, 1995.

Ambrose, Isaac. *Looking Unto Jesus.* Harrisonburg, VA: Sprinkle, 1988.

————. *The Works of Isaac Ambrose.* London: for Thomas Tegg & Son, 1701.

Ames, William. *The Marrow of Sacred Divinity.* London: Edward Griffin for Henry Overton, 1642.

Arnott, Anne. *He Shall with Giants Fight.* Eastbourne, UK: Kingsway, 1985.

Augustine. *Earlier Writings.* Library of Christian Classics, 6. Edited by John H. S. Burleigh. Philadelphia: Westminster, 1953.

Backus, Irena Dorota. *The Reformed Roots of the English New Testament: The Influence of Theodore Beza on the English New Testament.* Pittsburgh Theological Monograph Series, 28. Pittsburgh: Pickwick, 1980.

Bacon, Leonard W. *A History of American Christianity.* New York: Christian Literature Co., 1897.

Baird, Henry Martyn. *Theodore Beza: The Counsellor of the French Reformation, 1519–1605.* Burt Franklin Research & Source Works Series, 475. Eugene, OR: Wipf & Stock, 2004.

Baker, J. Wayne. *Heinrich Bullinger and the Covenant: The Other Reformed Tradition*. Athens, OH: Ohio University Press, 1980.

Balke, Willem. "Het Pietisme in Oostfriesland." In *Theologia Reformata* 21 (1978): 320–27.

———. "The Word of God and *Experientia* according to Calvin." In *Calvinus Ecclesiae Doctor*, edited by Wilhelm H. Neuser, 19–31. Kampen: Kok, 1978.

Ball, Thomas. *The Life of the Renowned Doctor Preston*. Edited by E. W. Harcourt. London: Parker and Co., 1885.

Balmer, Randall H. *A Perfect Babel of Confusion: Dutch Religion and English Culture in the Middle Colonies*. Oxford: Oxford University Press, 1989.

Barrett, Michael P. V. *Beginning at Moses: A Guide to Finding Christ in the Old Testament*. Grand Rapids, MI: Reformation Heritage Books, 2018.

Baxter, Richard. *The Dying Thoughts of the Reverend Learned and Holy Mr. Richard Baxter*. Abridged by Benjamin Fawcett. Salop: J. Cotton and J. Eddowes, 1761.

———. *The Practical Works of Richard Baxter*. 4 vols. Reprint, Ligonier, PA: Soli Deo Gloria, 1990–1991.

———. *The Reformed Pastor*. Edinburgh: Banner of Truth, 1974.

Baynes, Paul. *The Diocesans Tryall: Wherein All the Sinnewes of Doctor Dovvnhams Defence Are Bought into Three Heads, and Orderly Dissolved*. London: n.p., 1621.

Beck, Stephen Paul. "The Doctrine of *Gratia Praeparans* in the Soteriology of Richard Sibbes." PhD diss., Westminster Theological Seminary, 1994.

Beddome, Benjamin. *A Scriptural Exposition of the Baptist Catechism*. Birmingham, AL: Solid Ground, 2006.

Beeke, Joel R. "Calvin as an Experiential Preacher." In *Puritan Reformed Journal* 1, no. 2 (July 2009): 131–54.

———. *Gisbertus Voetius: Toward a Reformed Marriage of Knowledge and Piety*. Grand Rapids, MI: Reformation Heritage Books, 1999.

———. *Jehovah Shepherding His Sheep: Sermons on the Twenty-Third Psalm*. Sioux Center, IA: Netherlands Reformed Book and Publishing, 1982.

———. "Justification *by* Faith Alone." In *Justification by Faith Alone*, edited by Don Kistler, 53–105. Morgan, PA: Soli Deo Gloria, 2003.

———. *Living for God's Glory: An Introduction to Calvinism*. Lake Mary, FL: Reformation Trust, 2008.

———. *Portraits of Faith*. Bridgend, Wales: Bryntirion, 2004.

———. *Puritan Reformed Spirituality*. Darlington, England: Evangelical Press, 2006.

———. *The Quest for Full Assurance: The Legacy of Calvin and His Successors*. Edinburgh: Banner of Truth, 1999.

———. "Theodore Beza's Supralapsarian Predestination." In *Reformation and Revival Journal* 12, no. 2 (Spring 2003): 69–84.

———. "Thomas Goodwin on Christ's Beautiful Heart." In *The Beauty and Glory of Christ*, edited by Joel R. Beeke, 135–54. Grand Rapids, MI: Reformation Heritage Books, 2011.

———. "The Utter Necessity of a Godly Life." In *Reforming Pastoral Ministry: Challenges for Ministry in Postmodern Times*, edited by John H. Armstrong, 59–82. Wheaton, IL: Crossway, 2001.

———. *Walking as He Walked*. Grand Rapids, MI: Reformation Heritage Books; Bridgend, Wales: Bryntirion, 2007.

———. "William Perkins on Predestination, Preaching, and Conversion." In *The Practical Calvinist: An Introduction to the Presbyterian and Reformed Heritage: In Honor of D. Clair Davis*, edited by Peter A. Lillback, 183–213. Fearn, Ross-shire, Scotland: Christian Focus, 2002.

Beeke, Joel R., and James A. La Belle. *Living Zealously*. Grand Rapids, MI: Reformation Heritage Books, 2012.

Beeke, Joel R., and Mark Jones. *A Puritan Theology: Doctrine for Life*. Grand Rapids, MI: Reformation Heritage Books, 2012.

Beeke, Joel R., and Paul M. Smalley, eds. *Feasting with Christ: Meditations on the Lord's Supper*. Darlington, England: Evangelical Press, 2012.

Beeke, Joel R., and Randall J. Pederson. *Meet the Puritans: With a Guide to Modern Reprints*. Grand Rapids, MI: Reformation Heritage Books, 2006.

Beeke, Joel R., and Sinclair B. Ferguson, eds. *Reformed Confessions Harmonized*. Grand Rapids, MI: Baker, 1999.

Beeke, Joel R., ed. *Doctrinal Standards, Liturgy, and Church Order*. Grand Rapids, MI: Reformation Heritage Books, 2003.

———, ed. *Forerunner of the Great Awakening: Sermons by Theodorus Jacobus Frelinghuysen (1691–1747)*. The Historical Series of the Reformed Church in America, no. 36. Grand Rapids, MI: Eerdmans, 2000.

———, ed. *The Psalter with Doctrinal Standards, Liturgy, Church Order, and Added Chorale Section*. Grand Rapids, MI: Reformation Heritage Books, 2010.

————, ed. *The Soul of Life: The Piety of John Calvin.* Grand Rapids, MI: Reformation Heritage Books, 2009.

Belcher, Joseph. *George Whitefield: A Biography.* New York: American Tract Society, 1857.

Benoit, Jean-Daniel. *Calvin in His Letters: A Study of Calvin's Pastoral Counseling Mainly from His Letters.* Appleford, England: Sutton Courtenay, 1986.

Berkouwer, G. C. *Divine Election.* Translated by Hugo Bekker. Grand Rapids, MI: Eerdmans, 1960.

Berthoud, Jean-Marc. "John Calvin and the Spread of the Gospel in France." In *Fulfilling the Great Commission*, 44–46. London: Westminster Conference, 1992.

Beza, Theodore. *The Christian Faith.* Translated by James Clark. Lewes, UK: Focus Christian Ministries Trust, 1992.

Bèze, Théodore de. *A Little Book of Christian Questions and Responses in Which the Principal Headings of the Christian Religion Are Briefly Set Forth.* Princeton Theological Monograph Series, Issue 9. Translated by Kirk M. Summers. Allison Park, PA: Pickwick, 1986.

————. "The Potter and the Clay: The Main Predestination Writings of Theodore Beza." Translated by Philip C. Holtrop. Grand Rapids, MI: Calvin College, 1982.

Bickel, R. Bruce. *Light and Heat: The Puritan View of the Pulpit.* Morgan, PA: Soli Deo Gloria, 1999.

Billingsley, A. S. *The Life of the Great Preacher, Reverend George Whitefield, "prince of Pulpit Orators": With the Secret of His Success, and Specimens of His Sermons.* Philadelphia: P. W. Ziegler & Company, 1878.

Blackham, Paul. "The Pneumatology of Thomas Goodwin." PhD diss., University of London, 1995.

Blaikie, W. Garden. *The Personal Life of David Livingstone.* New York: Fleming H. Revell, 1880.

Blench, J. W. *Preaching in England in the Late Fifteenth and Sixteenth Centuries.* Oxford: Basil Blackwell, 1964.

Bolton, Robert. *A Treatise on Comforting Afflicted Consciences.* Ligonier, PA: Soli Deo Gloria, 1991.

Bonar, Andrew A., ed. *Memoir and Remains of Robert Murray M'Cheyne.* 1892. Reprint, Edinburgh: Banner of Truth, 1966.

Bonar, Horatius. *Words to Winners of Souls.* Boston: American Tract Society, n.d.

Boot, Izaäk. *De Allegorische Uitlegging van het Hooglied voornamelijk in Nederland: Een Onderzoek naar de Verhouding tussen Bernard van Clairvaux en de Nadere Reformatie.* Woerden: Zuijderduijn, 1971.

Boston, Thomas. *The Art of Manfishing: A Puritan's View of Evangelism.* Fearn, Ross-shire, Scotland: Christian Focus, 1998.

Bounds, E. M. *Preacher and Prayer.* Chicago: Christian Witness Co., 1907.

Bouwman, Harm. *Willem Teellinck en de Practijk der Godzaligheid.* Kampen: Kok, 1928.

Bouwsma, William. *John Calvin: A Sixteenth-Century Portrait.* New York: Oxford University Press, 1988.

Bowman, John C. "Calvin as a Preacher." In *Reformed Church Review*, no. 56 (1909): 251–52.

Boys, John. *The Works of John Boys: An Exposition of the Several Offices.* Morgan, PA: Soli Deo Gloria, 1997.

Bozell, Ruth Beatrice. "English Preachers of the 17th Century on the Art of Preaching." PhD diss., Cornell University, 1939.

Braga, James. *How to Prepare Bible Messages.* Rev. ed. Portland, OR: Multnomah, 1981.

Brakel, Wilhelmus à. *The Christian's Reasonable Service.* Edited by Joel R. Beeke. Translated by Bartel Elshout. 4 vols. Grand Rapids, MI: Reformation Heritage Books, 2012.

Bray, John S. *Theodore Beza's Doctrine of Predestination.* In Bibliotheca Humanistica et Reformatorica, 12. Nieuwkoop: De Graaf, 1975.

Brencher, John. *Martyn Lloyd-Jones (1899–1981) and Twentieth-Century Evangelicalism.* Carlisle, UK: Paternoster, 2002.

Breward, Ian. "The Life and Theology of William Perkins, 1558–1602." PhD diss., University of Manchester, 1963.

————. "The Significance of William Perkins." In *Journal of Religious History*, 4 (1966): 113–28.

Breward, Ian., ed. *The Westminster Directory: Being a Directory for the Publique Worship of God in the Three Kingdomes.* Bramcote, UK: Grove Books, 1980.

————, ed. Introduction to *The Work of William Perkins*, Courtenay Library of Reformation Classics, vol. 3. Abingdon, England: Sutton Courtenay, 1970.

Bridges, Charles. *The Christian Ministry.* London: Banner of Truth, 1967.

Brienen, Teunis. *De Prediking van de Nadere Reformatie.* Amsterdam: Ton Bolland, 1974.

———. "Jodocus van Lodenstein." In *De Prediking van de Nadere Reformatie*, 108–16. Amsterdam: Ton Bolland, 1974.

Broadus, John A. *A Treatise on the Preparation and Delivery of Sermons*. Edited by Edwin C. Dargan. New York: A. C. Armstrong & Son, 1898.

Brodrick, George C. *A History of the University of Oxford*. London: Longmans, Green, and Co., 1886.

Bromiley, Geoffrey W., ed. *Zwingli and Bullinger*, Library of Christian Classics, vol. 24. Philadelphia: Westminster, 1953.

Brook, Benjamin. *The Lives of the Puritans*. 3 vols. 1813. Reprint, Pittsburgh: Soli Deo Gloria, 1994.

Brooks, Phillips. *Lectures on Preaching*. New York: E. P. Dutton, 1891.

Brooks, Thomas. *The Works of Thomas Brooks*. 6 vols. Edited by Alexander B. Grosart. Edinburgh: Banner of Truth, 2001.

Brown, John (of Haddington). *Questions and Answers on the Shorter Catechism*. Grand Rapids, MI: Reformation Heritage Books, 2006.

Brown, John. *Christ: the Way, the Truth, and the Life*. 1677. Reprint, Morgan, PA: Soli Deo Gloria, 1995.

———. *Expository Discourses on the First Epistle of the Apostle Peter*. New York: Robert Carter and Brothers, 1855.

———. *Puritan Preaching in England: A Study of Past and Present*. New York: C. Scribner's Sons, 1900.

Brown, John., ed. *The Christian Pastor's Manual*. Ligonier, PA: Soli Deo Gloria, 1991.

Brown, Paul E. "The Principle of the Covenant in the Theology of Thomas Goodwin." PhD diss., Drew University, 1950.

Bullinger, Heinrich. *The Decades*. 2 vols. Edited by Thomas Harding. Grand Rapids, MI: Reformation Heritage Books, 2004.

Bunyan, John. *Pilgrim's Progress*. London: John Murray and John Major, 1830.

———. *The Works of John Bunyan*. Edited by George Offor. 1854. Reprint, Edinburgh: Banner of Truth, 1991.

Burgess, Anthony. *The Scripture Directory, for Church Officers and People*. London: Abraham Miller for T. U., 1659.

Burns, Robert. Introduction to *The Works of Thomas Halyburton*. London: Thomas Tegg, 1835.

Burroughs, Jeremiah. *The Evil of Evils*. Morgan, PA: Soli Deo Gloria, 1995.

———. *The Saints' Happiness*. London: by M. S. for Nathaniel Brook, 1660.

Bush, Michael. "Calvin and the Reformanda Sayings." In *Calvinus sacrarum literarum interpres: Papers of the International Congress on Calvin Research*, edited by Herman J. Selderhuis, 285–300. Göttingen: Vandenhoeck and Ruprecht, 2008.

Caiger, J. A. "Preaching—Puritan and Reformed." In *Puritan Papers, Volume 2, 1960–1962*, 161–85. Edited by J. I. Packer. Phillipsburg, NJ: P&R, 2001.

Calderwood, David. *The History of the Kirk of Scotland*. Edited by Thomas Thomson. Edinburgh: Wodrow Society, 1843.

Calhoun, David B. *Princeton Seminary*. 2 vols. Edinburgh: Banner of Truth, 1994.

Calvin, John. *Calvin's Commentaries*. 22 vols. Grand Rapids, MI: Baker, 1979.

———. *Commentaries on the Twelve Minor Prophets*. Translated by John Owen. Edinburgh: Calvin Translation Society, 1849.

———. *Commentary on the Book of Psalms*. Translated by James Anderson. Edinburgh: Calvin Translation Society, 1845.

———. *The Epistle of Paul the Apostle to the Hebrews and The First and Second Epistles of St. Peter*. Translated by William B. Johnston. Edited by David W. and Thomas F. Torrance. Edinburgh: Oliver & Boyd, 1963.

———. *Institutes of the Christian Religion*. Translated by Ford Lewis Battles. Edited by John T. McNeill. Library of Christian Classics, vols. 20–21. Philadelphia: Westminster, 1960.

———. *The Mystery of Godliness*. Grand Rapids, MI: Eerdmans, 1950.

———. "Opera quae supersunt omnia." In *Corpus Reformatorum*, vols. 29–87. Edited by Guilielmus Baum, Eduardus Cunitz, and Eduardus Reuss. Brunsvigae: C. A. Schwetschke, 1863–1900.

———. *Sermons from Job*. Grand Rapids, MI: Eerdmans, 1952.

———. *Sermons on Genesis, Chapters 1:1–11:4: Forty-Nine Sermons Delivered in Geneva Between 4 September 1559 and 23 January 1560*. Edinburgh: Banner of Truth, 2009.

———. *Sermons on the Epistle to the Ephesians*. Reprint, Edinburgh: Banner of Truth, 1973.

———. *Sermons on the Epistles to Timothy and Titus*. 1579. Facsimile reprint, Edinburgh: Banner of Truth, 1983.

———. *Tracts and Treatises*. 3 vols. Translated by Henry Beveridge. Grand Rapids, MI: Eerdmans, 1958.

Capill, Murray A. *The Heart Is the Target: Preaching Practical Application from Every Text*. Phillipsburg, NJ: P&R, 2014.

————. *Preaching with Spiritual Vigour: Including Lessons from the Life and Practice of Richard Baxter.* Fearn, Ross-shire, Scotland: Christian Focus, 2003.

Carlson, Eric Josef. "The Boring of the Ear: Shaping the Pastoral Vision of Preaching in England, 1540–1640." In *Preachers and People in the Reformations and Early Modern Period,* edited by Larissa Taylor, 249–96. Leiden: Brill, 2003.

Cartwright, Hugh. "Faith and Assurance in the Teaching and Experience of Thomas Halyburton (1674–1712)." In *Scottish Bulletin of Evangelical Theology* 11, no. 2 (Autumn 1993): 109–28.

Catherwood, Christopher. *Martyn Lloyd-Jones: A Family Portrait.* Eastbourne, UK: Kingsway, 1995.

Catherwood, Christopher, ed. *Martyn Lloyd-Jones: Chosen by God.* Westchester, IL: Crossway, 1986.

Chae, Choon-Gill. "Thomas Goodwin's Doctrine of the Sealing of the Holy Spirit: Historical, Biblical, and Systematic-Theological Analysis." ThM thesis, Toronto Baptist Seminary, 2010.

Chalker, William H. "Calvin and Some Seventeenth Century English Calvinists." PhD diss., Duke University, 1961.

Charnock, Stephen. *The Complete Works of Stephen Charnock.* 5 vols. Edinburgh: James Nichol, 1854.

————. *Discourses on the Existence and Attributes of God.* 2 vols. Grand Rapids, MI: Baker, 1996.

Christoffel, Raget. *Zwingli: Or, the Rise of the Reformation in Switzerland.* Translated by John Cochran. Edinburgh: T&T Clark, 1858.

Clap, Roger. *Memoirs of Captain Roger Clap.* Boston: D. Clapp, Jr., 1844.

Clark, M. Guthrie. *John Charles Ryle, 1816–1900: First Bishop of Liverpool.* London: Church Book Room Press, n.d.

Clark, Stephen. "Archibald Alexander: The Shakespeare of the Christian Heart." In *The Voice of God,* 103–20. London: Westminster Conference, 2003.

Clarke, Samuel. *The Marrow of Ecclesiastical History.* London: W. B., 1675.

Clarkson, David. *The Practical Works of David Clarkson.* Edinburgh: James Nichol, 1865.

Clifford, Alan. "The Westminster Directory of Public Worship (1645)." In *The Reformation of Worship,* 53–75. N.p.: Westminster Conference, 1989.

Clowney, Edmund P. *Preaching and Biblical Theology.* Phillipsburg, NJ: Presbyterian and Reformed, 1979.

Coalter, Milton J., Jr. *Gilbert Tennent, Son of Thunder: Case Study of Continental Pietism's Impact on the First Great Awakening in the Middle Colonies*. New York: Greenwood, 1986.

Collinson, Patrick. *The Elizabethan Puritan Movement*. London: Jonathan Cape, 1967.

Costello, William T. *The Scholastic Curriculum at Early Seventeenth-Century Cambridge*. Cambridge, MA: Harvard University Press, 1958.

Courvoisier, Jaques. *Zwingli: A Reformed Theologian*. Richmond, VA: John Knox Press, 1963.

Crompton, Gordon D. "The Life and Theology of Thomas Goodwin, D.D." ThM thesis, Greenville Theological Seminary, 1997.

Curtis, Mark. *Oxford and Cambridge in Transition 1558–1642*. Oxford: Oxford University Press, 1965.

Dallimore, Arnold. *George Whitefield: The Life and Times of the Great Evangelist of the 18th Century Revival*. 2 vols. Edinburgh: Banner of Truth, 2009.

Dargan, Edwin C. *A History of Preaching*. 3 vols. Grand Rapids, MI: Baker, 1954.

Darrow, Diane Marilyn. "Thomas Hooker and the Puritan Art of Preaching." PhD diss., University of California, San Diego, 1968.

Davies, Horton. *The Worship of the English Puritans*. Morgan, PA: Soli Deo Gloria, 1997.

Davies, Samuel. *Collected Poems of Samuel Davies, 1723–1761*. Edited by Richard Beale Davis. Gainesville, FL: Scholars' Facsimiles & Reprints, 1968.

———. *The Reverend Samuel Davies Abroad: The Diary of a Journey to England and Scotland, 1753–55*. Edited by George William Pilcher. Urbana: University of Illinois Press, 1967.

De Jong, Peter Y., ed. *Crisis in the Reformed Churches: Essays in Commemoration of the Great Synod of Dort, 1618–1619*. Grand Rapids, MI: Reformed Fellowship, 1968.

De Reuver, Arie. *Sweet Communion: Trajectories of Spirituality from the Middle Ages through the Further Reformation*. Translated by James A. De Jong. Grand Rapids, MI: Baker Academic, 2007.

De Vrijer, Marinus J. A. *Lodenstein*. Baarn: Ten Have, 1947.

DeBlois, Austin Kennedy. "England's Greatest Protestant Preacher." In *John Bunyan, the Man*. Philadelphia: Judson, 1928.

Denholm, Andrew Thomas. "Thomas Hooker: Puritan Preacher, 1568–1647." PhD diss., Hartford Seminary, 1972.

Dennison, James T., Jr., ed. *Reformed Confessions of the Sixteenth and Seventeenth Centuries in English Translation (1523–1693)*. 4 vols. Grand Rapids, MI: Reformation Heritage Books, 2008–2014.

Dering, Edward. *M. Derings Workes*. New York: Da Capo, 1972.

Dever, Mark. *Richard Sibbes: Puritanism and Calvinism in Late Elizabethan and Early Stuart England*. Macon, GA: Mercer University Press, 2000.

Dever, Mark, and Sinclair B. Ferguson. *The Westminster Directory of Public Worship*. Fearn, Ross-shire, Scotland: Christian Heritage, 2008.

Di Gangi, Mariano. *Great Themes in Puritan Preaching*. Guelph, ON: Joshua Press, 2007.

Dickie, Edgar Primrose. "Thomas Halyburton." In *Scottish Journal of Theology 5*, no. 1 (March 1952): 1–13.

Dowey, Edward. *The Knowledge of God in Calvin's Theology*. New York: Columbia University Press, 1965.

Durham, James. *Christ Crucified; or The Marrow of the Gospel in 72 Sermons on Isaiah 53*. 2 vols. Glasgow: Alex Adam, 1792.

———. *A Commentary Upon the Book of the Revelation*. Amsterdam: John Frederickszoon Stam, 1660.

———. *A Practical Exposition of the Ten Commandments*. Edited by Christopher Coldwell. Dallas: Naphtali, 2002.

Eby, David. *Power Preaching for Church Growth*. Fearn, Ross-shire, Scotland: Christian Focus, 1996.

Edwards, Jonathan. *The Salvation of Souls: Nine Previously Unpublished Sermons on the Call of Ministry and the Gospel by Jonathan Edwards*. Edited by Richard A. Bailey and Gregory A. Wills. Wheaton, IL: Crossway, 2002.

———. *The Sermons of Jonathan Edwards: A Reader*. Edited by Wilson H. Kimnach, Kenneth P. Minkema, and Douglas A. Sweeney. New Haven, CT: Yale University Press, 1999.

———. *The Works of Jonathan Edwards*. 2 vols. Edited by Edward Hickman. Edinburgh: Banner of Truth, 1974.

———. *The Works of Jonathan Edwards*. 26 vols. New Haven, CT: Yale University Press, 1957–2008.

———. *Works of Jonathan Edwards Online*, vol. 47, *Sermons, Series II, 1731–1732*. Jonathan Edwards Center at Yale University, 2008. "Great Guilt No Obstacle to the Pardon of the Returning Sinner." http://edwards.yale.edu/archive?path=aHR0cDovL2Vkd2FyZHMueWFsZS5lZHUvY2dpLWJpbi9uZXdwaGlsby9nZXRvYmplY3Qw/Yy40NTozOS53amVv.

Ella, George Melvyn. *Henry Bullinger (1504–1575): Shepherd of the Churches.* Eggleston, UK: Go Publications, 2007.

Ellis, Thomas Talbot. "Samuel Davies: Apostle of Virginia." In *Banner of Truth,* 235 (April 1983): 21–27.

———. "Samuel Davies: Apostle of Virginia." http://www.puritansermons .com/pdf/sdavies2.pdf.

———. "Samuel Davies: Characteristics of His Life and Message." In *Banner of Truth,* 236 (May 1983): 10–18.

———. "Samuel Davies: Characteristics of His Life and Message." http:// www.puritansermons.com/pdf/sdavies2.pdf.

Elshout, Bartel. *The Pastoral and Practical Theology of Wilhelmus à Brakel: A Brief Evaluation of* The Christian's Reasonable Service. Grand Rapids, MI: Reformation Heritage Books, 1997.

Emerson, Everett H. *English Puritanism from John Hooper to John Milton.* Durham, NC: Duke University Press, 1968.

Engelberts, Willem Jodocus Matthias. *Willem Teellinck.* Amsterdam: Ton Bolland, 1973.

Evans, M. F. "Study in the Development of a Theory of Homiletics in England from 1537–1692." PhD diss., University of Iowa, 1932.

Eveson, Philip H. *Martyn Lloyd-Jones: In the Footsteps of the Distinguished Welsh Evangelist, Pastor and Theologian.* Travel With Series. Leominster, UK: Day One, 2004.

Exalto, K. *De Zekerheid des Geloofs bij Calvijn.* Apeldoorn: Willem de Zwijgerstichting, 1978.

Familie Exercise, or The Service of God in Families. Edinburgh: Robert Bryson, 1641.

Farley, Ian D. *J. C. Ryle, First Bishop of Liverpool: A Study in Mission amongst the Masses.* Carlisle, UK: Paternoster, 2000.

Farner, Oskar. *Zwingli the Reformer: His Life and Work.* Translated by D. G. Sear. Hamden, CT: Archon, 1968.

Farrell, Frank E. "Richard Sibbes: A Study in Early Seventeenth Century English Puritanism." PhD diss., University of Edinburgh, 1955.

Feenstra, P. G. *Unspeakable Comfort: A Commentary on the Canons of Dort.* Winnipeg: Premier Printing, 1997.

Ferguson, Sinclair B. "Evangelical Ministry: The Puritan Contribution." In *The Compromised Church: The Present Evangelical Crisis,* edited by John H. Armstrong, 263–80. Wheaton, IL: Crossway, 1998.

Fienberg, Stanley. "Thomas Goodwin: Puritan Pastor and Independent Divine." PhD diss., University of Chicago, 1974.

Fieret, W. *Theodorus à Brakel, Wilhelmus à Brakel en Sara Nevius*. Houten: Den Hertog, 1988.

Firmin, Giles. *The Real Christian, or A Treatise of Effectual Calling*. London: for Dorman Newman, 1670.

Flavel, John. *The Mystery of Providence*. Edinburgh: Banner of Truth, 1963.

———. *The Works of John Flavel*. 6 vols. 1820. Reprint, London: Banner of Truth, 1968.

Foote, William Henry. *Sketches of Virginia: Historical and Biographical, First Series*. Richmond, VA: John Knox Press, 1966.

Ford, Simon. *The Spirit of Bondage and Adoption*. London: T. Maxey, for Sa. Gellibrand, 1655.

Foxgrover, David. "John Calvin's Understanding of Conscience." PhD diss., Claremont, 1978.

———. "'Temporary Faith' and the Certainty of Salvation." In *Calvin Theological Journal* 15 (1980): 220–32.

Franklin, Benjamin. *Autobiography, Poor Richard, Letters*. Edited by Ainsworth D. Spofford. New York: D. Appleton, 1904.

Frelinghuysen, Theodorus Jacobus. *Sermons*. New York: Board of Publication of the Reformed Protestant Dutch Church, 1856.

Fudge, Thomas A. "Icarus of Basel? Oecolampadius and the Early Swiss Reformation." In *Journal of Religious History* 21, no. 3 (October 1997): 268–84.

Fuhrmann, Paul T. "Calvin, Expositor of Scripture." In *Interpretation* 6, no. 2 (April 1952): 188–209.

Fuller, Thomas. *Abel Redevivus; or, The Dead Yet Speaking*. London: William Tegg, 1867.

———. *The Holy and Profane State*. London: William Tegg, 1841.

Furcha, Edward J., and H. Wayne Pipkin. *Prophet, Pastor, Protestant: The Work of Huldrych Zwingli after Five Hundred Years*. Allison Park, PA: Pickwick, 1984.

Garretson, James M. *Princeton and Preaching: Archibald Alexander and the Christian Ministry*. Edinburgh: Banner of Truth, 2005.

Garretson, James M. ed. *Princeton and the Work of the Christian Ministry*. 2 vols. Edinburgh: Banner of Truth, 2012.

———, ed. *"A Scribe Well-Trained": Archibald Alexander and the Life of Piety*. Grand Rapids, MI: Reformation Heritage Books, 2011.

Gerstner, John H. "Calvin's Two-Voice Theory of Preaching." In *Reformed Review* 13, no. 2 (1959): 15–26.

———. *The Rational Biblical Theology of Jonathan Edwards*. 3 vols. Powhatan, VA; Lake Mary, FL: Berea Publications; Ligonier Ministries, 1991.

Gerstner, Jonathan N. *The Thousand Generation Covenant: Dutch Reformed Covenant Theology and Group Identity in Colonial South Africa*. Leiden: Brill, 1991.

Geschiere, Charles L. "Taste and See That the Lord Is Good: The Aesthetic-Affectional Preaching of Jonathan Edwards." ThM thesis, Calvin Theological Seminary, 2008.

Goldsworthy, Graeme. *According to Plan: The Unfolding Revelation of God in the Bible*. Downers Grove, IL: InterVarsity Press, 2002.

Golverdingen, M. *Avonden met Teellinck: Actuele Thema's uit Zijn Werk*. Houten: Den Hertog, 1993.

Goodwin, Thomas. "Memoir of Thomas Goodwin, D.D." In *The Works of Thomas Goodwin*, vol. 1. Grand Rapids, MI: Reformation Heritage Books, 2006.

———. *The Works of Thomas Goodwin*. 12 vols. Edited by Thomas Smith. Edinburgh: James Nichol, 1861–1866. Reprint, Grand Rapids, MI: Reformation Heritage Books, 2006.

Gordon, Bruce, and Emidio Campi, eds. *Architect of Reformation: An Introduction to Heinrich Bullinger, 1504–1575*. Texts and Studies in Reformation and Post-Reformation Thought. Grand Rapids, MI: Baker Academic, 2004.

Gordon, T. David. *Why Johnny Can't Preach*. Phillipsburg, NJ: P&R, 2009.

Gouge, William. *Panoplia Tou Theou: The Whole-Armor of God, or, The Spiritvall Fvrnitvre which God Hath Prouided to Keepe Safe Euery Christian Sovldier from All the Assaults of Satan*. London: Printed by Iohn Beale, 1616.

Graafland, Cornelis. *De Zekerheid van het geloof: Een onderzoek naar de geloof-beschouwing van enige vertegenwoordigers van reformatie en nadere reformatie*. Wageningen: H. Veenman & Zonen, 1961.

———. "Jodocus van Lodenstein (1620–1676)." In *De Nadere Reformatie: Beschrijving van haar voornaamste vertegenwoordigers*, edited by Willem van't Spijker, 85–125. 's–Gravenhage: Uitgeverij Boekencentrum, 1986.

———. *Van Calvijn tot Barth: Oorsprong en ontwikkeling van de leer der verkiezing in het Gereformeerd Protestantisme*. 's-Gravenhage: Boekencentrum, 1987.

———. "'Waarheid in het Binnenste': Geloofszekerheid bij Calvijn en de Nadere Reformatie." In *Een Vaste Burcht*, edited by K. Exalto. Kampen: Kok, 1989.

Graafland, Cornelis, W. J. Op 't Hof, and F. A. Van Lieberg. "Nadere Reformatie: opnieuw een poging tot begripsbepaling." In *Documentatieblad Nadere Reformatie*, 19 (1995): 105–84.

Greidanus, Sidney. *Preaching Christ from the Old Testament: A Contemporary Hermeneutical Method*. Grand Rapids, MI: Eerdmans, 1999.

Greve, Lionel. "Freedom and Discipline in the Theology of John Calvin, William Perkins, and John Wesley: An Examination of the Origin and Nature of Pietism." PhD diss., Hartford Seminary Foundation, 1976.

Grosse, Alexander. *The Happiness of Enjoying and Making a True And Speedy Use of Christ*. London: Tho: Brudenell, for John Bartlet, 1647.

Grudem, Wayne. "Right and Wrong Interpretation of the Bible: Some Suggestions for Pastors and Bible Teachers." In *Preach the Word: Essays on Expository Preaching in Honor of R. Kent Hughes*, edited by Leland Ryken and Todd Wilson. Wheaton, IL: Crossway, 2007.

Gurnall, William. *The Christian in Complete Armour: A Treatise of the Saints' War Against the Devil*. London: Banner of Truth, 1964.

Guthrie, William. "Sermon on Isaiah 44:3." In *A Collection of Lectures and Sermons . . . mostly in the time of the Late Persecution*, edited by J[ohn] H[owie], 100–7. Glasgow: J. Bryce, 1779.

Hall, C. A. *With the Spirit's Sword: The Drama of Spiritual Warfare in the Theology of John Calvin*. Richmond, VA: John Knox Press, 1970.

Hall, Joseph. *The Works of the Right Reverend Joseph Hall*. 12 vols. Edited by Philip Wynter. Oxford: Oxford University Press, 1863.

Hall, Robert. *The Works of the Rev. Robert Hall*. 4 vols. New York: G. & C. & H. Carvill, 1830.

Hall, Stanley R. "The American Presbyterian 'Directory for Worship': History of a Liturgical Strategy." PhD diss., University of Notre Dame, 1990.

———. "The Westminster Directory and Reform of Worship." In *Calvin Studies VIII: The Westminster Confession in Current Thought*, edited by John H. Leith, 91–105. Colloquium on Calvin Studies. S.l.: Davidson College, 1996.

Haller, William. *The Rise of Puritanism: Or, The Way to the New Jerusalem as Set Forth in Pulpit and Press from Thomas Cartwright to John Lilburne and John Milton, 1570–1643*. New York: Columbia University Press, 1938.

Halyburton, Thomas. *Memoirs of Thomas Halyburton*. Edited by Joel R. Beeke. Introduction by Sinclair B. Ferguson. Grand Rapids, MI: Reformation Heritage Books, 1996.

———. *The Works of Thomas Halyburton*. 4 vols. Aberdeen: James Begg Society, 2000–2005.

Hamilton, James M. *God's Glory in Salvation through Judgment: A Biblical Theology*. Wheaton, IL: Crossway, 2010.

Harling, Frederick. "A Biography of John Eliot." PhD diss., Boston University, 1965.

Harris, John. "Moving the Heart: the Preaching of John Bunyan." In *Not by Might nor by Power*, 32–51. London: Westminster Conference, 1989.

Hasler, Richard A. "Thomas Shepard, Pastor-Evangelist (1605–1649): A Study in the New England Puritan Ministry." PhD diss., Hartford Seminary, 1964.

Hedges, Brian G. "Puritan Writers Enrich the Modern Church." In *Banner of Truth*, no. 529 (October 2007): 5–10.

Helm, Paul. *Calvin and the Calvinists*. Edinburgh: Banner of Truth, 1982.

———. "Christian Experience: Experimental Theology." In *Banner of Truth*, no. 139 (April 1975): 1–6.

Henry, Matthew. *An Account of the Life and Death of Mr. Philip Henry*. London: for J. Lawrence, J. Nicholson, J. and B. Sprint, N. Cliffe, and D. Jackson, 1712.

———. *The Communicant's Companion*. Philadelphia: Presbyterian Board of Publication, 1825.

Henry, Philip. *Christ All in All, or What Christ is Made to Believers*. 1676. Reprint, Swengel, PA: Reiner, 1976.

Heppe, Heinrich. *Geschichte des Pietismus und der Mystik in der reformierten Kirche namentlich in der Niederlande*. Leiden: Brill, 1879.

Herr, Alan F. *The Elizabethan Sermon: A Survey and a Bibliography*. New York: Octagon, 1969.

Heywood, Oliver. "Life of Rev. J. Angier." In *The Whole Works of the Rev. Oliver Heywood*. Edinburgh: by John Vint for F. Westley, et al., 1827.

Hildersham, Arthur. *CLII Lectures Upon Psalm LI*. London: J. Raworth, for Edward Brewster, 1642.

Hill, Christopher. *Society and Puritanism in Pre-Revolutionary England*. New York: Schocken, 1964.

———. *A Tinker and a Poor Man: John Bunyan and His Church, 1628–1688*. New York: Knopf, 1989.

Hodge, Archibald Alexander. *The Life of Charles Hodge: Professor in the Theological Seminary, Princeton, N.J.* New York: C. Scribner's Sons, 1880.

Hodge, Charles. *Princeton Sermons.* Edinburgh: Banner of Truth, 1958.

Hoeksema, Herman. *Reformed Dogmatics.* 2nd ed. Grandville, MI: Reformed Free Publishing Association, 2005.

Hoeksema, Homer C. *The Voice of Our Fathers: An Exposition of the Canons of Dordrecht.* Grand Rapids, MI: Reformed Free Publishing Association, 1980.

Holdt, Jonathan. "Wilhelmus a Brakel's Use of Doctrine in Calling Sinners to Repentance and Faith." In *Puritan Reformed Journal* 3, no. 2 (July 2011): 267–90.

Hollweg, Walter. *Heinrich Bullingers Hausbuch: Eine Untersuchung über die Anfänge der Reformierten Predigtliteratur.* Neukirchen, Kreis Moers: Verlag der Buchhandlung des Erziehungsvereins, 1956.

Hood, Paxton. *Christmas Evans: The Preacher of Wild Wales.* London: Hodder and Stoughton, 1881.

Hooker, Thomas. *The Application of Redemption, By the effectual Work of the Word, and Spirit of Christ, for the bringing home of lost Sinners to God, The First Eight Books.* 1657. Facsimile reprint, New York: Arno Press, 1972.

Hoornbeeck, Johannes. *Theologiae Practicae.* Utrecht: Versteegh, 1663.

Horton, Michael Scott. "Christ Set Forth: Thomas Goodwin and the Puritan Doctrine of Assurance, 1600–1680." PhD diss., Wycliffe Hall, Oxford and Coventry College, 1996.

Howe, John. *The Works of the Rev. John Howe.* 3 vols. New York: John P. Haven, 1838.

Howell, Wilbur Samuel. *Logic and Rhetoric in England, 1500–1700.* New York: Russell and Russell, 1961.

Howorth, H. H. "The Origin and Authority of the Biblical Canon According to the Continental Reformers: II. Luther, Zwingli, LeFevre, and Calvin." In *The Journal of Theological Studies* 9 (1908): 108–230.

Hudson, Winthrop S. "The Ministry in the Puritan Age." In *The Ministry in Historical Perspectives*, edited by H. Richard Niebuhr and Daniel D. Williams, 180–206. New York: Harper and Brothers, 1956.

Hughes, R. Kent. "Restoring Biblical Exposition to Its Rightful Place." In *Reforming Pastoral Ministry*, edited by John H. Armstrong, 83–95. Wheaton, IL: Good News Publishers, 2001.

Hulse, Erroll. *The Believer's Experience.* Haywards Heath, Sussex, UK: Carey, 1977.

Humphrey, Richard A. "The Concept of Conversion in the Theology of Thomas Shepard (1605–1649)." PhD diss., Drew University, 1967.

Hunter, A. Mitchell. "Calvin as a Preacher." In *Expository Times* 30, no. 12 (September 1919): 562–64.

Jay, William. *The Autobiography of William Jay*. London: Banner of Truth, 1974.

Jennings, John. "Of Particular and Experimental Preaching." In *The Christian Pastor's Manual*. Edited by John Brown. 1826. Reprint, Ligonier, PA: Soli Deo Gloria, 1991.

————. *Two Discourses: The First, Of Preaching Christ; The Second, of Particular and Experimental Preaching*. Boston: n.p., 1740.

Johnson, George. "Calvinism and Preaching." In *Evangelical Quarterly* 4, no. 3 (July 1932): 244–56.

Johnson, Thomas H., and Perry Miller. *The Puritans*. Rev. ed. 2 vols. New York: Harper, 1963.

Jones, James William. "The Beginnings of American Theology: John Cotton, Thomas Hooker, Thomas Shepard and Peter Bulkeley." PhD diss., Brown University, 1970.

Jones, John Morgan, and William Morgan. *The Calvinistic Methodist Fathers of Wales*. Translated by John Aaron. Edinburgh: Banner of Truth, 2008.

Jones, Mark. "Why Heaven Kissed Earth: The Christology of Thomas Goodwin (1600–1680)." PhD diss., University of Leiden, 2009.

Jones, Phyllis M., and Nicholas R. Jones, eds. *Salvation in New England: Selections from the Sermons of the First Preachers*. Austin: University of Texas Press, 1977.

Keddie, Gordon J. "'Unfallible Certenty of the Pardon of Sinne and Life Everlasting': The Doctrine of Assurance in the Theology of William Perkins." In *Evangelical Quarterly*, 48 (1976): 230–44.

Keep, David John. "Henry Bullinger and the Elizabethan Church: A Study of the Publication of His 'Decades,' His Letter on the Use of Vestments and His Reply to the Bull Which Excommunicated Elizabeth." PhD diss., University of Sheffield, 1970.

Kendall, Robert T. *Calvin and English Calvinism to 1649*. New York: Oxford University Press, 1979.

Kersten, G. H. *Reformed Dogmatics: A Systematic Treatment of Reformed Doctrine*. 2 vols. Translated by Joel R. Beeke and J. C. Weststrate. Grand Rapids, MI: Netherlands Reformed Book and Publishing Committee, 1980.

Kidner, Derek. *Genesis*. Downers Grove, IL: InterVarsity Press, 1967.

Kim-Van Daalen, Lydia. "Wilhelmus à Brakel's Spirituality of Virtues and Its Implications for Soul Care." In *Puritan Reformed Journal* 3, no. 1 (January 2011): 279–303.

Kimnach, Wilson H. Introduction to *The Works of Jonathan Edwards*, vol. 10, *Sermons and Discourses, 1720–1723*. Edited by Wilson H. Kimnach. New Haven, CT: Yale University Press, 1992.

Knappen, Marshall M. *Tudor Puritanism: A Chapter in the History of Idealism*. Chicago: University of Chicago Press, 1939.

Knight, George W., III. *Commentary on the Pastoral Epistles*, New International Greek Testament Commentary. Grand Rapids, MI: Eerdmans, 1992.

Koelman, Jacobus. *The Duties of Parents*. Edited by M. Eugene Osterhaven. Translated by John Vriend. Grand Rapids, MI: Baker Academic, 2003.

Kranendonk, David H. "Vital Balance: The Pursuit of Professors J. J. Van Der Schuit, G. Wisse, and L. H. Van Der Meiden." MDiv thesis, Puritan Reformed Theological Seminary, 2004.

Lake, Peter. *Moderate Puritans and the Elizabethan Church*. Cambridge, UK: Cambridge University Press, 1982.

Lamb, William. *M`Cheyne from the Pew: Being Extracts from the Diary of William Lamb*. Edited by Kirkwood Hewat. Belfast: Ambassador, 1987.

Lane, A. N. S. "Calvin's Doctrine of Assurance." In *Vox Evangelica*, 11 (1979): 32–54.

———. "The Quest for the Historical Calvin." In *Evangelical Quarterly*, 55 (1983): 95–113.

Larson, Barbara Ann. "A Rhetorical Study of the Preaching of the Reverend Samuel Davies in the Colony of Virginia from 1747–1759." PhD diss., University of Minnesota, 1969.

Lawrence, Thomas M. *Transmission and Transformation: Thomas Goodwin and the Puritan Project, 1600–1704*. Cambridge, UK: University of Cambridge, 2002.

Lawson, Steven J. *The Expository Genius of John Calvin*. Lake Mary, FL: Reformation Trust, 2015.

Lea, Thomas. "The Hermeneutics of the Puritans." In *Journal of the Evangelical Theological Society* 39, no. 2 (June 1996): 271–84.

Leahy, Frederick S. Review of Thomas Halyburton, *Faith and Salvation*. In *Banner of Truth* 475 (April 2003): 26.

Lehmberg, S. E. "Archbishop Grindal & the Prophesyings." In *Historical Magazine of the Protestant Episcopal Church* 24 (1965): 87–145.

Leishman, Thomas. *The Westminster Directory.* Edited by T. Leishman. Edinburgh: Blackwood and Sons, 1901.

Lesser, M. X. *Reading Jonathan Edwards: An Annotated Bibliography in Three Parts, 1729–2005.* Grand Rapids, MI: Eerdmans, 2008.

Letham, Robert. "Theodore Beza: A Reassessment." In *Scottish Journal of Theology* 40, no. 1 (1987): 25–40.

Levy, Babette May. *Preaching in the First Half Century of New England History.* New York: Russell & Russell, 1967.

Lewis, Peter. *The Genius of Puritanism.* Grand Rapids, MI: Reformation Heritage Books, 2008.

Lloyd-Jones, Bethan. *Memories of Sandfields: 1927–1938.* Edinburgh: Banner of Truth, 1983.

Lloyd-Jones, D. Martyn. *An Exposition of Ephesians.* 8 vols. Grand Rapids, MI: Baker, 1972.

———. *Expository Sermons on 2 Peter.* Edinburgh: Banner of Truth, 1983.

———. *Knowing the Times: Addresses Delivered on Various Occasions, 1942–1977.* Edinburgh: Banner of Truth, 1989.

———. *Old Testament Evangelistic Sermons.* Edinburgh: Banner of Truth, 1995.

———. *Preaching and Preachers.* Grand Rapids, MI: Zondervan, 1971.

———. *The Puritans: Their Origins and Successors.* Edinburgh: Banner of Truth, 1987.

———. *Romans.* 14 vols. Grand Rapids, MI: Zondervan, 1970–2003.

Loane, Marcus L. *John Charles Ryle, 1816–1900.* London: Hodder & Stoughton, 1983.

Locher, Gottfried Wilhelm. *Zwingli's Thought: New Perspectives.* Leiden: Brill, 1981.

Loetscher, Lefferts A. *Facing the Enlightenment and Pietism: Archibald Alexander and the Founding of Princeton Theological Seminary.* Westport, CT: Greenwood, 1983.

Logan, Samuel T. "Jonathan Edwards and the 1734–35 Northampton Revival." In *Preaching and Revival,* 57–85. London: Westminster Conference, 1984.

Los, F. J. *Wilhelmus à Brakel.* Leiden: Groen en Zoon, 1991.

Lunt, Anders Robert. "The Reinvention of Preaching: A Study of Sixteenth and Seventeenth Century English Preaching Theories." PhD diss., University of Maryland College Park, 1998.

Maclean, Iain S. "The First Pietist: An Introduction and Translation of a Communion Sermon by Jodocus Van Lodenstein." In *Calvin Studies*

VI, edited by John H. Leith, 15–34. Davidson, NC: Davidson College, 1992.

Macleod, John. *Scottish Theology in Relation to Church History since the Reformation*. Edinburgh: Banner of Truth, 1974.

Maclure, Millar. *The Paul's Cross Sermons, 1534–1642*. Toronto: University of Toronto Press, 1958.

Mallinson, Jeffrey. *Faith, Reason, and Revelation in Theodore Beza, 1519–1605*. Oxford Theological Monographs. Oxford: Oxford University Press, 2003.

Manetsch, Scott M. *Calvin's Company of Preachers: Pastoral Care and the Emerging Reformed Church, 1536–1609*. Oxford: Oxford University Press, 2012.

———. "Onus Praedicandi: The Preaching Ministry of Theodore Beza." N.p.: Calvin College and Seminary, n.d.: 1.

———. *Theodore Beza and the Quest for Peace in France, 1572–1598*. Leiden: Brill, 2000.

Manton, Thomas. *The Complete Works of Thomas Manton*. 22 vols. London: James Nisbet, 1874.

Marquit, Doris G. "Thomas Shepard: The Formation of a Puritan Identity." PhD diss., University of Minnesota, 1978.

Marsden, George M. *Jonathan Edwards: A Life*. New Haven, CT: Yale University Press, 2003.

Marshall, Walter. *The Gospel-Mystery of Sanctification Opened, in Sundry Practical Directions*. New York: Southwick and Pelsue, 1811.

Martin, Albert N. *What's Wrong with Preaching Today?* Edinburgh: Banner of Truth, 1967.

Martin, Stephen. *Izaak Walton and His Friends*. London: Chapman & Hall, 1903.

Maruyama, Tadataka. *The Ecclesiology of Theodore Beza: The Reform of the True Church*. In Travaux D'humanisme Et Renaissance, no. 166. Geneve: Droz, 1978.

Masson, David. *The Life of John Milton*. Cambridge: Macmillan and Co., 1859.

Mather, Cotton. *The Great Works of Christ in America: Magnalia Christi Americana*. 3 vols. London: Banner of Truth, 1979.

———. *Manuductio ad Ministerium: Directions for a Candidate to the Ministry*. Boston: for Thomas Hancock, 1726.

Mather, Increase. *The Life and Death of that Reverend Man of God, Mr. Richard Mather*. Cambridge, MA: S. G. and M. J., 1670.

Maze, Scott. *Theodore Frelinghuysen's Evangelism: Catalyst to the First Great Awakening*. Grand Rapids, MI: Reformation Heritage Books, 2011.

McClymond, Michael J., and Gerald R. McDermott. *The Theology of Jonathan Edwards*. Oxford: Oxford University Press, 2012.

McCoy, Charles S., J. Wayne Baker, and Heinrich Bullinger. *Fountainhead of Federalism: Heinrich Bullinger and the Covenantal Tradition*. Louisville: Westminster/John Knox Press, 1991.

McGiffert, Michael, ed. *God's Plot: Puritan Spirituality in Thomas Shepard's Cambridge*. Rev. ed. Amherst, MA: University of Massachusetts Press, 1994.

McGrath, Alister. *Roots That Refresh: A Celebration of Reformation Spirituality*. London: Hodder & Stoughton, 1991.

McKim, Donald K. "Ramism in William Perkins." PhD diss., University of Pittsburgh, 1980.

————. "William Perkins and the Theology of the Covenant." In *Studies of the Church in History*, edited by Horton Davies, 85–102. Allison Park, PA: Pickwick, 1983.

McNally, Alexander. "Some Aspects of Thomas Goodwin's Doctrine of Assurance." ThM thesis, Westminster Theological Seminary, 1972.

McNally, Frederick W. "The Westminster Directory: Its Origin and Significance." PhD diss., University of Edinburgh, 1958.

McPhee, Ian. "Conserver or Transformer of Calvin's Theology? A Study of the Origins and Development of Theodore Beza's Thought, 1550–1570." PhD diss., University of Cambridge, 1979.

Mead, Matthew. *The Almost Christian Discovered; Or the False Professor Tried and Cast*. Ligonier, PA: Soli Deo Gloria, 1988.

Messler, Abraham. *Forty Years at Raritan: Eight Memorial Sermons*. New York: A. Lloyd, 1873.

Miller, Ed L. "Oecolampadius: The Unsung Hero of the Basel Reformation." In *Iliff Review* 39, no. 3 (Fall 1982): 5–25.

Miller, Glenn T. "The Rise of Evangelical Calvinism: A Study in Jonathan Edwards and the Puritan Tradition." ThD diss., Union Theological Seminary, 1971.

Miller, Perry. *Errand into the Wilderness*. Cambridge, MA: Belknap Press, 1956.

————. *The New England Mind: The Seventeenth Century*. Boston: Beacon, 1961.

Mitchell, Alexander F. Introduction to *Minutes of the Sessions of the Westminster Assembly of Divines*. Edited by Alexander F. Mitchell and John Struthers. Edmonton: Still Waters Revival Books, 1991.

Moore, Jonathan. *English Hypothetical Universalism: John Preston and the Softening of Reformed Theology*. Grand Rapids, MI: Eerdmans, 2007.

Morgan, Irvonwy. *The Godly Preachers of the Elizabethan Church*. London: Epworth, 1965.

———. *Prince Charles's Puritan Chaplain*. London: Allen & Unwin, 1957.

———. *Puritan Spirituality: Illustrated from the Life and Times of the Rev. Dr. John Preston*. London: Epworth, 1973.

Morison, Samuel. *The Intellectual Life of Colonial New England*. 2nd ed. New York: New York University Press, 1956.

Motyer, J. Alec. *The Prophecy of Isaiah: An Introduction and Commentary*. Downers Grove, IL: InterVarsity Press, 1993.

Muller, Richard A. *After Calvin: Studies in the Development of a Theological Tradition*. Oxford Studies in Historical Theology. Oxford: Oxford University Press, 2003.

———. *Christ and the Decree: Christology and Predestination in Reformed Theology from Calvin to Perkins*. Grand Rapids, MI: Baker, 1988.

———. "The Use and Abuse of a Document: Beza's *Tabula Praedestinationis*, the Bolsec Controversy, and the Origins of Reformed Orthodoxy." In *Protestant Scholasticism: Essays in Reassessment*, edited by Carl R. Trueman and R. Scott Clark, 33–61. Carlisle, UK: Paternoster, 1999.

———. "William Perkins and the Protestant Exegetical Tradition: Interpretation, Style, and Method." In William Perkins, *A Commentary on Hebrews 11*. Edited by John H. Augustine. New York: Pilgrim Press, 1991.

Muller, Richard A., and Rowland S. Ward. *Scripture and Worship: Biblical Interpretation and the Directory for Public Worship*. Phillipsburg, NJ: P&R, 2007.

Mullinger, James Bass. *The University of Cambridge*. Cambridge, UK: Cambridge University Press, 1884.

Munson, Charles Robert. "William Perkins: Theologian of Transition." PhD diss., Case Western Reserve, 1971.

Murray, David. *Jesus on Every Page: Ten Simple Ways to Seek and Find Christ in the Old Testament*. Nashville: Thomas Nelson, 2013.

Murray, Iain H. *David Martyn Lloyd-Jones: The Fight of Faith, 1939–1981*. Edinburgh: Banner of Truth, 1990.

———. *David Martyn Lloyd-Jones: The First Forty Years, 1899–1939*. Edinburgh: Banner of Truth, 1982.

———. "The Directory for Public Worship." In *To Glorify and Enjoy God: A Commemoration of the 350th Anniversary of the Westminster Assembly*, edited by John L. Carson and David W. Hall, 169–91. Edinburgh: Banner of Truth, 1994.

———. *Jonathan Edwards: A New Biography*. Edinburgh: Banner of Truth, 1987.

———. *Lloyd-Jones: Messenger of Grace*. Edinburgh: Banner of Truth, 2008.

———. *Revival and Revivalism: The Making and Marring of American Evangelicalism 1750–1858*. Edinburgh: Banner of Truth, 1994.

Naborn, Robert A. "Eilardus Westerlo (1738–1790): From Colonial Dominee to American Pastor." PhD diss., Vrije Universiteit Amsterdam, 2011.

Neal, Daniel. *History of Puritans*. 3 vols. Stoke-on-Trent, UK: Tentmaker, 2006.

Nettleton, Asahel. *Remains of the Late Rev. Asahel Nettleton*. Edited by Bennet Tyler. Hartford, CT: Robins and Smith, 1845.

New, John F. H. *Anglican and Puritan: The Basis of Their Opposition, 1558–1640*. Stanford: Stanford University Press, 1965.

Nicholls, John D. "Thomas Halyburton, 1674–1712." In *Faith and Ferment*, 32–49. London: Westminster Conference,1982.

Niesel, Wilhelm. *The Theology of Calvin*. Translated by Harold Knight. Grand Rapids, MI: Baker, 1980.

Nixon, Leroy. *John Calvin: Expository Preacher*. Grand Rapids, MI: Eerdmans, 1950.

Oakes, Urian. *An Elegie Upon the Death of the Reverend Mr. Thomas Shepard*. Aiken, SC: W. L. Washburn, 1902.

Old, Hughes Oliphant. *The Reading and Preaching of the Scriptures in the Worship of the Christian Church, Volume 4: The Age of the Reformation*. Grand Rapids, MI: Eerdmans, 1998.

———. *The Reading and Preaching of the Scriptures in the Worship of the Christian Church, Volume 5: Moderatism, Pietism, and Awakening*. Grand Rapids, MI: Eerdmans, 2004.

———. "What Is Reformed Spirituality?" In *Perspectives* 9, no. 1. (January 1994): 8–10.

———. "What Is Reformed Spirituality? Played Over Again Lightly." In *Calvin Studies VII*, edited by John H. Leith, 61–68. Colloquium on Calvin Studies. Davidson, NC: Davidson College, 1994.

Onstenk, A. J. "Lodenstein, Jodocus van." In *Biografisch Lexicon voor de Geschiedenis van het Nederlandse Protestantisme*, 3:253–55. Edited by D. Nauta, et al. Kampen: Kok, 1988.

Op 't Hof, Willem Jan. *Engelse pietistische geschriften in het Nederlands, 1598–1622*. Rotterdam: Lindenberg, 1987.

————. *Willem Teellinck (1579–1629): Leven, Geschriften en Invloed*. Kampen: De Groot Goudriaan, 2008.

Op 't Hof, W. J., C. A. De Niet, and H. Uil. *Eeuwout Teellinck in Handschriften*. Kampen: De Groot Goudriaan, 1989.

Orton, Job. *Memoirs of the Life, Character, and Writings, of the Late Rev. Philip Doddridge*. Edinburgh: Waugh and Innes, M. Ogle, R. M. Tims, and James Duncan, 1825.

Owen, Charles. *Plain Reasons for Dissenting from the Church of England*. 3rd ed. London: n.p., 1736.

Owen, John. *An Exposition of the Epistle to the Hebrews*. 7 vols. Edited by William H. Goold. Reprint, Edinburgh: Banner of Truth, 1991.

————. *The Works of John Owen*. 16 vols. Edited by William H. Goold. Reprint, Edinburgh: Banner of Truth, 1965.

Packer, J. I. *An Anglican to Remember: William Perkins, Puritan Popularizer*. London: St. Antholin's Lectureship Charity, 1996.

————. *Collected Shorter Writings of J. I. Packer*. 4 vols. Carlisle, UK: Paternoster, 1998.

————. *Faithfulness and Holiness: The Witness of J. C. Ryle*. Wheaton, IL: Crossway, 2002.

————. Foreword to *Introduction to Puritan Theology: A Reader*. Edited by Edward Hindson. Grand Rapids, MI: Baker, 1976.

————. "Introduction: Why Preach?" In *The Preacher and Preaching: Reviving the Art in the Twentieth Century*, edited by Samuel T. Logan Jr., 1–29. Phillipsburg, NJ: Presbyterian and Reformed, 1986.

————. *A Quest for Godliness: The Puritan Vision of the Christian Life*. Wheaton, IL: Crossway, 1990.

Pang, Patrick. "A Study of Jonathan Edwards as a Pastor-Preacher." DMin thesis, Fuller Theological Seminary, 1990.

Park, Tae-Hyeun. *The Sacred Rhetoric of the Holy Spirit: A Study of Puritan Preaching in a Pneumatological Perspective*. Apeldoorn: Theologische Unversiteit Apeldoorn, 2005.

Parker, T. H. L. *The Oracles of God: An Introduction to the Preaching of John Calvin*. London: Lutterworth, 1947.

Parks, Kenneth Clifton. "The Progress of Preaching in England during the Elizabethan Period." PhD diss., Southern Baptist Theological Seminary, 1954.

Parratt, J. K. "The Witness of the Holy Spirit: Calvin, the Puritans and St. Paul." In *Evangelical Quarterly*, no. 41 (1969): 161–68.

Parson, Thomas. "Of Saving Faith." In *Puritan Sermons, 1659–1689*, 5:345–71. Reprint, Wheaton, IL: Richard Owen Roberts, 1981.

Partee, Charles. "Calvin and Experience." In *Scottish Journal of Theology*, no. 26 (1973): 169–81.

Pelkonen, J. P. "The Teaching of John Calvin on the Nature and Function of the Conscience." In *Lutheran Quarterly* 21 (1969): 24–88.

Perkins, William. *The Art of Prophesying*. Edited by Sinclair B. Ferguson. Edinburgh: Banner of Truth, 1996.

———. *A Commentary on Galatians*. Edited by Gerald T. Sheppard. 1617. Facsimile reprint, New York: Pilgrim Press, 1989.

———. *A Commentary on Hebrews 11*. Edited by John H. Augustine. New York: Pilgrim Press, 1991.

———. *William Perkins, 1558–1602, English Puritanist—His Pioneer Works on Casuistry: "A Discourse of Conscience" and "The Whole Treatise of Cases of Conscience."* Edited by Thomas F. Merrill. Nieuwkoop: B. De Graaf, 1966.

———. *The Workes of that Famovs and VVorthy Minister of Christ in the Vniuersitie of Cambridge, Mr. William Perkins*. 3 vols. London: John Legatt, 1612–1613.

Petto, Samuel. *The Voice of the Spirit: or, An Essay towards a Discovery of the Witnessings of the Spirit*. London: Livewell Chapman, 1654.

Pilcher, George W. *Samuel Davies: Apostle of Dissent in Colonial Virginia*. Knoxville: University of Tennessee Press, 1971.

Pipa, Joseph A., Jr. "Puritan Preaching." In *The Practical Calvinist*, edited by Peter A. Lillback, 163–81. Fearn, Ross-shire, Scotland: Mentor, 2002.

———. "William Perkins and the Development of Puritan Preaching." PhD diss., Westminster Theological Seminary, 1985.

Piper, John. *Brothers, We Are Not Professionals: A Plea to Pastors for Radical Ministry*. Nashville: Broadman & Holman, 2002.

———. *Expository Exultation: Christian Preaching as Worship*. Wheaton, IL: Crossway, 2018.

———. "Preaching as Expository Exultation for the Glory of God." In *Preaching the Cross*, edited by Mark Dever, et al., 103–15. Wheaton, IL: Crossway, 2007.

————. *The Supremacy of God in Preaching*. Grand Rapids, MI: Baker, 1990.

Poe, Harry Lee. "Evangelistic Fervency among the Puritans in Stuart England, 1603–1688." PhD diss., Southern Baptist Theological Seminary, 1982.

Porter, H. C. *Puritanism in Tudor England*. New York: MacMillan, 1970.

————. *Reformation and Reaction in Tudor Cambridge*. London: Cambridge University Press, 1958.

Potter, G. R. *Zwingli*. Cambridge, UK: Cambridge University Press, 1984.

Poythress, Diane. "Johannes Oecolampadius' Exposition of Isaiah, Chapters 36–37." PhD diss., Westminster Theological Seminary, 1992.

————. *Reformer of Basel: The Life, Thought, and Influence of Johannes Oecolampadius*. Grand Rapids, MI: Reformation Heritage Books, 2011.

Pratt, John H., ed. *The Thought of Evangelical Leaders: Notes of the Discussions of The Eclectic Society, London, During the Years 1798–1814*. 1856. Reprint, Edinburgh: Banner of Truth, 1978.

Praxis, John Mayer. *Theologica: or The Epistle of the Apostle St. James . . . Expounded*. London: R. Bostocke, 1629.

Preston, John. *The Breast-Plate of Faith and Love*. 1634. Facsimile reprint, Edinburgh: Banner of Truth, 1979.

————. *The Fullness of Christ for Us*. London: by M. P. for Iohn Stafford, 1639.

————. *Riches of Mercy to Men in Misery, or Certain Excellent Treatises Concerning the Dignity and Duty of God's Children*. London: J. T., 1658.

Priebe, Victor L. "The Covenant Theology of William Perkins." PhD diss., Drew University, 1967.

Prime, Derek. *Robert Murray McCheyne: In the Footsteps of a Godly Scottish Pastor*. Travel With Series. Leominster, UK: Day One, 2007.

Pronk, Cornelis. *Expository Sermons on the Canons of Dort*. St. Thomas, ON: Free Reformed Publications, 1999.

Proost, Pieter. *Jodocus van Lodenstein*. Amsterdam: J. Brandt, 1880.

Raitt, Jill. *The Eucharistic Theology of Theodore Beza: Development of the Reformed Doctrine*, AAR Studies in Religion, no. 4. Chambersburg, PA: American Academy of Religion, 1972.

————. "Lessons in Troubled Times: Beza's Lessons on Job." In *Calvin and the State*, edited by Peter De Klerk, 21–45. Colloquia on Calvin and Calvin Studies. Grand Rapids, MI: Calvin Studies Society, 1993.

Richardson, Caroline F. *English Preachers and Preaching 1640–1670*. New York: Macmillan, 1928.

Richey, Robert Alan. "The Puritan Doctrine of Sanctification: Constructions of the Saints' Final and Complete Perseverance as Mirrored in Bunyan's *The Pilgrim's Progress.*" ThD diss., Mid-America Baptist Theological Seminary, 1990.

Rilliet, Jean. *Zwingli, Third Man of the Reformation.* Translated by Harold Knight. London: Lutterworth, 1964.

Robertson, David. *Awakening: The Life and Ministry of Robert Murray McCheyne.* Milton Keynes, UK: Authentic Media, 2004.

Robinson, Ralph. *Christ All and In All: or Several Significant Similitudes by which the Lord Jesus Christ is Described in the Holy Scriptures.* 1660. Reprint, Ligonier, PA: Soli Deo Gloria, 1992.

Rogers, John. *A Godly and Fruitful Exposition Upon All the First Epistle of Peter.* London: by John Field, 1650.

Rogers, Nehemiah. *The True Convert.* London: George Miller for Edward Brewster, 1632.

Rogers, Richard. *A Commentary Vpon the Whole Booke of Ivdges.* London: by Felix Kyngston for Thomas Man, 1615. Reprinted as Richard Rogers, *A Commentary on Judges.* Edinburgh: Banner of Truth, 1983.

———. *Seuen Treatises, Containing Such Direction as Is Gathered Out of the Holie Scriptures, Leading and Guiding to True Happines, Both in This Life, and in the Life to Come: And May Be Called the Practise of Christianitie.* London: by Felix Kyngston, for Thomas Man, 1603.

Rogers, Richard, and Samuel Ward. "Two Elizabethan Puritan Diaries." In *Studies in Church History Vol. II.* Edited by M. M. Knappen. Chicago: American Society of Church History, 1933.

Roney, John B., and Martin I. Klauber, eds. *The Identity of Geneva.* Westport, CT: Greenwood Press, 1998.

Rooy, Sidney H. *The Theology of Missions in the Puritan Tradition: A Study of Representative Puritans, Richard Sibbes, Richard Baxter, John Eliot, Cotton Mather, and Jonathan Edwards.* Grand Rapids, MI: Eerdmans, 1965.

Ross, Michael F. *Preaching for Revitalization.* Fearn, Ross-shire, Scotland: Mentor, 2006.

Rupp, E. Gordon. *Patterns of Reformation.* London: Epworth, 1969.

Russell, Eric J. C. *Ryle: That Man of Granite with the Heart of a Child.* Fearn, Ross-shire, Scotland: Christian Focus, 2008.

Rutherford, Samuel. *Letters of Samuel Rutherford.* Edited by Andrew Bonar. London: Oliphants, 1904.

Ryken, Leland. *Worldly Saints: The Puritans as They Really Were.* Grand Rapids, MI: Academie Books, 1986.

Ryle, J. C. *Expository Thoughts on the Gospels.* 7 vols. 1856–1869. Reprint, Edinburgh: Banner of Truth, 2009.

———. *Holiness.* Darlington, England: Evangelical Press, 2011.

———. *J. C. Ryle, a Self-Portrait: A Partial Autobiography.* Edited by Peter Toon. Swengel, PA: Reiner, 1975.

———. *Simplicity in Preaching: A Few Short Hints on a Great Subject.* London: William Hunt, 1882.

———. *The True Christian.* Grand Rapids, MI: Baker, 1978.

Saldenus, Guilelmus, and Wilhelmus à Brakel. *In Remembrance of Him: Profiting from the Lord's Supper.* Edited by James A. De Jong. Translated by Bartel Elshout. Grand Rapids, MI: Reformation Heritage Books, 2012.

Sargent, Tony. *The Sacred Anointing: The Preaching of Dr. Martyn Lloyd-Jones.* Wheaton, IL: Crossway, 1994.

Schaefer, Paul R. *The Spiritual Brotherhood: Cambridge Puritans and the Nature of Christian Piety.* Grand Rapids, MI: Reformation Heritage Books, 2011.

Schaff, Philip. *The Creeds of Christendom: With a History and Critical Notes.* New York: Harper, 1877.

Schoneveld, C. W. *Intertraffic of the Mind.* Leiden: Brill, 1983.

Schortinghuis, Wilhelmus. *Essential Truths in the Heart of a Christian.* Edited by James A. De Jong. Translated by Harry Boonstra and Gerrit W. Sheeres. Grand Rapids, MI: Reformation Heritage Books, 2009.

Schrag, F. J. "Theodorus Jacobus Frelinghuysen, the Father of American Pietism." In *Church History* 14 (1945): 201–16.

Schroeder, Carl J. *In Quest of Pentecost: Jodocus Van Lodenstein and the Dutch Second Reformation.* Lanham, MD: University Press of America, 2001.

Seaver, Paul S. *The Puritan Lectureships: The Politics of Religious Dissent, 1560–1662.* Stanford: Stanford University Press, 1970.

Selderhuis, Herman J. *John Calvin: A Pilgrim's Life.* Downers Grove, IL: IVP Academic, 2009

Shaw, Mark R. "William Perkins and the New Pelagians: Another Look at the Cambridge Predestination Controversy of the 1590s." In *Westminster Theological Journal*, 58 (1996): 267–301.

Shelly, Harold Patton. "Richard Sibbes: Early Stuart Preacher of Piety." PhD diss., Temple University, 1972.

Shepard, Thomas. *The Parable of the Ten Virgins*. Ligonier, PA: Soli Deo Gloria, 1990.

———. *The Works of Thomas Shepard*. 3 vols. New York: AMS Press, 1967.

Shepherd, Victor A. *The Nature and Function of Saving Faith in the Theology of John Calvin*. Macon, GA: Mercer University Press, 1983.

Sibbes, Richard. *The Complete Works of Richard Sibbes*. 7 vols. Edited by Alexander B. Grosart. Edinburgh: Banner of Truth, 1977.

Slagboorn, D. *Jodocus van Lodenstein*. Utrecht: De Banier, 1966.

Smalley, Paul M. "Satisfied with the Lord's All-Sufficiency: Wilhelmus à Brakel on Joy." In *Puritan Reformed Journal* 3, no. 2 (July 2011): 235–66.

Smellie, Alexander. *Robert Murray McCheyne*. London: National Council of Evangelical Free Churches, 1913.

Smith, Henry. *The Works of Henry Smith*. 2 vols. Stoke-on-Trent, UK: Tentmaker, 2002.

Smith, John C. *Robert Murray M'Cheyne*. London: E. Stock, 1910.

Smith, John E. "Introduction to Jonathan Edwards." In *The Works of Jonathan Edwards*, vol. 2, *Religious Affections*. Edited by John E. Smith. New Haven, CT: Yale University Press, 1959.

Smylie, James H. "Samuel Davies: Preacher, Teacher, and Pastor." In *Colonial Presbyterianism: Old Faith in a New Land: Commemorating the 300th Anniversary of the First Presbytery in America*, edited by S. Donald Fortson, 181–97. Eugene, OR: Pickwick, 2007.

Song, Young Jae Timothy. *Theology and Piety in the Reformed Federal Thought of William Perkins and John Preston*. Lewiston, NY: Edwin Mellen Press, 1998.

Sorge, H. F. *Genadeverbond en Genaldeleven: Een Onderzoek naar de Inhoud en Betekenis van het Genadeverbond Volgens de 'Redilijke Godsdienst' van Wilhelmus à Brakel (1635–1711)*. N.p.: 1998.

Sprague, William B. "Memoir." In Samuel Davies, *Sermons of Samuel Davies*. 3 vols. Pittsburgh: Soli Deo Gloria, 1993.

Spring, Gardiner. *The Power of the Pulpit*. 1848. Reprint, Edinburgh: Banner of Truth, 1986.

Sprunger, Keith L. *Dutch Puritanism: A History of English and Scottish Churches of the Netherlands in the Sixteenth and Seventeenth Centuries*. Leiden: Brill, 1982.

Spurgeon, Charles H. *Lectures to My Students*. Pasadena, TX: Pilgrim Publications, 1990.

———. Sermon no. 101, "The Exaltation of Christ." Nov. 2, 1856. In *The New Park Street Pulpit*. 1857. Reprint, Pasadena, TX: Pilgrim Publications, 1975.

———. Sermon no. 221, "Comfort Proclaimed." Sept. 21, 1856. In *The Spurgeon Archive*, https://www.spurgeon.org/resource-library/sermons/comfort-proclaimed.

———. Sermon no. 239, "Jacob and Esau." Jan. 16, 1859. In *The New Park Street Pulpit*, vol 5. 1859. Reprint, Pasadena, TX: Pilgrim Press, 1975.

———. Sermon no. 369, "The First Sermon in the Tabernacle." March 25, 1861. In *The New Park Street and Metropolitan Tabernacle Pulpit*. 1865. Reprint, Pasadena, TX: Pilgrim Publications, 1969.

———. Sermon no. 597, "Preparation for Revival." Oct. 30, 1864. In *Metropolitan Tabernacle Pulpit*. 1865. Reprint, Pasadena, TX: Pilgrim Publications, 1976.

Stalker, James. *The Preacher and His Models*. New York: A. C. Armstrong & Son, 1891.

Steinmetz, David Curtis. *Reformers in the Wings: From Geiler von Kaysersberg to Theodore Beza*. 2nd ed. Oxford: Oxford University Press, 2001.

Stelten, Leo F. *Dictionary of Ecclesiastical Latin: With an Appendix of Latin Expressions Defined and Clarified*. Peabody, MA: Hendrickson, 1995.

Stephens, W. P. *The Theology of Huldrych Zwingli*. Oxford: Clarendon, 1986.

———. *Zwingli: An Introduction to His Thought*. Oxford: Clarendon, 1992.

Stevens, David Mark. "John Cotton and Thomas Hooker: The Rhetoric of the Holy Spirit." PhD diss., University of California, Berkeley, 1972.

Stoeffler, Fred Ernest. "Pietism—Its Message, Early Manifestation, and Significance." In *Contemporary Perspectives on Pietism: A Symposium*. Chicago: Covenant Press, 1976.

———. *The Rise of Evangelical Pietism*. Leiden: Brill, 1965.

Stoever, William K. B. *A Faire and Easie Way to Heaven: Covenant Theology and Antinomianism in Early Massachusetts*. Middletown, CT: Wesleyan University Press, 1978.

Stout, Harry S. *The New England Soul: Preaching and Religious Culture in Colonial New England*. Oxford: Oxford University Press, 1986.

Summers, Kirk M. *Morality after Calvin: Theodore Beza's Christian Censor and Reformed Ethics*. New York: Oxford University Press, 2017.

Sweeney, Douglas A. *Jonathan Edwards and the Ministry of the Word: A Model of Faith and Thought*. Downers Grove, IL: IVP Academic, 2009.

Swinnock, George. *The Works of George Swinnock*. 5 vols. Edinburgh: Banner of Truth, 1992.

Taffin, Jean. *The Marks of God's Children*. Edited by James A. De Jong. Translated by Peter Y. De Jong. Grand Rapids, MI: Baker Academic, 2003.

Tanis, James. *Dutch Calvinistic Pietism in the Middle Colonies: A Study in the Life and Theology of Theodorus Jacobus Frelinghuysen*. The Hague: Martinus Nijhoff, 1967.

Taylor, Thomas. *Christ Revealed: or The Old Testament Explained; A Treatise of the Types and Shadowes of our Saviour*. London: M. F. for R. Dawlman and L. Fawne, 1635.

Teellinck, Willem. *The Path of True Godliness*. Edited by Joel R. Beeke. Translated by Annemie Godbehere. Grand Rapids, MI: Baker Academic, 2003.

———. *Pauls Complaint Against His Naturall Corruption: With the Meanes How to Bee Deliuered from the Power of the Same: Set Forth in Two Sermons Vpon the 24 Verse of the 7 Chapter of His Epistle to the Romanes*. Translated by Christopher Harmar. London: by Iohn Dawson for Iohn Bellamie, 1621.

———. *The Resting Place of the Minde: That Is, A Propovnding of the Wonderfull Prouidence of God, Whereupon a Christian Man Ought to Rest and Repose Himself, Euen When All Outward Meanes of Helpe Are Cut Off from Him*. London: by Iohn Haviland for Edward Brewster, 1622.

Thomas, Geoffrey. "Samuel Davies and the God of Wonders." In *Triumph through Tribulation: Papers Read at the 1998 Westminster Conference*, 119–34. London: Westminster Conference, 1998.

Thomas, I. D. E., comp., *The Golden Treasury of Puritan Quotations*. Chicago: Moody Press, 1975.

Thompson, Ernest Trice. *Presbyterians in the South*. Richmond, VA: John Knox Press, 1963.

Tipson, Lynn Baird, Jr., "The Development of Puritan Understanding of Conversion." PhD diss., Yale University, 1972.

Toon, Peter, and Michael Smout. *John Charles Ryle: Evangelical Bishop*. Cambridge: J. Clarke, 1976.

Traill, Robert. *Select Practical Writings of Robert Traill*. Edinburgh: Printed for the Assembly's Committee, 1845.

———. *The Works of the Late Reverend Robert Traill*. 4 vols. Edinburgh: J. Ogle, M. Ogle, J. Steven, R. Ogle, T. Hamilton, and T. Johnson, 1810.

Trimp, J. C. *Jodocus van Lodenstein: Predikant en Dichter.* Kampen: De Groot Goudriaan, 1987.

Tufft, J. R. "William Perkins, 1558–1602." PhD diss., Edinburgh, 1952.

Tumbleson, Beth E. "The Bride and Bridegroom in the Work of Richard Sibbes, English Puritan." MA thesis, Trinity Evangelical Divinity School, 1984.

Twisse, William. *The Doctrine of the Synod of Dort and Arles, Reduced to the Practise.* Amsterdam: Successors of G. Thorp, 1631.

Udemans, Godefridus. *The Practice of Faith, Hope, and Love.* Edited by Joel R. Beeke. Translated by Annemie Godbehere. Grand Rapids, MI: Reformation Heritage Books, 2012.

Van der Ham, H. *Professor Wisse: Aspecten Van Leven En Werk.* Kampen: De Groot Goudriaan, 1993.

Van Dixhoorn, Chad. "Preaching Christ in Post-Reformation Britain." In *The Hope Fulfilled: Essays in Honor of O. Palmer Robertson,* edited by Robert L. Penny, 361–89. Phillipsburg, NJ: P&R, 2008.

Van Lieburg, Fred A. "From Pure Church to Pious Culture: The Further Reformation in the Seventeenth-Century Dutch Republic." In *Later Calvinism: International Perspectives,* edited by W. Fred Graham, 423–25. Kirksville, MO: Sixteenth Century Journal Publishers, 1994.

Van Lodenstein, Jodocus. *A Spiritual Appeal to Christ's Bride.* Edited by Joel R. Beeke. Translated by Bartel Elshout. Grand Rapids, MI: Reformation Heritage Books, 2010.

Van Valen, L. J. *Constrained by His Love: A New Biography on Robert Murray McCheyne.* Fearn, Ross-shire, Scotland: Christian Focus, 2002.

Vaughan, Alden T., and Francis J. Bremer, eds. *Puritan New England: Essays on Religion, Society, and Culture.* New York: St. Martin's, 1977.

Venema, Cornelis P. *But for the Grace of God: An Exposition of the Canons of Dort.* Grandville, MI: Reformed Fellowship, 2011.

———. *Heinrich Bullinger and the Doctrine of Predestination: Author of "the Other Reformed Tradition"?* Texts and Studies in Reformation and Post-Reformation Thought. Grand Rapids, MI: Baker Academic, 2002.

Veninga, James F. "Covenant Theology and Ethics in the Thought of John Calvin and John Preston." PhD diss., Rice University, 1974.

Voetius, Gisbertus. *Ta asketika sive Exercitia Pietatis.* Gorinchem: Vink, 1654.

Voetius, Gisbertus, and Johannes Hoornbeeck. *Spiritual Desertion.* Edited by M. Eugene Osterhaven. Translated by John Vriend and Harry Boonstra. Grand Rapids, MI: Baker Academic, 2003.

Vollmer, Philip. *John Calvin: Theologian, Preacher, Educator, Statesman.* Richmond, VA: Presbyterian Committee of Publication, 1909.

Wakefield, Gordon. *Bunyan the Christian.* London: HarperCollins, 1992.

Waldron, Samuel E. *The 1689 Baptist Confession of Faith: A Modern Exposition.* Darlington, England: Evangelical Press, 1989.

Waltke, Bruce K. *An Old Testament Theology: A Canonical and Thematic Approach.* Grand Rapids, MI: Zondervan, 2006.

Walton, Robert C. "Oecolampadius, Johannes." In *The Oxford Encyclopedia of the Reformation,* 3:170. Edited by Hans Joachim Hillerbrand. Oxford: Oxford University Press, 1996.

Walzer, Michael. *The Revolution of the Saints: A Study in the Origins of Radical Politics.* Cambridge, MA: Harvard University Press, 1965.

Wandel, Lee Palmer. "Zwingli, Huldrych." In *The Oxford Encyclopedia of the Reformation,* 4:321. Edited by Hans Joachim Hillerbrand. Oxford: Oxford University Press, 1996.

Warfield, B. B. *Biblical and Theological Studies.* Philadelphia: P&R, 1952.

———. *Calvin as a Theologian and Calvinism Today.* London: Evangelical Press, 1969.

Warfield, Benjamin B. *The Significance of the Westminster Standards as a Creed.* New York: Scribner, 1898.

Watkins, Owen C. *The Puritan Experience.* Studies in Spiritual Autobiography. London: Routledge & Kegan Paul, 1972.

Watson, Thomas. *A Body of Practical Divinity in a Series of Sermons on the Shorter Catechism.* London: A Fullarton and Co., 1845.

———. *The Duty of Self-Denial.* Morgan, PA: Soli Deo Gloria, 1995.

———. *The Godly Man's Picture.* Edinburgh: Banner of Truth, 1992.

———. *The Lord's Prayer.* Edinburgh: Banner of Truth, 1965.

———. "Man's Chief End to Glorifie God." In *A Body of Practical Divinity, Consisting of Above One Hundred Seventy Six Sermons on the Lesser Catechism Composed by The Reverend Assembly of Divines at Westminster: With a Supplement of Some Sermons on Several Texts of Scripture.* London: Thomas Parkhurst, 1692.

———. *The Select Works of the Rev. Thomas Watson.* New York: Robert Carter, 1855.

———. *The Ten Commandments.* Edinburgh: Banner of Truth, 1965.

Watts, Isaac. "Rules for the Preacher's Conduct." In *The Christian Pastor's Manual,* edited by John Brown, 198–243. 1826. Reprint, Ligonier, PA: Soli Deo Gloria, 1991.

Wayland, Francis. *Notes on the Principles and Practices of Baptist Churches.* New York: Sheldon, Blakeman, and Co., 1857.

Webster, Tom. *Godly Clergy in Early Stuart England: The Caroline Puritan Movement, c. 1620–1643.* Cambridge, UK: Cambridge University Press, 1997.

Weisiger, Cary Nelson, III. "The Doctrine of the Holy Spirit in the Preaching of Richard Sibbes." PhD diss., Fuller Theological Seminary, 1984.

[Westminster Divines]. *Westminster Confession of Faith.* Glasgow: Free Presbyterian Publications, 1994.

Whitefield, George. *George Whitefield's Journals.* London: Banner of Truth, 1960.

Whyte, Alexander. *The Spiritual Life: The Teaching of Thomas Goodwin as Received and Reissued.* London: Oliphants, 1918.

———. *Thomas Shepard, Pilgrim Father and Founder of Harvard: His Spiritual Experience and Experimental Preaching.* Grand Rapids, MI: Reformation Heritage Books, 2007.

Widmer, Sigmund. *Zwingli, 1484–1984: Reformation in Switzerland.* Zürich: Theologischer Verlag, 1983.

Williams, J. B., and Matthew Henry. *The Lives of Philip and Matthew Henry.* Edinburgh: Banner of Truth, 1974.

Williamson, G. I. *The Heidelberg Catechism: A Study Guide.* Phillipsburg, NJ: P&R, 1993.

Winchester, S. G. "The Importance of Doctrinal and Instructive Preaching." In *A Series of Tracts on the Doctrines, Order, and Polity of the Presbyterian Church in the United States of America.* 12 vols. Philadelphia: Presbyterian Board of Publication, 1840.

Winslow, Ola. *John Bunyan.* New York: MacMillan, 1961.

Wisse, Gerard. *Christ's Ministry in the Christian: The Administration of His Offices in the Believer.* Translated by Bartel Elshout and William Van Voorst. Sioux Center, IA: Netherlands Reformed Book and Publishing, 1993.

———. *Godly Sorrow.* St. Thomas, ON: Free Reformed Publications, 1998.

———. *Memoires: Onvergetelijke Bladzijden Uit Mijn Levensboek.* Houten/Utrecht: Den Hertog, 1982.

Witsius, Herman. *On the Character of a True Theologian.* Edited by J. Ligon Duncan III. Greenville, SC: Reformed Academic Press, 1994.

Won, Chong-ch'on. "Communion with Christ: An Exposition and Comparison of the Doctrine of Union and Communion with Christ in Calvin and the English Puritans." PhD diss., Westminster Theological Seminary, 1989.

Wright, Louis B. *Middle-Class Culture in Elizabethan England.* Chapel Hill: University of North Carolina Press, 1935.

———. "William Perkins: Elizabethan Apostle of 'Practical Divinity.'" In *Huntington Library Quarterly* 3, no. 2 (1940): 171–96.

Wright, Shawn D. *Our Sovereign Refuge: The Pastoral Theology of Theodore Beza.* Carlisle, UK: Paternoster Biblical and Theological Monographs. Paternoster, 2004.

———. "The Pastoral Use of the Doctrine of God's Sovereignty in the Theology of Theodore Beza." PhD diss., Southern Baptist Theological Seminary, 2001.

———. *Theodore Beza: The Man and the Myth.* Fearn, Ross-shire, Scotland: Christian Focus, 2015.

Yuille, J. Stephen. *Living Blessedly Forever: The Sermon on the Mount and the Puritan Piety of William Perkins.* Grand Rapids, MI: Reformation Heritage Books, 2012.

Zwingli, Ulrich. "Of the Clarity and Certainty of the Word of God." In *Zwingli and Bullinger*, Library of Christian Classics, vol. 24, edited by Geoffrey W. Bromiley, 49–95. Philadelphia: Westminster, 1953.

———. *Selected Writings of Huldrych Zwingli.* Edited by Edward J. Furcha and H. Wayne Pipkin. Allison Park, PA: Pickwick, 1984.

———. "Spiritus Est Qui Vivificate, Caro Nihil Potest." In *Biblical Interpretation in the Era of the Reformation: Essays Presented to David C. Steinmetz in Honor of His Sixtieth Birthday*, edited by John L. Thompson and Richard A. Muller, 156–85. Grand Rapids, MI: Eerdmans, 1996.

General Index

Scripture Index

Mary Telf

Best wishes

Charles J. Mossing